AutoLISP Programming
Principles and Techniques

by

Rod R. Rawls
Instructor
Autodesk Premier Training Center
Clackamas Community College, Oregon City, Oregon

President–CADNet1
Portland, Oregon

Mark A. Hagen
Instructor
Portland Community College, Portland, Oregon

Publisher
The Goodheart-Willcox Company, Inc.
Tinley Park, Illinois

Library of Congress Catalog Card Number 97-13891
International Standard Book Number 1-56637-417-0

2 3 4 5 6 7 8 9 10 98 00 01 99 98

Library of Congress Cataloging-in-Publication Data

Rawls, Rod R.
AutoLISP programming: principles and techniques / by Rod R. Rawls, Mark A. Hagen.
p. cm.
Includes index.
ISBN 1-56637-417-0
1. AutoLISP (Computer program language)
I. Hagen, Mark A. II. Title.
QA76.73.A84R38 1998
620'.0042'02855369--dc21 97-13891
CIP

Introduction

AutoLISP Programming provides practical and easy-to-follow instruction in mastering the AutoLISP programming language. A step-by-step approach is followed throughout the text to allow progressive learning, ranging from basic to advanced programming techniques. Many examples of AutoLISP applications are incorporated into this text to provide instruction both in learning the language, and in using it productively in a contemporary work environment.

AutoLISP Programming offers the following features throughout the text to enhance your learning experience:

- Begins at a level understandable to the novice AutoCAD user.
- Progresses in a step-by-step manner describing how to create useful and productive routines and programs with AutoLISP.
- *Professional Tips* provide information, insights, and guidelines on effective and efficient programming techniques in a professional work environment.
- Exercises interspersed throughout the chapters to reinforce the topics previously covered.
- Designed to give you a strong understanding of how AutoLISP works, and how to build your skills in designing, writing, and debugging programs.
- Helps you to learn the basic skills of AutoLISP programming without feeling intimidated.
- Chapter Tests and in-depth end-of-chapter Problems allow you to apply functions and key AutoLISP concepts.
- Stresses how to learn the strengths of AutoLISP, and where AutoLISP will and will not work.

AutoLISP is a version of a widely used programming language known as LISP. (LISP is an acronym for LISt Processing.) AutoLISP is used within AutoCAD, and has a tool set that includes many functions specifically designed for use in AutoCAD's graphic environment. Understanding AutoLISP will provide you with the knowledge to develop programs and functions that optimize your productivity.

One of the most fascinating things about AutoLISP is that you do not need to be an experienced programmer to master its use. In fact, AutoLISP is among the easiest of all programming languages to learn. Since this language works within AutoCAD, a good understanding of AutoCAD will provide you with a distinct advantage in learning to use AutoLISP.

This text is designed to be used with AutoCAD Release 14. A comprehensive appendix lists the initial AutoCAD release in which each function is available. The AutoLISP interpreter is embedded within AutoCAD, and is, therefore, accessible from within the AutoCAD drawing editor. An AutoLISP expression can be entered directly at the command line; AutoLISP program files can be loaded as applications; or even placed within the AutoCAD menu for ease of use. These features, combined with AutoLISP's special graphics applications provide what can be one of the most powerful productivity tools available within AutoCAD.

Many repetitive tasks can be handled by menu macros, which string individual commands one after another. However, this approach is merely accelerated command entry, and may not be suitable for custom applications. On the other hand, AutoLISP can test for required circumstances and vary results accordingly, reset system variables, access and use AutoCAD entity definition data, and even request user input to determine how to perform a given task.

Another common use for AutoLISP routines is to reduce your most frequently used command sequences to one or two keystrokes. For example, instead of typing "OFFSET", you could define a command named "O", which would invoke the OFFSET command within AutoCAD. In addition, macro style routines can be defined to "walk through" several prompts within a single command or even process multiple commands. This can minimize the number of keystrokes, as well as keyboard entry errors, thus reducing duplication of effort and thereby increasing productivity.

AutoLISP can be used to increase drafting productivity in many different ways. Because of this, many companies using AutoCAD are looking for operators with a basic knowledge of AutoLISP. Employees with these skills are likely to receive faster promotions and higher salaries, and enjoy an even greater sense of accomplishment on the job.

You do not need to be an expert in AutoCAD to use this text, however, a basic understanding is assumed. No previous knowledge of AutoLISP or any other programming language is required.

About the Authors...

Rod Rawls

Rod is the president and founder of CADNet1 in Portland, Oregon. CADNet1 is a progressive company providing a broad range of AutoCAD-related services and AutoCAD solutions at all levels, including development of AutoLISP programming applications. Rod's services include development of World Wide Web-based AutoCAD applications, parametric design applications, application-specific menu systems, and design-drafting services.

In addition to his responsibilities at CADNet1, Rod is also a Certified AutoCAD instructor at the Authorized Premier Training Center for AutoCAD at Clackamas Community College in Oregon City. Rod teaches basic and advanced AutoCAD classes, AutoCAD menu design, AutoLISP programming, web technologies, and virtual reality applications. His expertise in writing **AutoLISP Programming** draws directly from his classroom experience in teaching AutoLISP.

Mark Hagen

Mark is currently an instructor in the Drafting Technology Department at Portland Community College. He teaches a wide variety of AutoCAD-related courses including beginning, intermediate, and advanced level courses, as well as AutoLISP programming courses.

Prior to working at Portland Community College, Mark worked as an Applications Consultant for KETIV Technologies, Inc. in Portland, Oregon. His responsibilities at KETIV included serving as an AutoCAD trainer/programmer/consultant for a large Pacific Northwest AutoCAD dealer and CAD/CAM/CAE company.

Mark also has extensive experience in the drafting and design field. Before working for KETIV, Mark worked as a CAD Specialist for the Silver Eagle Manufacturing Company. His responsibilities primarily dealt with the design and drafting of steel fabrication weldments and assemblies.

Mark has an Applied Arts and Sciences degree in Engineering Technology from Clark College in Vancouver, Washington. In addition, he has a Bachelor of Arts degree in Sciences and Humanities from Iowa State University. Mark is also certified in Geometric Dimensioning and Tolerancing applications.

Contents

Chapter 1

Fundamentals of AutoLISP

Learning Objectives

After completing this chapter, you will be able to:

- ☐ Define the elements of an AutoLISP expression.
- ☐ Describe the construction of an AutoLISP expression.
- ☐ Enter an AutoLISP expression for evaluation.
- ☐ Manage simple error situations.
- ☐ Explain the difference between real numbers and integers in AutoLISP.
- ☐ Use AutoLISP's mathematical functions to solve simple equations.
- ☐ Use function nesting to solve complex equations.
- ☐ Set and use AutoLISP variables.

BUILDING AN AUTOLISP EXPRESSION

The fundamental structure for all data processed by AutoLISP is known as a *list*. The term *LISP* is an acronym for *LISt Processing*. In the AutoLISP programming language, a *list* is simply a collection of any number of data elements contained within parentheses, with the individual elements (also called *atoms*) separated by spaces.

There are two types of lists recognized by AutoLISP–*expressions* and *data lists*. An *expression* is the basic ingredient of all AutoLISP programs. This type of list contains an AutoLISP *function* name as its first element, and is *evaluated* by the AutoLISP interpreter. When an expression is evaluated, the specified function is performed.

Basic AutoLISP expressions are similar to mathematical equations in composition. See Fig. 1-1. Examine the mathematical equation of 1 + 2 = 3. The *function* is the action being performed, such as + (addition), – (subtraction), × (multiplication), or ÷ (division). In this case, the function is + (addition). The *arguments* are the values provided for the function to be performed on or with. Here, the arguments are 1 and 2. The *return*ed value is the result of the function acting upon the arguments. In the equation 1 + 2 = 3, the sum, or returned value, is the value of 3.

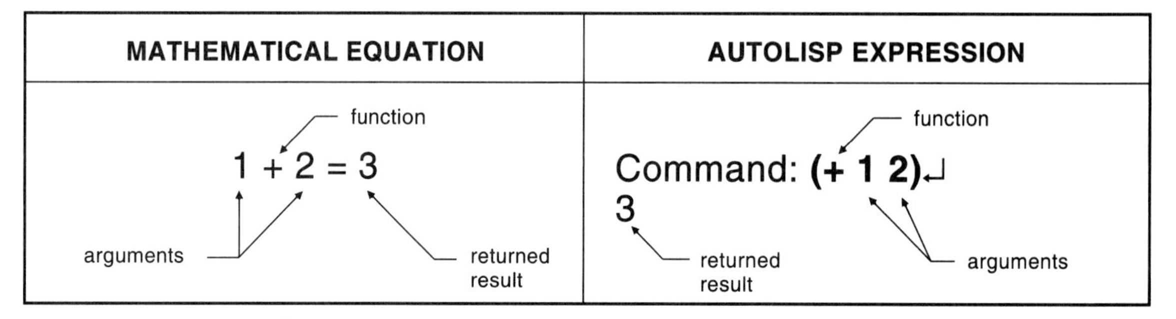

Fig. 1-1. Comparison of a mathematical equation and AutoLISP expression.

Similar to a mathematical equation, an AutoLISP expression applies a *function* to the supplied *arguments* and *returns* the resulting value. The *function* is the operation to be performed. The operation may be a mathematical function such as addition, or it may be any other function supported by AutoLISP. The *argument* is the supplied data that the function is applied to. When the function of addition is applied to the numerical arguments 1 and 2, the returned result is the sum of 3.

The main difference between a mathematical equation and an expression is that an AutoLISP expression requires you to enter the information in a different order and enclose it within parentheses. Using a simple calculator, a mathematical equation is entered as follows:

First:	1	*Argument*
Second:	+	*Function*
Third:	2	*Argument*
Fourth:	=	*Returns the result*

The first consideration when constructing an AutoLISP expression is that the expression is enclosed in parentheses. Therefore, the first entry is an *opening* parenthesis to begin the list. The first element of the list must be the function name, in this case the function name is **+**. The remaining elements of the list are interpreted as arguments (refer back to Fig. 1-1). Finally, the list must be closed with a *closing* parenthesis. Based on these requirements, the order of entry for the previous equation in AutoLISP format is as follows:

First:	(	*Opening parenthesis*
Second:	+	*Function*
Third:	1	*Argument*
Fourth:	2	*Argument*
Fifth:	)	*Closing parenthesis*

Final format: (+ 1 2)
The result of evaluation is then *returned:* 3

PROFESSIONAL TIP

AutoLISP uses blank spaces as a delimiter (separator) when evaluating input. Remember that both functions and arguments must be separated by blank spaces in order for AutoLISP to differentiate between individual atoms (elements) within a list. Therefore, all functions and arguments *must* be separated from each other by spaces. Note that the function name need not be separated from the opening parenthesis and likewise, the final argument in an expression need not be separated from the closing parenthesis.

Let's Review...

1. The fundamental data structure within AutoLISP is called a *list*.
2. The term *list* indicates any number of *atoms* (data elements) enclosed in parentheses.
3. An expression always contains a function name as its first element.
4. An expression consists of a function name and its required *arguments* enclosed in parentheses.
5. *Arguments* are the values supplied for the *function* to be applied to.
6. AutoLISP *returns* the result of the evaluation of an expression.

ENTERING AN EXPRESSION FOR EVALUATION

An AutoLISP expression can be entered at the AutoCAD Command: prompt just like any standard AutoCAD command, as long as you remember to enclose it in parentheses. Once AutoCAD encounters the parentheses, it recognizes the input as an AutoLISP expression and passes the information on to the AutoLISP interpreter for evaluation. An AutoLISP expression can be entered in any manner through which standard AutoCAD commands are entered, including direct entry via the keyboard, as a menu selection, or it may be loaded as an AutoLISP program file (covered in Chapter 2). Each of these methods will cause the expression to be evaluated, and will return the resulting value.

When entering AutoLISP expressions at the Command: prompt, use either the Text window (by pressing the F2 button) or size the floating command window so that at least six lines appear. This will help ensure that you see the returned value and any error messages that may have been issued.

Possible Problems

When performing exercises in this chapter, you will be entering your AutoLISP expressions directly at the AutoCAD Command: prompt. The result of evaluating your expression is returned immediately to the command line. If the final closing paren (paren*thesis*) is followed by typing a space bar, the returned result is on the same line. If the final closing paren is followed with an ENTER key, the result is displayed one line down. Examine the following example:

Using **SPACE BAR** following the closing paren:
Command: **(+ 2 4) 6**

Using **ENTER** key following the closing paren:
Command: **(+ 2 4)**
6

Keeping an eye on this returned value is critical when using or testing an expression at the command line. If the operation was successful, the returned value will verify the success. But, if for any reason the expression was incorrect, an appropriate *error message* is displayed, along with a copy of the offending expression. In the examples below, the first expression is entered correctly, and an appropriate value is returned. The remainder of the expressions are entered incorrectly and return appropriate error messages. These error messages may be encountered from time to time as you enter AutoLISP expressions for evaluation. The most common error messages encountered, and the necessary means of recovery are shown in the column on the right:

Command: **(+ 1 2)** ↵
3

1 and 2 are evaluated, the + function is applied; 3 is returned.

Command: **(+4 2)** ↵
error: bad function
(4 2)
****Cancel****

This expression needs a SPACE to separate the function name + from the first argument of 4. In this example, the first element is expected to be a function name, but instead, the first element is +4, which is read as a positive 4. Since 4 is a number, and not a function name, an error message is returned, the offending expression is printed to the screen and further evaluation is canceled.

Command: **(+ 4 .25)** ↵
error: invalid dotted pair
****Cancel****

The argument, .25, is incomplete. A number less than zero must start with a 0. Therefore, the correct way to specify this number in an AutoLISP expression is: 0.25. The message returned will be explained in later chapters, but as with any error, processing is canceled.

Command: **(+ 4 8** ↵
1〉 **)**
12

The expression is left open, since no closing parenthesis was used. The next line shows how many parentheses (and/or quotation marks) are required to properly close the expression. In this case, only one is required, as indicated by the number 1. Entering the closing parenthesis on the next line is acceptable (as shown). Once the expression is closed, it can be evaluated, and the result is returned.

Command: **(+ 4 8**
1〉 ***error: input aborted***
****Cancel****

Another way to "clean up" this situation is to cancel the operation using ESC. This cancels the operation and returns to a new Command: prompt.

ARITHMETIC, AUTOCAD, AND AUTOLISP

Although AutoCAD is a powerful tool, have you ever wondered why you have to use your calculator to solve mathematical equations? Within the program, a tremendous number of equations may be processed in order to perform a relatively simple command. This indicates that AutoCAD is capable of handling mathematical problems. However, AutoCAD does not allow a user to directly tap this power. Performance of arithmetic operations, along with many other powerful problem-solving techniques, become possible by using AutoLISP. In fact, if you have used AutoCAD's geometry calculator, you have already seen AutoLISP at work.

ARITHMETIC FUNCTIONS

Earlier in this chapter, you saw an example of a mathematical application of AutoLISP:

```
(+ 1 2)
```

The same format applies to all four basic mathematical AutoLISP functions. However, each of these functions has specific rules which govern its use.

The + Function

The + *(addition) function* accepts any number of numerical arguments, and returns the sum of all of the arguments. If only one argument is supplied, the result of adding that argument to zero is returned. The *syntax* (format) for the + function is:

```
(+ [NUMBER NUMBER] ...)
```

For example:

AutoLISP Expression		Standard Mathematical Equivalent
(+ 1 2)	returns 3	1 + 2 = 3
(+ 1 2 3)	returns 6	1 + 2 + 3 = 6
(+ 1 2 3 4 5)	returns 15	1 + 2 + 3 + 4 + 5 = 15
(+ 1 2 3 –2)	returns 4	1 + 2 + 3 + (–2) = 4
(+ 17)	returns 17	17 + 0 = 17

As discussed earlier, AutoLISP processes information provided in the form of a list. When a list is passed to the AutoLISP interpreter, each element (or atom) within the list is evaluated. If the first atom is a function name, the remaining atoms are presumed to be arguments and are evaluated prior to applying the function. In the examples above, the arguments are the NUMBERs to be added together.

Numerical arguments can be provided as either of two data types, *integer* or *real*. The term *integer* refers to a whole number (such as 1, 4, -38, or 72). Note that an integer does not have a decimal point. The term *real number* or *real* indicates a number with a "floating" decimal point (such as 1.25, 15.0, -19.002, or 357.14). Notice that there is a decimal point on all real numbers, even if there is no value beyond the decimal.

The data type of the arguments provided will determine the data type of the returned result. For example, integer math returns integer results. In other words, if all of the arguments are integers, the result will be returned as an integer. However, if all arguments are real numbers the returned result will also be a real. In the event that a combination of reals and integers are provided as arguments, then all of the integers will be *promoted* to real numbers and the result is likewise returned as a real. This rule of promoting integers to real numbers applies to addition, subtraction, multiplication and division. For example:

(+ 1 2)	returns	3
(+ 1 2.0)	returns	3.0
(+ 24 6 30)	returns	60
(+ 24.0 6 30.0)	returns	60.0
(+ 12 –24 4 7 –13)	returns	–14
(+ 1.553 2 7.1)	returns	10.653

The – Function

The – *(subtraction) function* subtracts the sum of the second through the last argument from the first argument and returns the difference. If only one argument is supplied, the result of subtracting that number from zero is returned. The syntax for this function is:

(– [NUMBER NUMBER] ...)

Examples of the subtraction function follow:

AutoLISP Expression			**Standard Mathematical Equivalent**
(– 4 2)	returns	2	4 – 2 = 2
(– 4.0 2)	returns	2.0	4.0 – 2 = 2.0
(– 20 5 5)	returns	10	20 – (5 + 5) = 10
(– 15)	returns	–15	–15 = –15
(– 100 25 25 50)	returns	0	100 – (25 + 25 + 50) = 0
(– 50 25 –15)	returns	40	50 – [25 + (–15)] = 40
(– 25 10.5 –15.5)	returns	30.0	25 – [10.5 + (–15.5)] = 30.0

The * Function

The * *(multiplication) function* multiplies all NUMBERs and returns the product. If only one NUMBER is supplied, the result is NUMBER multiplied by 1. The multiplication function's syntax is:

(* [NUMBER NUMBER] ...)

Examples of the multiplication function follow:

AutoLISP Expression		Standard Mathematical Equivalent
(* 1 2)	returns 2	1 × 2 = 2
(* 3)	returns 3	3 × 1 = 3
(* 2 5.0 6)	returns 60.0	2 × 5.0 × 6 = 60.0
(* 2 –5.0)	returns –10.0	2 × –5.0 = –10.0
(* 4 –2.5 –3.5)	returns 35.0	4 × (–2.5) × (–3.5) = 35.0
(* 2.25 6.375)	returns 14.3438	2.25 × 6.375 = 14.3438 (rounded off)
(* 13.75 3.625)	returns 49.8438	13.75 × 3.625 = 49.8438 (rounded off)

When working through the previous examples, you will notice that AutoLISP appears to round off the returned result. Actually, AutoLISP provides at least 14 digits of precision. However, only six *significant digits* will be *displayed* in the returned value. The tally of significant digits begins at the left side of the number and moves to the right. For example, the number 22,475.5 displays six significant digits. Trailing zeros are not considered to be significant digits. The number 755.3 does not display any trailing zeros since they are not considered to be significant digits.

The / Function

The */ (division) function* divides the first NUMBER by the product of the second through the last NUMBERs and returns the quotient. If only one NUMBER is supplied, the quotient is equal to NUMBER divided by 1. The format for the division function is:

```
(/ [NUMBER NUMBER] ...)
```

Examples of the division function follow:

AutoLISP Expression		Standard Mathematical Equivalent	
(/ 5)	returns 5	5 ÷ 1 = 5	
(/ 4 2)	returns 2	4 ÷ 2 = 2	
(/ 3 2)	returns 1	3 ÷ 2 = 1	*2 goes into 3 only 1 time, with a remainder of 1*
(/ 8 4.0)	returns 2.0	8 ÷ 4.0 = 2.0	
(/ 40 5 2)	returns 4	40 ÷ (5 × 2) = 4	
(/ 100 60)	returns 1	100 ÷ 60 = 1	*60 goes into 100 only 1 time, with a remainder of 40*
(/ 100 60.0)	returns 1.66667	100 ÷ 60.0 = 1.66667	
(/ 60 3 2 5)	returns 2	60 ÷ (3 × 2 × 5) = 2	
(/ 60 3 2 –5.0)	returns –2.0	60 ÷ [3 × 2 × (–5.0)] = –2.0	

Note that division performed strictly with integers returns only integer quotients. Division with real numbers yields a real number, and similar to the multiplication examples, AutoLISP only displays up to six significant digits. Division between real numbers and integers always returns a real number.

EXERCISE 1-1

☐ Using your computer, solve the following equations by entering the proper AutoLISP function and supplying the required arguments at the AutoCAD Command: prompt. Then write the expression used in the space provided.

A. $44 + 27$ ____________________

B. $6 + 33 + 12$ ____________________

C. $4.2 + 53 + 2.8$ ____________________

D. $5.25 + 19.375$ ____________________

E. $9 + 3 + 1.4 + 9$ ____________________

F. $14 - 4$ ____________________

G. $12 - 7.3$ ____________________

H. $6.77 - 3.02$ ____________________

I. $9.418 - 2.5 + 6.39$ ____________________

J. $43 - (7 + 4 + 77)$ ____________________

K. 6×9 ____________________

L. $4 \times 5 \times 3$ ____________________

M. 6.1×5 ____________________

N. 3.5×2.875 ____________________

O. 4×0.5 ____________________

P. $42 \div 7$ ____________________

Q. $14 \div 4$ ____________________

R. $14.0 \div 4$ ____________________

S. $28.5 \div 8.5 \times 1.25$ ____________________

T. $9 \div (0.3 \times 9)$ ____________________

☐ List any error messages you encountered (if any) when entering the AutoLISP expressions at the Command: prompt. Describe the solution you used to correct the problem.

____

____

____

____

SOLVING COMPLEX EQUATIONS

Simple expressions work well for simple mathematical operations, but what about complex equations? Several functions may be performed in a standard mathematical problem. In AutoLISP, *function nesting* is a technique used to solve such an equation. The term *nesting* means placing one expression inside another. The following example illustrates the nesting technique:

AutoLISP Expression	Standard Mathematical Equivalent
(– 40 (* 8 3))	40 – (8 × 3)

In this example, only one level of nesting occurs. Notice that there are two arguments provided for the subtraction function–the first is the integer 40 and the second is an expression. The inner expression is considered a *nested expression.* The order in which nested expressions are evaluated is from the deepest nesting outward to the top level. Another example follows:

AutoLISP Expression	Standard Mathematical Equivalent
(/ 100 (– 40 (* 3 5)))	100 ÷ (40 – (3 × 5))

Here, the most deeply nested expression is (* 3 5) and is evaluated by AutoLISP first. The returned result of 15 is brought up to the next nesting level:

AutoLISP Expression	Standard Mathematical Equivalent
(/ 100 (– 40 15))	100 ÷ (40 – 15)

Now, the nested expression of (– 40 15) is processed and the result is moved up to the top level:

AutoLISP Expression	Standard Mathematical Equivalent
(/ 100 25)	100 ÷ 25

The top level is then evaluated and a final value of 4 is returned.

The following is an example of how to translate a standard mathematical equation into an AutoLISP expression.

(720 ÷ 360) + (49 × 2)

Notice that the results of the two nested equations are being added together, with the top level function being addition and the two nested equations residing at the same level. Therefore, the translation is:

```
(+ (/ 720 360) (* 49 2))
```

Where the quotient of (/ 720 360) is added to the product of (* 49 2), the expression could be shown as:

(+ 2 98)	*when this expression is evaluated, the value of 100 is returned*

EXERCISE 1-2

☐ Solve the following equations by entering the proper AutoLISP functions and supplying the required arguments. Pay special attention to nesting techniques. Write the expression used in the space provided.

A. 15 + (6 × 4) ______

B. 100 ÷ [22 ÷ (10 + 1)] ______

C. 16 × 4 × (81 ÷ 9) ______

D. 45 ÷ (3 × 5) ______

E. 106 – (2 + 2 + 2 + 2) ______

F. (45 ÷ 5) × (13 – 4) ______

G. (357 ÷ 26) × 14 ______

H. 28 ÷ [14 × (6 × 0.3)] ______

I. 53 + (22 × 4) ______

J. 1 + 2 – (3 × 0.75) ______

When you work with very complex equations, it is usually easier to construct the AutoLISP expression from the inside out. In other words, find the deepest level of nesting and work your way up to the top level. Study the following example:

18 – [(3 + 6 + 9) ÷ (9 – 6)] – 12

Step 1.
Deepest level. **(+ 3 6 9) (– 9 6)**

Step 2.
Next level. **(/** (+ 3 6 9) (– 9 6)**)**

Step 3.
Top level. **(– 18** (/ (+ 3 6 9) (– 9 6))**)**

Step 4.
(– (– 18 (/ (+ 3 6 9) (– 9 6))) **12)**

Note that at the top level, AutoLISP proceeds from left to right in its evaluation process. As shown in Step 3, subtract the result of Step 2 from 18, and then subtract 12 from that value (Step 4). Here is another example:

[(55 – 10) × (3 × 6 × 9)] ÷ [(4 × 10) + 5]

Step 1.
Deepest level. **(– 55 10) (* 3 6 9) (* 4 10)**

Step 2.
Next level. **(*** (– 55 10) (* 3 6 9)**) (+** (* 4 10) **5)**

Step 3.
Top level. **(/** (* (– 55 10) (* 3 6 9)) (+ (* 4 10) 5)**)**

EXERCISE 1-3

☐ The best way to master the nesting technique is with practice. Solve the following equations by entering the proper AutoLISP expressions with the required arguments. Use the technique of constructing your expressions from the deepest level to the top level. Write the expression in the space provided.

A. $[21 \div (7 \times 3)] + (4 \times 5)$ ________

B. $(27 - 7) - [(2 \times 3) \div (3 \times 2)] - (3 \times 6)$ ________

C. $[(25 - 4 - 6) \div (3 \times 5)] + (4 \times 3)$ ________

D. $[256 \div (16 \times 16)] + [225 \div (15 \times 15)]$ ________

E. $(7 \times 6) \div \{142 - [10 \times (80 \div 8)]\}$ ________

F. $[697 - (47 + 50)] \div 6$ ________

G. $[(25 \div 5) \times 36] \div (4 \times 9 \times 5)$ ________

H. $27216 \div (7 \times 6 \times 18 \times 12.0)$ ________

I. $22 - \{12 \div [-5 \times (44.0 \div -22)]\}$ ________

J. $[31 + 15 + (-10)] \div (4.5 \times 2)$ ________

Let's Review...

1. When the first element of an AutoLISP expression is a function name, all additional elements are considered arguments and are evaluated prior to applying the function.
2. The four basic mathematical functions all have the same format: (⟨FUNCTION⟩ ⟨ARGUMENT⟩ ⟨ARGUMENT⟩ ...), but each has its own specific rules.
3. AutoLISP mathematical functions return an integer only if *all* arguments are integers. If any arguments are real numbers, then the result will be given as a real.
4. Nesting techniques are used to perform complex equations.
5. When translating a complex equation to an AutoLISP expression, it is best to work from the deepest nesting level up to the top level.

PROFESSIONAL TIP

The values returned by evaluated AutoLISP expressions can be used as input for many AutoCAD prompts. Mathematical expressions can be entered at most of AutoCAD's numerical prompts. For example, drafting standards in some industries specify that the drill diameter for a threaded hole is to be drawn at 75% of the nominal thread diameter. When using the CEN,DIA method to create a circle in AutoCAD, the Diameter: prompt could be answered with an AutoLISP expression to calculate the correct diameter. For example:

```
Command: CIRCLE ↵
3P/2P/TTR/⟨Center point⟩: pick center location
Diameter/⟨Radius⟩: D ↵
Diameter: (* 0.625 0.75) ↵
Command:
```

In this example, the value returned by the multiplication expression (0.46875) was accepted by the Diameter: prompt as input and the circle was drawn. Using AutoLISP to solve equations in this manner is often faster and more convenient than using AutoCAD's geometry calculator.

AUTOLISP VARIABLES AND SYMBOLS

In AutoLISP, *symbols* and *variables* are used to store and access values required for use within a program. The term *symbol* is used in reference to a static (unchanging) value, such as the name of a built-in AutoLISP function (for example, +, -, *, /, etc.), a user-defined function (discussed in Chapter 2) or an AutoLISP constant (such as *pi*). One example of a user-defined symbol could be a constant numerical value required for a formula. Such a value would be the same each time the program runs and is referred to as a symbol. The term *variable* is used in reference to program data, since these types of values often change depending on the parameters supplied to a program. An example of variables in a program that draws threaded holes might be diameter, depth, thread specification and hole center point based on user input. These values might change each time a program is used, and are therefore considered to be *variables*. For the most part, symbol names and variable names are created and handled the same in AutoLISP. Which term is used is dependent on whether the value represented is static or variable.

Setting Variables

Within AutoLISP, the value of a variable or symbol can be set using the SETQ function. The *SETQ function* assigns a value to a symbol name, and subsequent evaluation of the symbol name by AutoLISP returns its assigned value. A symbol may be used to represent any data type, including integers, real numbers, text strings, lists, and other data types discussed in subsequent chapters.

As discussed earlier, AutoLISP *evaluates* (determines the value of) each element within a list. Data items such as numbers and text strings evaluate to themselves, while variable names evaluate to their assigned values. An exception to this evaluation process is found within a SETQ expression. The symbol name argument is not evaluated and a new value is assigned regardless of any previous value associated with it.

The syntax for the SETQ function is as follows:

```
(setq SYMBOL1 VALUE1 [SYMBOL2 VALUE2] ...)
```

Any number of symbols or variables may be set at the same time within a single SETQ expression. The value of the last variable set is returned. In order to assign the symbol "X" a value of 3, the following expression would be used:

```
Command: (setq X 3) ↵
3
```

This expression sets the symbol X to the value 3 and returns 3. To set the symbol Y to 4 and Z to 9, use the following expression:

```
Command: (setq Y 4 Z 9) ↵
9
```

This sets the symbols to the shown values and returns 9, which is the value of the last symbol set.

A known value may be assigned to a symbol as shown in the previous examples, or a symbol may be set to the value returned from the evaluation of another expression or symbol. For example, this next SETQ expression sets the symbol A to the value of the symbol Z:

```
Command: (setq A Z) ↵
9
```

Since the evaluation of the symbol Z returns 9, this value is then assigned to the symbol A and returned as shown.

The returned result of an evaluated expression may also be used for setting symbol names. For example:

Command: **(setq X (+ 1 2))**↵
3

Here, the addition expression is the most deeply nested and is therefore evaluated first. The value of 3 is then returned to the top level SETQ expression and is assigned to the symbol X.

Another example shows the use of symbols and expressions in a SETQ expression:

Command: **(setq X (+ Y Z))**↵
13

Returned Values

An important point to remember is that a SETQ statement will return a value in the same manner that mathematical functions return a value. This is true of all AutoLISP statements. The value returned may be "nil" (no value), "T" (true), or data such as a real number, text string, or list, depending upon the expression being used. After you type in a SETQ expression, the value assigned to the symbol is returned by AutoLISP. Here are some examples of results returned by AutoLISP:

AutoLISP Expression	Result	
(setq a 14)	returns 14	*a was set equal to 14*
(setq X Y)	returns nil	*Y has no value in this example; X was set equal to Y*
(setq b A)	returns 14	*A was set equal to 14 (from the first example); the symbol is then evaluated and its value is returned; b is set equal to the result*
(setq z (* 3 4))	returns 12	*z was set equal to the returned result of the nested expression*
(setq X (– B Z))	returns 2	*since B is equal to 14 and Z is equal to 12, the result returned is 2, which is the value X was set equal to*
(setq M "XYZ")	returns "XYZ"	*M was set equal to the text string "XYZ"*

Note that a symbol may be a combination of two or more characters, as well as numbers. Additionally, AutoLISP is not *case sensitive,* which means that a symbol name may be uppercase, lowercase, or even a combination of both. This case insensitivity applies to both symbol names *and* function names, but does not apply to text strings. Be sure to see the section at the end of this chapter regarding rules for symbol names.

The following example helps demonstrate AutoLISP's case insensitivity:

Command: **(setq aBcd 40)** ↵
40

Command: **(setq X AbCD)** ↵
40

The symbol ABCD is set to 40 in the first expression. Even though the symbol was typed as **aBcd**, it was read by AutoLISP as **ABCD**. In the second expression, the symbol X is assigned to the result of evaluating the symbol **AbCD**, which AutoLISP again reads as **ABCD** and returns the assigned value of 40.

PROFESSIONAL TIP

AutoLISP allows integers and real numbers to possess a minus sign, symbolizing negative values. To reverse the sign of a symbol value, use a subtraction expression with the symbol as its only argument. The following example shows how this can be accomplished:

Command: **(setq A 15.0)** ↵	*A is set to 15.0*
Command: **(setq B (– A))** ↵	*The subtraction expression has a single argument, the variable A. Note that one space separates the subtraction function from its argument. B is now set to –15.0*
Command: **(setq C (+ (– B) (– A)))** ↵	*C is set to 0.0, where (– B) evaluates to 15.0 and (– A) evaluates to –15.0*

This technique is applicable only to symbols having numeric values.

Setting Multiple Symbols

It is often necessary to set the values of several different symbols within an AutoLISP expression. As shown earlier, instead of using several SETQ expressions to accomplish this, each symbol name and value combination may be listed sequentially in the same expression. Notice what is returned in the following examples:

(setq tx "ABC")	*sets tx equal to "ABC" and returns "ABC"*
(setq tx "ABC" FF 49)	*sets tx equal to "ABC", FF to 49, and returns 49*
(setq A 4 x "OK" B6L (* 14 pi) h 14.3)	*sets A equal to 4, x to "OK", B6L to 43.9823, h to 14.3, and returns 14.3*

As you can see from the previous examples, the SETQ function returns the value of the last variable set within the expression.

Using Variables

Once a value has been assigned to a symbol, AutoLISP evaluates the symbol name. So in effect, the symbol is read as its assigned value whenever it is encountered. Look closely at the following example:

(setq n 1)	*n was set equal to 1*
(+ 4 n)	*returns 5—the sum of 4 and 1*

AutoLISP also allows a symbol value to be altered. For example:

(setq n 1)	*n was set equal to 1*
(setq n (+ 2 n))	*The deepest expression adds 2 to the value of n and then returns 3. The top level expression sets the symbol n to the value returned by the deepest level, so n now equals 3 and this expression returns 3*

The only requirement for using variables as arguments is that the data type assigned to the symbol is the type of data required by the function. Some functions require an integer, some a real number, and others require text strings. (More data types will be discussed later.) Obviously, two text strings cannot be valid arguments for a math function.

Using variables on the Command: line

Like AutoLISP expressions, an AutoLISP symbol can be evaluated at the command line to answer AutoCAD prompts. To extract the value of an AutoLISP symbol, type an exclamation point "!" followed by the symbol name. The following example shows an AutoLISP variable being set and subsequently used to answer an AutoCAD prompt:

Command: **(setq X 5)** ↵ 5	*utilizes the AutoLISP SETQ function*
Command: **!X** ↵ 5	*returns the value assigned to "X"*

One application of using the exclamation point is as follows:

Command: **CIRCLE** ↵	*activates the AutoCAD CIRCLE command*
3P/2P/TTR/⟨Center point⟩**:** *(pick a point)*	*locate a center point for the circle*
Diameter/⟨Radius⟩: **!X** ↵	*Sets the circle radius to the assigned value of X, which is 5*

RULES AND HINTS FOR SYMBOL NAMES

There is only one general rule which AutoLISP enforces regarding symbol names. Symbols may consist of any printable character except the following:

( ) . ' " ; and blank spaces may not be used in a symbol name.

In addition, the following rules are highly recommended:

1. AutoLISP has certain built-in symbols such as pi for the real number 3.1415926, which are used as *constants* (unchanging values). These constants should not be assigned different values because AutoLISP will discard the original value, consequently making them inaccessible.
2. Do not use symbols that are also built-in function names in AutoLISP.
3. Avoid using long, complicated symbol names. Shorter names are easier to type, quicker to process, and less likely to contain typing errors.

PERSISTENT AUTOLISP

In versions of AutoCAD previous to Release 14, all AutoLISP variables and symbols are reset between drawing sessions. This means that all symbol and variable assignments are discarded and reset to defaults upon leaving a drawing session, and are therefore valid only in a single drawing session. This can be used to your advantage if you accidentally change the value of a built-in function or symbol name. Use the AutoCAD OPEN command to reopen the drawing you are working in or simply start a new drawing, whichever is most appropriate.

Beginning with AutoCAD Release 14, the AutoLISP variable and symbol assignments are only reset upon closing the AutoCAD program window. This means that the set values for AutoLISP symbols and variables *persist* from one drawing to the next until you exit AutoCAD. With this in mind, it is important to note that any AutoLISP assignments are local to the instance of AutoCAD in which they are set. AutoLISP symbols set in one AutoCAD window cannot be directly accessed by another AutoCAD window running at the same time.

When using Release 14, if you accidentally reassign some function names, you can temporarily disable persistent AutoLISP and restart the drawing session. This is done by adjusting the value of the AutoCAD LISPINIT system variable, either directly at the Command: prompt or by using the PREFERENCES command. In the Preferences dialog box, select the Compatibility tab and place a check in the toggle labeled "Reload AutoLISP between drawings." See Fig. 1-2. After opening another drawing session and resetting AutoLISP, you can then enable this feature again. It is best to keep persistent AutoLISP enabled in most cases.

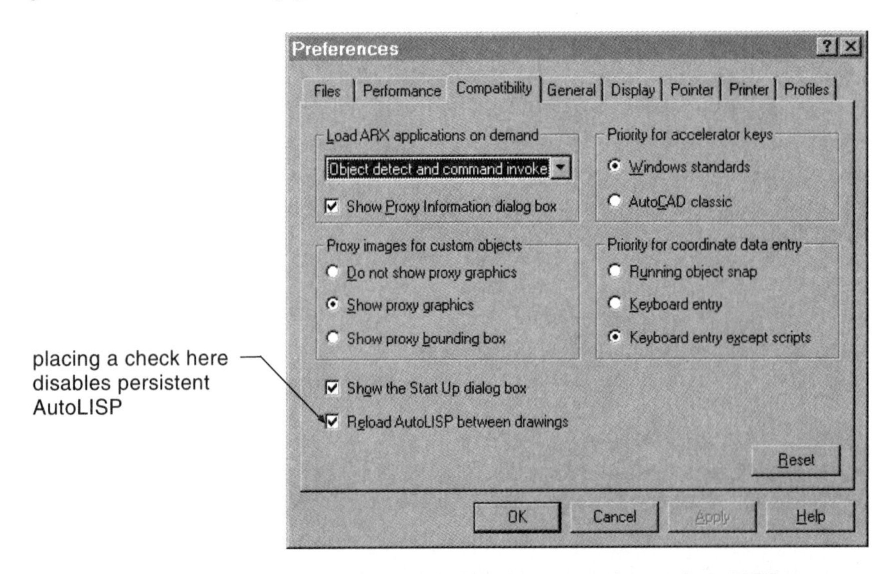

Fig. 1-2. Disabling persistent AutoLISP.

Let's Review...

1. The SETQ function is commonly used to assign values to symbols and variables.
2. The terms *symbol* and *variable* are basically the same, except *symbol* implies a static (constant) value and *variable* implies a changeable value.
3. The value associated with a symbol name can be changed at any time using the SETQ function.
4. Several variable values may be set in the same expression.
5. All AutoLISP expressions return a value.
6. Symbol names are evaluated when encountered in an expression.
7. Symbol names must not conflict with AutoLISP functions or constants.
8. AutoLISP has certain built-in symbols, such as pi (3.1415926).
9. AutoLISP values are reset when exiting AutoCAD, but they will persist between drawing sessions if persistent AutoLISP is not disabled.

EXERCISE 1-4

☐ Write an AutoLISP expression to perform each of the following tasks. Test your work at the AutoCAD Command: prompt, and record the expression in the space provided.

A. Assign the sum of 6, 22, and 14 to the symbol X.

____

B. Assign the quotient of 144 divided by the product of 4 and 3 to the symbol Y.

____

C. Subtract "Y" from "X" and assign the result to the symbol Z.

____

D. Set up the following symbols with their respective values:

Symbol Name	Value
A	42
B	15
C	144
D	88

____

____

E. Assign the value of 2 × (A + B) to the symbol E.

____

F. Assign the value of (D ÷ 4) + B – A to the symbol F.

____

____

G. Assign the value of Z – A + B to the symbol G.

____

H. Assign the value of [(4.0 × B) ÷ C] × A to the symbol H.

____

I. Translate the following mathematical equation into an AutoLISP expression:
$\{(A - B) \div [(C + D) - (E \times F)]\} \div 2$

____

J. Translate the following mathematical equation into an AutoLISP expression:
$(F - B) \div (G \div H) - [(3 + C) \times 1.75]$

____

CHAPTER TEST

Write your answers in the spaces provided.

1. What is the basic ingredient of any AutoLISP program?

____

____

2. Give an example of a list that is evaluated.

____

____

3. How is an expression different from any other list?

____

____

4. Explain the purpose of a "function" in AutoLISP.

____

____

____

5. If the first element of a list is a function, the remaining elements are considered to be ______________________________.

6. Define the term "argument."

____

____

____

7. How will AutoCAD treat an AutoLISP expression if you don't use parentheses?

____

____

8. What should you do if you see the prompt "1)"?

____

____

9. What is meant when AutoLISP "returns" a value?

____

____

10. What are the three ways an AutoLISP expression may be entered for evaluation?

____

____

____

11. How do you cancel when you are entering an expression?

____

12. An AutoLISP expression usually consists of _______________ and _______________.

13. The composition of an AutoLISP expression is similar to the construction of a _______________ _______________.

14. Define the term "list."

____

____

____

15. Define the term "integer" and list three examples.

____

____

16. Define "real number." List three examples of real numbers.

____

____

17. What is the first element of an AutoLISP mathematical expression?

____

____

18. When does AutoLISP return an integer value?

____

____

19. What is meant by "nesting"?

____

____

____

20. Write the following equations in the proper AutoLISP format:

    A. $[(22 + 14) - 6] \times 2$ _______________

    B. $43 - [(16 \times 4) \div (3 - 1)]$ _______________

    C. $[442 \times (64 \div 8)] - (14 \times 22)$ _______________

    D. $-12 + [(2 \times 4) \div (15 - 14)]$ _______________

    E. $155 \div [44 - (3 \times 12) - 7]$ _______________

21. What does the SETQ function do?

____

____

22. Define the terms "symbol" and "variable."

____

____

23. List three points that should be considered when assigning symbol names.

____

____

24. What is returned when the following expressions are evaluated?
    A. (setq NML (* 2 4)) _______________
    B. (setq AA AB) _______________
    C. (setq X 26 y "hello") _______________
    D. (setq X N) _______________
    E. (setq ABC (* (– 14 12) (/ 60 15))) _______________

25. How does the type of data supplied as arguments affect the operation of a function in an AutoLISP expression?

____

____

____

____

____

26. What is implied by the term "significant digit," and how many will AutoLISP actually display?

____

____

27. Explain how AutoLISP's handling of integers and reals could adversely affect the accuracy of division functions.

____

____

____

____

28. How are variables accessed and used as input for AutoCAD commands?

____

____

29. List several AutoLISP applications that could increase your AutoCAD productivity through using variables or mathematical expressions for input in AutoCAD commands.

____

____

____

____

____

30. Define "persistent AutoLISP."

____

____

____

____

PROGRAMMING PROBLEMS

1. Using the formula **1/2bh** where **b** is the length of the base and **h** is the height of a triangle, design an AutoLISP expression to find the area of the following triangles. Enter the expression at the Command: prompt of AutoCAD, then write your results and the expression used in the space provided.

1.0
1.25
1.13
0.5

Area: _______________

Expression: _______________

____

Area: _______________

Expression: _______________

____

2. Do problem 1 again, this time using symbols in the mathematical expression. For example, use SETQ to set a symbol named **b** to the length of the base and a symbol named **h** that represents the height. Then, enter the expression at the Command: prompt using the symbol names as arguments. The same expression works for either triangle, depending only on the values of the symbols. Write the expression in the space below:

____

____

____

3. Enter the following expressions for evaluation. Write the error message returned, then write a corrected version of the expression in the space provided. Be sure to test your work by entering the new expression for evaluation as well.

   (+4 4)

   Error message:____

   Corrected expression:____

   (– 6.25 .25)

   Error message:____

   Corrected expression:____

   (*8 2)

   Error message:____

   Corrected expression:____

   (/ 4.0 2.0

   Error message:____

   Corrected expression:____

   How did you return to the Command: prompt?____

Chapter 2
AutoLISP Program Files

Learning Objectives

After completing this chapter, you will be able to:

- ☐ Describe the format of an AutoLISP program file.
- ☐ Create and use AutoLISP program files.
- ☐ Define custom functions that may be used at the AutoCAD command line.

INTRODUCTION TO AUTOLISP PROGRAM FILES

A single, simple expression can be conveniently entered at AutoCAD's Command: prompt. However, this method is very slow and cumbersome when a series of functions must be performed or a complex expression is needed.

One way to handle such a situation is to type all of the desired AutoLISP expressions into a text file using a text editor. When needed, the file may be loaded and used as a single expression. By using this technique, any number of functions may be performed to produce the desired result. There are many advantages to using AutoLISP program files:

1. The expression only needs to be designed and written once, and may be used as necessary across any number of drawing sessions.
2. After the expression has been verified as being correct, there is no risk of troublesome typographical errors during later uses.
3. AutoCAD will read and evaluate the expressions much faster than they could be entered from the keyboard.

AUTOLISP FILENAMES

AutoLISP filenames abide by the rules governing your operating system. In Windows 95 and Windows NT, this means that a filename can be up to 256 characters in length. In versions of AutoCAD running in DOS-based or Windows 3.x environments, filenames are limited to eight characters in length (prior to the extension). AutoLISP files can use any desired file extension. However, the default and assumed file extension for an AutoLISP file is .LSP.

PROFESSIONAL TIP

The *.LSP* file extension is used for standard AutoLISP program files. This is the primary format used for most AutoLISP applications. In specialized applications where an AutoCAD menu is being created or modified, an AutoLISP support file may be used. Such a file will have a *.MNL* (MeNu Lisp) file extension, and will contain all of the AutoLISP code required by the customized menu. This type of file is discussed in later chapters. Note also, that *any* file extension is acceptable as long as both the filename and extension are specified when loading the program. Even so, in most cases it is best to use the .LSP extension for standard AutoLISP program files so that the file is easily identified.

EXERCISE 2-1

- ☐ Start the Windows Explorer.
- ☐ Using the Explorer, navigate to the \ACADR14 directory folder and open it.
- ☐ Now, open the BONUS folder, followed by opening the CADTOOLS folder.
- ☐ Pick the **Type** button at the top of the directory listing to sort the files.
- ☐ Using the scroll bar and arrows, if necessary, review the included AutoLISP filenames. Note that most of the names are very concise, and that many of the filenames seem to imply something about the function that they perform. This makes managing and using these files easier.

CREATING A PROGRAM FILE

One of the most efficient ways of executing AutoLISP statements is to compose them inside a program file. The file is then loaded into an AutoCAD drawing session for evaluation. Similar to the construction of other programming languages, AutoLISP utilizes a specific file format and a few special characters that affect the performance and readability of your programs. The following sections provide the necessary details concerning the creation and subsequent management of your program files.

Selecting a Text Editor

AutoLISP program files may contain only standard *ASCII* (American Standard Code for Information Interchange) characters. Only standard text characters can be used in AutoLISP files. No special page formatting codes, as used by many word-processing applications, is allowed. Although no specific text editing program is recommended or required, the program used must be able to create ASCII files.

When selecting a text editor, choose one with which you are comfortable. If you are used to using a specific program for editing text, it may be most productive to continue using it – as long as it can create ASCII files. If you are not experienced with text editors, you will want to select one that is easy to use. In Windows 95 and Windows NT, the Notepad program, Fig. 2-1, provides an excellent editor for creating and editing AutoLISP program files. To access Notepad, pick the **Start** button on the Windows taskbar and open Programs. Then, select the Accessories group and pick Notepad.

It is important to remember that some word-processing programs utilize special internal codes to control page formatting. These codes are used to indicate bold and italic text, as well as margins, indentations, and various other screen and printer formatting specifications. If these codes are found in an AutoLISP program file, they will not be understood and may cause unexpected errors when the file is loaded. If you are using a word processor such as MS Word or WordPerfect, be sure to specify a *non-document* mode (ASCII Text) when saving the file.

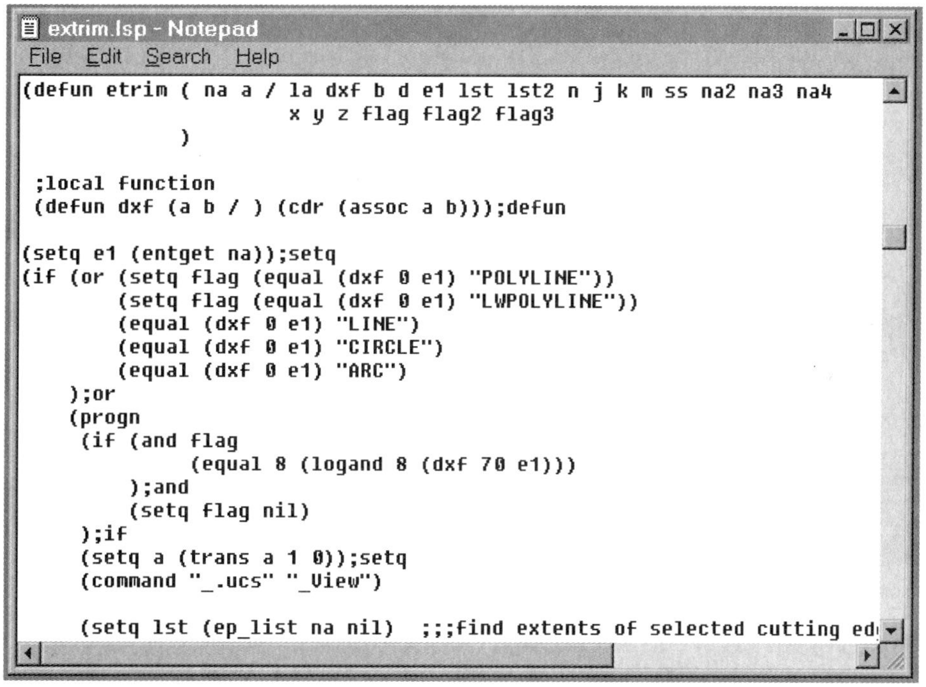

extrim.lsp - Notepad

File Edit Search Help

```
(defun etrim ( na a / la dxf b d e1 lst lst2 n j k m ss na2 na3 na4
                      x y z flag flag2 flag3
             )

 ;local function
 (defun dxf (a b / ) (cdr (assoc a b)));defun

(setq e1 (entget na));setq
(if (or (setq flag (equal (dxf 0 e1) "POLYLINE"))
        (setq flag (equal (dxf 0 e1) "LWPOLYLINE"))
        (equal (dxf 0 e1) "LINE")
        (equal (dxf 0 e1) "CIRCLE")
        (equal (dxf 0 e1) "ARC")
    );or
    (progn
     (if (and flag
              (equal 8 (logand 8 (dxf 70 e1)))
         );and
         (setq flag nil)
     );if
     (setq a (trans a 1 0));setq
     (command "_.ucs" "_View")

     (setq lst (ep_list na nil)  ;;;find extents of selected cutting ed
```

Fig. 2-1. Notepad can be used to create and edit AutoLISP files.

PROFESSIONAL TIP

When working in Windows and using NOTEPAD, you can have both AutoCAD and NOTEPAD active simultaneously. Setting up the AutoCAD and NOTEPAD windows such that both are visible at the same time allows greater programming speed and flexibility. By simply picking somewhere in the window you want active, you can switch from one application to the other instantly, without having to wait on the text editor to load or unload. In this manner, you can also view the effects of your AutoLISP code in AutoCAD, while viewing the program source code. This can be a big help when developing or "debugging" your AutoLISP program.

Parentheses

As discussed in Chapter 1, each individual AutoLISP expression must be enclosed within parentheses. The parentheses tell AutoCAD that the input is not a standard command, but rather an AutoLISP expression. AutoCAD then passes the input to the AutoLISP interpreter for evaluation. This occurs whether you are entering a single expression or loading a program file.

The most important aspect to remember regarding parentheses is to enclose an expression with an opening parenthesis "(" in front of the expression and a closing parenthesis ")" at the end. See Fig. 2-2.

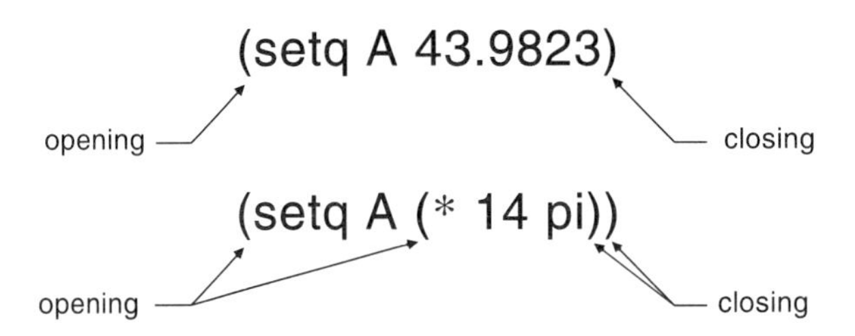

Fig. 2-2. Parentheses play a *critical* role in an AutoLISP expression.

When expressions are nested, each individual expression inside the overall expression must be properly enclosed. A quick method to check usage of parentheses is to "step" through the expression one character at a time and count the parentheses. Begin at zero, and *add 1* to your total each time an opening parenthesis is encountered. *Subtract 1* for each closing parenthesis. Fig. 2-3 illustrates this technique. The idea, of course, is to end up with a total of zero. If your total is not zero, then carefully check all of your parentheses for correct placement. This method works well for both individual expressions and program files, but will not show misplaced parentheses–just missing or extra ones.

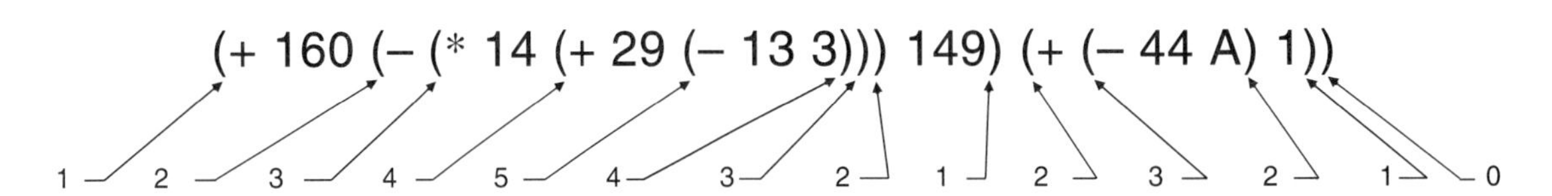

Fig. 2-3. A method of ensuring the proper number of parentheses are included in an expression.

AutoLISP File Format

As previously mentioned, only standard ASCII text characters can be used for AutoLISP expressions and program files. Other than this restriction, the data format within the file is very flexible.

- A long expression may be divided *as desired* and written on two or more consecutive lines.
- Indentation (spaces and tabs) may be used as desired, and will not affect the program's operation in any way.
- In most cases, uppercase and lowercase text may be used and even mixed in the same expression with few adverse results.

Quotation Marks

Quotation marks are used to indicate that the enclosed data is to be read as a text string, and not as a symbol or a function name. The first quotation mark is considered as an opening quotation mark, and all data following will be read as a text string until a closing quotation mark is encountered.

If the opening quotation marks are omitted (or none are used at all), the data is read as a function instead of a text string and an error is returned. Likewise, if a text string is not properly terminated with a closing quotation mark, an error will be created when AutoLISP attempts to evaluate the expression. The first example that follows shows the correct way to enter the expression. The remainder of the examples show error messages you may encounter from time to time.

Command: **(setq A "OK")** ↵
"OK"

Sets A to "OK" and returns "OK". Remember that if a spacebar is used to initiate an expression, the returned data begins on the same line as the expression. If an ENTER is used to initiate an expression, the ENTER keystroke denotes a carriage return and has the effect of starting a new line. (It is assumed here and in other examples in the book that the ENTER keystroke should be considered the standard.)

Command: **(setq A "OK)** ↵
1〉" ↵
1〉**)** ↵
"OK)\n"

The text string is still open, and the initial closing parenthesis is interpreted as part of the text string. Here, a closing quote is required to end the string, and a closing parenthesis is requested to close the entire expression. The returned string includes the misplaced parenthesis and a newline character.

In these examples, everything between quotation marks is read as a single text string and a single argument, and is assigned to the symbol A. AutoLISP has several of its own control codes for text characters. One of these appears in the second example, where the "\n" is shown. This control code indicates a *newline* and continues the text string on a new line. There are several other control codes that will be discussed later, along with AutoLISP's many text-related functions.

Let's Review...

1. In most cases (except for simple expressions), it is recommended that you create a text file, rather than typing the entire program at the AutoCAD Command: prompt.
2. An AutoLISP program file is an AutoLISP expression or sequence of several expressions saved as a text file for later use.
3. The text editor used to create AutoLISP programs must be able to output a standard ASCII text file.
4. Parentheses must be carefully managed when writing a complex expression. Similarly, quotation marks must be used correctly to avoid errors in the evaluation of an expression.

WRITING YOUR FIRST AUTOLISP PROGRAM

An AutoLISP program file is to AutoLISP as a script file is to AutoCAD. The file is read, and each complete and correct expression is evaluated sequentially until the end of the file is reached. If an error is encountered, the processing of the program file is halted (similar to an erroneous script file in AutoCAD) and an error message is displayed.

EXERCISE 2-2

- ☐ This exercise presents a sequence of simple mathematical expressions, which pass the returned results to the SETQ functions. This, in turn, sets values for the symbols A, B, and C.
- ☐ Use a text editor to create a program file with the following expressions. Name the file ABC.LSP.

```
(setq A (/ 100 4))
(setq B (+ A 75))
(setq C (/ B A))
```

- ☐ Check everything carefully to ensure that all characters are entered correctly. Save the file, exit your text editor, and re-enter AutoCAD.

USING AN AUTOLISP FILE

The *LOAD function* causes AutoLISP to read a program file, check for syntax errors, and evaluate the expressions. The LOAD expression in the following example is supplied with only one argument. The argument is FILENAME. The syntax for the LOAD function is:

```
(load FILENAME [ONFAILURE])
```

Note that when a LOAD expression is used, the AutoLISP filename is a string expression (enclosed within quotation marks). In addition, note that the .LSP file extension is *not* required. The LOAD function looks only for AutoLISP program files, so the .LSP extension is assumed and does not need to be supplied. If the file extension is anything other than .LSP, it must be specified. It is recommended that all AutoLISP files you generate have a .LSP file extension.

A drive letter and a directory prefix may also be supplied, if necessary. However, when indicating a directory prefix, a single backslash character " \" may not be used. Instead, a forward slash as in "C:/LISP/FILENAME" or a double backslash as in "C:\\LISP\\FILENAME" must be used. If a directory prefix is not specified, AutoLISP searches the AutoCAD *library path.* The library path includes the current directory, AutoCAD program files directory, and any other directories specified in the Support File Search Path set using the Preferences command. See your AutoCAD Command Reference for more information on using the Preferences command and setting up the support path.

Now use the LOAD function to run the ABC.LSP program file you created in Exercise 2-2:

Command: **(load "ABC")** ↵ 4	*the program file is read, the expressions are evaluated, and the result is returned*

Notice that the only value returned is that of the *final* expression evaluated within the file. Each expression has been evaluated and each function has been applied as specified, but when evaluating a series of functions, only the value of the last expression evaluated is returned to the command line by AutoLISP. If the LOAD function fails, check the following:

1. Was the LOAD function properly entered?
2. Is the file located on the AutoCAD library path?
3. Is the file named properly with an .LSP extension?
4. Is the file content exactly as specified?

An optional second argument–the ONFAILURE argument–may also be provided within a LOAD expression. In the following example, the LOAD expression contains a second argument that is returned when the LOAD fails:

Command: **(load "XYZ" "Error: File not loaded")**↵ "Error: File not loaded"	*the file was not found; the LOAD function failed and returned the value of the second argument*

PROFESSIONAL TIP

Reasons for a load failure might be due to either an internal error in the AutoLISP program code, or even that the specified file does not exist where the LOAD expression is looking for it. Depending on the reason for the load failure, the ONFAILURE argument may be used to do more than simply display an error message. Any expression may be placed here for evaluation in the event that the LOAD expression fails. For example, if a specific file fails to load, the ONFAILURE argument might specify an alternate path to search or even a different file to load, or it could be an expression that invokes a file dialog box to enable the user to find the program file manually. There are many ways to use the ONFAILURE argument to make the LOAD expression more forgiving of some error conditions.

Displaying a Symbol Value

In the last chapter, you learned that the exclamation mark (!) may be entered with a symbol at the Command: prompt to return the value of that symbol. Within the ABC.LSP file, values were assigned to the symbols A, B, and C. Now use the exclamation mark with each symbol to return the values of all three symbols. For example:

```
Command: !A ↵
25
```

Even though the result of each expression was not displayed, this shows that each of the expressions were evaluated.

IMPORTANCE OF DOCUMENTATION

Effective AutoLISP programming requires more than merely understanding the language. Several concepts must be mastered in order to become a skilled programmer. One of the most important of these concepts is proper documentation of your programs.

The depth of documentation in your programs will have a profound effect on both you *and* others who use your programs. Documentation supplies supportive information on how to interpret the file, thereby providing an effective means to debug your program. *Debugging* means to find and correct any trouble spots within the program, or to work out the "bugs." While learning to use AutoLISP, you will find that much of the time spent on any program you write will be debugging it. If you properly document the program, your debugging time will be much more productive because it will be easier to find the problem area.

Using Semicolons

The AutoLISP language provides the option of documenting a program within the program file itself. The only requirement for documentation is that it is clearly marked as being a *comment,* and not program data.

The character used to indicate a comment is the semicolon (;). When a semicolon is encountered in a program file, AutoLISP ignores any data following it on the same line. Therefore, whenever you wish to enter a comment in your file that is not an AutoLISP expression, simply precede it with a semicolon. Any text beyond the semicolon to the end of the line is considered a comment. Note that a comment may start at the beginning of a line *or* following an AutoLISP expression. If a comment uses more than one line in the file, be sure to begin *each* comment line with a semicolon. For example:

```
; SAMPLE.LSP written by R. Friend, January 19XX
; This program sets the value of "n" to 1, then doubles it.
(setq n 1)          ; set n to 1
(setq n (* n 2))    ; set n to 2n
```

This example is an illustration of the most efficient format for in-file documentation. First, a section is placed at the head of the file which states its overall purpose, followed by a line-by-line sequence of statements briefly describing what each line is intended to do. This way, you not only document *what* happens, but *when* and *where* in the program it occurs.

AutoCAD/AutoLISP Release 14 also offers in-line documentation. Any text found within the string ;| ... |; is considered to be a comment. Examples of this format include:

```
(setq R1   ;| A real number setting   |; 10.25)

(setq R2 230.5)   ;| The variable R2 is set to 230.5
This is a loading factor for calculating stresses in
high-rise rigid steel structures   |;

(setq R3   ;| Third setting |; 5.75)
```

Although it is difficult to see where the arguments for each SETQ expression are located, all three symbols R1, R2, and R3 are set to the real number values of 10.25, 230.5, and 5.75, respectively.

Exercise care when documenting your programs this way. By omitting semicolons within a program, or by placing random comments inside your expressions, the consistency of "clean" documentation is lost. In addition, you run the risk of AutoLISP halting due to improper marking of comments.

For good examples of proper documentation, examine some of the AutoLISP files found in the BONUS\CADTOOLS subdirectory of the AutoCAD directory.

The greatest advantage to effective documentation of your program is its use as a debugging tool. When you find something is not working correctly, it is much easier to locate the incorrectly constructed expression.

Another advantage of using proper documentation, which is not quite so obvious, will become evident when you revise a program written several months earlier. While the general purpose of the file may be understood, the finer details may be difficult to remember. If sufficient documentation has been included, the methods and purposes of each line will be much easier to follow.

Documentation is an important part of any AutoLISP program file. Develop the habit of inserting proper documentation into your programs as you write them.

PROFESSIONAL TIP

As you begin creating AutoLISP program files, refer frequently to Chapter 19 of this text for standards and guidelines on formatting your files. As you begin programming, learning to write easy-to-read programs that comply with accepted industry standards will build good habits and help you develop a solid and sensible programming style.

EXERCISE 2-3

- ☐ Revise the ABC.LSP program file developed in Exercise 2-2 to include the documentation previously described.
- ☐ Use the LOAD function to run your program after adding the documentation to ensure it has been done correctly.

Let's Review...

1. A program file is to AutoLISP as a script file is to AutoCAD.
2. The LOAD function causes AutoLISP to read a program file. The FILENAME argument must be specified as a text string by enclosing it within quotation marks.
3. After the file has been read, AutoLISP displays only the returned value of the last expression evaluated within the file.
4. Any data following a semicolon is considered to be a comment and is ignored by AutoLISP.
5. Documentation is extremely useful in both debugging and revising a program file.
6. Documentation should always be done as the program is written.

DEFINING CUSTOM FUNCTIONS

A powerful feature of AutoLISP is its ability to define custom functions. *User-defined functions* allow you to combine many of the capabilities of AutoLISP functions into a single custom function. These custom functions may request user input to determine the operating parameters, print information on the screen, or even create or modify AutoCAD entities. In addition, they may be used to define new AutoCAD commands.

Before user-defined functions can be fully covered, you will need to be introduced to a few supportive concepts. This section will introduce you to these new concepts and prepare you to begin creating your own user-defined functions in AutoLISP.

GETting User Input

One of the biggest advantages to utilizing AutoLISP rather than a script file or menu macro is the ability to request specific user input. Since operating parameters may vary, the program may produce different results based on the user's specific needs. For example, if an AutoLISP program were created to draw a threaded hole, the variable parameters might be the hole size and location. Using AutoLISP, you can request user input to specify these values. Consequently, a program may have a different outcome each time it is used.

There are several AutoLISP functions that request user input; one of them is the GETPOINT function. The *GETPOINT function* requires the user to input a coordinate location using any standard AutoCAD coordinate entry method. When "GETPOINT" is encountered in an expression, the evaluation process pauses until a point is picked or a point coordinate is specified.

The GETPOINT function has two optional arguments. One argument–PT–acts as the base point for a rubberband feature. The optional PROMPT argument is a built-in prompt. The syntax for the GETPOINT function is:

```
(getpoint [PT] [PROMPT])
```

Let's examine possible uses of this function. First, GETPOINT may be used with no arguments at all. In this case, AutoLISP will display no message, it will merely pause and go no further until a point is entered or the function is canceled with the Esc key. The following example illustrates this technique.

Command: **(GETPOINT)** ↵ (4.54743 6.98083 0.0)	*AutoLISP pauses here, awaiting a point entry. Even if only a 2D point is entered or picked, a 3D point is returned.*

- MODIFY FLIPLINE LISP ROUTINE. TO "SWAP" LISP ROUTINE
  - MAKE IT SO IT SWAPS THE OBJECTS THE USER SELECTS, BASED ON A POINT SELECTION ON EACH OBJECT

It is important to note that the point value is returned in the form of a list. Remember that a list uses spaces to separate each individual element. In the previous example, a point was picked with a pointing device. The X coordinate is 4.54743, the Y coordinate is 6.98083, and the Z coordinate is 0.0. Note that a point coordinate list uses spaces, not commas as delimiters to separate the X, Y, and Z values.

Using Data Storage Lists

As shown in the previous example, AutoLISP stores the coordinates of a point in a *data storage list.* This type of list differs from an expression in that the first element is not a function name. If AutoLISP takes this list through the standard evaluation process, it attempts to evaluate the first element to determine the specified function. However, since the first coordinate is *not* a function name, AutoLISP returns an error. Data storage lists are not intended to be evaluated; rather, they are a holding cell for data. To prevent AutoLISP from evaluating a data item, the *QUOTE function* is used. For example:

Command: **(2.0 2.0 0.0)** ↵ error: bad function (2.0 2.0 0.0) *Cancel*	*the list is evaluated as an expression, but the first element is not a valid AutoLISP function*
Command: **(quote (2.0 2.0 0.0))** ↵ (2.0 2.0 0.0)	*the list is not evaluated, but rather accepted at face value; this value is then returned*

As you can see, the QUOTE function returns its argument without evaluating it. This data may then be supplied as an argument for another function.

Another option for specifying the QUOTE function is to use an apostrophe (') at the beginning of the data item. This method is preferable since it involves less typing and contains fewer parentheses. For example:

```
(quote (A B C D E))
```

...is the same as:

```
'(A B C D E)
```

Both options work identically in AutoLISP. However, the apostrophe technique (second option) will not work as valid input for an AutoCAD prompt unless it is nested within another expression. Remember, the first character of the input at the AutoCAD Command: prompt must be an opening parenthesis or exclamation mark in order for it to be passed to the AutoLISP interpreter.

The GETPOINT Arguments

The PT argument causes AutoLISP to use AutoCAD's rubberband line to extend between a base point and the current crosshair location. The rubberband line is only for visual effect, and disappears when a point is finally indicated. Regardless of any arguments provided, GETPOINT returns the coordinates of the point entered. One advantage of using the base point argument is that the rubberband line responds to AutoCAD's ORTHO setting. An example of the GETPOINT function follows.

Command: **(getpoint '(2.0 2.0 0.0))** ↵
(4.33421 6.19034 0.0)

AutoLISP pauses, awaiting the point entry. As the cursor is moved around on the screen, a rubberband line is maintained between the point 2.0,2.0,0.0 and the cursor position until the point is indicated.

In this example, the base point was supplied as a list. However, the quote function prevented the list from being evaluated as an expression.

Another way to specify the base point is with a symbol name having a point value assigned to it. For example:

Command: **(setq PT1 (getpoint))** ↵
(8.03574 4.99524 0.0)

The symbol PT1 is set to a coordinate value. The value is then returned.

Command: **(getpoint PT1)** ↵
(6.30445 2.11894 0.0)

PT1 evaluates to a list containing a point specification. The rubberband line is maintained until the GETPOINT is answered.

The other optional GETPOINT argument allows a built-in prompt to accompany the point request, as shown in the next example:

Command: **(getpoint "Pick a point: ")** ↵
Pick a point: **4,2** ↵
(4.0 2.0 0.0)

When evaluated, this expression issues the prompt and pauses for you to enter a point. It then returns the coordinate value.

The two arguments–PT and PROMPT– can be used in the same expression as well.

Command: **(getpoint '(4 4) "Select next point: ")** ↵
Select next point: **5,5** ↵
(5.0 5.0 0.0)

this combination returns results in the same format as any other GETPOINT expression

Remember, the GETPOINT function may be used with one, two, or no arguments. Which option is used depends on how you want the function to appear. One enhancement to the PROMPT argument is to insert the newline code (\n) at the beginning. This keeps consecutive prompts from being displayed on the same line. The first example that follows does not include the newline code; the second example does.

Command: **(getpoint "First point: ")(getpoint "Second point: ")** ↵

...prompts as...

First point: Second point:

Command: **(getpoint "First point: ")(getpoint "\nSecond point: ")** ↵

...prompts as...

First point:
Second point:

You will note that rubberbanding is not in effect in the previous two examples because the base point argument (PT) is not used.

PROFESSIONAL TIP

It is recommended that you design an AutoLISP program to look as "built-in" is possible. If a program has the look and feel of a standard AutoCAD command, it will help an inexperienced operator to feel confident about using it. In addition, if the program is to be marketed as third-party software, the amount of technical support required will be much less for a program that has a built-in feel. For example, integrating features such as rubberbanding and designing your prompts to be similar to AutoCAD's will help a program have this feel. Refer to Chapter 19 for more information.

EXERCISE 2-4

- ☐ Design each of the AutoLISP programs as directed below. Be sure that each program is fully documented. Then, run each program using the LOAD function.
- ☐ Use the GETPOINT function with no arguments to get user input for two points–PT1 and PT2. Name this file GPT1.LSP.
- ☐ Use the GETPOINT function with PROMPT arguments to get user input for two points–PTA and PTB. Name this file GPT2.LSP.
- ☐ Use the GETPOINT function with the required arguments to force a rubberband line, supply appropriate prompts, and set user input values to P1 and P2. Name this file GPT3.LSP.
- ☐ Evaluate the operation of each program. They all perform the same task, but which one has the best appearance and feel?

Printing Messages to the Screen

The *PROMPT function* allows a message to be printed to the screen. The PROMPT function is commonly used to print supplementary messages to the screen for user information, and to supply prompts for input request expressions that do not provide their own.

This function requires one argument, which is the text string to be displayed. The syntax for the PROMPT function is:

```
(prompt MESSAGE)
```

The PROMPT function will print the argument (MESSAGE) and return nil. For example:

Command: **(prompt "OK")** ↵ OKnil	*the argument "OK" is printed to the screen and nil is returned*

If no expressions follow the PROMPT function, then no further evaluation is done, and nil is returned. However, if expressions follow the PROMPT function, the result of the last expression evaluated is returned. Therefore, AutoLISP does not display nil after the printed message:

Command: **(prompt "Select point: ")(getpoint)** ↵ Select point: **4,3.5** ↵ (4.0 3.5 0.0)	*These statements are evaluated consecutively. The prompt is issued, then the GETPOINT function awaits a point. The point is returned, and nil is not displayed.*

In addition, the PROMPT function will print the value of a variable if that value is a text string. For example:

Command: **(setq E "HELLO")** ↵ "HELLO"	*the text string "HELLO" is assigned to the symbol E and "HELLO" is returned*
Command: **(prompt E)** ↵ HELLOnil	*the symbol E is evaluated and its value is printed; nil is returned*

If the PROMPT function is used without an argument, an error message is returned. If more than one argument is provided, the function is only applied to the first argument. For example:

Command: **(prompt)** ↵ error: too few arguments (PROMPT)	*an argument has not been supplied so the function has nothing to print*
Command: **(prompt "OK" "ABC")** ↵ OKnil	*with more than one argument, the PROMPT function is only applied to the first argument*

EXERCISE 2-5

- ☐ Edit the GPT3.LSP program (from Exercise 2-4) so that it begins its operation with the following message. Be sure to document your revision.

  "This program will set the values for points P1 & P2."

- ☐ Load and run the program to ensure it is correct.

Using AutoCAD Commands in AutoLISP

A simple method for entity handling is to use standard AutoCAD commands via the AutoLISP *COMMAND function.* (An *entity* is any object such as a line, circle, arc, block, etc.) The COMMAND function accepts any number of arguments. Each consecutive argument is in turn entered in response to AutoCAD's standard prompts. Keep in mind, if an incorrect response is given to the AutoCAD prompt it will produce unexpected results or even an error. (Advanced entity-handling functions that create, modify, and delete entities are discussed in Chapter 13.)

The best way to design an expression using the COMMAND function is to "step through" the AutoCAD command one step at a time, making sure all prompts are being correctly answered, and writing down the sequence. This will ensure that the expression is correct the first time. The syntax for the COMMAND function is as follows:

```
(command [ARGUMENTS] ...)
```

An example of an expression utilizing the COMMAND function is shown below:

```
Command: (command "LINE" "2,2" "4,4" "") ↵
LINE From point: 2,2
To point: 4,4
To point:
Command: nil
```

The COMMAND function sends AutoCAD's LINE command to the prompt. The coordinate 2,2 is then sent to the prompt, followed by 4,4 being sent to the prompt. The "" represents a null string which is equivalent to pressing the ENTER key at the prompt, which finishes the command sequence for the LINE command. The COMMAND function always returns nil.

If the evaluation of an AutoLISP expression or data item returns the required command line input, then it may be used in place of a text string. For example:

```
Command: (setq PT1 '(4 2)) ↵
Command: (command "LINE" '(6 4) PT1 '(4 6) "c") ↵
LINE From point:
To point:
To point:
To point: c
Command: nil
```

The COMMAND function sends the LINE command to the prompt. '(6 4) evaluates to (6 4), a valid point specification. PT1 evaluates to (4 2). '(4 6) evaluates to (4 6). "c" is sent to the prompt, causing the line to close. The COMMAND function always returns nil.

Note that point specifications may be given in either a 2D or 3D format. If a 2D format is used, the Z axis value will default to the current elevation setting. Therefore, if the current elevation is zero, a point specified as (4.0 2.0) is interpreted as (4.0 2.0 0.0).

PROFESSIONAL TIP

The AutoLISP COMMAND function can be employed in a variety of forms. Aside from a "standard" AutoCAD command sequence shown below...

(command "circle" '(1 1 0) 2.5)	*center at 1,1,0 and Radius = 2.5*

...the COMMAND function can be used as follows:

(command "circle")	*Begin the CIRCLE command; user completes the sequence*
(command ".arc")	*Begin the ARC command; user completes the sequence. A period preceding any command instructs AutoCAD to use the true definition for that command. This safeguards against any conflict with commands that have been redefined (via AutoLISP), and that use the same name.*
(command ".line" pause pause "")	*Begin the standard LINE command, pausing twice to select two points, then return to end the sequence. The "pause" mechanism is a built-in AutoLISP feature, and awaits user input in the form of a pick or keyboard entry. The "pause" feature should not be quoted.*
(command "_circle" '(2 2) "_d" 4)	*Begin the CIRCLE command, with the center at 2,2 and a diameter of 4. Preceding AutoCAD commands and options with the underscore character (_) automatically translates them to English when using a foreign language version of AutoCAD.*

(command ".line" pause pause "" "_circle" '(2 2) "_d" 4)

The two COMMAND expressions above are combined into one expression. Multiple COMMAND sequences may be merged in this manner. Caution must be exercised in order to produce statements that function properly.

(command "") — *supplies a command line return*

(command) — *supplies a cancellation to the command line, and terminates nearly all command sequences in progress*

(command ".dim" ".leader" PT1 PT2 ^C ^C ".insert" ...)

In a command sequence that requires a cancel, the characters ^C can be used as a cancel keystroke. In this example, the LEADER option is canceled, then the DIM command is canceled so that the Command: prompt is available for the INSERT command.

Each COMMAND function expression, like those detailed above, can be used at any time to enhance your program files. Similar examples of the COMMAND function will be illustrated throughout this text.

Putting it All Together

When used individually, the functions discussed to this point have limited application. However, when these functions are combined, a useful program can be created. The following example shows the composition of a program file which, when loaded, will draw a line between two user-specified points.

```
; 1LINE.LSP 1/17/XX Created by P. Dexter
; Draws a line between two variable points, to be input by user.
(prompt "\nThis program draws a line between two points...")        ; opening message
(setq PT1 (getpoint "\nEnter the starting point: "))                 ; gets PT1 location
(setq PT2 (getpoint PT1 "\nEnter the ending point: "))               ; gets PT2 location
(command "LINE" PT1 PT2 "")                              ; draws a line between PT1 and PT2
(prompt "\nDone.\n")                                                  ; closing message
```

Note that the last expression in the file uses the PROMPT function, and its value (nil) is returned by the program.

PROFESSIONAL TIP

The PROMPT function is a simple means of getting a message to the screen, but is not always used in professional applications because of its lack of versatility. A more commonly used function is the PRINC function, discussed fully in Chapter 7. The simplest use of the PRINC function utilizes the same syntax as the PROMPT function:

```
(princ STRING)
```

The STRING argument is any number of text characters enclosed in quotation marks. The PRINC function prints its argument to the screen, and returns the text string instead of nil (as is returned by PROMPT). For standard printing operations, these two functions operate much the same.

When a printing function is the last expression in an application, using PROMPT always causes *nil* to be returned. By using a PRINC expression with no argument, this can be avoided. For example:

```
(princ)
```

This expression prints a *null* character (nothing) and likewise *returns* a null character. Therefore, if **(princ)** is the last expression within the DEFUN expression, rather than returning *nil*, the program exits quietly–returning nothing.

To test this, edit your 1LINE.LSP file and place a **(princ)** expression as the final expression within DEFUN. Now when you run the program, nothing is returned.

EXERCISE 2-6

- ☐ Create a program that displays appropriate messages and prompts for the three points of a triangle, and then draws it using a polyline. Make sure the file is fully documented.
- ☐ Name the program TRIANGLE.LSP.
- ☐ Load and run the program to ensure that it is correct.

Defining New Functions

AutoLISP's built-in functions are at the heart of every AutoLISP application. There are many situations, however, when a task requiring a sequence of several expressions must be performed more than once to produce the desired results. Entering the same series of expressions over and over within a program file quickly becomes redundant. To efficiently handle these circumstances, AutoLISP allows new functions to be defined.

Defining new functions is accomplished by first designing the expressions that perform the desired task. Then, these expressions are assigned to a symbol name using the *DEFUN (DEfine FUNction) function.* Whenever this symbol name is evaluated by AutoLISP, the expressions assigned to it are then executed.

As previously mentioned, DEFUN is an acronym for DEfine FUNction. Once a function has been defined, it may then be used freely throughout the current drawing session. However, upon exiting from the current drawing and entering a new one, the function will need to be defined again in order to be used. For this reason, the process of defining functions is usually accomplished by loading a program file containing the DEFUN expressions.

The format for a DEFUN expression is shown below:

```
(defun SYMBOL ARGUMENT-LIST EXPRESSION ...)
```

Note that any number of expressions may be supplied. The symbol name must adhere to the rules for naming symbols discussed in Chapter 1.

The ARGUMENT-LIST. The ARGUMENT-LIST has two parts. The first part is a listing of the required arguments that must be supplied when calling the function. The second part of the ARGUMENT-LIST is for specifying local variables. *Local variables* are maintained only while the AutoLISP program is operating. In other words, if a variable is specified as being "local," it exists only inside the program. If a *global variable* (not specified as local) is used, it will retain its identity even after the AutoLISP program is complete. In addition, a global variable will maintain its value regardless of any local variables of the same name. In Fig. 2-4, one argument is specified and no variables are used. Therefore, no local variables are declared.

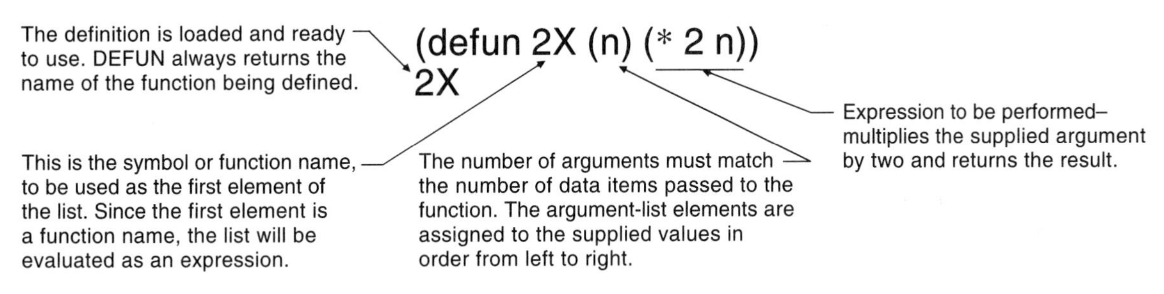

Fig. 2-4. Utilizing a DEFUN argument-list.

The format for using the 2X function in Fig. 2-4 is the function name followed by one required argument:

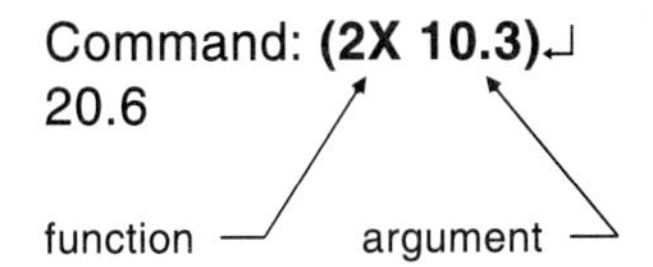

In this example, the 2X function is called and the real number 10.3 is assigned to the argument n. The function definition of (* 2 n) is then evaluated, which multiplies the required argument by 2, and returns the numerical result of 20.6. Another DEFUN application follows.

```
Command: (defun 2XADD (n1 n2) (+ (* 2 n1) n2)) ↵
2XADD
```

The 2XADD function requires two arguments; both must evaluate to numerical values. The first supplied argument will be multiplied by two, and its product will be added to the second supplied argument. There must be two arguments supplied or the function cannot perform properly. For example:

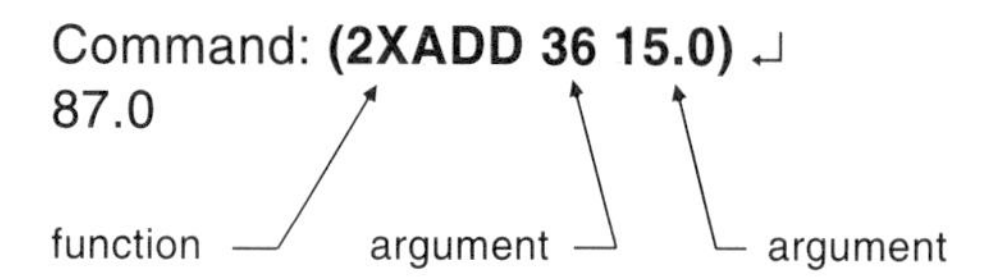

The integer 36 is assigned to n1, and the real number 15.0 is assigned to n2. The product of multiplying n1 and 2 is 72, and when added to n2 returns 87.0. Note that the value of the final expression is returned.

Local vs. Global Variables. All variables are global unless they are specified to be local. The value of a global variable is stored and remembered for the remainder of the current drawing session. It may be freely used or changed at any time.

Recall that specifying variables as being *local* means they are used exclusively within the function. Their values are not remembered after the function is complete. In addition, a local variable will not affect the value of a global variable using the same symbol name.

In most cases, it is recommended that you specify variables to be local. One exception is when a specific value associated with a variable will be used several times throughout a drawing session.

A variable is specified as being local to a function by including its symbol name in the ARGUMENT-LIST of the function definition. A forward slash (/) is used to separate the arguments from the local variables. Note that a function may not require any arguments or use any variables. Therefore, the ARGUMENT-LIST may contain both arguments and variables, arguments only, variables only, or even nothing at all. Consequently, an argument-list may appear as any of the following examples.

(ARGUMENT1 ARGUMENT2 ... / VARIABLE1 VARIABLE2 ...)
both arguments and variables are used

(ARGUMENT1 ARGUMENT2 ...) — *arguments only*

(/ VARIABLE1 VARIABLE2 ...) — *variables only*

() — *no arguments or variables are used*

EXERCISE 2-7

☐ Create a program file called 2X.LSP. Include the following expressions.

```
(setq w 14)
(defun 2X (n / w)
   (setq w "2X the value is: ")
   (prompt w)
   (* 2 n)
)
```

Symbol w is set globally to 14, and is then declared as a local variable within the defined function. A space is provided after the prompt to separate the text from the returned result.

☐ Load the file and enter an expression using the 2X function. Did the expression issue the prompt and return the proper result? Also, check the value of the variable **w** by entering "!w" at the Command: prompt. Even though **w** was reset to a text string within the function, the global value remains unchanged.

In Exercise 2-7, you will notice that a user-defined function always returns the value of the last expression evaluated. If the (* 2 n) expression were listed first, then this function would return the value of the PROMPT function. Keep this in mind when defining a new function so the desired result is returned.

Defining New AutoCAD Commands

AutoLISP provides two additional features that may be used to enhance user-defined functions. One of these features is the *C: option* for the function name. The other feature is the *S:: option.*

Using the C: Option. Preceding the user-defined function name with "C:" makes it accessible as an AutoCAD command. An important point here is that the C: indicates that it is an AutoCAD command. *It is not a reference to the computer's hard disk drive!*

In the following 1LINE.LSP program, the DEFUN function has been added using the command prefix option. It may now be used by entering "1LINE" at AutoCAD's Command: prompt. For example:

```
; 1LINE.LSP  1/17/XX  Created by P. Dexter
; Draws a line between two variable points, to be input by user.
; Revisions......2/17/XX–Changed program to a function definition with the C: option for
;                          command line accessibility.
(defun C:1LINE (/ PT1 PT2)                ; defines C:1LINE–PT1 & PT2 are local variables
  (prompt "\nThis program draws a line between two points...")     ; opening message
  (setq PT1 (getpoint "\nEnter the starting point: "))              ; gets PT1 location
  (setq PT2 (getpoint PT1 "\nEnter the ending point: "))            ; gets PT2 location
  (command "LINE" PT1 PT2 "")             ; draws a line between PT1 and PT2
  (prompt "\nDone.\n")                                              ; closing message
)
```

After creating this program, load it into AutoCAD using the LOAD function. AutoLISP returns the function name to the command line since the DEFUN expression is the last expression evaluated. If an error message is returned, go back and check your program against the example.

Once this command line function is defined, it can be used like any standard AutoCAD command. Type "1LINE" at AutoCAD's Command: prompt to invoke the function. For example:

Command: **(load "1LINE")** ↵
C:1LINE

Command: **1LINE** ↵
This program draws a line between two points...
Enter the starting point: *(pick a point)*
Enter the ending point: *(pick a point)*
Done.

This function can now be used as desired throughout the entire drawing session. Remember that when you exit this drawing session, this function definition will be forgotten by AutoCAD. You will have to load it again in the new drawing session in order to use it.

This particular aspect of AutoLISP is a great time-saving feature. Your productivity level will increase dramatically by finding those complex tasks (or even simple tasks that must be performed repeatedly), and defining a function that completes them with a single command entry.

PROFESSIONAL TIP

If a file named ACADR14.LSP exists on the library path, it will be loaded automatically each time you begin a drawing session. All of your most commonly used function definitions should be put into this file, so that each time you enter a drawing session, your custom functions will already be defined. If this file does not exist, simply create your own file with the desired function definitions and name it ACADR14.LSP. If it does exist, in most cases it can be freely modified as needed.

If you are using a third-party software package that has its own ACADR14.LSP file, be sure to check the documentation carefully prior to modifying the file.

In AutoCAD Release 10 or earlier versions, the C: option can be used for command line access to define keystroke options for AutoCAD's standard commands. For convenience, it is best to place these abbreviated command definitions in the ACAD.LSP file so that they are automatically loaded for each drawing session. For example:

```
(defun C:L () (command "LINE"))

(defun C:E () (command "ERASE"))
```

Beginning with AutoCAD Release 11, abbreviated commands can be defined within the ACAD.PGP file. These abbreviations, however, can only be used for invoking basic AutoCAD commands. For example, it is possible to define the keystroke "Z" to invoke the ZOOM command. On the other hand, it is not possible to construct an abbreviated ZOOM Previous command using this method.

For macros of this nature, AutoLISP's capabilities are needed. For example, to define a ZOOM Previous macro, the following AutoLISP code could be used:

```
(defun C:ZP () (command "ZOOM" "Previous"))
```

PROFESSIONAL TIP

As mentioned earlier in this chapter, a COMMAND function always returns *nil*. When defining new functions in AutoLISP, placing a **(princ)** expression as the last expression in the function definition allows a "quiet" exit from the function. For example, using the C:ZP function as defined above displays the following:

Command: **ZP** ↵
nil

The same function defined for a quiet exit appears as follows:

```
(defun C:ZP () (command "ZOOM" "Previous")(princ))
```

When using this version, *nil* is no longer returned:

Command: **ZP** ↵

Using the S::Startup Option. For AutoCAD Release 10 and later, only one automatically executed startup function exists–S::STARTUP. When S::STARTUP is included inside the ACADR14.LSP file, AutoLISP will evaluate any expressions contained within its definition. Since the function is automatically executed (hence the S:: prefix), no arguments to this DEFUN function are permitted.

A common use for this function is to do any desired setup operations upon beginning a drawing session. An example of the S::STARTUP program file is as follows:

```
(defun S::STARTUP ()
  (command ".limits" '(0 0) '(24 18)                   ; Set LIMITS
           ".zoom" "all"                                ; ZOOM all
           ".layer" "make" "Border" ""                  ; "Border" LAYER
           ".pline" '(0.5 0.5) '(23.5 0.5)              ; 1st and 2nd pts.
           '(23.5 17.5) '(0.5 17.5) "c"                 ; 3rd and 4th pts.
           ".layer" "make" "Draw" ""                    ; "Draw" LAYER
           ".text" '(1 1) 0.25 0.0 "PROJECT–1"          ; Supply TEXT
  ) ; End COMMAND
) ; ––( End of STARTUP )––
```

Upon entering the AutoCAD drawing editor, S::STARTUP would begin, and all expressions within it would be performed.

Note: Beginning with AutoCAD Release 12, there is another type of file that is automatically executed upon loading an AutoCAD menu file. This file has an .MNL extension, and must match the filename of the menu currently loaded in the AutoCAD drawing editor. AutoLISP statements may be contained within this .MNL file to assist the menu in its operations. For more information on .MNL files, see the *AutoCAD Customization Guide.*

Let's Review...

1. A great advantage of AutoLISP over script files and menu macros is the ability to request specific user input.
2. The GETPOINT function requests a coordinate point entry, and returns the point specification in the form of a list.
3. The GETPOINT function can issue a custom prompt and even draw a rubberband line if optional arguments are used.
4. The QUOTE function prevents AutoLISP from evaluating the data items immediately following it. This function may be abbreviated with an apostrophe.
5. It is important to give an AutoLISP program the look and feel of a built-in AutoCAD feature.
6. The PROMPT function is used to print a message to the screen. The PROMPT function always returns nil.
7. The DEFUN function can be used to define new function names in AutoLISP.
8. User-defined functions and variable values are lost upon leaving the drawing editor, and must be redefined in subsequent drawing sessions.
9. The ARGUMENT-LIST regulates the number of arguments to be supplied with a given function.
10. Arguments and local variables have value only within a function, and are immediately forgotten when the function is complete.
11. The C: option allows a function name to be used in the same manner as an AutoCAD command by entering its name at the Command: prompt.
12. The S::STARTUP function can be used in the ACADR14.LSP file to automatically perform a desired setup routine upon entering a drawing session.

CHAPTER TEST

Write your answers in the spaces provided.

1. What is the format for an AutoLISP program filename?

2. List the two most important factors in choosing a text editing program for AutoLISP program files.

3. What signals AutoLISP that certain data is to be read as a text string? Also, describe two potential errors associated with text strings.

4. What function causes AutoLISP to read a program file, and what is its principal argument?

5. What is the AutoCAD library path?

6. What are the acceptable ways to specify a path name when using the LOAD function?

7. When a program file is read, what value is returned?

8. Describe the advantages of proper documentation of AutoLISP program files.

9. What is the purpose of a semicolon in a program file?

10. Describe the use of the GETPOINT function and both of its optional arguments.

11. Describe the use of the QUOTE function. What are some possible applications?

12. Describe the PROMPT function. What are its most common uses?

13. What is the most important consideration when building an expression using the COMMAND function?

14. What circumstances would indicate a need for a custom user-defined function?

15. Explain the use of the ARGUMENT-LIST in the DEFUN function.

16. Explain the usage and purpose of the optional prefixes (C: and S::) when defining a function.

17. What is the difference between a local and a global variable? When should a variable be global?

18. What are the advantages of placing function definitions in the ACADR14.LSP file?

19. Why is it best to give a program a built-in look and feel? Describe some ways this can be accomplished.

20. Define the term "debug." Outline ways of making debugging easier.

PROGRAMMING PROBLEMS

1. Create an AutoLISP program file named CHAP2P1 which does the following. Be sure to include proper documentation.
   A. Defines a command function called EL, which erases the last entity drawn and displays a message when complete.
   B. Defines a command function called C3, which draws a 3-point circle using points input to the GETPOINT function.
   C. Displays a message when it has been loaded.
2. Create an AutoLISP file with three or more useful functions of your own design. It should be fully documented.
3. Modify your ACAD.PGP file to include a command to invoke your text editor.
4. Define a command line function called "TRI" that asks the user for three points, and then draws a closed polyline triangle using those point coordinates. Each of the point variables should be declared as local variables. Name the file TRI.LSP.
5. Define an AutoLISP function called "SQ" which squares a singular numerical argument. This user-defined function should appear as:

   ```
   (sq ARG)
   ```

   ...where ARG represents a numerical value that will be squared, and the result is returned to the user in combination with a text prompt.
6. Define at least 15 abbreviated commands, and incorporate them into your ACADR14.LSP file. Be sure to include full documentation.

BUBBLE.LSP

```
; BUBBLE.LSP  –  Bubble Lisp!
;
; Purpose:        This routine defines a command line access function C:BB
;                 that draws a callout bubble and leader.
;                 The user inputs the bubble location, 1 to 3 character
;                 alphanumeric designation, and leader line origin.
;
; Assumptions:    A block definition named BB exists in the current drawing or
;                 on the ACAD path.  This block consists of a 5/16" diameter
;                 circle with a single attribute– –the insertion point is the
;                 center of the circle.  The attribute definition is 1/8" text
;                 Middle-Center justified at the center of the circle.


(defun C:BB (/ BC PC PT1 PT2)                         ;Defun & local variables
  (setq BC (getpoint "\nPick bubble location: ")       ;Get Bubble Center point...
        PC (getstring "\nPart Callout: ")              ;Get Part Callout...
  )
  (command "INSERT" "BB" BC 1 1 0 PC)                  ;Insert block, specify attr.
  (setq PT1 (getpoint "\nLeader start point: ")        ;Get leader origin
        PT2 (polar BC (angle BC PT1) (/ 5.0 32))       ;Find intersection of leader
  )                                                    ;   and circle.
  (command "DIM" "LEADER" PT1 PT2 ^C ^C)               ;Draw leader, halt before
)                                                      ;   dog–leg and text entry.

;
;– –〈End of File〉– –
```

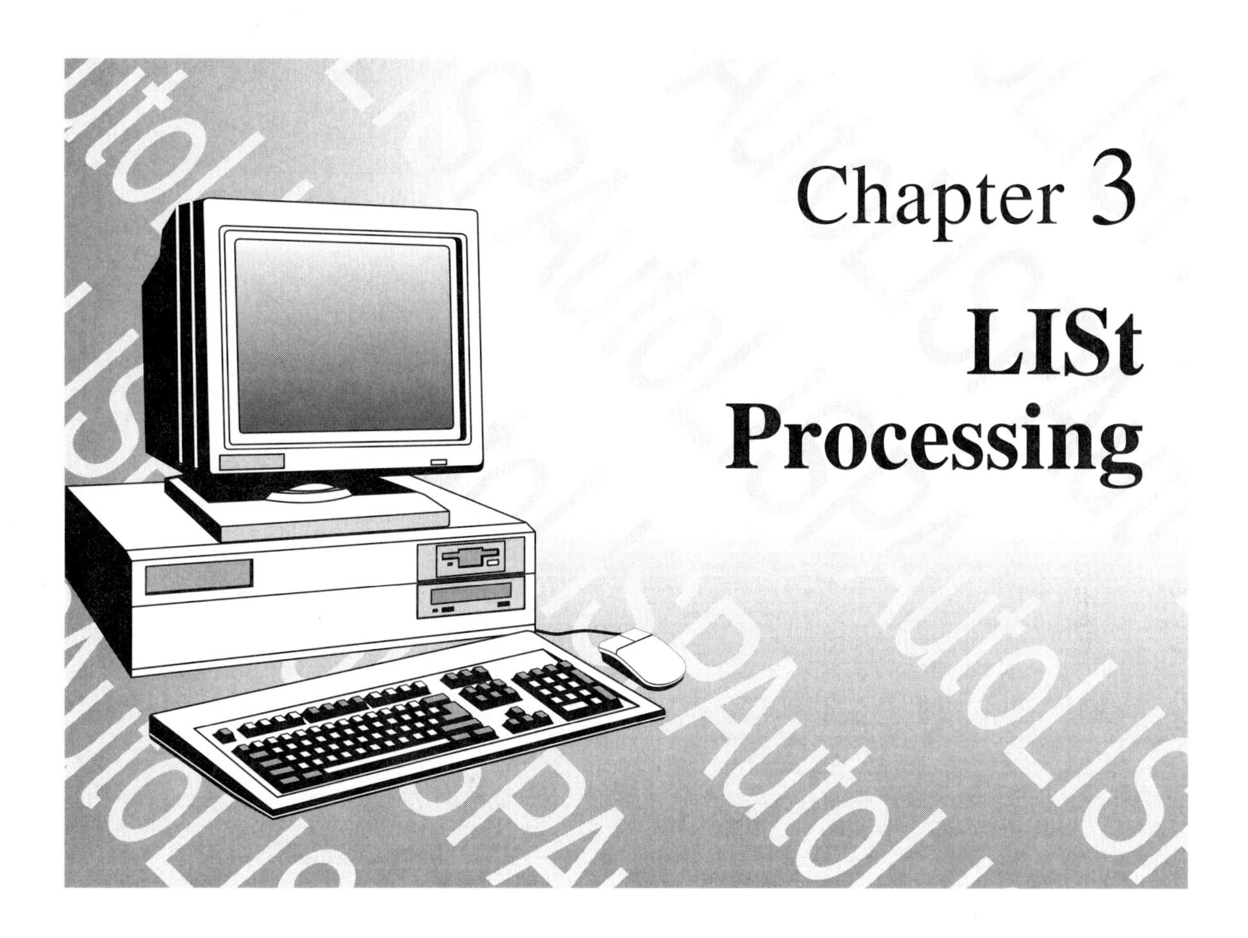

Chapter 3
LISt Processing

Learning Objectives

After completing this chapter, you will be able to:

- ☐ Define a list and explain its usage.
- ☐ Create data storage lists.
- ☐ Derive new point coordinates from existing point coordinate lists.
- ☐ Explain list manipulation through extracting elements and reconstructing lists for efficient data storage.

LISTS

The real processing power of AutoLISP originates in its ability to create, store, and manipulate lists. As previously discussed, there are three primary types of lists:

- **Expression List:** Contains a function as its first element, with all remaining elements utilized as arguments. This type of list requires evaluation.
- **Point Coordinate List:** A quoted list (to prevent evaluation) containing numbers representing either an X,Y or an X,Y,Z location. This list type is actually nothing more than a data storage list, but the information within must correspond to a point coordinate.
- **Data Storage List:** This quoted list may be a repository for any type of data. It is the fundamental information container within AutoLISP.

Creating Lists

Efficient data handling is an important part of productive programming with AutoLISP. Using individual variables for single data items (called *atoms*) may not always be a practical solution. In a situation where many separate atoms must be stored for future use, it can become quite a challenge to generate enough variable names, assign each one as required, and effectively manage them.

When it is necessary to handle large amounts of information, a better approach is to store the data in lists. A list with any number of elements may be assigned to a single variable name, thereby simplifying access and handling for each individual item. One method of creating a list is with the LIST function:

```
(list EXPRESSION ...)
```

Command: **(setq L1 (list "FLOOR1" "TABLE" 37.6 '(2.0 2.0 0.0) "CHAIR"))** ↵
("FLOOR1" "TABLE" 37.6 (2.0 2.0 0.0) "CHAIR")

In this example, list L1 has five elements. Note that these elements may be any data type. A list may also be an element of another list. In the previous example, one supplied argument to the LIST function is a quoted list containing three real numbers (which could be used as a point coordinate).

The LIST function evaluates each non-quoted argument prior to building the list. Expressions that are provided as arguments for the LIST function are evaluated, and the returned value is actually what is incorporated into the list. The following example demonstrates this concept:

Command: **(setq L2 (list (+ 14 24) (getpoint "\nPick a point: ")))** ↵ Pick a point: *(pick a point on the screen)* (38 (2.5633 6.051 0.0))	 *evaluation of the GETPOINT expression causes this prompt; both results are put into a list*

First, the arguments are evaluated. The results of the evaluations are then incorporated into a single list.

When a variable name is provided as an argument, the value of that variable will appear in the created list as shown in the following example:

Command: **(setq N 4 S "String")** ↵ "String"	*N is set to 4 and S is set to "String"; "String" is returned*
Command: **(setq L3 (list N S))** ↵ (4 "String")	*both variables are evaluated by the LIST function*

If it is necessary to evaluate some elements to be added to a list, while leaving others unevaluated, then use the QUOTE function as follows:

Command: **(setq L4 (list N 'S))** ↵ (4 S)	*N evaluates to 4, and S has not been evaluated; the variable (rather than its value) is put into the list*

Sometimes it will be necessary to assemble a list without first evaluating each element. The QUOTE function may be used to do this. Compare the following example to the previous setting of L2.

Command: **(setq L5 '((getpoint "\nPick a point: ") (+ 3 4)))** ↵
((getpoint "\nPick a point: ") (+ 3 4))

The QUOTE function has been abbreviated in this example, but the above expression could also be written as:

Command: **(setq L5 (quote ((getpoint "\nPick a point: ") (+ 3 4))))** ↵
((getpoint "n\Pick a point: ") (+ 3 4))

Note that the QUOTE function returns a single argument that is left unevaluated. In the previous example, the returned value is a list containing two unevaluated elements.

Instead of evaluating these two expressions, they are taken at face value and directly incorporated into the list. When using the QUOTE function to create a list, AutoLISP acts as though each element were quoted and performs no evaluation. Compare the next expression to the setting of L3 in one of the previous examples:

Command: **(setq L6 '(N S))** ↵
(N S)

Being able to store data in its unevaluated state allows for a great degree of flexibility in information management.

Point Coordinate Lists

A point coordinate list may be assembled automatically or manually. The *GETPOINT function* returns a selected point as a list of three real numbers automatically. If it is desirable to include the optional POINT argument, it may be provided by creating a list of real numbers:

```
(getpoint (list 2.0 4.0 0.0) "\nPick a point: ")

(getpoint (quote (2.0 4.0)) "\nPick a point: ")

(getpoint '(2.0 4.0 0.0) "\nPick a point: ")
```

Any of these methods are acceptable for point coordinate specification requirements within AutoLISP. Note that either an X,Y or an X,Y,Z coordinate location may be specified.

Let's Review...

1. There are three primary types of lists: expressions, point coordinate lists, and data storage lists.
2. By using a list, many different data items may be stored as a unit and given a single variable name.
3. The LIST function evaluates each of its arguments and assembles them as a list.
4. The QUOTE function returns a single argument that is unevaluated. If the argument consists of data items enclosed in parentheses, the returned value is a list.
5. Point coordinate lists are merely data lists with two or three real numbers as elements.

EXERCISE 3-1

☐ Using the variables and values provided, determine the returned result of each of the following expressions.

A = 15.0 B = "OK" C = '(2.0 1.5) D = "ABC" E = 23 X = E

A. (list "DEF" D) ______________________________
B. (list 4.5 8.2 A) ______________________________
C. (list "ABC" D "A" a) ______________________________
D. (list 5 6 (list 9 10)) ______________________________
E. (setq p '(a b c)) ______________________________
F. (quote (a b c d e x)) ______________________________
G. (list e x) ______________________________
H. (list (quote a)) ______________________________
I. (setq L8 '(e x a)) ______________________________
J. (setq L9 (list e x a)) ______________________________
K. (list c) ______________________________
L. (setq L10 '(c A (list d b))) ______________________________
M. (list (+ a E) x) ______________________________
N. (setq L11 '((+ a E) x)) ______________________________

BASIC LIST MANIPULATION

Elements or expressions assembled within lists allow for a variety of options for the user with regard to data storage. In the previous two chapters, variables were primarily regarded as having only one distinct value at a time:

Command: **(setq M "X")** ↵ — *variable M is assigned the string value of "X"*
"X"

On the other hand, variables that represent lists may contain any number of elements:

Command: **(setq N (list "X" "Y" "Z"))** ↵ — *variable N holds three specific elements*
("X" "Y" "Z")

Upon evaluation, the returned list of ("X" "Y" "Z") offers more input opportunities than does the single value "X." However, to use this to your advantage, certain methods must be employed to break down the contents of the variable N. One group of AutoLISP functions makes it possible to extract individual items such as real numbers or text strings from the original list. This provides a powerful means for managing data.

The CAR Function

The *CAR function* serves as the basic tool for returning the first element of a list. The format for this AutoLISP function is:

(car LIST)

The following examples illustrate the use of the CAR function:

AutoLISP Expression		
(car (list "A" "B" "C"))	returns "A"	*the function returns the first element of the list, which is "A"*
(car '(D E F))	returns D	*element D, which is a quoted and unevaluated variable in this list, is the first element*
(car (list 7.59 6.38 4.81))	returns 7.59	*this list of three real numbers has 7.59 as its first argument*
(car '())	returns nil	*the quoted list contains no members, and upon evaluation by the CAR function returns a value of nil*
(setq HUE (car '("RED" "BLUE")))	returns "RED"	*"RED" is the first element of the list, and is assigned to the variable HUE*

The following AutoLISP expression creates a variable called PTA by implementing the GETPOINT and SETQ functions:

Command: **(setq PTA (getpoint "\nPick any location in your drawing: "))** ↵
Pick any location in your drawing: (8.52 7.19 1.23) *X,Y,Z point (8.52 7.19 1.23) is chosen; (the SNAP value is set to 0.01)*

Applying the CAR Function. Use the CAR function to your advantage when writing programs. For example:

Command: **(car PTA)** ↵ *the function yields the X-axis coordinate*
8.52

This AutoLISP statement returns the first element of the list assigned to PTA, while the remaining elements within the list are "ignored." However, the variable PTA retains the value (8.52 7.19 1.23) until SETQed to something different. Check for the value of variable PTA by typing "!PTA" at the Command: prompt. The following program returns the X-axis coordinate of point list PTA:

```
; XCOORD.LSP written by R. Starr, Mar. 19XX
; This program prompts the user to input a coordinate,
; and retrieves the X–axis component of the point list.
(defun xcoord (/ PTA)
  (setq PTA (getpoint "\nPick any location in your drawing: "))
  (prompt "\nThe X–axis coordinate value is: ") (car PTA)
)
```

PROFESSIONAL TIP

Occasionally, a text string is required as a response for an AutoCAD request, such as one issued for the TEXT command. Make sure the AutoCAD TEXTEVAL system variable is set to 1. This provides evaluation for AutoLISP input at the Text: prompt. The following illustration applies the CAR function to a list:

Command: **SETVAR** ↵
Variable name or ?: **TEXTEVAL** ↵
New value for TEXTEVAL ⟨0⟩: **1** ↵

Command: **(setq ROOF '("SHINGLES" "SHAKES" "ALUMINUM"))** ↵
("SHINGLES" "SHAKES" "ALUMINUM")

Command: **TEXT** ↵
Justify/Style/⟨Start point⟩: *(pick a point)*
Height ⟨0.2000⟩: ↵
Rotation angle ⟨0⟩: ↵
Text: **(car ROOF)** ↵ *returns the first element "SHINGLES" to the screen*

With the TEXTEVAL system variable set to 0, the input is interpreted literally, and the returned text string is "(car ROOF)" instead of "SHINGLES".

The CDR Function

The *CDR function* returns a new list excluding the first element of the original list. The syntax for this AutoLISP function is as follows:

```
(cdr LIST)
```

The CDR function works opposite to the CAR function. Rather than extracting the initial member of a list as the CAR function does, the CDR function will ignore the first element and return the remainder of the list. Examine the following expressions.

AutoLISP Expression		
(cdr (list "A" 5.5 "10.75"))	returns (5.5 "10.75")	*the CDR function ignores the first element "A" leaving a remaining list of (5.5 "10.75")*
(cdr '((D E F G) H I))	returns (H I)	*the returned list of variables (H I) remains after the element (D E F G) is "dropped" from the quoted list*

AutoLISP Expression

(cdr '())	returns nil	*the quoted list contains no members, and upon evaluation by the CDR function, returns a value of nil*
(setq YZ (cdr '("x" "y" "z")))	returns ("y" "z")	*the list of ("y" "z") is returned and is assigned to the variable YZ*

The CDR function is typically used to omit an unwanted element from a list. The variable ROOF, from a previous CAR function example, may be altered in order to return a partial list:

Command: **(setq ROOF '("SHINGLES" "SHAKES" "ALUMINUM"))** ↵
("SHINGLES" "SHAKES" "ALUMINUM")

Command: **(setq ROOF (cdr ROOF))** ↵ — *the variable ROOF is reset to the CDR of the list*
("SHAKES" "ALUMINUM")

In this example, the first item SHINGLES is dropped, and the variable ROOF now represents a portion of the original list. Recycling symbols is a good practice that often returns values that are better suited for future programming applications.

AutoLISP variables that are recycled (reset to other values within the same routine) create less overhead for the programmer. Therefore, programs that employ only a small number of user-defined variables are easier to maintain and "track" the actual variable usage. The following example, which uses the C:ROOFLIST program shown below, demonstrates this concept by manipulating a data list (the variable ROOF) with the AutoLISP CAR and CDR functions:

```
; Program Name: ROOFLIST.LSP
; Author: A.S. Phalt
: January 3, 19XX
; Purpose: To print all text elements found inside
;          a list with the AutoCAD TEXT command.
;
(defun C:ROOFLIST (/ ROOF)
  (setq ROOF '("SHINGLES" "SHAKES" "ALUMINUM"))  ; List ROOF is assembled
  (prompt "\nPick Text start pt.: ")
  (command ".TEXT" pause)               ; Begin TEXT command–1st pause
                                        ;   allows user to select start point
  (prompt "\nText height: ")            ; Height is needed–this pause
  (command pause 0.0 (car ROOF))        ;   allows the user to set height.
                                        ; (car ROOF) is first text element of ROOF –
                                        ;   "SHINGLES"
  (setq ROOF (cdr ROOF))                ; Reset ROOF to CDR of ROOF.
  (command ".TEXT" "" (car ROOF))       ; (car ROOF) is first text element
                                        ;   of recycled variable ROOF – "SHAKES"
  (setq ROOF (cdr ROOF))                ; Reset ROOF to CDR of ROOF.
  (command ".TEXT" "" (car ROOF))       ; (car ROOF) is first text element
                                        ;   of recycled variable ROOF – "ALUMINUM"
)                                       ; End of C:ROOFLIST
```

Command: **SETVAR** ↵
Variable name or ?: **TEXTEVAL** ↵
New value for TEXTEVAL ⟨0⟩: **1** ↵

set TEXTEVAL = 1 to evaluate AutoLISP code

```
Command: (load "ROOFLIST") ↵                    load the ROOFLIST program file
C:ROOFLIST

Command: ROOFLIST ↵                             execute the program file
Pick Text start pt.: (pick a start point)
Text height: (specify a height)
```

The C:ROOFLIST program asks the user for two pieces of information–the starting point for placing text and the text height. Each data item from variable ROOF (a list of three text strings) is, in turn, written to the graphics screen. By using the CAR and CDR functions, only one symbol is utilized to complete this task–the variable ROOF.

Let's Review...

1. The CAR function extracts the first element of a list, typically returning a singular data type such as a real number, integer, string, or symbol.
2. The CDR function is commonly used when it is desirable to delete the first element of list. The returned value usually takes the form of a list.

EXERCISE 3-2

☐ Solve the following AutoLISP expressions and write the returned result in the spaces provided.

A. (car '("ONE" "TWO" "THREE")) ____________________

B. (car (list 9.77 4.61)) ____________________

C. (setq b (car '(8 "A-B-C"))) ____________________

D. (setq p (car '("GREEN" "BLUE"))) ____________________

E. (cdr (list "BOLTS" 3.0 4.25)) ____________________

F. (setq alpha (cdr '(ABC DEF))) ____________________

G. (cdr (list "ibeam" "bar" "wfbeam")) ____________________

H. (setq e (cdr '(m n o p))) ____________________

I. (car (cdr '(3.44 9.28 5.31))) ____________________

J. (setq w (cdr (car (list '(a b c) 'd)))) ____________________

K. (cdr (cdr '(lowpt midpt hipt))) ____________________

L. (setq q (car (cdr (list '(uv w) 'xy 'z)))) ____________________

LINKING THE CAR AND CDR FUNCTIONS

The CAR and CDR functions are valuable tools for data acquisition. Each function, in its own way, pulls information from given data lists, allowing the user to break down these lists into selected atoms or elements. In addition, AutoLISP *concatenates* (links) applications of CAR and CDR, creating variations to the CxxxxR group of functions. Each function may use up to four levels of A and D by substituting the desired letter ("A" for cAr or "D" for cDr) in place of the Xs. This concept is best demonstrated by the following derived functions.

The CADR Function

The *CADR function* returns the second element of a list. It does this by concatenating the CAR and CDR functions into one nested expression. The format for this function is as follows:

(cadr LIST)	*which is equivalent to (car (cdr ⟨LIST⟩))*

AutoLISP combines the CAR and CDR functions into the form of CADR. Notice that the order of the "A" and "D" in the spelling of CADR implies the manner in which these two basic functions are applied. (This is similar to the evaluation process of a nested expression; typically from right to left.) See Fig. 3-1. Pay close attention to the following examples:

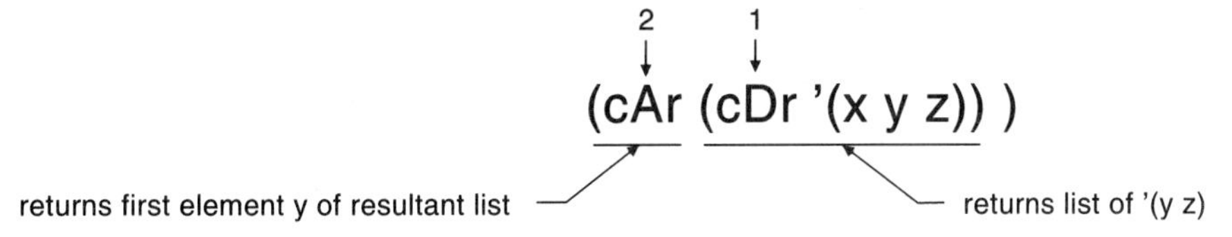

Fig. 3-1. The CADR function essentially combines the CAR and CDR functions.

AutoLISP Expression		
(cadr '(x y z))	returns y	*In this case, the CADR function could be broken down as follows:* *1. (cdr '(x y z))* *returns (y z)* *2. (car '(y z))* *returns y*
(setq P (cadr (list "A" "B")))	returns "B"	*For this AutoLISP statement, the CADR function is equivalent to:* *1. (cdr (list "A" "B"))* *returns ("B")* *2. (car (list "B"))* *returns "B"*
(cadr '(–3 (178 29)))	returns (178 29)	*The end result of applying the CADR function to this expression is a list:* *1. (cdr '(–3 (178 29)))* *returns ((178 29))* *2. (car '((178 29))* *returns (178 29)*
(cadr (list "v–weld"))	returns nil	*The list contains only one item and the CADR function will return a value of nil:* *1. (cdr (list "v–weld"))* *returns ()* *2. (car '())* *returns nil*

Applying the CADR Function. One application of the CADR function is to obtain the Y-axis coordinate of a point value. For example:

Command: **(setq Y (cadr '(1.63 5.74 7.81)))** ↵
5.74

The CADR expression returns the Y-axis coordinate:
1. *(cdr '(1.63 5.74 7.81))*
   returns (5.74 7.81)
2. *(car '(5.74 7.81))*
   returns 5.74

The CADDR Function

The *CADDR function* returns the third element of a list. Again, AutoLISP concatenates the CAR and CDR functions into one nested expression. Examine the diagram in Fig. 3-2 for a breakdown of the CADDR function. The format for this AutoLISP function is:

(caddr LIST)

which is equivalent to
(car (cdr (cdr ⟨LIST⟩)))

3 2 1
(cAr (cDr (cDr '(x y z))))
returns first element z of resultant list
2nd CDR returns list of (z)
returns list of (y z)

Fig. 3-2. The CADDR function returns the third element of a list.

Study the CADDR function in the following examples:

AutoLISP Expression

(caddr '(1.55 6.28 9.63)) returns 9.63

The 3D point list is evaluated by the CADDR function and the Z-axis coordinate is returned:
1. *(cdr '(1.55 6.28 9.63))*
   returns (6.28 9.63)
2. *(cdr '(6.28 9.63))*
   returns (9.63)
3. *(car '(9.63))*
   returns 9.63

(caddr (list "revA" "revB")) returns nil

The list contains only two elements and the CADDR function returns a value of nil:
1. *(cdr (list "revA" "revB"))*
   returns ("revB")
2. *(cdr (list "revB"))*
   returns ()
3. *(car ())*
   returns nil

AutoLISP Expression

(caddr (list 5 "x" (list "y" 6))) returns ("y" 6)

The nested list of ("y" 6) is the result of applying the CADDR function:

1. *(cdr (list 5 "x" (list "y" 6)))*
   returns ("x" (list "y" 6))
2. *(cdr (list "x" (list "y" 6)))*
   returns ((list "y" 6))
3. *(car ((list "y" 6)))*
   returns ("y" 6)

EXERCISE 3-3

- ☐ Assemble a new AutoLISP program similar to the XCOORD.LSP program (page 3-6). The program should include:
  - ☐ AutoLISP GETPOINT statements that ask for three random 3D points within the AutoCAD drawing editor, SETQing the points to variables PT1, PT2, and PT3.
  - ☐ A fourth point coordinate, variable 3DPT, is to be constructed, which combines the X-axis value of PT1, the Y-axis value of PT2, and the Z-axis value of PT3. The CAR, CADR, and CADDR functions will be used to return the X-axis, Y-axis, and Z-axis values, respectively.
  - ☐ AutoLISP COMMAND statements using the AutoCAD 3DPOLY command that draws four triangles between the combined points of PT1, PT2, PT3, and 3DPT.
- ☐ Properly document the file and name it XYZ-TRI.LSP.

Other CxxxxR Combinations

There are many possible CxxxxR combinations. Since they are all concatenations of the CAR and CDR functions, a little experimentation should be all that is needed to discover the possibilities. Three additional CxxxxR combinations are shown in the following examples, which are representative of the diversity achieved with regard to the CxxxxR family. In these examples, the variable N is a quoted list:

```
(setq N '((U V) (WX) Y Z))
```

The CADAR Function

(cadar LIST) *which is equivalent to (car (cdr (car N)))*

Examine the diagram in Fig. 3-3 for a breakdown of the CADAR function:

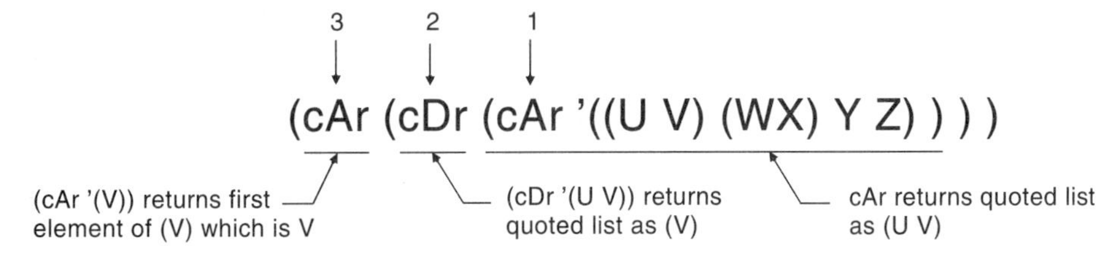

Fig. 3-3. Diagram of the CADAR function.

The CDDR Function

(cddr LIST) *which is equivalent to (cdr (cdr N))*

Examine the diagram in Fig. 3-4 for a breakdown of the CDDR function.

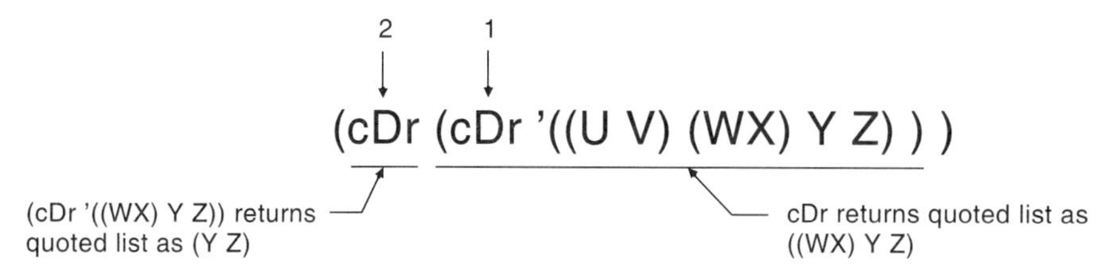

Fig. 3-4. The CDDR function.

The CADDDR Function

(cadddr LIST) *which is equivalent to (car (cdr (cdr (cdr N))))*

Examine the diagram in Fig. 3-5 for a breakdown of the CADDDR function:

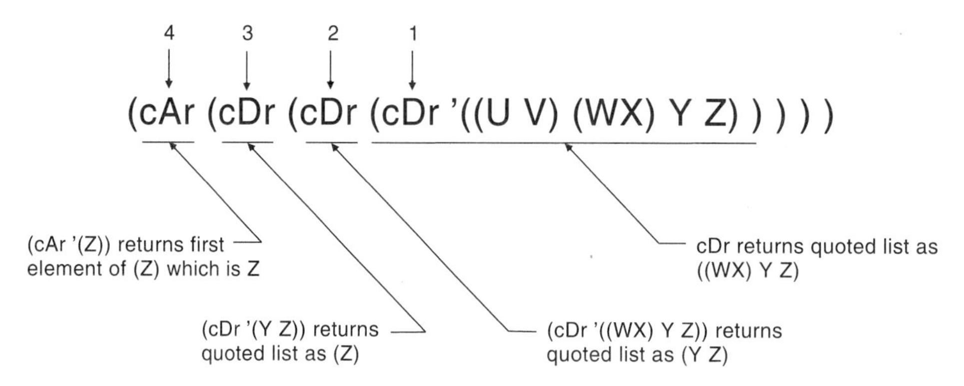

Fig. 3-5. Diagram of the CADDDR function.

By carefully inspecting the evolution of each of the previously listed functions, you should be able to arrive at the final values given. Four levels of "A" and "D" are utilized infrequently when applying the CxxxxR family of functions, but it is possible. Up to three levels is usually sufficient to handle the most basic lists. There are other AutoLISP functions available, (described later in this chapter) which assist in returning the desired element from a list.

EXERCISE 3-4

- ☐ Solve the following AutoLISP expressions and write the returned result in the spaces provided.
  A. (cadr '("FOUR" "FIVE" "SIX")) ______________________
  B. (cadr (list 5.39 9.48)) ______________________
  C. (setq h (cadr '(8 12 46 2))) ______________________
  D. (cadr (list 3 4 (cadr '(5 6)))) ______________________
  E. (caddr '("GREEN" "BLUE" "RED")) ______________________
  F. (setq beta (caddr '(AB CD EF))) ______________________
  G. (caddr '(a z)) ______________________
  H. (setq w (car (cddr '(m n o p)))) ______________________
  I. (cadar '((7.43 2.28 4.99) 8.92)) ______________________

- ☐ Use the following AutoLISP expressions, and the assignments provided for variables L1 and L2 to solve each of the following problems:

```
(setq L1 '(a b c (d e f)))

(setq L2 '((a b) (c d) (e f)))
```

- ☐ Extract atom c from list L1 by using the required concatenations of the CAR and CDR family of functions.
- ☐ Extract atom e from list L2 using the methods previously listed.
- ☐ Extract the list '(d e f) from list L1.
- ☐ Extract atom b from list L2.

THE GETCORNER FUNCTION

The GETPOINT function returns a selected point as a list of three real numbers. This allows the user to quickly locate 3D coordinates. When the GETPOINT function is provided with the optional base point argument (PT), AutoCAD displays a rubberband line and waits for the user to specify a second coordinate. A pick point concludes its operation.

Similar to the GETPOINT function, the *GETCORNER function* returns a 3D point, but its method of doing so is slightly different. A required base point argument–PT–locks in the first corner of a dynamic rectangle that the user manipulates until a final coordinate is picked. This operation resembles AutoCAD's windowing capability. The format for the GETCORNER function is:

```
(getcorner PT [PROMPT])
```

The GETCORNER function, when substituted for the GETPOINT function, provides a more natural way of choosing points (corners) in the drawing environment. The following program combines the usefulness of this function with the concepts of the CAR and CADR functions. The rectangle with identified points is shown in Fig. 3-6.

```
; RECTANGL.LSP written by Rick Tangal December 19xx
; This program prompts the user for beginning and
; ending corner points, then draws a rectangle
; constructed by the CAR and CADR functions.
(defun rectangl (/ CPT1 CPT2 CPT3 CPT4)
(setq CPT1 (getpoint "\nSelect first corner point: ")        ; CPT1 is first pick point
      CPT3 (getcorner CPT1 "\nSecond corner point: ")   ; CPT3 completes the box
      CPT2 (list (car CPT3) (cadr CPT1))                ; CPT2 is constructed
      CPT4 (list (car CPT1) (cadr CPT3))                ; CPT4 is constructed
)                                                       ; "Stacked" SETQed variables
(command ".line" cpt1 cpt2 cpt3 cpt4 "close")   ; Activates the AutoCAD LINE command and
                                                ;    uses both the corner and constructed points
)
```

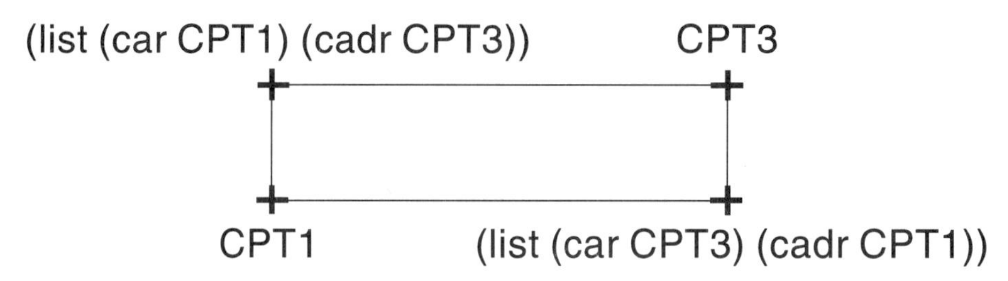

Fig. 3-6. A graphic representation of RECTANGL.LSP.

By uniting the GETCORNER, CAR, and CADR functions, a practical solution is reached for dynamically drawing rectangles. Take note of the two "constructed coordinates" by employing the CAR and CADR functions. The X coordinate of CPT3 and the Y coordinate of CPT1 are combined to create CPT2. Similarly, the X coordinate of CPT1 and Y coordinate of CPT3 are combined to create the constructed coordinate CPT4.

EXERCISE 3-5

☐ Using the AutoLISP GETCORNER, CAR, and CDR functions, design a program called FILLBOX.LSP that prompts the user for the first and second corner points and utilizes AutoCAD's SOLID command to create a solid (filled) rectangle.

ADDITIONAL BASIC LIST FUNCTIONS

Until now, the majority of discussion in this chapter has been devoted to explaining the effects of the CxxxxR group of functions. Two other functions will now be discussed since their operation is also related to basic list manipulation.

The LAST Function

The *LAST function* returns the last element within a list. The format for the LAST function is as follows:

```
(last LIST)
```

The LAST function can be extremely useful when interrogating long lists. Examine the following AutoLISP statement:

```
(setq LL (list "pt1" "pt2" "pt3" "pt4" "pt5" "pt6"))
```

Given the assignment of (list "pt1" "pt2" "pt3" "pt4" "pt5" "pt6"), retrieving the final element within lists such as this can be an overwhelming task when using the CxxxxR functions. However, when using the LAST function, the task of extracting element "pt6" is simple. For example:

```
Command: (setq LL (list "pt1" "pt2" "pt3" "pt4" "pt5" "pt6")) ↵
Command: (setq MM (last LL)) ↵
"pt6"
```

The LENGTH Function

References have been made regarding the number of elements present inside a list. There is also a function that returns this number as an integer. The *LENGTH function* returns the number of elements contained in a list. The format for the LENGTH function is:

```
(length LIST)
```

When applying the LENGTH function to variable LL (used in one of the previous examples), an integer value of 6 is obtained. For example:

```
Command: (setq LL (list "pt1" "pt2" "pt3" "pt4" "pt5" "pt6")) ↵
Command: (setq PP (length LL)) ↵
6
```

In complicated lists, it is often difficult to determine the number of items in them. For the following expression, the LENGTH function returns an integer value of 4:

```
(length '((aa bb cc) (dd ee) (ff gg hh) ii))
          ----------  -------  ----------  
              ↑          ↑         ↑      ↑
              1          2         3      4
```

Further discussion regarding the LAST and LENGTH functions will occur in later chapters, when each is used for specific program designs.

Let's Review...

1. The CxxxxR family of functions will extract various elements of a list, depending upon the linking of CAR and CDR, called concatenation. AutoLISP will allow up to four levels deep of "A" and "D" when assembling these particular functions.
2. The GETCORNER function is more useful than employing the GETPOINT function when constructing points in a rectangular configuration.
3. The basic list manipulating functions of LAST and LENGTH return the last element of a list and the corresponding length of a list, respectively.

EXERCISE 3-6

☐ Solve the following AutoLISP expressions and write the returned result in the space provided.

A. (last '("WOOD" "STEEL" "IRON")) ______________________

B. (last (list 1.23 4.56)) ______________________

C. (setq y (last (cdr '(1 3 5 7)))) ______________________

D. (setq s (last (car '((a b c) d)))) ______________________

E. (length '("RED" "GREEN" "BLUE")) ______________________

F. (length (last (list "BOLTS" 4.25))) ______________________

G. (setq gamma (length '(AB CD EF))) ______________________

H. (length (list "plate" "bar" "rod")) ______________________

I. (setq u (length (car (cdr '(9 5 1))))) ______________________

CHAPTER TEST

Write your answers in the spaces provided.

1. Give a general definition of list.

____

____

____

2. Specify the basic difference between the LIST and QUOTE functions.

____

____

3. Provide examples of lists using both the LIST and QUOTE functions. Remember the rules regarding the usage of each function.

   ____

   ____

   ____

   ____

4. Besides the GETPOINT function, how are lists created?

   ____

   ____

5. What data types can be stored in lists?

   ____

   ____

6. Use the SETQ function to assign an empty list to the variable MT.

   ____

7. What is the purpose of the CAR function? The CDR function? Give examples of each.

   ____

   ____

   ____

   ____

8. ______________________ refers to the linking of the CAR and CDR functions within the same expression.

9. Illustrate the breakdown of the AutoLISP CADDR function.

   ____

   ____

   ____

10. Besides constructing new coordinates from assigned point variables, what are other applications of lists?

    ____

    ____

    ____

    ____

11. Describe the format of the LAST function. Why should you use the LAST function on large lists instead of CAR and CDR?

    ____

    ____

    ____

12. Does the LENGTH function return an integer or real value upon evaluation?

    ____

13. Provide a few applications or situations where the LAST and LENGTH functions might be useful.

    ___

    ___

    ___

14. How many levels of concatenation are possible with the CxxxxR functions?

    ___

15. When dealing with 3D coordinates, what three AutoLISP functions are readily available to extract the X-, Y-, and Z-axis components?

    ___

    ___

PROGRAMMING PROBLEMS

1. Create a program file called 3D-RECT.LSP, which uses GETPOINT and GETCORNER to define a rectangular volume. Using list manipulation techniques, define each of the eight points necessary to construct a 3D rectangle 2 units thick. The program will then utilize the COMMAND function to draw six 3DFACEs using the defined points. (Until more advanced techniques have been discussed, this should be used only while the World Coordinate System is the current coordinate system.)
2. Create a program called 2L-BOX that uses the AutoLISP GETPOINT, GETCORNER, LIST and the CxxxxR functions to draw a double-line box. The user will specify the size of the rectangle, and the offset distance will be 0.1. The program will draw the user-specified rectangle, and then draw another one inside of the first using the specified offset distance. Locate the point coordinates for the inner rectangle by subtracting or adding the offset distance as required from the appropriate X and Y coordinate values. Assemble the derived values into new point coordinate lists, and complete the program. Be sure to document your file thoroughly.

Chapter 4

Requesting User Input

Learning Objectives

After completing this chapter, you will be able to:

- ☐ Alter program results based on numerical input.
- ☐ Prompt for input of both individual text strings and sentences.
- ☐ Find and change system variable values.

REQUESTING DATA

As discussed in earlier chapters, the ability to request specific user input makes the AutoLISP language much more versatile than simple menu macros and script files. An AutoLISP program may produce a different result each time it is used, based on variable information supplied by the user.

The most common method of acquiring data within AutoLISP is by using one of the GET functions. So far, examples have been given for the GETPOINT and GETCORNER functions. However, these functions only request coordinate input. There are other types of information that may be required to obtain the desired result for a program, including numerical data, text strings, and system variables.

Requesting Numerical Input

A common requirement for variations in a program is numerical input. Such input may determine a scale factor, the size an object is to be drawn, or even the number of times a task is to be repeated. The two potential forms for numerical values are integers and real numbers. Many functions accept real numbers as input; others do not.

Integers. Situations occur where integer input is the only applicable response. For example, when an operation is to be performed a certain number of times, an integer is required. A task cannot be repeated 0.3 times. The *GETINT function* is used to request integer input. For example:

Command: **(GETINT)** ↵
12 ↵
12

The GETINT function is entered like other GET functions. AutoLISP pauses its evaluation process until input is supplied, and then the expression returns the user-supplied value.

The GETINT function will accept only integers.

Command: **(GETINT)** ↵
12.0 ↵
Requires an integer value.
Try again: **12** ↵
12

The GETINT function is entered. If a non-integer response is given, a message is issued, followed by a new prompt. If no user prompt is specified, a default message "Try again:" is used.

Most GET functions allow a prompt to be issued to the user. In this manner, specific instructions may be provided as to the nature of the required input, as shown in the following examples:

Command: **(GETINT "\nEnter an integer: ")** ↵
Enter an integer: **43** ↵
43

Command: **(setq NUM (getint "\nEnter an integer: "))** ↵
Enter an integer: **122** ↵
122

Note in the first example that the returned value is lost if it is not immediately used. However, in the second example, the variable NUM may be used whenever it is needed. For example:

Command: **ARRAY** ↵
Select objects: *(pick the objects to array)*
Select objects: ↵
Rectangular or Polar array (⟨R⟩/P): **R** ↵
Number of rows (---) ⟨1⟩: **!NUM** ↵ — *NUM evaluates to 122*
Number of columns (¦¦¦) ⟨1⟩: **!NUM** ↵ — *NUM evaluates to 122*
Unit cell or distance between rows (---): *(input the desired row spacing and press ENTER)*
Distance between columns (¦¦¦): *(input the desired column spacing and press ENTER)*

There are certain limitations on input values when using the GETINT function, where the input must be between –32768 and +32767. The GETINT function is the only function affected by this restriction. It is important to note that AutoLISP can utilize integers falling outside of this range, but they cannot be acquired with the GETINT function.

Command: **(GETINT "\nEnter an integer: ")** ↵ Enter an integer: **32768** ↵ Requires an integer value between –32768 and 32767. Enter an integer: **32767** ↵ 32767	*The GETINT function is entered with a prompt. The input is out of range. A message is printed and the prompt is reissued. The input value is always returned.*

Requesting Real Numbers

Real numbers are usually more appropriate than integers for precise mathematical operations and refined numerical requirements. Real numbers are acquired by using the *GETREAL function.* The GETREAL function is used the same way as the GETINT function. However, the input value limitation does not apply.

Command: **(getreal)** ↵ **3.66** ↵ 3.66	*The function is entered, and input is awaited. A value is supplied and subsequently returned.*

With the GETINT function, input is restricted only to integers. The GETREAL function, however, allows its input to be either real numbers or integers. When an integer is provided, it is automatically promoted to a real number, and a real number is returned.

Command: **(getreal "\nEnter a number: ")** ↵ Enter a number: **43** ↵ 43.0	*an integer is entered, but a real number is returned*
Command: **(getreal "\nEnter a number: ")** ↵ Enter a number: **HELLO** ↵ Requires numeric value. Enter a number: **622** ↵ 622.0	*if a non-numeric response is given, a message is displayed and the prompt is reissued*

Applying GETINT and GETREAL. There are many applications possible with these two GET functions. The following two examples–QU and CONEVOL–illustrate the usage of both the GETINT and GETREAL functions. The GETINT function in the first routine assists in modifying the current AutoCAD UNITS settings. The linear units and linear units of precision are the only settings affected.

```
; QU (QuickUnit)   Created by Les Settam   12-27-xx
;
(defun C:QU (/ LUS LUP)
  (setq LUS (getint "\nEnter the Linear Units ⟨1–5⟩: ")
        LUP (getint "\nEnter the Precision: ")
  )
  (command "LUNITS" LUS "LUPREC" LUP)
)  ; – –⟨ End of QU ⟩– –
```

The next example uses the GETREAL function and returns the volume of a cone:

```
(defun C:CONEVOL (/ R H)
  (setq R (getreal "\nEnter radius of cone: ")
        H (getreal "\nEnter height of cone: ")
  )
  (prompt "\nThe volume of this cone is: ")
  (* (/ 1 3.0) PI (* R R) H)   ; Calculation for the conic volume
) ; --⟨ End of CONEVOL ⟩--
```

When invoked, this routine prompts for the radius and height of the cone, displays a message, and returns the result of the mathematical expression. Note that the values returned by the GET functions are immediately assigned to symbol names. This way, the returned values are still available for use in the expression at the end of the program.

```
Command: CONEVOL ↵
Enter radius of cone: 6.5 ↵
Enter height of cone: 15.75 ↵
The volume of this cone is: 696.844
```

This example has only a few real-world applications. More useful automated formulas might include the necessary calculations for determining physical data for load-bearing members in a structure, or any frequently utilized equation. The number of productive applications depends only on your needs and your ability to address those needs with AutoLISP.

PROFESSIONAL TIP

The phrase "Can't reenter AutoLISP." is a common error message encountered by new programmers. All of the GETxxxx functions, with the exception of the GETVAR and GETENV functions (discussed later in this text), require the user to physically supply "end result" data to the program. In other words, a GETxxxx function will not accept data requiring evaluation. Therefore, an AutoLISP expression would be an invalid response to a GETxxxx function prompt. Examine the following example:

```
Command: (setq NUM (getint "\nEnter an integer value: ")) ↵
Enter an integer value: (* 4 3) ↵
Can't reenter AutoLISP.
Requires an integer value.
Enter an integer value: 12 ↵
12
```

Note that the expression (* 4 3) is given as a response to the GETINT prompt. AutoLISP displays the error message and prompts again for an appropriate value. The integer 12 is entered, and the expression is completed successfully.

EXERCISE 4-1

- ☐ Use AutoLISP to define functions that will accomplish each of the following tasks. Name the programs as indicated.
- ☐ Create an AutoLISP program named CYL.LSP. Prompt for the necessary variable values and solve for the surface area of a cylinder. Hint: Use the equation: Surface Area = Pi × Diameter × Height. Be sure to include adequate documentation. Load the program file, and supply values for the prompts.
- ☐ Create an AutoLISP program named DEFL.LSP. Prompt for the necessary variable values and solve for the deflection of a structural member using the following equation. Be sure to include adequate documentation.

$$D = \frac{PL^3}{48EI}$$

Where:

D = Deflection (in inches)
P = Force in center of span (in pounds)
L = Length of beam span (in inches)
E = Modulus of elasticity
I = Moment of inertia, (beam width × height^3)/12

Load the program, and run it using the following values:

P = 4000 lbs.
L = 240″
E = 1,000,000
Beam width = 6.75″
Beam height = 13.5″

- ☐ Create an AutoLISP program named INTOMM.LSP. Prompt for a value in inches and return it in millimeters.
- ☐ Create an AutoLISP program named MMTOIN.LSP. Prompt for a value in millimeters and return it in inches. Load the program and supply values to ensure that it runs correctly.

Requesting Text Strings

Another data type that may be prompted for is a text string. The *GETSTRING function* is used to request string input, and similar to many other GETxxxx functions, pauses until the user responds with this data type. It will accept any alphanumeric character and return it as text. However, the input string may not exceed 132 characters in length. If this limit is exceeded, only the first 132 characters are returned. Note that if a number is entered in response to the GETSTRING function, the returned value is a string (enclosed in quotation marks), not an integer or real number.

```
Command: (getstring) ↵        the function pauses for user input
Hello ↵                       and returns the input value
"Hello"
```

Command: **(getstring)** ↵ **154.77** ↵ "154.77"	*even numerical input is returned as a text string*
Command: **(getstring "Enter text: ")** ↵ Enter text: **Material** ↵ "Material"	*an optional prompt may be supplied*

It may be necessary to allow the user to input more than one word at a time. When the GETSTRING function is used as previously shown, striking the space bar will produce the same result as pressing the ENTER key. When you want to allow spaces to be included in the text string, a non-nil argument must be provided. For example:

Command: **(getstring T "Enter text: ")** ↵ Enter text: **Notes (unless otherwise specified):** ↵ "Notes (unless otherwise specified):"	*an optional non-nil argument is supplied; therefore, spaces are allowed in the string*

Non-Nil Arguments

Several AutoLISP functions provide an option for a *non-nil argument,* which causes the function to perform in an alternate way. Non-nil arguments evaluate to any value, other than nil. (As discussed previously, nil indicates the absence of value.)

There are two common methods for providing a non-nil argument. The first method involves the use of the symbol T. The *symbol T* is one of AutoLISP's built-in symbols, and therefore, already has a value assigned to it. The predesignated value for T may be found (similar to other symbol names) by typing "!T" at the Command: prompt.

Command: **!T** ↵
T

This symbol evaluates to itself. The value of T should not be altered. Its value is often referred to as *true* because of its applications in AutoLISP test expressions. T is considered to be the opposite of nil, and is therefore commonly used when a non-nil argument is required.

Another technique used for non-nil arguments involves using any atom that has a value, such as an integer:

```
(getstring 2 "\nEnter text: ")
```

The 2 in this expression produces the same results achieved by using the symbol T.

EXERCISE 4-2

☐ Define an AutoLISP command line function (using the C: prefix) called LL. The function should prompt for an AutoLISP file name using GETSTRING then load that file using the LOAD function. Save the routine as LL.LSP.

CONTROLLING NUMERICAL AND TEXT INPUT

Many programming applications require the user to specify an option. For example, a circle is created in AutoCAD by implementing one of many different options, such as 3-Point or Cen/Rad. These options provide versatility, permitting the user to choose the desired course of action.

AutoLISP is no exception, and allows a valid option list to be specified. Only input that is found within the list is accepted. To handle this task, the AutoLISP *INITGET function* is used. The INITGET function is instrumental in controlling both numerical and text string input.

The next section demonstrates the usage of INITGET, and how it interrelates with the AutoLISP GETKWORD function.

The INITGET and GETKWORD Functions

The INITGET function allows the programmer to INITialize the next GETxxx expression by setting control flags and establishing a keyword list. This allows the programmer to specify what is to be considered valid input. All user input functions (with the exception of GET-STRING) respond to the control modes set by INITGET.

```
(initget [BITS] [STRING])
```

The first argument–BITS–is an optional integer specification given as a *bit code.* The bit codes may be used individually, or may be added together to activate more than one control mode. The table shown in Fig. 4-1 describes the available bit codes and their effect on user input.

Code	Effect
1	A value must be supplied; *null input* (pressing only ↵ with no value entered) not allowed.
2	Value of input may not be zero.
4	Numeric input may not be negative.
8	Limits are ignored for point picks even if the AutoCAD system variable LIMCHECK is on.
16	Not currently used. (Earlier releases used this to return 3D points rather than 2D points.)
32	Use dashed lines for rubberband line or box. If the system variable POPUPS is 0, this bit is ignored.
64	Used for GETDIST, ignores Z coordinate of 3D input to ensure that a 2D distance is returned.
128	Allows free input of text even if it is not a keyword. Other control bits are honored first, but if a bit value 1 and 128 are used together (129) then null input returns a null string ("").

Fig. 4-1. Bit codes for the INITGET function.

There are many possible combinations of control modes. By adding the bit values together, control modes can be simultaneously activated. The only limitations for control codes are those which are applicable for the particular GETxxxx function being used. For example, a flag value of 4 to disallow negative values has no effect on GETPOINT. The following example shows an application of multiple bit codes:

```
Command: (initget (+ 1 2 4)) ↵                    or (initget 7), non-null, non-zero,
                                                  non-negative
nil                                               always returns nil

Command: (setq NUM (getint "\nEnter a positive integer: ")) ↵
Enter a positive integer: ↵                       no null input allowed!
Value must be positive and nonzero.
Enter a positive integer: 0 ↵                     no zero input allowed!
Value must be positive and nonzero.
Enter a positive integer: –72 ↵                   no negative input allowed!
Value must be positive and nonzero.
Enter a positive integer: 14 ↵
14
```

For the GETINT expression shown above, the preceding INITGET specification of (+ 1 2 4) disallows null, zero, or negative input. A null response is gained by pressing the ENTER key without supplying any other keyboard characters. Note that the previous INITGET expression would typically be specified as **(initget 7)**. In this example, however, the component bits are shown separate for illustrative purposes.

The INITGET function can also be used to set up a list of acceptable *keywords* for the next GETxxxx function. The second argument is a text string that lists each of the keywords. If text input is given that is *not* found on the list, it is rejected and the prompt is repeated. Note that this keyword list can be used with numeric GETxxxx functions to expand the possible input options. For example:

```
Command: (initget 1 "Cancel") ↵                   null input disallowed plus
nil                                               keyword list defined

Command: (getint "\nCancel/⟨Floor #⟩: ") ↵
Cancel/⟨Floor #⟩: C ↵                             since unexpected input was
"Cancel"                                          received, the keyword list is
                                                  checked and C (for "Cancel")
                                                  is found

Command: (getint "\nCancel/⟨Floor #⟩: ") ↵
Cancel/⟨Floor #⟩: C ↵
Requires a numeric value.                         INITGET is only valid for one
Cancel/⟨Floor #⟩: 4 ↵                             subsequent GETxxxx function
4
```

Note that INITGET stays active only through one subsequent GETxxxx function; flags and keywords are automatically cleared for the next GETxxxx function. This eliminates the need for a second INITGET call to clear the control modes.

The GETKWORD function requests user input in the form of a keyword. Similar to other GETxxxx functions, all valid keywords are specified by using the INITGET function prior to initiating the GETKWORD expression. An optional prompt may also accompany the GETKWORD expression. The basic structure of this function is given as:

```
(getkword [PROMPT])
```

The GETKWORD function requires string input rather than numeric input, and the only functional control bits are 1 (Disallow null input) and 128 (Accept arbitrary keyboard input). If the input to GETKWORD matches an option within the keyword specification, then that keyword is returned. Any invalid input returns an "Invalid option keyword." message, and reissues PROMPT until an acceptable response is given. For example:

Command: **(initget 1 "Y N")** ↵	*null input disallowed + keyword list*
nil	*defined; INITGET returns nil*
Command: **(setq RES (getkword "\nCreate DIMension layer? ⟨Y/N⟩: "))** ↵	
Create DIMension layer? ⟨Y/N⟩: **LATER** ↵	*"Later" not included in the keyword*
Invalid option keyword.	*string*
Create DIMension layer? ⟨Y/N⟩: **N** ↵	*the keyword string includes "N"*
"N"	

If allowed by the INITGET function, a null response causes GETKWORD to also return nil. If no keyword string is specified by INITGET, the optional prompt is issued, but GETKWORD does not wait for a response. For these conditions, nil is automatically returned. For example:

Command: **(initget "Y N")** ↵	*null input allowed + keyword list*
nil	*defined; INITGET returns nil*
Command: **(setq INP1 (getkword "\nDefine new valve BLOCK? ⟨Y/N⟩: "))** ↵	
Define new valve BLOCK? ⟨Y/N⟩: ↵	*a valid null response is given*
nil	
Command: **(initget)** ↵	*no keyword list is defined; INITGET*
nil	*returns nil*
Command: **(setq INP2 (getkword "\nDefine new LType? ⟨Y/N⟩: "))** ↵	
Define new LType? ⟨Y/N⟩: nil	*nil is automatically returned*

When used in conjunction with each other, the GETKWORD and INITGET functions afford a convenient and effective means for limiting input to a specific set of options. An additional consideration is how much of the keyword is necessary to be typed. The only required portion is that which is capitalized, but the rest may also be used. For example, if the keyword string "LType" is supplied, valid responses would include "ltype," "ltyp," "lty," and "lt." However, simply entering "l" would not be satisfactory.

The following example demonstrates further the principle of controlling input for GETKWORD with the INITGET function:

```
(defun C:BYE (/ OPT)
  (initget 1 "Save Wblock Quit")
  (setq OPT (getkword "\nSave, Wblock or Quit drawing? ⟨S/W/Q⟩: "))
  (command OPT)
)
```

Here, null input is not allowed. Therefore, one of the available options must be supplied. An "S," "W," or "Q," (or up to the entire option keyword shown) can be entered. If the input is "S," the GETKWORD expression returns "Save" and the SETQ expression assigns this value to the symbol OPT. The AutoCAD SAVE command would then be issued.

PROFESSIONAL TIP

In Release 14, the INITGET function allows specification of localized keywords and an associated language-independent keyword for the GETKWORD function. The syntax for INITGET when used in this manner is as follows :

```
(initget [BITS] "local1 local2 localn _indep1 indep2 indepn")
```

When the user answers the GETKWORD prompt with "local1", "indep1" is returned. The same number of localized and language-independent keywords must be specified. The first language-independent keyword is prefixed with an underscore.

EXERCISE 4-3

- ☐ Revise the DEFL.LSP program that you developed in Exercise 4-1 to disallow null, zero, and negative input for all numerical data requests. Be sure to document your modifications.
- ☐ Load the program, and try using different values. Note messages that AutoLISP may provide.

AUTOLISP AND SYSTEM VARIABLES

AutoCAD system variables commonly are manipulated in AutoLISP programs in order to set the stage for the operations to be performed. AutoLISP allows the programmer to determine the current settings of any system variable, and to reset any which are not “read-only.” AutoCAD system variables include any values that may be listed using AutoCAD’s SETVAR command. It is important to remember that AutoCAD’s system variables are separate from AutoLISP’s variables, and therefore, may not be handled in the same manner.

A common application for acquiring system variable values might be accessing the LASTPOINT variable to begin or continue an operation. Other needs might include returning the current layer setting, limits, or even a fillet radius. Finding the value of a variable is accomplished using the *GETVAR function.* GETVAR requires one argument, which is the variable name specified as a text string. The syntax for the GETVAR function is:

```
(getvar VARNAME)
```

Examples of using the GETVAR function follow:

```
Command: (setq PT1 (getvar "LASTPOINT")) ↵
(6.626 3.92839 0.0)
```

```
Command: (setq CL (getvar "CLAYER")) ↵
"0"
```

Command: **(setq LM (getvar "LIMMAX"))** ↵
(44.0 34.0)

Command: **(setq FR (getvar "FILLETRAD"))** ↵
0.0625

In addition, system variables may be set to new values with the *SETVAR function.* The name of this function is the same as the AutoCAD command used for the same purpose. The format for SETVAR is as follows:

(setvar VARNAME VALUE)

The SETVAR function uses two arguments; the first is the VARiable NAME text string and the second is the new VALUE. As previously mentioned, the only restriction is that read-only variables cannot be changed using SETVAR. (A list of all system variables, indicating the use of each variable and whether or not it is read-only is provided in the Appendix of the *AutoCAD Reference Manual.*) Examples of the SETVAR function follow:

Command: **(setvar "LUPREC" 2)** ↵
2

Command: **(setvar "BLIPMODE" 0)** ↵
0

Command: **(setvar "DIMLFAC" 1)** ↵
1

Note that system variables are different than program variables. Also, the SETQ function is never used to change the value of a system variable.

PROFESSIONAL TIP

Some AutoCAD system variables may be used to enhance the appearance and performance of an AutoLISP routine. One such variable is CMDECHO, which controls the printing of AutoLISP's COMMAND function arguments to the screen as they are performed. If the value of CMDECHO is 1, this information will be echoed to the command line. Therefore, a simple expression at the beginning of an AutoLISP program setting CMDECHO to 0 will allow your programs to run more transparently. For example:

(setvar "CMDECHO" 0)

EXERCISE 4-4

- ☐ Design an AutoLISP function that may be invoked by typing "FR" at AutoCAD's Command: prompt. This function will prompt for a fillet radius value, set this value using SETVAR, and invoke the FILLET command.
- ☐ Design a command line function called BOR, which prompts for new limits values, sets the new values, and draws a .032 wide polyline around the defined limits.

THE COLOR SELECTION DIALOG BOX

The standard AutoCAD Select Color dialog box can be used to request a color number from the user. The function that calls this dialog box is *ACAD_COLORDLG*. The syntax for this function is shown here:

```
(acad_colordlg COLORNUM  [FLAG])
```

The COLORNUM argument is used to set the default color presented by the dialog box. The value returned represents the color number selected by the user. In the following example the default color is set to 7 and the user selects red (color number 1) and picks the OK button. The dialog box displayed is shown in Fig. 4-2.

Command: **(acad_colordlg 7)**
1

An optional [FLAG] argument allows you to disable the Bylayer and Byblock options, requiring a specific color selection from the user. If this argument is present and has a nil value, the Bylayer and Byblock buttons are disabled. If it is omitted, as in the previous example, or has a non-nil value, the Bylayer and Byblock options are enabled.

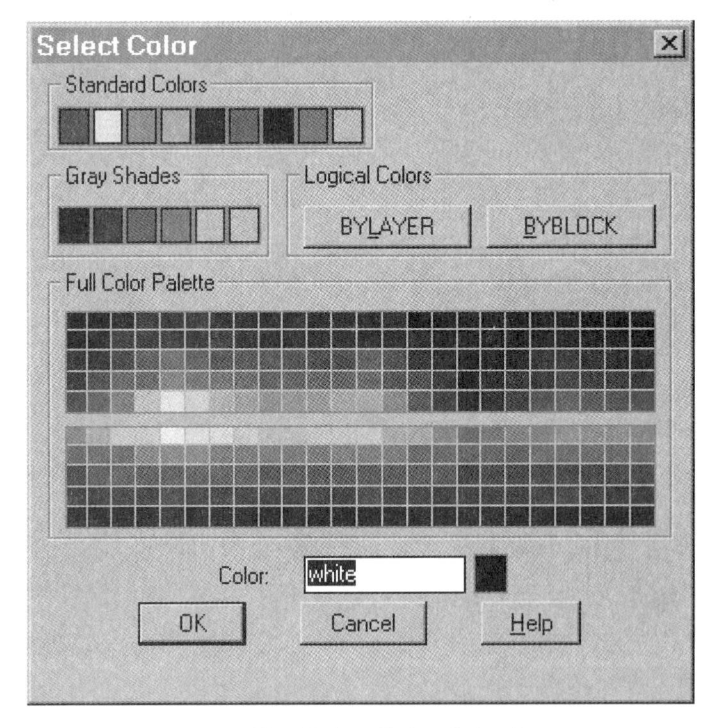

Fig. 4-2. The Select Color dialog box.

A useful example is shown in the following expression, where the DIMCLRT dimensioning system variable for the text color is set using the value returned by ACAD_COLORDLG. The COMMAND function is used to set the text color returned by ACAD_COLORDLG:

```
Command: (setq NC (acad_colordlg 7))(command "DIMCLRT" NC) ↵
DIMCLRT
New value for DIMCLRT ⟨0⟩: 1 ↵
Command: nil
```

Let's Review...

1. A GET function is the most common method for acquiring user input. There are GETxxxx functions for several different data types.
2. The GETINT function accepts only integer input between the range of -32768 and +32767.
3. The GETREAL function accepts numerical input as either an integer or a real number and returns a real number.
4. The GETSTRING function accepts a text string of up to 132 characters. If numerical input is provided, it is read and returned as a text string. An optional argument can allow spaces to be entered as well.
5. The INITGET function allows strict control of user responses when used in conjunction with GETxxxx functions.
6. The INITGET function must precede the GETKWORD function. INITGET allows the programmer to request input from a specified keyword list.
7. The AutoLISP functions GETVAR and SETVAR must be used when setting or retrieving AutoCAD system variable values within an AutoLISP program.
8. The ACAD_COLORDLG function can be used to request a color number from the user.

CHAPTER TEST

Write your answers in the spaces provided.

1. Describe a situation where integer input would be required instead of a real number.

   ____

2. What is the best way to provide specific instructions as to the nature of the required input?

   ____

   ____

3. The ______________________ function must be used to acquire numerical input if the supplied data is greater than 32,767.
4. How does AutoLISP respond when an expression is provided in response to a GETxxxx function? Why?

   ____

   ____

   ____

   ____

5. How does a GETREAL function treat integer input?

6. List some of the real-world applications for GETREAL and GETINT for your drafting discipline.

7. What happens if the maximum string length for GETSTRING of 132 characters is exceeded?

8. How can the GETSTRING function be used to acquire a text string consisting of more than one word?

9. What is a non-nil argument?

10. How does the GETSTRING function treat numerical input?

11. What symbol is commonly supplied as a non-nil argument?

12. Explain the usage of the INITGET function.

13. What occurs when irrelevant controls are specified for a GETxxxx expression?

____

____

____

14. Detail the input options in regards to the use of the INITGET and GETKWORD functions.

____

____

____

____

____

____

____

____

15. Describe the use of the GETVAR and SETVAR functions.

____

____

____

____

____

____

PROGRAMMING PROBLEMS

1. Create an AutoLISP program named CALC-IT.LSP. Define command line functions to prompt for necessary values and perform the following calculations:

   A. Determine the modulus of elasticity for a beam:

   $$E = \frac{L \times 12}{360}$$

   E = Modulus of elasticity
   L = Span of beam (in feet)

   B. Calculate the volume of a sphere.

   $$V = \frac{4}{3} \times \pi \times r^3$$

   C. Calculate the horizontal shear for a beam.

   $$F = \frac{3\left(\frac{W}{2}\right)}{2bd}$$

   F = Horizontal shear
   W= Uniformly distributed weight (in pounds)
   b = Width of beam (in inches)
   d = Height of beam (in inches)

   D. Calculate the perimeter of a rectangle.

   $$P = 2(a + b)$$

   P = Perimeter
   a = Horizontal size
   b = Vertical size

   E. Calculate the area of a triangle.

   $$A = \frac{1}{2}bh$$

   A = Area
   b = Base
   h = Height

   F. Calculate the lateral surface area of a cylinder.

   $$A = 2 \times \pi \times r \times h$$

   A = Area
   r = Radius
   h = Height

   G. Calculate the area of a circle.

   $$A = \frac{\pi \times d^2}{4}$$

   A = Area
   d = Diameter

H. Calculate the volume of a pyramid.

$$V = \frac{1}{3} bh$$

V = Volume
b = Area of base (base width × length)
h = Height of pyramid

Utilize all relevant input control options. Be sure to provide adequate documentation for the program.

2. Revise the programs from Chapters 1–3 listed below to turn off the CMDECHO system variable, and utilize INITGET wherever applicable. Be sure to include revision information in the documentation. The following AutoLISP programs have been created in Chapters 1–3:

ABC.LSP
SAMPLE.LSP
GPT1.LSP
GPT2.LSP
GPT3.LSP
1LINE.LSP
TRIANGLE.LSP
2X.LSP
RECTANGL.LSP
3D-RECT.LSP

GEO.LSP

```
; Filename: GEO.LSP
;
; Purpose: To determine the angle at A, given the three sides of an
;          oblique triangle. Points will be picked on a specified
;          vector to determine the length of one side. The remain-
;          ing sides will be picked by endpoints or input as reals.
;
(defun C:GEO (/ OSM PT1 PT2 S3 S1 S2 RTO RANG DANG)
  (setvar "cmdecho" 0)
  (setq OSM  (getvar "Osmode"))                 ; Current Object Snap mode
  (setvar “osmode” 1)
    (initget 1)
  (setq PT1  (getpoint "\nSelect 1st endpoint nearest angle A: "))
    (initget 1)
  (setq PT2  (getpoint "\nSelect 2nd endpoint away from angle A: ")
        S3   (distance PT1 PT2)                 ; Length of side c
        S1   (getdist "\nLength of side a: ")   ; Length of side a
        S2   (getdist "\nLength of side b: ")   ; Length of side b
        RTO  (/ (– (+ (expt S2 2) (expt S3 2)) (expt S1 2)) (* 2 S2 S3))
        RANG (atan (/ (sqrt (– 1 (expt RTO 2))) RTO))   ; Radian angle
        DANG (* RANG (/ 180 pi))                        ; Decimal angle
  )
  (if (minusp DANG)                             ; Convert angle if neg.
     (setq DANG (+ 180.0 DANG))
  )
  (princ "\nThe Decimal angle is: ")(princ DANG)
  (setvar "osmode" OSM)
  (setvar "cmdecho" 1)
  (princ)
)
; ––⟨ End of File ⟩––
```

Chapter 5 Identifying Distances and Angles

Learning Objectives

After completing this chapter, you will be able to:

- ☐ Use the basic elements of angular translation within AutoLISP.
- ☐ Retrieve angular and distance information within AutoCAD through specific GET and related AutoLISP functions.
- ☐ Apply AutoLISP functions to locate coordinates in the AutoCAD drafting environment using object snap, polar point entry, and intersection points.

AUTOCAD INQUIRY COMMANDS

AutoCAD inquiry commands are issued frequently in order to orient the user within the drawing environment. Commands such as ID or DIST are instrumental in obtaining locational data. The ID command produces the X,Y,Z coordinates of any chosen point. The DIST command reveals distance and angular details between two points:

```
Command: ID ↵
Point: X = 5.0000   Y = 9.0000   Z = 0.0000          an X,Y,Z location is chosen
```

```
Command: DIST ↵
First point: 5,9,0 ↵
  Second point: 17,3,0 ↵
Distance = 13.4164,   Angle in X-Y Plane = 333,   Angle from X-Y Plane = 0
Delta X = 12.0000,   Delta Y = –6.0000,   Delta Z = 0.0000
```

As shown here, location and distance data aid the user in determining spatial relationships within a drawing. The amount of feedback given by AutoCAD is important in determining fit and function of related drawing elements on screen.

The ID and DIST commands contain the data necessary to perform precision operations such as moving or copying entities. However, they merely display the data on screen, and allow limited access to the values displayed. When automating events during an editing session, it may be necessary to acquire this type of information. Therefore, AutoLISP has functions that extract this information and enable the user to utilize these values in a program.

PI AND AUTOLISP ANGLES

There are basic building blocks within the AutoLISP language that return values required to calculate angles and distances in AutoCAD. As presented in Chapter 1, the built-in AutoLISP constant *pi* is the real number 3.1415926. This constant expresses the ratio of a circle's circumference to its diameter.

circumference ÷ diameter = pi = 3.1415926r

In the previous formula, note that an "r", indicating *radians,* follows the numeric value. In angular measurement using radians (instead of degrees), the constant pi can be used to represent a measurement of 180° or 3.1415926 radians. Its value may be brought forward by typing "!PI" at the Command: prompt as follows:

```
Command: !PI ↵
3.14159
```

It is imperative that the programmer preserve the value of pi, and not assign any other value to this symbol. The following explanation will describe certain aspects of the use of pi in AutoLISP.

Two coordinates may be entered in order to render a compass direction or angular value within AutoCAD. The DIST command reveals the accessible data.

```
Command: DIST ↵
First point: 5,9,0 ↵
  Second point: 17,3,0 ↵
Distance = 13.4164,   Angle in X-Y Plane = 333,   Angle from X-Y Plane = 0
```

Note the "Angle in X-Y Plane" value of 333. This is the X-Y plane compass direction between the first and second points. Here, the chosen units reflect decimal degrees, which is familiar to all AutoCAD users. The calculated angle is written to the screen using the standard AutoCAD compass–East being the direction of 0° and a counterclockwise rotation. However, the X-Y plane angle of 333° is actually retained as the radian value 5.81954. AutoLISP utilizes radian angles rather than decimal degree angles. Use the following chart to determine other common radian angles.

Degrees	Equivalent Expression	Radians
0.0	(* 0.0 PI)	0.0
90.0	(* 0.5 PI)	1.5708
180.0	(* 1.0 PI)	3.14159
270.0	(* 1.5 PI)	4.71239
360.0	(* 2.0 PI)	6.28319

This cycle is repeated for angles specified greater than 360.0 degrees.

The CVUNIT Function

In many graphics languages, especially those which utilize complex drawing functions (such as AutoCAD), it may be necessary to convert angular values from degrees to radians (transform user input into AutoLISP format) and from radians to degrees (passing data from AutoLISP back to the user). The *CVUNIT (ConVert UNITs) function* is used to convert a value or point from one system of units to another.

```
(cvunit VALUE FROM TO)
```

Three arguments are required:

- VALUE–The value or number of units.
- FROM–The current unit of measure.
- TO–The desired unit of measure.

The VALUE argument can be supplied as an integer, a real number, or a 2D or 3D point. The FROM and TO arguments are given as text strings. This function retrieves its conversion factors from the ACAD.UNT file, which is a user-customizable file. If a specified unit name is not found in this file, nil is returned. In addition, if there is no basis for comparison of the units, such as hours and centimeters, the expression returns nil. For example:

```
(cvunit 180 "DEGREE" "RADIAN")             returns 3.14159
(cvunit PI "RADIANS" "DEGREE")             returns 180.0          either singular or plural
                                                                  forms can be used
(cvunit '(1.0 3.0) "FT" "IN")              returns (12.0 36.0)
(cvunit '(1 2) "FEET" "INCHES")            returns (12.0 24.0)
(cvunit '(4 2) "FOOT" "INCH")              returns (48.0 24.0)
(cvunit 10 "HOURS" "CENTIMETERS")          returns nil
(cvunit 4 "INCHES" "GALLONS")              returns nil
```

The CVUNIT function draws all of its information from the ACAD.UNT file. If this file is not found in the library path, a dialogue box is then displayed on the graphics screen in all releases supporting CVUNIT. The expression then returns nil, which is likely to produce an error when attempting to use the returned value.

Since there is the possibility of an AutoLISP program being entirely nonfunctional if the ACAD.UNT file is not found, it may be desirable to do these conversions with the method used in Release 10 and earlier versions. Since it is known that pi radians equals 180°, the following expressions may be used (substituting the desired angle for the argument angl):

```
(* PI (/ angl 180.0))                      converts degrees to radians

(/ (* angl 180.0) PI)                      converts radians to degrees
```

Since these expressions may be used frequently within a program, it is recommended that you create a user-defined function for each. The most commonly used names for these functions are RTD (Radians To Degrees) and DTR (Degrees To Radians). When necessary, each user-defined function should be placed at the top of the program file so they can be accessed at any time.

```
(defun dtr (A)
  (* PI (/ A 180.0))
)
```

Degrees To Radians. Argument A is an angular value in degrees. This returns the value of A expressed in radians.

```
(defun rtd (A)
  (/ (* A 180.0) PI)
)
```

Radians To Degrees. Argument A is an angular value in radians. This returns the value of A expressed in degrees.

Once loaded, the DTR function is executed as follows:

Command: **(dtr 180)** ↵ *180 degrees = pi radians*
3.14159

The RTD function is used the same as the DTR function:

Command: **(rtd 1.570796)** ↵ *(* 0.5 PI) radians = 90 degrees*
90.0

Note: The assumption is made that the vast majority of AutoCAD users employ decimal degrees rather than a radian system of angular measurement. References to these two functions will be made several times throughout this text.

The ANGLE Function

Many AutoLISP applications require that an existing angle between two reference points be derived. The *ANGLE function* determines the angle in the X-Y plane from one point to another in the current UCS. The syntax for the ANGLE function is:

```
(angle PT1 PT2)
```

The value is returned in radians, and represents the angle from the X axis (of the current construction plane) measured in a counterclockwise direction. If one or both of the arguments represent 3D points, they will be projected to the current construction plane before the angle is measured. In addition, each argument must take the form of a quoted list of coordinates, or be represented by a point variable. Text string input (such as "5,5") is not valid.

Command: **(angle '(0 0) '(0 4))** ↵
1.5708

Command: **(rtd (angle '(0 0) '(0 4)))** ↵ *note the use of the RTD function*
90.0

Command: **(cvunit (angle '(0 0) '(0 4)) "RADIANS" "DEGREES")**↵
90.0 *note the use of the CVUNIT function*

The DISTANCE Function

Many of the AutoLISP applications that utilize the angle between two reference points also require the distance to be determined. The *DISTANCE function* is used for this purpose. The syntax for the DISTANCE function is:

```
(distance PT1 PT2)
```

The 3D distance between PT1 and PT2 is returned by the DISTANCE function. Note that if one or both of the arguments represent 2D points, the Z coordinate is ignored. In such a case, the returned value depicts the 2D distance between the points as projected onto the current construction plane.

Command: **(distance '(0 0) '(0 4))** ↵ — *note the use of point coordinate lists*
4.0

Command: **(distance '(0 0 0) '(0 1 1))** ↵ — *Both arguments represent 3D points. A 3D distance is returned.*
1.41421

Command: **(distance '(0 0) '(0 1 1))** ↵ — *One 2D point and one 3D point are used. A 2D distance is returned.*
1.0

The POLAR Function

Values can be added or subtracted from existing coordinate list elements to achieve a relative displacement in a drawing. However, this method does not allow the specification of an angle and a distance for the displacement. The *POLAR function* is used to specify new points using polar coordinate entry. The format for the POLAR function is as follows:

```
(polar PT ANGLE DISTANCE)
```

The UCS 3D point located at the specified ANGLE and DISTANCE from the UCS PT (point) argument is returned by the POLAR function. If the PT argument represents a 2D point, the POLAR function returns a 2D point transformation. Note that the angle specification is in the X-Y plane of the current construction plane.

Command: **(polar '(1 0) 0 3)** ↵ — *angle is 0; distance is 3*
(4.0 0.0)

Command: **(polar '(1 0 0) 0 3)** ↵
(4.0 0.0 0.0)

Command: **(polar '(3.5 8.0 11.5) 0 -3)** ↵ — *angle is 0; distance is -3*
(0.5 8.0 11.5)

Command: **(polar '(3.5 8.0 11.5) Pi 3)** ↵ — *angle is Pi (180 degrees); distance is 3*
(0.5 8.0 11.5)

Command: **(setq PT1 '(1 0 9))** ↵ — *variable PT1 is a 3D point*
(1 0 9)

Command: **(polar PT1 (* 0.5 Pi) 7.25)** ↵ — *angle is (* 0.5 Pi); distance is 7.25*
(1.0 7.25 9.0)

Since the ANGLE argument is always referenced to the current construction plane, the value returned by the POLAR function retains the same Z coordinate as its PT (point) argument.

The POLAR function does not include the methods or techniques used for spherical or cylindrical coordinates.

Combining the ANGLE, DISTANCE, and POLAR Functions

The need to determine distances and angles arises frequently in AutoLISP programs, especially when the result is something being drawn. The following example incorporates the ANGLE, DISTANCE, and POLAR functions in a sequence, which results in an item callout balloon.

```
; BALLOON.LSP  written by B. Lunes  4/09/xx
;
; This program prompts for a balloon location, a part number, and a leader
; start point. It then draws a 5/16" balloon, fills in the part number, and
; draws the leader arrow.
;
; Local variables:  CC - Circle Center
;                   IN - Item Callout
;                   LS - Leader Start point
;
(defun C:BLN (/ CC IN LS)
  (setq CC (getpoint "\nCenter point for balloon: ")
        IN  (getstring "\nItem callout <max. 2 characters>: ")
        LS  (getpoint "\nLeader start point: ")
  )
  (command "CIRCLE" CC "D" 0.3125   ; Draw a 5/16" circle with center at CC
           "TEXT" "M" CC 0.125 0 IN ; Middle justified 1/8" text at circle center
           "DIM" "LEA" LS           ; Draw leader from LS
           (polar                   ; polar from
             LS                     ;   point LS
             (angle LS CC)          ;   at the angle between LS to CC
             (-                     ; distance for leader is
               (distance LS CC)     ;   distance from LS to CC minus
               0.15625              ;   circle radius of 0.15625
             )                      ; close – expression
           )                        ; close POLAR expression
           ^C ^C                    ; Cancel leader, Cancel DIM:
  )                                 ; close COMMAND expression
)                                   ; close DEFUN expression
```

In this example, two reference points were first established. Subsequently, all of the required data for the completion of this program could be derived.

The GETANGLE Function

The *GETANGLE function* is used when providing the option of either specifying an angle numerically or by picking it. The format for the GETANGLE function is as follows:

```
(getangle [PT] [PROMPT])
```

The GETANGLE function is used in a manner similar to the other GETxxxx functions. It awaits a response from the user in the form of a valid angle specification. This input may be in the form of a keyboard entry using any valid angular units format or by specifying 2D points in the current UCS.

The optional 2D PT (base point) argument works like the GETPOINT and GETCORNER functions; it supplies a rubberband line from the base point. The other optional argument allows a prompt to be supplied to the user. The angular value supplied to GETANGLE is measured in a counterclockwise direction, and returns a value expressed in radians. For example:

Command: **(getangle)** ↵ — *this expression awaits either a single numeric value or two valid 2D point coordinates*

Command: **(getangle '(5.0 7.0))** ↵ — *Here, the base point argument is used, and a rubberband line is drawn from the point indicated. A second 2D point entry is required. The 2D point may be indicated by picking, or by polar/relative/absolute coordinate specification.*

Command: **(getangle "\nSpecify the angle: ")** ↵ — *the PROMPT argument allows a custom message to be displayed*

Command: **(getangle '(5.0 7.0) "\nSpecify the angle: ")** ↵
both arguments can be used

An important concept to understand regarding the GETANGLE function is the difference between the *input angle* and the *angle returned by GETANGLE.* AutoCAD has settings available that modify the way it measures specified angles. The UNITS command allows the direction for angle 0 to be changed, as well as whether the angles are measured in a counterclockwise or clockwise direction. The AutoCAD system variables associated with these angular measurements are ANGBASE and ANGDIR.

Applying ANGDIR and ANGBASE

All angles that are supplied to the GETANGLE function are based on the current settings for ANGDIR and ANGBASE. The returned angle, however, is measured in a counterclockwise direction from the current ANGBASE, regardless of the value of ANGDIR. See Fig. 5-1.

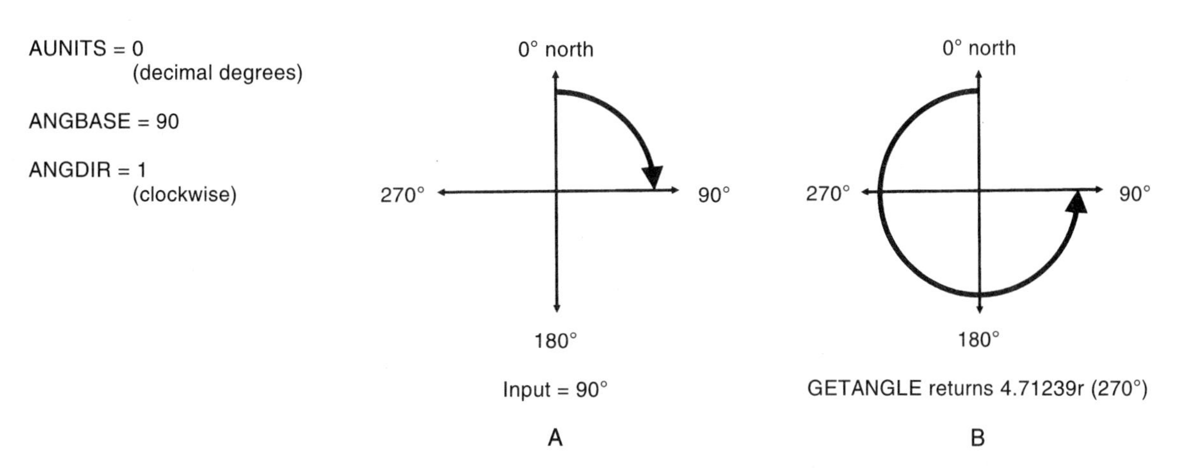

Fig. 5-1. All angles supplied to GETANGLE are based on the current ANGDIR and ANGBASE settings. However, the returned angle is measured in a counterclockwise direction.

Fig. 5-1A represents AutoCAD's measuring method for an input angle of 90° with the indicated settings. Fig. 5-1B shows the same angle as it is measured and returned by AutoLISP's GETANGLE function. Note that the same ANGBASE value is used for both input and output, but ANGDIR is ignored for the GETANGLE output. Therefore, given the settings in Fig. 5-1, an input angle of 90° causes GETANGLE to return 4.71239r (270 degrees).

This difference between input and output angles could be problematic to a program using GETANGLE to acquire a rotation angle specification. The following example utilizes an ANGBASE of 90 and an ANGDIR of 1:

```
Command: (rtd (getangle "Indicate rotation angle: ")) ↵
Indicate rotation angle: 90 ↵
270.0
```

In this case, the specified rotation of 90° actually results in a returned angle of 270°! There are a number of ways to avoid this predicament. First, realize that when specifying a rotation angle, it is more common for a user to input numeric data at the keyboard, rather than by picking points. Unless the situation requires points to be picked, the GETREAL function may be used to acquire numeric input of a rotation angle.

Another possible option would be to use a conditional function to test for the values of ANGBASE and ANGDIR, and adjust the value returned by GETANGLE appropriately. (Conditional functions are discussed in Chapter 8.)

The GETORIENT Function

The *GETORIENT function* is used when it is necessary to establish an absolute angle based on AutoCAD's default settings (ANGBASE = 0; ANGDIR = 0). The format for the GETORIENT function is:

```
(getorient [PT] [PROMPT])
```

The GETORIENT function is similar to the GETANGLE function with one significant difference–its output ignores *both* the ANGDIR and ANGBASE settings. Instead, AutoCAD's default values of 0° East, with angles measured counterclockwise, are always used for the returned angle.

Fig. 5-2 demonstrates the manner in which an input of 180° is interpreted by AutoCAD, given the settings shown. AutoLISP's output, using GETORIENT, is the absolute angle. This uses East ("true" 0°) as its angle base and measures in a counterclockwise direction, regardless

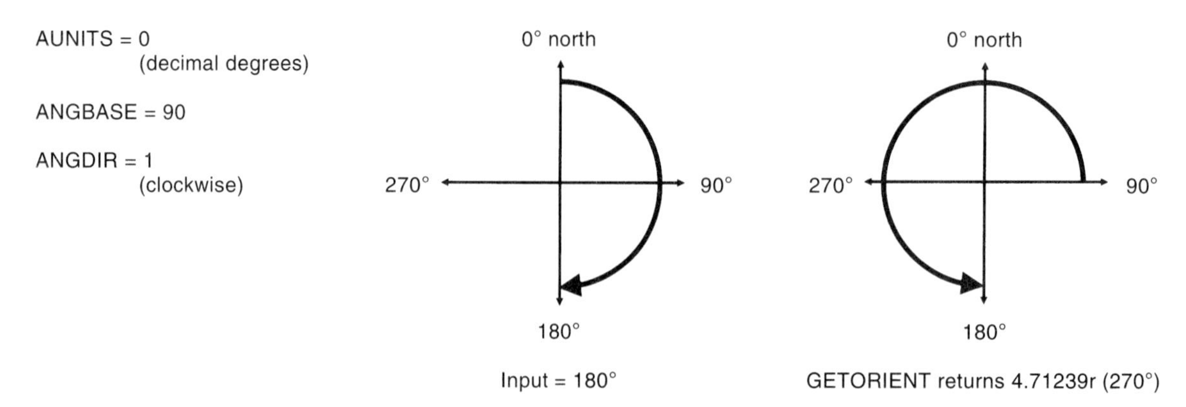

Fig. 5-2. The GETORIENT function uses East as its base angle, and measures in a counterclockwise direction, regardless of the ANGBASE and ANGDIR settings.

of the settings for ANGBASE and ANGDIR. When the 180° input is read, it is from the ANGBASE of 90°. With these settings, this denotes an angle pointing directly down. Based on the current ANGBASE setting, that angle would be interpreted as 180°. However, the GETORIENT function ignores the ANGBASE setting and returns the angle as equivalent to 270°.

(getorient)	*this expression awaits either a single numeric value or two valid 2D point coordinates*
(getorient '(4.0 2.0))	*Here, a rubberband line is drawn from the point indicated, and a second 2D point entry is required. The point may be indicated by picking, or by polar/relative/absolute coordinate specification.*
(getorient "\nOrientation angle: ")	*the PROMPT argument allows a custom message to be displayed*
(getorient '(5.0 7.0) "\nOrientation angle: ")	*both arguments can be used*

One application in which a 0° North orientation may be specified is a plat drawing. When placing text, it would be necessary to obtain the proper orientation angle. If horizontal text is desired, and the user picks a second point located horizontally to the right of the first, the following results are achieved:

Command: **ORTHO** ↵
ON/OFF ⟨current⟩: **ON** ↵
Command: **(rtd (getangle))** ↵
Second point: **270.0** ↵ — *The user picks a point, and then a second point to the right of the first. Note the results using GETANGLE.*

Command: **(rtd (getorient))** ↵
Second point: 0.0 — *The user picks a point, and then a second point to the right of the first. Note the results using GETORIENT.*

The following short routine reports the absolute angle between two picked coordinates using the GETORIENT function.

```
; ABSANGLE.LSP  written by H. Ford  Oct. 19xx
; This program defines the "rtd" function, prompts the user to
; input two X,Y,Z coordinates, and then issues the GETORIENT
; function to retrieve an absolute angle.
(defun rtd (A)
  (/ (* A 180.0) PI)
)
(setq AGL (getorient "\nChoose two X,Y,Z coordinates: "))
(prompt "\nThe absolute angle is: ") (rtd AGL)
```

The GETDIST Function

Similar to the relationship between ANGLE and GETANGLE, the DISTANCE function is complemented by the GETDIST function. The *GETDIST (GET DISTance) function* allows the user to input a distance or select two points. The format for the GETDIST function is as follows:

```
(getdist [PT] [PROMPT])
```

When a numeric value is typed in using the current units format as a response to GETDIST, the value is returned as a real number (for example, 1′ 3-1/4″ = 15.25). The optional base point argument–PT–can be either a 2D or 3D point. If either point argument is a 3D point, a 3D distance is returned. The optional PROMPT argument operates in the same manner as in the GETANGLE and GETORIENT functions.

(getdist)	*this expression awaits either a single numeric value or two valid 2D or 3D point coordinates*
(getdist '(3.5 1.0 0.0))	*Here, a rubberband line is drawn from the point indicated, and a second point must be entered. The point may be entered by picking or by specifying polar/relative/absolute coordinates.*
(getdist "\nSpecify the distance: ")	*the PROMPT argument allows a custom message to be displayed*
(getdist '(6.5 7.0) "\nSpecify the distance: ")	*both arguments can be used*

The GETDIST function is typically used only if the specified points are not previously referenced in the program. Otherwise, it is best to use the GETPOINT function, assign the points to variable names, and then use the DISTANCE function. This prevents the user from having to select the points more than once.

The following program allows for user input by implementing the GETDIST function and then displays the returned value. This program is an alternative to AutoCAD's DIST command, which eliminates the secondary list of information such as "Angle in X-Y Plane" and "Delta Z."

```
; DISTONLY.LSP  written by Howie Farr  May 19xx
; This program prompts the user to input a coordinate,
; and then issues the GETDIST function to retrieve a distance.
(defun C:DISTONLY (/ pt1 dst)
  (setq pt1 (getpoint "\nPick a starting point in your drawing: ")   ; Choose the 1st pt.
        dst (getdist pt1 "\nThe specified distance is ")              ; Choose a 2nd pt.
  )
)
```

EXERCISE 5-1

- ☐ Create a new program similar in style to DISTONLY.LSP, where this program includes a beginning SETQ statement, followed by a GETANGLE expression that prompts for the desired angle.
- ☐ Document the file accordingly, and name it ANGLONLY.LSP.

The next program incorporates the ANGLE, DISTANCE, GETDIST, and POLAR functions to create a door opening on a double-line wall. Note the usage of the OSMODE (Object Snap MODE) system variable to set the desired object snap. The OSMODE system variable is the subject of a Professional Tip found later in this chapter.

```
; DOOR.LSP  Written by O. Penit  11/29/xx
;
; Purpose: This program creates a door opening in a double-line wall,
;          and caps the loose ends. The user must select the nearest
;          intersection point on the wall lines for the opening, and
;          then select the opening start point nearest to that
;          intersection. The final selection indicates the parallel wall
;          line. The door width is requested as well. The following
;          Object Snap MODEs are set:
;                 OSMODE =   0 = NONe
;                 OSMODE =  32 = INTersection
;                 OSMODE = 128 = PERpendicular
;                 OSMODE = 512 = NEArest
;
(setvar "CMDECHO" 0)
(setq DORSIZ (getdist "\nSpecify door width: "))
(setvar "OSMODE" 32)
(setq PX (getpoint "\nPick intersection: "))
(setvar "OSMODE" 512)
(setq P1 (getpoint "\nPick opening start point (on same line): "))
(setvar "LASTPOINT" P1)
(setvar "OSMODE" 128)
(setq P2 (getpoint "\nPick second line: "))
(setvar "OSMODE" 0)
(setq ANG1 (angle PX P1)
      ANG2 (angle P1 P2)
      P3   (polar P1 ANG1 DORSIZ)
      P4   (polar P3 ANG2 (distance P1 P2))
)
(command ".break" P1 P3
         ".break" P2 P4
         ".line" P1 P2 ""
         ".line" P3 P4 ""
)
; --⟨ End of DOOR.LSP ⟩--
```

Let's Review...

1. The geometric constant pi evaluates to the real number 3.1415926, and must not be changed. It is a valuable tool for radian angle specification, and necessary for most angular conversions and calculations.
2. The ANGLE and GETANGLE functions return a user-specified angle in the form of radians. GETANGLE is influenced by the system variable ANGBASE, but always measures an angle counterclockwise.
3. The GETORIENT function returns a user-specified angle in the form of radians, and represents an absolute measurement based upon the "standard" AutoCAD compass. (The standard AutoCAD compass uses an ANGBASE of 0 and an ANGDIR of 0, with angles measured counterclockwise).
4. The DISTANCE and GETDIST functions return a user-specified distance in the form of a real number.
5. The POLAR function allows a new point to be derived by applying a distance and an angle from a specified reference point. Both 2D and 3D points may be obtained, but the change in the angle is restricted to the X-Y plane of the current construction plane.

EXERCISE 5-2

☐ Given the following assignments, solve the expressions given below. Assume the RTD and DTR conversion routines have been defined.

```
(setq PT1 '(3.0 5.0 0.0) PT2 '(12.0 23.0 0.0) M 90 N 270)
```

A. (angle PT1 PT2) ____________________
B. (rtd (angle PT1 PT2)) ____________________
C. (setq A (rtd (angle PT2 PT1))) ____________________
D. (setq B (dtr A)) ____________________
E. (setvar "ANGBASE" N) ____________________
F. (setq C (angle '(0.0 0.0 0.0) PT1)) ____________________
G. (distance PT1 PT2) ____________________
H. (setq D (distance PT2 PT1)) ____________________
I. (setq E (+ D (distance '(0 0 0) PT1))) ____________________
J. (setvar "ANGBASE" M) ____________________
K. (* B (/ 180.0 PI)) ____________________
L. (* PI (/ 180.0 PI)) ____________________

PROFESSIONAL TIP

Wherever appropriate, use the GETxxxx functions for both angle and distance manipulation. This enables the user to not only see a screen prompt, but it also affords a variety of options not found by the basic functions of ANGLE and DISTANCE. When using the GETxxxx functions in conjunction with standard AutoCAD commands in a menu file, remember to supply the correct number of backslashes when asking for user input. For example, when using the GETDIST function provide backslashes as follows:

```
[Pick dis]^C^C(setq d1 (getdist "Pick 2 points for distance: ")) \\+
.offset !d1 \\ ^C

[Type dis]^C^C(setq d1 (getdist "Type a distance value: ")) \+
.offset !d1 \\ ^C
```

Note that the first item utilizes two points as the specified offset distance (two backslashes), while the second item applies a typed distance value (one backslash). When two points have previously been established through AutoLISP input, then apply either ANGLE or DISTANCE.

OBJECT SNAP AND INTERSECTION POINTS

One method for increasing the accuracy in the drawing editor is to use object snap mode(s) when selecting points. AutoCAD allows the user to employ techniques such as object snap overrides and running object snap modes to enhance the accuracy within design drafting. Referencing entities by this process virtually guarantees proper alignment.

The OSNAP (Object SNAP) Function

AutoLISP is capable of accessing any applicable object snap modes through the OSNAP function. The format for this function is as follows:

```
(osnap PT MODE–STRING)
```

A point request modifier is applied to the PT argument based on the object snap modes listed in the MODE–STRING argument. The value returned is a 3D point that represents the nearest valid object snap point of those specified. If more than one object snap mode is utilized, they must be *delimited* (separated) with commas. Review the following examples as they apply to Fig. 5-3.

(osnap '(5 4) "CEN")	returns (3.0 4.0 0.0)	
(osnap '(6 3) "INT")	returns nil	*no INTersection was found within the aperture*
(osnap '(6 3) "MIDP,ENDP")	returns (6.0 2.0 0.0)	*the ENDPoint was the closest point*
(osnap '(6 4) "MIDP,ENDP")	returns (6.0 4.5 0.0)	*the MIDPoint was the closest point*
(osnap '(6 4) "MIDP,ENDP,NEA")	returns (6.0 4.0 0.0)	*NEArest is always the closest point of an entity*

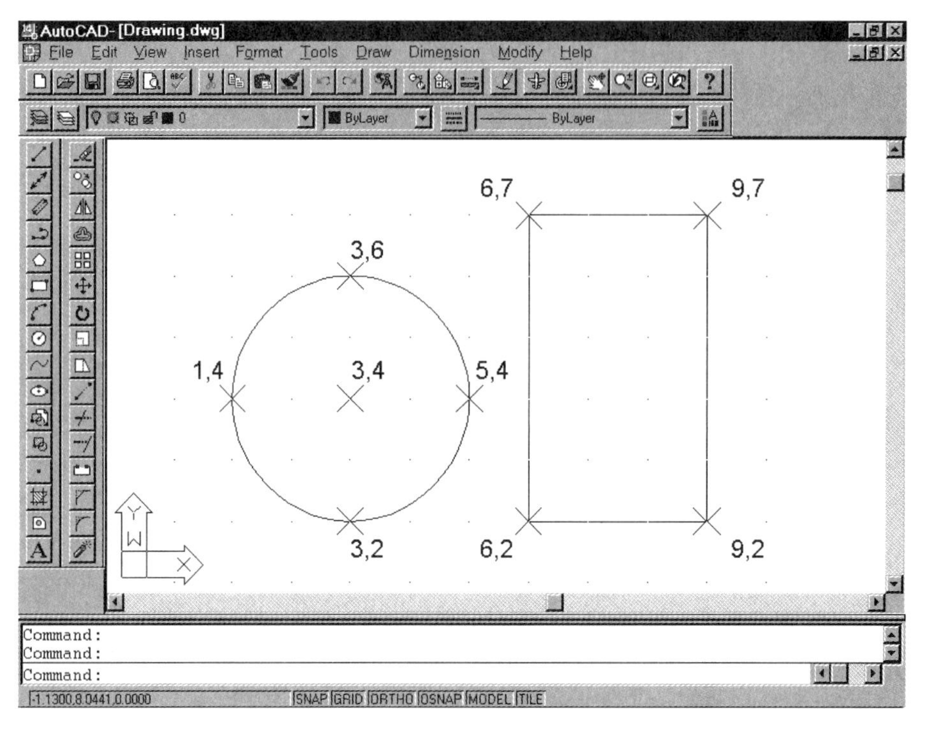

Fig. 5-3. Refer to the list of examples of OSNAP functions in conjunction with this illustration.

Certain restrictions apply to the use of the OSNAP function:

- As shown in Fig. 5-3, the target entity (or entities) must exist within the current aperture range of the point argument. The aperture size does not change as the view size changes. Therefore, an enlarged view will have a less effective aperture area than a reduced view. In the second example (shown at the bottom of the previous page), nil is returned since only one of the two entities creating the intersection is found in the aperture area. If the view were greatly reduced, the intersection might fall within the aperture area (along with several other candidates for selection). Be sure to give this consideration when using the OSNAP function.
- The OSNAP function only recognizes entities that are currently visible on the screen. Objects on layers that are frozen or turned off are not candidates for an object snap selection. In Release 14, locked layers are completely accessible with object snap modes and modifiers. Additionally, any entities outside of the current viewing area and pen-up portions of dashed lines cannot be accessed with the OSNAP function.
- The entity selected must support the object snap point specified in the MODE-STRING argument to be valid. For example, if a MIDP argument is specified and a circle is selected, nil is returned.
- The OSNAP function does not alter any running object snap modes, and does not consider them when making its selection.
- If the OSNAP function returns nil rather than a point, subsequent functions attempting to use the expected point will fail. Keep this in mind when designing an OSNAP expression.

PROFESSIONAL TIP

In many cases, setting the OSMODE system variable is preferable to using the OSNAP function. When a point is already known, use the OSNAP function. When allowing the user to supply a point, set the OSMODE variable and use a GETPOINT expression. This displays the familiar target box for the selection process.

The OSMODE settings are stored as *bit codes,* which means that multiple modes may be simultaneously activated by adding the numbers associated with specific modes. Remember that these are running modes and remain active until changed. Be sure to turn them off when not in use.

Use the following chart of associated bit codes for the OSMODE variable:

0 = NONE	8 = NODe	128 = PERPendicular	1024 = QUICK
1 = ENDPoint	16 = QUAdrant	256 = TANgent	2048 = APParent intersection
2 = MIDPoint	32 = INTersection	512 = NEArest	
4 = CENter	64 = INSertion		

The following examples illustrate the use of the OSMODE function:

(setvar "OSMODE" 32)	*sets the OSNAP INTersection mode*
(setvar "OSMODE" 3)	*sets the OSNAP ENDPoint and MIDPoint modes*
(setvar "OSMODE" 272)	*sets the OSNAP TANgent and QUAdrant modes*

The following AutoLISP program incorporates several of the functions discussed so far in this chapter. Study the usage of the OSNAP function versus the OSMODE function. Also, note the manipulation of pi for angular specifications, and the use of the POLAR function.

```
; Filename: MAKESLOT.LSP
; Programmer: Lotta Lines
; Date: 7/11/xx
;
; Purpose: Create a slot formation from two existing circles
;
; Prompts: Pick a point on the first circle:
;          Pick a point on the second circle:
;
; Restrictions: Completes operation only if circles are the same size.
;
; Local variables:    NP1 – First circle pick pt.
;                     NP2 – Second circle pick pt.
;                     CP1 – Center point 1
;                     CP2 – Center point 2
;                    ANGL – Lengthwise angle
;                    ANGW – Widthwise angle
;                    CRAD – Circle radius
;                     LP1 – Start for first line
```

```
;                          LP2 – End of first line
;                          OP1 – Offset point
;                          TP1 – Trim point 1
;                          TP2 – Trim point 2
;
(defun C:MAKESLOT (/ NP1 NP2 CP1 CP2 ANGL ANGW CRAD LP1 LP2 OP1 TP1 TP2)
  (setvar "OSMODE" 512)                                   ; osnap NEA
  (setq NP1 (getpoint "\nPick a point on the first circle: ")
        NP2 (getpoint "\nPick a point on the second circle: ")
  )
  (setvar "OSMODE" 0)                                     ; osnap NONE
  (setq CP1   (osnap NP1 "CEN")                           ; find CEN of circle 1
        CP2   (osnap NP2 "CEN")                           ; find CEN of circle 2
        ANGL  (angle CP1 CP2)                             ; angle lengthwise
        ANGW  (+ (* 0.5 pi) ANGL)                         ; angle lengthwise +90 degrees
        CRAD  (distance CP1 (NP1))                        ; radius circle 1
        LP1   (polar CP1 ANGW CRAD)                       ; first line start point
        LP2   (polar LP1 ANGL (distance CP1 CP2))         ; first line end point
  )
  (command ".line" LP1 LP2 ""
           ".select" "last" ""                            ; create Selection – set access to line
  )
  (setq OP1 (osnap LP1 "MID"))                            ; offset point – prohibits offset of circle
  (command ".offset" (* 2 CRAD) OP1 CP1 "")               ; offset line
  (setq TP1 (polar CP1 ANGL CRAD)                         ; trim point 1
        TP2 (polar CP2 (+ pi ANGL) CRAD)                  ; trim point 2
  )
  (command ".trim" "p" "last" "" TP1 TP2 "")              ; select lines for cut edges
  (prompt "\nDone.\n")                                    ; message when done
)
; – –< End of MAKESLOT.LSP >– –
```

EXERCISE 5-3

☐ Revise the MAKESLOT.LSP program to create a slot formation for two circles with different diameters. (Hint: The lines will need to be drawn TANgent to the circles.) Save the file as MAKSLOT2.LSP.

Finding Intersection Points

The *INTERS (INTERSection) function* is used to locate the intersection point of two nonparallel lines. The format for this function is as follows:

```
(inters PT1 PT2 PT3 PT4 [ONSEG])
```

The first two PT (point) arguments refer to the points on one line, and the last two PT (point) arguments are the points on the second line. Note that line entities are not required to exist at the specified points in order for the function to operate. If not all of the PT arguments represent 3D points, the lines are projected onto the current construction plane and INTERS searches for a 2D intersection point. Otherwise, a 3D intersection is searched for. Similar to the functions previously discussed, all coordinates are expressed in terms of the current UCS.

The optional ONSEG argument allows the user to check for a potential intersection point. If this argument is provided and has a nil value, the lines are treated as though they were of infinite length (in both directions). If the lines are not parallel, an intersecting point will be found–even if it falls beyond the endpoint of one or both lines. If this argument is not given, or has a non-nil value, the intersection point must be found on both line segments or nil is returned. For example:

```
(inters '(3 1) '(3 2) '(1 3) '(2 3) t)               returns nil
(inters '(3 1) '(3 2) '(1 3) '(2 3))                 returns nil
(inters '(3 1) '(3 2) '(1 3) '(2 3) nil)             returns (3.0 3.0)
(inters '(2 2 0) '(3 3 2) '(6 2 0) '(5 3 2) nil)     returns (4.0 4.0 4.0)
(inters '(2 2) '(3 3 2) '(6 2 0) '(5 3 2) nil)       returns (4.0 4.0)
```

Some of the possible applications for the INTERS function include finding intersections for trimming and extending operations. Potential intersection points can be found and the line endpoints subsequently changed to the new location. See Fig. 5-4.

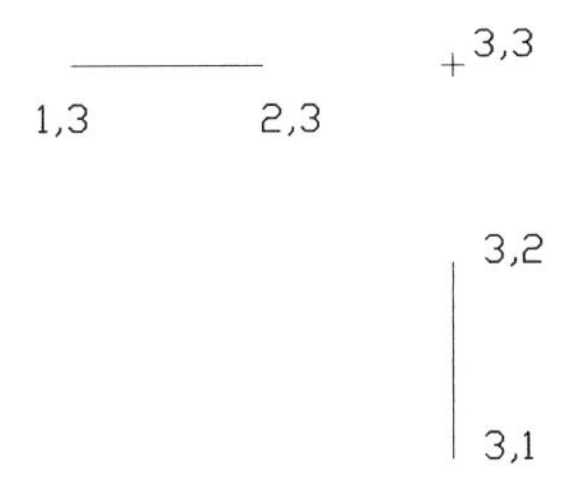

Fig. 5-4. If extended, the two lines would intersect at 3,3.

Let's Review...

1. The AutoLISP OSNAP function allows the programmer to have greater accuracy capabilities by utilizing the object snap modes. Several restrictions apply to its use, and many conditions can affect its usefulness, so OSNAP expressions should be considered and planned carefully.
2. In a situation that requires OSNAP reference to a user-supplied point, it is often best to use the GETPOINT function in conjunction with setting the OSMODE system variable. This method also supplies the familiar target box for the user, providing more of a built-in look and feel to the application.
3. The existing or potential intersection points of two lines can be found using the INTERS function. The point returned is expressed in terms of the current UCS. Remember, if the ONSEG argument is not supplied or has a non-nil value, the intersection point must lie on both of the lines, or the expression returns nil.

EXERCISE 5-4

☐ Given the following assignments, solve the expressions given below. Assume the RTD and DTR conversion routines have been defined. A polyline exists between endpoints PT1 and PT2.

```
(setq PT1 '(8.5 1.0 6.5) PT2 '(12.5 7.0 6.5) A 90 B 270)
```

A. (osnap PT2 "NEA") ____________________

B. (setq PT3 (osnap PT1 "MID")) ____________________

C. (polar PT1 (angle PT2 PT1) 2.5) ____________________

D. (setq PT4 (polar PT2 (dtr A) 5.5)) ____________________

E. (osnap PT1 "CEN") ____________________

F. (osnap PT1 "CEN,END") ____________________

G. (setq PT5 (polar PT1 (dtr B) 3.0)) ____________________

H. (polar PT2 PI (distance PT2 PT1)) ____________________

The following variables are also assigned:

```
(setq PTM '(1.5 9.0 6.5) PTN '(4.5 1.0 6.5))
```

I. (inters PT1 PT2 PTM PTN) ____________________

J. (inters PT1 PT2 PTM PTN nil) ____________________

K. (inters PT1 PTM PT2 PTN) ____________________

L. (inters PT1 PTM PT2 PTN nil) ____________________

CHAPTER TEST

Write your answers in the spaces provided.

1. What are the advantages of using AutoLISP functions such as GETANGLE and GETDIST versus AutoCAD inquiry commands such as ANGLE and DISTANCE?

____

____

____

____

____

2. Pi evaluates to the numeric value of ________. What is its significance in AutoLISP programming?

____

____

____

____

3. Provide the radian equivalents for each of the following decimal degree values using the pi constant in the middle column and a real number in the right column. The first example has been completed for you.

A. 90 degrees =	(* 0.5 pi)	=	1.5708	radians
B. 45 degrees =	________	=	________	radians
C. 15 degrees =	________	=	________	radians
D. 225 degrees =	________	=	________	radians
E. 30 degrees =	________	=	________	radians
F. 180 degrees =	________	=	________	radians
G. 135 degrees =	________	=	________	radians
H. 0.0 degrees =	________	=	________	radians
I. 270 degrees =	________	=	________	radians

4. If the pi constant is accidentally set to a different value, how can the original value be restored?

____

____

____

5. Explain the use of and importance of the RTD and DTR user-defined functions.

____

____

____

____

____

6. Explain the usage of both the AutoLISP ANGLE and GETANGLE functions. Also, under what circumstances would one be used instead of the other?

____

____

____

____

____

____

____

____

____

____

____

7. Detail the use of the CVUNIT function and list two possible error situations.

8. What AutoLISP function provides the capability of retrieving an absolute angle based upon the "standard" AutoCAD compass? How does this function's input differ from its output?

9. List the two functions that return distance information. Explain their usage and the difference in form for input and output.

10. Write a sample OSNAP expression.

11. When should the OSNAP function be used, and when should the OSMODE system variable be used with the GETPOINT function?

12. Describe two situations which affect the application of the AutoLISP OSNAP function.

13. Write the format for the AutoLISP POLAR function. Briefly describe each argument and its purpose.

____

____

____

____

____

____

____

14. Given the following assignments, provide the (x,y) or (x,y,z) coordinates for each POLAR expression.

    (setq PT1 '(1.0 1.5) PT2 '(12 5 4) PT3 '(6.5 3.5 11.0))

    A. (polar PT1 PI 3.0) = _______________
    B. (polar PT1 (* 0.5 PI) 3.0) = _______________
    C. (polar PT1 (* 1.5 PI) 8.5) = _______________
    D. (polar PT2 PI –1) = _______________
    E. (polar PT2 (* 0.0 PI) 9) = _______________
    F. (polar PT2 (* 3.0 PI) 7) = _______________
    G. (polar PT3 PI 2.5) = _______________
    H. (polar PT3 (* 1.5 PI) –4.0) = _______________
    I. (polar PT3 (* 0.5 PI) 0.0) = _______________

15. Detail the use of the AutoLISP INTERS function and list a few possible applications.

____

____

____

____

____

____

____

PROGRAMMING PROBLEMS

1. Study the following AutoLISP routine that creates a 3D pipe. The user is allowed to input a specified slope (drop per foot of pipe), as well as stipulate other construction criteria. Document all of the AutoLISP features within this program that pertain to the functions covered in Chapter 5. The documentation should include how and why the functions are used.

```
;   Filename:   PIPSLOPE.LSP
;   Author:   D. PLUMMER
;   Date:   10/10/xx
;
;   Purpose:  Calculates and draws a 3D pipe by slope/drop per foot.
;             The 3D pipe is created by an extruded circle.
;             User input should be in the form of Architectural units.
;
;   Local Variables:  SLP  RIS  P1  P2  DIS  ANG  SIZ  LU  LP  TH
;
(defun C:PIPSLOPE (/ SLP RIS P1 P2 DIS ANG SIZ LU LP TH)
  (setvar "cmdecho" 0)
;
;---< Store default units and precision >---
;
  (setq LP (getvar "luprec")
        LU (getvar "lunits")
        TH (getvar "thickness")
  )
  (setvar "lunits" 4)                       ; Set units to Architectural
  (setvar "luprec" 4)                       ; Set precision to 1/4"
;
;---<Retrieve parameters for constructing 3D pipe>---
;
  (setq P1     (getpoint "\nStart point for sloped 3D pipe: ")
        ANG    (getorient "\nEnter numeric X-Y angle from start point:")
        DIS    (getdist "\nEnter linear pipe distance in X-Y plane: ")
        SLP    (getreal "\nDecimal slope per foot [specify + or -]: ")
        SIZ    (getstring "\nDiameter size of pipe: ")
        P2     (polar P1 ANG DIS)
        RIS    (* (/ DIS 12.0) SLP)
        P2     (list (car P2) (cadr P2) (+ (caddr P2) RIS))
  )
  (setvar "thickness" (distance P1 P2))
  (command ".ucs" "za" P1 P2
           ".circle" "0,0,0" "d" SIZ
           ".ucs" ""
  )
  (setvar "lunits" LU)                      ; Reset default units
  (setvar "luprec" LP)                      ; Reset default precision
  (setvar "thickness" TH)                   ; Reset default thickness
  (setvar "cmdecho" 1)
  (prompt "\nDone.\n")
)
;---< End of PIPSLOPE.LSP >---
```

Chapter 6

Advanced Math Functions

Learning Objectives

After completing this chapter, you will be able to:

- ☐ Utilize AutoLISP functions to change the format of numerical data.
- ☐ Design programs that solve for unknown distances and angles using trigonometric functions.
- ☐ Explain the use of AutoLISP's advanced math functions.

APPLICATIONS OF MATH FUNCTIONS

AutoCAD is used in many different environments for a variety of drafting disciplines. The program is quite versatile, and is used as a productivity tool by drafters, engineers, and designers. One obvious need for a programming language used in these environments is a wide range of mathematical functions that can be drawn from. The AutoLISP programming language provides a wide range of math functions to meet almost any requirement. Having a strong understanding of these functions enables the programmer to solve complex equations by applying appropriate formulas within a program.

NUMERICAL FORMAT CONTROLS

Most programming applications require that the numerical arguments be presented in the proper format. Since information can be drawn from many different sources, these arguments may or may not be given in the required format. In response to this programming need, certain AutoLISP functions are used to alter numerical arguments to satisfy this requirement.

The FIX Function

The *FIX function* returns the integer value of a number. The returned integer is not a rounded value; rather, the number is merely truncated and everything to the right of the decimal point is discarded. The format for the FIX function is as follows:

```
(fix NUMBER)
```

Examples of the FIX function are:

```
(fix 23.4)          returns 23
(fix 23.99)         returns 23
(fix (/ 20 3))      returns 6          no remainder is given
(fix 33)            returns 33
```

If an integer argument is provided, the same integer is returned. This allows the FIX function to be used as a filter for functions requiring integer data where the input may be either a real number or an integer.

It is also possible to extract the decimal value of a number. Use the FIX function as follows. Note the use of the "–" (subtraction) function.

Command: **(setq N 6.375)(setq N (– N (fix N)))**↵ — *the integer value of N is subtracted, leaving only the decimal value*
0.375

When the argument provided for the FIX function is larger than the largest possible integer (+2,147,483,647 or -2,147,483,648 on a 32-bit platform), the value is returned as a truncated real number. For example:

```
(fix 2147483649.982224)          returns 2147483649.0
```

With numbers this large, the decimal value is discarded, but the data type of the returned value is not an integer, but a real.

The FLOAT Function

The *FLOAT function* returns the real number value of a number. The format for the FLOAT function is:

```
(float NUMBER)
```

The NUMBER argument is promoted to a floating point decimal (real) number. Similar to the FIX function, the supplied argument can be either a real number or an integer. For example:

```
(float 19)          returns 19.0
(float 24.045)      returns 24.045
(float (/ 4 2))     returns 2.0
```

The ABS Function

The *ABS (ABSolute) function* returns the absolute value (magnitude) of a number. In other words, a positive value is always returned whether a negative or positive value is supplied as an argument. The format for the ABS function is:

```
(abs NUMBER)
```

The supplied argument can be either a real number or an integer. For example:

```
(abs 56)            returns 56
(abs –56)           returns 56
(abs –56.0)         returns 56.0
(abs (* –2.0 2.0))  returns 4.0
(abs (– 12 15))     returns 3
```

As shown in the last example, one useful application for the ABS function is in determining the absolute difference between two numbers. When a cube root must be extracted, and the number is either positive or negative, the ABS function is used to ensure that the value is positive. In addition, this function is vital whenever a number is required as a magnitude since these values are always positive.

EXERCISE 6-1

☐ Provide the answers for the following FIX, FLOAT, and ABS expressions. Attempt to solve each statement without using the AutoLISP interpreter.

A. (fix (– 33.0 30)) ____________

B. (float (– 24)) ____________

C. (fix (+ 1.5 2.5)) ____________

D. (abs (– 18.5 19)) ____________

E. (abs (– 19 18.5)) ____________

F. (float (+ 3 4 5)) ____________

G. (fix (* 8.0 7.0)) ____________

H. (abs (* 4 5 6)) ____________

I. (fix (/ 25.0 5)) ____________

J. (float (/ 18 5)) ____________

MISCELLANEOUS MATH FUNCTIONS

The AutoLISP FIX, FLOAT, and ABS functions are quite basic in nature, and are simple to apply. The next section deals with mathematical functions that defy easy categorization, and are considered to be “miscellaneous” in their programming usage. Similar to those functions previously examined, the miscellaneous math functions deal with both integers and real numbers.

The REM Function

The *REM function* is similar to the division (/) function, except that it returns only the remainder. The format for the REM function is:

```
(rem NUMBER NUMBER ...)
```

REM divides the first NUMBER by the second NUMBER. The *remainder* is then divided by the third NUMBER (if an argument is provided). This remainder is then divided by the fourth NUMBER, and so on. When all division is complete, the remainder of the last step is returned. If there is no remainder, zero is returned.

```
(rem 7 2)                  returns 1
(rem 6 2)                  returns 0
(rem 6.0 2)                returns 0.0
(rem 24 5.0)               returns 4.0
(rem 121.0 64)             returns 57.0
(rem 121.0 64 10)          returns 7.0
(rem 621.0 500 64 10 3)    returns 1.0
```

In this example, 621.0 ÷ 500 = 1 with a remainder of 121.0. 121.0 is then divided by 64 (the next NUMBER) to obtain 1 with a remainder of 57.0. The 57.0 remainder is then divided by 10 to obtain 5 with a remainder of 7.0. The 7.0 value is finally divided by 3 to obtain 2 with a remainder of 1.0. The value 1.0 is then returned.

Applying the FIX and REM Functions. By combining the FIX and REM functions, both the quotient and remainder of an equation can be derived. Applying the FIX function to the result of a division expression returns an integer that represents the whole number portion of the quotient. Then, the REM function can find the remainder, as shown in the following example:

```
(setq Q (fix (/ 27.5 5)))
(setq R (rem 27.5 5))
```

The first expression sets Q equal to 5. The symbol R is then set to 2.5. Therefore, it is found that dividing 27.5 by 5 equals 5 with a remainder of 2.5.

The GCD Function

The *greatest common denominator* is the largest value that can be divided into other values without obtaining a remainder or a decimal value. The *GCD (Greatest Common Denominator) function* is used to determine the greatest common denominator of two integers. The format for this function is as follows:

```
(gcd NUMBER1 NUMBER2)
```

The greatest common denominator of two supplied integer arguments is returned by the GCD function. For example:

```
(gcd 32 48)            returns 16
(gcd 10 14)            returns 2
(gcd 27 9)             returns 9
(gcd 2 4 359.295)      returns 2      any number, whether integer or
                                      real, that follows the second
                                      integer argument is ignored
```

The MAX Function

The *MAX (MAXimum) function* returns the value of the largest NUMBER argument found within the expression. The format for the MAX function is:

```
(max NUMBER NUMBER ...)
```

Any number of arguments can be supplied–both real numbers and integers. The standard rules of promotion apply. If all arguments are integers, then an integer is returned. If any real numbers are specified, then the result will be a real number. For example:

```
(max 14 22)        returns 22
(max 3 994 16)     returns 994
(max 4.0 66)       returns 66.0
(max "A" "AB")     returns error: bad argument type    text strings are not permitted
```

The MIN Function

The *MIN (MINimum) function* performs the exact opposite function of the MAX function. MIN returns the NUMBER argument with the lowest value. The format for the MIN function is:

```
(min NUMBER NUMBER ...)
```

Examples of the MIN function follow:

```
(min 2 434 88)       returns 2
(min 39.03 46 8)     returns 8.0
```

EXERCISE 6-2

- ☐ Create a short program that uses the MAX function to find the largest numeric value between the following AutoCAD system variables:
  A. Chamfera
  B. Chamferb
  C. Filletrad
  D. Circlerad
  (Hint: Use the GETVAR function to return the variable values.) Report the MAXimum value to the screen.
- ☐ Name the file EX6-2.LSP.

TRIGONOMETRIC FUNCTIONS

Since drafters and designers frequently work with distances and angles, a need arises for the use of trigonometry. See Fig. 6-1. Three basic trigonometric functions are provided within AutoLISP–sine (SIN), cosine (COS), and arctangent (ATAN).

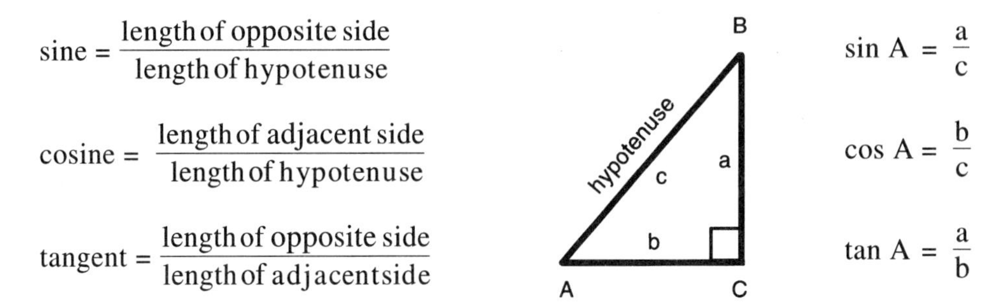

Fig. 6-1. Trigonometric functions.

The SIN Function

The *SIN (SINe) function* returns the sine of an ANGLE argument. The proper format for the SIN function is:

```
(sin ANGLE)
```

The value returned by the SIN function is always returned as a real number. Note that ANGLE must be specified in radians.

```
(sin 0.2618)                              returns 0.25882
(sin (* pi 0.25))                         returns 0.707107
(sin (cvunit 60 "DEGREES" "RADIANS"))     returns 0.866025
(sin (dtr 30.0))                          returns 0.5
```

Remember that the DTR (Degrees to Radians) function is a user-defined function; the last example works only if DTR has previously been defined.

The SIN function, applied in the following program, utilizes trigonometric ratios to solve for the amount of rise of an angled line. This could be useful for many types of engineering projects.

```
; RISE.LSP written by A. Line
; Date: 6-22-xx
; (sin (angle PT1 PT2)) is the sine of the included angle
; (distance PT1 PT2) is the hypotenuse
; Multiplying these two arguments returns the opposite side (rise)
(defun C:RISE (/ PT1 PT2)
  (setvar "OSMODE" 1)                          ; OSnap MODE – Endpoint
  (setq PT1 (getpoint "\nPick highest endpoint: "))
  (setq PT2 (getpoint "\nPick lowest endpoint: "))
  (setvar "OSMODE" 0)                          ; OSnap MODE – None
  (prompt "\nThe total rise of this line is: ")
  (abs (* (distance PT1 PT2) (sin (angle PT1 PT2))))
)
```

The COS Function

AutoLISP's *COS (COSine) function* returns the cosine of an ANGLE argument. The format for this function is:

```
(cos ANGLE)
```

As with the SIN function, COS requires that its ANGLE argument be expressed in radians. For example:

```
(cos (* PI 0.125))                          returns 0.92388
(cos (cvunit 30 "DEGREES" "RADIANS"))       returns 0.866025
(cos (dtr 60.0))                            returns 0.5
```

The previous program uses the SIN function to return the total *rise* of an angled line. By replacing the SIN function with the COS function, the program returns the total *run* of the selected line. For example:

```
; RUN.LSP  written by B. Line
; Date: 6-30-xx
; (cos (angle PT1 PT2)) is the cosine of the included angle
; (distance PT1 PT2) is the hypotenuse
; Multiplying these two arguments returns the adjacent side (run)
(defun C:RUN (/ PT1 PT2)
  (setvar "OSMODE" 1)                           ; OSnap MODE – Endpoint
  (setq PT1 (getpoint "\nPick highest endpoint: "))
  (setq PT2 (getpoint "\nPick lowest endpoint: "))
  (setvar "OSMODE" 0)                           ; OSnap MODE – None
  (prompt "\nThe total run of this line is: ")
  (abs (* (distance PT1 PT2) (cos (angle PT1 PT2))))
)
```

The ATAN Function

According to trigonometric ratios, the *tangent* of an angle is equal to the length of the side opposite the angle divided by the length of the side adjacent to the angle. (Refer back to Fig. 6-1.) Once the tangent has been determined, the *arctangent* (inverse tangent) can be found, which represents the value of the angle. *ATAN (ArcTANgent)* is AutoLISP's arctangent function. The ATAN function syntax is:

```
(atan NUM1 [NUM2])
```

When the optional NUM2 argument is *not* supplied, the ATAN function returns the arctangent of NUM1. In this situation, NUM1 represents the quotient of the length of the opposite side divided by the length of the adjacent side. The angle is returned in radians, and will be in the range of pi/2 radians (+90°) to –pi/2 radians (–90°). Examples follow:

```
(rtd (atan 1))                              returns  45.0        both legs are equal
(rtd (atan 4.0))                            returns  75.9638
(atan –1)                                   returns –0.785398
(cvunit (atan –1) "RADIANS" "DEGREES")      returns –45.0
```

If the optional argument NUM2 *is* specified, then NUM1 represents the opposite side and NUM2 represents the adjacent side. The quotient of NUM1/NUM2 is derived, and the ATAN function is applied. Note that if NUM2 is 0, there is rise but no run. Therefore, the angle will be plus or minus pi/2 radians (+90° or –90°) depending on the sign of the NUM1 argument.

```
(atan 1 1)                                   returns 0.785398
(cvunit (atan 60 15) "RADIANS" "DEGREES")    returns 75.9638
(cvunit (atan 11 0) "RADIANS" "DEGREES")     returns 90.0
```

The following sample routine uses the ATAN function. The purpose of the function is to allow a user to input the rise and run of a line, and then return the slope angle in degrees.

```
; R_AND_R.LSP
; By: Up'n Down
; Date: 7-1-xx
; (atan D1 D2) is the arctangent of the opposite side/adjacent side
; (cvunit (atan D1 D2) "RADIANS" "DEGREES") converts atan radians to degrees
(defun C:R_AND_R (/ D1 D2)
  (setq D1 (getdist "\nWhat is the rise?: "))
  (setq D2 (getdist "\nWhat is the run?: "))
  (prompt "\nThe angle in the X-Y plane [in degrees] is: ")
  (cvunit (atan D1 D2) "RADIANS" "DEGREES")
)
```

The SIN, COS, and ATAN functions represent all of the fundamental trigonometry tools provided within AutoLISP, but virtually all trigonometric functions can be derived from them. This represents a very powerful group of functions for geometric problem solving.

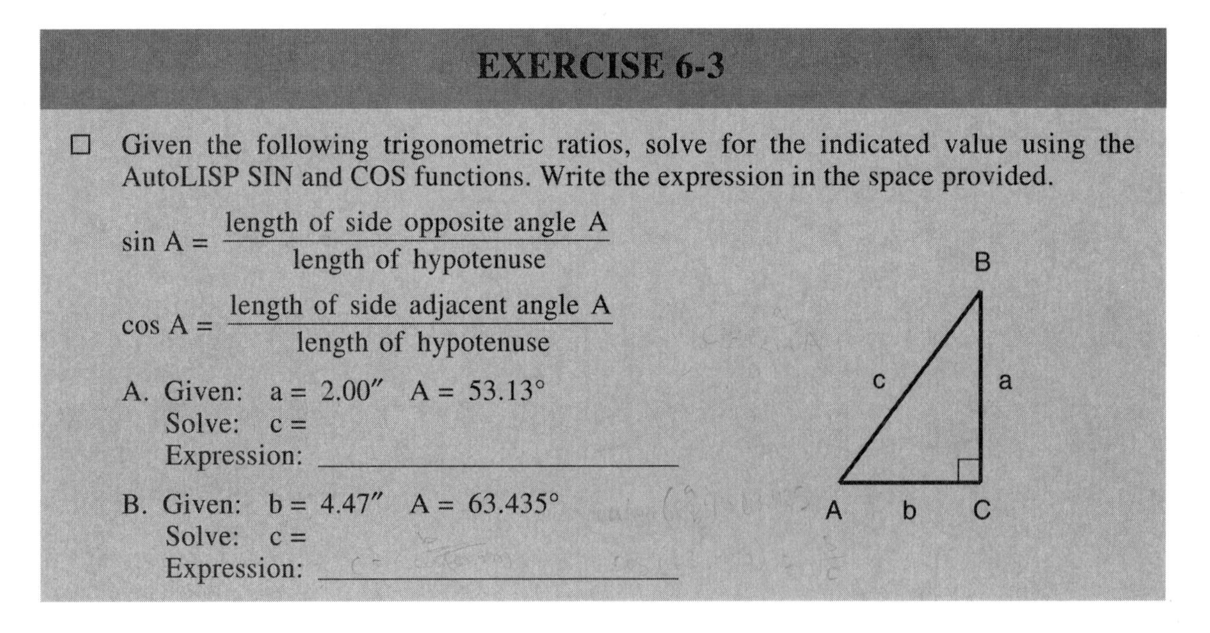

EXERCISE 6-3

☐ Given the following trigonometric ratios, solve for the indicated value using the AutoLISP SIN and COS functions. Write the expression in the space provided.

$$\sin A = \frac{\text{length of side opposite angle A}}{\text{length of hypotenuse}}$$

$$\cos A = \frac{\text{length of side adjacent angle A}}{\text{length of hypotenuse}}$$

A. Given: a = 2.00″ A = 53.13°
Solve: c =
Expression: ______________

B. Given: b = 4.47″ A = 63.435°
Solve: c =
Expression: ______________

EXPONENTS, ROOTS, AND LOGS

The next group of functions addresses the requirements of more complex mathematical equations. The use of exponents, derived roots, and natural logs, combined with basic math functions, allows for the solution of many useful formulas using AutoLISP.

The EXPT Function

The *EXPT (EXPonenT) function* allows you to use base numbers and exponents to express values. The format for the EXPT function is:

```
(expt BASE POWER)
```

The number returned represents the result of raising BASE to the specified POWER. Each argument may be presented as either a real number or an integer. If one or both of the supplied arguments are real numbers, then the returned value will also be a real number. For example:

```
(expt 2 2)        returns 4
(expt 3.0 2)      returns 9.0
(expt 1.5 4)      returns 5.0625
(expt 6 3)        returns 216
```

When applying more advanced exponential functions, the option is also available to specify decimal values and negative exponents. For example:

```
(expt 2 –4.0)     returns 0.0625
(expt 2 0.5)      returns 1.41421
(expt 2 2.5)      returns 5.65685
```

PROFESSIONAL TIP

The use of exponents can often result in very large numbers. Handling large numbers requires that you take into account certain limitations of your computer system. As discussed in Chapter 4, integer values have specific restrictions depending on whether the computer being used is a 16-bit or 32-bit system. For MS-DOS®, OS/2® 1.1 and 1.2, and PC-DOS computer systems, integers are 16-bit signed numbers, and therefore fall between –32768 and +32767. On DOS systems using the 386|DOS-Extender from Phar Lap® Software, Inc. and 32-bit systems, the range for AutoLISP integers is between –2,147,483,648 and +2,147,483,647. Even on 32-bit systems, any integer exchanged between AutoCAD and AutoLISP is limited to a 16-bit value.

When it becomes necessary to utilize numbers with values beyond the limitations of your system, then they must be real numbers. The restrictions for integers do not apply to real numbers:

```
(expt 500 4)      returns –1924509440
(expt 500.0 4)    returns  6.25e+10
```

When attempting to derive integer values that exceed the capacity of the system, negative or zero values may be returned. To avoid this problem, always use real numbers when the result has the potential of going beyond the integer limits.

The SQRT Function

The square root of a number is returned by the *SQRT (SQuare RooT) function.* The NUMBER argument can be specified as a real number or an integer. The result is always given as a real number. The format for the SQRT function is:

```
(sqrt NUMBER)
```

Examples of the SQRT function follow:

```
(sqrt 2.0)          returns 1.41421
(sqrt 16)           returns 4.0
(sqrt –4)           returns error: function undefined for argument
(sqrt (abs –4))     returns 2.0
```

The NUMBER argument must be positive or an error results. If there is a question as to whether the supplied number will be positive or negative, use the ABS function to avoid any problems.

The LOG Function

The *LOG (LOGarithm) function* returns the natural log of the supplied NUMBER argument. The result is always returned as a real number. The format for the LOG function is:

```
(log NUMBER)
```

```
(log 6)             returns 1.79176
(log 9.33)          returns 2.23324
(log 21)            returns 3.04452
(log –2)            returns error: function undefined for argument
```

The EXP Function

Logarithmic functions are inverse to exponential functions. The *EXP function* is the inverse of the LOG function. The format for the EXP function is as follows:

```
(exp NUMBER)
```

The EXP function returns the natural antilog of NUMBER, or e raised to the NUMBER power. The value *e* (equal to 2.71828182845905...) is an irrational number similar to pi, and is fundamental to technical and scientific work. Examples of the EXP function follow:

```
(exp 1.79176)       returns 5.99904
(exp (log 6))       returns 6.0          the antilog is the inverse of the log
(exp 4.2)           returns 66.6863
(exp 1)             returns 2.71828      the value of e (2.71828)
```

Applying the LOG and EXP Functions. The application that follows uses both the LOG and EXP functions, and allows any root to be drawn from a number. The only intrinsic root extraction function in AutoLISP is for square roots, but the following program can extract any root.

```
(defun C:ROOT (/ NUM R)
  (setq NUM (abs (getreal "\nBase: ")))
  (setq R (getreal "\nRoot level: "))
  (prompt "\nThe specified root is: ")
  (exp (/ (log NUM) R))
)
```

For evaluation purposes, only the last expression is used by substituting numbers for symbol names:

```
Command: (setq N (exp (/ (log 2) 16))) ↵        extract the 16th root of 2
1.04427
```

To verify the expression, use the EXPT function as follows:

```
Command: (expt N 16) ↵
2.0
```

A strong understanding of the mathematical functions discussed in this chapter enables the programmer to design routines that solve complex mathematical formulas. Such programs not only automate drawing procedures, but can also aid in the design process by supplying necessary engineering data.

Let's Review...

1. The FIX, FLOAT, and ABS functions allow the programmer to handle numerical data with more flexibility by providing a means to alter the format as required.
2. AutoLISP offers three basic trigonometric functions–SIN, COS, and ATAN. Any of the remaining trigonometric formulas can be derived using these three functions.
3. Several advanced mathematical functions are supplied for solving more complex equations. These include the SQRT, EXP, and LOG functions.

CHAPTER TEST

Write your answers in the spaces provided.

1. Explain the use of the FIX function.

____

____

____

____

____

2. How does FIX respond if its argument is already an integer?

____

____

3. The ______________ function is used to convert integers into floating point decimal (real) numbers.
4. What is the purpose of the ABS function? List some possible applications.

____

____

____

____

5. Explain the use of the REM function and describe one possible application.

6. What is the purpose of the GCD function?

7. Describe the MIN and MAX functions. Do these functions return integers or real numbers?

8. How are exponent values specified within AutoLISP? Explain the use of this function.

9. When working with potentially very large numbers, what precautions should be taken by the programmer? Explain your answer.

10. Describe the use of the SQRT function. What type of number produces an error situation? How can such errors be avoided?

11. What is the number e and which function is based on this number? Detail its use.

____
____
____
____
____
____
____
____

12. What function is inverse to exponential functions? Describe the use of this function.

____
____
____
____
____
____
____

PROGRAMMING PROBLEMS

1. Create an AutoLISP program file named HYP.LSP that defines a command line function called C:HYP to solve for the hypotenuse of a right triangle when given the lengths of the other two legs. Prompt for the required values and use the Pythagorean Theorem to find the solution:

   $$C = \sqrt{a^2 + b^2}$$

2. Create an AutoLISP program file named TRI-AREA.LSP that defines a command line function named C:TA which solves for the area of a triangle. It will prompt for the lengths of all three sides and return the result. The formula to use is:

   $$A = \sqrt{s(s - a)(s - b)(s - c)}$$

   Where $s = 0.5 \times (a + b + c)$, and a, b, and c are the lengths of the three sides.
3. Design a program called COS.LSP that solves for the length of one of the three sides of a right triangle. Use the following formula:

   $$\cos \text{angle} = \frac{\text{length of side adjacent to angle}}{\text{length of hypotenuse}}$$

   Prompt the user for the required information.

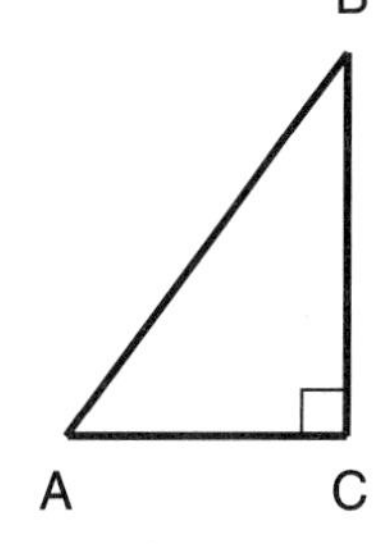

4. Design a simple routine that prompts for a base and a power and returns the base number raised to the specified power. Name the program EXPONENT.LSP.
5. The following programming problem involves a number of advanced math functions. To summarize, the goal for this problem is to combine two factors–an internal area measurement and the number of sides–to create a polygon. Rather than asking the user to supply radius or length of one of the sides (as with the AutoCAD POLYGON command), this routine will solve for these elements. The following diagram shows a regular polygon circumscribing a circle: Note that two elements are represented by this figure–an inscribed radius (R) and the length of one side (S). The radius can be found by implementing the equation shown below:

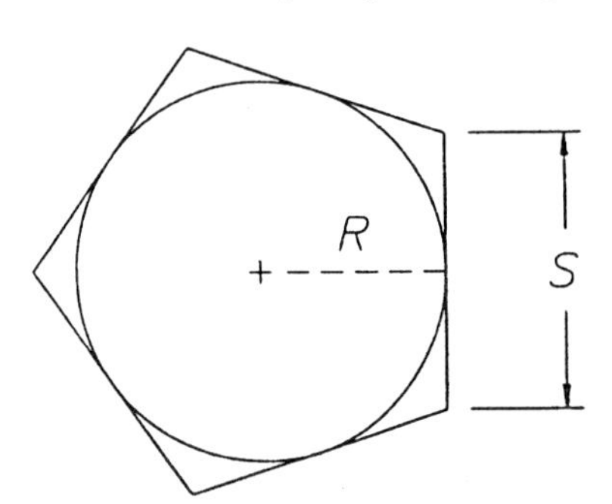

$$\sqrt{\frac{A}{N * (\sin\frac{pi}{N} / \cos\frac{pi}{N})}} = R$$

where,

A = Area of the POLYGON
N = Number of sides
R = Radius of inscribed circle
sin = Sine function
cos = Cosine function
pi = 180° (as radians)

Reformatting the equation yields:

$$\sqrt{[A / \{N * (\sin\frac{pi}{N} / \cos\frac{pi}{N})\}]} = R$$

In AutoLISP code, this statement would be written as:

```
(setq R (sqrt (/ AREA (* NUM (/ (sin (/ pi NUM)) (cos (/ pi NUM)))))))
```

Note the use of AutoLISP functions in lowercase, and user-assigned symbols in uppercase. Compare the two expressions for similarity.

Based upon the information given, develop a program that creates an AutoCAD polygon using the steps listed below:

A. Ask the user for the following three pieces of information:
   - The number of sides for the polygon (symbol NUM).
   - The internal area measurement for the polygon (symbol AREA).
   - The starting point for one edge of the polygon (symbol SP).
B. Implement the AutoLISP statement shown above to solve for the radius of the inscribed circle. Assign the radius to symbol RAD.

C. Rewrite the equation shown below in a format that is understandable to AutoLISP.

$$[2 * R * (\sin \frac{pi}{N} / \cos \frac{pi}{N})] = S$$

where,

A = Radius of inscribed circle
sin = Sine function
cos = Cosine function
pi = 180° (as radians)
S = Length of one side

For this expression, the length of one side of the polygon is derived. Assign this length to the symbol SIDE.

D. Find a complementary ending point to symbol SP. Finally, draw the new POLYGON. Document and name this file POLYAREA.LSP.

BP.LSP

```
; BP.LSP  -  Block Pick LiSP
; Purpose: Allows the user to pick a block on screen for insertion.
;             Uses the VWL (VoWeL) function below for message displayed.
;
(defun C:BP (/ ET EG BN)
   (prompt "\nSelect block to insert: ")
   (while (null (setq ES (entsel)))
          (princ "\nYou missed!")
   )
   (if (= "INSERT" (setq ET (cdr (assoc 0 (setq EG (entget (car ES)))))))
          (cond
                 ((= "*" (substr (cdr (assoc 2 EG)) 1 1))
                  (princ "\nEntity selected is not a USER block.")
                  (princ)
                 )
                 (T
                  (setq BN (cdr (assoc 2 EG)))
                  (command "INSERT" BN)
                  (princ)
          )      )
          (progn
                  (if (VWL ET) (setq N "n") (setq N ""))
                  (if (= "TEXT" ET) (setq ET (strcat ET " entity.")))
                  (princ (strcat "\nEntity selected is a "N " " ET))
   ) ) (princ)
)

; VWL function. Returns T if string argument is a vowel, nil otherwise.
; Usage = (VWL 〈arg〉)           {used in C:BP 〈Block Pick〉}
(defun VWL (X))
   (member (substr X 1 1))
            '("A" "a" "E" "e" "I" "i" "O" "o" "U" "u" "X" "x")
   )
)
```

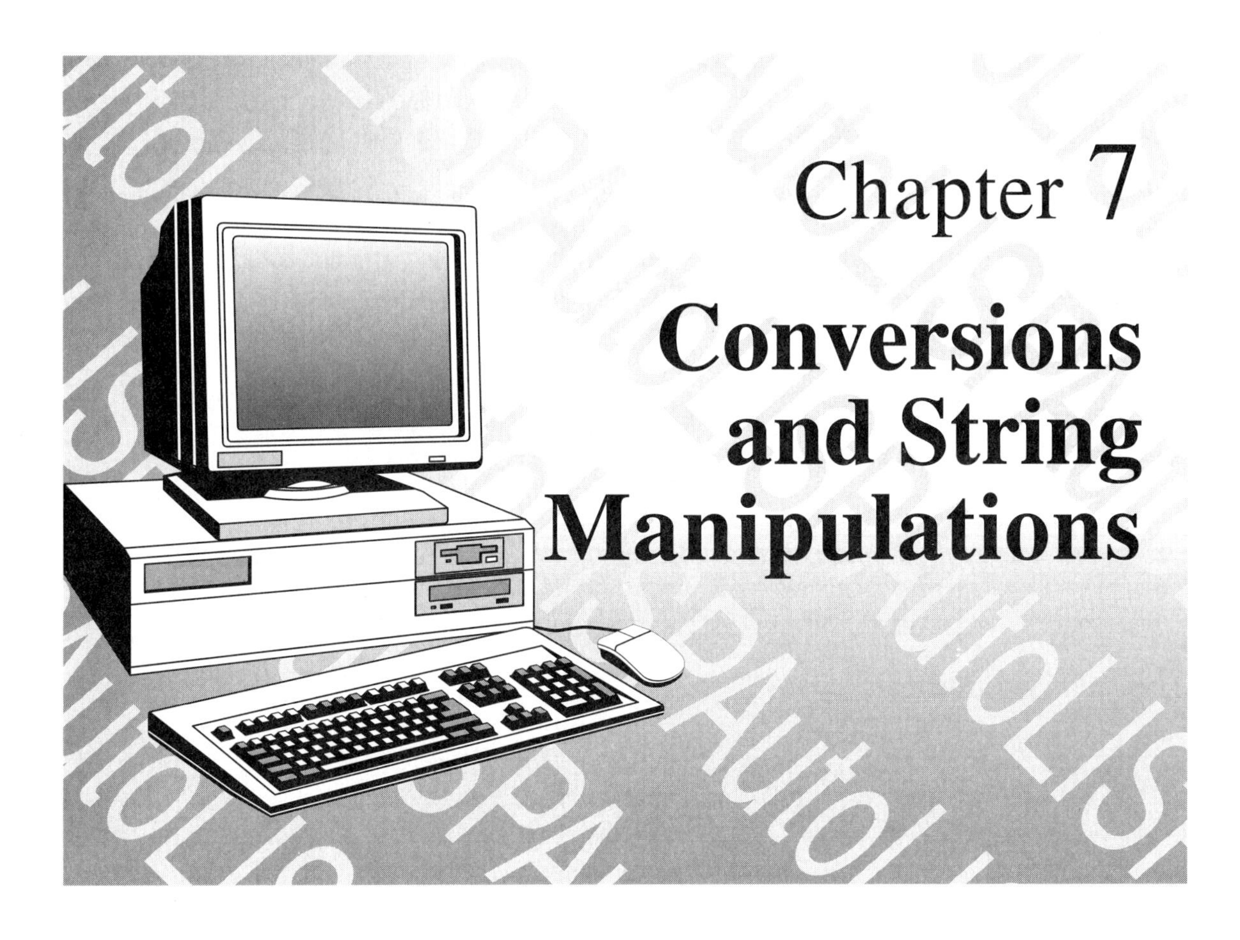

Chapter 7

Conversions and String Manipulations

Learning Objectives

After completing this chapter, you will be able to:

- ☐ Recognize the need for data conversions and string manipulations.
- ☐ Implement AutoLISP conversion functions to modify data types.
- ☐ Supply text strings with functions other than the PROMPT function.
- ☐ Apply a variety of AutoLISP functions that change the appearance of strings, concatenate strings, and create substrings.

AUTOLISP DATA CONVERSION AND STRING MANIPULATION

AutoLISP data types such as real numbers and strings can be retrieved by using functions such as GETREAL and GETSTRING, respectively. These values can then be used to complete either mathematical or text-based operations. Once an answer is supplied, it can then be applied to the appropriate AutoLISP function or AutoCAD command.

While this practice is the basis for many AutoLISP programs, there are occasions when a data item must be retrieved from a source that does not supply it in the proper format. An example of this might be attempting to print a message to the screen listing the current limits of a drawing. The source of this information–the LIMMAX and LIMMIN system variables–are lists of real numbers. Supplying a real number as an argument to some printing functions, such as PROMPT, results in a "bad argument type" error message. Under these and other similar circumstances, numbers and text strings must be modified in order to provide acceptable arguments to AutoLISP functions, and avoid potential error situations.

AutoLISP offers many data conversion and string manipulation functions that provide additional programming flexibility, such as merging integers with text strings to form user prompts with number defaults. This capability provides the programmer with many new options for providing an intuitive and user-friendly program that has the "built-in" look and feel. This, in turn, helps the user to feel more comfortable in using an application, and tends to reduce erroneous entries. Understanding the concepts of data conversion and string manipulation is a prerequisite to creating programs which are truly "user-friendly."

CONVERTING TEXT STRINGS INTO NUMERICAL DATA AND NUMERICAL DATA INTO TEXT STRINGS

Values returned by basic AutoLISP GETxxxx expressions, without conversion, are typically used for a single purpose and then "discarded." When the AutoLISP conversion functions are applied, these elements become multifunctional tools for various programming tasks, making them more conducive to problem solving.

The ATOF Function

The *ATOF (Ascii TO Floating point decimal) function* converts string data into a real number. The syntax for the ATOF function is as follows:

```
(atof STRING)
```

Basically, the ATOF function strips the set of quotation marks from the STRING argument, thus returning a real number. A real number is returned regardless of whether STRING represents a real number or an integer. Given the following variable assignments, several examples are used to illustrate the use of the ATOF function.

```
(setq A "5.25"   B "45"   C "CAPSCREW"   D "24x18 BORDER")
```

(atof "33.75")	returns 33.75	
(atof "21")	returns 21.0	
(atof "1.")	returns 1.0	
(atof ".56")	returns 0.56	
(atof A)	returns 5.25	
(atof B)	returns 45.0	
(atof "33.2E–09")	returns 3.32e–08	*the ATOF function employs exponential notation*
(atof "7–1/2")	returns 7.0	*the ATOF function does not recognize fractions*
(atof C)	returns 0.0	*no numerical value was found*
(atof D)	returns 24.0	*the first numerical atom that is found is evaluated*
(atof "")	returns 0.0	
(atof "3.15" "62")	returns error: too many arguments	*the ATOF function uses only one argument*

Using the values previously set for A and B, the next expression shows the combination and conversion of data types:

Command: **(prompt "\nThe product of [A * B] is: ")(* (atof A)(atof B))** ↵
The product of [A * B] is: 236.25

In this case, the text values of A and B are not valid arguments for the multiplication function. The values returned by the ATOF expressions are multiplied instead. Note that this conversion process does not actually alter the original variable setting. Examine the following example:

```
(setq A (atof A))
```

This expression reassigns the value returned by (atof A) to the variable possessing the same name.

The DISTOF Function

The *DISTOF (DIStance TO Floating point decimal) function* converts string data into a real number, similar to the ATOF function. The syntax for the DISTOF function is:

```
(distof STRING [MODE])
```

The STRING argument must be written in the format specified by the MODE argument, the system of linear units. If the MODE argument is not present in the expression, the DISTOF function uses the current value of the AutoCAD LUNITS system variable. When the STRING argument is written improperly, DISTOF returns nil. The chart in Fig. 7-1 lists the available integer assignments for the MODE argument.

Mode	Format
1	Scientific
2	Decimal
3	Engineering (feet and decimal inches)
4	Architectural (feet and fractional inches)
5	Arbitrary fractional units

Fig. 7-1. Available integer assignments for DISTOF and RTOS MODE argument.

Within the chart shown in Fig. 7-1, modes 3 and 4 are treated the same, where the STRING argument can be presented in either format and return the correct real number value. The following examples illustrate the usage of the DISTOF function:

```
(distof "8.2500E+01" 1)      returns  82.5      MODE 1 = Scientific
(distof "82.50" 2)           returns  82.5      MODE 2 = Decimal
(distof "6'–10.50\"" 3)      returns  82.5      MODE 3 = Engineering
(distof "6'–10 1/2\"" 4)     returns  82.5      MODE 4 = Architectural
(distof "82 1/2" 5)          returns  82.5      MODE 5 = Fractional
```

Note that each expression returns the same real number value. The inclusion of the \" substring (modes 3 and 4) forces an inch mark to be part of the overall STRING argument. This technique is similar to the control codes used for both newlines and tabs.

The ATOI Function

While some functions require real numbers as arguments, others can only utilize integer values. The *ATOI (Ascii TO Integer) function* converts string data into an integer. The format for the ATOI function is:

```
(atoi STRING)
```

Like the ATOF function, the ATOI function strips the set of quotation marks from the STRING argument, thus returning an integer. If the numbers represented are real numbers, they are FIXed (returned as integers). Given the same variable assignments as previously used for the ATOF function, the following examples illustrate the ATOI function:

(atoi "33.75")	returns 33	
(atoi "21")	returns 21	
(atoi A)	returns 5	
(atoi "4.3e03")	returns 4	*the ATOI function ignores exponential notation*
(atoi C)	returns 0	*no numerical value was found*
(atoi D)	returns 24	*symbol d begins with "24"*

If you want to return an integer from the exponential format, the following expression serves as an alternative:

(fix (atof "4.3e03"))	returns 4300	*invoke the ATOF function first, then truncate the decimals*

The RTOS Function

Many programming applications are required to supply data to the user. In cases where numerical data is supplied, standard screen printing functions (such as PROMPT) will not accept it as an argument; it must first be converted into string data. The *RTOS (Real TO String) function* returns a string that represents the given number argument. The format for the RTOS function is as follows:

```
(rtos NUMBER [MODE [PRECISION]])
```

The MODE and PRECISION settings are optional integer arguments, which relate to the AutoCAD system variables LUNITS (Linear UNITS) and LUPREC (Linear Units of PRECision), respectively. This function is also affected by the DIMZIN (DIMension Zero INches) and UNITMODE system variables. The chart shown in Fig. 7-1 lists the available integer assignments for the MODE argument.

If the MODE and PRECISION arguments are not present within the expression, the current units and units precision are used. UNITMODE applies only to the RTOS MODE values of 3, 4, or 5, and assists in returning string values that are compatible with actual AutoCAD number responses, such as 11'6–3/4" for architectural format. (Note the absence of spaces in this value.)

With the AutoCAD dimensioning variable DIMZIN = 0, and provided with the following variable assignments:

```
(setq F 21.5   G 963   H "36.5 x 24.5")
```

The examples below show the RTOS function at work. Note that NUMBER values are rounded either up or down before being converted to a string.

(rtos F 1 2)	returns "2.15E+01"	*scientific format*
(rtos G 2 1)	returns "963.0"	*decimal format*
(rtos (atof H) 2 1)	returns "36.5"	*the ATOF function returns 36.5*
(rtos F 6 3)	returns "1'–9 1/2""	*defaults to arbitrary fractional units if MODE argument is over 5*
(rtos F 3 20)	returns "1'–9.500000000000000"	*only 15 decimal places are supported*

The LUNITS and LUPREC system variables also have an impact on the returned value of the RTOS function. The following examples demonstrate the effect of the LUNITS and LUPREC settings:

(rtos 54.75)	returns "54.7500"	*LUNITS = 2, LUPREC = 4*
(rtos 54.75)	returns "54.75"	*LUNITS = 2, LUPREC = 2*
(rtos 54.75 4)	returns "4–6 3/4""	*LUNITS variable is set by the RTOS function; LUPREC = 2*
(rtos 54.75)	returns "55"	*LUNITS = 2, LUPREC = 0*
(rtos 54.5)	returns "55"	*LUNITS = 2, LUPREC = 0*
(rtos 54.49)	returns "54"	*LUNITS = 2, LUPREC = 0*
(rtos 54)	returns "54"	*LUNITS = 2, LUPREC = 0; for precision*

When the AutoCAD UNITMODE variable takes effect (RTOS MODE argument = 3, 4, or 5), the differences in the report formats are subtle.

	UNITMODE = 0	**UNITMODE = 1**
(rtos F 3 3)	returns "1'–9.500""	"1'9.500""
(rtos F 4 3)	returns "1'–9 1/2""	"1'9–1/2""
(rtos F 5 3)	returns "21 1/2"	"21–1/2"

As previously mentioned, the UNITMODE system variable (UNITMODE = 1) assigns the appropriate number format, which is considered to be a valid AutoCAD response. In addition, a string is formed. If UNITMODE = 0 (default), the returned string value may contain spaces or misplaced characters.

The ITOA Function

The *ITOA (Integer TO Ascii) function* converts an integer into string data. Unlike the RTOS function, the ITOA function does not allow the presentation format to be specified. The integer data is simply returned as a text string. The syntax for the ITOA function is:

```
(itoa INTEGER)
```

Given the following variable assignments, inspect the examples illustrating the use of the ITOA function:

```
(setq K 9.45   J 69   M "FLOORPLN")
```

(itoa 21)	returns "21"	
(itoa K)	returns error: bad argument type	*real numbers are not valid arguments*
(itoa J)	returns "69"	
(itoa M)	returns error: bad argument type	*strings are not valid arguments*
(itoa 16 2145)	returns error: too many arguments	*only one argument is evaluated at a time*

PROFESSIONAL TIP

When using AutoLISP to control command line operations of AutoCAD commands, any request for numerical data can be answered through the use of numerical data or a text string consisting of a number. The following example illustrates this concept:

Command: **(setq VALUE1 2.0 VALUE2 "2.0" DWGSCALE 4.0 BLK "CAPSCREW")** ↵
"CAPSCREW"
Command: **INSERT** ↵
Block name (or ?): **!BLK** ↵
Insertion point: *(pick a point)*
X scale factor ⟨1⟩ / Corner / XYZ: **!VALUE1** ↵ — *the real number, 2.0, which was previously assigned*
Y scale factor (default=X): ↵
Rotation scale ⟨0⟩: ↵

or use

X scale factor ⟨1⟩ / Corner / XYZ: **!VALUE2** ↵ — *the string "2.0" is acceptable*
Y scale factor (default=X): ↵
Rotation angle ⟨0⟩: ↵

When employing overall drawing scale factors such as the user-defined variable "DWGSCALE," remember to use data conversion functions where applicable:

X scale factor ⟨1⟩ / Corner / XYZ: **(* VALUE1 DWGSCALE)** ↵

or use

X scale factor ⟨1⟩ / Corner / XYZ: **(* (atof VALUE2) DWGSCALE)** ↵

In this situation, each scaling factor expression works equally well. Typically, it is easiest to combine similar data types. However, the AutoLISP data conversion process, as seen in the second expression, poses a valid solution.

The ANGTOS Function

The *ANGTOS (ANGle TO String) function* returns a string that represents the given ANGLE argument. The ANGLE argument is in the form of a real number expressed as a radian measurement. The format for the ANGTOS function is as follows:

```
(angtos ANGLE [MODE [PRECISION]])
```

The MODE and PRECISION settings are optional integer arguments, which relate to the AutoCAD system variables AUNITS (Angular UNITS) and AUPREC (Angular Units of PRE-Cision), respectively. The ANGTOS function, like the RTOS conversion, is also affected by the DIMZIN (DIMension Zero INches) dimensioning variable and UNITMODE system variable. The chart in Fig. 7-2 lists the available integer assignments for the MODE argument.

Mode	Format
0	Degrees
1	Degrees/minutes/seconds
2	Grads
3	Radians
4	Surveyor's units

Fig. 7-2. Available integer assignments for the ANGTOS and ANGTOF MODE argument.

If the MODE and PRECISION arguments are not included in the expression, the current angular units (AUNITS) and angular units of precision (AUPREC) are used. The UNITMODE variable applies only to the ANGTOS MODE value of 4, returning string values in surveyor's units without intermittent spaces. By applying UNITMODE to the ANGTOS function, values are created that are compatible with actual AutoCAD angle responses. For example, when UNITMODE = 1 and surveyor's units are current, the ANGTOS function forces "N 30d E" to read "N30dE".

With the AutoCAD dimemsioning variable DIMZIN = 0, using the "standard" AutoCAD compass (East = 0; counterclockwise rotation), and provided with the following variable assignments:

```
(setq ANG (cvunit 60 "DEGREES" "RADIANS") PT1 '(2 2) PT2 '(4 4))
```

...the following results are returned when utilizing the ANGTOS function:

(angtos 0.0)	returns "0"	*AUNITS = 0, AUPREC = 0*
(angtos (/ pi 2))	returns "90d0'"	*AUNITS = 1, AUPREC = 2*
(angtos (* pi 1.5))	returns "270.0000"	*AUNITS = 0, AUPREC = 4*
(angtos ANG 0 4)	returns "60.0000"	
(angtos ANG 1 4)	returns "60d0'0""	
(angtos ANG 2 4)	returns "66.6667g"	
(angtos ANG 3 4)	returns "1.0472r"	
(angtos ANG 4 4)	returns "N 30d0'0" E"	
(angtos (angle PT1 PT2) 0 2)	returns "45.00"	

As mentioned during the discussion of the RTOS function, the UNITMODE system variable (when equal to 1) assigns the appropriate number format, which is considered to be a valid AutoCAD response. In addition, the ANGBASE and ANGDIR system variables also have a direct impact upon the use of the ANGTOS function. If you assign ANGBASE = 90 (North for base angle 0) and ANGDIR = 1 (clockwise rotation), the next example reveals slightly different results:

(angtos (/ pi 2) 0 4)	returns "0.0000"	*derived angle ends at compass 0.0*
(angtos (/ pi –2) 0 4)	returns "180.0000"	*derived angle ends at compass 180.0*

A negative number within the (/ pi –2) expression sets the angle in motion opposite to the ANGDIR setting, reinstating a counterclockwise rotation. The value returned by (/ pi –2) is –1.570796. Taking this radian measurement and applying it to the current compass settings yields 180.0000 degrees. The ANGTOS function finally returns the string "180.0000" according to the AUNITS (0 = Decimal) and the AUPREC (4 = 4 decimal places) system variables.

The ANGTOF Function

The *ANGTOF (ANGle TO Floating point decimal) function* converts string data, in the form of an angular measurement, into a real number. The syntax for the ANGTOF function is shown below:

```
(angtof STRING [MODE])
```

The STRING argument must be written in the format specified by the MODE argument, which is the system of angular units. If the MODE argument is not present within the expression, the ANGTOF function uses the current AutoCAD AUNITS system variable value. When the STRING argument is written improperly, ANGTOF returns nil. The chart in Fig. 7-2 lists the available integer assignments for the MODE argument. Several examples are given below to help illustrate the usage of the ANGTOF function:

```
(angtof "90" 0)              returns 1.5708     MODE 0 = Degrees
(angtof "90d0'0\"" 1)        returns 1.5708     MODE 1 = Degrees/min/sec
(angtof "100.0000g" 2)       returns 1.5708     MODE 2 = Grads
(angtof "1.5708r" 3)         returns 1.5708     MODE 3 = Radians
(angtof "N" 4)               returns 1.5708     MODE 4 = Surveyor's units
```

Note that each expression returns the same radian real number value. The inclusion of the \" substring (mode 1) forces an inch mark to be part of the overall STRING argument. This technique is similar to the control codes used for both newlines and tabs, and is utilized much like the syntax found in the DISTOF function.

The ASCII Function

The *ASCII function* converts the first character of a string into its corresponding ASCII character code, which is returned as an integer. The format for the ASCII function is:

```
(ascii STRING)
```

The ASCII (American Standard Code for Information Interchange) codes represent a standard for defining keyboard and extended characters. The ASCII character code chart is found in Appendix D.

When the following variable assignments are declared:

```
(setq U "90.0"   V 451   W "Stove Bolt"   X "radians")
```

...the following examples return these values when using the ASCII function:

```
(ascii "A")              returns 65
(ascii "A DWG FILE")     returns 65
(ascii "a")              returns 97
(ascii "9")              returns 57
(ascii U)                returns 57       takes only first character of "90.0"

(ascii (itoa V))         returns 52       first character is 4

(ascii W)                returns 83       first character is S

(ascii X)                returns 114      first character is r
```

The CHR Function

The *CHR (ascii CHaRacter to string) function* converts the given ASCII code (INTEGER argument) and returns a single-character string. The syntax for CHR is:

```
(chr INTEGER)
```

Basically, the CHR function is the reciprocal of the ASCII function. The ASCII character code chart is found in Appendix D. Provided with the following variables and their respective values:

```
(setq AA 65   BB "42"   CC   109.66)
```

...the following examples illustrate the CHR function:

```
(chr 65)          returns "A"
(chr AA)          returns "A"
(chr (+ AA 1))    returns "B"
(chr (+ AA 2))    returns "C"
(chr 42)          returns "*"
(chr BB)          returns error: bad argument type     need to use the ATOI function
(chr (atoi BB))   returns "*"
(chr CC)          returns error: bad argument type     need to use the FIX function
(chr (fix CC))    returns "m"
```

As shown in the previous examples, the CHR function returns the single-character string that corresponds to the supplied ASCII integer argument. While the standard ASCII code chart supports an integer argument range of 32 to 126, the remaining integer values of 1 to 31 and 127 to 256 are denoted by *octal codes* (or extended characters). For example:

```
(chr 12)          returns "\014"
(chr 30)          returns "\036"
```

Finally, the CHR function is incorporated in the user-defined function shown below, as a suffix of " (chr 34) is applied to the "dimpost" dimensioning variable.

```
(defun c:dimprep (/ DSF)
   (setvar "cmdecho" 0)
   (setq DSF (getreal "\nDimension Scale Factor: "))
   (command ".layer" "make" "DIM" ""    ; Make the DIMension layer
            ".dim" "dimunit" 5          ; Dim. Arbitrary Fractional Units
                  "dimdec"  4           ; 16ths / inch for Dim. Precision
                  "dimscale" DSF        ; Dim. Scale Factor
                  "dimpost" (chr 34)    ; (chr 34) is " for inch marks
   )                                    ; end command
   (setvar "cmdecho" 1)
)
;---( End of Dimprep )---
```

The READ Function

The *READ function* returns the first atom or list from its STRING argument. While many of the functions previously discussed are capable of interrogating one specific element, the READ function takes the first item encountered within a string composed of "multiple" elements, and returns that item converted into its corresponding data type. The format for the READ function is as follows:

```
(read STRING)
```

Given the following variable assignments, the ensuing examples highlight the use of the READ function:

```
(setq DD "DIM BLOCKS"   EE "(x y) (z)"   FF 109.66   GG "12 vars")
```

(read "the paper")	returns	the	*SYMBOL*
(read "1 2 3")	returns	1	*INTEGER*
(read "1.5 2.5 3.5")	returns	1.5	*REAL*
(read DD)	returns	DIM	*SYMBOL*
(read EE)	returns	(X Y)	*LIST*
(car (read EE))	returns	X	*SYMBOL*
(read FF)	returns	error: bad argument type	*need to use the RTOS function*
(read (rtos FF 2 2))	returns	109.66	*REAL*
(read GG)	returns	12	*INTEGER*
(read "A" "B")	returns	error: too many arguments	*only one argument is evaluated at a time*

Let's Review...

1. The following summary is provided as a reference for the conversion functions previously discussed.

ATOF	(Ascii TO Floating point)–Converts string data into a real number.
DISTOF	(DIStance TO Floating point)–Converts string data, specified by MODE, into a real number.
ATOI	(Ascii TO Integer)–Converts string data into an integer.
RTOS	(Real TO String)–Returns a string that represents the given real number argument.
ITOA	(Integer TO Ascii)–Converts an integer into string data.
ANGTOS	(ANGle TO String)–Returns a string that represents the given angle argument.
ANGTOF	(ANGle TO Floating point)–Converts angular string data, specified by MODE, into a real number.
ASCII	(string to ASCII character)–Converts the first character of string into its corresponding ASCII character.
CHR	(ascii CHaRacter to string)–Converts ASCII integer code to a single-character string.
READ	(READ string)–Returns the first atom or list from the string argument.

EXERCISE 7-1

☐ Given the following variable assignment:

```
(setq A "7th Chapter – Conversions and Strings")
```

...determine the returned result of each expression.

A. (atof A) ____________________

B. (atoi A) ____________________

C. (rtos (atof A) 2 1) ____________________

D. (itoa (atoi A)) ____________________

E. (angtos (/ pi 24) 0) ____________________

F. (ascii "\010") ____________________

G. (chr 56) ____________________

H. (read A) ____________________

FUNCTIONS THAT PRINT TEXT STRINGS

Thus far, the PROMPT function has been used for printing information to the screen. There are three other AutoLISP functions–PRIN1, PRINC, and PRINT–that provide additional support in this area. Each function is similar to the others, yet different in the way that the data is ultimately written to the screen. These functions provide the means to communicate effectively with the user and utilize text files for data storage.

The PRIN1 Function

The *PRIN1 function* prints the EXPR argument on the screen and also returns EXPR. The format for the PRIN1 function is:

```
(prin1 [EXPR [FILE–DESC]])
```

Note that the EXPR argument may be a variety of data types, and is not confined only to text strings. The optional FILE-DESC argument represents an open operating system file that receives the returned value of EXPR. (Reading and writing to text files is covered in detail in Chapter 14.) Supplied with the following variable assignments:

```
(setq KK "BLOCKS"   MM 29.75   NN '(A B C)   PP "36x24 BORDER")
```

...the PRIN1 function returns:

```
(prin1 "33.75")      prints "33.75"     returns "33.75"
(prin1 KK)           prints "BLOCKS"    returns "BLOCKS"
(prin1 MM)           prints 29.75       returns 29.75
(prin1 'a)           prints A           returns A
(prin1 nn)           prints (A B C)     returns (A B C)
(prin1 (car NN))     prints A           returns A
(prin1 (atoi PP))    prints 36          returns 36
(prin1 (chr 63))     prints "?"         returns  "?"
(prin1 "\n")         prints "\n"        returns "\n"
(prin1 (chr 9))      prints "\t"        returns "\t"
```

The final two expressions illustrate that strings possessing control codes are printed literally.

The PRINC Function

The *PRINC function* handles data in much the same manner as the PRIN1 function. The format for the PRINC function is as follows:

```
(princ [EXPR [FILE-DESC]])
```

Examples of the PRINC function in use follow:

```
(princ "\n")         prints newline         returns "\n"
(princ (chr 9))      prints a tab           returns "\t"
(princ (chr 75))     prints K               returns "K"
(princ 50)           prints 50              returns 50
```

The PRINC function can also be used without arguments. This has the effect of printing a null character, and returning the same. Every time AutoLISP evaluates an expression, it returns the result of the evaluation. This means that when a program completes its run, the value of the last expression is returned to the command line. By using (PRINC) as the last expression in a program, the null character is printed and subsequently returned. Since a null character is no character, nothing is printed and nothing is returned. Try this next example:

```
Command: (defun C:PR (/ TS) ↵
1> (setq TS (getstring T "\nEnter string to print: ")) ↵
1> (princ "\n\n") ↵
1> (princ TS) ↵
1> ) ↵
C:PR
Command: PR ↵
Enter string to print: AutoLISP Programmer's Reference ↵

AutoLISP Programmer's Reference"AutoLISP Programmer's Reference"
```

Note that the string is first printed to the screen, and then the text data is returned. By adding a PRINC function without any arguments as the last expression, the returned value is effectively suppressed:

```
Command: (defun C:PR (/ TS) ↵
1〉(setq TS (getstring T "\nEnter string to print: ")) ↵
1〉(princ "\n\n") ↵
1〉(princ TS) ↵
1〉(princ) ↵
1〉) ↵
C:PR
Command: PR ↵
Enter string to print: AutoLISP Programmer's Reference ↵

AutoLISP Programmer's Reference
Command:
```

Using the PRINC function in this manner allows any program to be exited from "quietly," without returning any visible value to the screen.

The PRINT Function

The *PRINT function* handles data in the same manner as the PRIN1 function. However, the PRINT function prints a newline before the EXPR argument, and a space following it. The syntax for the PRINT function is:

```
(print [EXPR [FILE–DESC]])
```

The PRINT function can be used in a number of ways. The following examples illustrate this function:

(print "AutoLISP")(princ "Programming")(princ) "AutoLISP" Programming	*Prints newline, then "AutoLISP" with a space, and finally adding Programming. (princ) nullifies echoing.*
(print "The current area value is:")(getvar "AREA") "The current area value is:" 15.0	*assumes "Area" is currently set to 15.0 square inches*

Determining which function to use depends on the desired appearance of the data printed. Here is a simple comparison of the output of the PRIN1, PRINC, and PRINT functions when provided with the same argument:

Command: **(prin1 "OK")** ↵ "OK""OK"	*prints "OK" and returns "OK"*
Command: **(princ "OK")** ↵ OK"OK"	*prints OK and returns "OK"*
Command: **(print "OK")** ↵ "OK" "OK"	*prints newline, prints "OK", and returns "OK"*

The following user-defined function manipulates string and real number data, and prints that information to the screen. The PRIN1, PRINC, PRINT, and PROMPT functions combine to create a useful routine for examining polyline boundaries.

```
; Program:  Archarea.lsp
;
; Purpose:  Input the rate/square foot, and the program calculates the
;           basic total cost of a closed polyline floor plan.
;
; Assumptions:  The closed polyline is present within the drawing.
;
(defun C:AA (/ RATE)
   (setvar "cmdecho" 0)
      (print "Setting units to Architecture")        ; Print message
      (command ".lunits" 4)                          ; Linear UNITS to arch.
      (setq RATE (getreal "\nRate per s.f.: "))      ; Rate per square foot
      (prompt "\nSelect area for calculation: ")     ; Prompt for selection
      (command ".area" "entity" pause)               ; Select polyline entity
      (princ "\nThe estimated cost is: $")           ; Princ message
      (prin1 (* (/ (getvar "area") 144.0) RATE))     ; Prin1 cost per s.f.
   (setvar "cmdecho" 1)
   (princ)                                     ; Quietly exit
)
;---< End of Archarea >---
```

MANIPULATING STRING DATA WITH AUTOLISP

Since string data is used primarily for communicating with the user, a great deal of versatility is provided for manipulating and modifying string data. It is often necessary to alter the format of a string or extract a small portion of a greater string. Occasionally, it is more convenient to work with one long text string as opposed to several shorter ones. All of these requirements can be met with AutoLISP's STRing manipulation functions.

The STRCASE Function

The *STRCASE (STRing CASE) function* is a conversion process in which the STRING argument is returned in either uppercase or lowercase characters. The format for the STRCASE function is as follows:

```
(strcase STRING [WHICH])
```

The STRING may include more than one character or word. The optional WHICH argument, if it is not present or evaluates to nil, returns a copy of STRING in uppercase characters. When this argument is present and is non-nil, all characters in STRING are converted to lowercase characters. The STRCASE function is intended for use with the standard letters of the alphabet, and has no effect on other ASCII characters. When the following variable assignments are made:

```
(setq QQ "Patterns"  RR 15.5  TT "17x11 BORDER")
```

...the STRCASE function returns:

```
(strcase "33.75")    returns  "33.75"
(strcase QQ)         returns  "PATTERNS"
```

```
(strcase QQ T)        returns  "patterns"
(strcase RR)          returns  error: bad argument type      needs a string
(strcase (rtos RR))   returns  "15.5000"
(strcase TT nil)      returns  "17X11 BORDER"
(strcase TT T)        returns  "17x11 border"
```

In these examples, several printing functions may be required when more than one individual data element is to be printed to the screen. It is more convenient to use a single printing function and one string argument. AutoLISP allows separate strings to be combined into one string using the STRCAT function.

The STRCAT Function

The *STRCAT (STRing conCATenate) function* is used to concatenate (link) several strings, and thereby forming one string. The format for the STRCAT function is:

```
(strcat STRING1 [STRING2] ...)
```

The STRCAT function can be demonstrated by the examples that follow. Again, supplied with the following variable assignments:

```
(setq QQ "Patterns"   RR 15.5   SS '("A" "B" "C")   TT "17x11 BORDER")
```

...the STRCAT function produces these results:

```
(strcat "5" QQ)                   returns  "5Patterns"
(strcat "5 " QQ)                  returns  "5 Patterns"
(strcat "5 " (strcase QQ))        returns  "5 PATTERNS"
(strcat (itoa (fix RR)) " " QQ)   returns  "15 Patterns"
(strcat (car SS) (cadr SS))       returns  "AB"
(strcat "The choice is: " TT)     returns  "The choice is: 17x11 BORDER"
```

Utilizing the appropriate conversion function along with the STRCAT function allows the programmer greater versatility. The next example illustrates this concept:

```
; Filename:  CV.LSP
;
; Author:  Cher E. Picken
;
; Purpose:  Draws a radial line from the center of an arbitrary circle,
;           at a user-specifed angle.  The user chooses the circle and
;           subsequently enters the angle of choice.  Radial distance,
;           starting center point, and angled line are automatically
;           derived.  Finally, the angled line is arrayed within the
;           circle at equal divisions, again specified by the user.
;
(defun C:CV (/ PT1 CPT DIS AGL DIV)
   (setvar "cmdecho" 0)
   (setq PT1   (osnap (getpoint "\nSelect circle: ") "nea")   ; Find nearest pt
         CPT   (osnap PT1 "cen")                              ; Center of circle
         DIS   (distance PT1 CPT)                             ; Radius of circle
         AGL   (getstring "\nAngle for radial line: ")        ; Angle of vector
         DIV   (getint "\nNumber of equal divisions: ")       ; Circle divisions
```

```
        )                                          ; End setq
        (command ".line" CPT (strcat "@"           ; Start string concatenation
                              (rtos DIS 2 8)       ; Convert real to string
                              "<<"                 ; Standard AutoCAD angle
                              AGL                  ; User-specified rotation
                         ) ""                      ; End of strcat, and return
                 ".array" "L" "" "p" CPT DIV 360 "y"    ; Array radial line
        )                                          ; End command
        (setvar "cmdecho" 1)
        (princ)
)
;---< End of Cv >---
```

The STRLEN Function

The *STRLEN (STRing LENgth) function* returns the numerical length of the supplied STRING arguments as an integer. The syntax for the STRLEN function is:

```
(strlen [STRING] ...)
```

When more than one STRING is specified, the STRLEN function returns the total number of characters contained in all strings. Given the following variable assignments:

```
(setq QQ "Patterns"  SS '("A" "B" "C"))
```

...the STRLEN function produces these results:

```
(strlen "AA")                  returns 2
(strlen "AA ")                 returns 3          spaces are counted
(strlen QQ)                    returns 8
(strlen "Hatch " QQ)           returns 14
(strlen (car SS) (cadr SS))    returns 2
```

The STRLEN function has many useful applications, several of which involve the use of looping techniques and other advanced functions that are introduced in later chapters.

The SUBSTR Function

The *SUBSTR (SUBSTRing) function* allows the user to extract any portion of the contents of a specified STRING argument. Note that a single string is used. The syntax for the SUBSTR function is:

```
(substr STRING START [LENGTH])
```

The SUBSTR function returns a partial string, called the *substring,* beginning at a positive integer START point, and continues through the string for LENGTH characters. The START argument must be specified for the function to operate properly. If the LENGTH argument is omitted, the SUBSTR function returns the substring from the start point to the end of the string. Given the following assignments:

```
(setq VV "Acad Directory"   WW '("Red Layer" "Blue Layer")   XX "45 degrees")
```

...the SUBSTR function yields the following values:

```
(substr 44 2)                           returns  error: bad argument type
(substr "OK")                           returns  error: too few arguments
(substr VV 1 4)                         returns  "Acad"
(substr VV 6)                           returns  "Directory"
(substr (car WW) 1 3)                   returns  "Red"
(substr (cadr WW) 6)                    returns  "Layer"
(substr "Directory Information" 11 4)   returns  "Info"
```

User-defined functions that automatically write text information to the graphics screen present a distinct advantage over manual typing. The next routine not only accomplishes this task, but also registers the current date stored in the AutoCAD CDATE system variable.

```
; Filename: Date.lsp
;
; Author: Cal Endar
;
; Date: December 21, 19xx
;
; Purpose: Write the current date to the screen
;
(defun C:DATE (/ TODAY YEAR MONTH DAY MDY INSPT HGT)
  (setvar "cmdecho" 0)
  (setq TODAY  (rtos (getvar "CDATE") 2 0)                     ; current date into string
        YEAR   (substr today 1 4)                              ; year
        MONTH  (substr today 5 2)                              ; month
        DAY    (substr today 7 2)                              ; day
        MDY    (strcat "TODAY'S DATE: " MONTH "–" DAY "–" YEAR)  ; date string
        INSPT  (getpoint "\nStart pt. for Today's Date: ")     ; text ins pt
        HGT    (getreal "\nText height: ")                     ; text height
  )
  (command ".text" INSPT HGT 0.0 MDY)
  (princ)
)
; – –⟨ End of Program ⟩– –
```

The ACAD_STRLSORT Function

The *ACAD_STRLSORT (AutoCAD STRing List SORT) function* accepts a single list argument containing any number of text strings, and returns the list in an alphabetized order. If the list size exceeds the amount of memory available to do the sort, or if the list contains elements that are not text strings, ACAD_STRLSORT returns nil. The syntax for the ACAD_STRLSORT function is:

```
(acad_strlsort LIST)
```

Given the following variable assignments:

```
(setq LST1   '("a" "w" "A" "k")   LST2   '("3/4" "Screw" "5/8" "Bolt"))
```

...the ACAD_STRLSORT function produces these results:

```
(acad_strlsort   '("c" "b" "a"))              returns  ("a" "b" "c")
(acad_strlsort   '("b" "a") '("d" "c"))       returns  ("a" "b")
(acad_strlsort   '("abcd" "abc"))             returns  ("abc" "abcd")
(acad_strlsort   (list 4 3 2 1))              returns
                                              Usage: (strlsort <of strings>)
                                              nil
(acad_strlsort LST1)                          returns  ("A" "a" "k" "w")
(acad_strlsort LST2)                          returns  ("3/4" "5/8" "Bolt" "Screw")
(acad_strlsort '("BOLT" "BOLt"))              returns  ("BOLT" "BOLt")
```

The ACAD_STRLSORT function adheres to the character heiarchy set forth in the ASCII code chart found in Appendix D. As shown in the previous examples, number values expressed as text entries are listed first, followed by uppercase letters, with lowercase letters listed last in the sort. The following program demonstrates the basic usage of the ACAD_STRLSORT function, where four names are presented, sorted, and written as text within AutoCAD. Note the application of the STRCAT function as well.

```
; Filename: A-TEAM.LSP
;
; Purpose: Compiles the names of 4 team members, alphabetizes the
;          team list, and produces the team list as text within the
;          current drawing. Order of entry is not important.
;
(defun C:ATEAM (/ ST M1 M2 M3 M4 LST)
   (setvar "cmdecho" 0)
   (setq ST    "\nEnter Team Member #"                ; Lead text string
         M1    (getstring T (strcat ST "1: "))        ; 1st Team Member
         M2    (getstring T (strcat ST "2: "))        ; 2nd Team Member
         M3    (getstring T (strcat ST "3: "))        ; 3rd Team Member
         M4    (getstring T (strcat ST "4: "))        ; 4th Team Member
         LST   (acad_strlsort (list M1 M2 M3 M4))     ; Alphabetized list
   )
   (princ "\nPick Text start pt.: ")
      (command ".text" pause)               ; Begin text command...
   (princ "\nText height: ")
      (command pause 0.0 (car LST))         ; Continue text command...1st member
   (setq LST (cdr LST))                     ; ....reset LST
      (command ".text" "" (car LST))        ; Continue text command...2nd member
   (setq LST (cdr LST))                     ; ....reset LST
      (command ".text" "" (car LST))        ; Continue text command...3rd member
   (setq LST (cdr LST))                     ; ....reset LST
      (command ".text" "" (car LST))        ; Continue text command...4th member
   (setvar "cmdecho" 1)
   (princ)
)
;---< End of A-TEAM >---
```

The GETCNAME Function

The *GETCNAME (GET Command NAME) function* retrieves the localized or English name of the specified AutoCAD command. The syntax for the GETCNAME function is:

```
(getcname CNAME)
```

The CNAME argument specifies the localized or underscored English command name, where the name cannot exceed 64 characters in length. If CNAME is not preceded by an underscore (assumed to be the localized or native language command name), the GETCNAME function returns the underscored English command name. Where CNAME is preceded by an underscore (the English command name), GETCNAME returns the localized command name. The function returns nil if the CNAME argument is not a valid command. For example, in a French version of AutoCAD, the following example holds true:

```
(getcname "ETIRER")              returns "_STRETCH"
(getcname "_STRETCH")            returns "ETIRER"
```

The next sample routine could be used as a tool for verifying the existence of, or correct spelling for, the included string argument:

```
(defun c:intl (/ CMD)
   (setq CMD (getstring "\nCheck for command: "))
   (princ (getcname CMD))
   (princ)
)
```

This routine would check to see if the command actually exists within the body of available AutoCAD commands.

EXERCISE 7-2

- ☐ Design a program that returns the values stored in the following AutoCAD system variables:
  - ☐ Acadver
  - ☐ Dwgprefix
  - ☐ Dwgname
  - ☐ Loginname
  - ☐ Menuname
  - ☐ Platform
- ☐ Utilize the PRINC and STRCAT functions to report the value of each returned string. The format for the STRCAT expression should appear as:

  ```
  (strcat "\nThe value for " VAR " is: " X)
  ```

  ...where "VAR" represents the system variable, and "X" represents its stored value. Document the file accordingly, and name it VARSOUT.LSP.

Let's Review...

1. The AutoLISP family of PRINx functions–PRIN1, PRINC, and PRINT–print information for a variety of data types, allowing greater formatting capabilities than the PROMPT function.
2. The STRCASE function initiates a conversion process where the string argument is returned in either uppercase or lowercase letters.
3. The STRCAT function is used for concatenating or linking multiple strings together, and thereby forming one string.
4. The STRLEN function returns the number of intergers in a string argument. When more than one string is specified, STRLEN returns the total number of characters contained within all strings.
5. The SUBSTR function returns a substring, beginning at a positive integer start point, and continuing through the argument for LENGTH characters.
6. The ACAD_STRLSORT function alphabetically sorts one list argument containing any number of text strings. The string list is sorted according to the hierarchy established by the ASCII code chart.
7. The GETCNAME function returns the localized or English name of an AutoCAD command.

CHAPTER TEST

Write your answers in the spaces provided.

1. What is the problem when AutoLISP returns the "error: bad argument type" message?

____

____

2. What function returns the floating point decimal number represented by the first numerical atom within a text string? Describe the use of this function.

____

____

____

____

3. What limitations affect the values returned by the ATOI function?

____

____

4. List the value returned by AutoLISP for each of the following expressions:

   A. (rtos 430.2 1 2) _______________

   B. (rtos 430.2 3 2) _______________

   C. (rtos 430.2 5 8) _______________

   D. (rtos 0.1875 5 6) _______________

   E. (rtos 430.2 2 0) _______________

   F. (rtos 430.2 4) _______________

   G. (rtos 430.2 5 2) _______________

   H. (rtos 0.1875 5 2) _______________

5. Which of AutoCAD's dimensioning and system variables have an affect on the output of RTOS? Explain your answer.

6. What are AutoCAD's requirements for data types when answering command line prompts?

7. Name the function used for converting integer data into string data and describe its use.

8. List the value returned by AutoLISP for each of the following expressions:
   A. (angtos (/ pi 2) 0 4) ______
   B. (angtos (/ pi 2) 2 4) ______
   C. (angtos (/ pi 2) 4 4) ______
   D. (angtos pi 3 0) ______
   E. (angtos (/ pi 2) 1 4) ______
   F. (angtos (/ pi 2) 3 4) ______
   G. (angtos (* pi 1.5) 4 2) ______
   H. (angtos (* pi 1 2 2) ______

9. Detail the use of the ASCII function.

10. What is one valuable use for the CHR function? Explain.

____

____

____

11. For each of the following expressions, list the value returned and its data type.

Expression	Value	Data type
A. (read "ABC")	_______	_______
B. (read "185.5")	_______	_______
C. (read "185")	_______	_______
D. (read "(z)")	_______	_______

12. Given the following symbol assignments, provide the returned values for each conversion function:

```
(setq A 5.0   B 24.7   C "36 inches"   D "12th AutoCAD Release")
```

A. (atof C) _______________
B. (atoi C) _______________
C. (+ (atoi C) (atoi D)) _______________
D. (itoa A) _______________
E. (rtos A) _______________
F. (atof D) _______________
G. (chr (atoi D)) _______________
H. (chr (fix B)) _______________
I. (ascii "ABC") _______________

13. What data types can be utilized by the PRIN1 function?

____

____

14. What happens when PRINC is used without arguments? How is this commonly used?

____

____

____

____

____

15. Name the function that is able to control the uppercase and lowercase presentation of text strings. Detail its use.

 ____

 ____

 ____

 ____

16. Detail the use of the STRCAT function.

 ____

 ____

 ____

 ____

17. Design an expression using the SUBSTR function, which returns the word "for" from the string "AutoLISP is used for automating many tasks."

 ____

 ____

PROGRAMMING PROBLEMS

1. Create a program that sets a symbol to the AutoCAD FILLETRAD system variable, and reports that value to the screen. Initiate the FILLET command after displaying the current system variable. Use the RTOS conversion function, the PRINC function, and the STRCAT function to complete this task. Name the file FR.LSP.
2. Create a program that accomplishes the following:
   A. Sets the variable to a real number greater that 2.5 and less than 4.0.
   B. Draws a circle with a radius equal to the variable value given above.
   C. Draws a text entry displaying the circle radius, beginning with the string "Circle radius = " and ending with the real number variable. The text entry is to be located in the center of the circle with a middle justification.

   These assignments/constructions are to be user-defined, using functions such as GETREAL and GETPOINT. As in Problem 1, use the RTOS conversion function and the STRCAT function to complete this task. Name the file CIR-LABL.LSP.

3. Study the following AutoLISP program that performs flat pattern computations. List the variables used in the routine that assist in formulating a report to the screen. Use AutoLISP functions such as RTOS and PRINT to help generate the Materials Report in the specified area.

```
; Filename: Steel.lsp
;
; Author: J. Brown
;
; Date: December 27, 19xx
;
; Purpose: Basic flat pattern computations program.
;
; Restrictions: Selected features must be valid for "AREA" command in entity mode
;                (pline or circle).
;
; Program inputs: 1. Select major feature for overall area, etc. (pline)
;                 2. Select hole to be subtracted (circle)
;                 3. Results will reveal overall area data and resultant area and weight data
;
(defun C:STEEL (/ PT1 TPL PT2 VOID TH WT TOTA TOTW)
  (setvar "cmdecho" 0)
;
; --( Template Area )--
;
  (prompt "\nSelect template for area/weight calculation: ")
  (setq PT1 (getpoint))
    (command ".area" "e" PT1)
  (setq TPL (getvar "area"))
;
; --( Voided Area )--
;
  (prompt "\nSelect hole in template to be subtracted: ")
  (setq PT2 (getpoint))
    (command ".area" "e" PT2)
  (setq VOID (getvar "area"))
;
; --( Computations )--
;
  (setq TH    (getreal "\nThickness of material: ")
        WT    (getreal "\nWeight of material/cubic in. : ")
        TOTA  (- TPL VOID)              ; Composite Area
        TOTW  (* TOTA TH WT)            ; Composite Weight
  )
;
; --( Material Report )--
)
; --( End of Program )--
```

Chapter 8

Conditional Expressions

Learning Objectives

After completing this chapter, you will be able to:

- ☐ Differentiate between linear and non-linear flow in a program.
- ☐ Use AutoLISP's built-in test functions to check for specific conditions.
- ☐ Create simple branches in a program using conditional and test functions.
- ☐ Enhance the operation of conditional expressions using AutoLISP's logical functions.
- ☐ Design complex branches with conditional functions.

PROGRAM FLOW AND PROBLEM-SOLVING TECHNIQUES

The programming applications discussed in earlier chapters have been primarily task-oriented, as opposed to being problem-oriented. *Task-oriented* means that the applications have a linear flow, or merely follow a step-by-step movement from the beginning to the end of a program. Even with user-supplied input, the program follows the same path each time it is used. If programs were only capable of linear flow, a user would always be required to analyze the circumstances, decide on an appropriate solution, and initiate the correct AutoLISP program.

AutoLISP provides a variety of test functions that enable a programmer to check for particular conditions. In addition, conditional functions are provided to allow an alternate course of action to be taken based on the outcome of specific test expressions. In this manner, a program may be designed to find the best solution under any given set of conditions. This allows

AutoLISP to make logical decisions consistently without requiring further effort or information from the user. Such a design creates a program suitable for problem-solving applications.

This chapter describes the creation of programs with non-linear flow capabilities. A program may be designed with many different branches to follow. Each branching point has a *flow director*–a conditional expression and applicable test expressions that guide the program to the correct branch. An example of this concept is expressed with the familiar "IF test condition, THEN do this, ELSE do that" format.

TEST EXPRESSIONS

AutoLISP provides a great diversity of built-in test functions. These functions return *T* (a non-nil value) if a condition is met, or *nil* if the condition is not met. The returned values of T and nil can be compared to "true" and "false," where T is true and nil is false. In this sense, a condition is checked to determine whether or not it is true. Another name for a function that affirms these qualities or attributes is called a *predicate.*

A common basis for testing is to determine the relationship between two items. In the following section, you will see that various predicates are used in the evaluation of atoms, but only a few utilize lists as arguments. An *atom* is any data item that is not a list. Pay close attention when each function is used, and which data types are valid arguments.

Relational Predicates

Predicates are used to determine whether or not a specific relationship exists between data items. These predicates, called *relational predicates,* include:

- =
- EQ
- EQUAL
- /=
- <
- >
- <=
- >=

The = Function. The = *(equal to) function* returns T if all atoms are numerically equal, or nil if they are not equal. The format for the = function is as follows:

```
(= ATOM ATOM ...)
```

Only numbers and text strings are valid arguments. The = function, in reference to text strings, is case sensitive. (The basis for testing string arguments is detailed later in this chapter.) Use the following symbol assignments to evaluate the examples below:

```
(setq A "OK"   B 4   X 12   Y 12)

(= 1 1)              returns T
(= 1 2)              returns nil
(= 1 1 2 1)          returns nil
(= A "OK")           returns T
(= A "ok")           returns nil        note that text is case sensitive
(= 4 B)              returns T
(= X Y 12)           returns T
(= B X 4)            returns nil
(= '(0 0) '(0 0))    returns nil        lists are not valid arguments
```

The EQ Function. The *EQ function* determines whether or not the arguments evaluate to the exact data item. The format for the EQ function is:

```
(eq EXPR1 EXPR2)
```

If EXPR1 and EXPR2 are identical, T is returned. The following symbol assignments are used to explain the examples below:

```
(setq PT1 '(2.0 2.0 0.0))
(setq PT2 '(2.0 2.0 0.0))

(eq PT1 PT2)        returns nil

(setq PT3 PT1)

(eq PT1 PT3)        returns T
```

In this example, a list of three real numbers is assigned to the symbol PT1. A second list, containing the same three reals, is assigned to symbol PT2. Although the same elements are contained in both lists, they are not the same list. In comparison, two tool boxes may each contain a pair of pliers, a hammer, and a screwdriver. Although the contents are the same, they are still two different tool boxes. Since PT1 was evaluated, and its value assigned to PT3, both of these symbols represent the same list.

The EQUAL Function. The *EQUAL function* provides greater versatility when it is necessary to evaluate expressions and determine whether the given arguments are equivalent. No limitations on data types apply to the use of the EQUAL function. Therefore, it can test the equality of numbers, text strings, and lists. The format for EQUAL is:

```
(equal EXPR1 EXPR2 [FUZZ])
```

Using the following symbol assignments, review the examples below:

```
(setq A 6.0 B "OK")
```

(equal '(0 0) '(0 0))	returns T	*the lists are equivalent*
(equal "OK" B)	returns T	*symbol B evaluates to "OK"*
(equal 5.0 A)	returns nil	*symbol A is 6.0; 6.0 is greater than 5.0*
(equal 6.0 A)	returns T	*symbol A evaluates to 6.0*

The optional *FUZZ argument* is a numeric argument used to specify the maximum amount in which two numbers may differ and still be considered equal. Note that this argument is only used when numbers are specified as test expressions. The numbers being tested may be individual numbers, returned values from expressions, or members of lists. The FUZZ argument is commonly used to verify point coordinate lists for equality. For example:

```
(setq X 1.1357   Y 1.1358   Z 15.0   PT1 '(0.123 0.123)   PT2 '(0.123 0.124))

(equal X Y)          returns nil
(equal X Y 0.0001)   returns T
(equal Z 15.1)       returns nil
(equal Z 15.1 0.1)   returns T
(equal Z 14.9 0.1)   returns T
(equal PT1 PT2)      returns nil
```

If lists of two or more real numbers are being tested, the difference must be less than FUZZ. Note that lists are compared in a manner such that the first element of one list is compared to the first element of the other list, the second element is compared to the second element, and so on until the end of a list is encountered. In addition, if the lists being compared each contain a different number of elements, they cannot be equal.

```
(equal PT1 PT2 0.001)               returns nil
(equal PT1 PT2 0.0011)              returns T
(equal PT2 '(0.122 0.123) 0.0011)   returns T
(equal '(0.1 0.2) '(0.1 0.2 0.3))   returns nil
```

The /= Function. The /= *(not equal to) function* is the opposite of the = function. The format for this function is:

```
(/= ATOM ATOM ...)
```

If all atoms are not numerically equal, it returns T. If they are equal, nil is returned. The /= function only accepts numerical and string arguments. The /= function returns the following for these symbol assignments:

```
(setq A 1   B 2   C "OK")

(/= 1 2)            returns T
(/= A 1)            returns nil
(/= C "OK")         returns nil
(/= "YES" "NO")     returns T
(/= A B)            returns T
```

The following relational functions apply only to numerical and string arguments. Each of the functions operate the same way, therefore, they have been grouped together here, with examples following the >= function.

The < Function. The < *(less than) function* returns T if each ATOM is less than the ATOM to its right. The format for the < function is:

```
(< ATOM ATOM ...)
```

The <= Function. The <= *(less than or equal to) function* returns T if each ATOM is less than or equal to the ATOM to its right. The syntax for the <= function is:

```
(<= ATOM ATOM ...)
```

The > Function. The > *(greater than) function* returns T if each ATOM is greater than the one to its right. The format for the > function is as follows:

```
(> ATOM ATOM ...)
```

The >= Function. The >= *(greater than or equal to) function* returns T if each ATOM is greater than or equal to the one to its right. The syntax for >= is:

```
(>= ATOM ATOM ...)
```

Relational Function Applications. The four relational functions previously discussed return the following when these symbol assignments are applied:

```
(setq X 4  Z -32  M 3  N 2)

(< X 16)          returns T
(< N M X 4)       returns nil        X is equal to 4
(<= 1 2 3 X 4)    returns T
(<= 9 11)         returns T
(> 14 8 M 1)      returns T
(> -1 N)          returns nil
(>= 4 4 2)        returns T
(>= 12 Z)         returns T
```

When text strings are used as arguments, evaluation is based on the ASCII value of each character. (ASCII values for alphanumeric characters are shown in Appendix D.) Beginning with the first character of each text string argument, the same character position in each argument is in turn evaluated and tested, until the condition is met or the end of the string is reached. Supplying text strings as arguments for > (greater than) and < (less than) is not a common application for these functions, but can be done when required. For example:

```
(> "b" "a")          returns T
(> "abcd" "abc")     returns T
(< "xyz" "a")        returns nil
(< "ABC" "ABD")      returns T
(> "ABC" "aBC")      returns nil
(<= "xy" "xy")       returns T
(> "xz" "xyz")       returns T
```

Let's Review...

1. Programs with linear flow are primarily task-oriented. Programs designed in a problem style must have branching capabilities in order to produce the appropriate results given alternate sets of circumstances.
2. AutoLISP's built-in test functions return T or nil (which can be compared to True or False). These functions, called predicates, are designed to support branching expressions, and have limited application when used by themselves.
3. Predicates that test for equality include functions such as EQUAL, /=, and >=. The supplied arguments can be numbers, text strings, or lists, depending on the equality function being applied.

Testing Data Types with Predicates

Data types may also require testing. If an improper data type is supplied as an argument to a function, an error will occur. Such an error is avoided by first testing the data item to ensure it is the proper data type before proceeding with the program. The following predicates are used to determine data types and specific attributes of the supplied arguments:

- ATOM
- LISTP
- NUMBERP
- MINUSP
- ZEROP
- BOUNDP
- NULL

The ATOM Function. The *ATOM function* determines whether or not the item is an atom. Any data item that is not a list is considered an atom. The syntax for the ATOM function is:

```
(atom ITEM)
```

When these symbol assignments are used, the ATOM function returns the following results.

```
(setq B nil   S "string"   N 1   LS '(a b))

(atom N)                    returns T
(atom S)                    returns T
(atom LS)                   returns nil
(atom B)                    returns T
(atom (car (list 'A 'B)))   returns T
```

The LISTP Function. When using the *LISTP function,* if the item being tested is a list, T is returned. Nil is returned if it is not a list. The format for the LISTP function is as follows:

```
(listp ITEM)
```

When the following symbol assignments are made,

```
(setq B nil   S "string"   N 1   LS '(a b))
```

...the following results are returned:

```
(listp N)         returns nil
(listp S)         returns nil
(listp LS)        returns T
(listp '(0 0))    returns T
(listp B)         returns T
```

Note that nil can also be considered a list by AutoLISP. It is an empty list and, therefore, has no value. However, the LISTP function returns T when nil is tested.

The NUMBERP Function. The *NUMBERP function* is used to test whether or not an item is a number. The syntax for the NUMBERP function is:

```
(numberp ITEM)
```

If the item is either an integer or a real number, T will be returned as shown in the following examples.

```
(setq A 14   B "ok")

(numberp 'A)                 returns nil    symbol A is unevaluated

(numberp A)                  returns T      symbol A evaluates to 14

(numberp B)                  returns nil    symbol B evaluates to a string

(numberp 0.556)              returns T
(numberp (cadr '(0 1 2)))    returns T
```

The MINUSP Function. The *MINUSP function* returns T if the item evaluates to a negative number. The format for the MINUSP function is:

```
(minusp ITEM)
```

The ITEM can be either a real number or an integer. The only valid data type that may be supplied as an argument is a numerical value.

```
(minusp 1)          returns nil
(minusp –1)         returns T
(minusp (+ 5 2 –8)) returns T
```

The ZEROP Function. When using the *ZEROP function,* T will be returned if the item is either an integer or a real and also evaluates to zero. The format for the ZEROP function is:

```
(zerop ITEM)
```

The ZEROP function also requires the item to be a numeric value.

```
(zerop 1)           returns nil
(zerop 0)           returns T
(zerop (– 14 14))   returns T
```

The BOUNDP Function. The *BOUNDP function* returns T if the atom is bound to a value. Otherwise, nil is returned. The format for BOUNDP is:

```
(boundp ATOM)
```

The BOUNDP function accepts any data item as an argument, but it will return T only if the atom is a symbol that has been assigned a non-nil value. Given the following symbol assignments:

```
(setq A 15   B nil   C 'B)
```

...the following results are returned when using the BOUNDP function.

(boundp 1)	returns nil	*1 is not a symbol*
(boundp A)	returns nil	*A evaluates to 15, which is not a symbol*
(boundp 'A)	returns T	*A is bound to 15*
(boundp 'B)	returns nil	*B is bound to nil*
(boundp 'C)	returns T	*C is bound to the symbol B*
(boundp C)	returns nil	*C returns the value of B, which is nil*

A symbol must be quoted in order to guarantee the proper result when using the BOUNDP function. Otherwise, the symbol is first evaluated, and then the BOUNDP function is applied. If the symbol is evaluated, then its value is used as the argument.

The NULL Function. The *NULL function* may be used to verify whether or not a symbol has been assigned a value or if a list is empty. The syntax for the NULL function is:

```
(null ITEM)
```

If the ITEM is bound to a value of nil, T is returned. Assume the following symbol assignments are made:

```
(setq A '(x y z)   B nil)
```

Then, the following results are returned:

```
(null A)            returns nil
(null B)            returns T
(null '())          returns T
```

The predicates shown above represent all of AutoLISP's primary test functions. They offer great flexibility regarding data types and attributes to be tested. Relationships can be tested, data types can be verified, and the current status of a list or symbol can be checked.

Since these predicates only have the capability of returning either T or nil, their individual applications are very limited. By themselves, they would be of little value without the ability to modify the flow within a program based on their results. In the next section, applications for these functions are shown using conditional functions.

CREATING SIMPLE BRANCHES WITH IF

The *IF function* is used when it is necessary to perform a task when only one specific condition exists. The format of an IF expression is as follows:

```
(if TESTexpr THENexpr [ELSEexpr])
```

An IF expression requires two arguments and allows an optional third argument. The required arguments are a TEST expression and a THEN expression. The optional argument is an ELSE expression, which will be evaluated if the TEST expression returns nil. If the TEST expression returns a value other than nil, the THEN expression will subsequently be evaluated and the ELSE expression will be ignored. Fig. 8-1 illustrates the evaluation flow within an IF expression. As shown in the figure, if the TEST condition returns T (or any non-nil value), the THEN expression is evaluated.

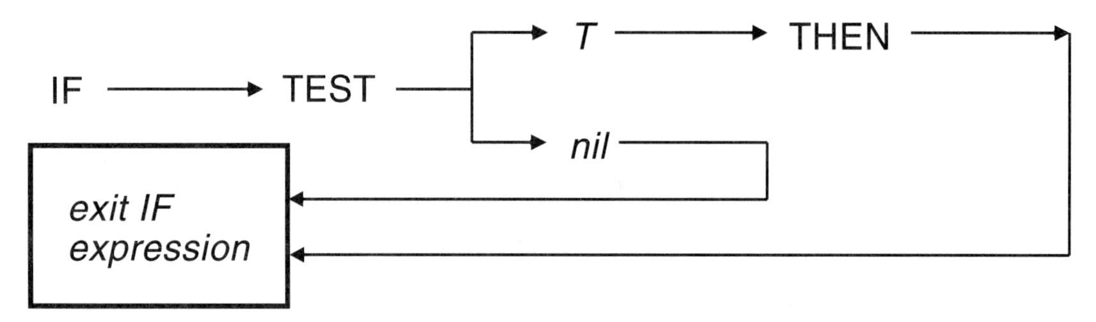

Fig. 8-1. Evaluation flow within an IF expression.

In cases where the optional ELSE expression is included, the flow proceeds as shown in Fig. 8-2. The THEN expression is evaluated if the TEST expression returns any non-nil value. If nil is returned, the ELSE expression will be evaluated instead. In the first example that follows, a string input is requested from the user, and action is taken only if a specific string is given in response to the prompt.

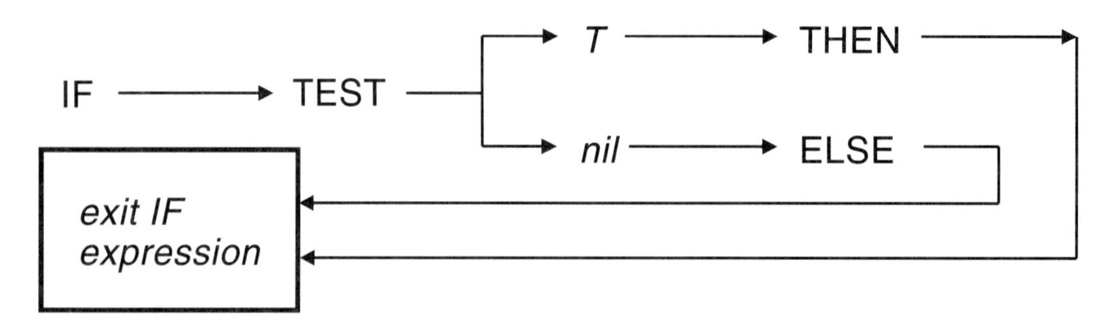

Fig. 8-2. Evaluation flow when the optional ELSE expression is included.

```
; If the "=" expression returns T, the THEN expression is evaluated and
; the CIRCLE command is issued.

(defun C:YC ()
    (initget 1 "Yes No")
    (if (= "Yes" (getkword "\nDraw a CIRCLE?⟨Y/N⟩: "))
          (command ".CIRCLE")
    )
    (princ)
)
```

If the user input meets the test criteria, the CIRCLE command is issued; otherwise, nil is returned by this expression and nothing else is done.

In the next example, an ELSE argument is provided.

```
(defun NUMTEST (NUM / INP)                ; Defun with one argument, NUM
  (if                                     ; Begin IF
    (numberp NUM)                         ;   If NUM is a number, T is returned
    (princ (setq INP (– NUM 32)))         ;   THEN is evaluated if test is T
    (princ "\nNUM is not a number.")      ; ELSE is evaluated if test is nil
  )                                       ; End IF
  (princ)
)
```

This user-defined function requires one argument–NUM. The NUMBERP function evaluates the NUM argument to see if it returns as a real number or integer. When this test expression passes, a subtraction expression is called. The ELSE expression is issued in the event that the test expression returns nil. Applying this user-defined function would yield results such as the following examples:

(numtest 48)	returns 16	*NUM is a number; THEN is evaluated*
(numtest 33.5)	returns 1.5	*NUM is a number; THEN is evaluated*
(numtest "A")	returns "NUM is not a number."	*NUM is not a number; ELSE is evaluated*

EXERCISE 8-1

- ☐ Write AutoLISP programs to fulfill the requirements of the following program descriptions:
  - ☐ C:DIV–Prompt for a divisor and dividend. If the divisor is not zero, return the quotient; otherwise display the message "ERROR: Cannot divide by zero!" Name the file DIV.LSP.
  - ☐ C:PTS–Prompt for user selection of two points. Use the EQUAL function with the FUZZ argument to determine if the points are within 0.1 unit of each other. If they are within the FUZZ value, give a message that the user picked the same point. If the points are not within 0.1 unit of each other, give a message that the points are not the same. Name the file PTS.LSP.

Expanding Possible Applications

As previously shown, an IF expression only evaluates one THEN or one ELSE expression. If additional arguments are supplied, an error message is returned. For example:

Command: **(if (= A "OK") (setq A 14) (setq D 43) (setq N 12))** ↵
error: too many arguments — *Four arguments are supplied. Therefore, an error message is returned.*

The PROGN Function. Being able to evaluate only one THEN expression or one ELSE expression can be problematic. In most cases, more than one function must be performed in order to achieve the desired results. Therefore, AutoLISP provides the *PROGN function,* which binds expressions together so that several may be evaluated where only one expression is expected. The syntax for the PROGN function is as follows:

```
(progn EXPRESSION ...)
```

The PROGN function allows any number of expressions to be supplied, evaluates each one, and returns the result of the last evaluated expression. For example:

```
(progn
  (setq A 14)
  (setq B 22)
  (setq C (– B A))
)                                        8 is returned
```

A common use of the PROGN function is within an IF expression to enable evaluation of more than one expression after a test is performed. Study the following example.

```
(defun C:LorC (/ ANS PT1 PT2 RAD)
    (setvar "cmdecho" 0)
    (initget  1 "L C")
    (setq ANS (getkword "\nDraw a Line or Circle?〈L/C〉: "))
    (if (= ANS "L")
     (progn                              ; begin THEN progn
     (setq PT1 (getpoint "\nStart point: ")
           PT2 (getpoint PT1 "\nEnd point: ")
      )
      (command ".LINE" PT1 PT2 "")
     )                                   ; end THEN progn
     (progn                              ; begin ELSE progn
      (setq PT1 (getpoint "\nCenter of Circle: ")
            RAD (getdist PT1 "\nRadius: ")
      )
      (command ".CIRCLE" PT1 RAD)
     )                                   ; end ELSE progn
    )                                    ; end IF
    (princ)
)                                        ; end DEFUN
```

In this example, several expressions must be evaluated in order to complete either the THEN or the ELSE option. To accomplish this, the PROGN function binds all of the supplied expressions together as one. The flexibility of an IF expression is greatly enhanced when using the PROGN function.

EXERCISE 8-2

- □ Design an AutoLISP program that accomplishes the following:
  - A. Use the symbols VAR1, VAR2, and VAR3 to store the values found in the AutoCAD system variables CIRCLERAD, FILLETRAD, and OFFSETDIST, respectively.
  - B. Report the values found in each of these system variables. Use the AutoLISP PRINC function to print these findings to the screen.

  Construct three IF expressions that ask the user if any of these values are to be modified (one IF expression per system variable).
- □ Each IF expression should include statements that both test the user's responses and also make the necessary changes. Name the file EX8-2.LSP.

LOGICAL FUNCTIONS

A *logical function* is used to increase the number of test conditions that may be handled by an IF expression, just like the PROGN function is used to enhance the result options. In addition, the test criterion may be modified through the use of one or more of these functions. The basic logical functions available in AutoLISP are AND, OR, and NOT.

The AND Function

The *AND function* returns T if all of its arguments evaluate to non-nil values. When the first nil value is encountered, the AND function does not evaluate the remaining arguments, and nil is returned. An AND expression is extremely useful when you need to run more than one test in a single test expression. The format for the AND function is as follows:

```
(and EXPRESSION ...)
```

When the following symbol assignments are made, the results shown in the examples are returned.

```
(setq A 1   B "OK"   C nil   D '(0 0)   E 25.4)
```

```
(and
  (> A 0)
  (< A 2)
)
```

T is returned

```
(and
  (> A 0)
  (= A 4)
  (< A 6)
)
```

nil is returned

```
(and
  (null C)
)
```

T is returned

```
(and)
```

T is returned. No nil arguments were found.

```
(and D E)
```

T is returned. Symbols D and E are bound to non-nil values.

The OR Function

The *OR function* returns T if at least one argument evaluates to something other than nil. In contrast to the AND function, the OR function evaluates each expression until a non-nil value is found. If a non-nil value is found, it ceases evaluation and returns T. The syntax for the OR function is:

```
(or EXPRESSION ...)
```

When the following symbol assignments are made, the results shown in the examples are returned.

```
(setq A nil   B nil   C 14)

(or
  (> C -20)
  (< C 20)
)                                       T is returned

(or A B)          returns  nil
(or A B C)        returns  T
(or)              returns  nil          no non-nil arguments were found

(or
  (setq A 1)
  (setq B 2)
)                                       T is returned
```

In the last example, the first argument returned a non-nil value, and therefore, the expression returns T. A quick check of the values of A and B will show that the second argument was not evaluated.

The NOT Function

The *NOT function* returns T if its argument evaluates to nil, or otherwise returns nil. The NOT function is commonly used to determine whether or not an item has any value. It may also be used in combination with the AND and OR functions to reverse their output (effectively creating a NAND or a NOR function) to meet the specific needs of the programmer. The format for the NOT function is:

```
(not ITEM)
```

Examples of the NOT function follow:

```
(not nil)         returns  T
(not T)           returns  nil

(not
  (and 1 2)
)                                       nil is returned. The AND function
                                        returned T, which is reversed by
                                        the NOT function to obtain nil.
```

Applications of Logical Functions

Logical functions are often used to gain a tighter control on the response to test conditions. The next example takes advantage of AutoLISP's logical functions. This program uses the OR function to help determine which program branch to follow. In addition, function nesting plays an important role in the sequence of evaluation. Each nested IF statement, with its own test expressions and subsequent outcomes, has the potential to return markedly different results each time the program is run.

```
; Filename:  Filetime.lsp
;
; Author:  T. Fortoo
;
; Date:  November 22, 19xx
;
; Purpose:  To initiate a beginning "dialogue" between the user and the new/current drawing file.
;           The AutoCAD system variables that are examined and modified include:
;
; DWGTITLED:  Reveals whether the current drawing is named. The bit codes for this
;             variable are as follows: 0 = Drawing has no name, 1 = Drawing has a name.
; DWGWRITE:   Controls the read–only toggle for opening drawings. The bit codes for
;             this variable are as follows: 0 = Drawing is read–only, 1 = Drawing is
;             read–write. Used for Release 13, no implication for Release 14.
; SAVETIME:   The automatic drawing file saver mechanism. The timer value is
;             expressed in minutes, from 0 to 32767.
; LOGINNAME:  The user's name as configured for AutoCAD (read–only).
;
;
;
(defun C:FILETIME (/ VAR1 VAR2 VAR3 VAR4 RES)
  (setvar "cmdecho" 0)
  (setq
    VAR1 (getvar "Dwgtitled")
    VAR2 (getvar "Dwgwrite")
    VAR3 (getvar "Savetime")
    VAR4 (getvar "Loginname")
  )
  (command ".textscr")                       ; Flip to the text screen
  (princ "\n         ")                      ; Return first, add 9 spaces
  (princ VAR4)                               ; After spaces, user Login placed on screen
;
  (if                                        ; Begin IF
    (or                                      ; Begin OR – TEST expression
      (= (getvar "Dwgname") "UNNAMED")       ;   Does drawing have name
      (= VAR1 0)                             ;   Does drawing have title
    )                                        ; End OR
;
      (progn                                 ; Begin PROGN – THEN expression
        (princ "\n\nThe current drawing file is unnamed...")
        (setq RES (strcase
          (getstring "\nWould you like to name this file? <Y/N>: "))
```

```
          )                                     ; End setq
          (if                                   ; Begin nested IF
            (= RES "Y")                         ; TEST expression
              (command ".saveas"  "R14"  "~"    ; THEN expression – SAVEAS in a
                       ".textscr" )             ;   dialogue box, then text screen
              (princ "\nNo file name given.")   ; ELSE expression
          )                                     ; End nested IF
        )                                       ; End PROGN
;
        (progn                                  ; Begin PROGN – ELSE expression
          (princ "\n\nThe current drawing file is: ")
          (princ (getvar "Dwgname"))
        )                                       ; End PROGN
;
  )                                             ; End IF
;
  (if                                           ; Begin IF
    (= VAR2 1)                                  ; TEST expression
;
        (progn                                  ; Begin PROGN – THEN expression
          (princ "\n\nThe read–only toggle is not enabled...")
          (setq RES (strcase
            (getstring "\nEnable the read–only feature? <Y/N>: "))
          )
          (if                                   ; Begin nested IF
            (= RES "Y")                         ;   TEST expression
              (setvar "Dwgwrite" 0)             ;   THEN expression
              (princ "\nRead–only not enabled.") ;  ELSE expression
          )                                     ; End nested IF
        )                                       ; End PROGN
;
  )                                             ; End IF
;
  (princ "\n\nThe automatic drawing file saver is set to: <")   ; PRINC time
  (princ VAR3)                                                  ; saver value
  (princ ">")
  (setq RES (strcase (getstring "\nWould you like to reset this? <Y/N>: ")))
;
  (if                                                           ; Begin IF
    (= RES "Y")                                                 ;   TEST expression
      (setvar "Savetime" (getint "\nNew setting <0–32767>: "))  ;   THEN expression
      (princ "\nNo change in Savetime.")                        ;   ELSE expression
  )                                                             ; End IF
;
  (princ)
)
; – –< End of Program >– –
```

The AutoCAD system variables DWGNAME and DWGTITLED, included within an OR test expression, reveal whether the current drawing has a name. In the event that the file is unnamed, the user has the opportunity to name the drawing via the SAVEAS command/dialogue box; named files are printed to the screen.

The read-only status of the drawing may also be changed, as well as the automatic drawing file-saver setting (system variable SAVETIME). Nearly all of the IF statements found in this program utilize the THEN and ELSE branching expressions, an essential aspect of program flow.

PROFESSIONAL TIP

An alternate (and faster) method for accessing AutoLISP functions is by entering the function names into the AutoCAD menu. The following example demonstrates this technique:

```
[Load WALLS]^C^C(load "E:/WALLS")
```

This AutoCAD menu macro, located in a pull-down menu, accesses the E: drive on the computer and loads the command line function named "WALLS".

In addition, the menu can be used to load the function definitions only on an "as needed" basis. In this manner, two different aspects of loading and using a function are controlled: function definitions are loaded only if needed, and they are only loaded once. By using the IF and NOT functions, a programmer is able to see whether the function is already defined:

```
[Load DIV]^C^C(if (not C:DIV) (load "DIV"))+
(C:DIV)
```

This AutoCAD menu macro, located in the screen menu area, loads the command line function named "DIV". Notice that this expression differs from the previous LOAD expression. If no command line function named "DIV" exists, this file will be loaded (on the AutoCAD library path). There is no ELSE expression needed. The next line invokes the C:DIV function.

Note that when entering AutoLISP expressions into the menu file, a backslash character requests a pause for user input. In file/path name specifications, use a forward slash as a directory name separator.

If the C:DIV function is not defined, its symbol has a nil value. As an argument for a NOT expression, the nil value of this symbol causes T to be returned. When the predicate test returns T, the THEN expression is evaluated, and the proper file is loaded. Once the file has been loaded, subsequent calls of the NOT function return nil, and the THEN expression is ignored. Consequently, the function is invoked without loading it each time.

An application of the AND expression is provided in the next example, along with another application of the NOT function. This program ensures that two points are picked prior to attempting to use them. If the ENTER key is pressed in response to a GETPOINT function, nil is returned. The AND expression guarantees that both PT1 and PT2 have values. Remember that the PROMPT function always returns nil. The NOT function reverses this value to T so the AND function can continue.

```
(if                                          ; Begin IF
  (and                                       ; Begin AND
    (not (prompt "\nPick two points: "))     ; PROMPT returns nil, so NOT returns T
    (setq PT1 (getpoint))                    ; Non-nil value (if a point is picked)
    (setq PT2 (getpoint PT1))                ; Non-nil value (if a point is picked)
  )                                          ; End AND
  (command ".POLYGON" "6" "E" PT1 PT2)       ; THEN expression
  (prompt "\nTwo points must be picked!")    ; ELSE expression
)                                            ; End IF
```

Let's Review...

1. When a simple "fork" is required in a program, the IF function should be used. The IF function is composed of at least two required arguments–a TEST expression and a THEN expression. An optional ELSE expression may also be supplied.
2. The PROGN function allows several expressions to be used where only one expression is expected. Any number of expressions may be incorporated within a PROGN expression.
3. AutoLISP's basic logical functions are AND, OR, and NOT. These functions greatly enhance a program's versatility by allowing more than one test within a TEST argument.

EXERCISE 8-3

- ☐ AutoCAD attribute editing is usually handled through the DDATTE dialogue box. On the other hand, text editing may be handled through the DDEDIT dialogue box. Design an AutoLISP program that asks the user to edit an attribute entry or a text entity using either of these two dialogue boxes. An IF expression should be used to accomplish this task. A block containing one attribute and one separate text item should be present on the screen when testing the program.
- ☐ Name the file EX8-3.LSP.

INTEGRATED TESTING PROCEDURES

The functions discussed so far in this chapter are only a few of the many test functions available in AutoLISP. However, almost any condition can be tested for by integrating test functions with customized expressions.

The TYPE Function

One example of a shortcoming in the built-in AutoLISP test functions is found in the NUMBERP function. This function indicates whether or not the item is a number. Certain situations may require that you know whether the number is a real number or an integer. One available building block for integrated tests is the TYPE function. The syntax for the TYPE function is:

```
(type ITEM)
```

The *TYPE function* returns the data type associated with the item. An ITEM evaluating to nil also returns nil. The following is a listing of the values returned by the TYPE function.

Returned Value	Explanation
REAL	Floating Point Numbers
INT	Integers
STR	Text Strings
SYM	Symbol Names
LIST	Lists
FILE	File Descriptors
PICKSET	AutoCAD Selection Sets
ENAME	AutoCAD Entity Names
SUBR	Internal AutoLISP Functions
EXSUBR	External (ADS) Functions
PAGETB	Function Paging Table

If the following symbol assignments are made:

```
(setq a 1.0   B 3   C "OK"   D '(0 0)   E nil)
```

...the following results are returned.

(type A)	returns REAL	*A evaluates to 1.0, a real number*
(type 'A)	returns SYM	*unevaluated; A is a symbol name*
(type B)	returns INT	*B evaluates to an integer*
(type C)	returns STR	*C evaluates to a text string*
(type D)	returns LIST	*D evaluates to a list*
(type E)	returns nil	*E evaluates to nil*

In order to use the TYPE function as a test expression, it can be combined with a predicate. In the situation previously described where it is desirable to determine whether an argument is an integer or a real number, the following expression would apply:

```
(setq A 1.0)
(if
  (numberp A)                        ; first, verify that argument is a number
  (if                                ; if it is an integer...
    (= 'INT (type A))                ; 'INT is quoted to prevent evaluation
    (prompt "\nIt is an integer!")
    (prompt "\nIt is a real number!")
  )
  (prompt "\nIt is not a number!")
)
```

First, note that the data type indicator returned is *not* a text string; it is returned as a symbol. That is why INT is quoted, rather than being enclosed within quotation marks. To support this, observe the following examples:

```
(type '(0 0))              returns LIST
(type (type '(0 0)))       returns SYM
```

The second expression shown here returns the data type associated with the value returned (the symbol LIST) by the nested TYPE expression. Almost any expression may be used as a test expression either by itself or in combination with a predicate.

PROFESSIONAL TIP

In a program where certain input data may be uncontrolled, unexpected data types may be returned. As one example, an uncontrolled GETINT function may return an integer or it may return nil. If an attempt is made to use a nil value in an expression expecting numeric data, it can cause errors within a program. The TYPE function allows the programmer to first test for a proper data type before attempting to use the returned value.

CREATING COMPLEX BRANCHES USING THE COND FUNCTION

The IF function works well when a simple branch is needed. An IF expression can be compared to a fork in the road, as it presents only two possible directions of flow. In a situation where several potential paths may be required, the *COND (CONDition) function* is used. The syntax for the COND function is as follows:

```
(cond (TEST1 RESULT1 ...) ...)
```

The COND function allows any number of lists to be supplied as arguments. The first element of each list is evaluated in the order encountered until one is found which has a non-nil value, or until there are no more test arguments. If a list is encountered where the first element evaluates to a non-nil value, the rest of the elements in that list (sublist) are processed, and no further evaluation is performed. The diagram in Fig. 8-3 illustrates the flow within a COND expression.

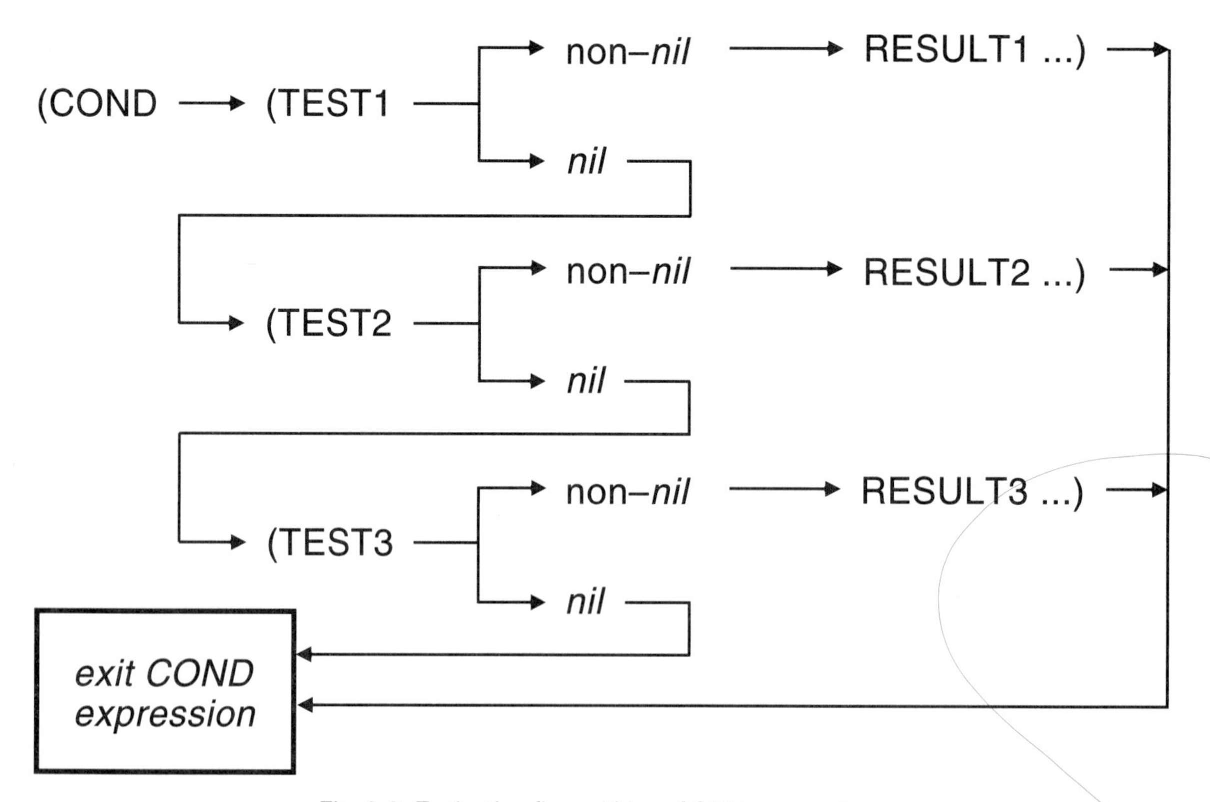

Fig. 8-3. Evaluation flow within a COND expression.

Notice that if TEST1 evaluates to anything other than nil, the sublist is evaluated, and AutoLISP immediately exits the COND expression. If, however, TEST1 returns nil, then TEST2 will be evaluated, and so on until no more arguments are found.

Carefully examine the following example. This routine instructs the user to pick a point on the screen. A different message is returned depending on where the point is located in relationship to the upper limits of the drawing.

```
(defun C:CHECKPLZ (/ CHKPT LM)
  (setvar "cmdecho" 0)
  (setq CHKPT (getpoint "\nSelect point to check: "))
  (setq LM (getvar "LIMMAX"))
  (cond                                ; Begin COND
    (                                  ; Begin first list
      (and                             ; Begin AND – TEST expression #1
        (> (car CHKPT) (car LM))       ;   compare X values...
        (> (cadr CHKPT) (cadr LM))     ;   compare Y values...
      )                                ; End AND
      (prompt "\nPoint exceeds upper limits on both axes. \n")  ; Sublist #1
    )                                  ; End first list
    (                                  ; Begin second list
      (> (car CHKPT) (car LM))         ; TEST expression #2 – compare X values...
      (prompt "\nPoint exceeds upper limits on X-axis.\n")  ; Sublist #2
    )                                  ; End second list
    (                                  ; Begin third list
      (> (cadr CHKPT) (cadr LM))       ; TEST expression #3 – compare Y values...
      (prompt "\nPoint exceeds upper limits on Y-axis.\n")  ; Sublist #3
    )                                  ; End third list
    (T                                 ; Begin last list – First item is T (True)
      (prompt "\nSelected point does not exceed upper limits.\n")  ; Sublist #4
    )                                  ; End last list
  )                                    ; End COND
  (princ)
)                                      ; End DEFUN
```

In this example, up to four conditions are tested. The list given as the first argument is an AND expression that returns T only if both the X and Y values of CHKPT exceed the upper limits. If nil is returned, the first item in the next list is evaluated. This continues until a non-nil value is found or the end of the COND expression is encountered. In the previous example, if none of the first three test expressions are true, then the upper limits are not exceeded. Therefore, in this particular example, the failure of the first three tests indicates that the point selected does not exceed the upper limits, so the final list requires no test expression. In such a case, a simple non-nil value may be used instead of a test expression to ensure that the entire list will be evaluated. (In the previous example, the value T is used.)

The next example uses the COND function to implement AutoCAD solid modeling commands. Detailed documentation for the program is provided at the end of the routine.

```
; Filename:  3Dsolmod.lsp
;
; Date:  July 23, 19xx
;
; Purpose: To combine a select group of AutoCAD solids commands into one
;          command window routine. The program lists primarily drawing
;          and modification tools for solids manipulation. The "startcom"
;          function provides the user with a single help prompt when using
;          the specified command.
;
; Note:    Setting the AutoCAD command window to 4 lines of text will permit
;          the user to view all prompts given.
;
(defun C:SOL (/ RES)
  (setvar "cmdecho" 0)
  (defun startcom (helpstring)                                          ; [1]
    (princ (strcat "\n3-D solids operation for: " RES  "\n" helpstring))  ; [2]
    (command (strcat "." RES))                                          ; [3]
  )
  (initget 1 "Extrude Revolve sLice seCtion Intersect Union Subtract eXit")
  (setq RES (getkword (strcat "3D tools - Extrude/Revolve/sLice/seCtion/"
                        "Intersect/Union/Subtract/eXit: ")
            )                                                           ; [4]
  )
  (cond ((= RES "Extrude")                                              ; [5]
      (startcom "Creates solid primitives by extruding 2-D objects 〈ie., Circles, Plines〉.")
     )
     ((= RES "Revolve")
      (startcom "Creates a circular solid by revolving a 2-D object about an axial path.")
     )
     ((= RES "sLice")
      (startcom "Slices a group of solids with a working or imaginary plane.")
     )
     ((= RES "seCtion")
      (startcom "Employs the intersection of a specified plane and solids to form a region.")
     )
     ((= RES "Intersect")
      (startcom "Calculates the common volume shared by two or more solids.")
     )
     ((= RES "Union")
      (startcom "Creates a composite solid by adding two or more existing solids.")
     )
     ((= RES "Subtract")
      (startcom "Composite solid created by subtracting voidable solids from base solids.")
     )
     ((= RES "eXit")
      (princ "\nExiting SOL routine")
     )
  ) ; End cond
  (princ)
)
```

Documentation for 3DSOLMOD.LSP

[1] **(defun startcom (helpstring)** The STARTCOM defined function is intended to assist the user with on-line help, after having selected from a variety of solid modeling commands. The HELPSTRING argument is a string that is printed in the command window, describing how the 3D solid function works.

[2] **(princ (strcat "\n3-D solids operation for: " RES "\n" helpstring))** Print the concatenation of 4 separate text strings. The RES variable stores the solids command about to be issued. The HELPSTRING argument is subsequently printed to the screen, and provides an on-screen tip as to the operation of the chosen command.

[3] **(command (strcat "." RES))** The RES variable, which stores the AutoCAD command, is concatenated with a "." so that the standard definition is activated.

[4] **(setq RES (getkword (strcat "3D tools - Extrude/Revolve/sLice/seCtion/" "Intersect/Union/Subtract/eXit: ")** A select number of solid modeling commands are provided as choices for the user. The preceding INITGET function forces the user to select from the list of key words.

[5] **(cond ((= RES "Extrude") (startcom "Creates solid primitives by extruding 2-D objects...)** The RES variable is examined to see which key word has been selected. Where the conditional test returns true, the STARTCOM function is then called. The indicated HELPSTRING argument is printed to the screen, and the appropriate AutoCAD command is then given.

Branching Function Applications

Branching functions have a variety of applications. In fact, they are the foundation of program versatility. Not only can error situations be carefully avoided, but input options can be controlled and several potential solutions can stem from the same program, depending on the specific conditions existing each time the program is used. Without the capabilities provided by conditional functions, a program would be nothing more than a script file–merely a list of tasks to be performed regardless of any differing circumstances. Utilizing branching functions brings the power of intelligent decision-making into your programs.

EXERCISE 8-4

- ☐ Using the conditional expression found in the C:CHECKPLZ program, which returned a message about the location of a point, create a revised version that ensures a point has been selected prior to checking for a location. If a point was not selected, display an appropriate message. Name the file CHKPT.LSP.

Let's Review...

1. Through integrating AutoLISP functions, a greater variety of test criterion may be examined. Many functions not designed for testing purposes may be used by themselves, or in conjunction with predicates to perform required tests.
2. When a program that has several potential branches is needed, the COND function is used. This allows several options to be available for any specific set of conditions. In addition, if none of the test conditions return T (True), the last expression can be supplied with a non-nil value. This forces the last expression to be evaluated.
3. Without the capabilities provided by CONDitional functions, a program would be nothing more than a script file. Utilizing these functions brings the power of intelligent decision-making to your programs.

CHAPTER TEST

Write your answers in the spaces provided.

1. Explain what is meant by a "non-linear flow" within a program.

____

____

____

____

2. Define the term "predicate."

____

____

3. List the data types that are valid arguments for the = function.

____

4. How does the EQ function differ from the = function?

____

____

____

____

5. Why is EQUAL considered to be the most versatile of the predicates that check equality?

____

____

____

____

6. Explain the use of the FUZZ argument within the EQUAL function. List at least two potential applications using different data types.

7. Given the two arguments shown in each of the following problems, indicate which one AutoLISP would consider to have a greater value than the other.

   A. "Hello" "hello"

   B. 12345 12346

   C. "abCde" "abcde"

   D. "XYZ" "XyZ"

   E. '(12 0.33) '(11 0.2 0)

8. Detail the method and order of evaluation in a >= expression.

9. Any item that is not a list is called a(n) ________________.

10. Describe all of the possible arguments for an IF expression. Also, indicate whether they are required or optional.

11. Detail the use of the PROGN function. List some possible applications.

12. Explain the use of the AND function. List some possible applications.

13. Describe the use of the OR function.

14. Show an example of how the NOT function is used to modify test results to meet the needs of a conditional expression.

15. Explain the purpose of an integrated test function. Give three examples.

16. What data type is associated with the values returned by the TYPE function?

17. How can a non-test function be used in a test expression?

18. Describe a situation when the COND function should be used rather than the IF function.

19. Detail the method and order of evaluation in a COND expression.

20. Explain how and when a simple non-nil value would be used in place of a test expression within a COND expression.

PROGRAMMING PROBLEMS

1. Design a program using an IF expression to accomplish the following:
   A. Use the AutoCAD SAVE command to store a drawing on the C: drive.
   B. Construct an IF expression that asks if the drawing is also to be saved on a floppy disk (A: or B: drive). If so, another nested IF expression will need to be used to handle this task. (Hint: The AutoLISP STRCAT function and AutoCAD DWGNAME system variable will be employed.)
   C. Use AutoLISP's prompting capabilities as needed to keep the user "on track" within the program. A statement should be issued when the program is complete.
   D. Thoroughly document the program. Save the file as P8-1.LSP.
2. Design a program using CONDitional expressions to accomplish the following:
   A. Control input and return a message for invalid input at the prompt.
   B. Draw a rectangle, square, or triangle based upon user selection.
   C. Use a polyline to draw the specified entity, making use of the POLAR function (or list manipulation techniques) to find necessary points.
   D. Make the program look and feel as built-in as possible. Name the file P8-2.LSP.

FILE–PRN.LSP

```
; Filename: FILE–PRN.LSP
;
; Purpose: To dispatch an AutoLISP file to the printer.
;
; Requirements: The printer is turned on, and on–line.
;               The file subdirectory is \ACADR14\ACADLISP.
;
(defun C:FILE–PRN (/ RES)
  (setvar "cmdecho" 0)
  (setq RES (getfiled "Lisp File to Print"  ; [1]
                      "/acadr14/acadlisp/"
                      "lsp"
                      (+ 2 8)))
  (if (null RES)                            ; [2]
     (princ "\nFunction cancelled.")
     (progn
       (princ RES) (princ " is printing...one moment please.")
       (command "sh" (strcat "Type "  RES  "  prn"))
     )
  )                                         ; end if
  (setvar "cmdecho" 1)
  (princ)
)
; ––⟨ End of File ⟩– –
;
; [1] (setq RES (getfiled "Lisp File to Print"
;                         "/acadr14/acadlisp/"
;                         "lsp"
;                         (+ 2 8)))
;
;     The title for the Standard File Dialogue box is "Lisp File to Print".
;     The file path to search is "/acadr14/acadlisp/". The file extension for
;     selection is "lsp". The flags argument is set to (+ 2 8) which dis-
;     ables the "Type it" button; the library path will also be searched.
;
; [2] (if (null RES)
;
;     If the user cancels the operation, a "Function cancelled." message
;     is issued to the screen. Otherwise, print the file stored in the
;     symbol RES.
```

Chapter 9 Looping Techniques

Learning Objectives

After completing this chapter, you will be able to:

- ☐ Explain the use and benefits of program loops.
- ☐ Utilize looping techniques to perform repetitive tasks.
- ☐ Assemble and process data lists with program loops.

LOOPING TECHNIQUES

AutoLISP provides several methods for creating program loops. A *program loop* allows one or more expressions to be executed in sequence. The program then returns to the beginning of the loop and executes the same expressions again. This is very useful for repetitive tasks, or when performing the same set of operations on several entities.

The most appropriate looping function for any given situation depends on the criterion used to designate the number of iterations (repetitions). The programmer can specify an exact number of iterations, or a loop can continue as long as a particular condition exists. In addition, a loop may be used to process each element contained within a list. By utilizing looping techniques, a programmer can incorporate greater processing power into a program.

THE BASIC LOOP

A variety of looping techniques can be used in AutoLISP. As previously mentioned, the circumstances will determine which function is most appropriate.

The REPEAT Function

In situations where a series of expressions are to be executed a predetermined (or otherwise specified) number of times, the *REPEAT function* can be used. The syntax for the REPEAT function is:

```
(repeat NUMBER EXPR ...)
```

The REPEAT function evaluates any quantity of EXPRESSIONs as many times as is indicated by NUMBER. Note that NUMBER must be a positive integer of any magnitude. When the NUMBER argument is zero or a negative value, this causes the REPEAT expression to immediately return nil, and no further evaluation is performed.

As previously mentioned, integers *must* be used for the NUMBER argument. Since a task cannot be performed 1.6 times, AutoLISP considers a real number to be a "bad argument type," even if it represents a whole number such as 1.0, 24.0, etc. A REPEAT expression always returns the value of the last expression contained within the loop.

When the symbols M and N are assigned the following values:

```
(setq M 1   N 5)
```

...the REPEAT function returns:

```
(repeat 10
  (setq M (+ 2 M))
  (setq N (+ 5 N))
)                                             55 is returned
```

In this example, the REPEAT function evaluates the enclosed expressions ten times. On the tenth round, M is equal to 21 and N is equal to 55. The last expression evaluated sets a new value for N, so in this case, 55 is returned.

The following program, which creates an evenly spaced and incremented row of numbers, is a variation of this idea. The last expression of the program does the "real work;" after the parameters have been set up, the REPEAT function does the rest.

```
; NUMROW.LSP  by Cal Clater
;
; 1/12/xx
;
; Purpose: To create an evenly spaced row of incremented numbers, such as might be
;          required for a chart or graph. The beginning number is zero and the last
;          number is as specified.
;
(defun C:NUMROW (/ PT1 DST DIR NN HN)
  (setvar "CMDECHO" 0)(setvar "BLIPMODE" 0)                 ; CMDECHO off is faster.
  (princ "\nText will be CENTER Justified.")                ; User information
  (setq PT1 (getpoint "\nStart point of number row: ")      ; Text start point.
        DST (getdist "\nDistance between numbers: ")        ; Spacing for text.
        DIR (getorient "\nAngle: ")                         ; Angle for text.
        NN  0                                               ; Next Number value
        HN  (getint "\nNumber sequence to be 0 through: ")  ; High Number value
  )                                                         ; close SETQ
  (command "TEXT" "C" PT1 "" "" "0")                        ; First text point
  (repeat HN                                                ; Repeat HN times
    (setq PT1 (polar PT1 DIR DST))                          ; Spacing
    (command "TEXT" "C" PT1 "" "" (itoa (setq NN (+ NN 1)))) ; itoa converts the
  )                                                       ; numeric argument NN to text.
)
```

In this example, a keyboard entry is the specifier for the number of iterations. Another method for indicating the number of iterations could be directly provided by the programmer. In addition, the specifier could be based on a variable number such as the number of elements in a list or the number of objects in a selection set. (These applications are discussed in later chapters since they involve the use of functions not yet covered in this text.)

The WHILE Function

The primary factor for determining the appropriate looping function is the criterion used to determine the number of iterations. For the REPEAT function, the number is an exact, specified amount. Another possibility, however, is that the program loop could be processed until a test condition is met. For this type of application, the *WHILE function* is more suitable. The syntax for the WHILE function is as follows:

```
(while TESTEXPR EXPR ...)
```

The WHILE function provides a conditional loop. If the TESTEXPR (test expression) returns a non-nil value, the enclosed EXPRs (expressions) are evaluated. This sequence is repeated until the test expression evaluates to nil. A WHILE expression returns the value of the last expression evaluated. Any number of expressions can be specified. Try the following:

```
(setq N 0)
(while (not (minusp N))                              while N is not negative...
  (setq N (getint "\nInput a negative integer: "))   ...prompt for new N value
)
```

In this manner, a process may be repeated until the test expression returns nil. Depending on the design of the conditional expression, this may indicate either that a condition exists, or that it no longer exists.

One effective application for using the WHILE function occurs when the user has several options to select from within the program, including one which will exit the program. Under such circumstances, a WHILE expression can continue until the user inputs the Exit option keyword. Study the following example:

```
(defun C:CHT (/ ANS NT)
  (setvar "CMDECHO" 0)
  (prompt "\nSelect TEXT entity...")
  (command "SELECT" pause)
  (while
    (or
      (initget 1 "Position Style Height Rotation Text Exit")
      (/= "Exit"
        (setq ANS
          (getKword "\nChange Position/Style/Height/Rotation/Text/Exit: ")
        )                              ; End SETQ
      )                                ; End /=
    )                                  ; End OR
    (cond
      ( (= "Position" ANS)
        (prompt "\nNew text location: ")
        (command "CHANGE" "P" "" "" pause "" "" "" "")
      )
      ( (= "Style" ANS)
        (prompt "\nNew text style: ")
        (command "CHANGE" "P" "" "" "" pause "" "" "")
      )
      ( (= "Height" ANS)
        (prompt "\nNew text height: ")
        (command "CHANGE" "P" "" "" "" "" pause "" "")
      )
      ( (= "Rotation" ANS)
        (prompt "\nRotation angle: ")
        (command "CHANGE" "P" "" "" "" "" "" pause "")
      )
      ( (= "Text" ANS)
        (setq NT (getstring T "\nNew text: "))
        (command "CHANGE" "P" "" "" "" "" "" "" NT)
      )
    )                                  ; End COND
  ))                     ; End while & end DEFUN
```

In this example, while the user response is not equal to "Exit," the program will continue to loop. Such an application greatly increases the convenience of using a program since it is not necessary to reload or invoke the program for each use; the option line returns, allowing subsequent selections until the user chooses to exit.

The next program also allows an operation to continue for as many iterations as required by the user. This example uses a slightly different approach than the previous program.

```
; TD.LSP  Written by Paul Kadot 1/11/xx
;
; Multiple Tie-Dot creation routine.
;
; Requires that a block named "TD" exists, which represents the proper size dot.
(defun C:TD (/ TDPT)
  (setq TDPT (getpoint "\nTie-Dot insertion point: "))
  (command "INSERT" "TD" TDPT 1 1 0)
  (while
    (setq TDPT
      (getpoint "\Next Tie-Dot insertion point (or [ENTER] when done): ")
    )
    (command "INSERT" "TD" TDPT 1 1 0)
  )                                       ; End WHILE
)                                         ; End DEFUN
```

When the ENTER key is pressed in response to a GETPOINT, nil is returned. Therefore, the GETPOINT expression serves a dual purpose; it prompts the user for data, plus it functions as a test expression for the WHILE expression. Building on this concept and utilizing some basic list manipulation functions, a simple routine may be designed that will continuously add user-supplied data items to a list for later use. A necessary element for this process is the APPEND function.

The APPEND Function

The *APPEND function* accepts any number of list arguments and combines them into a single list. It is important to remember that a list is the only valid argument for the APPEND function. The order of the elements in the returned list is the same as the supplied arguments. The format for the APPEND function is:

```
(append EXPR ...)
```

The APPEND function returns the following when supplied with the included lists:

```
(append '(2.5 33.066) '(6.0))          returns  (2.5 33.066 6.0)
(append (list "X" "Y") (list "Z"))     returns  ("X" "Y" "Z")
(append (list 1 2) 3)                  returns  error: bad argument type
(append (list 1 2) (list 3))           returns  (1 2 3)
```

Note the last two examples. In the second to last example, an element that is not contained within a list cannot be added to another list with APPEND. All arguments must be lists, as shown in the last example.

Utilizing the APPEND function within a WHILE loop allows existing lists to be combined in order to create larger lists. In the following examples, user-supplied data is continuously added to a list until the WHILE loop is exited. Here, the method of utilizing a GETxxxx function to both acquire data and serve as a test expression is used.

```
(setq RNLST nil)   ; Ensure that RNLST is an empty list
(while (setq RN (getreal "\nType a number (or [ENTER] when done): "))
  (setq RNLST (append RNLST (list RN)))
)
```

Numbers are APPENDed to the list until an ENTER is provided without a value:

```
Type a number (or [ENTER] when done): 1.0 ↵
Type a number (or [ENTER] when done): 5.5 ↵
Type a number (or [ENTER] when done): 0.6 ↵
Type a number (or [ENTER] when done): 91.375 ↵
Type a number (or [ENTER] when done): ↵
(1.0 5.5 0.6 91.375)                          the appended list RNLST is
                                              returned
```

In the next example, a list of points is constructed:

```
(setq PLST nil)
(while (setq P (getpoint "\nPick a point (or [ENTER] when done): "))
  (setq PLST (append PLST (list P)))
)
```

This technique may be applied using any of the GETxxxx functions requiring user input with the exception of GETSTRING, or if the INITGET function has disallowed null input.

COUNTING FUNCTIONS

Two simple math functions have been provided to facilitate counting within a loop. One increases a number by 1, while the other decreases a number by 1.

The 1+ Function

The *1+ function* returns the value of NUMBER increased by one. This is often used to count upward to a specific sum. The NUMBER supplied may be an integer or a real number. The syntax for the 1+ function is:

```
(1+ NUMBER)
```

When the following values are supplied, the 1+ function provides the returned results:

```
(1+ 4)          returns 5
(1+ –22.1)      returns –21.1
```

The 1– Function

The *1– function* returns the value of NUMBER decreased by one. The syntax is the same as used for the 1+ function. Once again, either integers or real numbers can be supplied. For example:

```
(1– 12)         returns 11
(1– 6.2)        returns 5.2
```

There is no difference in results between (1+ 4) and (+ 1 4)–both return 5. The primary difference is that the 1+ function only adds 1 each time it is used, and therefore, is most often applied for incrementing. The + (addition) and – (subtraction) functions may be used instead, but are not solely designed for incrementation. Similarly, if you had a choice of using a box end wrench or a crescent wrench, the box end would be the best choice. Even though the crescent is adjustable to fit many needs, the box end fits perfectly. Try the following routine:

```
(setq N 0)
(while (> 10 N)
  (setq N (1+ N))
)
```

Counters can be used for many effective applications within a program. Some of the more common uses for counters are in evaluating each member of a text string, each element of a list, or even for counting lines within a text file being read by AutoLISP. In the next example, the goal is to isolate the first word of a supplied text string:

```
(setq N 1 TXT "AutoLISP Programmer's Reference")
(while
  (and
    (/= " " (substr TXT N 1))          While a space is not found
    (/= (strlen TXT) N)                 and there are more characters...
  )
  (setq N (1+ N))                       Add one to position, look again.
)                                       ...now N is 1 greater than the
                                        number of characters in the
(setq WORD1 (substr TXT 1 (1- N)))     first word.
```

Now the value assigned to WORD1 is "AutoLISP."

Let's Review...

1. A loop allows one or more expressions to be executed in sequence a given number of times. Determining the appropriate looping function depends on the criterion used to indicate the number of iterations (repetitions).
2. The REPEAT function is used when the number of repetitions is a specified positive integer.
3. The WHILE function allows a loop to continue repeating until its test expression returns nil.
4. The APPEND function accepts any number of LIST arguments and combines them into a single list.
5. The counting functions 1+ and 1– are specifically designed for incrementing numbers within program loops.

EXERCISE 9-1

- ☐ Design a program using a WHILE loop (and the required counting functions) which will return the last word in a text string. As shown in the previous example, make sure that when you encounter the end of the string that the loop stops. This will help to avoid a possible error situation. Name the program LASTWORD.LSP.

PROCESSING EACH ELEMENT OF A LIST

As discussed in earlier chapters, the real power of AutoLISP is in its ability to process lists. This next section details a set of functions that provide great versatility in processing each element contained within a list. These functions allow the application of one or more expressions to each individual element found in a data storage list. The primary function for this purpose is the FOREACH function.

THE FOREACH FUNCTION

There are many possible applications for the FOREACH function, ranging from testing data to consolidating repetitious sequences of expressions. The syntax for the FOREACH function is:

```
(foreach NAME LIST EXPR ...)
```

The *FOREACH function* processes LIST one element at a time. In turn, each individual element of LIST is temporarily assigned to the symbol NAME. Then, each EXPR (expression) within FOREACH is evaluated. Thus, the expressions provided are evaluated once "for each" element found in the supplied LIST argument. Similar to the WHILE function, any number of expressions can be specified for evaluation.

The FOREACH function loops through its list of expressions, one time for each element in the list, regardless of the length of the list. If an empty list is provided as an argument, nothing further is evaluated and nil is returned.

Typically, all of the items found within a single list are somehow related; therefore, a single set of expressions can often be applicable for each list element. In the following example, note that each item contained in the specified list argument is a single-character text string:

```
(foreach LTR (list "A" "B" "C" "D" "E" "F" "G")     each cycle assigns the next
  (princ                                             element to LTR, which then has
    (strcat "\n" LTR)                                a newline added and is printed
  )                                                  to the screen
)
(princ)
```

THE SET FUNCTION

The *SET function* is a valuable tool for the handling of symbols and symbol names within a FOREACH expression. The *SET function* sets the value of SYM to the value of EXPR. The syntax for the SET function is:

```
(set SYM EXPR)
```

The difference between SET and SETQ is that the SET function will first evaluate SYM. Remember that the SETQ function does not evaluate its symbol name argument. That is because the SETQ function is actually a combination of the *SET* and *QUOTE* functions. Since the SET function first evaluates its symbol name (SYM) argument, it can be very useful when used in conjunction with the FOREACH function. Study the following example:

```
(foreach S '(a b c)
  (set S (getint "\nEnter an integer: "))
)
```

In this expression, the LIST argument is a list of quoted symbols. The SYMbol argument S temporarily carries each quoted symbol, which is then used in the SET expression. Subsequently, the SET function evaluates S and assigns the returned value of the EXPRession argument to the quoted symbol held as S. For example, in the first loop of the previous expression, S represents the quoted symbol 'a. Therefore, you could say that in this iteration, S = 'a. Since the SET function evaluates its argument, the SET expression is equivalent to the expression shown here:

```
(set 'a (getint "\nEnter an integer: "))
```

To take this one step further, the previous expression is also equivalent to:

```
(setq a (getint "\nEnter an integer: "))
```

In this manner, the FOREACH function repetitively applies the SET function to each of the symbols contained in the LIST argument. Such an application is especially useful when many variables need to be set within a program.

Note that the SET function can only be used when the SYMbol argument represents a quoted symbol. If the SYMbol it represents is not quoted, then it is also evaluated in the EXPRession. If the SYMbol has no value, it evaluates to nil, which is not a valid symbol name. Such an oversight causes AutoLISP to return the "bad argument type" error message.

THE EVAL FUNCTION

The *EVAL (EVALuate) function* returns the result of the evaluation of EXPR. The EXPR argument can be any AutoLISP expression. The format for the EVAL function is:

```
(eval EXPR)
```

When the following values are assigned to the variables:

```
(setq X "OK"   Y 15   Z 'X)
```

...the EVAL function returns:

```
(eval X)        returns "OK"
(eval Y)        returns 15
(eval Z)        returns "OK"        the symbol X (equal to "OK") is
                                    assigned to symbol Z
```

As shown, the EVAL function does not cease evaluation at the first level; rather, the expression or variable is completely evaluated. This allows the value of a temporary symbol to be extracted. For example, a simple evaluation of the symbol S in the first iteration of the previous FOREACH expression would return 'a. However, using the EVAL function on the symbol S would return the *value* of the symbol 'a. To demonstrate this, the previous FOREACH expression has been modified so that it places each symbol in list L followed by the symbol's value. The value is derived by using the EVAL function.

```
(foreach S '(a b c)
  (set S (getint "\nEnter an integer: "))
  (setq L (append L (list S)))           the value of S is quoted symbol
                                         (a b or c)
  (setq L (append L (list (eval S))))    eval returns the value of the symbol
)

Enter an integer: 1 ↵
Enter an integer: 2 ↵
Enter an integer: 3 ↵
Enter an integer: ↵
(A 1 B 2 C 3)
```

The ability to work creatively with symbols and symbol names greatly enhances the effectiveness of your programs. One additional aspect of working with symbols comes from being able to draw symbol names from text values. As discussed in Chapter 7, the READ function is used for this purpose.

The next example is part of a parametric drawing program. This application requests user-supplied values for each of eleven letter specifications for dimensional features on a part.

```
(setq LTRLST (list "A" "B" "C" "D" "E" "F" "G" "H" "J" "K" "L"))
(foreach VN LTRLST
  (set
    (read VN)
    (getreal
      (strcat "\nValue for dimension " VN ": ")
    )
  )
)
```

Carefully study the following example; it incorporates many of the functions discussed in this chapter. Note the use of the READ function to withdraw symbol names from text strings. Within the COND expression, the SET function is used so that an evaluation of the first argument occurs. (Since it is an expression, it must be evaluated to return the symbol name.) The FOREACH expression utilizes the EVAL function to extract the value of the variable name for printing to the screen.

```
(defun C:VAR (/ VNS VNL DT)
  (while (/= "" (setq VNS (getstring "\nEnter the variable name to assign: ")))
    (setq VNL (append VNL (list VNS)))              ; Append requires LIST arguments
    (initget 1 "Integer Real String Point")         ; Define the options keyword
    (setq DT (getkword "\nData type (Integer/Real/String/Point): "))
    (cond
      ( (= DT "Integer")      ; If DT is equal to "Integer"...
        (set (read VNS)       ; Use SET so argument is evaluated, READ returns a SYM
          (getint
            (strcat "\nInteger value for " VNS ": ")    ; String + SYM name
          )                                             ; End GETINT
        )                                               ; End SET
      )                                                 ; End of first COND argument
      ( (= DT "Real")
        (set (read VNS) (getreal (strcat "\nReal number value for " VNS ": ")))
      )                                                 ; End of second COND argument
      ( (= DT "String")
        (set (read VNS) (getstring T (strcat "\nString value for " VNS ": ")))
      )                                                 ; End of third COND argument
      ( (= DT "Point")
        (set (read VNS) (getpoint (strcat "\nPoint value for " VNS ": ")))
      )                                                 ; End last COND argument
    )                                                   ; End COND expression
  )                                                     ; End WHILE
  (princ "\nVariable assignments made: ")
  (foreach VN VNL             ; For each Variable Name in the Variable Name List
    (princ (strcat "\n" VN " = "))   ;   print Variable Name and equal sign
    (princ                    ; Print what is returned by...
      (eval                   ;   evaluating the...
        (read VN)             ;   variable name.
      )                       ; End EVAL
    )                         ; End PRINC
  )                           ; End FOREACH
  (princ)                     ; For a "quiet" exit
)                             ; End DEFUN
```

Many common programming requirements can be met only through the use of loops in a program. A strong understanding of looping techniques can help maximize your programming efforts. Further applications for these functions are found throughout the following chapters.

EXERCISE 9-2

- ☐ Design a parametric drawing routine using the following guidelines:
  GOAL: Draw a user-defined version of the part shown below.
  - ☐ An AutoCAD slide (.SLD) showing the following part will be available to define the letter specifications. The first prompt of the routine will provide an option to view this slide.
  - ☐ The program will then prompt for the six required dimensions using a FOREACH expression.
  - ☐ The LIST argument supplied to the FOREACH expression should consist of text characters A through F.
  - ☐ The entered dimensions are to be displayed for the user to verify. The user will have the option to terminate the program or continue at this point.
  - ☐ The routine will verify that the dimensions are possible; for example, "Dimension A is not greater than Dimension C," etc. If any impossible value has been specified, a message is displayed and the program terminates.
  - ☐ Document the routine appropriately. Save the file as PARA1.LSP.

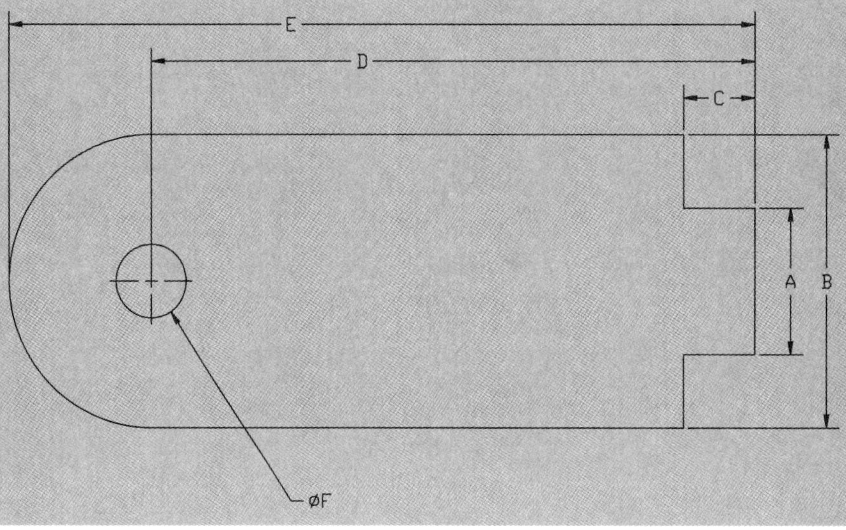

Let's Review...

1. Lists of data can be effectively processed using the FOREACH function.
2. The SET function provides the programmer with a means to define variable names other than by their individual specification. This can shorten variable setting sequences when used in conjunction with FOREACH for processing of a data list.
3. Any AutoLISP expression may be evaluated using the EVAL function. This evaluation is complete and derives the base value.
4. Loops are one of the most useful and powerful features of the AutoLISP programming language.

CHAPTER TEST

Write your answers in the spaces provided.

1. Define "program loop."

 ____

 ____

 ____

 ____

2. List the three looping functions. How is the determination made as to which function should be used in a given situation?

 ____

 ____

 ____

 ____

3. Name the basic looping function and describe its use.

 ____

 ____

 ____

 ____

4. Name and describe the use of the conditional loop.

 ____

 ____

 ____

 ____

 ____

5. The loop used to process a data list is _________ . Detail its use.

 ____

 ____

 ____

 ____

 ____

6. Besides AutoLISP's standard predicates, what other functions can be used for creating test expressions? Explain your answer.

7. Why isn't a real number an acceptable argument for the REPEAT function?

8. Within a looping expression, how many expressions can be evaluated?

9. Describe the advantages of using a loop to present an option line to the user.

10. How can the INITGET function adversely affect the use of GETxxxx functions as test expressions?

11. Why is the 1+ or 1– function used for simple counting purposes as opposed to the standard + (addition) or – (subtraction) functions?

12. List some possible applications of the FOREACH function.

13. Detail the difference between the SET and SETQ functions.

____

____

14. Describe a useful application involving the SET function.

____

____

____

15. What simple oversight on the part of the programmer results in the SET function returning a "bad argument type" error?

____

____

PROGRAMMING PROBLEMS

1. Design a program that uses an option line WHILE loop. The actual function of the program is left up to the programmer. The goal is to create a functional looping option line. Use four to seven options with one being the option to exit.
2. Design a custom multiple block insertion program. The user will be prompted for the name of the block, the number of insertions, and the insertion scale factor. Use the REPEAT function to execute a loop that asks only for the insertion point and rotation angle each time.
3. Design a parametric routine to draw the part shown below. As in previous problems, ensure that all dimensions are possible. Name the program PARA2.LSP.

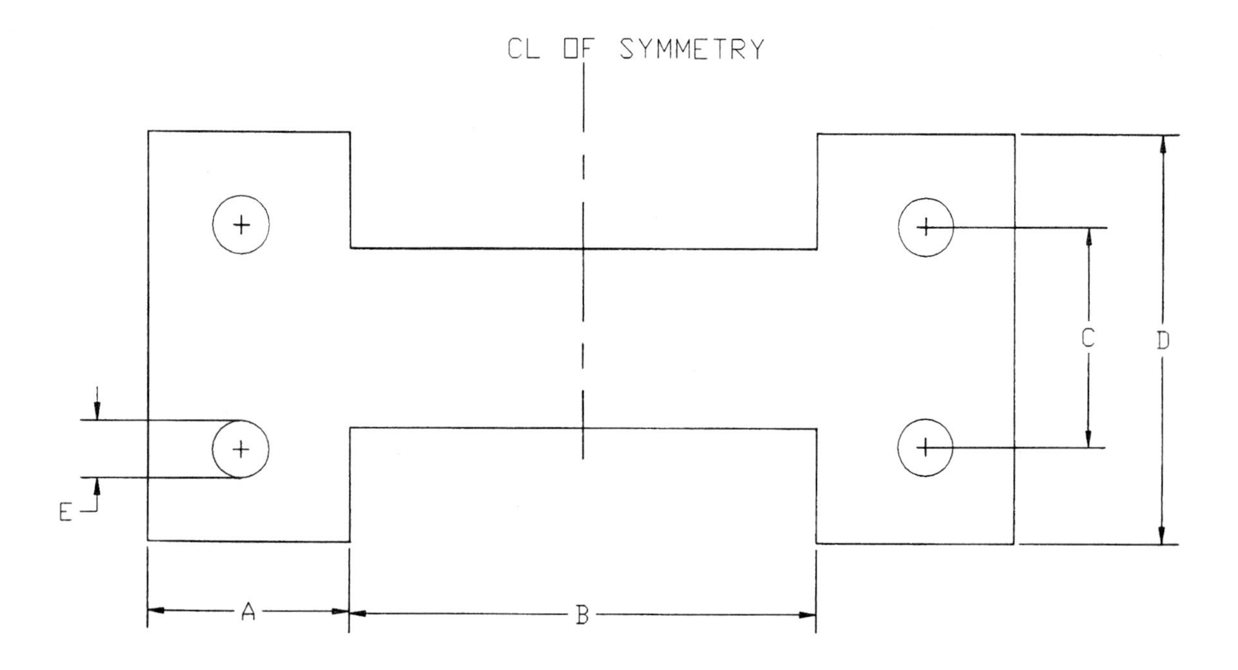

4. Design a program similar to TD.LSP (shown in this chapter) and call it TD2.LSP. However, the TD2.LSP will prompt for the number of tie-dots needed. The program will terminate when the requested number of dots have been placed.
5. Design a program that requests a text string, then count the number of words in the string. (Hint: Count spaces between words.) Name the program WORDCT.LSP.

Chapter 10

Advanced List Manipulation

Learning Objectives

After completing this chapter, you will be able to:

- ☐ Use advanced AutoLISP functions to create, modify, and manipulate lists.
- ☐ Execute functions that employ data list arguments.
- ☐ Create anonymous functions rather than defining functions.

ADVANCED LEVEL LIST MANIPULATION

Using lists for data storage and retrieval places a great deal of power at the programmer's fingertips. Lists are an efficient means for handling large quantities of data. As you might imagine, managing an individual variable for every stored piece of data in a large programming application can become very cumbersome.

Many of the drawing database records retrieved by AutoLISP are stored as lists. Therefore, it is essential that you have a strong understanding of the different types of lists, and the functions and methods provided for managing them.

REVIEW OF BASIC LIST-HANDLING FUNCTIONS

A brief review of the list-handling functions covered earlier in this text will help prepare you for the new information covered in this chapter.

The LIST Function

The *LIST function* takes any number of items of any data type and places them together in a single list. Remember that each element in a LIST expression is evaluated.

(list EXPR ...)

The QUOTE Function

The *QUOTE function*, which may also be written as ', provides another efficient method for generating lists. All items contained in a quoted list are *not* evaluated.

(quote EXPR)

The CxxxxR Functions

This *CxxxxR family of functions* allow the user to access individual items within a list. Even though these functions are commonly used with point coordinate lists, they are also useful with any type of data list.

(CxxxxR LIST)

The LAST Function

The *LAST function* returns the last item included in a list.

(last LIST)

The LENGTH Function

The *LENGTH function* returns the number of elements included in a list.

(length LIST)

The APPEND Function

The *APPEND function* combines any number of lists together as one list. Detailed information on APPEND is found in Chapter 9.

(append EXPR ...)

These functions will prove to be instrumental in many situations as the more-advanced functions are introduced in this chapter. If you are uncertain about the usage of any of these functions, review Chapters 2, 3, and 9 before proceeding.

DATA STORAGE LIST TYPES

Data lists within AutoLISP have two basic configurations–a simple data list and an association list. The simple data list consists of an opening and a closing parenthesis with "unformatted" data held inside. "Unformatted" refers to the concept that the included data items are not required to be of any specific type or in any particular order.

The second type of data list is an *association list.* This type of list contains any number of associated sublists. An association list allows the programmer to use special functions that make data management much easier.

The ASSOC Function

The *ASSOC (ASSOCiation) function* allows retrieval of specific data through association. The syntax for the ASSOC function is:

```
(assoc ITEM ALIST)
```

The ALIST argument must be an association list. The ASSOC function searches ALIST for ITEM, and then returns the ALIST entry. If ITEM is not found as the first element of a sublist in ALIST, nil is returned. To demonstrate this, an association list is created below:

```
(setq ALIST '( (1 "ONE" "UNO") (2 "TWO" "DOS") (3 "THREE" "TRES") ))
```

The following list is then returned:

```
((1 "ONE" "UNO") (2 "TWO" "DOS") (3 "THREE" "TRES"))
```

By accessing the *header* (first element of a sublist), the associated data can then be retrieved. A header can be compared to the tab on a file folder, which has a label written on it. All other elements of the sublist can be thought of as the information contained in that file. See Fig. 10-1.

(setq ALIST '((1 "ONE" "UNO") (2 "TWO" "DOS") (3 "THREE" "TRES")))

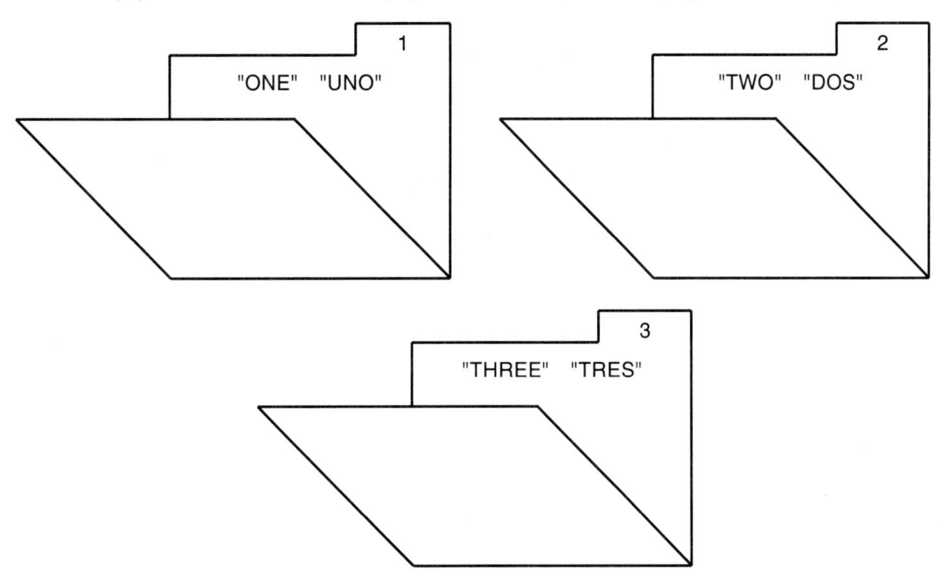

Fig. 10-1. Comparing an association list to a file folder.

The ASSOC function returns the entire record associated with the specified header:

```
(assoc 2 ALIST)              returns (2 "TWO" "DOS")
```

By applying the CDR function, the value can be separated from the header. (Remember, the CDR function returns all but the first element of a list.)

```
(cdr (assoc 2 ALIST))        returns ("TWO" "DOS")
```

Note that if the specified header is not found, nil is returned:

```
(assoc 4 ALIST)                         returns nil
```

The ASSOC function provides a convenient and efficient means of retrieving stored data. Study the following examples, which are based on the next list:

```
(setq FORM '((length 18.5) (width 7.5) (height 4.5) (volume 624.375)))

(cadr (assoc 'length FORM))             returns 18.5
(cadr (assoc 'width FORM))              returns 7.5
(cadr (assoc 'height FORM))             returns 4.5
(cadr (assoc 'volume FORM))             returns 624.375
```

The CONS Function

The sublists within an association list may take any form and contain any number of elements. One common form for a sublist is the dotted pair. A *dotted pair* is a special kind of list, which contains two elements separated by a dot (period). A dotted pair can be constructed by using the CONS function.

The *CONS (CONStruct) function* is a dual-purpose function. By supplying two arguments, where the second argument is a list, CONS returns a modified list with the NEW-FIRST-ELEMENT argument placed at the beginning. The format for the CONS function is:

```
(cons NEW-FIRST-ELEMENT LIST)
```

Study the following examples:

```
(cons 1 '(2 3 4))                       returns (1 2 3 4)
(cons 'x '(y z))                        returns (X Y Z)
(cons (quote "Red") '("Green" "Blue"))  returns ("Red" "Green" "Blue")
```

However, if the second argument is an atom, a dotted pair is returned. As shown in the following example, both elements are evaluated before the list is constructed:

```
(setq A 1  B "ONE")

(cons A B)              returns (1 . "ONE")
```

When it is only necessary to have a field header and one value within the sublist, the CONS function provides a very simple means of creating it. Note that the dotted pair is special in another way than just its appearance. It also produces varied results when assembling and accessing associated data. Given the following assignment:

```
(setq AL (list (cons 'COLOR 4) (cons 'LAYER "0") (cons 'PT1 '(2.4 9.0 0.0))))
```

The resulting list is:

```
((COLOR . 4) (LAYER . "0") (PT1 2.4 9.0 0.0))
```

Since the data supplied for PT1 was a coordinate list, a dotted pair was not created. Next, observe the differences when accessing this associated data:

```
(cdr (assoc 'COLOR AL))        returns 4
```

In the previous example, the CDR function returns a single atom from the dotted pair where the atom is not contained within a list.

```
(cdr (assoc 'PT1 AL))          returns (2.4 9.0 0.0)
```

When accessing the value for PT1, the CDR function returns the value as a list since PT1 is not a dotted pair.

The dotted pair is the primary format that AutoLISP uses for storing and retrieving data records within the drawing database. These functions are covered extensively in Chapter 13, which discusses entity database manipulation.

The MEMBER Function

The *MEMBER function* scans a LIST argument to determine if EXPR is an element of LIST. When EXPR is encountered within LIST, the remainder of the LIST (beginning with EXPR) is returned. If EXPR is not encountered, nil is returned. The format for the MEMBER function is:

```
(member EXPR LIST)
```

When provided with the following assignment:

```
(setq NEWLST '(u v w x y z))
```

...the MEMBER function returns:

```
(member 'u NEWLST)          returns (u v w x y z)
(member 'w NEWLST)          returns (w x y z)
(member 'x NEWLST)          returns (x y z)
(member 'a NEWLST)          returns nil
```

Many programming applications require that the user be prompted for a response and provided with several different options. In the following example, five options are available to the user for a simple setup routine. This program utilizes the MEMBER, ASSOC, and the CxxxxR functions in a way that allows the programmer to supply different parameters to the setup portion of the routine based on user input.

```
; SETUP.LSP by I.M. Reddy
;
; January 4, 19xx
;
; This routine pulls its parameters from an association list and performs
; a simple drawing setup.
;
; --( Get user input )--
;
; This section shows how the MEMBER function can be used as an efficient means of
; checking the validity of a user response...
;
;
(setq OPT (strcase (getstring "\nPaper size for drawing (A/B/C/D/E): ")))
(while
  (not (member OPT '("A" "B" "C" "D" "E")))         ; While OPT is not found in list
  (princ "\nInvalid paper size. Try again...")      ;   issue message and prompt again
  (setq OPT (strcase (getstring "\nPaper size for drawing (A/B/C/D/E): ")))
)                                                    ; End WHILE
;
; --( Define Parameter List )--
;
; Create an association list of parameters...
  (setq ALIST '(                                     ; Build association list
              ("A" 11 8.5 "TITLE-A")
              ("B" 17 11 "TITLE-B")
              ("C" 22 17 "TITLE-C")
              ("D" 34 22 "TITLE-D")
              ("E" 44 34 "TITLE-E")
              )                                      ; End QUOTE
  )                                                  ; End SETQ
;
; --( Setup Routine )--
;
; This routine is utilized for all paper sizes, but alternate parameters are
; used by ASSOCiation depending on the user response...
;
(setq PARALIST (assoc OPT ALIST))                        ; Get value associated with OPT
                                                         ; Assign value to PARALIST
(setvar "LIMMIN" '(0 0))                                 ; Lower left limits at 0,0
(setvar "LIMMAX" (list (cadr PARALIST) (caddr PARALIST))) ; 2nd & 3rd items found
                                                         ; in PARALIST
(command "INSERT" (cadddr PARALIST) '(0 0) 1 1 0)        ; 4th item in PARALIST
(command "ZOOM" "A")
```

In this example, if the user response is not a member of the list of options, the MEMBER function returns nil and the loop is repeated. Once a valid response is given, the ASSOC function accesses the parameters associated with that paper size. These parameters are subsequently supplied to the setup portion of this routine. The use of lists for data storage helps to eliminate redundancy within a program, and makes data management tasks much easier.

The REVERSE Function

The *REVERSE function,* as the name implies, returns LIST in reverse order. The syntax for REVERSE is:

```
(reverse LIST)
```

When supplied with the following values:

```
(setq L1 '(A B C D E) L2 (list (cons "LENGTH" 4) (cons "WIDTH" 2.5)))
```

...the REVERSE function returns the following results:

```
(reverse L1)        returns  (E D C B A)
(reverse L2)        returns  (("WIDTH" . 2.5) ("LENGTH" . 4))
```

The REVERSE function has the same effect regardless of the configuration of the supplied list. However, only lists are acceptable arguments.

By using the MEMBER and REVERSE functions, it is possible to remove an item from a list. The following program demonstrates this technique. The numbers shown in brackets, such as [1], [2], etc., are identifiers for the detailed documentation following the program.

```
; REMFMLST.LSP  by Tae Ki Tout
; Date:  December 29, 19xx
; Purpose:  Remove a given item from a specified list
;
; Usage:  (RFL ITEM LIST)
;
; Notes: This routine uses MEMBER to locate item in a REVERSEd list, then takes
;          the CDR of the returned list and REVERSEs it back to its proper order.
;          This generates the first portion of the new list. Then, the CDR of the
;          list returned by (MEMBER item list) supplies the second portion. Using
;          APPEND puts these two lists together as one – without ITEM.  This
;          function returns the modified list.
;
(defun RFL (I L / L1 L2)
  (setq L1                        ; [5]
    (reverse                      ; [4]
      (cdr                        ; [3]
        (member I                 ; [2]
          (reverse L)             ; [1]
        )
      )
    )
  )
  (setq L2                        ; [8]
    (cdr                          ; [7]
      (member I L)                ; [6]
    )
  )
  (append L1 L2)                  ; [9]
)
```

It may be helpful to track the previous program through every step with a specific example. As previously mentioned, the numbers enclosed in brackets within the program are now discussed in detail. The following assignment is used for the example:

```
(setq LST '(A B C D E F G H))
(setq LST (RFL 'E LST))
```

RFL is invoked using LST for list and 'E as the item to be removed

[1] **(reverse L)** The argument list specifies that L represents the list. The first step REVERSEs the list.
[1] returns (H G F E D C B A)

[2] **(member I** Now, locate the item (assigned to I within RFL) within the reversed list using the MEMBER function.
[2] returns (E D C B A)

[3] **(cdr** Since MEMBER returns a list with the specified search item as its first element, CDR is used to return that list without the first element.
[3] returns (D C B A)

[4] **(reverse** At this point, 'E has been successfully removed from the first portion of the list. In order to restore the ordering of this list, it is reversed again.
[4] returns (A B C D)

[5] **(setq L1** To hold this value, it is assigned to the local variable L1.
[5] returns (A B C D) ...after assigning L1 to this value.

[6] **(member I L)** Now the second portion of the list must be created. Using MEMBER locates item and returns a list with item as its first element.
[6] returns (E F G H)

[7] **(cdr** Once again, 'E must be removed by using CDR.
[7] returns (F G H)

[8] **(setq L2** The resultant list is then assigned to the local variable L2.
[8] returns (F G H) ...after assigning L2 to this value.

[9] **(append L1 L2)** Finally, the last expression appends L1 with L2. Since this is the last expression in the function, its result is also returned by the function.
[9] returns (A B C D F G H)

The following expression calls this function:

```
(setq LST (RFL 'E LST))
```

Note that the variable LST is assigned to the value returned by the RFL expression. The value in step [9] is returned by the expression, and the new list has 'E removed from it.

This function will be very useful for a variety of applications. The previous example has been written for ease of reading and understanding. A condensed version of the same program is as follows:

```
(defun RFL (I L)
  (append (reverse (cdr (member I (reverse L)))) (cdr (member I L)))
)
```

The NTH Function

In Chapter 3, the CxxxxR family of functions was examined. These functions work quite well for lists containing few elements, but would require an incredible number of concatenations to access, for example, the seventy-third element of a list. The *NTH function* enhances the programmer's ability to access an element within a list by its position number. The syntax for the NTH function is:

```
(nth N LIST)
```

The item found at position number N within LIST is returned by the NTH function. Within a list, the first element is located at position number zero, the second element at position number one, and so on. See Fig. 10-2.

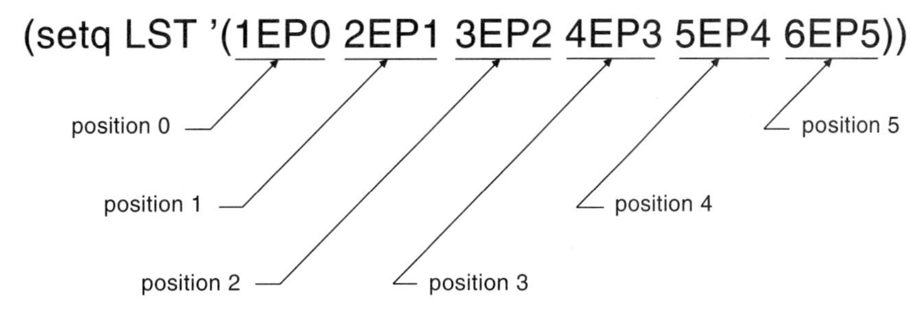

Fig. 10-2. Position numbers when using the NTH function.

Therefore, in the previous dialogue, the seventy-third element is found at position number 72. When the position number argument N is greater than the last position number found in the list, nil is returned. Note that NTH requires an integer argument. When LST is assigned the following list:

```
(setq LST '(1EP0 2EP1 3EP2 4EP3 5EP4 6EP5))
```

...these results are returned:

(nth 0 LST)	returns 1EP0	*first element, position zero*
(nth 5 LST)	returns 6EP5	*sixth element, position five*
(nth 6 LST)	returns nil	*last position is number 5*

Here is an example of a routine using the NTH function to access specific position numbers within a list:

```
; Filename:  PAPER.LSP
;
; Purpose:  Paper Space setup routine. Set snap and grid, choose between
;           C, D, or E–size limits, select quantity of mview Paper Space
;           entities, and specify scaling for each Paper Space entity.
;
; Assumptions:  Program is intended for a basic Architectural setup.
;               All details in Model Space are displayed and at full scale.
;               The REMFMLST.LSP [ REMove FroM LiST ] file is loaded.
;
; - - - - - - - - - - - - - - - - - - - - - - - - - - - - - - - - - - - - - -
;
(defun C:PAPER (/ SIZ ALIST T_R RES ALI VP CTR SCA)
  (setvar "cmdecho" 0)
  (setvar "tilemode" 0)                                  ; Enable Paper Space
  (princ "\nSnap setting: ")  (command ".snap" pause)    ; Snap setting
  (princ "\nGrid setting: ")  (command ".grid" pause)    ; Grid setting
;
;– – –⟨ Define parameter list for Paper Space drawing sizes ⟩– – –
;
  (initget 1 "C D E")
  (setq SIZ   (getkword "\nPaper Space drawing size – C/D/E: ")
        ALIST '(("C" 24 18) ("D" 36 24) ("E" 48 36))     ; Associated size list
        T_R   (cdr (assoc SIZ ALIST))                          ; [1]
  )
  (command ".limits"  '(0 0)  T_R
           ".zoom" "a"
           ".layer" "m" "pslayout" ""            ; Establish layer for Paper Space
           ".mview"                              ; Begin mview command...
  )
  (initget 1 "2 3 4")
  (setq RES   (getkword "\nMview creation - 2/3/4 viewports: "))  ; [2]
  (cond
    ((= "2" RES)
     (initget "Horizontal Vertical")
     (setq ALI   (getkword "\nHorizontal/⟨Vertical⟩: ")            ; [3]
           ALI   (if (null ALI) "Vertical" ALI)                    ; [4]
     )
    (command RES ALI '(0 0) T_R)                                   ; [5]
    )                                      ; End 1st cond list for 2 entities
;
    ((= "3" RES)
     (initget "Horizontal Vertical Above Below Left Right")
     (setq ALI (getkword (strcat "\nHorizontal/Vertical/Above"
                                 "/Below/Left/⟨Right⟩: "))          ; [6]
           ALI (if (null ALI) "Right" ALI)                         ; [7]
     )
     (command RES ALI '(0 0) T_R)                                  ; [8]
     )                                     ; End 2nd cond list for 3 entities
;
    (T (command RES '(0 0) T_R))           ; 4 entities...Finish mview
```

```
;
  )                                     ; End cond
  (command ".mspace")
  (setq VP     (vports)   ; [9]
        VP     (rfl (assoc 1 VP) VP)                                     ; [10]
        CTR    0                        ; Set CounTeR to 0 for next function
  )
  (repeat (atoi RES)                    ; Repeat for each Paper Space entity
    (setvar "cvport" (car (nth CTR VP)))                                 ; [11]
    (princ "\nViewport selected...Zoom window on details:")
    (command ".zoom" "w" pause pause)                                    ; [12]
    (initget 1 "2 4 8")
    (setq SCA (getkword "\nScaling [i.e. 2 = 1/2 scale] - 2/4/8: ")
          SCA (/ 1 (* (atoi SCA) 12.0))                                  ; [13]
    )
    (command ".zoom" (strcat (rtos SCA 2 8) "xp"))                       ; [14]
    (setq CTR (1+ CTR))
  )
  (command ".pspace")
  (princ)
)
;---⟨ End of PAPER ⟩---
```

For each of the numbered lines in the previous example, a brief explanation is given below. Documentation is a vital ingredient to effective programming.

[1] **(setq T_R (cdr (assoc SIZ ALIST)))** The ASSOC function retrieves the desired associated list, where SIZ [the user-specified size] is the header. The CDR function drops the first element of the associated list, the SIZ value, returning a coordinate pairing. Variable T_R becomes the Top Right corner.

[2] **(setq RES (getkword "\nMview creation – 2/3/4 viewports: "))** The variable RES stores a text string that represents the number of Paper Space viewport entities to be created by the Mview command.

[3] **(setq ALI (getkword "\nHorizontal/ ⟨Vertical⟩: "))** In a 2 entity configuration, the keyword options are Horizontal or Vertical.

[4] **(setq ALI (if (null ALI) "Vertical" ALI))** Where the user enters to accept the ⟨Vertical⟩ default, as shown by (null ALI), then set the keyword option to "Vertical", or else keep variable ALI set to the user-specified keyword.

[5] **(command RES ALI '(0 0) T_R)** Continue with the Mview command. The variable RES specifies the number of Paper Space viewport entities, variable ALI specifies the configuration, the coordinate '(0 0) is the lower-left corner of the configuration, and variable T_R is the upper-right corner.

[6] **(setq ALI (getkword (strcat "\nHorizontal/Vertical/Above"
"/Below/Left/⟨Right⟩: "))**
In a three entity configuration, the keyword options are displayed.

[7] **(setq ALI (if (null ALI) "Right" ALI))** Where the user enters to accept the ⟨Right⟩ default, as shown by (null ALI), then set the keyword option to "Right", or else keep variable ALI set to the user-specified keyword.

[8] **(command RES ALI '(0 0) T_R)** Continue with the Mview command. The variable RES specifies the number of Paper Space viewport entities, variable ALI specifies the configuration, the coordinate '(0 0) is the lower-left corner of the configuration, and variable T_R is the upper-right corner.

[9] **(setq VP (vports))** The VPORTS function creates a listing of all viewport entities within the Paper Space environment, and is then stored in variable VP. The VPORTS function is discussed in detail in Chapter 15 of this text.

[10] **(setq VP (rfl (assoc 1 VP) VP)** The associated listing (assoc 1 VP) references viewport display descriptor number 1. This viewport is not an actual viewport entity, and is subsequently removed from the VP listing by the RFL [Remove From List] routine.

[11] **(setvar "cvport" (car (nth CTR VP)))** On the first pass of the REPEAT function, the variable CTR is set to 0. The NTH function uses CTR as a position indicator, and retrieves the element found at that position. In this case, each element is a list that describes a single viewport entity. Since each sublist contained within variable VP gives the viewport number as its first atom, the CAR function returns this number. Set the AutoCAD current viewport variable "cvport" to this number, and toggle to that viewport. As the REPEAT function continues, the counter CTR is incremented, and all viewport entities are examined.

[12] **(command ".zoom" "w" pause pause)** Allow the user to zoom window on the drawing [per each viewport in mspace], producing a display that is eventually scaled by a second zoom command.

[13] **(setq SCA (/ 1 (* (atoi SCA) 12.0)))** The variable SCA, an ASCII text string representing an architectural scaling size, is converted to an integer by the ATOI function. Multiply this value by 12.0, use the product as the divisor for 1, and reset SCA.

[14] **(command ".zoom" (strcat (rtos SCA 2 8) "xp"))** Convert the real number stored in variable SCA to a string, with mode 2 specifying decimal units, and the precision set to 8. This string is then concatenated with "xp" to produce the correct zoom scaling in each respective viewport.

EXERCISE 10-1

- ☐ Use the indicated sample program in the previous section of the text as a guide for each of the following exercises:
- ☐ Use the SETUP.LSP program as a basis for your program design. Design a complete drawing setup routine that uses an association list to obtain the parameters based on user input. This routine will perform the following tasks:
  - A. Prompt for ARCHITECTURAL or MECHANICAL sheet size.
  - B. Use an association list with headers indicating sheet size and application. For example, "B-A" indicates B-size–Architectural, or "D-M" for D-size–Mechanical. Be sure that all necessary information is included in the list as appropriate data types.
  - C. Set limits and units, show the drawing limits on screen, and insert the appropriate title block.
  - D. Name the program DATALIST.LSP.
- ☐ Create a function that assigns a global variable called DATALIST, and presents an option line to the user with the following options:
  - A. Allows the user to insert associative values as dotted pairs into DATALIST by prompting for the HEADER and the VALUE.
  - B. Allows the user to display DATALIST when desired.
  - C. Allows the user to remove a specified dotted pair from DATALIST.
  - D. Allows the user to extract a value associated with a given HEADER.

Let's Review...

1. Association lists are an effective and simple means of data storage and retrieval, and are particularly useful when handling large numbers of data items.
2. The ASSOC function allows the programmer to find a sublist with the specified item as its first element. This function returns the entire sublist.
3. A dotted pair is a special kind of list that is created by CONSing two atoms. The CDR function evaluates differently when used on a dotted pair than when used on a simple list.
4. The MEMBER function returns a sublist of the specified list argument, beginning at the indicated member and continuing to the end of the list.
5. The REVERSE function returns the supplied list argument in a reversed order.
6. The NTH function is more appropriate than the CxxxxR family of functions when working with lists containing many elements.

USING LIST ARGUMENTS FOR NON-LIST FUNCTIONS

Another effective application of lists involves using individual elements of lists as arguments to AutoLISP functions. Certain functions accept lists as arguments; others do not. AutoLISP provides a means of supplying lists to even those functions that cannot normally use them by utilizing specialized list-handling tools.

In a given application, a programmer may need to add a series of user-supplied numbers to solve for an overall sum. Without the use of lists, it is necessary to either loop through an expression sequence once for each number input, or have a limited quantity of numbers assigned to individual variables. A more efficient approach to this would be to simply assemble a list from the user-supplied numbers, and then add them. The only potential problem is that the addition function requires numerical arguments, not a list.

The APPLY Function

The *APPLY function* allows the programmer to specify a list containing all of the arguments to be provided to an AutoLISP function. It is important to remember that the number of arguments and their respective data types within LIST *must* be consistent with the requirements of the specified FUNCTION. The syntax for the APPLY function is:

```
(apply FUNCTION LIST)
```

Examples of the APPLY function are as follows:

```
(apply 'strcat (list "H" "e" "l" "l" "o"))          returns  "Hello"
```

Note that the function name is quoted. Failure to do so results in a "bad argument type" error message. This is true whether the specified function is an internal AutoLISP function or one that is defined by the user.

```
(apply 'princ '("A" "B" "C"))                      returns  Error: incorrect number of arguments
(apply 'princ '("A"))              prints A        returns  "A"
(apply '+ (list 4 4 9 3 10))                       returns  30
```

The following routine allows the user to input any quantity of numbers and returns the sum. This is a prime example of being able to specify a list containing all of the arguments to be provided to an AutoLISP function.

```
; ADDEM.LSP  by Cal Clater
;
; Date:  6/28/xx
;
; Purpose:  Assemble a list of user specified numbers, and return the sum of all
;           members of the list.
;
(defun C:ADDEM (/ NEXNUM NUMLST)
  (while (setq NEXNUM (getreal "\nInput number or [ENTER] when done: "))
    (setq NUMLST (append NUMLST (list NEXNUM)))
  )
  (apply '+ NUMLST)
)
```

In this example, the loop continues to append new items to the list until the user strikes the ENTER key. Once the loop is broken, the APPLY function is evaluated and applies + (addition) to all elements of the list.

When utilizing functions that require a specific number of arguments, it is preferable to simply use the function itself. The only real advantage gained through using the APPLY function is the capability to store all supplied arguments in a list. However, APPLY gives added flexibility in that the list can continue to expand in size until all arguments have been entered.

The MAPCAR Function

The APPLY function allows its FUNCTION argument to be evaluated only once using elements supplied from a single list. In a situation where the function is to be evaluated more than once, while using different arguments each time, the *MAPCAR function* is used. The syntax for the MAPCAR function is:

```
(mapcar FUNCTION LIST1 ... LISTN)
```

When using MAPCAR, instead of supplying one list containing all necessary arguments (the APPLY function), a separate list is created for each argument required by the given function. On its first loop, MAPCAR applies FUNCTION using the first element of each LIST; the second loop uses the second element of each LIST, and so on. All results are assembled into another list, which is returned by MAPCAR. Here are a few examples:

Command: **(mapcar '+ (list 10 20 30) (list 1 2 3))** ↵
(11 22 33)

Command: **(mapcar 'strcat '("A" "X") '("B" "Y") '("C" "Z"))** ↵
("ABC" "XYZ")

The MAPCAR function can also be used when the function requires only one argument. The next example increments each element of the supplied list:

Command: **(mapcar '1+ (list 1 2 3 4 5))** ↵
(2 3 4 5 6)

The MAPCAR function is also commonly used for setting groups of system variables. For example:

Command: **(mapcar 'setvar '("BLIPMODE" "CMDECHO" "EXPERT") '(0 0 1))** ↵
(0 0 1) *sets BLIPMODE=0, CMDECHO=0, and EXPERT=1*

The MAPCAR function is primarily a step-saver, thus increasing productivity. To provide a basis for comparison, the previous example, which sets the system variables, incorporates three separate SETVAR functions into a single expression. The alternative to using the MAPCAR function would be to write out each full expression as follows:

```
(setvar "BLIPMODE" 0)
(setvar "CMDECHO" 0)
(setvar "EXPERT" 1)
```

The following example utilizes the APPLY, STRCAT, and MAPCAR functions.

Command: **(apply 'strcat** ↵
1⟩ **(mapcar 'substr '("HOME" "END" "SCROLL" "LOCK") '(1 1 5 2) '(1 1 2 1))** ↵
1⟩ **)** ↵
"HELLO"

This returns the same value as the following sequence:

Command: **(strcat** ↵
1⟩ **(substr "HOME" 1 1)** ↵ *returns "H"*

1⟩ **(substr "END" 1 1)** ↵ *returns "E"*

1⟩ **(substr "SCROLL" 5 2)** ↵ *returns "LL"*

1⟩ **(substr "LOCK" 2 1)** ↵ *returns "O"*

1⟩ **)** ↵
"HELLO"

One limitation of the MAPCAR function is that only one function can be specified. For programming applications where several functions must be performed, it may be necessary to define an anonymous function.

ANONYMOUS FUNCTIONS

Functions such as APPLY and MAPCAR require that a function name be specified to perform with the supplied list(s). If a built-in AutoLISP function is not sufficient for the programmer's purpose, a user-defined function name can be used instead. However, certain situations may not warrant the definition of a new function. Here, an *anonymous function* can be used. An anonymous function is defined using the LAMBDA function:

```
(lambda ARGUMENTS EXPR ...)
```

A *LAMBDA expression* is an on-the-spot function definition, which may be used where a function name is expected. It is frequently used in conjunction with an APPLY or a MAPCAR expression.

LAMBDA and DEFUN both define a function. The difference is that DEFUN requires a name for the function being defined, giving it accessibility throughout the drawing session. The

LAMBDA function, however, is for a single use and the definition is then forgotten. On releases of AutoCAD prior to Release 11, this can be a very important aspect of memory management.

These on-the-spot definitions are called "anonymous" because they have no name. The syntax for a LAMBDA expression requires that it be placed where a function name would normally be expected, and that the appropriate arguments follow. This first example shows LAMBDA being used where a function name is expected in an expression with two arguments:

```
(
  (lambda (P1 P2 / CL)  ; the syntax is identical to DEFUN without name specification
    (command ".line" P1 P2 "")                   ; These are the expressions that
    (setq CL (getint "\nColor number: "))        ;   comprise the function's
    (command ".chprop" "L" "" "C" CL "")         ;   definition.
  )                                              ; End LAMBDA
  '(2 2) '(8 2)            ; Two arguments as required (specified in argument list above)
)                          ; End top level expression

Color number: 12 ↵
```

The result of evaluating this expression is that a line is drawn, and subsequently changed to the color specified by the user. If DEFUN was to be used, the expressions would appear as follows:

```
(defun COLIN (P1 P2 / CL)
  (command "LINE" P1 P2 "")
  (setq CL (getint "\nColor number: "))
  (command ".chprop" "L" "" "C" CL "")
)
```

Having loaded this definition, the following expression would execute it:

```
(COLIN P1 P2)
```

List operators such as APPLY or MAPCAR can take full advantage of the LAMBDA anonymous function. A LAMBDA expression is often used as the function name argument for either APPLY or MAPCAR. This programming technique can be applied when the capability of a user-defined function is required, but the overhead of creating and cataloging the function is superfluous.

Three lists have been assembled for the following example–the first list contains layer names, the next list contains linetypes, and the final list stores colors. Each of the lists can be accessed using the MAPCAR function, with LAMBDA acting as the function name argument.

```
(setq LNLST '( "HID" "CEN" "PHAN" "DIM" "OBJ")
      LTLST '( "HIDDEN" "CENTER" "PHANTOM" "CONTINUOUS" "CONTINUOUS")
      COLST '( "CYAN" "YELLOW" "GREEN" "RED" "WHITE")
)

(mapcar
  '(lambda (LN LT CO)          ; LAMBDA acts as the function argument to MAPCAR
     (command ".layer" "new" LN "ltype" LT LN "color" CO LN "")
  )
  LNLST                        ; First list argument to MAPCAR
  LTLST                        ; Second list argument to MAPCAR
  COLST                        ; Third list argument to MAPCAR
)
```

On the first iteration of this function, the first element of each list is used. A new layer is created and named "HID", which uses a hidden linetype and cyan color. The MAPCAR function performs as it would in any other circumstance and repeats for each sequence contained in the supplied list arguments. Also, note that even a LAMBDA expression must be quoted.

Let's Review...

1. Lists are a more efficient means of handling large amounts of data than the use of individual variables. A single variable can virtually store an unlimited amount of data when stored in list format.
2. Association lists provide an efficient means of data retrieval. Any number of data items can be accessed by means of a key, which is the header for a given sublist. Thus, data retrieval is accomplished through association. Any information associated with a given data item can be quickly and easily accessed. In addition, this is the format in which AutoLISP presents much of the data retrieved from the drawing database.
3. List operators, such as APPLY and MAPCAR, allow entire lists of data to be used as arguments to AutoLISP functions that do not normally use list arguments.
4. The LAMBDA function provides a means for on-the-spot function definitions, which can be used in place of a function name in some expressions.

SAMPLE PROGRAM

The following program uses several of the concepts and functions discussed in this chapter. The purpose of the program is to obtain the weight and moment of inertia on hollow rectangular shafts made of various materials. List operators and association lists are employed to simplify the storage and retrieval of data.

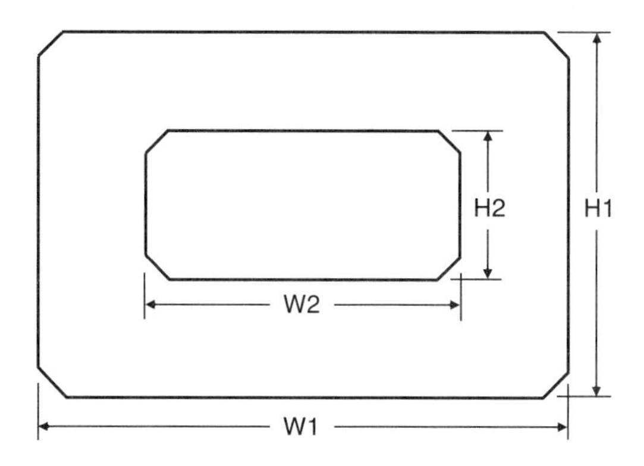


```
; File:   SQTUBE.LSP
;
; Author:  T.B. SQUARE
;
; Purpose:  Obtain weight and moment of inertia data on
;           hollow rectangular shafts of various materials.
;           The shaft is then drawn and hatched accordingly.
;
; Notes:  Results are best seen in a new drawing file.
(defun C:PARA (/ H1 W1 H2 W2 LEN ANS MATS)
  (setvar "cmdecho" 0)
  (setvar "gridmode" 0)
```

```
;
; Generate parametric information for hollow rectangular shaft calculations
;
  (mapcar
    '(lambda (PARMS DIMS)
      (initget (+ 1 2 4))
      (set PARMS (getreal DIMS))
    )                                  ; End LAMBDA
    (list 'H1 'W1 'H2 'W2 'LEN)        ; 1st list argument to MAPCAR – symbol names
;                                      ;    PARMS for LAMBDA
    '("\nHeight #1: " "\nWidth #1: "   ; 2nd list argument to MAPCAR – prompts
      "\nHeight #2: " "\nWidth #2: "   ;    DIMS for LAMBDA
      "\nLength of Beam in inches: "
    )                                  ;
  )                                    ; End MAPCAR
;
; Build 3–D shape within the drawing editor
;
  (defun lp ()                 ; User function to retrieve last point – nested in DEFUN above
    (getvar "lastpoint")
  )                            ; End nested DEFUN
  (setq PT1 '(0 0 0)
        PT2 (list (/ (– W1 W2) 2) (/ (– H1 H2) 2) 0)
  )                            ; End SETQ
  (command ".ucs" 3 "*0,0,0" "*0,1,0" "*0,0,1"
           ".vpoint" "–1,–1,1"
           ".ucsicon" "or"
           ".thickness" LEN
           ".pline" PT1 (polar PT1 0 W1)
                        (polar (lp) (* pi 0.5) H1)
                        (polar (lp) pi W1) "c"
           ".pline" PT2 (polar PT2 0 W2)
                        (polar (lp) (* pi 0.5) H2)
                        (polar (lp) pi W2) "c"
           ".zoom" "e"
           ".hide"
  )                            ; End COMMAND
;
; Print statistics to the screen for weight & inertia
;
  (mapcar
    '(lambda (MAT WTS)
      (princ (strcat "\nThe weight for "
                     MAT
                     " is: "
             )
      )
      (princ (* (– (* W1 H1) (* W2 H2)) LEN WTS)) (princ " lbs.")
    )                                                  ; End LAMBDA
    '("Steel " "Copper " "Brass " "Alum " "Iron ")     ; 1st list argument to MAPCAR
                                                       ;    MAT for LAMBDA
    '(0.28287 0.32118 0.31423 0.09751 0.28530)         ; 2nd list argument to MAPCAR
```

```
                                                    ;     WTS for LAMBDA
   )                                                ; End MAPCAR
 ;
   (princ "\n\n  The Moment of Inertia is: ")
   (princ (/ (– (* W1 (expt H1 3)) (* W2 (expt H2 3))) 12))
 ;
 (initget 1 "Steel Copper Brass Alum Iron")
   (setq ANS   (getkword "\n\nSelect one of the above materials: ")
         MATS '(("Steel" "ansi32") ("Copper" "ansi33") ("Brass" "ansi33")
                ("Alum" "ansi38") ("Iron" "ansi31"))      ; Association list
   )
   (command ".thickness" 0
              ".hatch" (cadr (assoc ANS MATS)) "3" "0" PT1 PT2 ""
   )
   (setvar "cmdecho" 1)
   (princ)
 )
 ; – –⟨ End of file ⟩– –
```

CHAPTER TEST

Write your answers in the spaces provided.

1. Why are lists a preferred method of data storage?

____

____

2. Describe an association list.

____

____

____

____

3. What function is provided to access data within an association list? Detail its use.

____

____

____

____

____

4. What is a dotted pair? How is it different from a regular list?

____

____

____

5. Detail the use of the CONS function.

6. What function scans a list to determine if a specified item is found within it?

7. What is the effect of the REVERSE function?

8. Describe the use and advantages of the NTH function.

9. What AutoLISP function allows the programmer to provide a single list containing all necessary arguments to a function that normally will not accept a list argument? Describe in detail its purpose and usage.

10. Why must the function name argument in an APPLY expression be quoted?

11. In what way does the APPLY function give the programmer added flexibility?

12. Which list operator allows a function to be evaluated more than once, each time using different arguments?

13. What data type is always returned by the MAPCAR function?

14. List some applications of the MAPCAR function.

15. What is a major limitation of the MAPCAR function? How can this be avoided?

16. Define the term "anonymous function."

17. Detail the purpose and use of the LAMBDA function.

18. How does the LAMBDA function differ from the DEFUN function?

19. Where is the most productive use of the LAMBDA function found? Why?

PROGRAMMING PROBLEMS

1. Generate a program called REPLACE.LSP that will replace an element of an existing list with a new element as specified by the user. Do *not* use the SUBST function introduced in Chapter 7. Instead use techniques similar to those shown in the REMFMLST.LSP program in this chapter, combined with the CONS function.
2. Create a program that will first ask the user for a name of an existing list. Then, the program will ask the user for a position number and show the element located at that position in the list. The position number interrogation should be in a loop offering an exit option, and should continue until the user specifies to exit. Name the program LISTPOS.LSP.
3. Design a program named SET-TOL.LSP that does the following:
   A. Allow an option to generate or modify a tolerance list. This list will be an association list, and will have three elements: an alphabetical header followed by a plus tolerance, then a minus tolerance. For example: ("A" 0.005 0.002).
   B. Allow an option for the user to display the assigned tolerance ranges and modify them as desired.
   C. Allow an option to select a tolerance range and set the appropriate dimension variables. For example, by using ("A" 0.005 0.002) and specifying tolerance range "A", then DIMTP and DIMTM would be set to 0.005 and 0.002, respectively.

Chapter 11
The Entity Database

Learning Objectives

After completing this chapter, you will be able to:

- ☐ Explain how AutoCAD stores data in the entity database.
- ☐ Describe AutoLISP's capabilities regarding manipulation of the entity database.
- ☐ List the advantages of direct access to entity information.

DATABASE MANAGEMENT

The biggest difference between AutoCAD and simple graphics programs is that AutoCAD is "object-oriented." A complete record is maintained of each object drawn. The user can invoke the LIST command to see a listing of part of this record. The following data is displayed by the LIST command when a line is selected:

```
LINE          Layer: 0
              Space: Model Space
from point, X=  2.0000   Y=  2.0000   Z=  0.0000
to point, X=  4.0000   Y=  4.0000   Z=  0.0000
Length =  2.8284,   Angle in X-Y Plane =        45
Delta X =  2.0000,    Delta Y =  2.0000,    Delta Z =  0.0000
```

Using these records, AutoCAD generates graphic representations of these object descriptions to the screen. The records themselves comprise what is known as a database. A *database* is defined as a collection of information arranged for ease of retrieval. AutoCAD is not usually thought of as a database management program, but in fact, that is exactly what AutoCAD is. Database managers are programs that allow the user to create, delete, organize, modify, and access the information contained within a database. Some database managers, such as *Dbase,* manipulate and display alphanumeric data types. A fairly common example of this is a mailing list. The database itself is stored as a file, which can be retrieved whenever needed. Many individual *records* are contained within the file, and within each record are one or more fields. The term, *field,* refers to a specific data area for a given record. The following example provides you with an idea of what might constitute the fields in a mailing list database:

NAME	COMPANY	ADDRESS	CITY	ST	ZIP
Anderson, John	Oregon Engineering	684 92nd Ave.	Portland	OR	97219
Berkely, Tim	ABC Construction	PO Box 010	Vancouver	WA	96114
Boardman, Frank	US Forest Service	2909 Percy St.	Eugene	OR	98261

This example shows three records, and six fields in each record. The records stored by AutoCAD contain as many fields as required to completely describe an object. Each object (e.g. line, arc, circle, etc.) in AutoCAD is called an *entity.*

Although AutoCAD graphically displays the vector data associated with the contents of its database, it stores information in a manner similar to other database managers. Each simple entity created in a drawing is stored as an individual record. The fields within each record contain all of the information relevant to that particular entity. A line, for example, includes the start and end point, the layer, color, linetype, etc.

An AutoCAD drawing database is stored as a *.DWG* file. These files are written in a very compact format for efficient storage and quick retrieval, and may not be read directly. The *DXF (Drawing eXchange File)* format is a means to output the file into a readable text file.

In a similar manner, AutoLISP can retrieve information on entities in the form of a list by using AutoLISP's basic entity-handling functions. Within this list are several sublists, which hold the value for each field, and a DXF *group code* is used to identify the field. A complete listing of these DXF group codes is provided in Appendix B. Here is an excerpt from this table showing a few of the codes:

Group Code	Value Type
0	Starts an entity. The type of entity is given by the text value that follows this group.
6	Line type name
8	Layer name
10	Primary point (start point of a line or text entity, center of a circle, etc.)

These group codes are assembled in an association list when the entity data is requested from the entity database. The following is an example of part of a record retrieved from the database using AutoLISP:

```
(
  (-1 . <Entity name: 3250500>)
  (0 . "LINE")
  (8 . "0")
  (10 2.0 2.0 0.0)
  (11 4.0 4.0 0.0)
  (210 0.0 0.0 1.0)
)
```

This list represents one record, and describes one entity. Within the sample record are six separate fields, each of which holds a DXF group code as a field descriptor and the value associated with that field.

The first field, the *entity name,* is a "pointer" into the database. The entity names are used solely for the purpose of specifying, or "pointing to" entities in the database file.

The second field, shown with a DXF Group Code of 0, indicates the entity type. In this case the entity is a line. The next field, group code 8, indicates that the entity resides on layer 0. The next two fields, the codes for the start and end point, are 10 and 11, respectively. The final listing in this record specifies the components of the extrusion direction.

Various entities can use these and other fields, depending on what information is necessary to completely describe them.

AUTOLISP AND THE ENTITY DATABASE

As a programmer, you are able to freely access the entity database for many different purposes. By utilizing AutoLISP selection techniques, the entity names can be obtained. An entity name is the key to unlocking the power of direct manipulation of the database. Once acquired, these entity names can then be assigned to symbols and used as desired.

An entity name can be used for subsequent selection of the entity for editing purposes. This can be done using individual entity names or even entire selection sets. Such practices allow the selection processes to be automated within a program, both enhancing the speed of the application and reducing the required amount of user interaction.

In addition, the entity name can be used to retrieve its record from the database. Any of the fields within this record can be examined, and the values can be used as needed. This includes start and end points of lines, center points of arcs and circles, vertex locations on a polyline, layer and color data, and virtually any other entity data available.

With advanced list manipulation techniques, the record can be reconstructed. New values can be supplied for certain fields, and the old record can then be replaced by the new one. The speed and versatility of direct modification of entities often proves to be both faster and more versatile than using AutoCAD commands.

Beyond this, direct entries can be made into the database. This gives the programmer the ability to create a completely new entity by describing it and entering the new record into the database. This is sometimes a desirable alternative to using the COMMAND function to invoke AutoCAD's entity creation commands.

Let's Review...

1. While working within AutoCAD, the drafter is performing drawing functions. Geometric shapes are described and drawn; existing elements of the drawing are modified or erased. This results in a visible drawing generated on the screen, modified elements are updated, and deleted objects disappear. However, this is nothing more than a graphic interface for the convenience of the user. The greatest amount of work is occuring in the background–extensive manipulation of the entity database. Records are being modified or deleted, and new records are being entered.
2. AutoCAD is a powerful drafting program. However, an AutoLISP programmer will benefit greatly by looking past the outward appearances and seeing AutoCAD for what it really is–a sophisticated and very comprehensive database management program. Approaching a program application from this standpoint opens many new doors for the programmer. Faster, more powerful, and much more intuitive programs can be developed.

The next few chapters will address the functions used for accessing and manipulating the entity database, from selecting objects to making new entities.

CHAPTER TEST

Place your answers in the spaces provided.

1. Define "database."

 ____

 ____

2. Compare AutoCAD with other "typical" databases.

 ____

 ____

 ____

3. Describe the relationship between "fields" and "records."

 ____

 ____

4. A .DWG file can be output to a readable text file via the ______________ format.

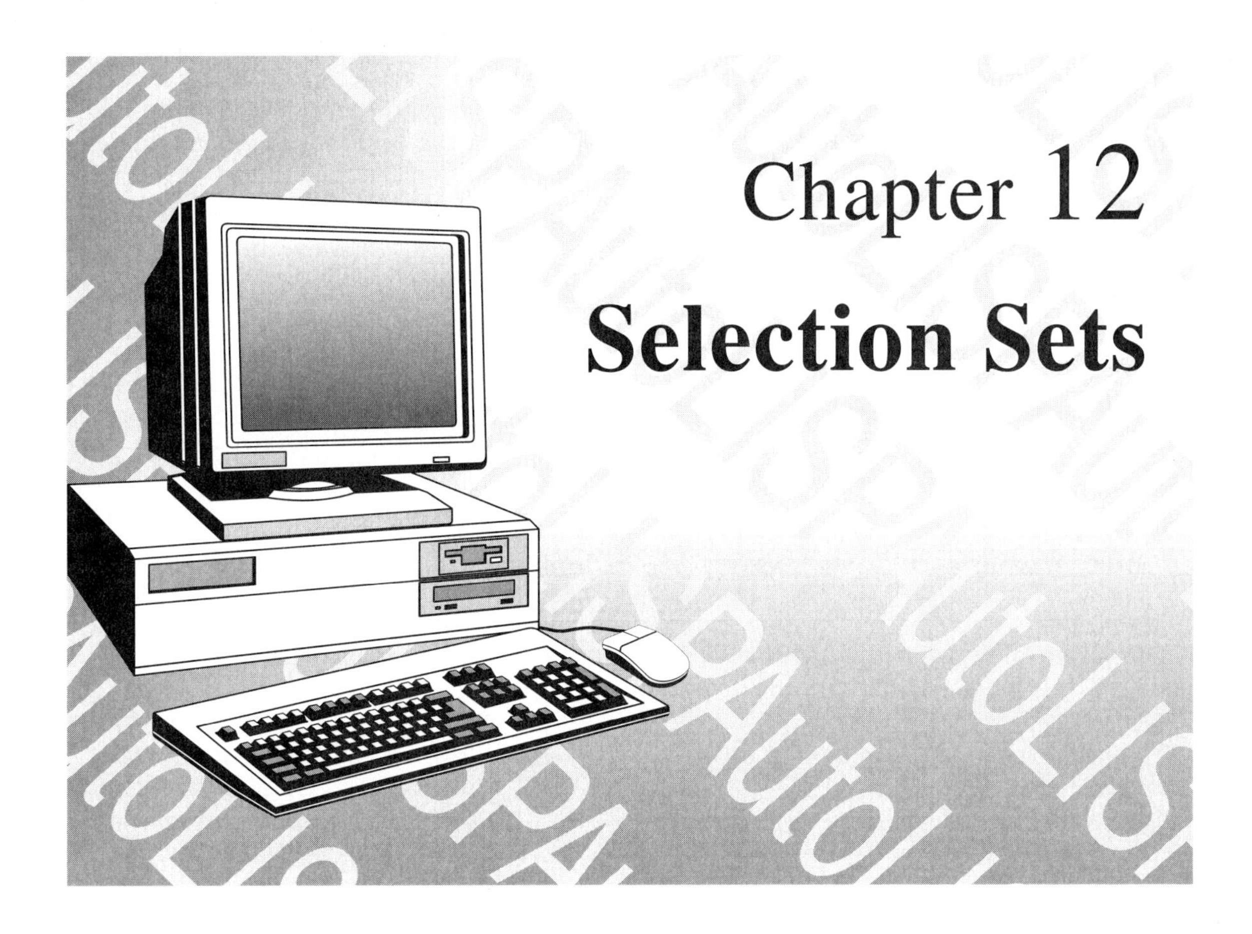

Chapter 12

Selection Sets

Learning Objectives

After completing this chapter, you will be able to:

- ☐ Create and utilize simple selection sets with the AutoLISP SSGET function.
- ☐ Form discrete selection sets by employing SSGET filter-lists.
- ☐ Manage selection set entity names by indexing.
- ☐ Add, delete, and test entities as they relate to specific selection sets.

BASIC AUTOLISP SELECTION SETS

Each AutoCAD editing command issues essentially the same "Select objects:" prompt. At that point, the desired drawing entities are picked and an AutoCAD selection set is created. This *selection set* is a collection of one or more entities that are grouped together for processing within the AutoCAD drawing editor. This process is repeated frequently during an editing session, and is a prerequisite to the use of all editing commands. For example:

Command: **MOVE** ↵	*AutoCAD editing command...*
Select objects: *(pick the desired objects)*	*...objects are chosen...*
Select objects: ↵	*...press the ENTER key to close the selection process...*
Base point or displacement:	*Utilize the new selection set. It is then stored as the Previous set.*

AutoCAD streamlines basic editing by reserving only Previous selection sets to memory. As the drawing increases in complexity, a large number of selection sets are manipulated and eventually "discarded" in favor of new sets. The AutoCAD FILTER and GROUP commands prove advantageous when creating and maintaining selection sets, but are dialog box intensive and may not be suitable for all editing applications. On the other hand, the programmer can build discrete and versatile selection sets by using a wide range of AutoLISP selection set functions.

THE SSGET FUNCTION

The *SSGET (Selection Set GET) function* returns a selection set consisting of any number of user-specified entities. These selection sets are used as collectors or storage cells for entity names. The syntax for the SSGET function is:

(ssget [MODE] [PT1 [PT2]] [PT-LIST] [FILTER-LIST])

When utilizing the SSGET function without the additional optional arguments, AutoLISP begins a general selection set process. For example:

Command: **(ssget)** ↵ — *Basic object selection begins...*
Select objects: *(pick the desired objects)* — *...desired entities are chosen by picking, windowing, crossing, etc...*
Select objects: ↵
⟨Selection set: 1⟩ — *...the selection set is closed when you press the ENTER key.*

This general selection set can now be used as the *Previous* set of objects:

Command: **(command ".move" "P" "" '(0 0) '(15 12))** ↵
SSGET objects are retrieved using the "P" (Previous) option

As with other AutoLISP functions, it is necessary to establish variable name and data element relationships. Here, a selection set is formed, given a variable name, and used repeatedly during editing:

Command: **(setq A (ssget))** ↵
Select objects: *(pick the desired objects)*
Select objects: ↵ — *selection set construction takes place*
⟨Selection set: 2⟩
Command: **(command ".array" A "" "R" 5 5 7.5 7.5)** ↵
Array objects found within selection set A. A 5 row/5 column array is used–spacing between both rows and columns is 7.5.

Command: **(command ".copy" A "" pause pause)** ↵
Copy the objects found within selection set A. Two pauses are used to establish a base point and a second point.

Command: **(command ".erase" A "")** ↵

Erase the objects found within selection set A. The objects can be restored to the drawing database by using OOPS.

When using the SSGET function as previously shown, selection sets may be created and then "cataloged" as AutoLISP variables. These variables can then be used freely for the rest of the editing session.

The following general rules and suggestions apply to the use of selection sets:

1. It is recommended that variable names be assigned to selection sets. By using this technique, selection sets can be called by name at any moment during the editing process.
2. Objects from one selection set can be members of another set. Thus, one object can be associated with many selection sets.
3. Main entities (excluding polyline vertices and block attributes) are counted as a *single* item, where no one entity is duplicated in the selection set.
4. AutoLISP tracks any modifications made while editing (e.g. moving, erasing, etc.) a selection set or its subset, and adjusts the set per the change. Therefore, if one item belonging to selection set A is erased, that set is reduced in length by one.
5. The AutoCAD OOPS and UNDO commands may restore selection sets to their original state.
6. Paper space and model space entries may be contained within a single set, but are *filtered* in accordance with the space that is currently in effect. If paper space is in use, then model space items are screened out, and visa versa.
7. While in the drawing editor, an unwanted selection set can be SETQed to nil at any time. Upon exiting the drawing editor, all existing selection sets are made null.

AutoLISP is only capable of manipulating a total of 128 selection sets during an individual editing session. Attempting to create more selection sets beyond this limit results in a null condition. At that point, AutoLISP disallows any additional selection sets.

PROFESSIONAL TIP

Selection sets are lost from one drawing session to the next even when persistent AutoLISP is enabled. Although any global variable names are remembered, the actual selection set is lost, so trying to access a selection set assigned in a prior drawing session results in no selection being made, which can cause your program to fail.

PROFESSIONAL TIP

Because of the limitation of 128 simultaneously open selection sets, selection set variables should always be local if possible. Otherwise, if too many selection sets are left open, a subsequent application may fail because it cannot create a required selection set.

Setting the variable name to nil does not clear the actual selection set, just the variable name. After setting the selection set variable name to nil, you can clear the unreferenced selection sets by using the GC function. The GC (Garbage Collection) function is called with no arguments:

```
(GC)
```

GC always returns nil.

The following program documents a fairly generic application of the SSGET function. Despite its relative simplicity, this routine can save time when rearranging items within a drawing file:

```
; Program: DXY.LSP
;
; Purpose: Move a selected group of objects orthogonally along the "X"
;          or "Y" axis.  A base point and target point are chosen, and
;          a third coordinate is formed along the axis of choice (aligned
;          with the target point).  Remember to use object snaps!
;
(defun C:DXY (/ OBJ AX BAS TAR)
   (setvar "cmdecho" 0)
   (princ "\nSelect objects for ortho move: ")
   (setq OBJ   (ssget))                              ; Selection set "OBJ"
   (initget 1 "X Y")
   (setq AX    (getkword "\nMove along X/Y axis:  ")  ; Ortho axis move
         BAS   (getpoint "\nSpecify base point: ")    ; Base Point location
         TAR   (getpoint "\nSpecify target point: ")  ; Target Point location
   )
   (command ".move" OBJ "" BAS          ; Begin move command from base...
      (if (= AX "X")
         (list (car TAR) (cadr BAS))    ; If X-axis...form x-axis third point
         (list (car BAS) (cadr TAR))    ; If Y-axis...form y-axis third point
      )
  )                          ; end command
  (setvar "cmdecho" 1)
  (princ)
)
;---<End of DXY>---
```

Other applications may require specific control when selecting entities. The optional MODE argument of the SSGET function specifies the method for entity selection. These modes more clearly define the intent of the user when creating new selection sets, and are outlined in the table in Fig. 12-1.

Mode	Selection Method	Syntax
none	User selection by any supported method	(ssget)
⟨point⟩	Select entity passing through ⟨point⟩	(ssget ⟨point⟩)
"L"	Select Last entity found in the database	(ssget "L")
"P"	Select Previous selection set entities	(ssget "P")
"W"	Select entities by Windowing	(ssget "W" pt1 pt2)
"C"	Select entities by Crossing	(ssget "C" pt1 pt2)
"I"	Select entities by Implied selection set	(ssget "I")
"F"	Select entities by Fence selection	(ssget "F" pt-list)
"WP"	Window Polygon selection method	(ssget "WP" pt-list)
"CP"	Crossing Polygon selection method	(ssget "CP" pt-list)
"X"	Select all entities in database of drawing	(ssget "X")

Fig. 12-1. The optional MODE argument of the SSGET function specifies the method for entity selection.

Several examples are given below to help illustrate the use of the various selection modes for the SSGET function. Assume that the following AutoLISP variables have been set:

```
(setq PT1 '(1.0 1.0 0.0)
      PT2 '(16.0 1.0 0.0)
      PT3 '(16.0 10.0 0.0)
      PT4 '(1.0 10.0 0.0)
)
```

Examples of SSGET function modes follow:

(ssget)

The user is free to select entities by any supported or valid AutoCAD selection method. The general AutoCAD "Select objects:" prompt is given, and the user completes the process.

(ssget '(18 12 0))

Select the entity that is found at '(18 12 0). Pickbox size and Last entity drawn at '(18 12 0) help to determine which object is selected.

(ssget PT1)

Select the entity that is found at PT1.

(setq A (ssget "W" PT1 PT3))

A selection set is constructed by using an AutoCAD standard window, with points PT1 and PT3 acting as the corners. Variable A is then set to the entities found inside the window.

```
(ssget "C" '(0 0) '(36 24))
```

Select entities by crossing box. Here, the two point arguments are quoted lists, and constitute the corners of the crossing box.

```
(while (setq G (ssget "L"))
  (command ".erase" G ""
           ".delay" 50
  )
)
```

While there are entities in the database (beginning with the "Last" item), erase each entity and delay briefly before continuing in sequence.

```
(setq W (ssget "P"))
(princ "\nErase Previous set? ")
  (if (= (getstring) "Y")
    (command ".erase" W "")
  )
```

The variable W represents the entities from the Previous selection set. If the user desires, erase the Previous selection set (stored as W).

```
(setq L (ssget "I")
      M (ssget PT2))
(command ".select" L M "")
(setq N (ssget "P"))
```

Retrieve objects in the Implied selection set. Retrieve the object at PT2, '(16.0 1.0 0.0). Create another selection set of both L and M with the AutoCAD SELECT command. This new set is accessed with the Previous mode.

```
(ssget "F" (list PT3 PT4))
```

Create a selection set of those objects that are crossed by the fence. In this application, the fence is defined by an imaginary line that runs from PT3 to PT4.

```
(ssget "WP" (list '(2.0 2.0)
                  '(4.0 2.0)
                  '(4.0 4.0)
                  '(2.0 4.0)
            )        ; End list
)                    ; End ssget
```

Create a selection set of the objects bounded by an imaginary polygon. The polygon is defined by the four points LISTed together, forming a window.

```
(ssget "CP" (list PT1 PT2 PT3 PT4))
```

Create a selection set of the items "crossed" over and bounded by an imaginary polygon. This mode is very similar to the "WP" mode.

The final SSGET mode is the letter "X", and signifies that a selection set is being created from a filter-list. In the absence of any filter-list argument(s), the mode "X" returns a selection set of the entire drawing, regardless of layer status and entity visibility within the current view.

Notice that the example shown on the next page creates an "overall" selection set before reinstating all layers back to full visibility. In addition, a second selection set is made with the SSGET "W" mode, where the corners of the standard window are formed with the LIMMIN (LIMits MINimum) and LIMMAX (LIMits MAXimum) system variables:

```
(defun C:EOL (/ SS1 SS2)
  (setvar "cmdecho" 0)
  (prompt "\nCreating selection set of entire drawing...")  ; Create SS1, the
    (setq SS1 (ssget "X"))                                   ;   entire drawing
;
  (command ".layer" "thaw" "*" "on" "*" "")                 ; All LAYERs visually activated
  (command ".zoom" "V")                                      ; ZOOM the virtual screen
;
  (prompt "\nCreating selection set within drawing limits...")      ; Create SS2
    (setq SS2 (ssget "W" (getvar "LIMMIN") (getvar "LIMMAX")))
;
  (prompt "\nErasing objects outside of drawing limits...")
    (command ".erase" SS1 "remove" SS2 "")    ; Erase all objects, but remove SS2 first
                                              ;   before erasing
;
  (command ".zoom" "P")                       ; Zoom to Previously stored view
  (setvar "cmdecho" 1)                        ; Restore command echo
  (princ)
)                                             ; End EOL
```

SSGET Filter-Lists

So far in this discussion, general selection sets have been created to do relatively easy tasks. It is usually more desirable to exercise control over the drawing database by choosing items that satisfy specific criteria. The SSGET *filter-list* capability allows for "customized" object selection, and is operable across the entire entity database, regardless of layer status. The filter-list calls out associated lists of information, taking the format of:

```
(ssget MODE FILTER-LIST)
```

The FILTER-LIST may be composed of one or more dotted pairs–group codes with their associated values. The group codes are shown in Fig. 12-2. The syntax for the filter-list is indicated by one of two methods. These methods are represented in the next two examples:

```
(ssget "X" (list (cons 6 "HIDDEN")))
```

In this example, a list (dotted pair) is CONStructed bearing the group code number 6 (linetype name) with its associated value "HIDDEN". A selection set is established after AutoLISP scans the entire drawing for entities that match this single filter-list. The resultant selection set might include entity names of circles, polylines, arcs, etc. In addition, those entities could reference many different layer and color assignments. As long as the entity possesses a "HIDDEN" linetype, the filter-list is then satisfied.

In the following example, the filter-list is supplied with more than one specification to control the selection of objects:

```
(ssget "X" '((0 . "TEXT") (7 . "STANDARD") (8 . "NOTES")))
```

This example calls out three criteria to search for: "TEXT" entity types, a "STANDARD" text style, and a layer named "NOTES". All specifications must be met in order to constitute a valid match. Any deviations from this list, such as SIMPLEX text style, layer 0, etc., will cause SSGET to pass over the entity being interrogated. Notice that this filter-list is already in the form of dotted pairs. This is a requirement for the SSGET function. All SSGET functions return nil if no entities match the specified filtering criteria.

Code	Meaning / Value
–5	Persistent reactor chain.
–4	Conditional operator (for use only with SSGET).
–3	Extended entity data (XDATA) sentinel (fixed value).
–2	Entity name (fixed entity name reference).
0	Entity type (fixed value).
1	Primary text value for an entity.
2	A name: Block name, Attribute tag, etc.
3–4	Miscellaneous text or name values.
6	Linetype name (fixed value).
7	Text Style or Attribute Definition name (fixed value).
8	Layer name (fixed value).
10	Primary entity point (Start of line, center of circle, etc.).
11–18	Other point values.
39	Thickness (fixed value).
40–48	Floating-point values (Block scale factors, text height, etc.).
49	Repeated value for an entity with variable length tables (such as a LTYPE's dash lengths). A 7x group appears before the first 49 group specifying the table length.
50–58	Angles.
62	Color number (fixed value; 0 = BYBLOCK, 256 = BYLAYER).
66	"Entities follow" flag (Attributes follow Block flag, etc.).
67	Drawing Space (0 = Paper Space, 1 = Model Space).
70–78	Integers for counters, flag bits, or other modes.
90–99	32-bit integer values.
100	Subclass data marker.
102	String followed by "{arbitrary name" or "}".
105	Dimension variable symbol table entry object handle.
210	3D extrusion direction vector (list of three real numbers).
280–289	8-bit integer values.
300–309	Arbitrary text strings.
310–319	Arbitrary binary chunks.
320–329	Arbitrary object handles.
330–339	Soft pointer handle (specifies pointer to other objects in the drawing).
340–349	Hard pointer handle (specifies pointer to other objects in the drawing).
350–359	Soft owner handle (specifies ownership to other objects in the drawing).
360–369	Hard owner handle (specifies ownership to other objects in the drawing).
999	Comments.

Notes: Wild cards are permitted for group codes 0, 2, 3, 6, 7, and 8. Group code –3 is reserved for extended entity data manipulation relative to programs outside of AutoCAD, and is not addressed in this book.

Fig. 12-2. Group codes accepted by SSGET "X".

A single group code number can be used only once within a single SSGET "X" call. Also, wild cards are permitted for the group codes 0, 2, 3, 6, 7, and 8. See Fig. 12-2. If there is any uncertainty about the use of wild cards in AutoLISP applications, please refer to Chapter 15 of this text.

As you can see, SSGET "X" filtering provides a distinct advantage when selecting only certain objects in a drawing database. Entities can be included (or excluded) within a selection set based exactly upon what the user desires. Note the following examples:

```
(setq K (ssget "X"))
```
when filter-list is absent, all objects within the drawing are selected

```
(command ".erase" K "")
```
erase all items within the drawing

```
(command ".chprop" (ssget "X" '((62 . 1))) "" "C" "5" "")
```
objects with color number 1 (red) are changed to color number 5 (blue)

```
(command ".chprop" (ssget "X" '((62 . 0))) "" "C" "Bylayer" "LA" "Hatch" "")
```
Color number is BYBLOCK and changed to BYLAYER. The Hatch layer is also designated. This is useful for exploded HATCH patterns.

Command: **CHPROP** ↵
Select objects: **(SSGET "X" '((0 . "CIRCLE") (8 . "0") (39 . 2)))** ↵
Select objects: **(SSGET "X" '((0 . "CIRCLE") (8 . "DRAW") (39 . 2)))** ↵
Select objects: ↵
Change what property (Color/LAyer/LType/ltScale/Thickness)? **LA** ↵
New layer ⟨varies⟩: **3D-CIRCLES** ↵

Multiple layer listings ("0" and "DRAW") become one for circles extruded by 2 units. AutoLISP and AutoCAD interact with each other as needed.

Following are more examples of the SSGET filter-list option. Remember that *all* filter-list specifications must be satisfied in order for an entity to be included in a selection set. Note that each example uses an SSGET function mode other than "X":

```
(ssget '(5 5) '((8 . "0")))
```
select the entity that is found at '(5 5) and resides on layer "0"

```
(setq J (ssget "W" '(0 0 0) '(17 11 0) '((0 . "TEXT") (62 . 256))))
```
A selection set is constructed by using an AutoCAD standard Window, with points '(0 0 0) and '(17 11 0) acting as the corners. Only text entities with a "BYLAYER" color (62 . 256) are chosen for inclusion within the set.

```
(setq H (ssget "I" '((0 . "CIRCLE") (10 7.5 11.5 0.0) (67 . 1))))
```

Retrieve objects in the Implied selection set. Those entities that are circles in paper space with center points at '(7.5 11.5 0.0) are selected. Note that the associated 10 coordinate is neither quoted nor placed within parentheses. This is true of all coordinate listings within associated pairs of information.

```
(setq M (ssget "L" (list (cons 0 "LINE") (cons 6 "HIDDEN"))))
```

If the Last object is a line with an assigned "HIDDEN" linetype, place it within a selection set. The CONS function is used here to construct the associated 0 pair and associated 6 pair.

```
(setq K (ssget "P" '((0 . "POLYLINE") (8 . "3D*") (39 . 2.75))))
```

*The variable K represents the entities from the Previous selection set. Acceptable objects, according to the filter-list, would include any polyline with an extrusion value of 2.75. Note that any layer starting with the two characters "3D" and continuing with any characters satisfies the associated 8 pair. In this case, the " * " acts as a wild card for any characters. Layer names may be up to 31 characters long.*

Code	Comment

`(ssget "WP" (list '(0.0 0.0)`
`'(8.0 0.0)`
`'(8.0 8.0)`
`'(0.0 8.0)`
	Create a selection set of the objects bounded by an imaginary polygon. The polygon is defined by the four points LISTed together, forming a "Window".

`)`	*end list*
`'((2 . "DOOR–68")`	*block named "DOOR–68"*
`(8 . "DOORS")`	*layer named "DOORS"*
`(66 . 1)`	*attributes are found within "DOOR–68"*
`)`	*end filter-list*
`)`	*end ssget*

The next program allows the user to remove existing block entities from the current editing session. Wild cards can be employed to make this application somewhat limited (or global) in its usage.

```
; Filename: BLOCKOUT.LSP
;
; Author:   L. Snuffo
;
; Purpose: To delete user-specified block entities. Those blocks
;          found on frozen or off layers will still be deleted.
;          Wild cards are permitted as valid block names.
;
; ------------------------------------------
;
(defun C:BLOCKOUT (/ BLK SET)
  (setvar "cmdecho" 0)
  (command ".textscr"                ; Flip to text screen and display
           ".block" "?" "*"          ; all block names
  )
;
;---( CONS is needed to combine group code with user-specified value )---
;
  (setq BLK  (strcase (getstring "\nDelete which block[s]: "))
        SET  (ssget "X" (list (cons 2 BLK)))
  )
;
;---( If no selection set, then tell user, else erase blocks )---
;
  (if (null SET)
     (princ (strcat "\nThere are no occurrences of block " BLK))
     (command ".erase" SET "")
  )
  (setvar "cmdecho" 1)
  (princ)
)
; ---( End of BLOCKOUT )---
```

Similar to the previous example, the next program illustrates the application of SSGET filter-lists. The user is asked to select an entity group to be modified. In addition, a target layer must be specified. A selection set is formed consisting of objects that match both the entity group and the desired layer. Those entities belonging to other layers are ignored. Detailed documentation follows the program.

```
; Program: EDIT–ENT.LSP
;
; Author: G.T. Out
;
; Date: December 28, 19xx
;
; Purpose: To modify one group of entities from the drawing editor. Entities selected
;          from include arcs, circles, lines, polylines, and text. Editing command
;          choices include COPY, ERASE, MOVE, ROTATE, and SCALE. Supplemental
;          documentation, designated by numbers in brackets, follows the program.
;
 (defun C:EDIT-ENT (/ RES LAY SS1 COM)
   (setvar "cmdecho" 0)
   (initget 1 "Arc Circle Line Polyline Text")                  ; [1]
;
   (setq RES (getkword "\nEdit ⟨Arcs/Circles/Lines/Plines/Text⟩: ")
         LAY (getstring "\nSelect layer by name: ")
         SS1 (ssget "X" (list (cons 0 RES) (cons 8 LAY)))       ; [2]
   )                                             ; End setq
;
   (if SS1                                                      ; [3]
     (progn
       (initget 1 "Copy Erase Move Rotate Scale")               ; [4]
;
       (setq COM (getkword "\nCommand ⟨Copy/Erase/Move/Rotate/Scale⟩: "))
       (command COM SS1 "")                                     ; [5]
     )                                           ; End progn
     (princ "\nNo objects found!")                              ; [6]
   )                                             ; End if
;
   (setvar "cmdecho" 1)
   (princ)
 )                                               ; End defun
; ---⟨ End of program ⟩---
```

Documentation for EDIT-ENT.LSP

[1] **(initget 1 "Arc Circle Line Polyline Text")** The first INITGET expression used in this program disallows a null string (initget 1), and states which strings are valid for the next GETxxxx expression. Here, the INITGET optional STRING argument defines a list of entities to choose from.

[2] **(setq SS1 (ssget "X" (list (cons 0 RES) (cons 8 LAY))))** This SETQ expression contains a nested SSGET expression. The SSGET statement creates a selection set based on the choices specified by the user. This criteria is CONStructed to form two associated pairs, 0 (entity group) and 8 (layer). AutoLISP scans the drawing database according to this filter-list specification.

[3] An IF expression is given. If the TEST expression returns T (the selection set SS1 actually exists), the THEN expression is executed. The THEN expression is the PROGN function shown here.

[4] **(initget 1 "Copy Erase Move Rotate Scale")** The second INITGET expression used in this program disallows a null string, and states which strings are valid for the next GETxxxx expression. Here, the INITGET optional STRING argument defines a list of editing commands to choose from.

[5] **(command COM SS1 "")** The AutoLISP COMMAND function uses the string assigned to variable COM, and begins the editing process. Selection set SS1 is chosen to be modified.

[6] **(princ "\nNo objects found!")** This PRINC expression constitutes the ELSE portion of the IF statement. In the event that selection set SS1 does not exist, issue a message to the user.

EXERCISE 12-1

☐ Design AutoLISP expressions that accomplish the following tasks. Each expression will be a single application of the SSGET function. Remember to use the appropriate SSGET MODE and FILTER-LIST arguments.

A. Set the variable VAR1 to a selection set that contains all AutoCAD circles with a radius of 1.0. (Hint: Use code 40 for radius.)

B. Set the variable BLK to a selection set that contains all AutoCAD blocks named "PART" residing on layer 0.

C. Set the variable RL to a selection set that contains all AutoCAD lines generated in red (color 1). Confine the search to the current limits of the drawing by utilizing a crossing box.

D. Set the variable TX to the Previous selection set that contains all AutoCAD text entities with a text style named "Simplex". (Hint: Use code 7 for text style.)

☐ Generate the necessary drawing entities on the graphics screen, and test each statement at the Command: prompt. Finally, store all of the expressions in the file: EX12-1.LSP.

The SSGET Function–Relational Tests

The SSGET function's FILTER-LIST argument is provided for specifying unique entity properties, such as text height values or block scaling factors. By employing a filter-list, the user effectively isolates a group of objects that match the given specification. Those entities that do not reflect the desired criteria (not equal to the filter-list) are simply ignored. It is by this method that a distinct selection set is formed.

When it is necessary to specify other numerical relationships for a set of objects, the special –4 group code is used. The *–4 group code* enlists a relational operator, such as > (greater than) or < (less than), to test for these numerical conditions. Integers, real numbers, point coordinates, and 3D vectors within the drawing database may be compared using these testing operators. For a concise review on relational operators and predicate tests, refer to Chapter 8. The table shown in Fig. 12-3 lists all of the available relational operators.

Operator	Meaning
"*"	Any value acceptable (always True)
"="	Equals
"!="	Not equal
"/="	Not equal
"<>"	Not equal
"<"	Less than
"<="	Less than or equal
">"	Greater than
">="	Greater than or equal
"&"	Bitwise AND (Integers only)
"&="	Bitwise masked equals (Integers only)

Fig. 12-3. Relational operators for the SSGET function.

Note that each operator is given in the form of a string. The string indicates the relational test to be applied to the next associated pair in the filter-list. There are a few restrictions when using relational operators, which are discussed below:

1. All relational operators, excluding the bitwise operators "&" and "&=", are valid for integer and real number-based group codes. For example:

```
(ssget "X" '((0 . "TEXT") (–4 . ">") (50 . 0.0)))
```

Create a selection set of all text entities that have rotational values greater than 0.0. The relational operator ">" is applied to group code 50, where the text rotation is 0.0, a real number.

Group codes using strings, such as (8 . "DIM") for the "DIM" layer, cannot use these relational operators. For example:

```
(ssget "X" '((0 . "LINE") (–4 . "<") (8 . "WINDOWS")))
```

Attempt to create a selection set of all line entities generated on layers with names less than "WINDOWS". In this case, AutoLISP returns nil (no selection set created). Group codes with strings may not be tested in this manner.

The bitwise operators "&" and "&=" are only valid for integer-based group codes.

2. When testing coordinates within point group codes, the X, Y, and Z values may be tested individually or all together. A single string defines the relational test, where each operator is separated by a comma. For example:

```
(ssget "X" '((0 . "CIRCLE") (-4 . ">,>,*") (10 0.0 0.0 0.0)))
```

Create a selection set of all circles that have X and Y center points greater than 0, and the Z coordinate may be any value. Group code 10 specifies the center point location.

Where a single axis value is omitted, as in the example "<=, <=" (Z-axis operator is missing), the "*" operator is assumed.

3. The group code 210 (a directional vector) can only be tested with the "*", "=", or "!=" (not equal group) relational operators. For example:

```
(ssget "X" '((0 . "SOLID") (-4 . "!=") (210 0.0 0.0 1.0)))
```

Create a selection set of all solids that are not generated within the WCS (World Coordinate System). The group code 210 specifies the directional vector relative to the WCS origin '(0.0 0.0 0.0).

More examples using relational tests are outlined below:

```
(ssget "W" '(0 0) '(36 24) '((0 . "CIRCLE") (-4 . "<") (40 . 1.0)))
```

Create a selection set of all circles found inside an AutoCAD window with corners '(0 0) and '(36 24), and that have radius values less than 1.0.

```
(ssget "P" '((0 . "POLYLINE") (-4 . "!=") (40 . 0.25)))
```

From the Previous AutoCAD selection set, create a new selection set of all polyline entities whose first vertex does not have a starting width value equal to 0.25.

```
(ssget "X" '((0 . "ARC") (-4 . ">=") (40 . 1.0) (-4 . "<>") (62 . 256)))
```

Create a selection set of all arcs whose radius values are greater than or equal to 1.0, and whose color assignments are not 256 ("BYLAYER").

```
(ssget "X" '((0 . "LINE")
     (–4 . "⟩,⟩,/=") (10 0.0 0.0 0.0)        ; Group code 10 – 1st endpoint.
     (–4 . "⟨,⟨,/=") (11 24.0 18.0 0.0)      ; Group code 11 – 2nd endpoint.
     )                                       ; End filter-list.
)                                            ; End ssget
```

Create a selection set of all 3D lines whose endpoints are held within a certain coordinate range. Included within the filter-list are specifications for group codes 10 and 11. If the group code 10 X and Y coordinates of each line are "⟩, ⟩" (greater than) 0.0, and the group code 11 X and Y coordinates are "⟨, ⟨" (less than) 24.0 and 18.0 respectively, a match is virtually guaranteed. Note: In this example, the Z-axis coordinate must "/=" (not equal) zero in all cases, either with the first or second points!

The SSGET Function–Logical Grouping Tests

Relational operators, such as ⟩ (greater than) or ⟨ (less than), are used to test for various numerical conditions. Each relational operator is contained inside a –4 group code, and influences the type of data returned by an SSGET filter-list.

When testing a *group* of filter-list specifications, logical operators are applied. Similar to the AutoLISP AND, OR, and NOT functions found earlier in Chapter 8, *logical operators* bind the arguments (group codes) together as one test. As opposed to testing a single associated pair in an SSGET filter-list specification (relational operators), logical operators nest multiple group codes together. The table shown in Fig. 12-4 lists all of the available logical grouping operators:

Starting Operator	Enclosed Operators and/or Filter-List Tests	Ending Operator
"⟨AND"	One or more operands are enclosed	"AND⟩"
"⟨OR"	One or more operands are enclosed	"OR⟩"
"⟨XOR"	Two operands are enclosed	"XOR⟩"
"⟨NOT"	One operand is enclosed	"NOT⟩"

Fig. 12-4. Available logical grouping operators for the SSGET function.

Note that each logical operator is given in the form of a string, which may be indicated in either upper- or lowercase letters. Like the relational operators, logical groupings use the –4 group code. Examples of each logical operator are illustrated below:

The "⟨AND" ... operands ... "AND⟩" logical grouping. For example:

```
(ssget "X" '((–4 . "⟨AND")
       (0 . "TEXT")
       (8 . "NOTES")
       (40 . 0.125)
     (–4 . "AND⟩")    ; End AND logical group
  )                   ; End filter–list
)                     ; End ssget
```

Create a selection set of all text entities that are present on layer "NOTES" and are 0.125 high. As indicated by the AND logical grouping, all nested group codes must be satisfied (return True) in order for the selection set to be created.

Note the pairing of the "⟨AND" and "AND⟩" logical operators. This format must remain consistent in order to properly execute any logical grouping(s).

The "⟨OR" ... operands ... "OR⟩" logical grouping. For example:

```
(ssget "X" '((–4 . "⟨OR")
       (0 . "CIRCLE")
       (39 . 1.0)
       (40 . 2.5)
     (–4 . "OR⟩")     ; End OR logical group
  )                   ; End filter–list
)                     ; End ssget
```

Form a selection set that includes any of the following entities:

A. All circles regardless of size, layer setting, etc.

B. Any entity that carries an extruded thickness of 1.0.

C. Any entity that has the group code 40 containing the real number value 2.5.

The pairing of the "⟨OR" and "OR⟩" logical operators opens up a variety of possibilities within the drawing editor. If any of the filter-list specifications return T (True), a non-nil selection set is formed.

The "⟨XOR" ... operands ... "XOR⟩" logical grouping. For example:

```
(ssget "X" '((0 . "INSERT")
     (2 . "XREF–1")
     (–4 . "⟨XOR")
       (–3 . ("EXTERNAL–APP1"))
       (–3 . ("EXTERNAL–APP2"))
     (–4 . "XOR⟩")    ; End XOR logical group
  )                   ; End filter–list
)                     ; End ssget
```

Create a selection set that gathers all external references (XREFs) named "XREF–1" (2 group code) that possess extended entity data (–3 group code). The external references that are chosen are from either "EXTERNAL–APP1" or "EXTERNAL–APP2", but not both.

The use of the "⟨XOR" and "XOR⟩" logical operators is limited to building selection sets containing extended entity data. This data is primarily for use with an external program outside of AutoCAD. This type of AutoLISP manipulation is not common with the typical programmer, and falls beyond the scope of this text.

The "⟨NOT" ... operands ... "NOT⟩" logical grouping. For example:

```
(ssget "X" '((0 . "INSERT")
     (2 . "PART–39")
     (–4 . "⟨NOT")    ; Begin first NOT logical group
       (8 . "0")
     (–4 . "NOT⟩")    ; End first NOT logical group
     (–4 . "⟨NOT")    ; Begin second NOT logical group
       (41 . 1.0)
     (–4 . "NOT⟩")    ; End second NOT logical group
  )                   ; End filter–list
)                     ; End ssget
```

Form a selection set that includes all inserted blocks named "PART–39", but with the following two restrictions:

A. The block(s) may not be inserted on layer "0".

B. The block(s) may not have an X scale factor of 1.0.

Using the "⟨NOT" and "NOT⟩" logical operators allows the user to create a selection set containing entities *not* found within the logical section of the filter-list.

Occasionally, the AutoCAD "Thickness" setting interferes with objects already created, like text. It is unusual for text entities to have extrusion values other than 0.0, and can be annoying when presenting 3D information. The next programming example demonstrates how AutoLISP relational tests and logical groupings can be linked together to overcome this obstacle.

```
; Program:  FLATTEXT.LSP
;
; Purpose:  To change all TEXT within a drawing to a thickness value of 0.0. A filter-list
;           is formed by scanning the drawing file for TEXT with extrusion values ⟨⟩
;           (not equal to) 0.0. All "offending" entities will be modified. A provision is
;           made to allow the user to choose a specific layer for keeping 3D TEXT.
;           Detailed documentation follows the program.
;
; Note:  Switching to a 3D VPOINT will assist in viewing the conversion process.
;
(defun C:FLATTEXT (/ LAY TXT)
    (setvar "cmdecho" 0)
    (prompt "\nRemove which Layer from processing ⟨ENTER for none⟩: ")
                                                    ; Keep this layer's 3D TEXT
;
    (if (= (setq LAY (strcase (getstring))) "")                  ; [1]
       (progn
          (prompt "\nLocating all TEXT entities with extrusions ⟨⟩ 0")
;
          (setq TXT (ssget "X" '((0 . "TEXT") (–4 . "⟨⟩") (39 . 0.0))))    ; [2]
;
          (if (null TXT)                                         ; [3]
             (prompt "\nNo objects found!")
             (command ".chprop" "P" "" "Thickness" 0.0 "")
          )                                         ; End nested if
       )                                            ; End progn – THEN expression
       (progn
          (prompt "\nLocating all TEXT entities with extrusions ⟨⟩ 0")
          (princ (strcat "\nExcluding layer " LAY))
;
```

```
          (setq TXT (ssget "X" (list '(0 . "TEXT")                        ; [4]
                                     '(-4 . "⟨⟩")          ; Relational test
                                     '(39 . 0.0)
                                     '(-4 . "⟨NOT")        ; Begin NOT logical group
                         (cons 8 LAY)
                                     '(-4 . "NOT⟩")        ; End NOT logical group
                    )                                      ; End filter-list
                 )                                         ; End ssget
          )                                                ; End setq
;
          (if (null TXT)                                                  ; [5]
             (prompt "\nNo objects found!")
             (command ".chprop" "P" "" "Thickness" 0.0 "")
          )                                                ; End nested if
       )                                                   ; End progn – ELSE expression
    )                                                      ; End if
    (setvar "cmdecho" 1)
    (princ)
)                                                          ; End defun
; – –⟨ End of program ⟩– –
```

Documentation for FLATTEXT.LSP

[1] **(if (= (setq LAY (strcase (getstring))) ""))** The nested SETQ expression returns the user's response to the previous prompt. The variable LAY could be either a layer name (string), or an ENTER keystroke (string), depending on what characters are passed to the GETSTRING function. If the user supplies an ENTER as a response, all text entries will be considered for the ensuing selection set.

[2] **(setq TXT (ssget "X" '((0 . "TEXT") (–4 . "⟨⟩") (39 . 0.0))))** A selection set is formed and the variable TXT is assigned. The SSGET filter-list searches for all text entities with a thickness value not equal to 0.0. The –4 group code supplies the “” test for the next associated pair within the specification (group 39).

[3]
```
(if (null TXT)
   (prompt "\nNo objects found!")
   (command ".chprop" "P" "" "Thickness" 0.0 "")
)
```

If there is no match for the previous filter-list (null TXT), then inform the user that the selection set is nil (prompt). Otherwise, issue the AutoCAD CHPROP command and modify the previous selection set accordingly.

[4]
```
(setq TXT (ssget "X" (list '(0 . "TEXT")
                           '(-4 . "⟨⟩")        ; Relational test
                           '(39 . 0.0)
                           '(-4 . "⟨NOT")      ; Begin NOT logical group
                      (cons 8 LAY)
                           '(-4 . "NOT⟩")      ; End NOT logical group
                      )
          )
)
```

After a prompt is issued to the user, a selection set is formed and the variable TXT is assigned. The SSGET filter-list searches for all text entities with a thickness value not equal to 0.0. Again, the –4 group code supplies the "〈〉" relational test for the next associated pair in the specification (group 39).

Furthermore, note the inclusion of the "〈NOT" ... operands ... "NOT〉" logical grouping. The relational operators handle only numeric data groups, while this logical grouping is employed to manipulate string data (group 8 layer name). This section of the expression excludes all text residing on layer LAY from the filter-list. Since there is evaluation of group code 8, the LIST function is used to assemble the filter-list.

```
[5] (if (null TXT)
      (prompt "\nNo objects found!")
      (command ".chprop" "P" "" "Thickness" 0.0 "")
    )
```

If there is no match for the previous filter-list (null TXT), then inform the user that the selection set is nil (prompt). Otherwise, issue the AutoCAD CHPROP command and modify the previous selection set accordingly. This expression, although written exactly as the one found in comment [3], excludes text from the user-specified layer (from the ELSE selection set).

EXERCISE 12-2

- ☐ Design AutoLISP expressions that accomplish the following tasks. Each expression will be a single application of the SSGET function, taking full advantage of the relational and logical operators.
  - A. Set the variable PNT to a selection set that contains all AutoCAD points with X and Y coordinate values "〉" (greater than) the LIMMAX system variable setting. (Hint: Use code 10 for point location.)
  - B. Set the variable VP to a selection set that contains all AutoCAD viewports with X-axis values "〈" (less than) 12.0, and Y-axis values "〈" (less than) 9.0. Remember that viewport entities are generated in paper space. (Hint: Use code 40 for X-axis, and code 41 for Y-axis.)
  - C. Set the variable CIR to a selection set that contains all AutoCAD circles with radii "〈=" (less than or equal to) 2.0, and are *not* found on layer 0. (Hint: Use code 40 for radius value.)
- ☐ Generate the necessary drawing entities on the graphics screen, and test each statement at the Command: prompt. Finally, store all of the expressions in the file: EX12-2.LSP.

Let's Review...

1. AutoLISP selection sets are generated by using the SSGET (Selection Set GET) function. The selection set stores each element by entity name, and is similar in action to AutoCAD's "Select objects:" editing feature.
2. The SSGET selection MODE is an optional argument that assists the user in choosing objects in a more discrete manner. Various selection modes, like "W" (Window selection), "P" (Previous selection), and "F" (Fence selection) are available. Refer to the selection modes table in this chapter for specific MODE values.
3. AutoLISP selection sets can be formed by matching specific criteria held within FILTER-LISTs. A filter-list calls out which entity properties to search for, called group codes, and creates a new selection set based upon this descriptive information. Together, these group codes make up an association list (filter-list specification), and are described in the group codes table placed within this chapter.
4. A relational operator, such as ⟩ (greater than) or ⟨ (less than), is used to test for numerical conditions within selection sets. Relational operators are included within a special –4 group code, and like all other group codes, are assembled in an SSGET filter-list. A relational operator table is found in this chapter.
5. When testing a group of filter-list specifications, logical operators are applied. Similar to the AutoLISP AND, OR, and NOT functions, logical operators bind the arguments (group codes) together as one test. Logical operators nest multiple group codes together, and can be seen in their respective table within this chapter.

USING GRIP SELECTION OPTIONS

When items on screen are *grip selected*, or selected while no command or function is active, an (ssget) call immediately returns a selection set consisting of the grip selected items. When you need to determine the specific status of grip selected objects, the *SSGETFIRST (Selection Set GET FIRST) function* is used. The syntax for the SSGETFIRST function is:

```
(ssgetfirst)
```

Only entities from the current drawing's model space and paper space database can be analyzed by this function. Nongraphical objects or entities in other block definitions cannot be acquired with SSGETFIRST.

SSGETFIRST returns a list of two selection sets. The first selection set consists of objects that are displaying grips, but are not currently selected. The second selection set consists of the objects which are both gripped and selected. In a drawing where some objects were gripped, and others were both gripped and selected, two selection sets are returned:

Command: **(ssgetfirst)** ↵
(⟨Selection set: 1⟩ ⟨Selection set: 2⟩)

In a drawing where objects are currently gripped but *not* selected, nil is returned as the second item in the list:

Command: **(ssgetfirst)** ↵
(⟨Selection set: 3⟩ nil)

Likewise, in a drawing where objects are gripped *and* selected (where none are merely gripped), nil is returned in the first position:

```
Command: (ssgetfirst) ↵
(nil ⟨Selection set: 4⟩)
```

Finally, if no objects are gripped *or* grip selected, nil is returned in both positions:

```
Command: (ssgetfirst) ↵
(nil nil)
```

This function should be used when the grip selection status affects how the objects are handled, or when you need to preserve the current grip selection. Using a standard SSGET selects only the currently gripped and selected objects. However, it also removes the grips after the selection is made. SSGETFIRST allows you to access and use both selections, but it does not alter the current grip state of any of the objects selected.

Various AutoCAD functions, such as the DDEDIT command, automatically clear grip selection. This means that even when PICKFIRST is enabled, you cannot grip select text to be edited with DDEDIT. In the following example, an AutoLISP shortcut is designed for the DDEDIT command, using the abbreviation of TE (for Text Edit).

```
(defun C:TE ()
 (command ".DDEDIT")
 (princ)
)
```

The problem with the previous method is that grip selected text is not automatically selected. Instead, the grips are cleared and the user is presented with a selection prompt.

In the next example, SSGETFIRST is used to retrieve the grip selected selection set. If more than one object is selected, the selection set is ignored and the normal selection method is used. If, however, a single text object is selected, the text editor is displayed using the grip selected text object:

```
; TE.LSP  (Text Editor)  by  Ed Eaton
; Short-cut for DDEDIT that allows grip selection
(defun C:TE ()                          ; begin DEFUN
 (if                                    ; begin IF
  (and                                  ; begin AND (test)
   (setq SS (cadr (ssgetfirst)))        ; First test checks for grip selected objects.
   (= 1 (sslength SS))                  ; Second test verifies only one item is grip selected.
  )                                     ; end AND
  (command ".DDEDIT" SS)                ; THEN- Start DDEDIT with selected object
  (command ".DDEDIT")                   ; ELSE- Start DDEDIT with no selection
 )                                      ; end IF
 (princ)                                ; quiet exit
)                                       ; end DEFUN
```

The compliment of the SSGETFIRST function is SSSETFIRST. The *SSSETFIRST (Selection Set SET FIRST) function* allows you to set the current grip selection state for objects in the drawing. The SSSETFIRST function syntax is as follows:

```
(sssetfirst [GRIPSET] [PICKSET])
```

The optional arguments are expected to be selection sets. The objects in the selection set specified as the GRIPSET argument are gripped. The objects in the selection set specified as the PICKSET argument are both gripped *and* selected. When called with no arguments whatsoever, SSSETFIRST clears all grips.

The following routine is a simple demonstration of using SSSETFIRST. Initially, SSGETFIRST is used to find the current grip selection status. Next, SSSETFIRST is used to reverse the status so that objects which were selected are now just gripped, and vice versa:

```
(defun C:SWITCH ()
  (setq GFL (ssgetfirst))                ; returns a list as (gripped  selected)
  (sssetfirst (cadr GFL) (car GFL))      ; selected presented as gripset, and
                                         ; gripped presented as pickset
  (princ)                                ; quiet exit
)
```

One common use for SSSETFIRST is to clear any existing grip selections and require the user to create a new selection set after starting an AutoLISP-defined function. To do this, call SSSETFIRST with no arguments:

```
(sssetfirst)
```

To set a gripset, but not a pickset, use only the first argument. The following example creates a selection set using a generic SSGET, then grips the objects:

```
(setq SS1 (ssget))
(sssetfirst SS1)
```

When you need to set a pickset but not a gripset, use nil as the gripset argument:

```
(setq SS2 (ssget))
(sssetfirst nil SS)
```

SSSETFIRST returns a list of the selection sets that were gripped or selected:

```
(sssetfirst)                 returns nil
(sssetfirst SS1)             returns (SS1)
(sssetfirst nil SS1)         returns (nil SS1)
(sssetfirst SS1 SS2)         returns (SS1 SS2)
```

SELECTION SET LENGTH

The *SSLENGTH (Selection Set LENGTH) function* is used to determine the number of data items (entity names) within a selection set. The number is returned as an integer if it is under 32,767; over this value, it is returned as a real number. The format for the SSLENGTH function is:

```
(sslength SS)
```

This function, where SS represents a selection set, may be helpful in controlling the AutoLISP looping environment or instrumental in obtaining number data for comparison. Like the SSGET function, SSLENGTH will *never* duplicate or count the same entity twice. For example:

```
(setq C (ssget "L"))          retrieve the Last object in the
                              database and store it within
                              selection set C

(sslength C)      returns 1
```

The following program provides a number comparison between the entities found on a user-specified layer and layer 0. The AutoLISP IF statement, as shown in previous SSGET routines, acts as a mechanism to inform the user of current drawing editor conditions.

```
; Filename: LAY–ENT.LSP
;
; Author: I.B. Three
;
; Date: October 31, 19xx
;
; Purpose: To report on the number of entities found on a user-
;          specified layer versus layer 0.
;
(defun C:LAY–ENT (/ LAY SET)
  (setvar "cmdecho" 0)
  (setq LAY (strcase (getstring "\nLayer for entities calculation: "))
        SET (ssget "X" (list (cons 8 LAY)))
  )
  (if (null SET)
    (princ (strcat "The layer " LAY " does not exist or is empty!"))
    (princ (strcat "The layer " LAY " has "
           (itoa (sslength SET))        ; SSLENGTH reports number of objects
           " entities."
           )
    )                                   ; End princ
  )                                     ; End if
  (princ (strcat "\nThe layer 0 has "
           (itoa (sslength (ssget "X" (list (cons 8 "0")))))
           " entities."
         )
  )                                     ; End princ
  (setvar "cmdecho" 1)
  (princ)
)
; ––⟨ End of program ⟩––
```

THE SSNAME FUNCTION

The *SSNAME (Selection Set NAME) function* returns the entity name that corresponds to the INDEX'th item held within selection set SS. Indexing begins with the integer 0. Negative INDEX numbers or numbers larger than the highest numbered entity in the selection set return nil. The syntax for SSNAME is:

```
(ssname SS INDEX)
```

As with the SSGET function, main entities are examined, but subentity structures are not. When the selection set exceeds 32,767 data items, the INDEX argument must be supplied as a real number. Examples of the SSNAME function follow:

```
(setq W (ssget "X" '((0 . "TEXT"))))                    all text chosen

(command ".change" (ssname W 0) "" "" "" "" "" "" "New Text")
                                                        first text element (index 0) within
                                                        selection set "W" is retrieved, and
                                                        changed to read "New Text"

(setq E (ssget "X" '((0 . "LINE"))))                    all lines chosen

(command ".erase" (ssname E 5) "")                      sixth line (index 5) within selection
                                                        set "E" is erased
```

The next AutoLISP program utilizes the features of the SSNAME function. This program, similar to the text program found in Chapter 12, allows the user to adjust the height of each text item contained within a named selection set. Note that the program uses the AutoLISP REDRAW function to highlight the text entity being modified. (The REDRAW function is covered in depth in Chapter 16.) The *REDRAW function* typically takes the form of:

```
(redraw [ENAME [MODE]])
```

...where *ENAME* is an optional entity name argument, and *MODE* is an optional integer argument that controls how the entity is displayed. The REDRAW modes shown in Fig. 12-5 are currently supported. An example of the REDRAW function is as follows:

```
(setq U (ssname L 0))                                   variable U represents entity name
                                                        (ename) from set L

(redraw U 1)                                            mode 1 shows the entity on screen
```

Mode	Action
1	Show entity on screen.
2	Hide entity (blank out).
3	Highlight entity (if display can).
4	Dehighlight entity (if display can).

Fig. 12-5. The MODEs available for the REDRAW function.

Now, the REDRAW function is incorporated into the following program. Here the AutoLISP REDRAW expressions assist the user in visualizing the entities being worked on.

```
; Filename: TEXTHGT.LSP
;
; Author: M.A. Kitshort
;
; Date: December 11, 19xx
;
; Purpose: To resize text within the drawing editor. Each text entry is individually
;          highlighted as the user is asked to change or ignore that entity.
;          All text should be visible to the screen and parallel to the UCS before beginning.
;
(defun C:TEXTHGT (/ RES TXTSET LAY HGT CTR ENT ANS)
  (setvar "cmdecho" 0)
  (setq RES (strcase
       (getstring "\nAdjust all text, or by layer <All/Layer>: ")))
;
; --< If All layers, then get all text, else get text per one Layer >--
;
  (if (= RES "A")
    (setq TXTSET (ssget "X" '((0 . "TEXT"))))
    (setq LAY (strcase (getstring "\nSpecify layer: "))
          TXTSET (ssget "X" (list (cons 0 "TEXT") (cons 8 LAY)))
    )
  )
;
; --< If no selection set, then tell user, else get new text height >--
;
  (if (null TXTSET)
    (princ (strcat "\nThe layer " LAY
                   " does not exist or there is no text!"))
    (progn
    (initget 1)
      (setq HGT (getreal "\nNew text height: ")
            CTR 0
      )
      (while (setq ENT (ssname TXTSET CTR))     ; While there are items
        (redraw ENT 3)                          ;   Highlight text
        (setq ANS (strcase
           (getstring "\nChange this text entry <Y>: "))
        )
        (if (or (= ANS "Y") (= ANS ""))
           (command ".change" ENT "" "" "" "" HGT "" "")
        )
        (redraw ENT 4)                          ; Dehighlight text
        (setq CTR (1+ CTR))
      )                                         ; Close while
    )                                           ; Close progn
  )                                             ; Close if
```

```
    (setvar "cmdecho" 1)
    (princ)
)
; --⟨ End of program ⟩--
```

THE SSNAMEX FUNCTION

While the SSNAME function can be used to access entity names, it can be useful to be able to access additional information such as how the object was selected. The *SSNAMEX (Selection Set NAME indeX) function* requires a selection set argument and allows an optional INDEX argument:

```
(ssnamex SS [INDEX])
```

When called with just a selection set argument, SSNAMEX returns information about all of the objects in the selection set. The optional INDEX argument can be used to specify a single object within the selection set. The list returned by SSNAMEX contains information that describes an entity or entities and the selection method used.

In the following example, a polyline drawn from 2,2 to 4,4 was selected by a pick at the coordinate 3,3:

```
Command: (setq SS (ssget)) ↵
Select objects: 3,3↵
1 found
Select objects: ↵
⟨Selection set: 25⟩

Command: (ssnamex SS 0) ↵
((1 ⟨Entity name: 3bb0508⟩ 0 (0 (3.0 3.0 0.0))))
```

In the returned list, the first sublist includes the single entity within the selection set. The first element of the list is a selection method ID (for example, 1 as in the previous example), which indicates the selection method used. See Fig. 12-6.

ID	DESCRIPTION
0	Nonspecific
1	Pick, or other single point coordinate entry
2	Window or WPolygon
3	Crossing or CPolygon
4	Fence
8	Group name

Fig. 12-6. Selection method ID and descriptions for the SSNAMEX function.

The individual elements of the list are shown in Fig. 12-7. The subentity code (other than 0 when selecting by picking) indicates that a complex entity, such as a polyline, was selected. If the first segment of the polyline was selected, this number is 1, if the second segment was picked, this number is 2, and so forth. A point descriptor ID of 0 precedes the point coordinate list.

Fig. 12-7. Identification of the individual elements returned with SSNAMEX.

PROFESSIONAL TIP

Throughout this text or in actual development, it is often necessary to enter the same bit of code many times. To reduce your text entry requirements, you can develop a function to do the entry for you. For example, to assist in researching the SSNAMEX function, the following routine creates a selection set and returns information on the first object within the selection set by specifying an INDEX value of 0:

```
(defun C:SNX ()
  (setq SS (ssget))
  (ssnamex SS 0)
)
```

When a polygon or fence selection method is used, a –1 appears after the sub-entity code. Next, a polygon description is provided as shown in the following example:

Command: **(setq SS (ssget))** ↵
Select objects: **C**↵
First corner: *(select first corner)*
Other corner: *(select other corner)*
1 found
Select objects:↵
⟨Selection set: 26⟩

Command: **(ssnamex SS 0)** ↵
((3 ⟨Entity name: 4240768⟩ 1 -1) (-1 (0 (1.52951 3.83902 0.0)) (0 (3.54235 3.83902 0.0)) (0 (3.54235 2.8086 0.0)) (0 (1.52951 2.8086 0.0))))

The returned list is rewritten here in a more easily readable format, and documented in the subsequent section for clarity:

```
(
 (3 ⟨Entity name: 4240768⟩ 1 –1)         ;[1]
 (–1                                      ;[2]
  (0 (1.52951 3.83902 0.0))               ;[3]
  (0 (3.54235 3.83902 0.0))
  (0 (3.54235 2.8086 0.0))
  (0 (1.52951 2.8086 0.0))
 )                                        ;[4]
)                                         ;[5]
```

[1] (3 ⟨Entity name: 4240768⟩ 1 –1) This shows 3 as the selection method, meaning a Crossing or Crossing Polygon. The entity name of the selected object is given, followed by a 1, indicating that a complex entity was selected. The final element of –1 indicates the ID number of the polygonal selection that was used.

[2] (–1 The –1 is a numerical identifier code for the subsequent selection polygon description. When more than one polygonal selection was used, each subsequent polygon is numbered as –2, –3, and so forth.

[3] (0 (1.52951 3.83902 0.0))... Each point comprising the selection polygon is now listed.

[4]) Ends the selection polygon description.

[5]) Ends the entity selection description.

The following is a list returned by a Fence selection:

```
((4 ⟨Entity name: 4240530⟩ 0 (0 (7.14286 2.28571 0.0)) (0 (8.07143 4.14286 0.0))))
```

In this previous example, the fence intersects the selected object at two separate points.

PROFESSIONAL TIP

Two behaviors of the SSNAMEX function in the initial shipping version of AutoCAD Release 14.0 are not documented. However, these behaviors may adversely affect your programs if you are not aware of them:

1. When an object being selected is a Group, the selection ID may return 8, regardless of the selection method. This does not occur when grip selection methods are used.
2. The points reported to describe the selection polygon used for Windows and Crossings are inaccurate by approximately ±0.012 units.

The SSNAMEX function can also be used to look at an entire selection set by omitting the optional INDEX argument, as follows:

Command: **(setq SS (ssget))**↵
Select objects: *(pick a line object)*
1 found
Select objects: **C**↵
First corner: *(cross a polyline object)*
Other corner: 1 found
Select objects: ↵
⟨Selection set: 275⟩

Command: **(ssnamex SS)**↵
((1 ⟨Entity name: 4240530⟩ 0 (0 (7.5 3.0 0.0))) (3 ⟨Entity name: 4240768⟩ 1 -1)
(-1 (0 (2.48773 5.01227 0.0)) (0 (5.01227 5.01227 0.0)) (0 (5.01227 2.98773
0.0)) (0 (2.48773 2.98773 0.0))))

The returned list is presented here in a more readable format:

```
(
 (1 ⟨Entity name: 4240530⟩ 0 (0 (7.5 3.0 0.0)))
 (3 ⟨Entity name: 4240768⟩ 1 -1)
  (-1
   (0 (2.48773 5.01227 0.0))
   (0 (5.01227 5.01227 0.0))
   (0 (5.01227 2.98773 0.0))
   (0 (2.48773 2.98773 0.0))
  )
)
```

By studying this list, it can be determined that the first object is a simple object such as a line, arc, or circle and that the pick point is 7.5,3.0,0.0. The second object is a complex object selected by either a Crossing or a Crossing Polygon, and the polygon is described by its point coordinates.

When more than one polygon is used, the numerical identifier code is referenced to find out which polygon was responsible for selecting each individual object. The next example uses two different selection polygons to generate the selection set:

Command: **(setq SS (ssget))** ↵
Select objects: Other corner: 1 found
Select objects: Other corner: 1 found
Select objects:
⟨Selection set: 276⟩

Command: **(ssnamex SS)** ↵
((2 ⟨Entity name: 4240788⟩ 0 -1) (2 ⟨Entity name: 4240780⟩ 0 -2) (-2 (0
(5.48773 1.51227 0.0)) (0 (7.51227 1.51227 0.0)) (0 (7.51227 -0.512267 0.0))
(0 (5.48773 -0.512267 0.0))) (-1 (0 (7.98773 1.51227 0.0)) (0 (10.0123
1.51227 0.0)) (0 (10.0123 -0.512267 0.0)) (0 (7.98773 -0.512267 0.0))))

The returned list is reformatted below:

```
(
 (2 ⟨Entity name: 4240788⟩ 0 -1)
 (2 ⟨Entity name: 4240780⟩ 0 -2)
 (-2
  (0 (5.48773 1.51227 0.0))
  (0 (7.51227 1.51227 0.0))
  (0 (7.51227 -0.512267 0.0))
  (0 (5.48773 -0.512267 0.0))
 )
 (-1
  (0 (7.98773 1.51227 0.0))
  (0 (10.0123 1.51227 0.0))
  (0 (10.0123 -0.512267 0.0))
  (0 (7.98773 -0.512267 0.0))
 )
)
```

The first object indicates that it was selected by the polygon identified as -1, and the second object was selected by the polygon designated as -2. In the subsequent data, each polygon is then described.

Let's Review...

1. The SSGETFIRST function is used to determine the specific status of grip selected objects.
2. The SSSETFIRST function allows a user to set the current grip selection state for objects in a drawing.
3. The SSLENGTH (Selection Set LENGTH) function reports the length (number) of items within a selection set. Like the SSGET function, SSLENGTH never processes the same data element twice.
4. The SSNAME (Selection Set NAME) function returns the entity name that corresponds to the index'th item held within a selection set. Indexing for the selection set begins with the integer 0.
5. The SSNAMEX function provides not only the entity names of selected objects, but also details how the objects were selected.

ADDING, DELETING, AND TESTING ENTITIES WITHIN SELECTION SETS

The final section of this chapter deals with selection set "editing" tools. These supplemental functions assist in modifying the basic selection set, where it is possible to add, delete, and test entities within sets.

THE SSADD FUNCTION

The *SSADD (Selection Set ADD) function* enables the user to add ENAMEs (entity names) to a given SS (selection set). This can be beneficial when an entity name must be included within a set, but the overhead of forming a new selection set is not justified. The syntax for the SSADD function is:

```
(ssadd [ENAME [SS]])
```

When SSADD is used without arguments, a new selection set is initialized (created) without any members. The SSADD function constructs a selection set with one member when only the ENAME argument is used.

The SSADD function incorporates the new entity name(s) into the selection set without having to SETQ (reassign) them a second time. In addition, attempting to add an existing ENAME to the selection set will be ignored. The following examples are some applications of the SSADD function:

(setq P (ssadd))	*when no arguments are used, a null (empty) selection set is constructed*
(setq Q (ssget))	*a general selection set is formed*
(command ".copy" (ssadd (ssname Q 0) P) "" '(1 1) '(5 5))	*selection set P now has one data element, supplied by set Q, and is then copied*
(ssadd (ssname P 5) L)	*since selection set P from above has only one item, this SSADD statement will return "error: bad argument type"*
(ssadd (ssname (ssget "P") 0) Q)	*add the first index'th element stored inside the "Previous" set to the selection set Q*

The following sample program is somewhat complex. However, study the program carefully, and you will be able to decipher it. The AutoLISP *atoms-family* (list of atoms) is scanned for selection sets, and a list is subsequently formed containing these sets. This generated list is then displayed. Eventually, the user chooses one drawing entity to add to the desired selection set.

Supportive documentation is provided at the conclusion of the program. However, in situations where the AutoLISP function usage seems too complicated, review those functions from previous chapters.

```
; Filename: ADDTOSET.LSP
;
; Purpose: To add a single or group of entities to an existing
;          selection-set. The available selection–sets from the
;          AutoLISP Atoms–family (function/atom "storage facility")
;          are displayed, and the user is asked to choose one from
;          the list. The target selection–set is then highlighted.
;          Unrelated objects are then selected and subsequently
;          added to the desired set.
;
; Note: Selection–sets are stored as PICKSETs in the Atoms–family.
;
;–––––––––––––––––––––––––––––––––––––––
```

```
;
(defun C:ATS (/ CTR ITEM LST SS CTR ENT DUMMY)
  (setvar "cmdecho" 0)
  (princ "\n\nWorking...")
  (setq LST '())                                       ; [1]
    (foreach ITEM (atoms-family 0)                     ; [2]
      (if (= (type (eval ITEM)) 'PICKSET)              ; [3]
         (setq LST (cons ITEM LST))                    ; [4]
      )                                                ; End if
    )                                                  ; End foreach
  (princ "Available selection-sets: \n\n")
  (if LST (princ LST))                                 ; If sets...then display them
  (cond
    (LST                                               ; [5]
      (setq SS (strcase
                (getstring "\n\nAdd entities to which selection-set: "))
      )
      (if (member (read SS) LST)                       ; [6]
         (progn
           (setq SS   (eval (read SS))                 ; [7]
                 CTR   0                               ; [8]
           )
           (while (setq ENT (ssname SS CTR))           ; [9]
             (redraw ENT 3)                            ; [10]
             (setq CTR (1+ CTR))                       ; [11]
           )
;
;---( After selection-set is redrawn, add new entities to that set)---
;
           (princ "\nSet is highlighted...Select entities to add:\n")
           (setq DUMMY   (ssget)                       ; [12]
                 CTR        0
           )
           (while (setq ENT (ssname DUMMY CTR))        ; [13]
             (ssadd ENT SS)                            ; [14]
             (setq CTR (1+ CTR))                       ; [15]
           )
           (princ (strcat "\nThis selection-set now has "
                          (itoa (sslength SS))
                          " data elements.")
           )                                           ; End princ
           (setq DUMMY  nil                            ; Null DUMMY set
                 CTR   0
           )
           (while (setq ENT (ssname SS CTR))           ; While objects in SS...
             (redraw ENT 4)                            ; Unhighlight entities
             (setq CTR (1+ CTR))
           )
         )                                             ; End progn
         (princ "\nNot a selection-set!")
      )                                                ; End if
    )                                                  ; End 1st cond list
```

```
      (T                                                        ; [16]
        (princ "\nThere are no selection–sets currently available.")
      )                                                         ; End 2nd cond list
    )                                                           ; End cond
    (redraw)
    (setvar "cmdecho" 1)
    (princ)
  )
  ;– – –( End of program )– – –
```

For each of the numbered lines in the previous example, a brief explanation is given below. These documented steps may be helpful in understanding the program.

[1] **(setq LST '())** Initialize variable name LST as a null (empty) list.

[2] **(foreach ITEM (atoms–family 0)** The FOREACH function uses ITEM as a name when stepping through the AutoLISP Atoms-family, one element at a time. Here, the expression (atoms-family 0) returns the entire list of AutoLISP functions and atoms. The FOREACH function returns each consecutive atom found within Atoms-family, and in turn, stores this data under ITEM. FOREACH will continue to process each atom as long as ITEM exists (elements are found within Atoms-family).

[3] **(if (= (type (eval ITEM)) 'PICKSET)** The variable, ITEM, is EVALuated. A selection-set data type is called a 'PICKSET. If ITEM being examined matches this data type, then...

[4] **(setq LST (cons ITEM LST))** CONStruct a list called LST that includes selection-set ITEM. The first pass of this expression uses empty list LST, which ultimately allows for future additions of data elements. If ITEM being examined does not match the 'PICKSET data type, no addition to the list is made.

[5] **(cond (LST** Under the condition that variable LST exists (returns True), process the IF function that follows.

[6] **(if (member (read SS) LST)** READ the argument SS (selection-set name as string) and return an atom. This has the effect of converting SS into its corresponding data type. If this atom is a member of list LST, then...

[7] **(setq SS (eval (read SS))** READ the argument SS and return an atom. EVALuating the data type returns a selection-set, and reassigns variable SS.

[8] **(setq CTR 0)** Initialize the counter CTR to 0, and use the returned integer value as an increment for the upcoming WHILE loop.

[9] **(while (setq ENT (ssname SS CTR))** The variable SS is the selection-set argument for the SSNAME function. On the first pass, CTR is set to 0 and the entity name at the 0 index is stored under the variable ENT. WHILE the variable ENT is not null, proceed with the loop.

[10] **(redraw ENT 3)** The REDRAW function highlights the entity that is stored in the variable named ENT.

[11] **(setq CTR (1+ CTR))** Increment the counter CTR, and use the returned integer value for consecutive WHILE function testing. Eventually, all entities with set SS will be highlighted.

[12] **(setq DUMMY (ssget))** As the user selects entities to add to set SS, store the entities in variable DUMMY. This "dummy" local variable eventually passes its contents to set SS.

[13] **(while (setq ENT (ssname DUMMY CTR))** The variable DUMMY is the selection-set argument for the SSNAME function. On the first pass, CTR is set to 0 and the entity name at the 0 index is stored under variable ENT. WHILE the variable ENT is not null, proceed with the loop.

[14] **(ssadd ENT SS)** Add the entity stored in variable ENT to set SS.

[15] **(setq CTR (1+ CTR)** Increment the counter CTR, and use the returned integer value for consecutive WHILE function testing. Eventually, all entities within set DUMMY will be passed to set SS.

[16] **(T (princ "\nThere are no selection-sets currently available."))** Where the first CONDition returns nil, this expression returns True. The PRINC statement tells the user that no selection-sets have been defined.

THE SSDEL FUNCTION

The *SSDEL (Selection Set DELete) function* enables the user to delete ENAMEs (entity names) from a given SS (selection set). The syntax for the SSDEL function is:

```
(ssdel ENAME SS)
```

The arguments for SSDEL are identical to the SSADD function. However, unlike the SSADD function, the arguments for SSDEL are required. In contrast to the SSADD function, an entity name is removed from the desired set when using the SSDEL function.

Similar to the SSADD function, SSDEL deletes the target entity name(s) without having to SETQ (reassign) the values a second time. In addition, attempting to delete a nonexistent ENAME from SS will be ignored. The following are some examples of the SSDEL function:

(setq R (ssget))	*a general selection set is formed*
(sslength R) 15	*the selection set "R" returns 15. There are 15 items in the selection set*
(ssdel (ssname R 0) R)	*set "R" now has one less data element*
(ssdel (ssname R 22) R)	*Since selection set "R" has less than 22 items, the nested (ssname R 22) statement returns nil, and the remaining AutoLISP expression would return "error: bad argument type."*

THE SSMEMB FUNCTION

The *SSMEMB (Selection Set MEMBer) function* tests for ENAME (entity name) inside of SS (selection set). If ENAME is found, ENAME is returned; otherwise, nil is returned. The format for the SSMEMB function is as follows:

```
(ssmemb ENAME SS)
```

The arguments for this function, like the SSDEL function, are required. Examples of SSMEMB follow:

(setq J (ssget "C" '(0 0) '(12 9)))	*selection set "J" is formed*
(setq ENT1 (ssname J 0))	*the entity name is then returned*
⟨Entity name: 85c0500⟩	
(ssmemb ENT1 J)	*returns ENT1 name*
⟨Entity name: 85c0500⟩	
(setq ENT2 (ssname R 0))	
⟨Entity name: 85c0508⟩	
(ssmemb ENT2 J)	
nil	*returns nil when ENT2 is not a member of "J"*

Let's Review...

1. The AutoLISP SSADD (Selection Set ADD) and SSDEL (Selection Set DELete) functions add and delete entity names from specified selection sets, respectively. The primary purpose behind these two functions is to have a method for modifying existing selection sets.
2. The SSMEMB (Selection Set MEMBer) function tests to see whether an entity name exists within a specified selection set. If one does exist, the entity name is returned.

EXERCISE 12-3

- ☐ Produce a program that forms a selection set of all blocks within a drawing file. Individually highlight each block using the REDRAW function. If the highlighted block appears with embedded text or attributes, ask the user if the item should be deleted from the selection set. After looping through the entire selection set and removing certain blocks with the SSDEL function, erase the resultant selection set.
- ☐ Make sure that all layers are visible before the routine continues with the selection process. Study the TEXTHGT.LSP program found earlier in this chapter for ideas to construct this new program. Document the file, and name the program EX12-3.LSP.

CHAPTER TEST

Write your answers in the space provided.

1. What are the advantages to using AutoLISP selection sets versus AutoCAD selection sets?

____

____

____

2. Cite at least four general rules and suggestions that apply to the use of selection sets.

____

____

____

____

____

____

3. Name five of the possible options for specifying MODE arguments when using the SSGET function. Give brief examples for each.

____

____

____

____

____

4. During a typical editing session, how many selection sets can be open at any one time? What does AutoLISP do beyond this point?

____

____

5. Detail the use of SSGET filter-lists.

____

____

____

6. How many SSGET filter-list codes are supported? Describe at least three filter-list codes, and provide examples of each.

____

____

____

____

7. What is the reason for using the CONS function to create a filter-list?

 ___

 ___

 ___

8. What AutoLISP function reports the number of items held in a selection set? Other than counting entities on a specified layer, how might a programmer use this function?

 ___

 ___

 ___

 ___

9. If a selection set contains 19 entities, the highest index the selection set can have is _____. What AutoLISP function employs this capability? Cite examples of the function.

 ___

 ___

 ___

 ___

 ___

10. Does AutoLISP consider block attributes to be main entities when forming a selection set? Why or why not?

 ___

 ___

 ___

11. If selection set Z contains only one entry, what will the AutoLISP statement (setq ABC (ssname Z 1)) return?

 ___

12. Which two AutoLISP functions allow for additions and deletions within a named selection set? Provide a brief example for each.

 ___

 ___

13. Describe the purpose and use of the AutoLISP SSMEMB function.

 ___

 ___

14. Can paper space and model space entities be combined within a selection set? What are the restrictions?

15. What is the purpose of the SSGETFIRST function?

16. Name the six possible selection method ID numbers for the SSNAMEX function and briefly describe each.

PROGRAMMING PROBLEMS

1. Occasionally, AutoCAD associated dimension entities are placed on an incorrect layer. Produce a program that forms a selection set of these items, and transfers them to a different layer. The routine will ask the user for a new layer name. Generate a variety of associated dimension entities (on differing layers) for testing. Name the file: P12-1.LSP. (Hint: "DIMENSION" is the correct entity type.)
2. Create a small rectangle measuring 1″ x 3″ using the AutoCAD LINE command. Next, place the text string "DESK" in the middle of the rectangle, with a height of 1/2″, and a rotation of 0. Finally, group these objects into an AutoCAD block named "DESK", with an insertion point at one corner of the rectangle. Randomly insert the block onto LAYER 0 at least 15 times, with scaling factors ranging from 1-5 (Scale overall size; keep X=Y=Z).
   After completing this task, design an AutoLISP program that will accomplish the following:
   A. Create a selection set that includes all drawing objects. Assign the symbol SS1 to this set.
   B. Create a selection set that includes all blocks named "DESK", with X,Y,Z scaling factors ranging from 1-3. Assign the symbol SS2 to this set.
   C. Erase all drawing objects, excluding the selection set named SS2.
   D. Make a layer called "FURNITURE", and transfer all of the blocks in SS2 to this layer.
   In addition to the inserted blocks, generate a variety of drawing entities on the graphics screen, and test the program. Name the file: P12-2.LSP.
3. Draw ten circles on a blank graphics screen, where seven of the circles have a radius of 1.0, and the remaining circles have a radius of 0.5.
   After completing this task, design an AutoLISP program that will accomplish the following:
   A. Create a selection set that includes all circles with radius values "<>" (not equal to) 1.0. Assign the symbol SS-SET1 to this set.
   B. Construct a looping environment that cycles through each individual circle within SS-SET1, and asks the user if the radius value needs to be changed. Circle highlighting will need to be used here for clarity.
   C. Use the AutoCAD CHANGE command (while in the loop) to modify the desired items. Document the file accordingly, and name it P12-3.LSP.

HAPPYBOY.LSP

```
; Filename:  HAPPYBOY.LSP
;
; Purpose:  The proper way to end your day. Demonstrates motion with
;           the AutoCAD DVIEW command. Start in a clean screen.
;
(defun C:HAPPYBOY (/ A)
  (mapcar 'setvar (list "cmdecho" "elevation" "thickness"
                        "blipmode" "ucsicon")
          (list 0 0 0 0 0)
  )
  (setq A 0)
  (command ".limits"  '(0 0) '(12 9)                    ; Drawing area
           ".zoom"    "a"
           ".circle"  '(6 4.5)   3.0                    ; Circles, Arc make face
           ".circle"  '(4.5 5.5) 0.5
           ".circle"  '(7.5 5.5) 0.5
           ".circle"  '(6.0 4.5) 0.5
           ".arc"     '(4.5 3.0) '(6.0 2.5) '(7.5 3.0)
           ".ucsicon" "off"
  )
  (command ".dview" "c" '(0 0) '(12 12) "" "ca")        ; Begin dview of face
    (repeat 30                                          ; Angle upwards by 3
      (command (setq A (+ A 3)) "–90" "ca")             ; degrees each frame
    )
  (command ^c "exit"                                    ; Cancel dview
           ".line"   '(5.5 2.5) '(5.5 1.0) ""           ; Lines, Arc make tongue
           ".line"   '(6.5 2.5) '(6.5 1.0) ""
           ".arc"    '(5.5 1.0) '(6.0 0.5) '(6.5 1.0)
           ".trim"   '(5.5 2.0) '(6.5 2.0) "" '(6.0 1.5) ""
           ".delay"  250
           ".erase"  "all"  ""
  )
  (setvar "cmdecho" 1)
  (princ)
)
; ––⟨ End of File ⟩––
```

Learning Objectives

After completing this chapter, you will be able to:

- ☐ Retrieve data from AutoCAD's entity database for any objects in a drawing.
- ☐ Modify entity data records and update the drawing.
- ☐ Access subentity definition data.
- ☐ Create new objects in a drawing without using the COMMAND function.

AUTOCAD ENTITIES

Direct manipulation of the entity database is a powerful capability for the AutoLISP programmer. This chapter discusses the fundamental concepts and techniques of working with entity definition data. Many techniques discussed in earlier chapters surface again in this chapter. This is especially true of the advanced list manipulation functions, since entity definition data retrieved by AutoLISP is provided as a list. Basic list construction methods are equally as important for handling entity data.

By mastering entity-manipulation techniques, you gain the ability to make direct alterations to the database, including additions and deletions. When the COMMAND function is used to edit or create an object, both the AutoLISP interpreter and AutoCAD's command processor must be accessed. Making these changes directly increases both the speed and efficiency of an application.

RETRIEVING ENTITY DATA

Selection set functions can be used to select entities and store the entity names for later use. Selection sets are especially useful when more than one user-specified entity must be manipulated. There are several other methods available to gain access to entities, which are discussed later in this chapter. Some of these functions require the user to select the entities, while others allow for direct searching of the entity database.

The ENTNEXT Function

The *ENTNEXT (ENTity NEXT) function* allows the programmer to extract main entity and subentity names from the database. ENTNEXT returns the name of the *next* non-deleted entity following ENAME, where ENAME is a valid entity name found within the database. The syntax for the ENTNEXT function is:

(entnext [ENAME])

If the optional ENAME argument is omitted, the name of the first non-deleted entity in the database is returned. When a next entity is not found, nil is returned. Note that the ENTNEXT function also finds entities on frozen layers.

To explore the ENTNEXT function, load AutoCAD and begin a new drawing session named CHAPT13A. Next, "walk through" the following command sequence.

Command: **(entnext)** ↵
nil — *no entities are found*

Command: **LINE** ↵
From point: **2,2** ↵
To point: **4,4** ↵
To point: ↵

Command: **LINE** ↵
From point: **2,4** ↵
To point: **4,6** ↵
To point: ↵

Command: **CIRCLE** ↵
3P/2P/TTR/⟨Center point⟩: **6,6** ↵
Diameter/⟨Radius⟩: **1** ↵
Command:

At this point, three entities exist in your drawing. AutoCAD automatically assigns each of these a unique entity name as they are entered into the database. Now, an ENTNEXT expression is used to access the entity names:

Command: **(setq E1 (entnext))** ↵
⟨Entity name: 8f0505d0⟩ — *the name of the first entity drawn*

Command: **(setq E2 (entnext E1))** ↵
⟨Entity name: 8f0505d8⟩ — *the "next" entity following E1*

```
Command: (setq E3 (entnext E2)) ↵
<Entity name: 8f0505e0>                  the "next" entity following E2

Command: (setq E4 (entnext E3)) ↵
nil                                      only three entities exist, therefore,
                                         nil is returned
```

The entity names returned may differ from those shown here depending on the release of AutoCAD you are using as well as the status of the current drawing.

As you can see, it is possible to progress through the entity database one entity at a time, starting at the beginning. Since nil is returned when no more entities are found in the database, an ENTNEXT expression can also be used as a test in a conditional loop. The following routine employs this concept and prints all of the entity names in the database to the text screen.

```
; PR-ENAME.LSP by N.T. Teenayme
;
; Date: December 12, 19xx
;
; Prints out entity names contained in database.
;
(if (setq E (entnext))                       ; IF an entity is found...
  (progn                                     ;   THEN...
    (print E)                                ;   print the entity name to screen and...
    (while (setq E (entnext E))              ;   WHILE subsequent entities are found...
      (print E)                              ;   print the entity name to screen.
    )                                        ; end WHILE
  )                                          ; end PROGN for THEN expression.
  (princ "\nNo entities found in database!") ; ELSE print this message.
)                                            ; end IF
(princ)                                      ; "Clean" exit.
```

Note the techniques used in this routine. First, a test is performed to ensure that at least one entity exists. If none exist, then a simple message is printed to the screen. If at least one entity is found, the entity name returned by ENTNEXT is printed. The WHILE expression is designed to check for an entity name following the one currently assigned to "E." Each iteration resets the variable "E" to the next entity in the database. As long as entities are found, the loop continues. When one is not found, ENTNEXT returns nil, which stops the processing of the loop.

Now load the PR-ENAME.LSP program:

```
Command: (load "PR-ENAME") ↵
<Entity name: 8f0505d0>
<Entity name: 8f0505d8>
<Entity name: 8f0505e0>
Command:
```

The names of all entities in the database are printed to screen.

Using these techniques, it is now possible to gain access to all entity names contained in the database. The next step is to acquire the data record for an entity name.

The ENTGET Function

The *ENTGET (ENTity GET) function* returns a list representing the definition record of the entity having the name ENAME. The optional APPLIST argument enables the programmer to access extended entity data. The format for the ENTGET function is:

```
(entget ENAME [APPLIST])
```

The individual fields for each of the entity's characteristics are presented as association lists, which are sublists of the overall record. The first element of each association list is the DXF group code representing a specific property of the entity. The second element of the association list is the value for that property.

Now, make sure you are in the drawing session previously described. The following example demonstrates the use of the ENTGET function:

```
Command: (entget (entnext))↵
((–1 . ⟨Entity name: 8f0505d0⟩) (0 . "LINE") (5 . "42") (100 . "AcDbEntity")
(67 . 0) (8 . "0") (100 . "AcDbLine") (10 2.0 2.0 0.0) (11 4.0 4.0 0.0) (210
0.0 0.0 1.0))
Command:
```

The name of the first non-deleted entity in the database is returned by the ENTNEXT function. The ENTGET function then returns the entity definition data list for the ENAME argument supplied to it. The following data list has been slightly reformatted for readability. The notations explain each record.

(	
(–1 . ⟨Entity name: 8f0505d0⟩)	*the field name –1 holds the entity name*
(0 . "LINE")	*the 0 field holds the object type data.*
(5 . "42")	*the 5 field holds the entity handle—(entity handles are discussed later in this chapter)*
(100 . "AcDbEntity")	*this field is a "subclass data marker."*
(67 . 0)	*space field (Model/Paper)*
(8 . "0")	*the 8 field is a layer name field.*
(100 . "AcDbLine")	*this is another "subclass data marker."*
(10 2.0 2.0 0.0)	*the 10 field holds the line's start point.*
(11 4.0 4.0 0.0)	*the 11 field holds the line's end point.*
(210 0.0 0.0 1.0)	*this field shows the extrusion direction.*
)	

Remember that the entity names returned may vary somewhat from the examples shown. In addition, the entity data itself may vary depending on the entity creation mode settings when the entity was drawn.

The list returned will vary somewhat, depending on the entity type represented. When you apply the ENTGET function to the circle, the following list is returned. To retrieve the entity data on the circle (remember the symbol E3 was assigned to the circle's entity name), enter the following expression:

Command: **(entget E3)** ↵

Once again, the list is reformatted and annotated for clarity.

(

(–1 . ⟨Entity name: 8f0505e0⟩)	*the entity name*
(0 . "CIRCLE")	*object type*
(5 . "44")	*handle*
(100 . "AcDbEntity")	*subclass data marker*
(67 . 0)	*space*
(8 . "0")	*layer*
(100 . "AcDbCircle")	*subclass data marker*
(10 6.0 6.0 0.0)	*center point*
(40 . 1.0)	*radius*
(210 0.0 0.0 1.0)	*extrusion direction*

)

Many of these associative records are common to all entity types, but others may only apply to specific entities. Certain fields, such as entity color and linetype settings, will be present only if the value is other than the standard default. If the entity has a default value of "BYLAYER" for these types of fields, entries are not included. When the values are different than the default, the field is shown. For example:

Command: **CHPROP** ↵
Select objects: **(entnext)** ↵ *entity names are valid selections*
1 found
Select objects: ↵
Change what property (Color/LAyer/LType/ltScale/Thickness) ? **C** ↵
New color ⟨BYLAYER⟩: **5** ↵
Change what property (Color/LAyer/LType/ltScale/Thickness) ? **LT** ↵
New linetype ⟨BYLAYER⟩: **CENTER** ↵
Change what property (Color/LAyer/LType/ltScale/Thickness) ? **LTS** ↵
New linetype scale ⟨1.0000⟩: **1.3125** ↵
Change what property (Color/LAyer/LType/ltScale/Thickness) ? ↵

Command: **(entget (entnext))** ↵
((–1 . ⟨Entity name: 8f0505d0⟩) (0 . "LINE") (5 . "42") (100 . "AcDbEntity")
(67 . 0) (8 . "0") **(62 . 5) (6 . "CENTER") (48 . 1.3125)** (100 . "AcDbLine") (10
2.0 2.0 0.0) (11 4.0 4.0 0.0) (210 0.0 0.0 1.0))

Note that three additional fields appear in the record. The field specification of 48 represents linetype scale, 6 is for the entity linetype, and 62 is for the entity color. It is important to remember that such variations can occur within entity records for identical entity types. A complete listing of all of the DXF group codes is given in Appendix B.

The association list returned by ENTGET allows for easy extraction of any field value stored within it through the ASSOC function. (Chapter 10 provides a complete description of the ASSOC function.) The ASSOC function is the principal method for retrieving values of individual data fields. The following simple example shows how to retrieve an entity type value using the ASSOC function:

```
(assoc 0 (entget (entnext)))          returns (0 . "LINE")
(cdr (assoc 0 (entget (entnext))))    returns "LINE"
```

SUBENTITY ACCESS

Unlike the selection set functions, ENTNEXT can also provide access to subentities. A *subentity* is one of the subordinate entities comprising a complex entity. Examples of subentities include a polyline *vertex* or a block *attribute*. To understand the processing of subentities, the structure of a complex entity's database record must be explored.

The initial entry of a polyline or a block record is for the main entity, followed by individual records for the subentities. The final entry is for a SEQEND entity. The *SEQEND (SEQuence END)* record indicates that no more subentity records are given for this entity. In the case of a polyline, the SEQEND record follows the entry for the last vertex. For block attributes, the SEQEND record follows the last attribute.

NOTE

By default, AutoCAD Release 14 uses lightweight polylines, which are described as single objects that contain no vertex subentities. To force the creation of old-format polylines, as required by the examples in this section, set the system variable PLINETYPE to 0 as follows:

Command: **PLINETYPE** ↵
New value for PLINETYPE⟨2⟩: **0** ↵

If your preference is to use lightweight polylines, be sure to set PLINETYPE back to 2 when you are finished working in this section.

For the next few examples, begin a new drawing named CHAPT13B. Then, enter the command sequences as shown below:

Command: **PLINE** ↵
From point: **0,0** ↵
Current line-width is 0.0000
Arc/Close/Halfwidth/Length/Undo/Width/⟨Endpoint of line⟩: **12,9** ↵
Arc/Close/Halfwidth/Length/Undo/Width/⟨Endpoint of line⟩: **4,8** ↵
Arc/Close/Halfwidth/Length/Undo/Width/⟨Endpoint of line⟩: **C** ↵
Command:

Since a vertex is also an entity, the entity database should now hold more than one entity record. The SSGET functions, however, only recognize and can only access *main* entities. For example:

```
Command: (sslength (ssget "x")) ↵        the number of entities in a global
1                                         selection set
Command:
```

However, there are actually five separate entity records currently in the database. By using a slightly modified version of PR-ENAME.LSP, which also utilizes the ENTGET function, each of these entries can be printed to the screen.

```
; PR-EDATA.LSP by D.B. Raycards
;
; Date:  January 13, 19xx
;
; Prints out entity data records contained in database.
;
(if (setq E (entnext))                        ; IF an entity is found...
   (progn                                     ;    THEN...
      (print                                  ;    print the...
         (entget E)                           ;    entity data record to the screen.
      )                                       ; end PRINT.
      (while (setq E (entnext E))             ; WHILE subsequent entities are found...
         (print (entget E))                   ; print the entity data record to screen.
      )                                       ; end WHILE
   )                                          ; end PROGN for THEN expression.
   (princ "\nNo entities found in database!") ; ELSE print this message.
)                                             ; end IF
(princ)                                       ; "Clean" exit.
```

Now, load PR-EDATA.LSP and examine the results:

```
Command: (load "PR-EDATA") ↵
((–1 . <Entity name: 8f0505d0>) (0 . "POLYLINE") (5 . "42") (100 .
"AcDbEntity") (67 . 0) (8 . "0") (100 . "AcDb2dPolyline") (66 . 1) (10 0.0 0.0
0.0) (70 . 1) (40 . 0.0) (41 . 0.0) (210 0.0 0.0 1.0) (71 . 0) (72 . 0) (73 .
0) (74 . 0) (75 . 0))
((–1 . <Entity name: 8f0505d8>) (0 . "VERTEX") (5 . "43") (100 . "AcDbEntity")
(67 . 0) (8 . "0") (100 . "AcDbVertex") (100 . "AcDb2dVertex") (10 0.0 0.0 0.0)
(40 . 0.0) (41 . 0.0) (42 . 0.0) (70 . 0) (50 . 0.0))
((–1 . <Entity name: 8f0505e0>) (0 . "VERTEX") (5 . "44") (100 . "AcDbEntity")
(67 . 0) (8 . "0") (100 . "AcDbVertex") (100 . "AcDb2dVertex") (10 12.0 0.0
0.0) (40 . 0.0) (41 . 0.0) (42 . 0.0) (70 . 0) (50 . 0.0))
((–1 . <Entity name: 8f0505e8>) (0 . "VERTEX") (5 . "45") (100 . "AcDbEntity")
(67 . 0) (8 . "0") (100 . "AcDbVertex") (100 . "AcDb2dVertex") (10 4.0 8.0 0.0)
(40 . 0.0) (41 . 0.0) (42 . 0.0) (70 . 0) (50 . 0.0))
((–1 . <Entity name: 8f0505f0>) (0 . "SEQEND") (5 . "46") (100 . "AcDbEntity")
(67 . 0) (8 . "0") (-2 . <Entity name: 8f0505d0>))
```

An explanation of the main entity field follows:

```
(
  (–1 . <Entity name: 8f0505d0>)      entity name
  (0 . "POLYLINE")                    object type
  (5 . "42")                          handle
  (100 . "AcDbEntity")                subclass data marker
  (67 . 0)                            space
  (8 . "0")                           layer name
  (100 . "AcDb2dPolyline")            subclass data marker
  (66 . 1)                            "Subentities follow..." flag
  (10 0.0 0.0 0.0)                    start point
  (70 . 1)                            PLINE Flags: 1=closed
  (40 . 0.0)                          starting width
  (41 . 0.0)                          ending width
  (210 0.0 0.0 1.0)                   extrusion direction
  (71 . 0)                            M-vertex count (meshes only)
  (72 . 0)                            N-vertex count (meshes only)
  (73 . 0)                            smooth surface M density (meshes
                                        only)
  (74 . 0)                            smooth surface N density (meshes
                                        only)
  (75 . 0)                            curve (or smooth surface) type
)
```

Many of the same field specifications previously shown are applicable to a vertex entity. The final entry for a complex entity is the SEQEND record. Remember, the SEQEND record signifies the end of an overall record and identifies the main entity name. The identification of the main entity is needed because of the possibility of nesting, for example, a polyline within a block entity. Now the breakdown of the SEQEND record is presented:

```
(
  (–1 . <Entity name: 8f0505f0>)      entity name
  (0 . "SEQEND")                      object type
  (5 . "46")                          handle
  (100 . "AcDbEntity")                subclass data marker
  (67 . 0)                            space
  (8 . "0")                           layer name
  (–2 . <Entity name: 8f0505d0>)      main entity name
)
```

Using basic test and conditional expressions, the programmer can access the record for each subentity. Once the main entity record is returned, a WHILE expression using ENTNEXT can be used to obtain all of the subentity names. In the following program, the SSGET function is used to select the main entity, then a WHILE loop continues finding subentity names until a SEQEND entity is encountered.

```
; SUBLST.LSP  by V.R. Jayrmun
;
; Date:  February 1, 19xx
; Lists entity names for a selected polyline entity and its subentities
```

```
;
; Assumptions: Entity selected is indeed a polyline!
;
(defun C:SUBLST (/ SS EN EL ME SN SE)          ; define function and local variables
 (princ "\nSelect a polyline: ")               ; user instructions
 (setq SS (ssget)                              ; user selection process
       EN (ssname SS 0)                        ; sets EN to first entity name (ename)
                                               ;   in SS
       EN (entnext EN)                         ; sets EN to next entity in database
       EL '()                                  ; sets EL to an empty list
 )                                             ; end SETQ
 (while                                        ; Begin WHILE...
  (/= "SEQEND"                                 ;   Test:SEQEND is not...
   (cdr                                        ;        the value in...
    (assoc 0                                   ;        field 0 of the...
     (entget EN)                               ;        entity record for EN.
    )                                          ;   end ASSOC
   )                                           ;   end CDR
  )                                            ;   end /= [end test]
  (setq EL (append EL (list EN))               ;   appends and redefines EL
        EN (entnext EN)                        ;   sets EN to subsequent ename
  )                                            ;   end SETQ
 )                                             ; End WHILE
 (setq SE EN                                   ; sets SE to ename EN
       ME (cdr (assoc -2 (entget EN)))         ; sets ME to main entity name
 )                                             ; end SETQ
 (princ "\nMain entity name: ")                ; print message
 (princ ME)                                    ; print main entity name
 (foreach SN EL                                ; for each Subentity Name in EL,
  (princ "\nSubentity name: ")                 ;   print message and
  (princ SN)                                   ;   Subentity Name
 )                                             ; end FOREACH
 (princ "\nSEQEND entity name: ")              ; print user message
 (princ SE)                                    ; print SEQEND entity name
 (princ)                                       ; quiet exit
)                                              ; end DEFUN
```

Using this program in the CHAPT13B drawing returns the following results:

```
Main entity name: <Entity name: 8f0505d0>
Subentity name: <Entity name: 8f0505d8>
Subentity name: <Entity name: 8f0505e0>
Subentity name: <Entity name: 8f0505e8>
SEQEND entity name: <Entity name: 8f0505f0>
```

Although this routine only prints the entity names to the screen, it demonstrates a very important concept. By using loops, it is possible to search through the entire entity database until any given condition or conditions are met. This could include searching for all entities possessing a specific attribute or property not covered in the SSGET "X" function.

THE ENTLAST FUNCTION

The *ENTLAST (ENTity LAST) function* simply returns the name of the last non-deleted main entity found in the database. It does not use any arguments, as shown in the following syntax.

(entlast)

In programming applications, the ENTLAST function is commonly used to access data on an entity that has just been created. Similar to the ENTNEXT function, the ENTLAST function can access entities that are placed on layers that are frozen or turned off.

In the current drawing (CHAPT13B), the ENTLAST function returns the following:

Command: **(entlast)** ↵
⟨Entity name: 8f0505d0⟩
Command:

As you can see, this represents the name of the main polyline entity. When it is necessary to access subentities of the last entity, the ENTNEXT function would also be required. Since ENTNEXT returns the name of the next entity, the following expression would return the name of the first vertex of the polyline:

Command: **(entnext (entlast))** ↵
⟨Entity name: 8f0505d8⟩

Through the use of looping techniques, all subentity names can then be found.

HANDLES AND THE HANDENT FUNCTION

In certain applications, it may be necessary to access the same entity through more than one drawing session. Entity names may change from one drawing session to the next, but an entity's *handle* remains the same for its entire life.

Handles are a convenient means to access entities across multiple drawing sessions. The *HANDENT function* returns the name of the entity (within the current drawing session) whose HANDLE is specified. The format for the HANDENT function is:

(handent HANDLE)

For example, begin a new drawing named CHAPT13C. Do the following:

Command: **LINE** ↵
From point: **2,2** ↵
To point: **4,4** ↵
To point: ↵

Command: **LIST** ↵
Select objects: **L** ↵
Select objects: ↵

In the listing provided, a handle is specified. Similar to entity names, entity handles in your drawing may vary slightly from the examples shown, depending on the prototype drawing referenced. Entities are given handles in a hexadecimal order, but the data type is actually a string. In this drawing (CHAPT13C), now do the following:

Command: **(entnext)** ↵
⟨Entity name: 8f0505d0⟩

Command: **(handent "1")** ↵
⟨Entity name: 8f0505d0⟩

In older releases of AutoCAD, handles can be disabled or destroyed. If handles are not active, or a handle that is not used in the drawing is passed to HANDENT, then nil is returned.

Let's Review...

1. The ENTNEXT function provides for direct searches of the database.
2. The ENTNEXT function returns an entity's name, and is able to find the names of both entities and subentities.
3. The data record for the supplied entity name is returned by the ENTGET function.
4. The SEQEND entity is solely for marking the end of the subentity sequence.
5. Conditional loops can be used to effectively search the entire database, or to return the names of all the subentities of a selected complex entity.
6. The ENTLAST function accesses the last entity drawn, but is only able to access main entity names.
7. The HANDENT function returns the name of the entity which has the handle specified as the supplied argument.

INTERACTIVE ENTITY SELECTIONS

Many applications require that the user select the entities for a given operation. For most of these situations, the SSGET function can be used. This approach, however, allows the user to select any number of entities and gives no information about the points that were selected.

The direct entity-selection functions permit the programmer to exercise greater control over the selection process. In addition, the coordinates of the point picked on the entity are also available.

AutoLISP has two direct entity-selection functions; one is for selecting only main entities, the other allows user selection of subentities as well.

THE ENTSEL FUNCTION

The *ENTSEL (ENTity SELect) function* permits the user to select one entity with a single pick by specifying a point coordinate. If no entity is found at the specified location, nil is returned. Otherwise, a list is returned containing two elements. The first element is the entity name and the second element is the point picked. The syntax for the ENTSEL function is:

(entsel [PROMPT])

PROMPT is an optional string argument, which allows the display of a custom prompt. If PROMPT is not supplied, the standard "Select objects:" prompt is issued.

Command: **(setq ES (entsel))** ↵
Select objects: *(select an entity)*
(⟨Entity name: 8f0505d0⟩ (4.28306 3.21572 0.0))
Command:

When the optional PROMPT argument is supplied, the ENTSEL function issues a custom prompt:

```
Command: (entsel "\nPick a line entity: ") ↵
Pick a line entity:
```

By employing simple list-manipulation functions, either of the elements in this list can be extracted. The entity name is the first element, and can be retrieved with the CAR function:

```
(car ES)            returns  〈Entity name: 8f0505d0〉
```

The selection point is returned by the CADR function:

```
(cadr ES)           returns  (4.28306 3.21572 0.0)
```

Since the ENTSEL function returns both the entity name and the point picked, the ENTSEL expression is acceptable input to any of AutoCAD's object selection prompts. This includes the TRIM and EXTEND commands, which require point selection and, therefore, reject input given by an SSGET function.

PROFESSIONAL TIP

Another useful feature of the ENTSEL function is that it allows only for the selection of a single entity. If no entity is found, then nil is returned. This makes ENTSEL usable as a test expression for a conditional loop. For example:

```
(while (null (setq ES (entsel)))       ; While ES is bound to nil,
  (princ "\nNo object found!")         ;   print this message and loop again...
(princ)
)
```

This loop makes it possible to continue to prompt the user until an entity is selected. Once the ENTSEL function returns a value other than nil, the loop is discontinued and the program can proceed. Such tactics allow many common error conditions to be effectively avoided.

THE NENTSEL FUNCTION

The *NENTSEL function* allows the user to directly select an attribute within a block or a specific vertex of a polyline. Similar to ENTSEL, an optional PROMPT argument can be supplied if desired. If an argument is not supplied, the standard "Select objects:" prompt is used. The format for the NENTSEL function is:

```
(nentsel [PROMPT])
```

For simple entities, such as lines, arcs, etc., the NENTSEL function returns the same data as ENTSEL. However, when a complex entity is selected, the NENTSEL function returns the name of the subentity selected and the coordinates of the pick point.

NENTSEL and Polylines

When NENTSEL is used to select a polyline, the returned list contains the entity name of the starting vertex of the selected polyline segment and the coordinates of the point picked. Note that the SEQEND entity name for a polyline is never returned by NENTSEL.

Open CHAPT13B if it is not already on your screen. Use the NENTSEL function to select the first segment of the polyline:

```
Command: (nentsel) ↵
Select objects: (pick the first segment)
(⟨Entity name: 8f0505d8⟩ (2.59312 1.98138 0.0))
```

Extracting the database record for the entity name returned by NENTSEL gives the following results:

```
Command: (entget (car (nentsel))) ↵
Select objects: (pick the first segment)
((–1 . ⟨Entity name: 8f0505d8⟩) (0 . "VERTEX") (8 . "0") (10 0.0 0.0 0.0) (40 .
0.0) (41 . 0.0) (42 . 0.0) (70 . 0) (50 . 0.0) (71 . 0) (72 . 0) (73 . 0) (74 .0))
```

NENTSEL does not return the name of the main polyline entity; instead, the name of the selected vertex entity is returned. When it is necessary to obtain the name of the main polyline entity, it can be found by "stepping" through the entity database using ENTNEXT until the SEQEND entity listing is found. The SEQEND entity listing contains the name of the main entity. For example:

```
(setq EN (car (nentsel "\nPick a polyline entity: ")))
  (while (/= "SEQEND" (cdr (assoc 0 (entget EN))))
  (setq EN (entnext EN))
)
```

This routine assumes that the entity selected is a polyline and provides no error checking. However, when a polyline is selected, the entity name of the SEQEND is returned:

```
⟨Entity name: 8f0505f0⟩
```

Now use ENTGET to return the entity data record:

```
(entget EN)
```

...returns...

```
((–1 . ⟨Entity name: 8f0505f0⟩) (0 . "SEQEND") (8 . "0") (–2 . ⟨Entity name: 8f0505d0⟩))
```

Note the –2 field entry. This denotes the name of the main polyline entity for this SEQEND. Using the CDR and ASSOC functions allows the extraction of this name:

```
(cdr (assoc –2 (entget EN)))    returns ⟨Entity name: 8f0505d0⟩
```

Now the main entity data records may be accessed as needed.

NENTSEL and Blocks

Attributes, like vertices, are actually subentities and cannot be found with the SSGET functions or by ENTSEL. The NENTSEL function allows the user to directly select and find any attribute subentity within a block entity.

To further explore this function, begin a new drawing named CHAPT13D. Then follow these command sequences.

Command: **CIRCLE** ↵
3P/2P/TTR/⟨Center point: **4,4** ↵
Diameter/⟨Radius⟩: **.5** ↵

Command: **ATTDEF** ↵
Attribute Modes – Invisible:N Constant:N Verify:N Preset:N
Enter (ICVP) to change, RETURN when done: ↵
Attribute tag: **TAG** ↵
Attribute prompt: **Prompt?** ↵
Default attribute value: **DEFAULT** ↵
Justify/Style/⟨Start point⟩: **4,4** ↵
Height ⟨0.2000⟩: **.125** ↵
Rotation angle ⟨current⟩: **0** ↵

Command: **BLOCK** ↵
Block name (or ?): **CIR** ↵
Insertion base point: **4,4** ↵
Select objects: **W** ↵
First corner: **2,2** ↵
Other corner: **6,6** ↵
2 found
Select objects: ↵

Command: **VPOINT** ↵
Rotate/⟨view point⟩⟨0.0000,0.0000,1.0000⟩: **2.5,2.5,–1.0** ↵
Regenerating drawing.

Command: **UCS** ↵
Origin/ZAxis/3point/Entity/View/X/Y/Z/Prev/Restore/Save/Del/?/⟨World⟩: **V** ↵

Command: **INSERT** ↵
Block name (or ?): **CIR** ↵
Insertion point: **4,4** ↵
X scale factor ⟨1⟩ / Corner / XYZ: **1** ↵
Y scale factor (default=X): **1** ↵
Rotation angle: **0** ↵
Prompt? ⟨DEFAULT⟩: ↵

Command: **ZOOM** ↵
All/Center/Dynamic/Extents/Previous/Scale(X/XP)/Window/⟨Realtime⟩: **E** ↵
Regenerating drawing.

When NENTSEL is used to select a block, it returns varying information, depending on what part of the block is selected. If an attribute is picked, the returned list consists only of the subentity name and the coordinates of the pick point:

Command: **(nentsel)** ↵
Select objects: *(pick the attribute)*
(⟨Entity name: 8f030610⟩ (4.73481 4.05054 0.0))

Using the ENTGET function on this entity name returns the attribute's entity record:

Command: **(entget (car (nentsel)))** ↵
Select objects: *(pick the attribute)*
((–1 . ⟨Entity name: 8f030610⟩) (0 . "ATTRIB") (5 . "4A") (100 . "AcDbEntity") (67 . 0)
(8 . "0") (100 . "AcDbText") (10 4.0 4.0 2.22045e–016) (40 . 0.125) (1 . "DEFAULT") (50 . 0.0)
(41 . 1.0) (51 . 0.0) (7 . "STANDARD") (71 . 0) (72 . 0) (210 0.680414 0.680414
–0.272166) (100 . "AcDbAttribute") (2 . "TAG") (70 . 0) (73 . 0) (74 . 0))

The data returned by NENTSEL is very different when a component (other than an attribute) of a block is selected:

Command: **(nentsel)** ↵
Select objects: *(pick the circle)*
((⟨Entity name: 8f0305f8⟩ (4.27151 4.41683 0.0) ((–0.707107 0.707107 0.0) (0.19245
0.19245 0.96225) (0.680414 0.680414 –0.272166) (2.05863 3.59823 3.849)) ((⟨Entity
name: 8f030608⟩))

The list returned has four separate elements. The first two elements are the subentity's name and the coordinates of the pick point. The third element is a list containing four sublists, known as the *Model to World Transformation Matrix.* The last item is a list including the entity name of the block containing the selected entity. If the item selected is a component of a nested block, the list will also contain the entity name of each block in which the entity is nested. This list begins with the most deeply nested block and works its way outward. The final entity name refers to the main entity, which was inserted into the drawing. Here is a descriptive breakdown of the entire list that was previously returned.

((⟨Entity name: 8f0305f8⟩	*name of selected entity*
(4.27151 4.41683 0.0)	*coordinates of the pick point*
((–0.707107 0.707107 0.0) (0.19245 0.19245 0.96225) (0.680414 0.680414 –0.272166) (–2.05863 3.59823 3.849))	*Model to World Transformation Matrix*
((⟨Entity name: 8f030608⟩))	*entity name of block containing the selected subentity*

In a nested block, the final element of this list would be a list of the names of each block within which the selected subentity is nested:

((⟨Entity name: 8f030630⟩	*name of the most deeply nested block*
⟨Entity name: 8f030670⟩... ⟨Entity name: 8f0306c0⟩	
⟨Entity name: 8f0306d0⟩)	*name of top level block (main entity)*

Since the first element of the list returned by NENTSEL is the name of the selected entity, the entity record can be obtained in the same manner as before:

Command: **(entget (car (nentsel)))** ↵
Select objects: *(pick the circle)*

```
((-1 . <Entity name: 8f0305f8>) (0 . "CIRCLE") (5 . "47") (100 . "AcDbEntity") (67 . 0)
(8 . "0") (100 . "AcDbCircle") (10 0.0 0.0 0.0) (40 . 0.5) (210 0.0 0.0 1.0))
```

The entity name of a block component (other than attributes) is the same in each occurrence of the block. This is because the entity database references the same component record for each occurrence of the same block definition. The main entity data, such as insertion point, scale factors, and rotation angle, is then applied to the block description for displaying each occurrence within the drawing.

Model to World Transformation Matrix

The third element of a list returned by the NENTSEL function provides the necessary data for the transformation of entity definition data points from the internal coordinate system called the Model Coordinate System (MCS) to the World Coordinate System (WCS).

As presented by the NENTSEL function, the transformation matrix references are as follows:

```
(
  (X0 Y0 Z0)
  (X1 Y1 Z1)
  (X2 Y2 Z2)
  (X3 Y3 Z3)
)
```

Using this matrix, it is possible to transform entity definition data points from the MCS to the WCS. Note that this is a 4x3 matrix passed as an array of four points. By extracting the third element from the list returned by NENTSEL, the values for this matrix can be established:

```
Command: (setq MATRIX (caddr (nentsel))) ↵
Select objects: (pick the circle)
( (–0.707107 0.707107 0.0) (0.19245 0.19245 0.96225) (0.680414 0.680414 –0.272166)
(–2.05863 3.59823 3.849) )
```

Here is the same data presented in a more readable format:

```
(
  (–0.707107 0.707107 0.0)
  (0.19245 0.19245 0.96225)
  (0.680414 0.680414 –0.272166)
  (–2.05863 3.59823 3.849)
)
```

The ASSOC function can be used to return any entity data points. In Fig. 13-1, ASSOC is used to extract the center point of the circle. Note that the MCS establishes its origin at the insertion point of the block it references. Since the insertion point of the CIR block is the center point, that point's coordinate listing is (0.0 0.0 0.0). Now that all of the necessary data has been obtained, solve for the following equation using these values:

```
XWCS = (+ (* X1 XMCS) (* X2 YMCS) (* X3 ZMCS) X4)
YWCS = (+ (* Y1 XMCS) (* Y2 YMCS) (* Y3 ZMCS) Y4)
ZWCS = (+ (* Z1 XMCS) (* Z2 YMCS) (* Z3 ZMCS) Z4)
```

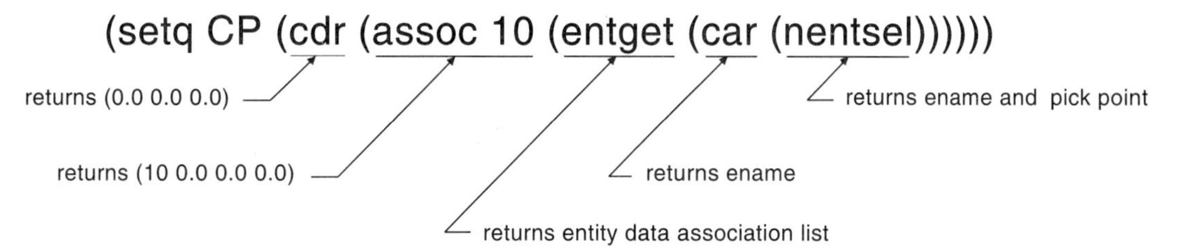

Fig. 13-1. Using the ASSOC function to return entity data points.

Given the previous variable settings, an expression solving for the value of the WCS X coordinate appears as follows:

```
(setq WX
  (+
    (* (car (nth 0 MATRIX)) (car CP))
    (* (car (nth 1 MATRIX)) (cadr CP))
    (* (car (nth 2 MATRIX)) (caddr CP))
    (car (nth 3 MATRIX))
  )
)
```

To find the WCS Y or Z coordinate of this point, the same basic expression can be used. A simple substitution of the second and third elements (respectively) of the MATRIX sublists gives the desired results:

```
(setq WY
  (+
    (* (cadr (nth 0 MATRIX)) (car CP))
    (* (cadr (nth 1 MATRIX)) (cadr CP))
    (* (cadr (nth 2 MATRIX)) (caddr CP))
    (cadr (nth 3 MATRIX))
  )
)

(setq WZ
  (+
    (* (caddr (nth 0 MATRIX)) (car CP))
    (* (caddr (nth 1 MATRIX)) (cadr CP))
    (* (caddr (nth 2 MATRIX)) (caddr CP))
    (caddr (nth 3 MATRIX))
  )
)
```

By applying these equations and storing the results in a list, the following point coordinates are derived:

```
Command: (setq W–XYZ (list WX WY WZ)) ↵
(–2.05863 3.59823 3.849)
```

This can be verified by making the WCS active, and using the ID command. Specify the center point of the circle at the prompt, and the same coordinates are displayed.

THE NENTSELP FUNCTION

Similar to NENTSEL, the NENTSELP function provides access to entity definition data contained within a block. However, NENTSELP provides additional options and features. The format for this function is:

```
(nentselp [PROMPT] [PT])
```

This function issues the standard "Select objects: " prompt, or the optional PROMPT argument can be used:

Command: **(nentselp "\nPick a subentity: ")** ↵
Pick a subentity:

If no entity is picked, the NENTSELP expression returns nil. To ensure that an entity has been selected, placing the NENTSELP expression within a loop will help to prevent an error situation.

```
(while (null (setq NSP (nentselp "\nPick a subentity: ")))
  (princ "\nYou missed!")
)
```

The second optional argument allows specification of a point coordinate, which allows entity selection without user input.

Command: **(nentselp '(0 0))** ↵
nil *no entity was found at 0,0*

The list returned by NENTSELP differs somewhat from the list returned by NENTSEL. The entity name information is composed just like NENTSEL, but a 4x4 transformation matrix is returned.

Command: **(NENTSELP "\nPick an entity: ")** ↵
Select object: *(pick the desired entity)*
(⟨Entity name: 8f0305f8⟩ (3.53554 4.1817 0.0) ((–0.707107 0.19245 0.680414 –2.05863) (0.707107 0.19245 0.680414 3.59823) (0.0 0.96225 –0.272166 3.849) (0.0 0.0 0.0 1.0)) (⟨Entity name: 8f030608⟩))

The transformation matrix is isolated below and reformatted for clarity:

```
(
  (–0.707107 0.19245 0.680414 –2.05863)
  (0.707107 0.19245 0.680414 3.59823)
  (0.0 0.96225 –0.272166 3.849)
  (0.0 0.0 0.0 1.0)
)
```

Since this matrix differs from the one returned by NENTSEL, the equation used to transform a point is also different:

```
XWCS = (+ (* X1 XMCS) (* Y1 YMCS) (* Z1 ZMCS) )
YWCS = (+ (* X2 XMCS) (* Y2 YMCS) (* Z2 ZMCS) )
XWCS = (+ (* X3 XMCS) (* Y3 YMCS) (* Z3 ZMCS) )
```

Using the same sequence of developing the CIR block as described earlier in the section on NENTSEL, the center point "CP" could be derived as follows:

```
(setq WX
  (+
    (* (car (nth 0 MATRIX)) (car CP))
    (* (cadr (nth 0 MATRIX)) (cadr CP))
    (* (caddr (nth 0 MATRIX)) (caddr CP))
    (cadddr (nth 0 MATRIX))
  )
)

(setq WY
  (+
    (* (car (nth 1 MATRIX)) (car CP))
    (* (cadr (nth 1 MATRIX)) (cadr CP))
    (* (caddr (nth 1 MATRIX)) (caddr CP))
    (cadddr (nth 1 MATRIX))
  )
)

(setq WZ
  (+
    (* (car (nth 2 MATRIX)) (car CP))
    (* (cadr (nth 2 MATRIX)) (cadr CP))
    (* (caddr (nth 2 MATRIX)) (caddr CP))
    (cadddr (nth 2 MATRIX))
  )
)
```

It can be difficult to enter this much code directly at the Command: prompt, due to the high possibility of typographical errors. The following example is used only to illustrate the step-by-step sequence utilizing the transformation matrix:

Command: **(setq WX (+ (* (car (nth 0 matrix))(car CP))(* (cadr (nth 0 matrix))(cadr cp))(* (caddr (nth 0 matrix))(caddr cp))(cadddr (nth 0 matrix))))**↵
–2.05863

Command: **(setq WY (+ (* (car (nth 1 matrix))(car CP))(* (cadr (nth 1 matrix))(cadr cp))(* (caddr (nth 1 matrix))(caddr cp))(cadddr (nth 1 matrix))))**↵
3.59823

Command: **(setq WZ (+ (* (car (nth 2 matrix))(car CP))(* (cadr (nth 2 matrix))(cadr cp))(* (caddr (nth 2 matrix))(caddr cp))(cadddr (nth 2 matrix))))**↵
3.849

Command: **(setq W-XYZ (list WX WY WZ))**↵
(–2.05863 3.59823 3.849)

The accuracy of the transformation can be easily verified:

Command: **UCS↵**
Origin/ZAxis/3point/OBject/View/X/Y/Z/Prev/Restore/Save/Del/?/⟨World⟩: **W↵**
Command: **PLAN↵**
⟨Current UCS⟩/Ucs/World: Regenerating drawing.

Command: **ID↵**
Point: **CEN↵**
of *(select the circle)*
X = –2.0586 Y = 3.5982 Z = 3.8490

The NENTSEL and NENTSELP functions both provide the same capabilities. The important difference is that NENTSELP returns a 4x4 transformation matrix similar to those used by other AutoLISP and ADS functions. The 4x3 matrix returned by NENTSEL is passed as an array of four points, using the convention that a point is a row rather than a column.

MODIFYING ENTITY DATA RECORDS

Direct editing of AutoCAD entities by modifying their database records can be both faster and more efficient than working through the COMMAND function. Greater versatility is also possible by making several modifications simultaneously.

The entity record is presented as a list, and can be manipulated using standard list-handling functions. Some of the key functions have been introduced in earlier chapters, and additional functions are discussed in the following section.

EDITING FIELD VALUES

It is possible to directly manipulate the entity database using AutoLISP functions. While these methods may or may not be the best answer to any given situation, they do provide the programmer with some exceptionally powerful editing tools.

When AutoCAD is thought of as a database program with a graphic user interface, AutoLISP then becomes an even greater productivity tool. The aspect of making direct entries, changes, and deletions of database records greatly increases the potential scope of AutoLISP program applications.

THE SUBST FUNCTION

Rather than create an entirely new listing for an entity record that is to be edited, a new value can simply be substituted for an existing value within the record. The *SUBST (SUBSTitute) function* is used to make substitutions within a list. The syntax for SUBST is:

```
(subst NEWitem OLDitem LIST)
```

Every occurrence of OLDitem within LIST is replaced with NEWitem and the resulting list is returned. If LIST does not contain any OLDitems, the original LIST is returned. The SUBST function may be used with any type of list, but is particularly valuable for altering entity data records.

The first example shows the results of using the SUBST function on a simple data storage list:

```
(setq DLST '(A 1 3 "OK" 3 B 1))

(subst 2 1 DLST)              returns  (A 2 3 "OK" 3 B 2)
(subst 6 'A DLST)             returns  (6 1 3 "OK" 3 B 1)
(subst "XYZ" "OK" DLST)       returns  (A 1 3 "XYZ" 3 B 1)
(subst "STOP" "GO" DLST)      returns  (A 1 3 "OK" 3 B 1)      "GO" was not found
```

Next, review the following examples, which illustrate how the SUBST function is used on an association list. The list being used is the record of a line drawn as the first entity in a drawing.

```
Command: (setq EL (entget (entnext)))↵
((–1 . <Entity name: 8f0305d0>) (0 . "LINE") (5 . "42") (100 . "AcDbEntity")
(67 . 0) (8 . "0") (100 . "AcDbLine") (10 2.0 2.0 0.0) (11 4.0 4.0 0.0) (210
0.0 0.0 1.0))
```

To create an alternate entity record, simply substitute the new value for the old value:

```
Command: (setq EL (subst '(8 . "NEWLAYER") '(8 . "0") EL))↵
((–1 . <Entity name: 8f0305d0>) (0 . "LINE") (5 . "42") (100 . "AcDbEntity")
(67 . 0) (8 . "NEWLAYER") (100 . "AcDbLine") (10 2.0 2.0 0.0) (11 4.0 4.0 0.0)
(210 0.0 0.0 1.0))
```

This is the first step of entity modification using AutoLISP. The entity itself has not yet been modified, but the new entity data record has been assigned to the variable EL for use with the ENTMOD function.

THE ENTMOD FUNCTION

Next, the entity record must be physically changed within the database. The *ENTMOD (ENTity MODify) function* must be used to actually alter the record in the drawing database. The format for ENTMOD is as follows:

```
(entmod ELIST)
```

The ENTMOD function requires an entity data list (ELIST) as an argument. It then uses this list as the new database record for the entity whose name is found in the –1 DXF group code record in ELIST.

After using the SUBST function to create a new entity-defining list (EL from the previous example), the ENTMOD function must be used to activate the changes:

```
Command: (entmod EL)↵
((–1 . <Entity name: 8f0305d0>) (0 . "LINE") (5 . "42") (100 . "AcDbEntity")
(67 . 0) (8 . "NEWLAYER") (100 . "AcDbLine") (10 2.0 2.0 0.0) (11 4.0 4.0 0.0)
(210 0.0 0.0 1.0))
```

ENTMOD returns a list representing the modified data record. If the modification was not successful, nil is returned. An unsuccessful modification effort can be attributed to either supplying an unusable value to a field or attempting to change something that AutoLISP cannot modify. The limitations of ENTMOD include the following:

- You cannot change an entity name record (DXF group code –1 or –2).
- You cannot change an entity type record (group code 0).
- You cannot change an entity handle record (group code 5).
- You cannot modify a viewport entity.
- You cannot use any linetypes, shapes, text styles, or block references not already defined in the current drawing session.

One exception to the last limitation deals with layer names. If a non-existent layer name is specified in a list used by the ENTMOD function, that layer name is created using the default settings of color–WHITE and linetype–CONTINUOUS.

NOTE

Note that if ENTMOD is used to modify entities within a block definition, *all* instances of that block in the current drawing will be affected. Another potential problem that can be encountered when modifying the entities in a block definition is creating a self-referencing block. If such a block is inadvertently created, it can cause AutoCAD to crash.

When supplying the ELIST argument for ENTMOD, it is important to ensure that the proper data types are given for fields requiring string or numeric values. One common mistake involves specifying layer names, such as layer 0, as integers. However, layer names are all string values. All numeric fields accept either real numbers or integers; the numerical value is simply converted to the required data type. Note that when a real number is given for a field that uses integers, such as color, the supplied value is truncated–not rounded.

EXERCISE 13-1

- ☐ Begin a new drawing. Draw a line from coordinate 2,2 to 4,4.
- ☐ Use the SUBST and ENTMOD functions to change the start point of the line (group code 10) to coordinate 2,4.

When working with subentities of complex entities, the ENTMOD function does not cause an update of the entity on the screen. This allows the user to modify several vertices or attributes without having to wait for the screen image to be updated each time a change is made. This can be especially useful when modifying several vertices in one operation. Once the required modifications have been completed, the image is then updated using the ENTUPD function.

THE ENTUPD FUNCTION

The *ENTUPD (ENTity UPDate) function* regenerates the complex entity whose name is ENAME. The syntax for the ENTUPD function is:

```
(entupd ENAME)
```

When modifications are made to a polyline vertex entity, ENTMOD is first used to enter the changes into the database file. This leaves an image on the screen which does not yet represent the new data record. The modifications to the image will only be shown after a regeneration. The entire drawing can be regenerated using (command "REGEN"), but this may take too long. A time-saving option is to use ENTUPD to regenerate only the named entity. Note that ENTUPD will regenerate any entity type, but it is primarily intended for polylines and blocks.

The ENAME argument can be the name of the main entity *or* the name of a subentity. If ENAME is the name of a subentity, the head of the entity will be found and regenerated. In cases where the entity is nested in a block, the REGEN command *must* be used to ensure that the entire block and all of its nested entities have been regenerated.

Begin a new drawing named CHAPT13E for the following example. Next, draw a polyline from coordinate 2,2 to 4,2 to 4,4 to 2,4, and then close it. Now, find the name of the first vertex entity of the polyline using the ENTNEXT function:

Command: **(setq EN1 (entnext))** ↵ *the polyline main entity name*
⟨Entity name: 8f0305d0⟩

If you wish to verify that this is the polyline main entity name, use the ENTGET function as follows:

Command: **(entget EN1)** ↵
((–1 . ⟨Entity name: 8f0305d0⟩) (0 . "POLYLINE") (5 . "42") (100 . "AcDbEntity") (67 . 0) (8 . "0") (100 . "AcDb2dPolyline") (66 . 1) (10 0.0 0.0 0.0) (70 . 1) (40 . 0.0) (41 . 0.0) (210 0.0 0.0 1.0) (71 . 0) (72 . 0) (73 . 0) (74 . 0) (75 . 0))

The individual vertex records follow the main entity listing. The next entity encountered in the database is the name of the first vertex in the polyline:

Command: **(setq en2 (entnext EN1))** ↵ *the first vertex name*
⟨Entity name: 8f0305d8⟩

In order to change an entity data record, it must first be retrieved:

Command: **(setq EG2 (entget EN2))**↵
((–1 . ⟨Entity name: 8f0305d8⟩) (0 . "VERTEX") (5 . "43") (100 . "AcDbEntity") (67 . 0) (8 . "0") (100 . "AcDbVertex") (100 . "AcDb2dVertex") (10 2.0 2.0 0.0) (40 . 0.0) (41 . 0.0) (42 . 0.0) (70 . 0) (50 . 0.0))

Now use the SUBST function to change the record of the vertex location:

Command: **(setq EG2 (subst '(10 1.0 1.0 0.0) (assoc 10 EG2) EG2))**↵
((–1 . ⟨Entity name: 8f0305d8⟩) (0 . "VERTEX") (5 . "43") (100 . "AcDbEntity") (67 . 0) (8 . "0") (100 . "AcDbVertex") (100 . "AcDb2dVertex") (10 1.0 1.0 0.0) (40 . 0.0) (41 . 0.0) (42 . 0.0) (70 . 0) (50 . 0.0))

The ENTMOD function updates the entity database and vertex location:

Command: **(entmod EG2)**↵
((–1 . ⟨Entity name: 8f0305d8⟩) (0 . "VERTEX") (5 . "43") (100 . "AcDbEntity") (67 . 0) (8 . "0") (100 . "AcDbVertex") (100 . "AcDb2dVertex") (10 1.0 1.0 0.0) (40 . 0.0) (41 . 0.0) (42 . 0.0) (70 . 0) (50 . 0.0))

Note that the screen image has changed. The polyline segment containing the changed vertex is no longer displayed. This is where the ENTUPD function must be used:

Command: **(entupd EN2)** ↵
⟨Entity name: 8f0305d8⟩

The entity name is returned, and the screen image is regenerated and now reflects the previously made changes.

Let's Review...

1. The ENTSEL function returns a list with two elements–the entity name and the coordinates of the pick point. The basic expression that returns the name of a user-selected entity is:

   (car (entsel))

   An optional prompt can be supplied as an argument to ENTSEL.
2. The NENTSEL function allows the user to directly select a subentity such as a vertex of a polyline, a block attribute, or even a block component. When NENTSEL is used on a simple entity, it acts like the ENTSEL function.
3. The SUBST function can be used to alter the data within an entity-definition list.
4. Once a new entity-definition list has been generated, the ENTMOD function must be used to enter the changes into the database file and update the screen image.
5. The ENTUPD function regenerates a single entity in a drawing. Even though the ENTMOD function makes the changes to the entity database, changes to any subentity data will not be reflected on the screen until the ENTUPD function is used.

SAMPLE PROGRAM

This sample program is intended to show useful applications for entity-manipulation functions discussed in this chapter, as well as demonstrate some of the basic techniques associated with these operations.

This example changes any number of entities to the same layer as any existing entity selected by the user. First, the user specifies a selection set and subsequently picks an entity already on the target layer:

```
; CHL.LSP – Change Layer – by Chan Jalayer
; Date: December 21, 19xx
; Allows user to specify target layer by picking an entity residing on it.
(defun C:CHL (/ SS1 ENAM EGET EN EG COUNT)
  (princ "\nChange Layer...\nSelect entities to change: ")  ; message/prompt
  (setq SS1 (ssget))                        ; assign selected entities to SS1
  (while
    (null (setq ENAM (car (entsel "\nPick an entity on the target layer: "))))
    (princ "\nYou missed.")                 ; Error checking ensures that an entity is selected
  )                                         ; end WHILE
  (setq EGET (entget ENAM))                 ; assign entity data list to EGET
  (setq COUNT 0)                            ; sets counter to 0 to start with first entity in SS1
  (repeat (sslength SS1)                    ; do once for each entity found in SS1
    (setq EN (ssname SS1 COUNT)             ; sets EN to entity name indicated by COUNTER
          EG (entget EN)                    ; sets EG to entity data list
          EG (subst (assoc 8 EGET)          ; substitute target layer record found in EGET
```

```
                    (assoc 8 EG)         ; for existing layer record found in EG
                              EG         ; in the list EG
               )                         ; end SUBST
               COUNT (1+ COUNT)          ; then add one to counter
        )                                ; end SETQ
        (entmod EG)                      ; modify data record!
      )                                  ; end REPEAT
    )                                    ; end DEFUN
```

EXERCISE 13-2

☐ Design a program that allows the user to change the location of a circle by selecting a new center point. Name the file CHCIR.LSP.

ENTITY CREATION

In Release 10 and prior releases of AutoCAD, the only means provided to create entities was the COMMAND function. The ENTMAKE function, incorporated into Release 11 and later releases, allows AutoLISP to make direct entries into the drawing database.

The ENTMAKE Function

The *ENTMAKE (ENTity MAKE) function* allows the programmer to make a direct entry into the drawing database. The ELIST argument is a list containing the entity-definition data needed to completely describe the new entity. The format for the ENTMAKE function is:

```
(entmake [ELIST])
```

The ENTMAKE function will not accept an argument that is incorrect or missing a required data field. In addition, ENTMAKE requires that either the first or second field in ELIST be the entity type field specification (DXF group code 0). The remaining entries are accepted without regard to the order of presentation.

When using the ENTMAKE function in a program, it is recommended that you first obtain a sample data list for an existing entity of the same type as an example. In the following example, the data record for a line has been extracted from the entity database:

```
Command: (entget (entlast))↵
((–1 . <Entity name: 8f0305d0>) (0 . "LINE") (5 . "42") (100 . "AcDbEntity")
(67 . 0) (8 . "0") (100 . "AcDbLine") (10 2.0 2.0 0.0) (11 4.0 4.0 0.0) (210
0.0 0.0 1.0))
```

This data record is representative of a line on layer 0, which is drawn from coordinate 2,2 to 4,4. This record shows all of the fields maintained in the entity record by AutoCAD. Some fields, such as layer, dimstyle, text style names, etc., are considered optional. When optional fields are omitted, default values are used. Here are some common defaults:

Layer name: *CURRENT* LAYER
Dimstyle name: *UNNAMED
Text style name: STANDARD
Extrusion Direction: 0,0,1
Point coordinate Z value: 0

The entity name is assigned by AutoCAD as it is created, and cannot be specified by the programmer. The extrusion direction and layer name will accept default values if they are not specified. Therefore, there are only three fields required by the ENTMAKE function to make a simple line entity as shown in the following example.

The following expression creates a line from coordinates 4,4 to 5,6:

```
(entmake
  '(
    (0 . "LINE")
    (10 4 4)
    (11 5 6)
  )
)
```

Now, retrieving the entity data for the last entity created yields these results:

```
Command: (entget (entlast))↵
((–1 . ⟨Entity name: 8f0305d8⟩) (0 . "LINE") (5 . "43") (100 . "AcDbEntity") (67 . 0) (8 . "0")
(100 . "AcDbLine") (10 4.0 4.0 0.0) (11 5.0 6.0 0.0) (210 0.0 0.0 1.0))
```

Note that the optional entity data has been filled in with the default values. Therefore, unless it is desired to use the default values, these optional fields must also be supplied. Also, similar to ENTMOD, when integer values are supplied where a real number is expected, they are automatically promoted. Notice that since Z-axis values were not supplied, the default of zero in the WCS was used. The WCS was the default since no extrusion direction field was supplied (group code 210). These are important points to remember, especially when working within a 3-D environment.

An alternate means of supplying the entity data is to use the record of an existing entity, and substitute the values to be changed. In the following example, the record from the previously created entity is used to create another line:

```
(setq EG (entget (entlast))                    Assigns the entity record to EG...
      EG (subst (cons 10 '(9 7))               ...SUBSTitutes 9,7 for the existing
                (assoc 10 EG)                    start point in the list EG...
                EG
         )                                     Close SUBST...
      EG (subst (cons 11 '(6 6))               ...the coordinates 6,6 is
                (assoc 11 EG)                    SUBSTituted for the existing
                EG                               end point in the list EG.
         )                                     ...close SUBST...
)                                              ...close SETQ...
(entmake EG)                                   ...makes a new line from 9,7,0 to
                                                 6,6,0.
```

While this example might seem like a little more work for a simple line than by specifying the data fields, it can be an effective time-saver when creating complex entities such as polylines or meshes.

For polyline entities, the ENTMAKE function becomes a bit more involved. The programmer is required to define the main entity record first. At this time, a temporary file is opened for storage of the supplied data until the entity definition is complete. Note that the DXF group code 66, which indicates that entities follow, is forced to a value of 1 for a polyline main entity definition. The only allowable entity record to follow this listing is one for a vertex entity. Attempting to enter any other entity type results in an "Out of Context Entity" error.

As each subsequent entity record is entered, it is stored in the temporary file, but nothing is displayed. The following example demonstrates the creation of a polyline entity:

```
(entmake
  '( (0 . "POLYLINE") )
)
(entmake
  '( (0 . "VERTEX") (10 2 2 0) )
)
(entmake
  '( (0 . "VERTEX") (10 4 2 0) )
)
(entmake
  '( (0 . "SEQEND") )
)
```

Once the SEQEND entity is specified, AutoLISP knows that the ENTMAKE sequence has ended, and it then enters the record into the database, thereby causing the entity to be drawn. The resultant entity for this sequence is a single polyline segment from the coordinate location 2,2,0 to 4,2,0.

Since the ENTMAKE arguments contained only the minimum information required to create the polyline, many other fields accepted default values. To see each of these fields, enter the following expression:

Command: **(setq EN (entlast))** ↵
Command: **(while EN (print (entget EN))(setq EN (entnext EN)))** ↵

The results below show the *optional* fields in bold print:

((–1 . ⟨Entity name: 8f0305e8⟩) (0 . "POLYLINE") **(5 . "45") (100 . "AcDbEntity") (67 . 0) (8 . "0") (100 . "AcDb2dPolyline") (66 . 1) (10 0.0 0.0 0.0) (70 . 0) (40 . 0.0) (41 . 0.0) (210 0.0 0.0 1.0) (71 . 0) (72 . 0) (73 . 0) (74 . 0) (75 . 0))**
((–1 . ⟨Entity name: 8f0305f0⟩) (0 . "VERTEX") **(5 . "46") (100 . "AcDbEntity") (67 . 0) (8 . "0") (100 . "AcDbVertex") (100 . "AcDb2dVertex")** (10 2.0 2.0 0.0) **(40 . 0.0) (41 . 0.0) (42 . 0.0) (70 . 0) (50 . 0.0))**
((–1 . ⟨Entity name: 8f0305f8⟩) (0 . "VERTEX") **(5 . "47") (100 . "AcDbEntity") (67 . 0) (8 . "0") (100 . "AcDbVertex") (100 . "AcDb2dVertex")** (10 4.0 2.0 0.0) **(40 . 0.0) (41 . 0.0) (42 . 0.0) (70 . 0) (50 . 0.0))**
((–1 . ⟨Entity name: 8f030600⟩) (0 . "SEQEND") **(5 . "48") (100 . "AcDbEntity") (67 . 0) (8 . "0") (-2 . ⟨Entity name: 8f0305e8⟩))**
nil

In many cases, the default values are the ones that are needed. However, remember if any other value is required, it *must* be specified.

If it is desired to discontinue the creation of a complex entity and close the temporary file, ENTMAKE is used with no arguments:

```
(ENTMAKE)          returns nil
```

Blocks can also be created using the ENTMAKE function. This differs greatly from creating a block reference–which is an *INSERT* entity, not a BLOCK entity. A block is created by first specifying the block entity itself, then each of the component entities, and finally an *ENDBLK entity.* The following sequence creates a block named SQR which is defined as a polyline with four vertices that represents a two-unit square:

```
(entmake '( (0 . "BLOCK") (2 . "SQR") (70 . 64) (10 0 0 0)))
(entmake '( (0 . "POLYLINE") (70 . 1)))
(entmake '( (0 . "VERTEX") (10 0 0 0)))
(entmake '( (0 . "VERTEX") (10 2 0 0)))
(entmake '( (0 . "VERTEX") (10 2 2 0)))
(entmake '( (0 . "VERTEX") (10 0 2 0)))
(entmake '( (0 . "SEQEND")))
(entmake '( (0 . "ENDBLK")))
```

The *Block type flag* (group code 70) must be supplied whenever a block is to be created. For a user block, the value is 64. This bit value indicates that the block is referenced. Even though the block has just been created and is not yet referenced, this value is still used.

Now, to create an instance of the SQR block within the drawing, it is necessary to ENTMAKE an *INSERT* entity:

```
(entmake '((0 . "INSERT") (2 . "SQR") (10 2 2 0)))
```

A block reference now exists at 2,2,0 which has the default insertion factors of 1,1,1 and a rotation of 0.

Be careful when defining user blocks because it is possible to accidentally redefine an existing block if the appropriate checks are not performed. After defining the previous block in the same drawing, enter the following:

```
Command: (entmake '((0 . "BLOCK") (2 . "SQR") (70 . 66) (10 0.0 0.0 0.0))) ↵
Command: (entmake '((0 . "CIRCLE") (10 0 0 0) (40 . 0.5))) ↵
Command: (entmake '((0 . "ENDBLK"))) ↵
```

No change is yet evident. Enter "REGEN" at the Command: prompt and observe the effect. The insertion of the SQR block at 2,2 is now represented as a circle!

The DIMENSION entity is even more complex. Each of the component entities must be defined. If the dimension is associative, the component entity must be defined within a block definition. Such an entity is defined as an *anonymous (unnamed) block* by setting the Block type flag (group code 70) to 1. After creating the block which it references, the dimension entity itself is then defined.

Here, the anonymous block definition is created:

```
Command: (entmake '((0 . "BLOCK") (2 . "*Uxx")(70 . 1) (10 0.0 0.0 0.0))) ↵
Command: (entmake '((0 . "LINE")(10 0 0.0625 0) (11 0 2 0))) ↵
Command: (entmake '((0 . "LINE")(10 0 1.875 0) (11 1.75 1.875 0))) ↵
Command: (entmake '((0 . "LINE")(10 2.25 1.875 0) (11 4 1.875 0))) ↵
Command: (entmake '((0 . "LINE")(10 4 0.0625 0) (11 4 2 0))) ↵
Command: (entmake '((0 . "SOLID")(10 0 1.875 0) (11 0.12 1.905 0)(12 0.12 1.845 0)
  (13 0.12 1.845 0))) ↵
Command: (entmake '((0 . "SOLID")(10 4 1.875 0) (11 3.88 1.905 0)(12 3.88 1.845 0)
  (13 3.88 1.845 0))) ↵
Command: (entmake '((0 . "TEXT")(10 1.84 1.94 0)(40 . 0.12)(1 . "4.00")(50 . 0.0)(41 . 1.0)
  (51 . 0.0) (71 . 0) (72 . 1) (11 2 1.875) (73 . 2))) ↵
Command: (entmake '((0 . "POINT") (8 . "DEFPOINTS")(10 0 0 0) (50 . 0.0))) ↵
Command: (entmake '((0 . "POINT") (8 . "DEFPOINTS")(10 4 0 0) (50 . 0.0))) ↵
Command: (entmake '((0 . "POINT") (8 . "DEFPOINTS")(10 4 1.875 0) (50 . 0.0))) ↵
Command: (entmake '((0 . "ENDBLK"))) ↵
```

After encountering the ENDBLK entity, the name of the block is returned. This name must be indicated in field 2 of the dimension entity record. Since this is the first unnamed block created in this drawing, the name returned should be *U0. AutoCAD assigns these names. The names may not remain the same from one drawing session to another, so be sure that your applications take this into consideration. The name is then indicated in the entity description for the dimension:

```
(entmake '((0 . "DIMENSION")(2 . "*U0")(10 4 1.875 0)(11 2 1.875 0)(12 0 0 0)
(13 0 0)(14 4 0 0)(40 . 0)(50 . 0)(52 . 0)(53 . 0)(1 . "")(51 . 0)(70 . 0)))
```

The dimension should now appear on screen.

SAMPLE PROGRAM

```
; AutoPL.LSP
;
; Date: November 29, 19xx
;
; Purpose: Demonstrate the use of the ENTMAKE function by creating a polyline.
;
(entmake '( (0 . "POLYLINE")))
(setq VP (getpoint "\nFrom point: "))
(entmake (list (cons 0 "VERTEX") (cons 10 VP)))
(while (setq VP (getpoint VP "\nTo point or [ENTER] if done: "))
  (entmake (list (cons 0 "VERTEX") (cons 10 VP)))
)
  (entmake '( (0 . "SEQEND")))
```

EXERCISE 13-3

☐ Design a program that uses the ENTMAKE function in a loop to create a line sequence where each line segment is a different color. The color number for the first line should be 1. The color number for each additional line segment should then increase by 1. When color 16 is reached, reset the color to 1 again. Name the program COLINE.LSP.

A SPECIALIZED ENTITY FUNCTION

While most entity-handling functions can be used with all entity types, the TEXTBOX function is a specialized function pertaining only to text and attribute or attribute definition entities. The syntax for the TEXTBOX function is as follows:

```
(textbox ELIST)
```

The TEXTBOX function returns the diagonal coordinates (lower-left and upper-right corners) of the bounding box for the text described by ELIST. A *bounding box* is a rectangle which encompasses the entire text string. Note that ELIST must define a text entity (or an "attribute" text entity). In order to use TEXTBOX with an attribute, the attribute must be selected through either the NENTSEL or NENTSELP function.

When a partial entity data list is provided, a default value is assumed if any fields are missing. The default values will be the current settings within the drawing (text height, style, etc.). The minimum acceptable data list accepted by TEXTBOX is the text string itself (group code 1).

To demonstrate the use of this function, first use AutoCAD's STYLE command to define a text style named "STANDARD" using the font file TXT.SHX. All other parameters will be default values. Then enter text as shown here:

```
Command: TEXT ↵
Justify/Style/〈Start point〉: 2,2 ↵
Height 〈0.200〉: 0.125 ↵
Rotation angle 〈0〉: 0 ↵
Text: abc ↵
```

Next, use ENTGET and ENTLAST to return the entity data record:

```
Command: (entget (entlast))↵
((–1 . 〈Entity name: 8f0306f8〉) (0 . "TEXT") (5 . "67") (100 . "AcDbEntity")
(67 . 0) (8 . "0") (100 . "AcDbText") (10 2.0 2.0 0.0) (40 . 0.125) (1 . "abc")
(50 . 0.0) (41 . 1.0) (51 . 0.0) (7 . "STANDARD") (71 . 0) (72 . 0) (210 0.0
0.0 1.0) (100 . "AcDbText") (73 . 0))
```

Now use TEXTBOX to return the bounding box for the text:

```
Command: (textbox (entget (entlast))) ↵
((0.0 0.0 0.0) (0.333333 0.125 0.0))
```

The first set of coordinates in the list denotes the X, Y, and Z distances from the insertion point (group code 10) of the text. The second set gives the X, Y, and Z distances of the upper-right corner from the lower-left corner of the bounding box. The first list returned will generally be (0.0 0.0 0.0) except in cases where the text is vertical, oblique, or contains letters with descenders, such as "g," "p," and "q." This next string shows an example of this:

Command: **TEXT** ↵
Justify/Style/⟨Start point⟩: **2,1** ↵
Height ⟨0.200⟩: **0.125** ↵
Rotation angle ⟨0⟩: **0** ↵
Text: **efg** ↵

Command: **(textbox (entget (entlast)))** ↵
((0.0 –0.0416667 0.0) (0.333333 0.125 0.0))

On the Y axis, the text string falls 0.0416667 units below the Y-axis value of the insertion point of the text. The second list shows that the text string is 0.333333 units long and 0.125 units high.

As mentioned previously, the minimum entity data list required by TEXTBOX is the text string value. For example:

Command: **(textbox '((1 . "abc")))** ↵
((0.0 0.0 0.0) (0.333333 0.125 0.0))

The missing fields are assumed to be default values. To check this, change the TEXTSIZE system variable as follows, then perform the TEXTBOX function again:

Command: **(setvar "TEXTSIZE" 0.25)** ↵
Command: **(textbox '((1 . "abc")))** ↵
((0.0 0.0 0.0) (0.666667 0.25 0.0))

Note that regardless of the text orientation, the returned list always refers to the lower-left and upper-right corners of the text. If TEXTBOX is not successful, it returns nil.

Let's Review...

1. The ENTMAKE function allows entries to be made directly to the drawing database.
2. Many of the entity record fields can be omitted, and default values will be assigned. If any non-optional fields are specified, an error is encountered and no entity is created.
3. Complex entities may require several ENTMAKE calls, where nothing is drawn until a SEQEND entity is created. In order to close the temporary file used by AutoLISP while creating complex entities, use the ENTMAKE function without any arguments.
4. Sometimes it is advantageous to create a new entity record by accessing an existing record and SUBSTituting new values where required.

CHAPTER TEST

Write your answers in the spaces provided.

1. What is the primary AutoLISP function used for direct searching of the entity database? Describe its use.

2. What is an entity name and what is it used for?

3. Detail the use of the AutoLISP function that retrieves the entity data record from the drawing database.

4. Define the term "subentity."

5. What is the purpose of a SEQEND entity?

6. What data is held in the –2 field of a SEQEND entity record?

7. Why are loops valuable when using entity data functions? Give an example.

8. Detail the use of the ENTLAST function.

9. What function is provided for direct entity-selection by the user? Describe its use.

10. Write an expression that prompts the user to select an entity, and then returns the data record for the selected entity.

11. When should ENTSEL be used instead of SSGET? Explain your answer.

12. Why is it a good idea to use the ENTSEL function as a test in a loop?

13. How does NENTSEL differ from ENTSEL?

14. What is returned by NENTSEL when each of the following entities is picked?
    A. Polyline ______
    B. Block ______

15. What is the "Model to World Transformation Matrix"? Explain its use.

16. List the equation for finding the WCS coordinates through the Model to World Transformation Matrix.

17. Detail the use and purpose of the SUBST function.

18. After an entity data list has been modified, which function causes the database to be updated? What argument is supplied to this function?

19. List the restrictions applicable to the ENTMOD function.

20. Detail the purpose and use of the ENTUPD function.

21. Describe the use of the ENTMAKE function.

22. List at least five optional data fields (and their respective default values) for the ENTMAKE function.

____

____

____

____

____

____

23. What means is provided to stop the ENTMAKE process for a complex entity and properly close the temporary files?

____

____

____

24. After defining a block with the ENTMAKE function, what must be done before the block will appear in the drawing?

____

____

____

____

25. Describe the use of the ENDBLK entity.

____

____

____

____

PROGRAMMING PROBLEMS

1. Create a program named LAYPICK.LSP that defines a command line function called C:LP. The program will prompt the user to select an entity, find the layer that the entity is on, and make that the current layer.
2. Design a program named 16COLINE.LSP that defines a command line function called C:CL. The program will prompt the user to pick points and will use the ENTMAKE function to create lines between these points. The first line segment will have a color value of 1, the second a value of 2, and so on. The color sequence will begin again after number 16. Therefore, the user will be able to draw a 16-color line by simply picking points.
3. Create a program called ENTCOUNT.LSP that uses looping techniques and ENTNEXT to count all entities and subentities in the drawing and return the total number to the user.

4. Create a program called ENTLIST.LSP that defines a command line function called C:ELS. This function will allow the user to select either a line, arc, or circle entity and return a listing of that entities data as shown here:

LINE	**ARC**	**CIRCLE**
Entity Type ____________	Entity Type ____________	Entity Type ____________
Layer ________________	Layer ________________	Layer ________________
Start Point ____________	Center Point ___________	Center Point ___________
End Point _____________	Radius ________________	Radius ________________
In WCS? ______________	In WCS? ______________	In WCS? ______________

   For the "In WCS?" listing, provide a Yes or No value. (Remember to check the DXF group code 210 for this information.)
5. Design a program named P-LIST.LSP that prompts the user to pick a polyline and returns a list of all vertex point coordinates.
6. Create a program named TEXTFILL.LSP that does the following:
   A. Prompts the user for a text string.
   B. Draws a rectangle around the text, offset from the bounding box by 1 unit.
   C. Draws a temporary rectangle defining the bounding box of the text and fills between the two rectangles with a user-specified hatch pattern.
   D. Erases the temporary rectangle.

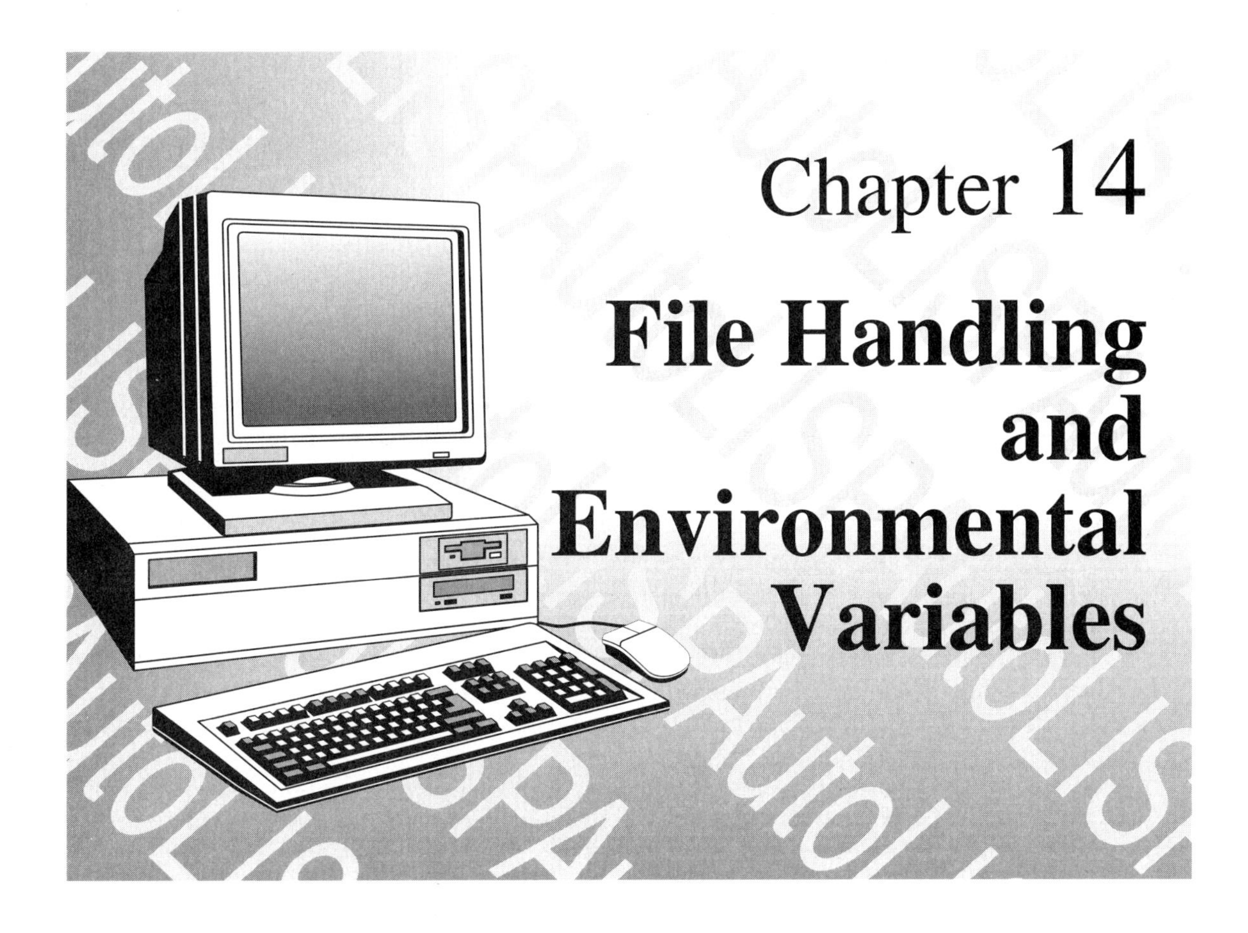

Chapter 14

File Handling and Environmental Variables

Learning Objectives

After completing this chapter, you will be able to:

- ☐ Find files on disk using AutoLISP functions.
- ☐ Read and write data to text files.
- ☐ Access environmental variable values.

FILE-HANDLING OPERATIONS

A great deal of this text has been dedicated to various methods of data storage and retrieval. This should not be surprising, since data manipulation is the primary function of AutoCAD. With the large amounts and various types of information used, it is necessary to support a variety of techniques for handling all of the data. The methods to be explored in this chapter involve reading from and writing to text files.

There are various reasons that you might want to store information in a text file. One situation is when data, such as construction notes held in the current drawing session, is to be dispatched to other drawings. Storing the text entries in a file provides access to these notes in future drawing sessions.

There are various AutoLISP file-handling functions available for manipulating large quantities of text file data. Additional possibilities include supplying output to and receiving input from other applications, and even generating or modifying AutoCAD support files.

Locating Files

One common source of program errors occurs when trying to load an AutoLISP file that is not present in the expected location. The typical "error: load failed" message is displayed, and if the LOAD statement is embedded within another application, everything comes to a screeching halt. When an attempt is made to load an AutoLISP file, the current directory is first searched. If the file is not found there, the rest of the library path is searched. If the indicated file is not found, the error message is returned.

The FINDFILE Function. If a preliminary check is performed before attempting to load an AutoLISP file, many potential errors can be avoided. The *FINDFILE function* is used to determine the location of the intended file. The syntax for FINDFILE is:

```
(findfile FILENAME)
```

The FINDFILE function searches for FILENAME along the library path, as previously discussed. The FILENAME specification must be correct and complete; both the filename and extension must be supplied. If a drive and directory are indicated in the FILENAME argument, then no other directories are searched. Otherwise, the search continues along the entire library path or until a matching filename is found. When FINDFILE locates the file, it returns the entire file specification–drive, full directory path, filename, and extension. If no match is found, nil is returned.

When specifying the directory path, the separators must either be the double backslash (\\) or a forward slash (/). The results shown in the following examples may vary, depending on where the files are actually located at your workstation.

```
(findfile "ACAD.EXE")          returns "C:\\PROGRAM FILES\\AUTOCAD R14\\ACAD.EXE"
(findfile "NEVER.WAS")         returns nil
```

One common method used to verify whether a file exists in the expected location prior to loading is shown in the following example. Since the FINDFILE function returns nil when a file is *not* found, and returns a value when the file *is* found, it can be used as a test expression:

```
(defun C:LL (/ FN)
  (setq FN (getstring "\nAutoLISP file name to load: "))  ; Set FN to filename
  (if
    (findfile
      (strcat FN ".LSP")                  ; If the AutoLISP file named FN is found...
    )                                     ;   End FINDFILE
    (load FN)                             ; Then load FN
    (princ                                ;   Else print a message to the screen
      (strcat "\n" FN ".LSP not found!")
    )
  )
  (princ)                                 ; Clean exit
)
```

Whenever an application depends on the existence of a specific file, the FINDFILE function should be used to ensure that it is found where expected.

Prompting the User to Find a File

Certain applications may require the user to specify a filename for a specific operation. This can be done by using GETSTRING and then FINDFILE to verify the existence of the file before proceeding. A dynamic search can also be performed using AutoCAD's dialog box features. The *GETFILED (GET FILE dialog box) function* invokes a dialog box that displays a list of existing files of a specified extension type. The syntax for the GETFILED function is:

```
(getfiled TITLE DEFAULT EXT FLAGS)
```

The TITLE argument specifies the text string that appears at the top of the dialog box. A DEFAULT text string is used to specify the default filename, or this can be a null string (""). The extension type is indicated by the EXT argument, and a variety of FLAGS can be specified to control the features of the dialog box. As with most flags, these integer values correspond to bit values. The table in Fig. 14-1 explains the effect of each code.

Value	Meaning
1	Indicates a request for a new file to be created.
2	Disables the "Type it" button.
4	Lets the user enter an arbitrary filename extension.
8	Performs a library search for the filename entered.

Fig. 14-1. GETFILED flags.

If the user indicates a valid and existing filename, the dialog box returns a string bearing that filename; otherwise, nil is returned by GETFILED. For example, if it was necessary for the user to specify a font file name, the following GETFILED expression could be used:

```
(getfiled "Select a font file:" "/Program Files/AutoCAD R14/Fonts/simplex" "shx" 8)
```

This expression invokes the dialog box shown in Fig. 14-2.

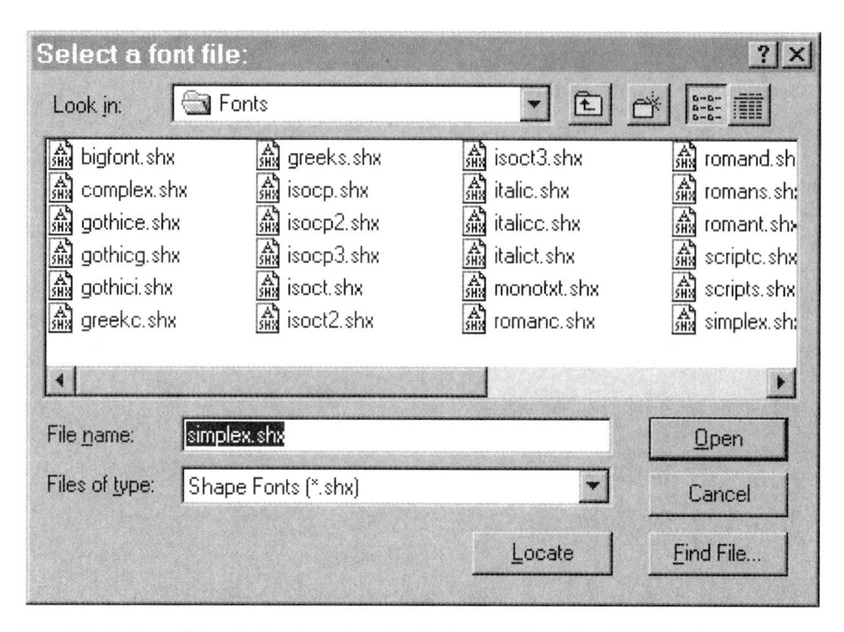

Fig. 14-2. Possible dialog box invoked when using the GETFILED function.

Note that if a nonexistent filename is entered by typing, a message appears at the bottom of the dialog box indicating that the file was not found. In some cases it may be best to force the user to pick an existing file rather than allowing it to be typed. Adding the 2 bit greys out (deactivates) the "Type it" button. In this next example the 2 bit is used together with the 8 bit:

```
(getfiled "Select a font file:" "/Program Files/AutoCAD R14/Fonts/simplex" "shx" 10)
```

Each flag has its own specific applications and may be used together or separately to produce the desired results. The 1 bit is used only when the filename being prompted for is a new file to be created. If the user indicates the name of a file that already exists, a dialog box is displayed, and asks if the user wants to replace the existing file.

The 2 bit disables the "Type it" button and is automatically set if the dialog box is called while another is already present on screen. Since the TYPE IT option dismisses the currently visible dialog boxes, this prevents the previous dialog box from disappearing.

If an arbitrary filename extension can be used, the 4 bit should be set. When it is not set, GETFILED only accepts the extension indicated by the EXT argument.

The 8 bit is used to strip the directory path information from the returned filename if it is found on the library path. Since any file on the library path can be found by its name alone, this removes the extraneous information. If the 8 bit is used and the file is found outside of the library path, the directory path information is returned with the filename. Also, if a filename is found in more than one directory on the library path the directory path will not be stripped.

Reading from Files

The process of reading from and writing to files involves combining several functions. The first three functions discussed in this next section can be used to read from a text file.

The OPEN Function. In order to access a file for AutoLISP I/O (Input/Output) functions, it must first be opened using the *OPEN function.* The syntax for OPEN is:

```
(open FILENAME MODE)
```

This function opens a FILENAME for I/O as indicated by the MODE argument. The MODE argument must be a single *lowercase* letter presented as a string (enclosed in quotation marks). The following effects are produced by the MODE argument.

"r" Open FILENAME for reading. The *file pointer* is initially placed at the first line of the file. (The term "file pointer" refers to the way in which a position within a file is maintained.) Nil is returned if the file is not found.

"w" Open FILENAME for writing. If the file already exists, its data is overwritten, otherwise a new file is created. The file pointer is placed at the beginning of the file.

"a" Open FILENAME for appending. If the file exists, new data can be appended to it. In this situation, the pointer is placed at the end of the file. If the file does not exist, a new file is created, and the pointer is placed at the beginning.

When a file has been successfully opened, a unique file descriptor is returned. This *file descriptor* is simply a handle; something by which the file can be accessed. The handle must be immediately assigned to a variable in order for it to be supplied as an argument to AutoLISP's reading and writing functions.

The READ-LINE Function. The *READ-LINE function* is the basic function for reading a text file. The format for READ-LINE is:

```
(read-line [FILE-DESC])
```

The READ-LINE function works two ways, depending on whether the optional FILE-DESC argument is supplied. If no file descriptor is indicated, the function reads a string from the keyboard. Otherwise, the function will read a line from the file whose handle is FILE-DESC.

READ-LINE begins with the first line of a file. Each ensuing use of the READ-LINE function will read the second, third, fourth, etc., lines of the file, respectively. When no more lines remain in the file, nil is returned.

Before a line can be read using the READ-LINE function, the file must be opened (using the OPEN function) and a file descriptor must be obtained. For the following example, make sure that the AutoCAD's ACADR14.LSP file is in the AutoCAD support directory.

```
Command: (setq PR (open "c:/program files/autocad r14/support/acadr14.lsp" "r")) ↵
⟨File: #2b43bd8⟩

Command: (read-line PR) ↵
"; Next available MSG number is    86"

Command: (read-line PR) ↵
"; MODULE_ID ACADR13_LSP_"

Command: (read-line PR) ↵
";;;    ACADR14.LSP Version 14.1 for Release 14 "
```

Using this method, an entire file can be read one line at a time. The data retrieved from the file may be printed to the screen, or used for computations or other operations.

A common method for reading an entire file is to use a WHILE loop. The following routine reads and prints the remainder of the ACADR14.LSP file that was previously opened.

```
(while (setq RL (read–line PR))
  (princ RL)
)
```

Since a READ-LINE expression returns nil when the end of a file is encountered, it makes a perfect test expression. As long as (while) READ-LINE returns a non-nil value, the loop can continue.

Once a file is opened, it uses one of the available file handles from the operating system. The maximum number of available file handles is set in the CONFIG.SYS file with the "FILES=nn" statement. In order to release the handle, the file must be closed using the CLOSE function.

The CLOSE Function. The *CLOSE function* closes the file referenced by FILE-DESC, resulting in its handle being released. Nil is always returned by CLOSE. The format for the CLOSE function is:

```
(close FILE-DESC)
```

You must close all open files prior to leaving AutoCAD. A directory entry is not created or maintained for a file until it is closed, but space is allocated in the file allocation table by the operating system. Therefore, if a file is left open, it will not show up on a directory listing and is inaccessible by normal means. In addition, when disk space is allocated but no directory entry is found, it becomes a *lost cluster.*

Another potential problem encountered when not closing files is the possibility of running out of file handles altogether. The CLOSE function uses the variable assigned to the file descriptor that was obtained by the OPEN function. To close the ACADR14.LSP file that was previously opened, the following expression is used:

Command: **(close PR)** ↵
nil *the CLOSE function always returns nil*

EXERCISE 14-1

- ☐ Using the OPEN, READ-LINE, and CLOSE functions, generate a routine with a loop which will print the contents of a user-specified file to the screen. Use GETFILED for user specification, and FINDFILE to ensure that the file exists prior to attempting to open and read it. Be sure to provide your program with a "clean" exit.
- ☐ Name the file TYPE-IT.LSP.

Writing to Files

Whether a file is opened with the "w" (write) or an "a" (append) MODE flag (argument), it is for the purpose of writing new data to a text file. The WRITE-LINE function is used primarily for writing data to a file.

The WRITE-LINE Function. The *WRITE-LINE function* is similar to READ-LINE in that it is a dual-purpose function. Note the syntax of the WRITE-LINE function:

```
(write-line STRING [FILE-DESC])
```

If the optional FILE-DESC argument is omitted, the STRING is written at the Command: prompt. When a FILE-DESC argument is included, the specified STRING is written to the indicated file. It returns STRING enclosed in quotation marks. However, the STRING written to file is not enclosed in the quotation marks. Like the OPEN function, the file descriptor for WRITE-LINE is returned as a handle. In addition, the file must be closed after writing is complete.

The next example assigns the file descriptor returned by OPEN to the variable PW, which points to the file named RITE-IT.TXT. The WRITE-LINE function is then used to enter data into the file.

```
(setq PW (open "RITE–IT.TXT" "w"))

(write–line "OK" PW)          returns  "OK"          writes OK to the file represented by
                                                     PW
```

The WRITE-LINE function also acts similar to READ-LINE in that after writing a line, it moves the file pointer to the next line. Therefore, another WRITE-LINE expression will write its string to the new position and again move the file pointer down one line.

Now close the file:

```
(close PW)                    returns  nil
```

Compare your TYPE-IT.LSP program (created in Exercise 14-1) with the following solution.

```
; TYPE–IT.LSP
;
(defun C:TYP ()
  (if (not
      (setq FN
        (getfiled "Indicate file to type: " "" "" 10)
    ))
    (princ "\nFunction cancelled.")
    (progn
      (command ".textscr")
      (setq PR (open FN "r"))
      (while (setq RL (read–line PR))
           (princ RL)
           (princ "\n")
      )
      (close PR)
    )
  )
  (princ)
)
```

Use TYPE-IT.LSP to list the contents of the RITE-IT.TXT file.

When a file has been opened for appending, each new line is written at the end. The next expression reopens RITE-IT.TXT with an “a” (append) flag, writes a line, and closes the file:

```
(setq PA (open "RITE–IT.TXT" "a"))
(write–line "Appendix 1" PA)
(close PA)                                        returns  nil
```

Again, use TYPE-IT.LSP to list the contents of the file.

Another common need for a programmer is the ability to add a new line to the middle of a file. Even though AutoLISP does not provide any single internal function for doing this, it is easily accomplished using a combination of functions. The following routine writes a new linetype definition into the ACAD.LIN file and explains each step. (It is assumed that the ACAD.LIN file exists in the current directory.)

```
(command "SHELL" "RENAME ACAD.LIN ACADSAV.LIN")   ; Rename source file
(setq PR (open "ACADSAV.LIN" "r"))               ; Open source file to read
(setq PW (open "ACAD.LIN" "w"))                  ; Open new target file to write
(setq RL (read–line PR))                         ; Read first line of source
;
;
(while (/= (substr (strcase RL) 1 7) "*HIDDEN")  ; While RL not HIDDEN line variation
  (write–line RL PW)                             ;   write data to target and
  (setq RL (read–line PR))                       ;   read next line of source
)                                                ; End WHILE
;
;
(while                                           ; Read until last entry of HIDDEN
  (or                                            ;   variations is passed
    (= (substr (strcase RL) 1 7) "*HIDDEN")
    (= (substr RL 1 1) "A")
  )
  (write–line RL PW)
  (setq RL (read–line PR))
)
                              ; Write new definition to target
(write–line "*HIDDEN4,_ _ _ _ _ _ _ _ _ _ _ _ _ _ _ _ _ _ _ _ _ _ _ _ _ _ _ _ _ _" PW)
(write–line "A,.125,–.125" PW)
                              ; Transcribe rest of file
(write–line RL PW)
(while (setq RL (read–line PR))
  (write–line RL PW)
)
(mapcar 'close (list PR PW))       ; Close files. Note the use of MAPCAR that
                                   ;   consolidates two CLOSE expressions.
```

The search criterion will vary, but the concept is the same when inserting data into any file. A source and a target (destination) file must be used. While it is possible to read from and write to the same file, it is recommended that you use separate files. By using two files, if the write is unsuccessful and the file is closed, the original file remains intact.

The following program produces a Bill of Material file for drawings that contains attributed blocks. The single attribute pertains to the price of the item, and in this case, relates to a "Bush", "Shrub", or "Tree". A costing summation is also provided.

```
; Filename: BOM.LSP
;
; Purpose:  A) Conduct a keyword search for attributed blocks:
;              "Bush", "Shrub", or "Tree". Each block has one
;              attribute pertaining to price of vegetation.
;           B) Export cost and location data to a BOM file.
;
(defun C:BOM (/ TYP GREEN FIL DATE TOT CTR ENT E-LST LOC VAL)
  (setvar "cmdecho" 0)
  (initget 1 "Bush Shrub Tree")
  (setq TYP     (getkword "\nB.O.M. for <Bush/Shrub/Tree>: ")
        GREEN   (ssget "X" (list '(0 . "INSERT") (cons 2 TYP) '(66 . 1)))  ; [1]
  )
  (cond
    (GREEN
      (setq FIL     (open (strcat (getvar "dwgname") ".bom") "a")         ; [2]
            DATE    (rtos (getvar "cdate") 2)            ; Current date as String
            TOT     0                                    ; Initialize TOTal value
            CTR     0                                    ; Initialize CounTeR
      )
      (write-line  (strcat "\nBilling for: " (getvar "dwgname")            ; [3]
                      " "
                      (substr DATE 5 2) "-"
                      (substr DATE 7 2) "-"
                      (substr DATE 1 4)
                      "\n- - - - - - - - - - - - -\n"
                 ) FIL)
      (repeat (sslength GREEN)                           ; Repeat for # of Plants
        (setq ENT     (ssname GREEN CTR)                 ; Entity name of Plant at CTR
              E-LST   (entget ENT)                       ; Entity associated list
              LOC     (cdr (assoc 10 E-LST))             ; LOCation of Plant
              E-LST   (entget (entnext ENT))             ; Attribute associated list
              VAL     (cdr (assoc 1 E-LST))              ; Attribute VALue as string
              TOT     (+ TOT (read VAL))                 ; Running $ TOTal for all
        )
        (write-line
          (strcat "    " VAL "    "                      ; Write VALue and LOCation
                  (rtos (car  LOC)) ","                  ; to open FILe
                  (rtos (cadr LOC)))
           FIL)
        (setq CTR (1+ CTR))                              ; Increment CounTeR
      ) ;end repeat
      (write-line (strcat "\n" "< " TYP " >- - - - -< Qty: "              ; [4]
                     (itoa (sslength GREEN)) " >- - - - -< Cost: $"
                     (rtos TOT 2 2) "\n")
                  FIL
      )
      (close FIL)
    ) ;end sublist
  ) ;end cond
  (princ)
)
;- - -<End of File>- - -
```

Documentation for BOM.LSP

[1] **(setq GREEN (ssget "X" (list '(0 . "INSERT") (cons 2 TYP) '(66 . 1))))** The variable GREEN stores a selection set of inserted blocks, where the associated list (cons 2 TYP) specifies which block name to search. The associated listing (66 . 1) indicates that each block is to contain attributes.

[2] **(setq FIL (open (strcat (getvar "dwgname") ".bom") "a"))** Append an open file with an extension of ".bom", using the same name as the current drawing. As blocks are continually added to the open drawing, its associated ".bom" file can also be updated.

[3] **(write-line (strcat "\nBilling for: " (getvar "dwgname") ...** Write a heading and compiled date for the open file.

[4] **(write-line (strcat "\n" " " TYP " ⟩-----⟨ Qty: " ...** Write the quantity and total cost of the target vegetation.

Additional READ and WRITE Functions

Depending on the format of the data being read or written, it may be necessary to read or write data one character at a time without moving the file pointer down a line. The READ-CHAR and WRITE-CHAR functions are provided for this purpose.

The READ-CHAR Function. The *READ-CHAR (READ-CHARacter) function* reads one character from the keyboard or from the open file specified as FILE-DESC. The syntax for READ-CHAR is:

```
(read-char [FILE-DESC])
```

If the optional FILE-DESC argument is included, READ-CHAR reads one character from the indicated (and opened) file and returns the ASCII code for that character. If the FILE-DESC argument is omitted, READ-CHAR reads one character from the keyboard. To explore this function, reopen ACADR14.LSP for reading:

```
Command: (setq PR (open "c:/program files/autocad r14/support/acadr14.lsp" "r")) ↵
<File: #22004a2>                          the file handle will vary; yours will
                                          probably be different
```

Now use the READ-CHAR function to read the first character in the file:

```
Command: (setq LTR (read-char PR)) ↵
59
```

Remember that the ASCII code is returned; in this case, 59 is returned. Since the first character of this file is a semicolon, the ASCII code for the semicolon is returned. To return the actual character represented, the CHR function is used:

```
Command: (chr LTR) ↵
";"
```

READ-CHAR will advance through the file one character position each time it is used. The following loop demonstrates this as it prints the remainder of the first line to the screen:

```
Command: (repeat 36 (princ (chr (setq LTR (read-char PR))))) ↵
Next avaliable MSG number is 86.

"\n"
```

The WRITE-CHAR Function. The *WRITE-CHAR (WRITE-CHARacter) function* writes the character represented by the ASCII code NUM to the indicated open file. If the optional FILE-DESC argument is omitted, the character is written to the screen. The format for the WRITE-CHAR function is:

```
(write–char NUM [FILE-DESC])
```

For example:

```
(write–char 65)              writes A (to the screen)              returns 65
```

When using WRITE-CHAR, it may be helpful to use the ASCII function:

```
(write–char (ascii "A"))     writes A (to the screen)              returns 65
```

When the optional FILE-DESC argument is supplied and points to a file opened with a "w" (write) or "a" (append) flag, the character represented by NUM is written to that file. The following example writes the alphabet in uppercase characters to the open file:

```
(setq PW (open "ALPHA.BET" "w") N 65)  ; Open file/set N to ASCII code for "A"
(repeat 26                             ; Do once for each letter of alphabet...
  (write–char N PW)                    ; Write character to file
  (setq N (1+ N))                      ; Increment N
)                                      ; End REPEAT
(close PW)                             ; Close file
```

Now use TYPE-IT.LSP to list the contents of the ALPHA.BET file.

EXERCISE 14-2

- ☐ Create a program that will copy the contents of a file using read and write functions. This routine should prompt for an input filename and an output filename.
- ☐ Name the program file FILECOPY.LSP.

HANDLING APPLICATION DATA IN THE ACAD14.CFG FILE

The ACAD14.CFG file is AutoCAD's primary configuration tool for establishing an automated drawing environment. This important file contains the necessary instructions for "talking" to devices such as displays or plotters, as well as manipulates drawing setup features like file-locking and default drawing filenames. In AutoCAD, it is possible to store and retrieve extraneous application data contained in this file, adding a new dimension of data aquisition capabilities.

The SETCFG Function

The *SETCFG (SET ConFiGuration) function* writes various application data to the AppData section contained in the AutoCAD acad14.cfg file. The syntax for the SETCFG function is as follows:

```
(setcfg CFGNAME CFGVAL)
```

The required CFGNAME argument is a string that specifies the desired section name and associated parameter name when setting the value of CFGVAL. Where the section name does not exist within the acad14.cfg file, SETCFG creates the new section with its respective value. On the other hand, SETCFG appends the new value to an existing applications data section. The CFGNAME argument takes on this particular form:

```
"AppData/application_name/section_name/.../parameter_name"
```

The CFGVAL argument is also required, and must be presented as a text string. Note the following example:

```
Command: (setcfg "AppData/SurveyCoords/Quad9/Latitude" "78.754 N") ↵
"78.754 N"
Command: (setcfg "AppData/SurveyCoords/Quad9/Departure" "62.139 E") ↵
"62.139 E"
```

Calling the acad14.cfg file would then yield the following partial results:

```
[AppData/SurveyCoords/Quad9]
Latitude=78.754 N
Departure=62.139 E
```

The following test routine takes advantage of the SETCFG function, as new application data is added to the acad14.cfg file. Be aware that the acad14.cfg file does not need to be opened with the AutoLISP OPEN function in order to pass data between the operator and this configuration file.

```
; Program:   SETDATA.LSP
;
; Purpose:   Writes user-specified data to the acad14.cfg file.
;
(defun C:SETDATA (/ AN SN PN CV)
  (setvar "cmdecho" 0)
  (while (/= "" (setq AN (getstring T "\nApplication Name [ENTER to exit]: ")))
    (setq SN (getstring T "\nSection Name: ")
          PN (getstring T "\nParameter Name: ")
          CV (getstring T "\nConfiguration Value: ")
    )
    (setcfg (strcat "AppData/" AN "/" SN "/" PN) CV)
  )
  (princ)
)
;---⟨End of File⟩---
```

The GETCFG Function

The *GETCFG (GET ConFiGuration) function* is the complement to the SETCFG function and retrieves application data from the AppData section contained in the AutoCAD acad14.cfg file. The syntax for the GETCFG function is:

```
(getcfg CFGNAME)
```

The required CFGNAME argument is a string that specifies the desired section name and associated parameter name when retrieving the stored value. The CFGNAME argument takes on this particular form:

```
"AppData/application_name/section_name/.../parameter_name"
```

Examine the following expressions. Assume that the SETCFG example previously given has already transpired.

```
(getcfg "AppData/SurveyCoords/Quad9/Latitude")  returns "78.754 N"
(getcfg "AppData/SurveyCoords/Quad9/Departure") returns "62.139 E"
```

ACCESSING ENVIRONMENTAL INFORMATION

The environment in which your applications are used can have an unexpected impact on how well they run. The version of AutoLISP being used is of particular importance. If programs using Release 14-specific functions are run on earlier versions of the programming language, error situations will result. Tables which itemize the AutoLISP functions and their applicable release are found in Appendix A.

The VER Function

The *VER (VERsion) function* is provided to allow the programmer to determine what version of AutoLISP is currently being used. No arguments are required, as shown in the following syntax:

```
(ver)
```

A string is returned when the VER function is used:

```
"AutoLISP Release X.X"
```

...where "X.X" indicates the current version number of AutoLISP.

When *extended* AutoLISP is being used, the string will indicate this also:

```
"Extended AutoLISP Release X.X"
```

As an example, if a program were only compatible with Release 10 and more recent releases, the following expression could be used:

```
(if (and
      (< (atof (substr (ver) (– (strlen (ver)) 9 4))))
      (/= (substr (ver) (– (strlen (ver)) 4)) "(en)")
    )
    (princ (strcat "\nThis program not compatable with " (ver)))
    (RUNPROG)
)
```

...where RUNPROG is the name of a user-defined function. This expression converts the last four characters of the string to a real number and tests whether or not the result is less than 10. If so, a message is issued. If the result is 10 or more, the program is run.

EXERCISE 14-3

- ☐ Write an expression that tells the programmer whether Extended AutoLISP is being used.

Environmental Variables

Another aspect of the environment is contained in the environmental variable settings. *Environmental variable settings* are maintained by the operating system. These are set prior to entering AutoCAD, and include the ACAD, ACADMAXMEM, and other variables detailed in the *AutoCAD Interface, Installation and Performance Guide.* When it is necessary to obtain the value of one of these variables, the GETENV function is used.

The GETENV Function. The *GETENV (GET ENvironmental Variable) function* returns a string representing the value assigned to VARIABLE-NAME. If the variable does not exist (or has not been assigned a value), then nil is returned. The format for the GETENV function is:

```
(getenv VARIABLE-NAME)
```

If the ACAD variable, which contains the user-specified portion of the library path, is set to D:\ACADR14\SUPPORT;D:\ACADR14\LISP then the GETENV expression returns the following:

```
Command: (getenv "ACAD") ↵
D:\\ACADR14\\SUPPORT;D:\\ACADR14\\LISP
```

In a situation where the ACADPAGEDIR variable has not been assigned a value, the following is returned:

```
Command: (getenv "ACADPAGEDIR") ↵
nil
```

Let's Review...

1. The FINDFILE function searches the current directory and the library path for the specified file. Since FINDFILE returns nil when the file is not found, it also serves as a test expression.
2. For any file I/O (Input/Output) operations to be successful, the file must be opened using the OPEN function. One of three available MODEs can be specified for the opened file: "r" to read, "w" to write, or "a" to append. The MODE flag *must* be specified by a lowercase letter.
3. The READ-LINE function will read a line from a file opened for reading, and advance the file pointer down one line in the file. When no more lines are found, nil is returned.
4. When I/O operations are complete with a file, its file handle must be released using the CLOSE function. Failure to do so will result in lost clusters being formed on the disk drive.
5. Similar to READ-LINE, the WRITE-LINE function will move the file pointer down one line after writing the specified text to the file. When WRITE-LINE is used without a file-descriptor argument, the specified string is written to the screen.
6. The ASCII value of the character read (from a file or the keyboard) is returned by the READ-CHAR function.
7. The WRITE-CHAR function will write the character corresponding to the specified ASCII code either to the screen or to a specified file opened for a write operation.
8. The SETCFG and GETCFG functions are essential when storing and retrieving information within the AutoCAD acad14.cfg file, respectively.
9. A programmer can determine what environment and parameters an application is running under by using the VER and GETENV functions.

CHAPTER TEST

Write your answers in the space provided.

1. List at least three reasons why information would be written to a text file.

____

____

____

____

____

2. Define the term "library path."

____

____

____

3. Which environmental variable affects the library path?

4. Describe in detail the use of the FINDFILE function.

5. When using FINDFILE, what directory path separators can be used?

6. What purpose is served by the OPEN function? Also, detail the use of each of the three available MODE arguments.

7. Define the term “file descriptor.”

8. Name the function used for reading text strings from files. What is the significance of its optional argument?

9. When does the READ-LINE function return nil?

10. What controls the number of available file handles?

11. What function releases file handles?

12. Why is a lost cluster formed when a file is not properly closed?

13. Explain how and why READ-LINE works well in a loop.

14. Name the primary function for writing data to a file. Detail its use.

15. Explain the technique used to add text to the middle of an existing file.

16. Detail the use of the READ-CHAR function both with and without its optional argument.

17. What function can be used to convert an ASCII code to a text character?

18. Describe the use of the WRITE-CHAR function.

19. Why is the VER function important?

20. What function is used to interrogate environmental variables? Detail its use.

21. Describe the use of the GETFILED function.

22. Detail the effects of each of the four flag bits for the GETFILED function.

PROGRAMMING PROBLEMS

1. Design a program named LISPLOAD.LSP that defines a command line function named C:LSP. It will allow the user to select an AutoLISP file, which will then be loaded into the drawing editor. Use the GETFILED function for the file selection process.
2. Create a program called TEXTIN.LSP that allows a user to specify a text file to be read, and then prints each line of text to the graphics screen using the AutoCAD TEXT command. Again, use GETFILED for the file selection process. (Note that the FLAG argument may need to be set differently than in Problem 1.)
3. Create an AutoLISP program called TEXTOUT.LSP that allows the user to select any number of text strings, and have them written to a specified text file. A selection-set will be needed in order to process all entities to be exported. Note that when selecting by a window or a crossing, unexpected results may be encountered in the target file. An "entity-at-a-time" procedure may be desirable in order to maintain the proper text sequence within the target file. (When necessary, use the NENTSEL function.)

4. Create a revised version of the program TEXTIN.LSP (found in Problem 2), and call it TEXTIN2.LSP. Follow the same steps in Problem 2, but find an alternate method for file selection other than the GETFILED function. This routine is intended for use on versions of AutoCAD prior to Release 12.
5. Design a program called STORSET.LSP that writes the current settings for the following AutoCAD system variables to a user-specified file: ORTHOMODE, GRIDMODE, SNAPMODE, LUPREC, AUPREC, LUNITS, AUNITS, BLIPMODE, APERTURE, PICKBOX, ANGDIR, ANGBASE. Use the GETFILED function to specify the new file, and force the set-up file extension to be ".SET".
6. Design a program called GETSET.LSP that reads files written by STORSET.LSP, and uses the stored values to set up the current drawing environment. The program should only accept ".SET" files to read.

```
; LOOP for retrieving each line of FILE–R, SUB is first character of STRING
(defun LOOP ()
  (setq STRING (read–line FILE–R))
  (if STRING (setq SUB (substr STRING 1 1))
  )
)
; STRIP comments from an .lsp file – Not intended for in–line documentation
(defun C:STRIP ()
  (setvar "cmdecho" 0)
  (setq RES     (getstring "\nStrip comments from which file: ")
        FILE–R  (open (strcat "c:/acad/acadlisp/" res ".lsp") "r")
        FILE–W  (open (getstring "\nSave to what file name: ") "w")
        CTR     1
  )
  (princ "\nProcessing – one moment...")
  (LOOP)
  (while STRING
    (cond ( (or (= SUB ";")                        ; Entire STRING is comment
                (= SUB (chr 0))                    ; Blank line in FILE–R
            )
            (LOOP)                                 ; If test is T, LOOP to next line
          )                                        ; End 1st test
          ( T                                      ; 2nd test – "Trap" AutoLISP code
            (while SUB                             ; While SUBstring exists...
              (if (and (/= SUB ";")
                       (< CTR (strlen STRING))
                  )                                ; End test
                  (setq CTR (1+ CTR)
                        SUB (substr STRING CTR 1)
                  )                                ; End then
                  (progn
                    (if (= SUB ";")
                      (setq SUB (substr STRING 1 (1– CTR)))
                      (setq SUB (substr STRING 1 CTR))
                    )
                    (write–line SUB FILE–W)        ; Write code to new file
                    (setq CTR 1 SUB nil)           ; Reset CTR and SUBstring
                    (LOOP)                         ; LOOP to next line in file
                  )                                ; End else
              )                                    ; End if
            )                                      ; End while
          )                                        ; End 2nd test
    )                                              ; End cond
  )                                                ; End while
  (close FILE–R)                                   ; Close opened file – for Reading
  (close FILE–W)                                   ; Close opened file – for Writing
  (princ "Done")
  (setvar "cmdecho" 1)
  (princ)
)
```

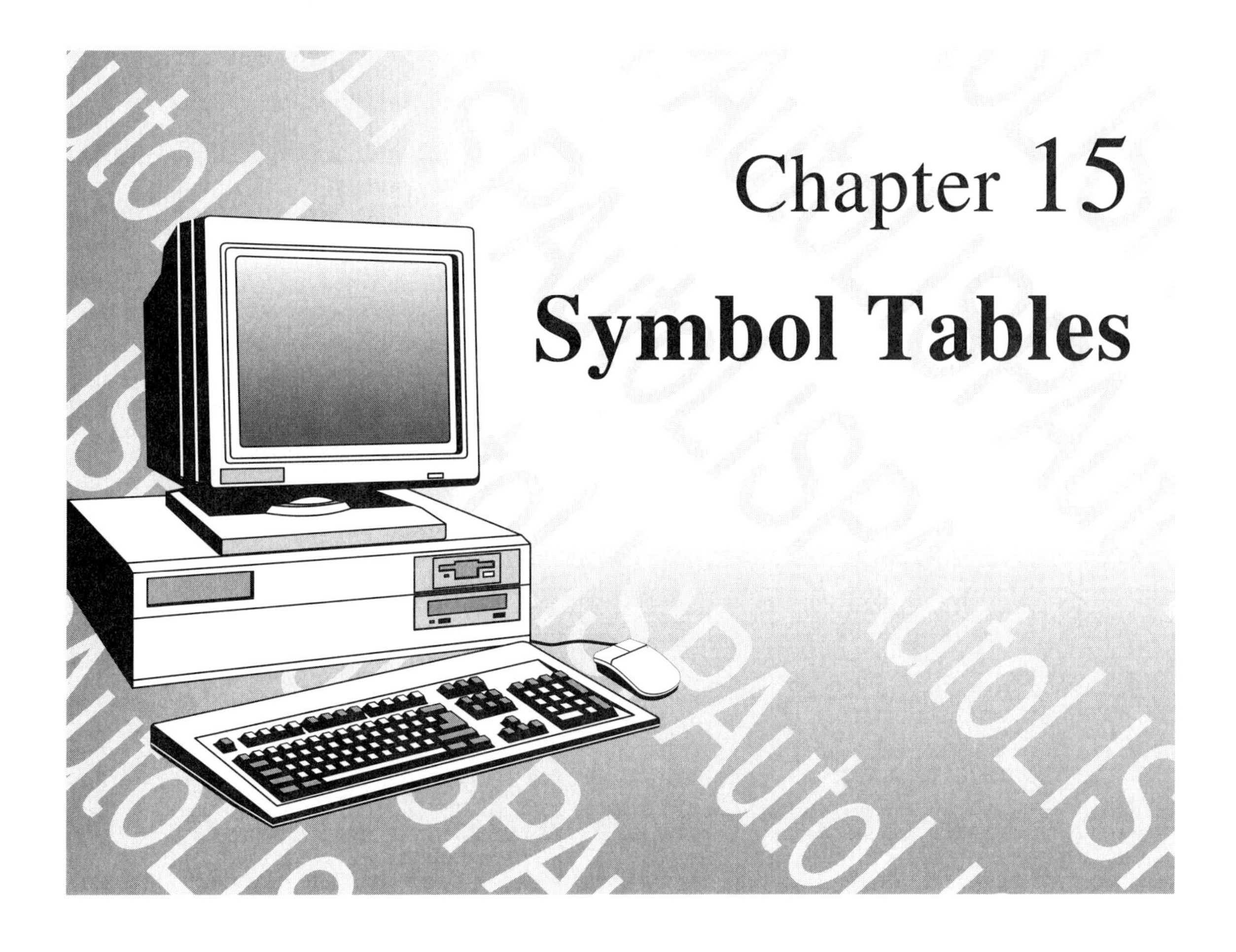

Chapter 15
Symbol Tables

Learning Objectives

After completing this chapter, you will be able to:

- ☐ Utilize the primary symbol table functions–TBLNEXT and TBLSEARCH–to examine and manipulate elements within AutoCAD's symbol tables.
- ☐ Scan object dictionaries for information stored in Mline styles and AutoCAD entity groups.
- ☐ Utilize DICTRENAME, DICTADD, and DICTREMOVE functions to affect object dictionaries.
- ☐ Take advantage of AutoLISP's wild card matching capabilities.
- ☐ Recognize the structural differences between viewports as configurations and viewports as entities.
- ☐ Utilize the SETVIEW function to establish a view.

AUTOCAD SYMBOL TABLES

The AutoCAD entity database contains structured and detailed information, which can be accessed through the use of AutoLISP entity-handling functions. This group of functions utilizes associated data lists–records that "describe" every technical aspect of an entity. As demonstrated in Chapter 13, entity data can be extracted and manipulated in a variety of ways. The returned results are oftentimes beyond the scope of standard AutoCAD commands.

As a complement to the entity name and data functions, AutoLISP provides a number of functions that enable access to AutoCAD's *symbol tables,* such as blocks, layers, and linetypes. Symbol tables can be viewed as inventory managers, where the contents are defined and numbered. Each unique item in a symbol table can be referenced quickly and easily.

Entity-handling functions are used for accessing and modifying the entity database. However, symbol table functions are required for accessing the data that comprises the framework of a drawing file.

Introduction to Symbol Table Functions

Access to AutoCAD's symbol tables is provided by the AutoLISP TBLNEXT and TBLSEARCH functions. The TBLNEXT function allows scanning of entire symbol tables, while TBLSEARCH locates a specified symbol within a given table. To introduce and describe the nature of AutoCAD symbol tables, several examples and basic guidelines are given in the following section.

The TBLNEXT Function

The *TBLNEXT (TaBLe NEXT) function* is the primary function for scanning an entire symbol table. Access is allowed to the following AutoCAD symbol tables:

- "APPID" (APPlication IDentification)
- "BLOCK"
- "DIMSTYLE"
- "LAYER"
- "LTYPE"
- "STYLE"
- "UCS"
- "VIEW"
- "VPORT"

The syntax for the TBLNEXT function is:

```
(tblnext TABLE-NAME [REWIND])
```

The TABLE-NAME string argument specifies the desired symbol table, and is written in either uppercase or lowercase characters. The optional REWIND argument returns the symbol table pointer to the beginning (first element) upon evaluating to a non-nil value. When the REWIND argument is nil or is omitted, AutoLISP returns the next consecutive entry within the symbol table.

The following examples utilize the TBLNEXT function. Each entry is returned in a DXF-type dotted pair format.

Command: **(tblnext "LAYER" T)** ↵ *set to the first layer table entry*
((0 . "LAYER") (2 . "0") (70 . 0) (62 . 7) (6 . "CONTINUOUS"))

The DXF code translation for each dotted pair is as follows:

0 = Symbol type	*"LAYER" symbol table.*
2 = Name of symbol	*Layer named "0".*
70 = Layer status flag	*0 means layer status is "On" and "Thawed".*
62 = Color number	*Color is 7 (white); negative when layer is "Off".*
6 = Linetype name	*"CONTINUOUS" is default linetype.*

For the following example, create a view named FULLSCREEN in your current drawing. Some of the values returned at your workstation will be different than those shown here.

```
Command: (tblnext "VIEW" T) ↵                    set to the first view table entry
( (0 . "VIEW") (2 . "FULLSCREEN") (70 . 0) (40 . 18.0) (10 . 14.7213 9.0) (41 . 29.4426)
(11 . 0.0 0.0 1.0) (12 . 0.0 0.0 0.0) (42 . 50) (43 . 0.0) (44 . 0.0) (50 . 0.0) (71 . 0) )
```

When reformatted for readability, the returned result appears as follows:

```
( (0 . "VIEW")                    Symbol type.
  (2 . "FULLSCREEN")              Name of symbol.
  (70 . 0)                        Standard flag.
  (40 . 18.0)                     View height.
  (10 . 14.7213 9.0)              View center point.
  (41 . 29.4426)                  View width.
  (11 . 0.0 0.0 1.0)              WCS view direction from target.
  (12 . 0.0 0.0 0.0)              WCS target point.
  (42 . 50)                       Lens length.
  (43 . 0.0)                      Front clipping plane.
  (44 . 0.0)                      Back clipping plane.
  (50 . 0.0)                      Twist angle.
  (71 . 0)                        View mode.
)
```

This entry, because of its many screen attributes and ties with the WCS, is obviously more complex than the preceeding example. When there are no named views within the drawing, the (tblnext “VIEW” T) expression returns nil.

In the following example, the linetype symbol table (“LTYPE”) is accessed. The results have been reformatted for readability.

```
Command: (tblnext "LTYPE" T) ↵    Set to the first linetype table entry.
                                    (The LTYPE table holds only the
                                    currently "loaded" linetypes.)
( (0 . "LTYPE")                   Symbol type.
  (2 . "CONTINUOUS")              Name of symbol.
  (70 . 0)                        Standard flag.
  (3 . "Solid line")              Descriptive text.
  (72 . 65)                       Alignment code.
  (73 . 0)                        Number of dash length items.
  (40 . 0.0)                      Total pattern length.
)
```

As mentioned earlier, if the next consecutive table entry is needed, the TBLNEXT function is applied *without* the REWIND argument. This is the case with any symbol table, and is the mechanism used to cycle through an entire table. After all table entries have been evaluated, AutoLISP returns nil. Again, the results have been reformatted for clarity.

```
Command: (tblnext "LTYPE") ↵         Set to the next linetype table entry.

( (0 . "LTYPE")                      Symbol type.
  (2 . "HIDDEN")                     Name of symbol.
  (70 . 0)                           Standard flag.
  (3 . "__ __ __")                   Description (shortened in this exam-
                                       ple).
  (72 . 65)                          Alignment code.
  (73 . 2)                           Number of dash length items (1
                                       segment, 1 space)
  (40 . 0.375)                       Total pattern length (0.25 + 0.125).
  (49 . 0.25)                        Dash length 1 (pen down for 0.25).
  (49 . –0.125)                      Dash length 2 (pen up for 0.125).
)

Command: (tblnext "LTYPE") ↵         Set to the next linetype table entry,
                                       and if no more linetypes have
                                       been loaded...
nil                                  All linetype table entries have been
                                       processed.
```

Since each table entry is unique, there is no duplication within any symbol table. Furthermore, regardless of the number of times that an identical block is inserted within the drawing editor, only one definition appears for that entity in the block symbol table. Consequently, this reduces the amount of memory needed to store the table and its respective elements. The following is an example of a "block" definition. Once again, the results have been reformatted for clarity.

```
Command: (setq A (tblnext "BLOCK" T)) ↵    Set to the first block table entry.
( (0 . "BLOCK")                            Symbol type.
  (2 . "PART–1A")                          Name of symbol.
  (70 . 66)                                Block-type flag–has attribute(s).
  (10 . 0.0 0.0 0.0)                       Origin (X,Y,Z).
  (–2 . <Entity name: bfe538>)             Name of primary entity.
)
```

Notice that the primary entity name is composed of an associated –2 group code. This particular association group, present only in the block symbol table, is accepted by ENTGET and ENTNEXT, but is invalid with any of the other entity-access functions.

To clarify the difference, block entities interrogated by entity data functions begin with the associated –1 group code (entity name).

For the following example, create a block that includes line segments named "PART-1A." When the block is selected using ENTSEL and retreived with ENTGET, these results would be returned. (The results have been reformatted for clarity.)

Command: **(setq S (entget (car (entsel))))** ↵	*The block "PART-1A" must be picked.*
((–1 . ⟨Entity name: bfe5d8⟩)	*Name of first entity.*
(0 . "INSERT")	*Entity type (INSERTed block reference).*
(5 . "3B")	*Entity handle.*
(100 . "AcDbEntity")	*Subclass data marker (class as string).*
(67 . 0)	*Model Space = 0 ; Paper Space = 1.*
(8 . "0")	*Layer designation.*
(100 . "AcDbBlockReference")	*Subclass data marker (class as string).*
(66 . 1)	*Attributes-follow flag ; present if = 1.*
(2 . "PART-1A")	*Name of symbol.*
(10 5.98779 7.61083 0.0)	*Insertion point (X,Y,Z).*
(41 . 1.0)	*X scale factor.*
(42 . 1.0)	*Y scale factor.*
(43 . 1.0)	*Z scale factor.*
(50 . 0.0)	*Angular rotation.*
(70 . 0)	*MINSERT column count.*
(71 . 0)	*MINSERT row count.*
(44 . 0.0)	*MINSERT column spacing.*
(45 . 0.0)	*MINSERT row spacing.*
(210 0.0 0.0 1.0)	*3D extrusion vector.*
)	

A few major distinctions between the prior two lists require further detail.

1. Primary entity names contained within block tables, such as ⟨Entity name: bfe538⟩, are reference designations only and are tied to individual block table definitions.

   The name found with ENTGET–⟨Entity name: bfe5d8⟩–is actually a pointer into the entity database records, making it a valid "Select objects:" candidate.

2. The symbol type for block tables is "BLOCK," and is a reference to a particular table. The entity extraction symbol type is "INSERT," and is a reference to a specific entity type.

3. The associated 10 group code for the symbol table is (10 . 0.0 0.0 0.0), and remains static. The WCS insertion point (10 5.98779 7.61083 0.0) given for the entity changes as the block is moved inside the drawing editor. In addition, coordinate data returned by NENTSEL are resolved via the Model to World Transformation Matrix. (The Model to World Transformation Matrix is detailed in Chapter 13.)

4. Block tables carry attribute definition data, and are referenced as an "ATTDEF" (ATTribute DEFinition–group code 0). Block tables include the associated 3 group (attribute text prompt) within the attribute definition data.

   The entity extraction listing carries the same attribute definition data. However, the associated 3 group (attribute text prompt) is excluded from the list. Attributes that are examined by entity extraction are referenced as an "ATTRIB" (ATTRIBute–group code 0).

5. The associated –2 group in the block table contains the primary entity name. Subentities are listed under the primary entity name, and include the sequence of drawing primitives (such as lines, arcs, circles, etc.) that comprise the defined block. These elements also possess entity names that refer only to block table definitions.

   The NENTSEL function must be used to inquire about separate block parts (drawing primitives such as lines, arcs, circles, etc.) during a single AutoLISP entity selection process.

Note the following lists, and compare the entity names for each. The first list represents an associated list acquired by using ENTGET and ENTNEXT on the block table entry, as in the following:

```
Command: (setq B (entget (entnext (cdr (assoc –2 A)))))↵   Variable A is the first
                                                           block
  (assoc –2 A)            returns     Associated –2 entity list from variable A
  (cdr (assoc –2 A))      returns     Extract primary entity name
  (entnext . . .)         returns     Next entity name (1st subentity)
  (entget . . .)          returns     Subentity definition data

  ( (-1 . <Entity name: bfe5b8>)            Next entity definition name.
    (0 . "LINE")                            Symbol type.
    (5 . "37")                              Entity handle.
    (100 . "AcDbEntity")                    Subclass data marker (string).
    (67 . 0)                                Model Space = 0 ; Paper Space = 1.
    (8 . "0")                               Layer designation.
    (100 . "AcDbLine")                      Subclass data marker (string).
    (10 0.5625 1.625 0.0)                   Start point.
    (11 1.0625 1.875 0.0)                   End point.
    (210 0.0 0.0 1.0)                       3D extrusion vector.
  )
```

The second list is returned by using NENTSEL on the block entity:

```
Command: (setq V (nentsel)) ↵                Select the line entity corresponding
                                               to the one in the previous
                                               associated list.
( <Entity name: bfe5b8>)                     Entity name.
 (6.28585 6.01509 0.0)                       Pick point of entity in drawing editor.
 ( (1.0 0.0 0.0)                             Model to World Transformation
                                               Matrix.
   (0.0 1.0 0.0)
   (0.0 0.0 1.0)
   (5.98779 7.61083 0.0)
 )
 (<Entity name: bfe5d8>)                     Name of "parent" block containing
                                               selected entity.
)
```

Each list has the same entity name–a reference to the block table! This symbol table provides the entities that comprise a block definition, which may be easily accessed with the ENTGET and ENTNEXT functions.

The following AutoLISP program takes advantage of the capability of the TBLNEXT function. This routine cycles through the "LTYPE" symbol table, and reports all loaded linetypes within the current drawing session. The numbers shown in brackets [] refer to the documentation following each program.

```
; Filename: LOADTYPE.LSP
;
; Author: Dot N. Dash
;
; Date: December 17, 19xx
;
; Purpose: This routine reports all loaded linetypes.
;          The report is generated to the text screen nearly
;          identical to the "?" option of the AutoCAD LINETYPE
;          command. This program helps to illustrate how table
;          information can be presented.
(defun C:LOADTYPE (/ LTYP LST TYP DES GAP CTR SPA NAME CHECK)
  (setvar "cmdecho" 0)
  (setq LTYP (tblnext "ltype" T) LST '() )                      ; [1]
  (while LTYP                                                   ; [2]
    (setq TYP  (cdr (assoc 2 LTYP))
          LST  (cons TYP LST)
          DES  (cdr (assoc 3 LTYP))
          LST  (cons DES LST)
          LTYP (tblnext "ltype")
    )                                   ; End setq
  )                                     ; End while
  (setq LST (reverse LST) GAP 19 CTR 0 SPA " ")                 ; [3]
  (command ".textscr")
  (princ "\n_ _ _ _ _Linetype_ _ _ _ _   _ _ _Description_ _ _\n")  ; [4]
;
  (while (setq NAME (nth CTR LST))                              ; [5]
    (princ (strcat "\n"                                         ; [6]
                NAME
                (repeat (- GAP (strlen NAME))
                        (setq SPA (strcat " " SPA))
                )
                (nth (1+ CTR) LST)
           )                            ; End strcat
    )                                   ; End princ
    (setq CHECK (+ CTR 2))                                      ; [7]
    (if (= (gcd CHECK 10) 10) (princ "\n"))                     ; [8]
    (if (= (gcd CHECK 30) 30) (getstring "\n- -<Enter> for More- -"))  ; [9]
    (setq SPA " " CTR CHECK)                                    ; [10]
  )                                     ; End while
;
  (setvar "cmdecho" 1)
  (princ)
)
; - -< End of File >- -
```

Documentation for LOADTYPE.LSP

[1] (setq LTYP (tblnext "ltype" T) LST '()) Set the "LTYPE" symbol table to the beginning, and initialize an empty list called LST. The list LST will eventually contain all linetypes with their respective descriptions.

[2] **(while LTYP**
```
(setq TYP  (cdr (assoc 2 LTYP))
      LST  (cons TYP LST)
      DES  (cdr (assoc 3 LTYP))
      LST  (cons DES LST)
      LTYP (tblnext "ltype")
```

While there are LTYPes to process, add the TYPe (assoc 2 LTYP) and DEScription (assoc 3 LTYP) to the new list LST. Each associated list from the "LTYPE" symbol table contains a linetype name and character description. The CONS function is instrumental in constructing the list LST, adding each TYPe and DEScription from the symbol table to the list. The variable LTYP is reset to the next consecutive entry in the "LTYPE" symbol (tblnext "ltype"), and will evaluate to nil after all entries are encountered. The returned nil value forces the program to drop out of the WHILE loop.

[3] **(setq LST (reverse LST) GAP 19 CTR 0 SPA " ")** Since the list LST is assembled backwards, reverse LST. Initialize variables GAP, CTR, and SPA. GAP is used for overall gap size. The counter CTR is established as an increment for marking. SPA will assist in determining the correct number of spaces between NAME and DEScription.

[4] **(princ "\n_ _ _ _Linetype_ _ _ _ _ _ _ _Description_ _ _\n")** Print the headers for Linetype and Description.

[5] **(while (setq NAME (nth CTR LST))** While there are linetype NAMEs to process (setq NAME (nth CTR LST)), print the following information within the loop. The NTH function begins with the first element contained in the list LST.

[6] Concatenate the linetype NAME (nth CTR LST) with its DEScription (nth (1+ CTR) LST) from LST, and print the string to the screen. The REPEAT function is used for inserting the appropriate number of spaces between the NAME and its DEScription. The two are separated by (– GAP (strlen NAME)) spaces. The longer the string length of NAME, the shorter the GAP.

[7] **(setq CHECK (+ CTR 2))** After each pair of NAME and DEScription are printed, then set the variable CHECK to (+ CTR 2)...

[8] **if (= (gcd CHECK 10) 10)**, then print a blank line (princ "\n"). This test ensures that five pairs of items have been processed through LST before printing a blank line. Note the use of the GCD [Greatest Common Denominator] function to return the desired results–when the variable CHECK eventually reaches 10, the IF test returns true, and a newline is printed to the screen.

[9] **if (= (gcd CHECK 30) 30)**, then issue a prompt to the user stating that there is more (getstring "\n– –⟨Enter⟩ for More– –"). After printing 15 pairs of linetype names and descriptions, it makes sense to stop and let the user view the page. Note the usage of the GETSTRING function that not only prints a message to the screen, but also awaits user input in the form of an ⟨Enter⟩.

[10] **(setq SPA " " CTR CHECK)** The symbol SPA is reset in order to process the appropriate number of spaces for the next NAME. The counter CTR is set to CHECK in order to maintain the proper position for processing each element within the list LST.

The TBLSEARCH Function

The *TBLSEARCH (TaBLe SEARCH) function* searches an entire symbol table for a specified symbol. All tables supported by the TBLNEXT function are also valid for TBLSEARCH. The format for the TBLSEARCH function is:

```
(tblsearch TABLE-NAME SYMBOL [SETNEXT])
```

The TABLE-NAME string argument indicates the desired symbol table, and is written in either uppercase or lowercase characters. The SYMBOL string argument is the element to be located within the TABLE-NAME. In addition, the optional SETNEXT argument, when present and evaluates to a non-nil value, sets the table entry counter. When adjusted, the entry counter points to the next element in the symbol table, thus affecting the next TBLNEXT call.

The following example illustrates the use of the TBLSEARCH function. Like TBLNEXT, the result is returned in a DXF-type dotted pair format. Once again, the results have been reformatted for readability.

```
Command: (setq Q (tblsearch "STYLE" "MARK")) ↵   The text style "MARK" is retrieved.

( (0 . "STYLE")                  Symbol type="STYLE".
  (2 . "MARK")                   Name of symbol="MARK".
  (70 . 0)                       Flag Linked with group code 71.
  (40 . 0.5)                     Fixed text height=0.5 drawing units.
  (41 . 1.0)                     Width factor=1.0.
  (50 . 0.261799)                Obliquing angle=15 degrees as radians.
  (71 . 0)                       Generation flags; 0=Normal generation.
  (42 . 0.759487)                Last text height used=0.759487 drawing units.
  (3 . "simplex.shx")            Primary font file="simplex.shx" .
  (4 . "")                       Bigfont file name; "" represents none.
)
```

The following AutoLISP program exploits the capabilities of the TBLSEARCH and TBLNEXT functions. The SEARCH.LSP program cycles through each AutoCAD symbol table, looking for the given string argument. After the search is complete, a report is generated to the text screen. Detailed documentation follows the program.

```
; Filename:  SEARCH.LSP
;
; Author:  F.I. Ndit
;
; Date:  January 12, 19xx
;
; Purpose:  This routine searches for string DOG in all AutoCAD symbol
;           tables. A search report is generated to the text screen.
;
(defun SEARCH (DOG)
  (setvar "cmdecho" 0)
  (setq LST '("Layer" "Ltype" "Style" "Dimstyle" "Block"        ; [1]
              "Ucs" "Appid" "View" "Vport")
  )
```

```
    (command ".textscr")
    (foreach TNAME LST                              ; [2]
      (cond ((null (setq ITEM (tblnext TNAME T)))   ; [3]
              (princ (strcat "\nThere are no entries in the " TNAME " Table!"
                     )                              ; End strcat
              )                                     ; End princ
            )
            ((setq ITEM (tblsearch TNAME DOG))
              (princ (strcat "\n" DOG " was found in the " TNAME " Table."
                     )                              ; End strcat
              )                                     ; End princ
            )
            (T
              (princ (strcat "\n" DOG was NOT found in the " TNAME " Table."
                     )                              ; End strcat
              )                                     ; End princ
            )
      )                                             ; End cond
    )                                               ; End foreach
    (setvar "cmdecho" 1)
    (princ)
)
; --( End of File )--
```

Documentation for SEARCH.LSP

[1] (setq LST '("Layer" "Ltype" "Style" "Dimstyle" "Block" "Ucs" "Appid" "View" "Vport")) The variable LST is a list containing all AutoCAD symbol table names. Each name, in turn, is eventually passed to TBLSEARCH and TBLNEXT for interrogation.

[2] The FOREACH function takes each symbol TNAME [Table NAME] within list LST and passes it to the COND function. When FOREACH has exhausted the entire list, nil is returned, and the remainder of the program is evaluated.

[3] Three conditions could arise when searching for TNAME within the symbol tables:

A. **(null (setq ITEM (tblnext TNAME T)))**–The TNAME symbol table is rewound to the first entry, shown by the nested expression (tblnext TNAME T). In the event that variable ITEM, the first table entry, is nil, print a message that there are no elements present in this symbol table.

B. **(setq ITEM (tblsearch TNAME DOG))**–Search for DOG, the user-specified string argument, within the TNAME symbol table. If this conditional test returns T (true), the PRINC function is employed:

```
(princ (strcat "\n" DOG " was found in the " TNAME " Table."))
                                  ; Print message – DOG was found!
```

C. T (True)–When conditional tests 1 and 2 return nil, at least do the final test. Print a message that string DOG was not found in this symbol table. Again, the search for DOG continues until the FOREACH expression has used all elements within LST.

Since the SEARCH.LSP program in not an AutoCAD command line function, it must be placed within parenthesis. Futhermore, include the required string argument when running the program. An example of this program's syntax might be:

Command: **(search "Part1")** ↵

The text string "Part1" is the required argument to search for in the symbol tables.

EXERCISE 15-1

- ☐ Write a program that generates the following information:
- ☐ Report all views found in the drawing editor.
- ☐ For each view, display its View name, View height, and View center point.
- ☐ Establish labels for each part of the report.
- ☐ Test the effectiveness of this program using a drawing that contains at least six named views.
- ☐ Name the program VIEWREP.LSP.

The TBLOBJNAME Function

The *TBLOBJNAME (TaBLe OBJect NAME) function* searches the specified symbol table for a given symbol name, and returns the entity name of that symbol table entry. All tables supported by the TBLNEXT and TBLSEARCH functions are also valid for TBLOBJNAME. The format for the TBLOBJNAME function is:

(tblobjname TABLE-NAME SYMBOL)

Similar to the TBLSEARCH function, the TABLE-NAME string argument is written in either upper or lowercase characters, and indicates the desired symbol table to search. The SYMBOL string argument is the element to be located within the TABLE-NAME. If the symbol name is found, its respective entity name is returned, otherwise TBLOBJNAME returns nil.

Take note of the following examples, where symbol names are accessed through the application of the TBLOBJNAME function. Entity names are subsequently returned and are explored via the use of the ENTGET function. It is assumed that a layer named "CENTER" with a "CENTER" linetype is present within the current drawing.

Command: **(setq LC (tblobjname "LAYER" "CENTER"))** ↵
⟨Entity name: bfa650⟩
Command: **(entget LC)** ↵

((-1 . ⟨Entity name: bfa650⟩)	*Entity name.*
(0 . "LAYER")	*Entity type.*
(5 . "4A")	*Entity handle.*
(100 . "AcDbSymbolTableRecord")	*Subclass data marker – Symbol Table.*
(100 . "AcDbLayerTableRecord")	*Subclass data marker – Layer Table.*
(2 . "CENTER")	*Name of symbol.*

```
   (70 . 4)                                  Layer status flag.
   (62 . 7)                                  Layer color.
   (6 . "CENTER")                            Layer linetype.
)

Command: (entget (tblobjname "STYLE" "STANDARD")) ↵
( (-1 . <Entity name: bfa480>)               Entity name.
   (0 . "STYLE")                             Entity type.
   (5 . "10")                                Entity handle.
   (100 . "AcDbSymbolTableRecord")           Subclass data marker – Symbol
                                               Table.
   (100 . "AcDbTextStyleTableRecord")        Subclass data marker – Text Style.
   (2 . "STANDARD")                          Name of symbol.
   (70 . 0)                                  Text style standard flag.
   (40 . 0.0)                                Fixed text height.
   (41 . 1.0)                                Width factor.
   (50 . 0.0)                                Obliquing angle.
   (71 . 0)                                  Generation flags.
   (42 . 0.2)                                Last text height used.
   (3 . "txt")                               Primary font file.
   (4 . "")                                  Bigfont file name.
)

Command: (tblobjname "UCS" "NO_SUCH_NAME") ↵
nil                                          There is no UCS named
                                             "NO_SUCH_NAME".
```

The SNVALID Function

The *SNVALID (Symbol Name VALID) function* checks the given string argument for valid characters. The argument may include all alphanumeric characters, dollar signs ($), underscores (_), and hyphens (–). The syntax for SNVALID is as follows:

```
(snvalid SYM_NAME [FLAG])
```

The SYM_NAME string argument may be up to 31 characters long. Where this symbol name is valid, the SNVALID function returns T; otherwise, nil is returned. The optional FLAG argument can be set to 1 or 0 (default). Where the optional FLAG argument is set to 1, text strings that represent external references and their dependent symbol names return T. Conversely, if the FLAG argument is set to the default value of 0, the identical text strings return nil.

The SNVALID function is intended for use with all AutoCAD symbol tables and their respective symbol names, and should not be considered as a spelling checker within AutoLISP. Examine the following examples using the SNVALID function.

```
(snvalid "part1")                 returns T
(snvalid "part1 a")               returns nil. No spaces are allowed
(snvalid "part1-a")               returns T
(snvalid "$500--Assembly")        returns T
(snvalid "Xref|LayerName")        returns nil. The "|" is disallowed.
(snvalid "Xref|LayerName" 1)      returns T. The "|" is now allowed.
(snvalid "Xref_Block")            returns T
(snvalid 3D–UCS)                  returns error: bad argument type
(snvalid "3D–UCS")                returns T
(snvalid "Ext_App_45-A")          returns T
```

The following AutoLISP program takes advantage of the SNVALID function, creating a user interface for changing user coordinate systems within the drawing editor.

```
; Filename: SELUCS.LSP
;
; Author:     U. C. Ess
;
; Purpose:   After presenting the current drawing's named user coordinate
;            systems (by dialog and displaying on screen), ask the user
;            to select the ucs of choice.
;
(defun C:SELUCS (/ NEXT_UCS UCS_SET SETS NAME RES)
  (setvar "cmdecho" 0)
  (defun SHOW ()                              ; Defined function for
    (foreach ITEM UCS_SET                     ;   displaying all named
      (princ (strcat "\nShowing UCS: " ITEM)) ;   ucs's to the screen.
      (command ".ucs" "restore" ITEM          ; Foreach will cycle
               ".delay" 2000)                 ;   through all ucs's in
    )                                         ;   the "UCS" table, restore
  )                                           ;   and display each one.
  (setq NEXT_UCS (tblnext "ucs" t)      ; Rewind the UCS symbol table
        UCS_SET '()                     ; Initialize empty list UCS_SET
        SETS      "Current UCS's"       ; Text heading for ALERT box
  )
  (if (null NEXT_UCS)                         ; If no named ucs's exist...
    (princ "\nNo named UCS's at this time")   ; Tell the user...else...
    (progn
      (while NEXT_UCS                         ; While there is a NEXT_UCS
        (if
          (snvalid (setq NAME (cdr (assoc 2 NEXT_UCS))))   ; Ucs NAME
          (setq SETS      (strcat SETS "\n" NAME)          ; Add NAME to string
                UCS_SET   (cons NAME UCS_SET)              ; Add NAME to set
                NEXT_UCS  (tblnext "ucs")                  ; NEXT_UCS becomes
          )                                                ; the next "ucs"
          (princ (strcat "\nInvalid name: " NAME))
        )
      )
      (alert SETS)                            ; Display the ucs's
      (setq UCS_SET (reverse UCS_SET))        ; Reorder the set
      (command ".ucs" "world")
      (SHOW)                                  ; Run SHOW function
      (if (= ""                               ; If RES = 〈 enter 〉...
        (setq RES (getstring "\nSelect named UCS/Display 〈 enter 〉: "))
        )
        (progn                                ; SHOW, and select ucs
          (SHOW)
          (alert SETS)
```

```
            (setq RES (getstring "\nSelect named UCS: "))
            (command ".ucs" "restore" RES)
          )
          (command ".ucs" "restore" RES)       ; Else, restore ucs
        )
      ) ; end progn
    ) ; end if
    (princ)
  ) ; end defun
```

The WCMATCH Function

The *WCMATCH (Wild Card MATCH) function* makes it possible to search for any matching combination of strings or substrings. Not only are wild card strings applicable to AutoCAD, they are also important in AutoLISP programming. The syntax for the WCMATCH function is as follows:

```
(wcmatch STRING PATTERN)
```

The matching process is performed on the STRING argument. The PATTERN argument specifies what sequence of characters (or groups of characters) is used to test against the STRING argument. The maximum limit for each argument is approximately 500 characters. If you exceed this limit, the remainder of the characters are ignored.

The comparison between STRING and PATTERN is case-sensitive (uppercase or lowercase characters must match). If a match is made between STRING and PATTERN (STRING = PATTERN), the WCMATCH function returns T (true).

Several wild card options are available, Fig. 15-1. These wild card options enable a programmer to include or exclude characters found in STRING.

Character	Definition
# (pound)	Matches any single numeric digit.
@ (at)	Matches any single alphabetic character.
. (period)	Matches any single nonalphanumeric character.
* (asterisk)	Matches any character sequence, including an empty one. It can be used anywhere in the search pattern–beginning, middle, or end.
? (question mark)	Matches any single character.
~ (tilde)	If the tilde is the first character in the pattern, then it matches anything except the pattern.
[...]	Matches any one of the characters enclosed.
[~...]	Matches any single character not enclosed.
– (hyphen)	Used inside brackets to specify a range for a single character.
, (comma)	Separates two patterns.
‘ (reverse quote)	Escapes special characters (reads next character literally).

Fig. 15-1. Wild card characters and definitions.

String searches can be conducted in a variety of places: selection set filter lists, symbol tables, attribute definitions, and so on. Furthermore, both the STRING and PATTERN arguments can take the form of either AutoLISP variables or returned values.

A single PATTERN argument can be applied, as shown in the following example:

```
(wcmatch "PART–1A" "P*")                          returns T
```

In this example, the STRING argument "PART–1A" starts with a capital "P" and has other alphabetic characters behind it (denoted by "*").

A multiple PATTERN argument can also be specified. Note how the commas are used in the following example:

```
(wcmatch "PART–1A" "S*,?????,~*Z*,PART–##")      returns T
```

In the second example, the PATTERN argument is specified as four conditions. If *any* of the four conditions are met, the WCMATCH function returns T. In this case, the STRING argument "PART–1A":

- Does not begin with an "S". (nil)
- Is not made up of five characters. (nil)
- Does not contain the letter "Z". (true)
- Does not end with two numbers. (nil)

Note that third conditional test returns true, therefore, the entire expression returns "T".

When either argument takes the form of an AutoLISP variable, the appearance of the WCMATCH function is slightly altered:

```
(setq STG (cdr (assoc 2 (tblnext "layer")))        Return layer name.
      PAT (getstring "\nPattern argument: ")       Pattern for comparison.
)
(if (wcmatch STG PAT) (setq NUM 5))                If the next layer name STG matches
                                                   variable PAT (the PATtern string
                                                   argument), set variable NUM to 5.
```

When matching elements contained within associated lists, the WCMATCH function is often used. The following example applies the AutoLISP ENTGET and ENTLAST functions to return data on the last entity placed in the drawing editor. The WCMATCH function provides a pattern test for the object being examined:

```
(setq OBJ (entget (entlast)))                      Associated list for entity OBJ.
(if (wcmatch (cdr (assoc 8 OBJ)) "~0")
   (command ".chprop" "last" "" "la" "0" "")
)                                                  CDR of group code 8 is OBJ's layer
                                                   designation–the WCMATCH string.
                                                   Does the string match anything not
                                                   equal to "0"–the WCMATCH pattern.
                                                   If the test is T (true), change the
                                                   last entity's layer to "0."
```

In certain situations, it becomes necessary to *escape* individual characters, such as testing for a wild card or searching for a backslash. The single reverse quote character (‘) allows WCMATCH to read the next single character literally:

(wcmatch "C:\\ACAD\\ACADLISP\\" "*‘*")	returns T	*In AutoLISP programming, it is required to supply two backslashes in directory prefixes to produce one actual backslash. The prefix shown above actually translates as "C:\ACAD\ACADLISP\", a DOS convention that most users are familiar with. The test pattern, "*‘*", allows any characters to be present before a single backslash, and any characters may follow. The reverse quote allows the embedded string "\\" to be read as a single backslash, an AutoLISP convention.*
(wcmatch "LISPFILE" "*‘*")	returns nil	*Again, the test pattern "*‘*" allows any characters to be present before a single backslash, and any characters may follow. The supplied string argument "LISPFILE" does not have a backslash, and consequently, the expression returns nil.*

There are two additional points that require mention in reference to the WCMATCH function:

1. The tilde character (~) is read literally when it is inside the pattern string (e.g. "dog~fight" or "car~chase").
2. The hyphen character (–) is read literally when it becomes the initial or ending bracketed character in a pattern string (e.g. "[-XYZ]" or "[abc-]").

The following AutoLISP program takes advantage of the WCMATCH function, returning matching elements within symbol tables.

```
; Filename: WC.LSP
;
; Author: Count Ting
;
; Date: November 18, 19xx
; Purpose: Scans any AutoCAD symbol table for wild card matching. More
;          than one wild card may be specified. Remember that wild cards
;          are case-sensitive. A report is generated to the text screen.
;
(defun C:WC (/ RES TBL TLST NAMELST LST NAME)
  (setvar "cmdecho" 0)
  (setq RES (getstring "\nSpecify wild card search string: "))
;
  (initget 1 "LAyer LType Style Dimstyle Block Ucs Appid VIew VPort")   ; [1]
;
  (prompt "\nSymbol table to search...")
  (setq TBL      (strcase (getkword
                  "\nLAyer/LType/Style/Dimstyle/Block/Ucs/Appid/VIew/VPort: "))
        TLST     '("LAYER" "LTYPE" "STYLE" "DIMSTYLE" "BLOCK"
                   "UCS" "APPID" "VIEW" "VPORT")
        NAMELST '()
  )
  (cond ((null (setq LST (tblnext TBL T)))                                ; [2]
         (princ (strcat "\nNo entries found in the " TBL " table!"))
        )
;
        (T                                                                ; [3]
         (while LST                                                       ; [4]
           (setq NAME (cdr (assoc 2 LST)))                                ; [5]
           (if (wcmatch NAME RES)                                         ; [6]
             (setq NAMELST (cons NAME NAMELST))
           )
           (setq LST (tblnext TBL))                                       ; [7]
         )                                  ; End while
         (if (null NAMELST)                                               ; [8]
           (princ (strcat "\nNo W.C. matches for the " TBL " table!"))
           (progn
             (command ".textscr")
             (princ "\nMatching list\n-------------\n")
             (foreach N NAMELST
               (princ N)
               (princ "\n")
             )                              ; End foreach
           )                                ; End progn
         )                                  ; End if
        )                                   ; End T
  )                                         ; End cond
  (setvar "cmdecho" 1)
  (princ)
)
; --< End of File >--
```

Documentation for WC.LSP

[1] **(initget 1 "LAyer LType Style Dimstyle Block Ucs Appid VIew VPort")** The INITGET function controls the user's next GETxxxx response, by allowing only those strings present in the INITGET string argument.
After having established the user wild card string and symbol table, there are two possible conditions.

[2] **(null (setq LST (tblnext TBL T)))** When there are no entries found within a valid symbol table, tell the user. Note that the table is wound to the beginning, and variable LST is set to the first entry. If there are items found within that table...

[3] **T (True)** Process the table for wild card matches.

[4] **(while LST** While LST exists...

[5] **(setq NAME (cdr (assoc 2 LST)))** Set NAME to the symbol name found in the associated 2 list.

[6] **(if (wcmatch NAME RES)** If NAME matches the wild card, CONS the NAME to the NAMELST. Variable NAMELST increases in size with each new addition of NAME.

[7] **(setq LST (tblnext TBL))** Set LST to the next entry in the symbol table, and continue testing if LST exists.

[8] **(if (null NAMELST)** If there were no matches to be found, then NAMELST is nil. Report this to the user. Where NAMELST contains matching elements, print this information to the test screen. The FOREACH function assists in printing all items from NAMELST.

THE AUTOCAD OBJECT DICTIONARY

Each AutoCAD drawing file contains a variety of graphical and nongraphical tables, including "BLOCK", "LAYER", and "VPORT." Access to this group of database managers is made possible by employing AutoLISP table functions, such as TBLNEXT and TBLSEARCH. For example, the TBLOBJNAME function may be used to modify AutoCAD "LTYPE" table definitions. Subsequently, AutoLISP's entity-handling functions are called to update the target data within the entire drawing. With this capability in mind, the programmer can implement a number of sweeping changes in the editor.

With AutoCAD Release 13 and later versions, it is now possible to work with data tied to an Object Dictionary. Similar to the nongraphical data stored in the AutoCAD "STYLE" table [parameters for text creation], information that originates from the Object Dictionary lists relative data entries that support either AutoCAD entity groups or mline styles. Each data entry, specifically entities found in the associated 350 groupings, is a pointer into a deeper nesting of information. From here, construction data may be extracted and interrogated by entity handling functions. The NAMEDOBJDICT function is the gateway into each drawing's Object Dictionary.

The NAMEDOBJDICT Function

The *NAMEDOBJDICT (NAMED OBJect DICTionary) function* returns the entity name of the current drawing's object dictionary. The *object dictionary* contains information relative to the nongraphical data present within the current drawing file. For each drawing, a unique object dictionary exists that details the specifics of entity groups and mline styles. The format for the NAMEDOBJDICT function is:

```
(namedobjdict)
```

The following illustration will help to demonstrate the use of the NAMEDOBJDICT function, where the ENTGET and ASSOC functions are instrumental in obtaining nested data associated with the object dictionary:

```
Command: (setq OD (namedobjdict)) ↵
⟨Entity name: bf9460⟩                Entity name–Object Dictionary.

Command: (setq DICT (entget OD)) ↵
(  (–1 . ⟨Entity name: bf9460⟩)       Entity name–Object Dictionary.
   (0 . "DICTIONARY")                 Entity type–"DICTIONARY".
   (5 . "C")                          Entity handle.
   (100 . "AcDbDictionary")           Subclass data marker–Dictionary.
   (280 . 0)                          8-bit integer value.
   (3 . "ACAD_GROUP")                 Group marker.
   (350 . ⟨Entity name: bf9468⟩)      Primary entity name for Groups.
   (3 . "ACAD_MLINESTYLE")            Mline style marker.
   (350 . ⟨Entity name: bf9470⟩)      Primary entity name for Mline styles.
)

Command: (setq G–AND–M (member (assoc 3 DICT) DICT)) ↵
(  (3 . "ACAD_GROUP")                 Group marker.
   (350 . ⟨Entity name: bf9468⟩)      Primary entity name for Groups.
   (3 . "ACAD_MLINESTYLE")            Mline style marker.
   (350 . ⟨Entity name: bf9470⟩)      Primary entity name for Mline styles.
)

Command: (setq GROUP–ENT (cdr (assoc 350 G-AND-M))) ↵
⟨Entity name: bf9468⟩                Primary entity name for Groups.

Command: (setq MLINE–AS (cddr G–AND–M)) ↵
(  (3 . "ACAD_MLINESTYLE")            Mline style marker.
   (350 . ⟨Entity name: bf9470⟩)      Primary entity name for Mline styles.
)

Command: (setq MLINE–ENT (cdr (assoc 350 MLINE-AS))) ↵
⟨Entity name: bf9470⟩                Primary entity name for Mline styles.

Command: (entget GROUP-ENT) ↵
(  (–1 . ⟨Entity name: bf9468⟩)       Entity name–Primary ename for Groups.
   (0 . "DICTIONARY")                 Entity type–"DICTIONARY".
   (5 . "D")                          Entity handle.
   (102 . "{ACAD_REACTORS")           Arbitrary control string.
   (330 . ⟨Entity name: bf9460⟩)      Entity name for Object Dictionary.
   (102 . "}")                        Arbitrary control string.
   (100 . "AcDbDictionary")           Subclass data marker–Dictionary.
   (280 . 0)                          8-bit integer value.
   (3 . "PARTS")                      Group name in current drawing file.
   (350 . ⟨Entity name: bf9700⟩)      Ename for preceeding group–"PARTS".
   (3 . "WIDGETS")                    Group name in current drawing file.
   (350 . ⟨Entity name: bf96f0⟩)      Ename for preceeding group–"WIDGETS".
   (3 . "GIZMOS")                     Group name in current drawing file.
   (350 . ⟨Entity name: bf96f8⟩)      Ename for preceeding group–"GIZMOS".
)
```

```
Command: (entget MLINE–ENT) ↵
(  (–1 . ‹Entity name: bf9470›)           Entity name–Primary ename for Mlines.
   (0 . "DICTIONARY")                     Entity type–"DICTIONARY".
   (5 . "E")                              Entity handle.
   (102 . "{ACAD_REACTORS")               Arbitrary control string.
   (330 . ‹Entity name: bf9460›)          Entity name for Object Dictionary.
   (102 . "}")                            Arbitrary control string.
   (100 . "AcDbDictionary")               Subclass data marker–Dictionary.
   (280 . 0)                              8-bit integer value.
   (3 . "BOUNDARY")                       Mline style name in current drawing.
   (350 . ‹Entity name: bf9728›)          Ename for mline style–"BOUNDARY".
   (3 . "STANDARD")                       Mline style name in current drawing.
   (350 . ‹Entity name: bf9498›)          Ename for mline style–"STANDARD".
)

Command: (entget (cdr (assoc 350 (entget MLINE–ENT)))) ↵
(  (–1 . ‹Entity name: bf9728›)           Entity name–"BOUNDARY".
   (0 . "MLINESTYLE")                     Entity type–"MLINESTYLE".
   (5 . "75")                             Entity handle.
   (102 . "{ACAD_REACTORS")               Arbitrary control string.
   (330 . ‹Entity name: bf9470›)          Primary entity name for Mline styles.
   (102 . "}")                            Arbitrary control string.
   (100 . "AcDbMlineStyle")               Subclass data marker–MlineStyle.
   (2 . "BOUNDARY")                       Mline style name.
   (70 . 272)                             Flag—Bit code for mline construction.
   (3 . "")                               Style description.
   (62 . 0)                               Fill color.
   (51 . 1.5708)                          Start angle in radians (default=90 deg).
   (52 . 1.5708)                          End angle in radians (default=90 deg).
   (71 . 5)                               Start cap attributes–Bit code.
   (49 . 0.5)                             Element offset value.
   (62 . 256)                             Element color value.
   (6 . "BYLAYER")                        Element linetype.
   (49 . 0.25)                            Element offset value.
   (62 . 1)                               Element color value.
   (6 . "DASHED")                         Element linetype.
   (49 . 0.0)                             Element offset value.
   (62 . 4)                               Element color value.
   (6 . "PHANTOM")                        Element linetype.
   (49 . -0.25)                           Element offset value.
   (62 . 1)                               Element color value.
   (6 . "DASHED")                         Element linetype.
   (49 . -0.5)                            Element offset value.
   (62 . 256)                             Element color value.
   (6 . "BYLAYER")                        Element linetype.
)
```

The preceeding expression, (entget (cdr (assoc 350 (entget MLINE-ENT)))), returns the first mline style located within the object dictionary. The mline elements, beginning with the first associated 49 group, provide the technical description for the mline:

```
(49 . 0.5)            1st line offset from center by +0.50
(62 . 256)               * Color value is 256–"BYLAYER"
(6 . "BYLAYER")          * Linetype value is –"BYLAYER"
(49 . 0.25)           2nd line offset from center by +0.25
(62 . 1)                 * Color value is 1–"RED"
(6 . "DASHED")           * Linetype value is–"DASHED"
(49 . 0.0)            3rd line is located on center 0.0
(62 . 4)                 * Color value is 4–"CYAN"
(6 . "PHANTOM")          * Linetype value is–"PHANTOM"
(49 . -0.25)          4th line offset from center by -0.25
(62 . 1)                 * Color value is 1–"RED"
(6 . "DASHED")           * Linetype value is–"DASHED"
(49 . -0.5)           5th line offset from center by -0.50
(62 . 256)               * Color value is 256–"BYLAYER"
(6 . "BYLAYER")          * Linetype value is –"BYLAYER"
```

When examining the object dictionary, the following concept generally applies to its internal structure:

1. The object dictionary is an established hierarchy based primarily upon its included AutoCAD groups and mline styles. The dictionary entity name sits at the top of this hierarchy, and acts as a doorway to the primary entity names for groups and mline styles.
2. The primary entity names for groups and mline styles are returned by the first ENTGET function call. These entity names are positioned at the second level of the hierarchy.
3. Individual or discrete entity names for groups and mline styles are returned by the second ENTGET function call. Similar to the entries given in AutoCAD's symbol tables, such as "STANDARD" for the AutoCAD "STYLE" symbol table, the programmer can now examine the available entries for each group or mline style.
4. Technical details for each group or mline style may be investigated at this point by employing a final ENTGET function call.

Currently, the object dictionary retains information pertaining only to AutoCAD entity groups and mline styles. Future releases of AutoCAD will presumably consolidate other data tables now found in the drawing editor, and place them within the object dictionary.

The next two functions, DICTNEXT and DICTSEARCH, allows for discrete viewing of material found in the object dictionary. When used in tandem with the entity-handling functions, as well as NAMEDOBJDICT, these two tools provide an efficient means for manipulating object dictionary entries.

The DICTNEXT Function

The *DICTNEXT (DICTionary NEXT) function* works similarly to the AutoLISP TBLNEXT function, where dictionary items are scanned for information according to entity name and symbol arguments. The syntax for the DICTNEXT function is:

```
(dictnext ENAME SYMBOL [REWIND])
```

The ENAME argument specifies a dictionary object to search. Valid symbol names include ACAD_MLINESTYLE and ACAD_GROUP. Where DICTNEXT is dispatched repeatedly, by using the expression (dictnext ENAME), the function returns the next consecutive entry as specified by the dictionary symbol name.

The optional REWIND argument, upon evaluating to a non-nil value, sets the dictionary to the first entry. Take note of the following example:

```
Command: (setq OD (namedobjdict)) ↵
⟨Entity name: bf9460⟩

Command: (setq GRPS (dictnext OD "acad_group")) ↵
(  (–1 . ⟨Entity name: bf9468⟩)          Entity name—Primary ename for Groups.
   (0 . "DICTIONARY")                    Entity type–"DICTIONARY".
   (5 . "D")                             Entity handle.
   (102 . "{ACAD_REACTORS")              Arbitrary control string.
   (330 . ⟨Entity name: bf9460⟩)         Entity name for Object Dictionary.
   (102 . "}")                           Arbitrary control string.
   (100 . "AcDbDictionary")              Subclass data marker—Dictionary.
   (280 . 0)                             8-bit integer value.
   (3 . "PARTS")                         Group name in current drawing file.
   (350 . ⟨Entity name: bf9700⟩)         Ename for preceeding group–"PARTS".
   (3 . "WIDGETS")                       Group name in current drawing file.
   (350 . ⟨Entity name: bf96f0⟩)         Ename for preceeding group–"WIDGETS".
   (3 . "GIZMOS")                        Group name in current drawing file.
   (350 . ⟨Entity name: bf96f8⟩)         Ename for preceeding group–"GIZMOS".
)

Command: (setq GRP-1 (entget (cdr (assoc 350 GRPS)))) ↵
(  (–1 . ⟨Entity name: bf9700⟩)          Entity name–Group "PARTS".
   (0 . "GROUP")                         Entity type–"GROUP".
   (5 . "70")                            Entity handle.
   (102 . "{ACAD_REACTORS")              Arbitrary control string.
   (330 . ⟨Entity name: bf9468⟩)         Groups Primary entity name.
   (102 . "}")                           Arbitrary control string.
   (100 . "AcDbGroup")                   Subclass data marker–Group.
   (300 . "")                            Arbitrary text string.
   (70 . 0)                              Selectability flag.
   (71 . 1)                              Flag.
   (340 . ⟨Entity name: bf96e0⟩)         1st entity within group.
   (340 . ⟨Entity name: bf96d8⟩)         2nd entity within group.
   (340 . ⟨Entity name: bf96d0⟩)         3rd entity within group.
   (340 . ⟨Entity name: bf9670⟩)         4th entity within group.
   (340 . ⟨Entity name: bf96e8⟩)         5th entity within group.
)
```

```
Command: (setq ENT1_GRP–1 (entget (cdr (assoc 340 GRP–1)))) ↵
(  (–1 . <Entity name: bf96e0>)       Entity name–1st entity within group.
   (0 . "LINE")                       Entity type–"LINE".
   (5 . "6C")                         Entity handle.
   (100 . "AcDbEntity")               Subclass data marker–Entity.
   (67 . 0)                           Space–Model or Paper.
   (8 . "PART")                       Layer name.
   (100 . "AcDbLine")                 Subclass data marker–Line.
   (39 . 2.0)                         Entity thickness.
   (10 8.0 5.875 0.0)                 Start point.
   (11 5.75 7.0 0.0)                  End point.
   (210 0.0 0.0 1.0)                  Extrusion direction.
)
```

The DICTNEXT function immediately returns group/entity name data that provides quick access to this part of the AutoCAD file structure. Further exploration takes place by using the ENTGET function to procure each object within the target entity group. Compare this usage of AutoLISP programming code with those expressions listed for NAMEDOBJDICT.

The DICTSEARCH Function

The *DICTSEARCH (DICTionary SEARCH) function* works similarly to the AutoLISP TBLSEARCH function, where dictionary items are searched for according to the entity name and symbol arguments. The syntax for the DICTSEARCH function is:

```
(dictsearch ENAME SYMBOL [SETNEXT])
```

The ENAME argument specifies a dictionary object to search. Like DICTNEXT, valid symbol names include ACAD_MLINESTYLE and ACAD_GROUP. If DICTSEARCH locates an entry for the specified item, the function returns that entry in the format described for DICTNEXT. The optional SETNEXT argument, upon evaluating to a non-nil value, adjusts the DICTNEXT entry counter to the next entry after the one returned by the current DICTSEARCH call.

Study the following AutoLISP program that takes advantage of the DICTSEARCH and NAMEDOBJDICT functions.

```
; Program: DICTGRP.LSP
;
; Purpose: Utilize the AutoLISP DICTSEARCH function–specifically for "group"
;                                                  selection sets.
;          User selects a group to reveal its included entities.
;          No provision is made for paging large listings of groups/entities.
;          Examination of group contents is best visualized in the text screen.
;
```

```
(defun C:DG (/ MASTER GRP GRP–LIST NE–LIST ARCH–LIST RES LST ENTS AS–340)
   (setvar "cmdecho" 0)
   (setq MASTER (namedobjdict)                          ; MASTER dictionary for dwg.
          GRP    (dictsearch MASTER "acad_group")       ; Search MASTER for groups
   )
   (if GRP                                              ; If entity "groups" exist...
      (progn
         (setq GRP–LIST (member (assoc 3 GRP) GRP)  ; Lists group names/enames
               NE–LIST '()                          ; Empty Name_Entity LIST
         )
         (foreach ITEM  GRP–LIST                                  ; [1]
           (setq NE–LIST (cons (cdr ITEM) NE–LIST))
         )
         (setq NE–LIST  (reverse NE–LIST)   ARCH–LIST  NE–LIST)   ; [2]
         (princ (strcat "\nGROUP names / Entity names: "
                      "\n– – – – – – – – – – – – – – – – – – –\n"))
         (while NE–LIST                                           ; [3]
            (princ (strcat "\tGroup Name: " (car NE–LIST) "\t"))
            (princ (cadr NE–LIST))
            (princ "\n")
            (setq NE–LIST (cddr NE–LIST))
         )
         (setq RES   (strcase (getstring "\n\nGroup for Entity listing: "))
               LST   (entget (cadr (member RES ARCH–LIST)))       ; [4]
               ENTS (member (assoc 340 LST) LST)                  ; [5]
         )
         (while (setq AS_340 (car ENTS))                          ; [6]
            (setq LST (entget (cdr AS_340)))
               (princ (strcat "\tEntity type: " (cdr (assoc 0 LST))))
               (princ (strcat "\tLayer desig: " (cdr (assoc 8 LST)) "\n"))
            (setq ENTS (cdr ENTS))
         )
      ) ; end progn
   ) ; end if
   (princ)
) ; end defun
;– –〈End of File〉– –
```

Documentation for DICTGRP.LSP

[1] **(foreach ITEM GRP–LIST (setq NE–LIST (cons (cdr ITEM) NE–LIST))** For each ITEM that is found within the GRouP LIST [a compilation of associated group codes, entity group names, and their respective entity name designations], cons the last element found in each ITEM [either the group name or its entity name] to the Name Entity LIST variable. After processing the entire group list, the NE-LIST variable should include only group and related entity names. This is done to strip away the unneeded associated group code number.

[2] **(setq NE–LIST (reverse NE–LIST) ARCH–LIST NE–LIST)** Reverse the list held in the NE-LIST variable. This is done to reorder its contents to a Name/Entity sequence. Variable ARCH-LIST archives the new structure now found in NE-LIST.

[3] **(while NE–LIST (princ (strcat "\tGroup Name: " (car NE–LIST)...** While there is a list to process, print the name of the entity group and its respective entity name on a single line. The expression (setq NE-LIST (cddr NE-LIST)) removes the first two elements from the original Name Entity LIST, and resets the variable to this new list. Each pair of elements represents an entity group name and an associated entity name.

[4] **(setq LST (entget (cadr (member RES ARCH–LIST))))** The user is asked to select an entity group for interrogation, which is then stored in variable RES. The MEMBER function uses the name stored in RES as a pointer, and returns a partial listing of ARCH-LIST starting at RES. The CADR element found in this new listing is the associated entity name for group RES. Get the entity data contained within the name, and set variable LST to it.

[5] **(setq ENTS (member (assoc 340 LST) LST))** Variable LST is a repository for a wealth of information. The only section that is required for study is the complete listing of all entities found within LST. The first associated 340 listing marks the beginning of all the included group entities. The variable ENTS is now set to that discrete entity listing.

[6] **(while (setq AS_340 (car ENTS)) (setq LST (entget (cdr AS_340)))....** While there are associated 340 groupings stored in variable ENTS, process each grouping separately, and print its related Entity type (cdr (assoc 0 LST)) and Layer designation (cdr (assoc 8 LST)).

The DICTRENAME Function

The *DICTRENAME (DICTionary RENAME) function* renames a dictionary entry's key name from the current symbol to a new symbol, as specified within the function arguments. The syntax for the DICTRENAME function is as follows:

```
(dictrename ENAME OLDSYM NEWSYM)
```

Where the DICTSEARCH function utilizes the ENAME argument to call upon the drawing file dictionary (the "master" named object dictionary), the ENAME (Entity NAME) argument for DICTRENAME typically refers to either an ACAD_MLINESTYLE entry or an ACAD_GROUP entry. Once the entity name has been obtained, the OLDSYM (OLD SYMbol) name argument can be modified to the NEWSYM (NEW SYMbol) name argument. If any one of the three required arguments is invalid or do not exist, DICTRENAME returns nil.

Study the following example to witness the progression from old symbol name to new symbol name. Take note of the associated 3 grouping, where the DICTRENAME function changes the old symbol name "PARTS" to the new symbol name "ASSEMBLY".

Command: **GROUP**↵ *select objects on screen to create a group called "PARTS"*

Command: **(setq MASTER (namedobjdict))**↵
⟨Entity name: 2050460⟩

Command: **(setq GROUP (dictsearch MASTER "acad_group"))**↵
((-1 . ⟨Entity name: 2050468⟩) (0 . "DICTIONARY") (5 . "D") (102 . "{ACAD_REACTORS") (330 . ⟨Entity name: 2050460⟩) (102 . "}") (100 . "AcDbDictionary") (280 . 0) (3 . "PARTS") (350 . ⟨Entity name: 2050588⟩))

Command: **(setq GROUP-ENAME (cdr (assoc -1 GROUP)))**↵
⟨Entity name: 2050468⟩

Command: **(setq NEWNAME (getstring "\nNew name for acad_group PARTS: "))**↵

New name for acad_group PARTS: **Assembly**↵
"Assembly"

Command: **(dictrename GROUP-ENAME "PARTS" NEWNAME)**↵
"ASSEMBLY"

Command: **(setq GROUP (dictsearch MASTER "acad_group"))**↵
((-1 . ⟨Entity name: 2050468⟩) (0 . "DICTIONARY") (5 . "D") (102 . "{ACAD_REACTORS") (330 . ⟨Entity name: 2050460⟩) (102 . "}") (100 . "AcDbDictionary") (280 . 0) (3 . "ASSEMBLY") (350 . ⟨Entity name: 2050588⟩))

Examine the next AutoLISP program that uses the DICTSEARCH and DICTRENAME functions. Flipping to the AutoCAD text screen will provide the best results when viewing the program in action.

```
; Program:  DICTREN.LSP
;
; Purpose:  Utilize the AutoLISP DICTRENAME function.
;           User selects an object group or mline style to rename.
;           No provision is made for paging large listings of groups/styles.
;           Examination of group/mline contents is best visualized in the text screen.
;
;
(defun C:DREN (/ MASTER GRP MLS GRP–E MLS–E FINAL OBJ–LIST OLD NEW)
  (setvar "cmdecho" 0)
  (setq MASTER  (namedobjdict)                          ; MASTER dictionary
        GRP     (dictsearch MASTER "acad_group")        ; Search for groups
        MLS     (dictsearch MASTER "acad_mlinestyle")   ; Search for styles
        GRP–E   (cdr (assoc –1 GRP))                    ; [1]
        MLS–E   (cdr (assoc –1 MLS))                    ; [2]
```

```
        FINAL  '()                                ; Initialize FINAL list
  )
  ;
  ;– – –⟨NAMES function for storing and printing Group/Mline entries⟩– – –
  ;
  (defun NAMES (S–NAME S–STR)             ; [3]
    (setq OBJ–LIST  '() )                 ; Initialize OBJect LIST for string storage
    (foreach ITEM S–NAME                  ; [4]
      (if (= (car ITEM) 3)
        (setq OBJ–LIST (cons (cdr ITEM) OBJ–LIST))
      )
    )
    (setq OBJ–LIST (reverse OBJ–LIST))     ; Reset order of OBJ–LIST
    (princ (strcat "\n AutoCAD "  S-STR     ; Princ heading for Group/Mlines
            " names:\n – – – – – – – – – – – – – – – – – – – – –\n"))
    (foreach ITEM  OBJ–LIST  (princ (strcat "\t" ITEM "\n")))      ; [5]
    (setq FINAL (append OBJ–LIST FINAL))                         ; [6]
  )
  ;
  ;– – –⟨End of NAMES⟩– – –
  ;
  (NAMES GRP "Group")                                            ; [7]
  (NAMES MLS "Mline")                                            ; [8]
  (setq OLD (strcase (getstring "\nName to change: ")))
  (while (not (member OLD FINAL))                                ; [9]
    (princ "\nIncorrect name, please try again...")
    (setq OLD (strcase (getstring "\nName to change: ")))
  )
  (setq NEW (strcase (getstring "\nNew name: ")))
  (if (null (dictrename GRP–E OLD NEW))                          ; [10]
     (dictrename MLS–E OLD NEW)
  )
  (princ)
) ; end defun
;– – –⟨End of File⟩– – –
```

Documentation for DICTREN.LSP

[1] **(setq GRP-E (cdr (assoc –1 GRP)))** The variable GRP represents the "acad_group" section of the named object dictionary. The nested expression returns the last element of (assoc -1 GRP), which is the entity name for "acad_group". Variable GRP-E now stores the entity name and is subsequently used for further interrogation.

[2] **(setq MLS-E (cdr (assoc –1 MLS)))** The variable MLS represents the "acad_mlinestyle" section of the named object dictionary. Similar to item [1] listed above, the nested expression returns the last element of (assoc -1 MLS), which is the entity name for "acad_mlinestyle". Variable MLS-E now stores the entity name and is subsequently used for further interrogation.

[3] **(defun NAMES (S-NAME S-STR)** The NAMES defined function is created in order to store and print the names of both AutoCAD groups and multiline styles. The S-NAME argument is employed as a symbol name, pertaining to the "acad_group" section, for example. The S-STR argument represents the symbol name as a string, such as "Group".

[4] **(foreach ITEM S-NAME**
(if (= (car ITEM) 3) For each ITEM that is found within S-NAME [the "acad_group" section, for example], if the car of ITEM is equal to 3 [the associated group code that represents a named AutoCAD group or a multiline style], cons the last element found in each ITEM [the string name] to the OBJect LIST variable. The OBJect LIST will grow to contain all string names.

[5] **(foreach ITEM OBJ-LIST (princ (strcat "\t" ITEM "\n")))** For each ITEM found within the compiled OBJect LIST, print the string concatenation of "\t" [a tab], ITEM [the string name], and "\n" [a new line]. This looping technique will exhaust all string names of AutoCAD groups or multiline styles held within variable OBJ-LIST.

[6] **(setq FINAL (append OBJ-LIST FINAL))** The FINAL variable is instrumental in storing symbol names from each category–AutoCAD groups and multiline styles. Since the NAMES defined function is used eventually more than once inside the overall program, each call to NAMES appends more symbol strings to FINAL. Note that variable OBJ-LIST is reset to a null or empty set each time that NAMES is called. This allows for new strings to be printed to the screen, while FINAL archives all strings from each call to NAMES.

[7] **(NAMES GRP "Group")** Initiate the NAMES defined function, utilize the variable GRP as an argument [AutoCAD "acad_group" listing of associated pairs], and display the string argument "Group" to the screen [the princ function].

[8] **(NAMES MLS "Mline")** Initiate the NAMES defined function, utilize the variable MLS as an argument [AutoCAD "acad_multiline" listing of associated pairs], and display the string argument "Mline" to the screen [the princ function].

[9] **(while (not (member OLD FINAL))**
(princ "\nIncorrect name, please try again... ") The variable OLD contains a text string that references the target "acad_group" name or "acad_multiline" name. If the user has supplied an incorrect name [not a member of FINAL, the archive of names], then continue asking the user to supply one that resides within FINAL.

[10] **(if (null (dictrename GRP-E OLD NEW))**
(dictrename MLS-E OLD NEW)) The expression [dictrename GRP-E OLD NEW] will replace the OLD name with the NEW user-specified name in the "acad_group" section. If this expression is null [change is not targeted at this dictionary section], then replace the OLD name with the NEW user-specified name in the "acad_multiline" section.

The DICTADD Function

The *DICTADD (DICTionary ADD) function* adds a new nongraphical data entry to the user-specified dictionary. The syntax for the DICTADD function is indicated below:

```
(dictadd ENAME SYMBOL NEWOBJ)
```

Where the DICTSEARCH function utilizes the ENAME argument to call upon the drawing file dictionary (the "master" named object dictionary), the ENAME (Entity NAME) argument for DICTADD typically refers to either an ACAD_MLINESTYLE entry or to an ACAD_GROUP entry. The NEWOBJ (NEW OBJect) argument corresponds to the entity name of the new dictionary entry.

Once the ENAME and NEWOBJ entity name arguments are established, the SYMBOL text string argument is added to complete the expression. Take note that the SYMBOL argument must be a unique name, and not duplicate any other dictionary names. If any one of the three required arguments are invalid or do not exist, DICTADD returns nil. Where all arguments are valid, DICTADD returns the NEWOBJ entity name, and the new dictionary nongraphical entry is added.

Examine the following illustration to see how the DICTADD function adds a new dictionary entry. The AutoLISP ENTMAKEX function, which is identical in syntax to the ENTMAKE function found in Chapter 13, assists in returning a nongraphical entity name for DICTADD:

Command: **GROUP**↵ *create two groups–one called "LINES" and the other called "CIRCLES"*

Command: **(setq MASTER (namedobjdict))**↵
⟨Entity name: c0a860⟩

Command: **(setq GROUP-SECTION (dictsearch MASTER "acad_group"))**↵
((-1 . ⟨Entity name: c0a868⟩) (0 . "DICTIONARY") (5 . "D") (102 . "{ACAD_REACTORS") (330 . ⟨Entity name: c0a860⟩) (102 . "}") (100 . "AcDbDictionary") (280 . 0) (3 . "LINES") (350 . ⟨Entity name: c0a968⟩) (3 . "CIRCLES") (350 . ⟨Entity name: c0a970⟩))

Command: **(setq GROUP-ENAME (cdr (assoc -1 GROUP-SECTION)))**↵
⟨Entity name: c0a868⟩

At this point, the variable GROUP-SECTION contains all entries pertinent to the "acad_group" section of the object dictionary. Variable GROUP-ENAME secures the "acad_group" entity name. The example continues:

Command: **(setq GROUP1 (entget (cdr (assoc 350 GROUP-SECTION))))**↵
((-1 . ⟨Entity name: c0a968⟩) (0 . "GROUP") (5 . "2D") (102 . "{ACAD_REACTORS") (330 . ⟨Entity name: c0a868⟩) (102 . "}") (100 . "AcDbGroup") (300 . "") (70 . 0) (71 . 1) (340 . ⟨Entity name: c0a950⟩) (340 . ⟨Entity name: c0a940⟩) (340 . ⟨Entity name: c0a948⟩))

Command: **(setq NEWENT (entmakex GROUP1))**↵
⟨Entity name: c0a978⟩

At this point, the variable GROUP1 stores the first "acad_group" entry data list, as returned by (entget (cdr (assoc 350 GROUP-SECTION))). The first associated 350 pair found in GROUP-SECTION is a reference to the "LINES" entity name. Variable NEWENT is then created by applying the expression (entmakex GROUP1), where a nongraphical entity is generated for the object dictionary. The example continues:

```
Command: (dictadd GROUP-ENAME "newgroup" NEWENT)↵
<Entity name: c0a978>

Command: (entget GROUP-ENAME)↵
((-1 . <Entity name: c0a868>) (0 . "DICTIONARY") (5 . "D") (102 . "{ACAD_REACTORS")
(330 . <Entity name: c0a860>) (102 . "}") (100 . "AcDbDictionary") (280 . 0) (3 . "LINES")
(350 . <Entity name: c0a968>) (3 . "CIRCLES") (350 . <Entity name: c0a970>) (3 . "NEW-
GROUP") (350 . <Entity name: c0a978>))
```

Employing the DICTADD function, the new entity is added under the heading "NEWGROUP", and is located within the "acad_group" section as directed by the GROUP-ENAME argument.

The next specialized programming example further demonstrates the use of the DICTADD function. In this case, an AutoCAD group of all external references has been formed. The task of the program is to scan all of the references, collect them by name, and add them as individual groups with the DICTADD function.

```
; Program: DICTXREF.LSP
;
; Purpose: Specialized demonstration for the AutoLISP DICTADD function.
;          Target "acad_group" is the group selection set named "XREFS".
;          The group "XREFS" contains all external references placed
;          within the current drawing file. Scale and location of each
;          xref is not important to the operability of the function.
;
;          All external references are subsequently categorized by name,
;          and placed by DICTADD, as individual entries into the object
;          dictionary. For example, all external references that are
;          named "BOXES" will be collected into a single group with the
;          same name. Caution must be exercised so as not to duplicate
;          existing group names.
;
(defun C:DXREF (/ MASTER GRP-SEC GRP-ENT XR-ALL XR-340
                  XR-REV E-HEAD NAME NAME-L ENTSET)
  (setvar "cmdecho" 0)
  (setq MASTER   (namedobjdict)                      ; MASTER dictionary
        GRP-SEC  (dictsearch MASTER "acad_group")    ; GRouP-SECtion
        GRP-ENT  (cdr (assoc -1 GRP-SEC))            ; GRouP-ENTity name
        XR-ALL   (entget (cdr (nth 1 (member (cons 3 "XREFS") GRP-SEC)))) ; [1]
        XR-340   (member (assoc 340 XR-ALL) XR-ALL)                       ; [2]
        XR-REV   (reverse XR-ALL)                                         ; [3]
        E-HEAD   (member (nth (length XR-340) XR-REV) XR-REV)             ; [4]
```

```
            E–HEAD  (reverse E–HEAD)                          ; [5]
            NAME–L  '()
            NAME    (cdr (assoc 2 (entget (cdr (car XR–340))))) ; [6]
            NAME–L  (cons NAME NAME–L)                        ; [7]
  )
  (foreach ITEM XR-340    ; For each ITEM within XR–340's list of entities...
    (if (not (member                                          ; [8]
          (setq NAME (cdr (assoc 2 (entget (cdr ITEM)))))
           NAME–L)
        )
        (setq NAME–L (cons NAME NAME–L))
    )
  )
  (repeat (length NAME–L)     ; Repeat the length (integer value) of list NAME–L
    (setq ENTSET '() )        ; Empty ENTity SET for depositing "like" entities
    (foreach ITEM XR–340      ; For each ITEM within XR–340's list of entities...
      (if (=  (setq NAME (cdr (assoc 2 (entget (cdr ITEM)))))          ; [9]
              (car NAME–L)
          )
          (setq ENTSET (cons ITEM ENTSET))
      )
    )
    (dictadd GRP–ENT (car NAME–L) (entmakex (append E–HEAD ENTSET))) ; [10]
    (setq NAME–L (cdr NAME–L))
  )
  (princ)
  ) ; end defun
  ;– – –⟨End of File⟩– – –
```

Documentation for DICTXREF.LSP

[1] **(setq XR-ALL (entget (cdr (nth 1 (member (cons 3 "XREFS") GRP-SEC)))))** The nested portion of this expression, (member (cons 3 "XREFS") GRP-SEC) isolates the "XREFS" group entry name as the 1st element within the GRouP-SECtion. The (nth 1 ...) expression then concentrates on the 2nd element found in the resultant list. This element holds the entity name for the "XREFS" group entry, and is secured with the CDR function. The returned entity name is further interrogated by ENTGET, and the entire xref group data record is stored in variable XR-ALL.

[2] **(setq XR-340 (member (assoc 340 XR-ALL) XR-ALL))** The variable XR-ALL contains miscellaneous associated pairs, as well as, all entity names for the external references in the drawing. Starting at the first entity name record (assoc 340 XR-ALL), create a listing of all entity records (member (assoc 340 XR-ALL) XR-ALL), and store this in XR-340.

[3] **(setq XR-REV (reverse XR-ALL))** Reverse the original "XREFS" group data record, and set XR-REV to it. This is done for the benefit of the next expression.

[4] **(setq E-HEAD (member (nth (length XR-340) XR-REV) XR-REV))** The length of list XR-340 supplies the exact number of xref entity records in the original "XREFS" group data record. Using this integer as a locational argument for the NTH function, and applied to the reversed list found in XR-REV, extracts all the essential "heading" data minus the entities section. By doing so, the "heading" which is now stored in variable E-HEAD can be appended to each unique category of xref entity groups. This is done in preparation for the ENTMAKEX function.

[5] **(setq E-HEAD (reverse E-HEAD))** The "heading" section is reversed to its proper order before applying the ENTMAKEX function.

[6] **(setq NAME (cdr (assoc 2 (entget (cdr (car XR-340))))))** This expression starts off by returning the first element in XR-340–a list of all xref entity records. The (cdr (car XR-340)) expression retrieves the entity name, and the ENTGET function returns the entity data listing. The associated 2 pair contains the string NAME of the target xref, and the CDR function yields this.

[7] **(setq NAME-L (cons NAME NAME-L))** Add the xref string NAME to the open list of NAME-L.

[8] **(if (not (member**
(setq NAME (cdr (assoc 2 (entget (cdr ITEM))))) If the NAME held within the associated 2 listing of ITEM is not a member of the NAME-List, then cons that NAME to the list. Eventually, all external references will be represented by the NAME-List. Names found within NAME-L are not duplicated, and only listed once.

[9] **(if (= (setq NAME (cdr (assoc 2 (entget (cdr ITEM)))))** If the NAME held within the associated 2 listing of ITEM is equal to the (car NAME-L) element, the 1st atom of NAME-L being a text string that represents an xref name, then cons the ITEM to the ENTSET list. As long as NAME and (car NAME-L) are equal, ITEM entity names will accumulate in list ENTSET.

[10] **(dictadd GRP-ENT (car NAME-L) (entmakex (append E-HEAD ENTSET)))** To create the nongraphical entity, the ENTMAKEX function receives the appended data "heading" [variable E-HEAD] and all similar entity data records [variable ENTSET]. The expression (car NAME-L) returns the appropriate xref name, and variable GRP-ENT, specifies the GRouP ENTity name for storing this new entry in the object dictionary.

The DICTREMOVE Function

The *DICTREMOVE (DICTionary REMOVE) function* removes an entry from the specified dictionary section. The syntax for the DICTREMOVE function is as follows:

```
(dictremove ENAME SYMBOL)
```

Where the DICTSEARCH function utilizes the ENAME argument to call upon the drawing file dictionary (the "master" named object dictionary), the ENAME (Entity NAME) argument for DICTREMOVE typically refers to either an ACAD_MLINESTYLE entry or an ACAD_GROUP entry. Once the entity name has been obtained, the SYMBOL name argument can be applied for removing. If any one of the two required arguments is invalid or do not exist, DICTREMOVE returns nil.

An mlinestyle currently in use within the drawing file, as referenced by an mline in the database, cannot be removed with DICTREMOVE.

Examine the next AutoLISP program that uses the DICTSEARCH and DICTREMOVE functions. Flipping to the AutoCAD text screen will provide the best results when viewing the program in action.

```
; Program: DICTREM.LSP
;
; Purpose: Utilize the AutoLISP DICTREMOVE function.
;          User selects an object group or mline style to remove.
;          No provision is made for paging large listings of groups/entities.
;          Examination of group/mline contents is best visualized in the text screen.
;
;
;
(defun C:DREM (/ MASTER GRP MLS GRP-E MLS-E FINAL OBJ-LIST SEL)
  (setvar "cmdecho" 0)
  (setq MASTER (namedobjdict)                          ; MASTER dictionary
        GRP    (dictsearch MASTER "acad_group")        ; Search for groups
        MLS    (dictsearch MASTER "acad_mlinestyle")   ; Search for styles
        GRP-E  (cdr (assoc -1 GRP))                    ; [1]
        MLS-E  (cdr (assoc -1 MLS))                    ; [2]
        FINAL  '()                                     ; Initialize FINAL list
  )
  ;
  ;---(NAMES function for storing and printing Group/Mline entries)---
  ;
  (defun NAMES (S-NAME S-STR)           ; [3]
    (setq OBJ-LIST '() )                ; Initialize OBJect LIST for string storage
    (foreach ITEM S-NAME                ; [4]
      (if (= (car ITEM) 3)
        (setq OBJ-LIST (cons (cdr ITEM) OBJ-LIST))
      )
    )
    (setq OBJ-LIST (reverse OBJ-LIST))      ; Reset order of OBJ-LIST
    (princ (strcat "\n AutoCAD " S-STR      ; Princ heading for Group/Mlines
           " names:\n---------------------\n"))
    (foreach ITEM OBJ-LIST (princ (strcat "\t" ITEM "\n")))    ; [5]
    (setq FINAL (append OBJ-LIST FINAL))                       ; [6]
  )
  ;
  ;---(End of NAMES)---
  ;
  (NAMES GRP "Group")                                          ; [7]
  (NAMES MLS "Mline")                                          ; [8]
  (setq SEL (strcase (getstring "\nSelect entry to remove/Exit: ")))
  (cond
    ((or (= SEL "E") (= SEL "EXIT"))     ; "E" or "EXIT" means no change
     (princ "\nNo changes at this time")
```

```
      )
      (T
       (while (not (member SEL FINAL))                          ; [9]
         (princ "\nIncorrect name, please try again...")
         (setq SEL (strcase (getstring "\nSelect entry to remove: ")))
       )
      (if (null (dictremove GRP–E SEL))                         ; [10]
         (dictremove MLS–E SEL)
      )
     )
    ) ; end cond
    (princ)
  ) ; end defun
  ;– – –⟨End of File⟩– – –
```

Documentation for DICTREM.LSP

[1] **(setq GRP–E (cdr (assoc –1 GRP)))** The variable GRP represents the "acad_group" section of the named object dictionary. The nested expression returns the last element of (assoc -1 GRP), which is the entity name for "acad_group". Variable GRP-E now stores the entity name and is subsequently used for further interrogation.

[2] **(setq MLS–E (cdr (assoc –1 MLS)))** The variable MLS represents the "acad_mlinestyle" section of the named object dictionary. Similar to item [1] listed above, the nested expression returns the last element of (assoc -1 MLS), which is the entity name for "acad_mlinestyle". Variable MLS-E now stores the entity name and is subsequently used for further interrogation.

[3] **(defun NAMES (S–NAME S–STR)** The NAMES defined function is created in order to store and print the names of both AutoCAD groups and multiline styles. The S-NAME argument is employed as a symbol name, pertaining to the "acad_group" section, for example. The S-STR argument represents the symbol name as a string, such as "Group."

[4] **(foreach ITEM S–NAME**
(if (= (car ITEM) 3) For each ITEM that is found within S-NAME, the "acad_group" section, for example, if the car of ITEM is equal to 3 [the associated group code that represents a named AutoCAD group or a multiline style], cons the last element found in each ITEM [the string name] to the OBJect LIST variable. The OBJect LIST will grow to contain all string names.

[5] **(foreach ITEM OBJ–LIST (princ (strcat "\t" ITEM "\n")))** For each ITEM found within the compiled OBJect LIST, print the string concatenation of "\t" [a tab], ITEM [the string name], and "\n" [a new line]. This looping technique will exhaust all string names of AutoCAD groups or multiline styles held within variable OBJ-LIST.

[6] (setq FINAL (append OBJ–LIST FINAL)) The FINAL variable is instrumental in storing symbol names from each category–AutoCAD groups and multiline styles. Since the NAMES defined function is used eventually more than once inside the overall program, each call to NAMES appends more symbol strings to FINAL. Note that variable OBJ-LIST is reset to a null or empty set each time that NAMES is called. This allows for new strings to be printed to the screen, while FINAL archives all strings from each call to NAMES.

[7] (NAMES GRP "Group") Initiate the NAMES defined function, utilize the variable GRP as an argument [AutoCAD "acad_group" listing of associated pairs], and display the string argument "Group" to the screen [the princ function].

[8] (NAMES MLS "Mline") Initiate the NAMES defined function, utilize the variable MLS as an argument [AutoCAD "acad_multiline" listing of associated pairs], and display the string argument "Mline" to the screen [the princ function].

[9] (while (not (member SEL FINAL))
(princ "\nIncorrect name, please try again...") The variable SEL contains a text string that references the target "acad_group" name or "acad_multiline" name. If the user has supplied an incorrect name [not a member of FINAL, the archive of names], then continue asking the user to supply one that resides within FINAL.

[10] (if (null (dictremove GRP–E SEL))
(dictremove MLS–E SEL)) The expression (dictremove GRP-E SEL) will delete the user-specified name in the "acad_group" section. If this expression is null [change is not targeted at this dictionary section], then delete the user-specified name in the "acad_multiline" section.

Viewports as Configurations and Entities

In a typical editing session, a single viewport is shown and the AutoCAD system variable TILEMODE is set to 1 (1=ON, which establishes standard or "tiled" viewports). With the exception of two other system variables–CVPORT (Current ViewPORT) and MAXACTVP (MAXimum ACTive ViewPorts), and the AutoCAD VIEWPORTS "?" display listing–little is documented within the drawing that explains the technique behind viewport construction. This section of Chapter 15 will explain the use of AutoCAD viewports, both in model space and paper space.

The VPORTS Function. The AutoLISP *VPORTS (ViewPORTS) function* renders a unique list that details the current viewport configuration. The syntax for VPORTS is:

```
(vports)
```

The "read-only" list returned by VPORTS is composed partially of coordinate pairs that express how the screen is subdivided. With the system variable TILEMODE set to 1 (1=ON [model space]), the VPORTS function might produce the following results:

```
Command: (vports) ↵
((2 (0.0 0.0) (1.0 1.0)))
```

The single viewport descriptor shown here lists an identification number 2, along with two coordinate pairs that constitute the viewport's lower-left and upper-right corners. The identification numbers are assigned *as needed,* where there is one required per newly created viewport. These viewport "tags" are managed (reassigned or discarded) solely by the AutoCAD editor, and are not references to named configurations.

In this example, the corners can be perceived as "X,Y" coordinates and are listed as (0.0 0.0) and (1.0 1.0)–simulating a window and forming a single viewport. In addition, the *minimum* viewport lower-left corner for any AutoCAD display is (0.0 0.0), while the *maximum* upper-right corner is (1.0 1.0).

When configuring the screen to four equal-size viewports, note the resultant list returned by the VPORTS function, where the current viewport is denoted *first:*

```
Command: VIEWPORTS ↵
Save/Restore/Delete/Join/SIngle/?/2/<3>/4: 4 ↵
Command: (vports) ↵
((2 (0.5 0.0) (1.0 0.5)) (3 (0.5 0.5) (1.0 1.0)) (4 (0.0 0.5) (0.5 1.0)) (5 (0.0 0.0) (0.5 0.5)))
```

When reformatted for readability, the resultant list can be interpreted as follows:

```
( (2 (0.5 0.0) (1.0 0.5))        Viewports are listed with
  (3 (0.5 0.5) (1.0 1.0))        corresponding identification
  (4 (0.0 0.5) (0.5 1.0))        numbers (2-5) and coordinate
  (5 (0.0 0.0) (0.5 0.5))        definitions. The viewport listed first
)                                is the current (active) viewport.
```

The diagram shown in Fig. 15-2 illustrates how the display is subdivided when using these coordinate pairs. In this situation, viewport number 2 is current (active) since it is listed first.

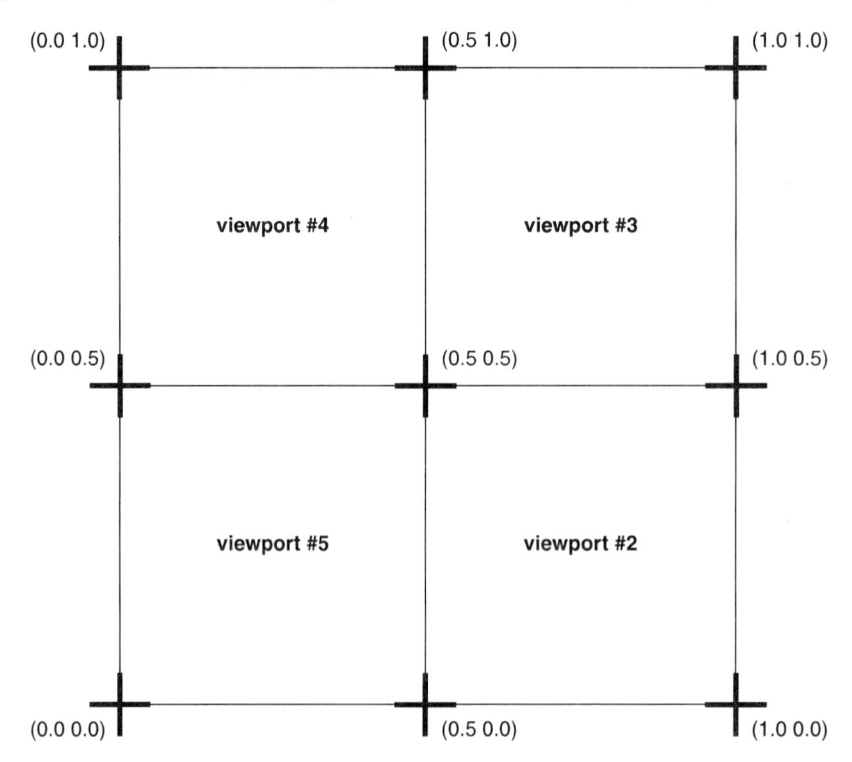

Fig. 15-2. Screen viewport configuration containing four viewports.The viewport listed first, in this case viewport #2, is the current viewport.

Viewport number 3 has its lower-left corner in the exact middle of the screen, and its upper-right corner located top right. Viewport numbers 4 and 5 are also positioned accordingly. Remember, on DOS platforms the maximum number of active viewports is sixteen. You can imagine the complex list of viewport descriptors returned when the VPORTS function is used for sixteen viewports! When viewport number 5 is split into four equal-size viewports, Fig. 15-3, the VPORTS function returns the following:

```
( (5 (0.25 0.0) (0.5 0.25))
  (2 (0.5 0.0) (1.0 0.5))
  (3 (0.5 0.5) (1.0 1.0))
  (4 (0.0 0.5) (0.5 1.0))
  (6 (0.25 0.25) (0.5 0.5))
  (7 (0.0 0.25) (0.25 0.5))
  (8 (0.0 0.0) (0.25 0.25))
)
```

Total of seven viewports, again listed with identification numbers and coordinate definitions. Note the change for viewport number 5. In addition, notice that viewports 2-4 remain unchanged.

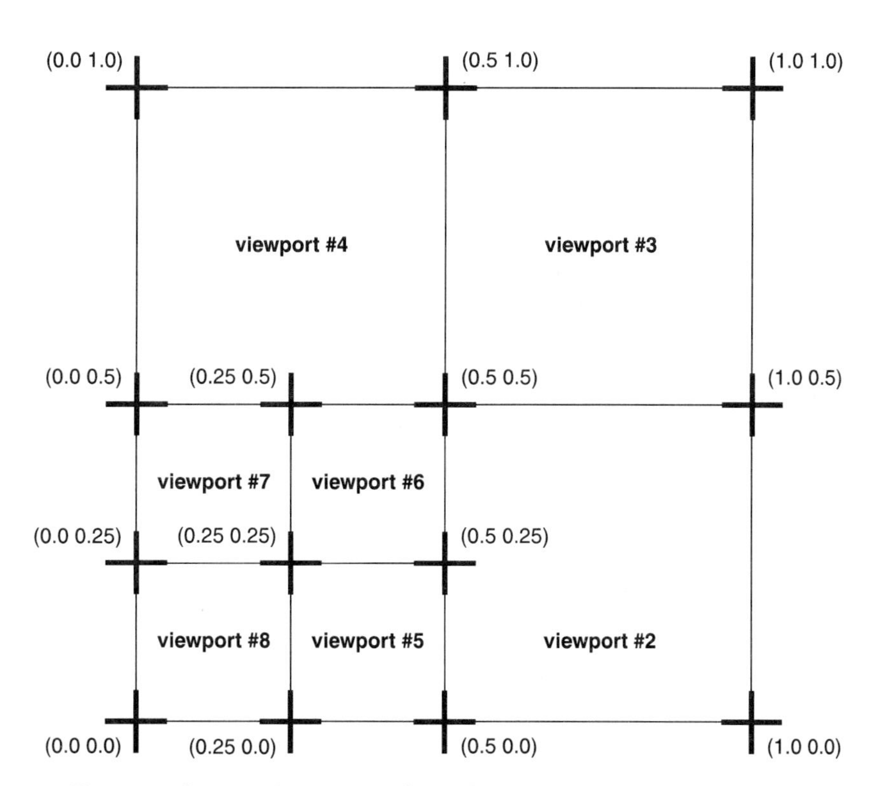

Fig. 15-3. Screen viewport configuration containing seven viewports.

AutoLISP tracks each viewport configuration as it is created. This is indicated by the entries found in the "VPORT" symbol table, and applies to *tiled* viewports only. Viewport entities (represented in paper space) can be solicited by using the entity-handling functions.

The following AutoLISP program shows an application for the VPORTS function. The purpose of this program is to search for the lower-left viewport and make it active.

```
(defun LL (/ CTR VP)
  (setq CTR 0
        VP (nth CTR (vports))          ; Initialize first element
```

```
    )
    (while (not (equal (cadr VP) '(0.0 0.0)))  ; While loop until the lower
      (setq CTR (1+ CTR)                       ;   left corner of (0.0 0.0)
            VP   (nth CTR (vports))            ;   is found. Setq VP to that
      )                                        ;   viewport descriptor
    )
    (setvar "cvport" (car VP))                 ; Car of VP returns the lower
    (princ)                                    ;   left corner identification number
)
```

The following program also takes advantage of the VPORTS function, while integrating the AutoCAD VPOINT command to establish one plan view and three distinct three-dimensional views of a simple box. Examine the use of the AutoLISP LAMBDA function that combines each unique viewport with its user-defined 3D viewpoint.

```
; Filename:  PORTS.LSP
;
; Author:  Dee Vide
;
; Date:  January 3, 19xx
;
; Purpose:  Allows for 3D configuration of each of four viewports.
;
; Assumptions:  The routine works best in a new drawing file.
;               The TILEMODE system variable is set to 1.
;
(defun C:PORTS (/ RES VPLIST PT)
(setvar "cmdecho" 0)
;
; --⟨ Construct a simple 3D box with label ⟩--
;
  (command ".limits" '(0 0) '(15 9)
           ".zoom" "a"
           ".elev" 0 3
           ".pline" '(5 3) '(10 3) '(10 6) '(5 6) "c"
           ".elev" 3 0
           ".text" "m" '(7.5 4.5) 0.75 0 "3D–BOX"
           ".elev" 0 0
  )
;
; --⟨ End of construction – ask user for desired configuration ⟩--
;
  (initget "Specify")
  (setq RES (getkword "\nSpecify 3 vpoints/⟨ENTER⟩ for standard cfg: ")
        VPLIST (list '(0 0 1))             ; Initial viewpoint list
  )
;
```

```
; --( If user-specified, get three unique viewpoints and form viewpoint list )--
;
  (if (= RES "Specify")                     ; If "Specify", then user selects three viewpoints
    (repeat 3
      (command ".vpoint" "" pause           ; Pause, then display chosen viewpoint
               ".delay" 500
      )
      (setq PT (getvar "viewdir")
            VPLIST (append VPLIST (list PT))  ; Add viewpoints to VPLIST
      )
    )                                       ; End repeat
  )                                         ; End if
  (command ".vports" 4)                     ; Establish four viewports
;
; --( Combine desired viewpoints with current viewports configuration )--
;
    (mapcar
      '(lambda (VPCFG VPLST)
         (setvar "cvport" (car VPCFG))      ; Cycle through all four vports
         (command ".vpoint" VPLST)          ; Use viewpoint from list below
      )
      (vports)
      (if (= RES "Specify")   ; If "Specify", then VPLIST, else standard configuration
         VPLIST
         (list '(0 0 1) '(1 -1 1) '(-1 -1 1) '(1 1 1))
      )                                     ; End if
    )                                       ; End mapcar
  (setvar "cmdecho" 1)
  (princ)
)
; --( End of File )--
```

When the AutoCAD system variable TILEMODE is set to 0 (0=OFF [paper space]), viewport entity creation is allowed via the AutoCAD MVIEW command. The list returned by the VPORTS function under these conditions is very different than the list produced in model space. For example:

```
Command: (vports) ↵
( (1 (0.0 0.0) (24.5335 15.0)) (4 (2.0 10.0) (14.0 14.0)) (3 (2.0 2.0) (9.0 9.0)) (5 (12.0 3.0)
(18.0 9.0)) )
```

When reformatted for readability, the previous list can be easily interpreted.

```
(  (1 (0.0 0.0) (24.5335 15.0))
   (4 (2.0 10.0) (14.0 14.0))
   (3 (2.0 2.0) (9.0 9.0))
   (5 (12.0 3.0) (18.0 9.0))
)
```

Each coordinate pair is coupled with a viewport entity identification number. The coordinate pair represents the actual WCS paper space coordinates (corners) in the drawing editor. See Fig. 15-4. The list that is identified as number 1 is always present, and indicates the lower-left and upper-right corners of the display. In this case, the coordinates read:

```
(1 (0.0 0.0) (24.5335 15.0))
```

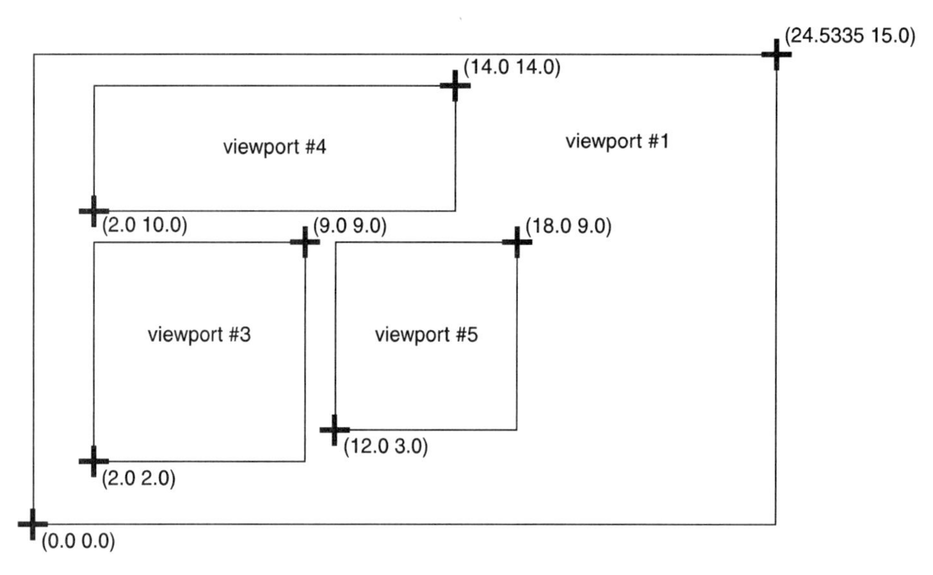

Fig. 15-4. Screen viewport configuration for four viewports in paper space. Note that the coordinate pair represents the actual WCS paper space coordinates (corners) in the drawing editor.

This coordinate pair for this configuration–(0.0 0.0) (24.5335 15.0)–reveals the WCS lower-left and upper-right corners of the current display. The remaining viewport entities are subsequently referenced by their "real world" WCS positioning.

The next AutoLISP program deletes all viewport entities in paper space. This may be helpful when a "clean" screen is needed. System variable checking is enabled to guarantee that deleting takes place in paper space mode.

```
(defun C:DELPORTS (/ PLST)
  (setvar "cmdecho" 0)
  (setq PLST (ssget "X" '((0 . "VIEWPORT"))))
  (if (= (getvar "TILEMODE") 0)
    (command ".erase" PLST "")
    (princ "\nSorry – Not in Paper Space!")
  )
  (setvar "cmdecho" 1)
  (princ)
)
```

EXERCISE 15-2

- ☐ Create a program that conforms to the following criteria:
- ☐ Search the "LAYER" and "BLOCK" symbol tables for all entries, excluding those names that begin with "FURN*" (the string "FURN" with any character sequence following). The objective is to create lists of those items that do not match this wild card pattern. Subsequently print each list (LAYER and BLOCK) to the screen.
- ☐ Form a selection set that includes the items found in the previous step (e.g. SSGET 'X), and erase them from the drawing editor. Entries starting with the string sequence "FURN" should be preserved.
- ☐ In order to test the effectiveness of this routine, initiate a drawing that contains at least fifteen layers and ten blocks, some with names that begin with "FURN". Name the program SAVEFURN.LSP.

The SETVIEW Function

The *SETVIEW (SET display VIEW) function* establishes a view for either the current display or a specified viewport. The syntax for the SETVIEW function is as follows:

```
(setview VIEW_DESCRIPTOR [VPORT_ID])
```

The required VIEW_DESCRIPTOR argument is composed of an entity definition list. That list contains all the essential associated codes needed to build a view, and is similar in structure to those held within the "VIEW" symbol table. There are subtle differences, however, between the data stored in a "VIEW" symbol table and the associated list used by the SETVIEW function. Examine the following:

```
Command: View↵
?/Delete/Restore/Save/Window: W↵
View name to save: Model-View1↵
First corner: 3,3↵
Other corner: 10,10↵

Command: (tblsearch "view" "Model-View1")↵
((0 . "VIEW") (2 . "MODEL-VIEW1") (70 . 0) (40 . 7.0) (10 6.5 6.5) (41 . 7.0) (11 0.0 0.0
1.0) (12 0.0 0.0 0.0) (42 . 50.0) (43 . 0.0) (44 . 0.0) (50 . 0.0) (71 . 0))

Command: (setview (tblsearch "view" "Model-View1"))↵
error: AutoCAD rejected function
(SETVIEW (TBLSEARCH "view" "Model-View1"))
*Cancel*

Command: (setq VIEW1 (tblsearch "view" "Model-View1"))↵
((0 . "VIEW") (2 . "MODEL-VIEW1") (70 . 0) (40 . 7.0) (10 6.5 6.5) (41 . 7.0) (11 0.0 0.0
1.0) (12 0.0 0.0 0.0) (42 . 50.0) (43 . 0.0) (44 . 0.0) (50 . 0.0) (71 . 0))
```

Command: **(setq VIEW1 (member (assoc 70 VIEW1) VIEW1))↵**
((70 . 0) (40 . 7.0) (10 6.5 6.5) (41 . 7.0) (11 0.0 0.0 1.0) (12 0.0 0.0 0.0) (42 . 50.0) (43 . 0.0) (44 . 0.0) (50 . 0.0) (71 . 0))

Command: **(setview VIEW1)↵**
((70 . 0) (40 . 7.0) (10 6.5 6.5) (41 . 7.0) (11 0.0 0.0 1.0) (12 0.0 0.0 0.0) (42 . 50.0) (43 . 0.0) (44 . 0.0) (50 . 0.0) (71 . 0))

The AutoCAD "View" command provides a named view called "Model-View1". The TBLSEARCH function locates this view, and returns an associated list that completely describes this symbol table entry. As this data list is passed directly to the SETVIEW function, AutoCAD rejects the attempt and cancels the function.

Variable "VIEW1" is then used to warehouse the same data list. In the next sequence, the expression (setq VIEW1 (member (assoc 70 VIEW1) VIEW1)) resets the variable "VIEW1" to include only the associated pairs starting at (assoc 70 VIEW1) within the original listing. The SETVIEW function is then provided with the new listing (under variable "VIEW1"), and in turn, renders the new display. Note the absence of entity type code, and view name code, when constructing an associated list for SETVIEW.

The VPORT_ID integer argument is optional, and identifies the viewport that is to display the submitted view. If this argument is 0, the current viewport shows the new view. Continuing with the illustration given above, the AutoCAD "CVPORT" system variable is instrumental in directing the view:

(setview VIEW1 (getvar "cvport"))	*Use VIEW1 associated data list within the current viewport*

Examine the next AutoLISP program that uses the TBLNEXT, TBLSEARCH, VPORTS, and SETVIEW functions to establish new views in the drawing editor.

```
; Filename: SVIEW.LSP
;
; Purpose:  Utilize the AutoLISP SETVIEW function.
;           View and Viewport selection routine. Where no named views
;           exist, a message is produced. Views are made available
;           according to the current drawing environment, either Paper
;           Space or Model Space. For example, no named Paper Space
;           views can be employed while operating in Model Space.
;
;           If more than 1 viewport exists in Model Space, the program
;           cycles through each viewport, stopping to allow the user to
;           specify the view of choice, or skip to the next viewport.
;
(defun C:SV (/ NEXT_VIEW VIEW_SET TM SETS NAME NEW_VIEW V_DATA VP)
 (setvar "cmdecho" 0)
 (setq NEXT_VIEW  (tblnext "view" t)          ; Rewind the VIEW symbol table
       VIEW_SET   '()                          ; Initialize empty list VIEW_SET
       TM         (getvar "tilemode")          ; Get "tilemode" setting
       SETS       (strcat "Current "                              ; [1]
                  (if (= TM 1) "Model" "Paper")
                   " Space VIEWS:\n")
 ) ; end setq
 ;
```

```
;– – –⟨DISPLAY function for storing names of Views⟩– – –
;
(defun DISPLAY ()                ; Defined function for DISPLAYing views
  (while NEXT_VIEW               ; While there is a NEXT_VIEW to process
    (if
      (/= (cdr (assoc 70 NEXT_VIEW)) (getvar "tilemode"))          ; [2]
      (setq NAME      (cdr (assoc 2 NEXT_VIEW))                    ; [3]
            SETS      (strcat SETS "\n" NAME)                      ; [4]
            VIEW_SET (cons NAME VIEW_SET)                          ; [5]
      )
    )
    (setq NEXT_VIEW (tblnext "view"))  ; NEXT_VIEW becomes the next "view"
  ) ; end while
  (alert SETS)                  ; Alert dialog to show views
)
;
;– – –⟨End of DISPLAY⟩– – –
;
;– – –⟨Select 1 function for selecting the desired named View⟩– – –
;
(defun SELECT1 ()
  (cond
    ( (/= ""                                                       ; If /= to enter
       (setq NEW_VIEW (strcase
             (getstring "\nView name / ⟨Enter⟩: ")))               ; Ask for view
      )
      (while (not (member NEW_VIEW VIEW_SET))                      ; [6]
       (princ "\nIncorrect name, please try again...")
       (alert SETS)
       (setq NEW_VIEW (strcase (getstring "\nView name: ")))
      )
      (setq V_DATA (tblsearch "view" NEW_VIEW)                     ; [7]
            V_DATA (member (assoc 70 V_DATA) V_DATA)               ; [8]
      )
      (setview V_DATA)                                             ; [9]
    )
  ) ; end cond
)
;
;– – –⟨End of SELECT1⟩– – –
;
(cond  ( (null NEXT_VIEW)                      ; If no named views exist...
         (alert "\nNo named VIEWS exist!")     ; Tell the user
       )
       ( (= TM 0)                              ; Where "tilemode" = 0...
         (DISPLAY)                             ; Run the DISPLAY function
         (if VIEW_SET        ; If VIEW_SET has views to select from...
            (SELECT1)        ; ...then run the SELECT1 function to choose
         )
       )
```

```
      ( (= TM 1)                                  ; Where "tilemode" = 1...
        (DISPLAY)                                 ; Run the DISPLAY function
        (if VIEW_SET                              ; If VIEW_SET has views to select from...
          (repeat (length (setq VP (vports)))     ; [10]
            (command ".cvport" (car (car VP)))    ; [11]
            (SELECT1)                             ; Run SELECT1 function
            (setq VP (cdr VP))                    ; [12]
          )
        ) ; end if
      )
    ) ; end cond
    (princ)
  ) ; end defun
;– – –⟨End of File⟩– – –
```

Documentation for SVIEW.LSP

[1] **(setq SETS (strcat "Current "**
(if (= TM 1) "Model" "Paper")
" Space VIEWS:\n")) The variable SETS serves as the text heading for an ALERT dialog box. Its initial setting includes the beginning text string "Current" and the ending text string "Space VIEWS:". If the AutoLISP variable TM is equal to 1, where this variable represents the AutoCAD "TILEMODE" system variable, then return the string "Model". Otherwise, the IF expression returns the string "Paper".

[2] **(if (/= (cdr (assoc 70 NEXT_VIEW)) (getvar "tilemode"))** The associated 70 pair of variable NEXT_VIEW contains the view flag for either Model Space or Paper Space. The CDR function returns the integer value of that flag. For Model Space, the flag is 0; for Paper Space, the flag is set to 1. This is the opposite of what AutoCAD's "TILEMODE" variable reports, where Model Space is 1, and Paper Space is 0. If these two returned values are /= to each other, then...

[3] **(setq NAME (cdr (assoc 2 NEXT_VIEW)))** The associated 2 pair of variable NEXT_VIEW contains the view name. The CDR function returns just the view name, and is stored in NAME.

[4] **(setq SETS (strcat SETS "\n" NAME))** Add this name string to the original SETS variable. With each pass of the DISPLAY user-defined function, SETS will increase in string length to include all names of views relative to either Model Space or Paper Space. Note that the return code "\n" is used to separate each view name onto its own line.

[5] **(setq VIEW_SET (cons NAME VIEW_SET))** The NAME text string is constructed to variable VIEW_SET in order to achieve a comprehensive listing of views.

[6] **(while (not (member NEW_VIEW VIEW_SET))**
(princ "\nIncorrect name, please try again... ") The variable NEW_VIEW contains a text string that references the target view. If the user has supplied an incorrect name [not a member of the VIEW_SET list], then continue asking the user to supply one that resides within VIEW_SET.

[7] **(setq V_DATA (tblsearch "view" NEW_VIEW))** Search the "VIEW" table for the text entry stored in variable NEW_VIEW.

[8] **(setq V_DATA (member (assoc 70 V_DATA) V_DATA))** In this next sequence, the above expression resets variable V_DATA to include only the associated pairs starting at (assoc 70 V_DATA) within the original listing.

[9] **(setview V_DATA)** The SETVIEW function is then provided with the new listing [under variable V_DATA], and in turn, renders the new display. Note the absence of entity type code and view name code when constructing an associated list for SETVIEW.

[10] **(repeat (length (setq VP (vports)))** Each singular data element within the (vports) expression holds an associated listing of one viewport. The variable VP stores these individual listings, and the LENGTH function returns how many lists are contained therein. Each data record bears a viewport ID number. Repeat the ensuing process until all records are exhausted.

[11] **(command ".cvport" (car (car VP)))** Set the current AutoCAD viewport to (car (car VP)), the viewport ID number stored in the data record.

[12] **(setq VP (cdr VP))** Reset variable VP to the next data record, and continue processing.

Let's Review...

1. Read-only access to AutoCAD's symbol tables is provided by the AutoLISP TBLNEXT and TBLSEARCH functions. The TBLNEXT function allows scanning of entire symbol tables, while TBLSEARCH locates a specified symbol within a given TABLE-NAME. Valid symbol tables include:
   "APPID"
   "BLOCK"
   "DIMSTYLE"
   "LAYER"
   "LTYPE"
   "STYLE"
   "UCS"
   "VIEW"
   "VPORT"
   TBLSEARCH's optional SETNEXT argument, when non-nil, marks the symbol position within its respective table, and accordingly adjusts the entry counter for the next TBLNEXT function call.
2. The WCMATCH function provides wild card pattern testing for a given string argument. A variety of testing procedures are available to the user (as specified in the chart found earlier in this chapter).

3. The DICTNEXT and DICTSEARCH functions enlist entity names that specify a dictionary object to search. A required symbol argument specifies the item within the dictionary. Valid symbol names include ACAD_MLINESTYLE and ACAD_GROUP. The DICTRENAME, DICTADD, and DICTREMOVE functions rename, add, and remove entries from the object dictionary, respectively.
4. The VPORTS function, like the AutoCAD VPORTS command, derives the current viewport configuration. Viewport descriptors contain special identification numbers and coordinate information that define the viewports within the drawing editor.
5. The SETVIEW function establishes a view for either the current display or a specified viewport.

CHAPTER TEST

Write your answers in the spaces provided.

1. Name at least three AutoCAD symbol tables. What purpose do they serve in an AutoCAD drawing?

   ____
   ____
   ____

2. What basic AutoLISP function allows the user to scan the AutoCAD symbol tables? Detail its use.

   ____
   ____
   ____
   ____

3. What is the purpose of TBLNEXT's REWIND argument? What advantage does this argument offer the programmer?

   ____
   ____
   ____
   ____

4. Provide the syntax and use of the TBLSEARCH function.

   ____
   ____
   ____
   ____

5. When examining the identical block definition, does TBLNEXT and TBLSEARCH return the same data list? If so, why?

____

____

____

____

6. If there are no entries present in a specified symbol table, what is returned by the TBLNEXT function?

____

____

7. Is it valid to use the AutoLISP table functions to retrieve data on a viewport entity? If not, what functions are valid?

____

____

8. Briefly describe the difference between symbol table entity names, and those names produced by the entity-handling functions.

____

____

____

9. External references belong to the _______________ symbol table.
10. What additional attribute information is brought forward by TBLSEARCH as opposed to the entity-handling functions?

____

____

____

11. The symbol table definition for the "HIDDEN2X" linetype is given below. Provide the DXF code translation for each associated pair.

(0 . "LTYPE") _______________

(2 . "HIDDEN2X") _______________

(70 . 64) _______________

(3 . "__ __") _______________

(72 . 65) _______________

(73 . 2) _______________

(40 . 0.75) _______________

(49 . 0.50) _______________

(49 . –0.25) _______________

12. Name four wild card matching character patterns, and cite examples of each.

____

____

____

____

13. Is it possible to list more than one criterion for wild card matching? If so, give an example.

____

____

____

14. What data type is returned by the VPORTS function? Who assigns the identification numbers for each viewport entry?

____

____

____

15. State the basic similarities and differences between viewport entities and viewport configurations, as "described" by the VPORTS function.

____

____

____

16. Provide the necessary documentation for the following AutoLISP program. (This program appeared earlier in this chapter.)

```
(defun DELPORTS (/ PLST)                              ; [1]
  (setvar "cmdecho" 0)
  (setq PLST (ssget "X" '((0 . "VIEWPORT"))))       ; [2]
  (if (= (getvar "TILEMODE") 0)                     ; [3]
    (command ".erase" PLST "")                      ; [4]
    (princ "\nSorry – Not in Paper Space!")         ; [5]
  )
  (setvar "cmdecho" 1)
  (princ)
)
```

[1] _______________

[2] _______________

[3] _______________

[4] _______________

[5] _______________

PROGRAMMING PROBLEMS

1. For each TBLNEXT expression shown below, enter the expression at the AutoCAD command line, and write down all associated group codes that appear. Attach a brief description for each group code. The DXF code chart appearing in Appendix B should help in completing this task.

   (tblnext "DIMSTYLE" T)

   ____

   ____

   ____

   ____

   ____

   (tblnext "UCS" T)

   ____

   ____

   ____

   ____

   ____

   If either the "DIMSTYLE" or "UCS" symbol table returns nil, run the appropriate AutoCAD commands (DIM or UCS) to create a named DIMSTYLE or UCS. After this is done, complete the TBLNEXT expressions shown above.
2. Compose an AutoLISP program that does the following:
   A. In a new editing session, construct a 2.0 wide x 6.0 long box with the AutoLISP GETPOINT and POLAR functions. All corners of the box should be assigned symbol names. The box should reside on layer 0.
   B. Use the TBLSEARCH function to verify the existence of a layer named "DIM". If this operation returns nil, make a new layer named "DIM" with the color red; otherwise, set to this layer.
   C. Implement AutoLISP statements that apply the AutoCAD DIM command to the new box on screen–one vertical and one horizontal dimension each. This part of the program should be as automated as possible.

   Name the file P15-2.LSP. Load and test the program for errors.

3. Create a BOM (Bill Of Materials) AutoLISP program that follows each step given below:
   A. Set a symbol named BL-ITEM to the first entry found within the "BLOCK" symbol table (TBLNEXT function).
   B. If there are no BLOCK entries within the table (NULL function test), then tell the user (PRINC function). The else expression will be composed of an AutoLISP WHILE loop that:
      - Retrieves each block name (CDR of group code 2).
      - Creates a selection-set of those blocks matching the name (SSGET "X" – CONS code 2 with block symbol name).
      - Counts the objects within the set (SSLENGTH function).
      - Prints the block name and quantity to the text screen (PRINC and STRCAT functions).

   Remember to increment the "BLOCK" symbol table for each consecutive entry. Name the file BLK-BOM.LSP.

Chapter 16

Graphics Screen and Input Device Functions

Learning Objectives

After completing this chapter, you will be able to:
- ☐ Implement the basic AutoLISP text and graphics screen functions to switch between the text and graphics screen.
- ☐ Redraw selected entities using a variety of methods.
- ☐ Call specific menu sections by name to enhance the menuing process.
- ☐ Manipulate the graphics screen and input devices through the use of the GRxxxx family of functions.

THE DRAWING EDITOR

The AutoCAD drawing editor displays a significant amount of information, and is continuously changing during any one drawing session. This dynamic capability has at least two implications:

- The user is constantly made aware of the AutoCAD environment, such as the status line and submenu pages, which govern the editing process. These settings have a profound effect on the user's course of action.
- The graphical interface can be modified to suit the special needs of the programmer, and in turn, provides a "tailored" look for the end-user.

If the drawing editor were static, and did not allow any manipulation to its text or graphics screen areas, productivity would obviously be hampered. Fortunately, however, AutoLISP enables the programmer to customize these sections in order to streamline editing procedures.

The TEXTSCR Function

The *TEXTSCR (TEXT SCReen) function* enables the user to switch from the graphics screen to the text screen, simulating the F2 function key (flip screen). TEXTSCR is applicable to single-screen workstations, and always returns nil. The syntax for TEXTSCR is:

```
(textscr)
```

Similar to most AutoLISP functions, TEXTSCR can be issued at the Command: prompt.

(textscr)	*when in the graphics screen, flip to the text screen*

The (textscr) expression is most commonly used in place of (command ".textscr"), and provides a more logical solution to screen manipulation.

The TEXTPAGE Function

The *TEXTPAGE function* operates under the same conditions as the TEXTSCR function, but also clears any remaining text in the text window (for DOS versions of AutoCAD). The format for the TEXTPAGE function is:

```
(textpage)
```

Similar to most AutoLISP functions, TEXTPAGE can also be issued at the Command: prompt.

(textpage)	*when in the graphics screen, flip to the text screen and clear any remaining data in the text window*

The GRAPHSCR Function

When you need to return to the graphics screen from the text screen, the *GRAPHSCR (GRAPHics SCReen) function* is utilized. Essentially, the GRAPHSCR function is the opposite of the TEXTSCR function. The syntax for GRAPHSCR is:

```
(graphscr)
```

Once again, using the GRAPHSCR function simulates the action produced by pushing the F2 function key (flip screen). Like TEXTSCR, the GRAPHSCR function is most commonly used in place of (command ".graphscr").

GRAPHSCR is applicable to single-screen workstations, and always returns nil.

(graphscr)	*when in the text screen, flip to the graphics screen*

The following AutoLISP program exploits the capability of the TEXTPAGE and GRAPHSCR functions. Take note of how simple, yet important, these functions are to the operation of this routine.

```
; Filename: STATS.LSP
;
; Author: Seymour Stuff
;
; Date: February 28, 19xx
;
; Purpose: This routine reveals the "vital" statistics of a drawing.
;
(defun STATS (/ DATE)
  (setvar "cmdecho" 0)
  (setq DATE (rtos (getvar "cdate") 2)               ; The current date as string
        DATE (strcat (substr DATE 1 4) "–"           ; Substrings of DATE, the
                     (substr DATE 5 2) "–"           ;   variable DATE is reset
                     (substr DATE 7 2)
             )                                       ; End strcat
  )                                                  ; End setq
  (textpage)                                         ; Go to "clean" text screen
  (mapcar 'princ (list                               ; Print the vitals...
                  "\nDrawing info...\n\n"
                  "Current Date:      " DATE "\n"
                  "Drawing Name:      " (getvar "Dwgname") "\n"
                  "Drawing Prefix:    " (getvar "Dwgprefix") "\n"
                  "Directory Path:    " (getvar "Acadprefix") "\n\n"
                  "L. L. Corner:      " (getvar "Limmin") "\n"
                  "U. R. Corner:      " (getvar "Limmax") "\n"
                  "The Last Point:    " (getvar "Lastpoint") "\n\n"
                  "Current Layer:     " (getvar "Clayer") "\n"
                  "Drawing Color:     " (getvar "Cecolor") "\n"
                  "Drawing Ltype:     " (getvar "Celtype") "\n\n"
                  "Text Style Name: " (getvar "Textstyle") "\n"
                  "Current Menu:      " (getvar "Menuname") "\n\n"
                  )                                  ; End list
  )                                                  ; End mapcar
  (getstring "Press ENTER to continue: ")
  (graphscr)                                         ; Return to graphics screen
  (setvar "cmdecho" 1)
  (princ)
)
; – –⟨ End of File ⟩– –
```

EXERCISE 16-1

- ☐ Return to previous chapters of this text, and select at least three programs that would benefit by applying TEXTSCR, TEXTPAGE, and GRAPHSCR. It would be preferable to modify programs developed from the chapter exercises. Make the appropriate changes to these routines and save them to disk.
- ☐ Save the programs with new filenames.

REDRAWING SINGLE AUTOCAD ENTITIES

As demonstrated in the C:TEXTHGT programming example from Chapter 12, the AutoLISP *REDRAW function* is invoked to highlight or redraw selected entities. This feature can assist the user in identifying certain items within the drawing editor. The syntax for the REDRAW function is relatively easy and straightforward.

```
(redraw [ENAME [MODE]])
```

The REDRAW function always returns nil.

The AutoLISP REDRAW function is a unique graphics display tool. When called without any supportive arguments, REDRAW will clear blip markers and temporary display vectors (i.e., those created by GRVECS) from the current viewport:

(redraw) *clears the current display*

If you want to redraw a specific entity by ENAME (Entity NAME), then the REDRAW function is used in a different way:

(redraw ENAME) *redraw a single entity only*

The optional ENAME and MODE arguments may be used concurrently to return distinct results. The REDRAW modes shown in Fig. 16-1 are supported.

Mode	Action
1	Show entity on screen.
2	Hide entity (blank out).
3	Highlight entity (if display can).
4	Dehighlight entity (if display can).

Fig. 16-1. Optional MODES for the REDRAW function.

When presented with the expression:

```
(setq A (entlast))
```

...the REDRAW function will perform in the following manner:

(redraw A 1) *Redraw the entity assigned to variable A. This process is very quick and difficult to detect, especially in a large group of entities.*

(redraw A 2)	*Blank out the entity assigned to variable A. The entity seems to be erased and disappears from the screen. The REDRAW MODE arguments of 1, 3, or 4 will restore the entity to the display. Also, the next REDRAW or REGENeration will achieve the same results.*
(redraw A 3)	*Highlight the entity assigned to variable A. Highlighting will remain until the next REDRAW or REGENeration.*
(redraw A 4)	*Dehighlight or "turn on" the entity assigned to variable A. This REDRAW process is the opposite of highlighting.*

Note: When the MODE argument is a negative integer, only the header entity of a complex object, such as a block with attributes, is manipulated.

The following AutoLISP program illustrates one of many techniques when using the REDRAW function. The user-defined function BLKBLINK will find the last occurrence of a specified block, and reveal its location on screen by making the block blink three times.

```
(defun C:BLKBLINK (/ RES SET BLK)
  (setvar "cmdecho" 0)
  (setq RES (getstring "\nHighlight last insert of which block: "))
  (if (null (setq SET (ssget "X" (list (cons 2 RES)))))   ; Create SET
    (princ "\nSorry – No block with that name was found!")
    (progn
      (setq BLK (ssname SET 0))                           ; Last block added to SET
      (repeat 3                                           ; Repeat sequence 3 times
        (redraw BLK 3)                                    ; Highlight block
        (command ".delay" 50)                             ; Slight delay for highlighting
        (redraw BLK 4)                                    ; Dehighlight block
        (command ".delay" 50)                             ; Slight delay before repeating
      )                                                   ; End repeat
    )                                                     ; End progn
  )                                                       ; End if
  (setvar "cmdecho" 1)
  (princ)
)
; – –⟨ End of File ⟩– –
```

CALLING SPECIFIC MENU SECTIONS BY NAME

By calling the appropriate menu page (such as the OSNAP submenu) within an AutoLISP program, the interaction between the user and the drawing editor can be greatly enhanced. The following examples will assist in understanding this versatile concept.

The MENUCMD Function

The *MENUCMD (MENU CoMmanD) function* gives the programmer, and consequently the user, a clear advantage over general menu usage. Rather than having to "explore" the current AutoCAD menu to help complete a certain task, MENUCMD streamlines user input by activating (displaying) the required submenu. As a result, entity handling and data acquisition is dramatically improved by reducing the number of menu picks.

If the submenu does not exist within the menu file, no error message is given and AutoLISP ignores the expression. In addition, the status of the drawing editor is not altered. The MENUCMD function always returns nil. The syntax for the MENUCMD function is:

```
(menucmd STRING)
```

The required STRING argument calls out a valid submenu or the menu section of choice. Supported menu sections include the ones shown in Fig. 16-2.

Menu_area String	Menu Section
B1–B4	Buttons menus 1 through 4
P0–P16	Pull-down menus 0 through 16
I	Image title menus
S	Screen menu
T1–T4	Tablet menus 1 through 4
A1–A4	Auxiliary menus 1 through 4
M	DIESEL string expressions
Gmenugroup.nametag	Specifies a menugroup and nametag

Fig. 16-2. STRING arguments for the MENUCMD function.

Examples of the MENUCMD follow:

(menucmd "S=EDIT") — *Display the EDIT submenu in the screen area*

(menucmd "B1=BUTTON4") — *Activate BUTTON4, making it the current Buttons menu. This works well for multibutton pucks. Multiple Buttons menus are beneficial–one for drawing, editing, osnapping, etc.*

(menucmd "T1=BLOCKS") — *Set Tablet section 1 to the "BLOCKS" submenu. Various submenus can be loaded into Tablet sections, so that each section is "redefined" to suit the user's needs.*

(menucmd "P5=LAYERS")	*Pull-down menu 5 loads the "LAYERS" submenu*
(menucmd "P5=*")	*For Pull-down menus, as well as image menus, the "*" is a valid submenu call. This expression displays Pull-down menu 5.*

For AutoCAD Release 12 and above, the AutoLISP MENUCMD function has been enhanced to include the following capabilities:

- A new pull-down cursor menu (initially defined as ***POP0) is added to the AutoCAD menuing system. Sample MENUCMD function calls include:

(menucmd "P0=*")	*Display the Cursor menu (defined as ***POP0) to the graphics screen. The standard AutoCAD cursor menu produces a list of OSNAP/Filters selections.*
(menucmd "P0=DRAW")	*Initialize (install) the AutoCAD DRAW menu at P0.*
(menucmd "P0=*")	*Display Cursor menu; now showing DRAWing commands.*

- Pull-down menu labels may be active (full color) or inactive (grayed-out). The MENUCMD function takes full advantage of this:

(menucmd "P3.14=#?")		*Retrieve the current state of the 14th label in pull-down menu P3. AutoLISP will return:*
"P3.14="	*(Label 3.14 is active)*	*This MENUCMD technique is available for all pull-down menus within the current menu file. Cascading menu labels are also counted in this process. Label numbering begins from the top of the pull-down menu being used.*
or		
"P3.14=~"	*(Label 3.14 is inactive)*	
(menucmd "P6.2=")		*Regardless of its current state, enable label "P6.2"–the 2nd label in pull-down menu P6.*
(menucmd "P8.3=~")		*Regardless of its current state, disable label "P8.3"–the 3rd label in pull-down menu P8.*

- *DIESEL (Direct Interpretively Evaluated String Expression Language)* is a feature that was introduced in Release 12. Essentially, this module provides the user with an alternative macro-building language to AutoLISP. Examples of DIESEL string expressions (combined with MENUCMD) are shown at the top of the following page:

```
(menucmd "M=$(edtime,$(getvar,date),DDDD DD MONTH YYYY)")
```

Note the use of the "M" section label to denote a DIESEL expression. This DIESEL expression returns the current date, provided by the string $(edtime,TIME,PICTURE). The TIME argument is $(getvar,date), and returns the AutoCAD DATE system variable. The PICTURE argument is DDDD DD MONTH YYYY, and potentially would return a value such as "Wednesday 27 January 19XX".

```
(menucmd "M=$(<,$(getvar,filletrad),0.50)")
```

This DIESEL expression employs the "<" predicate test. Where the AutoCAD FILLETRAD system variable is less than the value 0.50, this MENUCMD statement returns "1" (True condition). Otherwise, a "0" (Zero–nil condition) is returned. Further information on DIESEL is found in the AutoCAD Customization Manual.

The following AutoLISP program employs the MENUCMD function. Extensive documentation is provided at the conclusion to explain its application throughout the routine.

```
; Filename:  HOLEDRIL.LSP
; Author:  In D. Middle
; Date:  January 12, 19xx
;
(defun C:HOLEDRIL (/ PT1 SIZE CLAY FAC)
  (setvar "cmdecho" 0)
  (mapcar 'menucmd '("S=OSNAP" "P0=POP0" "P0=*"))               ; [1]
  (setq PT1 (getpoint "\nSpecify hole–center location: "))      ; [2]
  (menucmd "S=REALS")                                           ; [3]
  (setq SIZE  (getreal "\nSpecify size for drill hole: ")       ; [4]
        CLAY (getvar "clayer")                                  ; [5]
  )
  (if (setq FAC (getreal "\nScaling [e.g. 0.25;   default = 1]: "))
     (setq SIZE (* FAC SIZE))                                   ; [6]
  )
  (command ".layer" "s" "drill" ""                              ; [7]
           ".insert" "thehole" PT1 SIZE SIZE 0
           ".layer" "s" CLAY ""
  )
  (menucmd "S=S")                                               ; [8]
  (setvar "cmdecho" 1)
  (princ)
)
; – –< End of File>– –
```

Documentation for HOLEDRIL.LSP

[1] **(mapcar 'menucmd '("S=OSNAP" "P0=POP0" "P0=*"))** The MAPCAR function executes the MENUCMD function with the individual arguments found within the quoted list. Here, two submenu sections are loaded and ready; one is the Object Snap screen menu, the other is the Release 14 Cursor menu where POP0 is loaded ("P0=POP0"), and then it is displayed ("P0=*"). The Cursor menu is shown in Fig. 16-3.

```
***POP0
**SNAP
              [&Object Snap Cursor Menu]
ID_Tracking        [Trac&king]_tracking
ID_From            [&From]_from
ID_MnPointFi       [->Point Fi&lters]
ID_PointFilx       [.X].X
ID_PointFily       [.Y].Y
ID_PointFilz       [.Z].Z
              [--]
ID_PointFixy       [.XY].XY
ID_PointFixz       [.XZ].XZ
ID_PointFiyz       [<-.YZ].YZ
              [--]
ID_OsnapEndp       [&Endpoint]_endp
ID_OsnapMidp       [&Midpoint]_mid
ID_OsnapInte       [&Intersection]_int
ID_OsnapAppa       [&Apparent Intersect]_appint
              [--]
ID_OsnapCent       [&Center]_cen
ID_OsnapQuad       [&Quadrant]_qua
ID_OsnapTang       [&Tangent]_tan
              [--]
ID_OsnapPerp       [&Perpendicular]_per
ID_OsnapNode       [No&de]_nod
ID_OsnapInse       [In&sert]_ins
ID_OsnapNear       [Nea&rest]_nea
ID_OsnapNone       [&None]_non
              [--]
ID_Osnap           [&Osnap Settings...]'_osnap
```

A

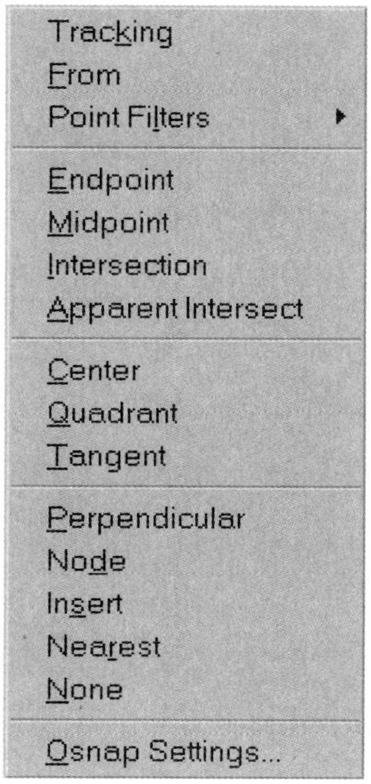

Tracking
From
Point Filters
Endpoint
Midpoint
Intersection
Apparent Intersect
Center
Quadrant
Tangent
Perpendicular
Node
Insert
Nearest
None
Osnap Settings...

B

Fig. 16-3. All Object Snap modes and XYZ Filters are represented. It works to the user's advantage to have the Object Snaps and Filters Cursor menu positioned next to the "active" area of the drawing. A–The POP0 Cursor menu as it appears in the menu file. B–Appearance of the POP0 Cursor menu as it is displayed on screen.

[2] **(setq PT1 (getpoint "\nSpecify hole–center location: "))** The user is asked for the hole–center location. Since the Object Snap menus are in place from the previous expression, this will help to speed up picking the center point.

[3] **(menucmd "S=REALS")** A customized submenu called "REALS" is presented to the screen. This submenu is a compiled list of real numbers, and has its applications in a variety of programming/drafting environments. Take note of the additional submenus for 32NDS of an inch, 64THS of an inch, and INTEGERS. A comparison of the REALS submenu as it appears in the menu and on screen is shown in Fig. 16-4.

```
**REALS
[16THS–IN]
[* * * *]$S=OSNAP
[1/16]0.0625
[  1/8]0.125
[3/16]0.1875
[  1/4]0.25
[5/16]0.3125
[  3/8]0.375
[7/16]0.4375
[  1/2]0.5
[9/16]0.5625
[  5/8]0.625
[11/16]0.6875
[  3/4]0.75
[13/16]0.8125
[  7/8]0.875
[15/16]0.9375
[INTEGERS]$S=INTEGER
[32NDS–IN]$S=32ND
[64THS–IN]$S=64TH
```

A

```
16THS-IN
* * * *
1/16
  1/8
3/16
  1/4
5/16
  3/8
7/16
  1/2
9/16
  5/8
11/16
  3/4
13/16
  7/8
15/16
INTEGERS
32NDS-IN
64THS-IN
```

B

Fig. 16-4. A–The REALS submenu as it appears in the menu file. B–When invoked, this is the way the REALS screen menu is displayed.

[4] **(setq SIZE (getreal "\nSpecify size for drill hole: ")** The drill hole size can be selected from the REALS screen menu quickly and easily. If these sizes are unsatisfactory, larger and smaller sizes can be retrieved from the INTEGERS, 32NDS–IN, and 64THS–IN screen menus.

[5] **(setq CLAY (getvar "clayer")** The current layer name is stored in a variable called CLAY. This layer will be restored after the routine has run its course.

[6]
```
(if (setq FAC (getreal "\nScaling [e.g. 0.25;  default = 1]: "))
   (setq SIZE (* FAC SIZE))
)
```

Again, the REALS screen menu is available if a scaling factor is needed. If a factor is given, multiply SIZE by that FACtor. Otherwise, if the user presses the ENTER key, the variable SIZE remains unchanged.

[7] Set the layer to “drill,” insert a block called “thehole” at the designated location with the correct size, and restore the previous layer. The block called “thehole” is a one-unit circle with center marks.

[8] **(menucmd "S=S")** Recall the previous screen with "S=S".

The MENUGROUP Function

The *MENUGROUP (loaded MENU GROUP) function* is a simple tool that verifies that a menugroup is loaded. The syntax for the MENUGROUP function is:

```
(menugroup GROUPNAME)
```

The GROUPNAME argument is a string that specifies the target menugroup name. Where the GROUPNAME argument matches a loaded menugroup (within the current drawing session), the function returns the GROUPNAME string. If the menugroup is not loaded, nil is returned. For example:

Command: **(menugroup "acad")** ↵ "acad"	*the standard AutoCAD menugroup is currently loaded*
Command: **(menugroup "custom")** ↵ nil	*a customized menugroup is specified, but is not loaded*

PROFESSIONAL TIP

Customized menu sections and submenus, as well as standard AutoCAD submenus, should be called whenever necessary within AutoLISP programs. Not only will this increase productivity, but it also focuses on the intent of the routine. Become familiar with the content and structures present in the standard AutoCAD menu file.

The TABLET Function

Many AutoCAD users “communicate” with the drawing editor via a digitizer. This electronic pointing device allows quick and accurate entry of X,Y,Z coordinates. In addition to inputting upper and lower X,Y boundaries (defined by LIMITS), a digitizer is often used in the Tablet mode to chart maps, facilities, and surveying data.

The AutoLISP TABLET function is primarily a tool used to retrieve or establish digitizer calibrations (digitizer coordinate data). TABLET employs several arguments as shown in the following syntax:

```
(tablet CODE [ROW1 ROW2 ROW3 DIRECTION])
```

The required CODE argument is specified as an integer, possessing either a value of 0 (return the current calibration) or 1 (set a new calibration).

When the CODE argument is 1, the ROW1, ROW2, and ROW3 arguments are required and are expressed as three-dimensional points. The X and Y values of each ROWx argument are axial motion components. These components provide the numerical data essential to synchronizing the X,Y axis of the digitizer to the X,Y axis of the AutoCAD drawing editor. Here, congruity is established between the digitizing device and the program.

The third value in each ROWx argument stipulates the amount of scaling necessary when locating points relative to the origin (0,0). Adjustments to this value can be made to reposition coordinate data within the editor. All three values contained in the ROWx arguments make up a 3X3 transformation matrix:

$$\begin{bmatrix} X' \\ Y' \\ D' \end{bmatrix} = \begin{bmatrix} M_{00} & M_{01} & M_{02} \\ M_{10} & M_{11} & M_{12} \\ M_{20} & M_{21} & 1.0 \end{bmatrix} * \begin{bmatrix} X \\ Y \\ 1.0 \end{bmatrix}$$

The 3X3 matrix transforms the required ROWx arguments into a 2D point. The goal is to solve for X', Y', and D' in order to establish a valid X,Y axial link (etc.) between the device and the program.

The DIRECTION argument, shown as the column vector (X Y 1.0), specifies a direction vector that is normal (perpendicular) to the current UCS. Its coordinates are expressed in the World Coordinate System (WCS). Combined with the ROWx arguments, a new tablet calibration can be attained where the tablet's (X,Y) surface is assumed to lie in congruence with the current UCS. This final argument must be supplied if the CODE argument evaluates to the integer 1. The DIRECTION argument is the final entry into the 3X3 transformation matrix, where the final formula is derived:

$$X' = M_{00}X + M_{01}Y + M_{02}$$
$$Y' = M_{10}X + M_{11}Y + M_{12}$$
$$D' = M_{21}X + M_{21}Y + 1.0$$

The following examples will assist in your understanding of the TABLET function:

(tablet 0) returns nil *no calibration has been established*

(setq CAL1 (tablet 1 '(1 0 0) '(0 1 0) '(0 0 1) '(0 0 1))) returns (1 '(1 0 0) '(0 1 0) '(0 0 1) '(0 0 1))

The calibration has been set to the absolute limits of the digitizing tablet. Points that are picked in this configuration are seen as absolute coordinates within AutoCAD.

After setting the AutoCAD TABLET command to CAL (CALibrate), and establishing the active digitizing area for the lower-left corner at (0,0) and the upper-right corner at (500,500), the following sample results are returned:

Command: **(setq CAL2 (tablet 0))** ↵

```
(1 (0.246452 –0.0259779 –587.981)        ROW1–M00, M01, M02
   (0.0259779 0.246452 –431.277)         ROW2–M10, M11, M12
   (0 0 1)                               ROW3–M20, M21, 1.0
   (0 0 1)                               DIRECTION argument (0 0 1)
)
```

The calibration is returned in the form of ROW1, ROW2, ROW3, and DIRECTION. This tablet configuration is considered to be an orthogonal transformation, a matrix that preserves length and distance in both the X and Y directions. Not only are M_{20} and M_{21} equal to 0, but $M_{00} = M_{11}$ and $M_{10} = -M_{01}$. This data listing is indicative of orthogonal transformations.

The following expressions modify the M_{02} and M_{12} values of ROW1 and ROW2, respectively. Each value is incremented by 50, providing equal changes to both the X and Y axis. The symbol CAL2 (from the previous expression) is used in this example:

```
(setq INC     50               ; INCrement is set to 50
      CAL2–A (cadr CAL2)       ; First list in CALibration 2, set to CAL2–A
      M02    (last CAL2–A)     ; Last value of CAL2–A, set to M02 (X' scaling)
      CAL2–B (caddr CAL2)      ; Second list in CALibration 2, set to CAL2–B
      M12    (last CAL2–B)     ; Last value of CAL2–B, set to M12 (Y' scaling)
      CAL2–C (cadddr CAL2)     ; Third list in CALibration 2, set to CAL2–C
      CAL2–D (last CAL2)       ; Last list in CALibration 2, set to CAL2–D
)
(setq CAL2–A (subst (+ INC M02) M02 CAL2–A))     ; SUBSTitute (+ INC M02)
(setq CAL2–B (subst (+ INC M12) M12 CAL2–B))     ; SUBSTitute (+ INC M12)
(tablet 1 CAL2–A CAL2–B CAL2–C CAL2–D)           ; Establish a new tablet calibration
```

The new tablet calibration increments the existing tablet coordinate system by 50 in both the X and Y directions. This does not change the amount of active digitizing area established by the AutoCAD TABLET command. Rather, it shifts the current coordinate system uniformly by 50 units. Where the old origin of (0,0) used to be, now it appears as (50,50).

Let's Review...

1. The three basic AutoLISP functions of TEXTSCR, TEXTPAGE, and GRAPHSCR are instrumental in giving the look and feel of a "responsive" interface. TEXTSCR and TEXTPAGE switch to the text screen, while GRAPHSCR flips to the graphics screen.
2. The AutoLISP REDRAW function highlights or redraws selected entities within the drawing editor. This feature assists the user in identifying certain items on screen.
3. The MENUCMD function streamlines user input by activating (displaying) the required submenu within the current menu file. This decreases the amount of time needed to find the appropriate submenu.
4. The MENUGROUP function is a tool that verifies whether a menugroup is loaded or not present.
5. The AutoLISP TABLET function is primarily a tool used to retrieve or establish digitizer calibrations. This function employs a number of arguments. The CODE argument (0 or 1) either returns or sets a calibration. The ROW1, ROW2, ROW3, and DIRECTION arguments define the tablet configuration as it relates to the current UCS of the AutoCAD drawing editor.

EXERCISE 16-2

- ☐ Create a program that fulfills the following criteria:
  - ☐ Establish new limits for the drawing editor, and then ZOOM All. Limits should be B– through D–size, and be either Mechanical or Architectural.
  - ☐ Place a circle in the middle of the drawing, with a radius of 1.000. The center point location may be derived from applying the CAR and CDR family of functions (or with the VIEWCTR system variable, if desired).
  - ☐ Place one more circle on the drawing with a radius of 0.500. Place this new circle 4 drawing units to the right of the first circle.
  - ☐ Create a polar array of the last circle, making eight circles total.
- ☐ Assume that a new drawing file is being used. Use the MENUCMD function and insert the standard AutoCAD submenu sections of OSNAP, CIRCLE, and ARRAY wherever needed.
- ☐ Save the program as PICKME.LSP.

ADDITIONAL GRAPHICS SCREEN AND INPUT DEVICE FUNCTIONS

The final section of this chapter deals with AutoLISP functions that allow direct access to and modification of the AutoCAD graphics screen, (for example, the status line) and input devices (such as the cursor and digitizing tablet). Although the application of the GRxxxx family of functions is not widespread, it provides a "gateway" into areas most often encountered by experienced AutoCAD developers. With some practice, the next five AutoLISP functions can give the programmer a foothold into another aspect of the AutoCAD interface.

The GRCLEAR Function

The *GRCLEAR (GRaphics CLEAR) function* clears the current viewport (for Release 13 and previous versions). However, this does not mean that the drawing database is discarded and a new drafting environment is created. GRCLEAR only "wipes clean" the entire screen, masking the drawing vectors (drawing entities such as lines, etc.) from view. The status and command lines, as well as the screen menu, are unaffected. The format for the GRCLEAR function is:

```
(grclear)
```

New entities may be generated in the drawing editor after the screen has been cleared, although these items may overlay existing entities. The AutoLISP REDRAW function (or AutoCAD REDRAW or REGEN commands) returns the graphics screen to its original state.

The following routine utilizes the GRCLEAR function, and is used primarily to conceal the contents of the drawing editor:

```
(defun C:OTL ()
  (setvar "cmdecho" 0)
  (setvar "blipmode" 0)
  (grclear)                                     ; Clear the viewport
  (command ".text" "m" (getvar "viewctr")       ; Center of screen
        (/ (getvar "viewsize") 10.0)            ; Vertical size / 10.0
        0.0                                     ; Rotation angle
```

```
        "BREAK TIME"                               ; Text string
    )                                              ; End command
    (getstring "\Press ENTER to continue editing: ")
    (command ".erase" "last" ""
             ".redraw"
    )
    (setvar "cmdecho" 1)
    (princ)
)
; --⟨ End of File ⟩--
```

The GRDRAW Function

The *GRDRAW (GRaphics DRAW) function* draws a vector between two specified locations in the current UCS. The GRDRAW syntax is:

```
(grdraw FROM TO COLOR [HIGHLIGHT])
```

The FROM and TO arguments are required, and constitute the 2D or 3D endpoints for the vector in the current UCS. Information regarding the required COLOR and optional HIGHLIGHT arguments are outlined in the following guidelines:

- The vector that is constructed using the GRDRAW function is only *temporary,* and is not included within the drawing database. In other words, the vector cannot be erased, copied, moved, etc. Any action that resets the viewport, such as a regeneration or zoom, will remove the vector(s).
- The required COLOR argument specifies the color for the vector (similar to the color assignments for "Layer"). The argument value must be an integer. A color number of –1 signifies XOR ink, and will complement any vector it comes in contact with, as well as disappear when drawn over.
- When present and non-zero, the optional HIGHLIGHT argument specifies that the vector is to be highlighted using the method common to the graphics display. The vector is usually dashed, but can vary in appearance depending upon the display. Highlighted and dehighlighted vectors may exist simultaneously on the same screen. The HIGHLIGHT argument, when specified, must be an integer.
- If the vector length exceeds the viewport size, the ends of the vector are "trimmed" to fit the screen.

Examples of the GRDRAW function follow:

```
(grdraw '(1 1) '(2 2) 1)
```

A vector is drawn between the 2D coordinates of (1 1) and (2 2) in the current UCS. The vector color is red (specified as 1).

```
(grdraw '(3 3 3) '(7 7 7) 3)
```

A vector is drawn between the 3D coordinates of (3 3 3) and (7 7 7) in the current UCS. The vector color is green (specified as 3).

```
(grdraw '(9.2 5.3) '(2.8 4.1) 6 –1)
```

A vector is drawn between (9.2 5.3) and (2.8 4.1) with a magenta color (specified as 6), and is also highlighted.

The next AutoLISP program uses the GRDRAW function to trace over a basic polyline within the drawing editor (line vectors only, polyarcs not included). Remember that any action that resets the viewport, such as a regeneration or zoom, will remove the GRDRAW vectors:

```
(defun C:CONTOUR (/ ENT CLR SPL PT1 PT2 CP1 CP2 VER BEG FINAL)
 (setvar "cmdecho" 0)
;
; --⟨ While a polyline is not selected, prompt user and try again ⟩--
;
 (while (/= (cdr
             (assoc 0
               (setq ENT (entget (car (entsel "\nSelect contour: "))))
             )                          ; End assoc
           )                            ; End cdr
       "POLYLINE")                      ; End /=
       (princ "\nNot a Contour/Polyline...Try Again")
 )                                      ; End while
;
 (initget (+ 1 2 4))
 (setq CLR (getint "\nContour tracing color number: ")    ; [1]
       SPL (cdr (assoc 70 ENT))                           ; [2]
       ENT (entget (entnext (cdr (assoc -1 ENT))))        ; [3]
       PT1 (cdr (assoc 10 ENT))                           ; [4]
       CP1 (cdr (assoc 70 ENT))                           ; [5]
       ENT (entget (entnext (cdr (assoc -1 ENT))))        ; [6]
       PT2 (cdr (assoc 10 ENT))                           ; [7]
       CP2 (cdr (assoc 70 ENT))                           ; [8]
       VER (cdr (assoc 0 ENT))                            ; [9]
       BEG PT1                                            ; [10]
 )
;
; --⟨ Vector looping function - cycle through polyline drawing vectors ⟩--
;
 (defun VECLOOP ()
   (while (/= VER "SEQEND")                               ; [11]
     (if (and                                             ; [12]
           (/= CP1 16)
           (/= CP2 16)
         )
         (grdraw PT1 PT2 CLR)                             ; [13]
     )                                                    ; End if
     (setq PT1  PT2                                       ; [14]
           CP1 CP2
           ENT (entget (entnext (cdr (assoc -1 ENT))))
           PT2 (cdr (assoc 10 ENT))
           CP2 (cdr (assoc 70 ENT))
           VER (cdr (assoc 0 ENT))
     )                                                    ; End setq
     (if (/= CP1 16)                                      ; [15]
         (setq FINAL PT1)
     )
   )                                                      ; End while
```

```
    )                                   ; End VECLOOP defun
;
    (cond ( (or
              (= SPL 0)                 ; No Spline curving – open polyline
              (= SPL 4)                 ; Spline curving – open polyline
            )
            (VECLOOP)                   ; Run VECLOOP to generate vectors
          )                             ; End test/list 1
          ( (= SPL 1)                   ; No Spline curving – closed polyline
            (VECLOOP)                   ; Run VECLOOP to generate vectors
            (grdraw BEG FINAL CLR)      ; Generate final vector
          )                             ; End test/list 2
          ( (= SPL 5)                   ; Spline curving – closed polyline
            (setq BEG PT2)              ; 1st vertex – Not a control point
            (VECLOOP)                   ; Run VECLOOP to generate vectors
            (grdraw BEG FINAL CLR)      ; Generate final vector
          )                             ; End test/list 3
    )                                   ; End cond
    (setvar "cmdecho" 1)
    (princ)
)
; – –⟨ End of File ⟩– –
```

Documentation for CONTOUR.LSP

[1] **(setq CLR (getint "\nContour tracing color number: ")** Get the color number for tracing and set it to symbol CLR.

[2] The value returned by this expression is passed to symbol SPL. The associated 70 group, after the first interrogation of the primary entity list, contains an integer that breaks down as follows:

(= SPL 0)	*No Spline curving–open polyline*
(= SPL 1)	*No Spline curving–closed polyline*
(= SPL 4)	*Spline curving–open polyline*
(= SPL 5)	*Spline curving–closed polyline*

[3] The symbol ENT is reset to the second interrogation of the primary entity list. This establishes the entry point into the sequence of polyline vertices.

[4] The symbol PT1 is set to the first vertex of the polyline, which is held in the associated 10 group.

[5] The symbol CP1 is set to the integer value which is held in the associated 70 group. This is done in order to verify if the coordinate value stored in PT1 is actually a control point for spline curving.

[6] The symbol ENT is reset to the third interrogation of the primary entity list. This establishes an entity list that contains the second vertex in the sequence of polyline vertices.

[7] The symbol PT2 is set to the second vertex of the polyline, which is held in the associated 10 group.

[8] The symbol CP2 is set to the integer value which is held in the associated 70 group. This is done in order to verify if the coordinate value stored in PT2 is actually a control point for spline curving.

[9] The symbol VER is set to the string value stored in the associated 0 group, the subentity name. The first name held in this group is "VERTEX".

[10] The symbol BEG stores the value [first coordinate] held in PT1. Since the symbol PT1 is eventually redefined in the ensuing loop, the symbol BEG is a static point marker that allows a final vector to be drawn to it.

[11] **(while (/= VER "SEQEND")** A WHILE loop begins the VECLOOP defined function. While the subentity name stored in symbol VER is not "SEQEND" [SEQuence END of the polyline], cycle through all vertices of the polyline.

[12] An IF expression tests the values stored in both CP1 and CP2. If the values of CP1 and CP2 are not 16 [an integer denoting a control point], execute the THEN expression. This test is provided so that stray graphics vectors are not drawn between control points and vertices on the polyline.

[13] **(grdraw PT1 PT2 CLR)** Employ the AutoLISP GRDRAW function to draw a graphics vector from PT1 to PT2 in the CLR color. This is the THEN expression for the IF statement.

[14] The values stored in PT2 and CP2 are passed to symbols PT1 and CP1, respectively. This recycling process allows the program to step through each consecutive vertex of the polyline, analyzing a new pair of coordinates each time through the WHILE loop. Note that PT2 and CP2 are then set to the next vertex of the polyline, providing a different set of coordinate data for testing. The symbol VER is also reset, and will eventually evaluate to "SEQEND". This allows a mechanism for dropping out of the WHILE loop.

[15] An IF expression tests the value stored in symbol CP1. If the value of CP1 is not 16, set the symbol FINAL to the coordinate stored in PT1. The value of PT1 is continually updated in the WHILE loop, and will return the last coordinate location of the polyline before the "SEQEND".

The GRVECS Function

The *GRVECS (GRaphics VECtorS) function* draws multiple vectors on the graphics screen. Its operation is very similar to the GRDRAW function, but includes additional enhancements. The GRVECS syntax is:

```
(grvecs VLIST [TRANS])
```

The VLIST (Vector LIST) argument is required, and is composed of a series of color integers and two-point lists. The color integer portion of the vector list is optional, where integers range in value from 0–255. Like the GRDRAW function, these color values are patterned (duplicated) after the AutoCAD color chart. Vectors generated with integers exceeding this range are drawn in XOR ink, and will complement any vector they come in contact with, as well as disappear when drawn over.

Each vector list must contain at least one pair of coordinates, either two-dimensional or three-dimensional. The point lists are expressed in the current UCS, and constitute the starting and ending points for each graphics vector.

Here is a basic example of the GRVECS function:

```
(grvecs '(
        3 (2.75 2 0) (7 7.25 0)
        1 (8.25 3.5) (2.75 1.5)
        )                ; end vector list
)                        ; end grvecs
```

Two temporary vectors are drawn. The first vector has a color of 3 (green), and the second is in the color red (1). Both 2D and 3D points are represented here.

Here are a few additional guidelines to utilize when using the GRVECS function:

- The vectors that are constructed using the GRVECS function are only temporary, and are not included within the drawing database. In other words, the vectors cannot be erased, copied, moved, etc. Any action that resets the viewport, such as a regeneration or zoom, will remove the vectors.
- When present and less than zero, the optional color value specifies that the vectors are to be highlighted using the method common to the graphics display. The vectors are usually dashed, but can vary in appearance depending upon the display. Highlighted and dehighlighted vectors may exist simultaneously on the same screen. Remember that the color value must be in the form of an integer.
- If the vector length exceeds the viewport size, the ends of the vector are "trimmed" to fit the screen.

Note the use of the GRVECS function in the following examples:

```
(grvecs '(
        -5 (6.5 2.5) (8.75 7.25)
        15 (4.25 1.5) (6.75 3.5)
        )
)
```

Two temporary vectors are drawn. The first vector has a color of –5 (highlighted blue), and the second is the color gray (15).

```
(grvecs '(
        1 (1 1 0) (3 3 0)
          (1 2 0) (3 4 0)
        6 (1 3 0) (3 5 0)
          (1 4 0) (3 6 0)
        )
)
```

Four temporary vectors are drawn. The first and second vectors have a color of red (1). The third and fourth vectors have a color of magenta (6). Despite the "missing" color code for vectors two and four, their assignments are determined by the previous color value.

```
(grvecs '( (2.5 2.5) (8.5 2.5)  (8.5 2.5) (8.5 6.5)      ; Point lists 1 & 2
           (8.5 6.5) (2.5 6.5)  (2.5 6.5) (2.5 2.5)      ; Point lists 3 & 4
         )                                               The given point lists make up the
)                                                        corners of a vector rectangle. Note
                                                         that the color argument is
                                                         completely omitted. In a case such
                                                         as this, GRVECS defaults to the
                                                         color assignment of the current
                                                         layer. This default value is then
                                                         held in memory, and is now
                                                         dynamically linked to this one
                                                         specific layer. As the color
                                                         assignments change for the layer,
                                                         each call to GRVECS (that totally
                                                         excludes color integers) aquires
                                                         the layer's color assignment.

(initget 1)                                              disallow null input

(setq COL (getint "\nColor integer: ")
      PT1 (getpoint "\nFirst point: ")
      PT2 (getpoint "\nSecond point: ")
      PT3 (getpoint "\nThird point: ")
)
(grvecs (list
         COL  PT1 PT2          ; A color integer and point locations are
         COL  PT2 PT3          ; determined by the user, and substituted
         COL  PT3 PT1          ; into the GRVECS expression.
   )
)
```

The optional TRANS (TRANSformation) argument of the GRVECS function specifies a transformation matrix that allows the programmer to change the location or proportion of the point lists inside VLIST. This transformation matrix is comparable to matrices found for other AutoLISP functions, like NENTSELP.

The following example uses the required format of four lists of four real numbers to complete the matrix:

```
'(                                                       This matrix has a uniform scaling of
  (1.0 0.0 0.0 7.0)                                      1.0 and a translation of 7.0,7.0,0.0.
  (0.0 1.0 0.0 7.0)                                      This translation provides an offset
  (0.0 0.0 1.0 0.0)                                      of 0.0,7.0,0.0 for the supplied
  (0.0 0.0 0.0 1.0)                                      vector list.
)
```

The following example applies both arguments, VLIST and TRANS, to the GRVECS function. The user is asked to select four random corners in order to build a four-sided LINE figure. The figure is then highlighted with the color and point-list arguments contained within VLIST. The user is allowed to cycle through any number of colors desired, choosing the final color with ENTER. Finally, a user-defined X,Y,Z transformation matrix is input to the program.

```
; Program: GRBOX.LSP
;
; Author: Bilda Box
;
; Date: November 14, 19xx
;
; Purpose: Demonstrate the VLIST and TRANS arguments within the AutoLISP
;          GRVECS function. It is best to run this program on a layer
;          with the color white and the continuous linetype. Entity
;          properties should be "BYLAYER".
;
(defun C:GRBOX (/ PT1 PT2 PT3 PT4 COL FCOL X-TRANS Y-TRANS Z-TRANS)
  (setvar "cmdecho" 0)
  (setq PT1 (getpoint "\nFirst corner: ")                  ; Four corners of the
        PT2 (getpoint "\nSecond corner: ")                 ;   four–sided figure.
        PT3 (getpoint "\nThird corner: ")
        PT4 (getpoint "\nFourth corner: ")
  )
  (command ".line" PT1 PT2 PT3 PT4 "c")
  (while
    (setq COL (getint "\nColor integer/⟨ENTER⟩ when done: "))
    (grvecs (list
              COL  PT1 PT2          ; The color integer COL and point lists
              COL  PT2 PT3          ;   are determined by the user, and placed
              COL  PT3 PT4          ;   within GRVECS.
              COL  PT4 PT1
            )
    )
    (setq FCOL COL)                 ; Final COLor integer, after dropping out of loop.
  )
  (setq X-TRANS (getreal "\nX–transformation value: ")  ; User–defined
        Y-TRANS (getreal "\nY–transformation value: ")  ;   transformation
        Z-TRANS (getreal "\nZ–transformation value: ")  ;   values
  )
  (grvecs (list
            FCOL  PT1 PT2           ; The color integer FCOL and point lists
            FCOL  PT2 PT3           ;   are determined by the user, and placed
            FCOL  PT3 PT4           ;   within GRVECS.
            FCOL  PT4 PT1
          )
          (list
            (list 1.0 0.0 0.0 X–TRANS)                     ; The transformation matrix
            (list 0.0 1.0 0.0 Y–TRANS)                     ;   established by the user.
            (list 0.0 0.0 1.0 Z–TRANS)                     ; The LIST function lists
            (list 0.0 0.0 0.0 1.0)                         ;   together each element of
          )                                                ;   the X,Y,Z transformation.
  )                                                        ; End grvecs
  (setq SS  (ssget "F" (list PT1 PT2 PT3 PT4))             ; Select LINEs by "Fence"
        CTR 0                                              ; CounTeR is set to 0
  )
  (while (setq ENT (ssname SS CTR))                        ; While there are ENTities to process
    (redraw ENT 1)                                         ;   in SS (selection-set), redraw each
```

```
      (setq CTR (1+ CTR))                    ; Entity back into its original form
    )
    (setvar "cmdecho" 1)
    (princ)
  )
  ; --( End of File )--
```

The GRTEXT Function

The *GRTEXT (GRaphics TEXT) function* places a user-supplied text string into one of the text areas of the AutoCAD drawing editor. The syntax for GRTEXT is:

```
(grtext [BOX TEXT [HIGHLIGHT]])
```

The GRTEXT function is used primarily for placing the required TEXT argument into a screen menu cell, or BOX. Valid screen menu BOX numbers are between 0 and the highest screen menu BOX number minus 1. The SCREENBOXES system variable assists in determining the highest BOX number.

The optional HIGHLIGHT argument, when present, must be a positive integer. Using a negative integer value for the HIGHLIGHT argument is ignored. An example of the GRTEXT function follows:

```
(grtext 0 "RootMenu")
```

The text string "RootMenu" is placed in screen menu cell 0, which is the top of the menu. Picking this menu cell still returns the macro found in this position of the loaded menu. Always place text strings first before doing any optional highlighting.

The following guidelines will assist you in putting the GRTEXT function to use:

- On many systems, a null text string may be used when highlighting a screen menu box. For example:

```
(grtext 0 "" 1)
```

Null string "" is acceptable during highlighting. Note the positive integer for highlighting. If dehighlighting is desired, use 0.

- It is a good policy to use the *exact* text string when highlighting screen menu boxes. This not only guarantees upward compatibility for future AutoLISP programs, but also yields the same results despite differences in graphics cards/workstations.
- Paging through a loaded menu file will clear out any GRTEXT entries shown in the screen menu portion.
- If the BOX number argument is –1, the TEXT argument is placed in the mode status line. Writing strings to the mode status line will *not* intrude into the coordinate status line. If longer strings are supplied, they are truncated.

- The only other negative BOX number argument is –2. This places the TEXT argument into the coordinate status line (for DOS versions of AutoCAD). For example:

```
(grtext –2 (getvar "Dwgname"))
```

writes the drawing name into the coordinate status line

- Highlighting for the GRTEXT function applies *only* to screen menu box applications.
- The expression:

```
(grtext)
```

...will restore all graphics text areas to their standard values, except the coordinate status line. If coordinate tracking is enabled (Coords "On"), any cursor activity will remove the graphics text. The AutoCAD REDRAW or REGEN commands will not restore this area.

The following program utilizes the GRTEXT function, as well as, other AutoLISP functions found in earlier chapters.Note the use of the READ function to withdraw variable names from text strings.Variable values are, in turn, created by using the SET function. Numbered documentation is also provided.

```
;   Filename: SCRVARS.LSP
;
;   Purpose: The SCReen VARiableS program offers the user a customized screen
;            menu interface for establishing Variable name / AutoLISP function
;            relationships. After entering a new AutoLISP variable name, the
;            user selects the desired AutoLISP function from the screen menu
;            area, such as "getint" or "entsel". Each screen menu box entry
;            is the result of applying the AutoLISP GRTEXT function.
;
;   ----------------------------------------------------------
;
(defun C:SV (/ LST1 LST2 VN CTR BOX FIL)
   (setvar "cmdecho" 0)                                ; [1]
   (setq LST1 '("getInt" "getReal" "getStrng" "getPoint" "getDist" "getAngle"
                "ssGet" "entSel" "nentSel" "findFile" "loadFile" "wordProc")
;
         LST2 '( (getint     (strcat "\nInteger value for "  VN  ": "))
                 (getreal    (strcat "\nReal number value for "  VN  ": "))
                 (getstring T (strcat "\nText string value for "  VN  ": "))
                 (getpoint  (strcat "\nPoint value for "  VN  ": "))
                 (getdist    (strcat "\nDistance value for "  VN  ": "))
                 (getangle (strcat "\nAngular value for "  VN  ": "))
                 (ssget)   (entsel)   (nentsel)
               )                                       ; End LST2 list
         VN    (getstring "\nVariable Name: ")         ; New Variable Name
         CTR   3                                       ; [2]
   )
;
   (grtext 0 "–Quick–") (grtext 1 "AutoLISP") (grtext 2 "––––––––") ; [3]
;
   (repeat 12
      (grtext CTR (nth (– CTR 3) LST1))                ; [4]
      (setq CTR (1+ CTR))
```

```
    )                                              ;end REPEAT function
;
    (grtext 15 "– – – – – – – –") (grtext 16 "PrevMenu") (setq CTR 17)  ; [5]
;
    (repeat (– (getvar "screenboxes") 16)          ;[6]
      (grtext CTR " ")
      (setq CTR (1+ CTR))
    )
;
    (setq BOX (cadr (grread)))                     ;[7]
    (cond
      ( (wcmatch (itoa BOX) "[0–2],15")             ;[8]
        (princ "\nInvalid box – exit function.")
        (grtext)
      )
      ( (= BOX 12)                                  ;[9]
        (setq FIL  (getstring "\nFile to search for: "))
        (set (read VN) (findfile FIL))
        (grtext)
      )
      ( (= BOX 13)                                  ;[10]
        (setq FIL  (getstring "\nAutoLISP File to load: "))
        (load FIL)
        (grtext)
      )
      ( (= BOX 14)                                  ;[11]
        (setq FIL  (getstring "\nFile to edit: "))
        (command "edit" FIL)
        (grtext)
      )
      ( (= BOX 16)                       ; If BOX = 16, clear menu
        (grtext)                         ;  with GRTEXT function
      )
      ( T                                           ;[12]
        (setq BOX (nth (– BOX 3) LST2))
        (set (read VN) (eval BOX))
        (grtext)
      )
   )
   (princ)
 )
 ;– –〈End of SCRVARS.LSP〉– –
```

[1] (setq LST1 ... LST2 ...) The AutoLISP function names found in LST1 represent a random sampling of those available through the AutoLISP programming language. As demonstrated later in the program, each function name in the list is placed within its own screen menu box, via the GRTEXT function. Variable LST2 contains the majority of those functions cited in LST1, and includes various prompts. Note that LST2 is a quoted list, where each element is an expression waiting to be evaluated.

[2] **(setq CTR 3)** The first three menu cell boxes [numbered 0, 1, and 2] are to be occupied with labels; therefore, establish the CounTeR with a value of 3. The CounTeR is now set to the first open slot for the ensuing REPEAT function.

[3] **(grtext 0 "–Quick–") (grtext 1 "AutoLISP") (grtext 2 "– – – – – – – – –")** GRTEXT places the text "–Quick–", "AutoLISP", and "– – – – – – – – –" into screen menu cell boxes 0, 1, and 2 respectively.

[4] **(repeat 12 (grtext CTR (nth (– CTR 3) LST1))** The variable LST1 contains a total of 12 different AutoLISP function names, so REPEAT 12 times in order to capture each name. The CounTeR is initially set to 3, the first open menu cell box for GRTEXT. The NTH function takes the CounTeR, minus 3, and returns the 0 element from its list argument. As the CounTeR is incremented, all elements from LST1 are exhausted and placed within consecutive screen menu cell boxes.

[5] **(grtext 15 "– – – – – – – – –") (grtext 16 "PrevMenu") (setq CTR 17)** GRTEXT places the text "– – – – – – – – –" and "PrevMenu" into screen menu cell boxes 15 and 16 respectively. The variable CTR is reset to 17 in order to capture the next open menu cell.

[6] **(repeat (– (getvar "screenboxes") 16) (grtext CTR " ")** The AutoCAD "screenboxes" system variable returns an integer that denotes the highest cell number in the screen menu.This number, minus 16 cells already occupied, represents the remaining menu cells. The REPEAT function now continues to loop until each remaining cell is altered, where GRTEXT supplies a null text string. This procedure starts at cell 17, the number stored in CTR.

[7] **(setq BOX (cadr (grread)))** The GRREAD function, found later in this chapter, reads AutoCAD input from the pointing device and returns a list containing 2 values. The first value is the device type, and the second value is the screen menu box number. The CADR function secures the second value and stores it in variable BOX.

[8] **(wcmatch (itoa BOX) "[0–2],15")** The variable BOX is converted from its default integer value to a string.The WCMATCH function then compares this string to the given pattern.If the string matches either "0", "1", "2", or "15", the user has selected an incorrect cell and an error message is displayed.

[9] **(= BOX 12) (setq FIL (getstring "\nFile to search for: "))** Where the user has selected menu cell BOX number 12, ask for the file to search for. READ the string stored by variable VN [the specified variable name], and SET the new variable to the results of FINDFILE.

[10] **(= BOX 13) (setq FIL (getstring "\nAutoLISP File to load: "))** Where the user has selected menu cell BOX number 13, ask for the file to load. If variable FIL returns a valid AutoLISP file, then load it.

[11] **(= BOX 14) (setq FIL (getstring "\nFile to edit: "))** Where the user has selected menu cell BOX number 14, ask for the file to edit. The editor, in this case, originates from the Acad.pgp file.

[12] **(T (setq BOX (nth (– BOX 3) LST2))** Where the user has selected a valid menu cell other than those described above, set the variable BOX to BOX minus 3. Since the first three menu cells are occupied by labels, BOX is now adjusted to the correct position when compared to list LST2. READ the variable VN, which converts the string to a symbol, and SET it to the EVALuation of the expression in (eval BOX).

EXERCISE 16-3

- ☐ Identify at least four system variables that return text strings.
- ☐ Use the GRTEXT function to place the resultant strings into one (or more) of the graphics portions of the screen.
- ☐ Save the program as GROUT.LSP.

The GRREAD Function

The *GRREAD (GRaphics READ) function* is quite different from the AutoLISP functions mentioned previously in this chapter. GRREAD reads (receives input from) AutoCAD input devices such as a pointing device or digitizing tablet. The syntax for the GRREAD function is shown below:

```
(grread [TRACK] [ALLKEYS [CURTYPE]])
```

The optional TRACK argument, when not nil, allows the user to track a pointing device without pressing any buttons. The optional ALLKEYS and CURTYPE arguments are explained in detail later in this section.

The chart in Fig. 16-5 provides the type of output seen when using the GRREAD function. The returned values, displayed in the form of a list, are composed of two elements:

- The first element relates to the type of input device.
- The second element is returned either as an integer or a coordinate list.

Input Code		Second Element	
Value	**Device / Input Used**	**Value**	**Significance**
2	Keyboard	varies	Returns character code
3	Point	3D point	Returns 3D pt. coordinate
4	Screen / Pull-down menus (Selection made from a screen pointing device– up to 16 POP menus)	0–999 1001–1999 2001–2999 3001–3999 ... 16001–16999	Screen menu box number POP1 menu box number POP2 menu box number POP3 menu box number ... POP16 menu box number
5	Pointing device	3D point	Drag mode coordinate
6	BUTTONS menu	0–999 1000–1999 2000–2999 3000–3999	BUTTONS1 menu button no. BUTTONS2 menu button no. BUTTONS3 menu button no. BUTTONS4 menu button no.
7	TABLET1 menu	0–32767	Digitized box number
8	TABLET2 menu	0–32767	Digitized box number
9	TABLET3 menu	0–32767	Digitized box number
10	TABLET4 menu	0–32767	Digitized box number
11	AUXILIARY menu	0–999 1000–1999 2000–2999 3000–3999	AUXILIARY1 menu button no. AUXILIARY2 menu button no. AUXILIARY3 menu button no. AUXILIARY4 menu button no.
12	Pointer Button	3D point	Returns 3D pt. coordinate

Fig. 16-5. Applications of the GRREAD function.

Examples of the GRREAD function follow:

(2 87)	*the keyboard character "W", ASCII value 87*
(3 (8.25 9.17 3.44))	*selected coordinate (8.25 9.17 3.44)*
(4 5001)	*pull-down #5, first cell in Pull-down menu*
(4 6)	*screen menu area, Box number 6*
(6 1)	*buttons device, Button number 1*
(9 23)	*tablet section 3, Cell number 23*

The final section of this discussion investigates the application of the ALLKEYS and CURTYPE arguments for GRREAD. Similar to the TRACK argument, ALLKEYS is an optional value, and influences the responses given by GRREAD. The ALLKEYS argument takes the form of a positive integer, and if present, behaves as shown in Fig. 16-6.

ALLKEYS Value	GRREAD Function
1	Return drag mode 3D coordinates.
2	Return all keyboard values, including cursor keys.
4	Use CURTYPE argument to control cursor display.
8	Do not display the cancellation message: error: console break
16	Disable the pull-down menu.

Fig. 16-6. Results of using the ALLKEYS argument.

When using the ALLKEYS argument, the TRACK argument must be set to nil. Otherwise, ALLKEYS returns drag mode coordinates regardless of the positive integer's value. Examine the following two GRREAD expressions:

(grread T) — *TRACK the cursor position, returning a list containing input code #5, and the drag mode coordinates.*

(grread T 2) — *Despite the ALLKEYS argument (the integer 2) calling for keyboard input, the cursor is TRACKed, and a list is returned containing input code #5, and the drag mode coordinates.*

By setting the TRACK argument to nil, GRREAD can now properly utilize the ALLKEYS argument:

(grread nil 2) — *The ALLKEYS argument (the integer 2) calls for keyboard input. The GRREAD function pauses until a key is selected. For example, the list (2 200) would be returned if the up-arrow cursor key is chosen.*

There are a few additional guidelines that will help describe the usage of the ALLKEYS argument:

- When the ALLKEYS argument is set to the integer 1, the GRREAD expression reacts in much the same manner as if a non-nil TRACK argument were present. Consequently, the following two expressions are identical:

(grread T)	*the non-nil TRACK argument allows GRREAD to scan the current cursor position*
(grread nil 1)	*the ALLKEYS argument is set to 1, allowing GRREAD to scan the cursor position. Notice the TRACK argument is set to nil.*

Here, the following list might be returned by either function call:

(5 (2.34912 17.39745 0.0))	*the input code is 5, and the remaining coordinate values constitute the 3D cursor position*

- When the ALLKEYS argument is set to the integer 2, the GRREAD expression pauses until a keyboard key is selected. For example:

(grread nil 2)	*GRREAD pauses until a key is chosen. The returned list always contains the integer 2 as the input code element.*

Here, the following list might be returned when using the integer 2 for the ALLKEYS argument:

(2 194)	*the input code is 2, and the selected key is 194 (F8 key)*

The following keyboard keys are not valid (do not respond) when the ALLKEYS argument is set to 2:

- Ctrl
- Pause
- Alt
- Num Lock
- Caps Lock
- Print Screen
- Shift
- Scroll Lock

- When the ALLKEYS argument is set to the integer 4, the GRREAD expression pauses until a point is picked, or a menu selection is made. The returned list takes the form of one of the elements found in the previous chart, depending upon the action taken by the user.

In addition, when ALLKEYS is set to 4, this argument enables a CURTYPE (CURsor TYPE) argument. The CURTYPE argument influences the appearance of the cursor display, as shown in Fig. 16-7.

CURTYPE Value	GRREAD Function
0	Display normal crosshairs.
1	No cursor is displayed (no crosshairs).
2	Display the entity-selection "target" cursor.

Fig. 16-7. CURTYPE values and their results.

The next few examples take advantage of the CURTYPE argument:

(grread nil 4) — *The ALLKEYS argument is set to 4, but no CURTYPE argument is listed. Display the normal crosshairs, despite the absence of CURTYPE.*

(grread nil 4 0) — *The ALLKEYS argument is set to 4, and the CURTYPE argument is set to 0. Display the normal crosshairs.*

(grread nil 4 1) — *The ALLKEYS argument is set to 4, and the CURTYPE argument is set to 1. Do not display any crosshairs on the screen. Even though the crosshairs do not appear on screen, the cursor is tracked as it moves within the drawing editor.*

(grread nil 4 2) — *The ALLKEYS argument is set to 4, and the CURTYPE argument is set to 2. Display the "target" cursor (pickbox).*

This example is an excerpt from a routine that changes the layer of objects. The interface must allow the user to select a single object, or to press ENTER by any accepted means (e.g. Enter, Space-bar, or right mouse button). GRREAD provides this kind of flexibility to your applications.

```
(princ "\nPick object on target layer (or [ENTER] for current layer): ")  ;[1]
(while                                                                     ;[2]
 (and                                                                      ;[3]
  (setq GRVAL (grread T 4 2))                                              ;[4]
  (/= 3 (car GRVAL))                                                       ;[5]
  (not (equal '(2 13) GRVAL))                                              ;[6]
  (not (equal '(2 32) GRVAL))                                              ;[7]
  (/= 11 (car GRVAL))                                                      ;[8]
))
```

[1] (princ "\nPick object on target layer (or [ENTER] for current layer): ") User prompt specifies options. User can either select an object or press Enter.

[2] **(while** Begins a while loop. This loop has only a test argument, and serves only to test input and continue when input is acceptable.

[3] **(and** Begins the AND function to allow each expression to be tested. When any of the tests fail, an appropriate entry has been made and the routine continues upon exiting the loop.

[4] **(setq GRVAL (grread T 4 2))** Sets a variable named GRVAL to the value returned by GRREAD. GRREAD is called with the following parameters: The first argument (T) enables active tracking so that a coordinate point can be returned. Since active tracking is enabled, each incremental cursor movement causes GRREAD to return a value. This is why the while loop is necessary–to test the returned value until it is acceptable. The second argument is the ALLKEYS argument, and the value of 4 specifies that the CURTYPE argument should be used to control cursor display. The third argument is the CURTYPE argument, and a value of 2 indicates that a pickbox is used. The pickbox simulates a selection mode for the user.

[5] **(/= 3 (car GRVAL))** The test fails if the user selected a point, whether or not it was on an object.

[6] **(not (equal '(2 13) GRVAL))** The test fails if the user pressed Enter.

[7] **(not (equal '(2 32) GRVAL))** The test fails if the user pressed the spacebar.

[8] **(/= 11 (car GRVAL))** The test fails if the user pressed the right mouse key.

Once this loop exits, the routine takes the appropriate action. Another approach might be to use ENTSEL, but then it would not be possible to determine if the user simply missed a pick or actually pressed enter, because both situations cause ENTSEL to return nil. Using GRREAD in the previous example allows the user input to be more accurately monitored.

The next programming example demonstrates the usage of the GRREAD function, where a WHILE function continually tests the cursor position until a "valid" location is found (inside a highlighted box generated by GRVECS). After the selection process is complete, the user is asked to reposition the items within the highlighted box. Pay close attention to the use of the TRACK argument (grread T) within the second WHILE loop:

```
; Filename: SCAN.LSP
;
; Author: Feign Dit
;
; Date: March 12, 19xx
; Purpose: After selecting any number of visible objects that reside inside the drawing
;          editor, the user is asked to reposition the items within a highlighted
;          box. The box is approximately 1/10 the size of the drawing limits.
;
;          This program helps demonstrate the usage of the GRREAD function.
;          A WHILE function continually tests the cursor position until the
;          user has placed the cursor inside the highlighted box (generated
;          by GRVECS). Picking inside the box is not needed – GRREAD will
```

```
;             scan for a location inside it.
;
(defun C:SCAN (/ CTR SET LST LL UR CPT LR UL PIC ENT PT IT)
   (setvar "cmdecho" 0)
   (setvar "blipmode" 1)
   (setq CTR 0                                  ; Initialize CounTeR to 0
         SET (ssadd)                            ; Initialize selection–SET
         LST '()                                ; Initialize empty LiST
         LL   (getvar "Limmin")                 ; LIMITS – Lower–Left corner
         UR   (getvar "Limmax")                 ; LIMITS – Upper–Right corner
         CPT (list (/ (+ (car LL) (car UR)) 2)  ; Center PoinT of LIMITS
              (/ (+ (cadr LL) (cadr UR)) 2)
              )
         LL   (list (– (car CPT) (/ (car CPT) 10.0))     ; Lower–Left corner
              (– (cadr CPT) (/ (cadr CPT) 10.0))         ;    of highlighted box
              )
         UR   (list (+ (car CPT) (/ (car CPT) 10.0))     ; Upper–Right corner
              (+ (cadr CPT) (/ (cadr CPT) 10.0))         ;    of highlighted box
              )
         LR   (list (car UR) (cadr LL))         ; Lower–Right corner of box
         UL   (list (car LL) (cadr UR))         ; Upper–Left corner of box
   )
;
   (prompt "\nSelect objects from screen/<ENTER> when done...")
   (while (setq PIC (entsel "\nSelect object: "))   ; PICk objects
     (setq ENT (car PIC)                        ; ENTity name
           PT   (cadr PIC)                      ; Pick PT. of entity
           LST  (cons PT LST)                   ; Cons PT. to LiST
     )
     (ssadd ENT SET)                            ; Add ENTity name to SET
   )                                            ; End while
   (setq LST (reverse LST))      ; Reverse LiST so pick pts. match correct entity
;
   (prompt "\nReposition cursor inside highlighted box...")
   (grvecs (list                 ; GRaphics VECtorS function
       (1– CTR) LL LR            ; List 4 box corners: LL LR UR UL
                LR UR            ;    with highlighted color –1 to
                UR UL            ;    generate graphics box to screen
                UL LL
       )
   )
;
; – –< WHILE loop cycles continuously until a "valid" location is found. >– –
; – –< Note the usage of (grread T) to track the cursor movement. >– –
;
   (while
     (or (> (car  (cadr (grread T))) (car  UR))     ; As long as the cursor
         (> (cadr (cadr (grread T))) (cadr UR))     ;    remains outside the
         (< (car  (cadr (grread T))) (car  LL))     ;    corners of the box,
         (< (cadr (cadr (grread T))) (cadr LL))     ;    WHILE continues...
     )
```

```
  )                                             ; End while
;
  (while (setq IT (ssname SET CTR))             ; Loop until no entities found in SET
    (command ".move" IT "" (nth CTR LST) (cadr (grread 5)))  ; MOVE entities
    (setq CTR (1+ CTR))                         ; From pick pt.
  )                                             ; To cursor pt.
  (setvar "cmdecho" 1)
  (princ)
)
; --( End of File )--
```

Let's Review...

1. The GRCLEAR function clears the current viewport, but does not discard the AutoCAD database. A redraw or regeneration restores the graphics screen.
2. The GRDRAW function draws a graphics vector between two specified locations in the current UCS. Any action that resets the viewport, such as a regeneration or zoom, will remove the GRDRAW vectors.
3. The GRVECS (GRaphics VECtorS) function draws multiple graphics vectors on the graphics screen. Its operation is very similar to the GRDRAW function. The VLIST (Vector LIST) argument is required, and is composed of a series of color integers and two-point lists. The optional TRANS (TRANSformation) argument specifies a transformation matrix that allows the programmer to change the location or proportion of the point lists inside VLIST.
4. The GRTEXT function places a user-supplied text string into one of the text areas of AutoCAD's graphics screen, such as the coordinate status line or screen menu. The expression (grtext) restores all graphics text areas to their standard values, except the coordinate status line. Coordinate tracking will remove the graphics text in this area.
5. The GRREAD function reads AutoCAD input devices such as a pointing device or digitizing tablet. The optional TRACK argument, when not nil, allows the user to track a pointing device without pressing any buttons. The optional ALLKEYS argument, if present, allows further modification to the graphics environment. When ALLKEYS is set to 4, this argument enables the CURTYPE (CURsor TYPE) argument. The CURTYPE argument influences the appearance of the cursor display.

CHAPTER TEST

Write your answers in the spaces provided.

1. What three basic AutoLISP functions control the switching from text screen to graphics screen, and back again?

   ____

   ____

2. How does the TEXTSCR function differ from the TEXTPAGE function?

   ____

   ____

   ____

3. Write the syntax for the AutoLISP REDRAW function.

____

____

   Is the ENAME argument intended for single or multiple entities?

____

4. The following expressions return the same result:

```
(redraw)
```

   and

```
(command ".redraw")
```

   However, the AutoLISP REDRAW function has four additional MODE arguments. Provide a brief description of each of the MODE arguments.

____

____

____

____

5. What will happen if the REDRAW function's MODE argument is a negative integer?

____

____

6. What is the major reason for using the MENUCMD function?

____

____

7. If a specified submenu does not exist within the menu file, what will be returned by the MENUCMD function?

____

____

8. List all of the available menu sections that are accessible with the MENUCMD function.

____

____

____

9. What is the significance of using the "*" when related to Pull-down and Image submenus?

____

____

10. Provide a brief description of the TABLET function.

11. Describe what happens after using a (grclear) expression.

    How can the graphics screen be restored to its original state?

12. List all arguments for the AutoLISP GRDRAW function, and provide a brief explanation for each. Compare this structure to the GRVECS function.

13. If a GRDRAW vector is too large for the size of screen, what will happen?

14. Will GRDRAW vectors always appear the same on different graphics cards and workstations?

15. What three graphics areas are affected by the GRTEXT function?

16. Describe the highlighting process of the GRTEXT function.

17. If the GRTEXT text string argument is too long for the graphics cell (box), what does AutoLISP do?

18. What AutoLISP function allows the user to track AutoCAD input devices?

19. Name at least four input devices that can be tracked by the GRREAD function.

20. Give a brief description of each of the GRREAD arguments.

PROGRAMMING PROBLEMS

1. For each AutoLISP expression shown below, describe what will happen when they are entered at the AutoCAD Command: prompt. A quick review of each function in Chapter 16 will assist you in this process.
   A. (textscr)

   B. (redraw (entlast) 3)

   C. (menucmd "T4=LAYERS")

   D. (grdraw '(2 2) '(9 9) 4 –1)

   As an option, store all expressions shown above (with descriptions) in a documentation file. Name the file CHAP16.DOC.

2. Create an AutoLISP program that follows each step given below:
   A. Construct a WHILE function loop that allows the user to continually add numbers together. Pressing only the ENTER key escapes the WHILE loop. Set the variable SUM to the final number summation. The inputs to the WHILE loop should be made in the graphics screen.
   B. PRINC the resultant SUMmation to the text screen. In addition, tell the user what the value is actually for (for example, "The summation is: ").
   Name the file NUM–TXT.LSP. Be sure to include appropriate documentation.
3. Create an AutoLISP program that follows each step given below:
   A. Ask the user to state a preference for the following graphics vector information:
      - Vector color
      - Highlighting (Yes or No)

      An AutoLISP IF statement will be needed when determining the highlighting value.
   B. Using either the GRDRAW or GRVECS AutoLISP functions, generate vectors that outline the current AutoCAD drawing LIMITS with the user settings. Be sure to check the syntax for GRDRAW and GRVECS so that the program runs properly.
   Name the file P16-3.LSP. Be sure to include documentation.
4. Utilize the following AutoCAD dimensioning variables and apply them in the manner described below:
   - DIMASZ
   - DIMCEN
   - DIMDLI
   - DIMSCALE
   - DIMTXT

   A. For each system variable shown in the list, create an AutoLISP variable that stores the system variable's value.
   B. Using the AutoLISP GRTEXT function, print the variables and their respective values to the screen menu area. The screen menu should look something like the information shown below (shown with header):

   DIMVARS   ⟨– – Screen menu cell 0

   – – – – – – – –

   Dimasz
   0.1800

   – – – – – – – –

   Dimcen
   0.0900

   – – – – – – – –

   Dimdli
   0.3800

   – – – – – – – –

   Dimscale
   1.0000

   – – – – – – – –

   Dimtxt
   0.1800

   Name the file P16-4.LSP. Be sure to include appropriate documentation.

DA.LSP

```
; Program:  DA.LSP
;
; Purpose:  The user provides polar entry for Distance and Angle without
;           having to enter the "@" or "<" symbols.
;
; Note:  While the DIStance variable is not equal to an enter and is
;        not equal to "C", ask for an ANGle value and complete a line
;        segment.  If the user enters, the line command halts.  If the
;        user types a "C", the line command closes back to the beginning.
;
(defun C:DA (/ DIS ANG)
  (setvar "cmdecho" 0)
  (princ "\nFrom point: ")     ; Beginning prompt for ".line" command
  (command ".line" pause)
  (while (and (/= "" (setq DIS (strcase
                        (getstring "\nClose/<Distance>: "))
                    )
                 )
          (/= DIS "C")
        )
      (setq ANG (getstring "\nAngle: "))
      (command (strcat "@" DIS "<" ANG))     ; Combine entry for line
  )
  (if (= DIS "") (command "") (command "c"))
  (princ)
)
```

Chapter 17

Programmable Dialog Boxes

Learning Objectives

After completing this chapter, you will be able to:

- ☐ Explain the advantages of a dialog interface.
- ☐ Define the various types of DCL tiles.
- ☐ Create dialog box definitions in DCL files.
- ☐ Use tile attributes to control the layout of a dialog box.

Programmable dialog boxes make it possible to completely customize the user interface for AutoCAD. Dialog boxes allow a much more intuitive user interface than can be provided by text prompts at the AutoCAD command line. Default values, popdown lists, edit boxes, and image tiles can be combined to effectively provide users with an easy and convenient way to supply a program with the needed parameters. This graphical interface helps minimize the typing requirements for the user. Since much of AutoCAD's built-in interface utilizes these same dialog boxes, it is familiar ground to users of all skill levels.

The actual appearance of a dialog box is platform dependent. The term *platform dependent* refers to the particular operating system you are using. In other words, dialog boxes displayed in a Windows environment will look different than the same dialog box in a DOS enviroment. However, dialog boxes displayed in AutoCAD will look like the dialog boxes displayed in most other Windows applications. Fig. 17-1 shows the appearance of a standard dialog box in a Windows 95/Windows NT 4.0 environment.

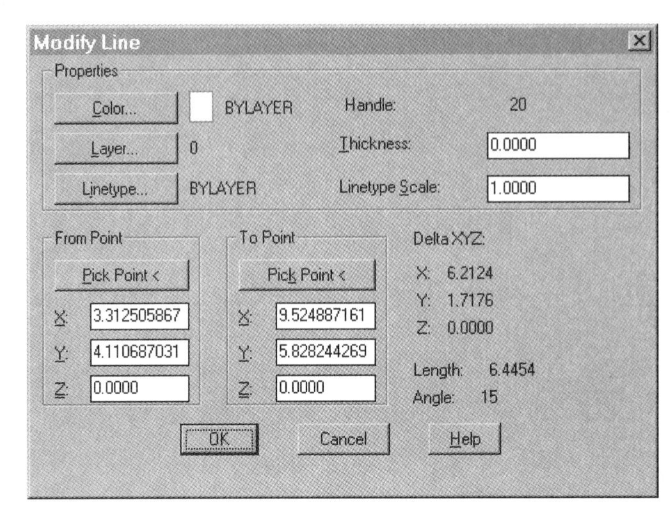

Fig.17-1. Dialog boxes created using DCL appear similar to other standard dialog boxes in the Windows environment.

Programmable dialog boxes cannot be created using the AutoLISP programming language. AutoLISP can be used to manage dialog functions and return the acquired information, but the dialog boxes must first be defined using *Dialog Control Language (DCL).* With DCL, you describe the layout of a dialog box by specifying such parameters as labels, locations, and defaults for each of the features of a dialog box. A button may only require a label and an action to be specified, whereas an edit box or radio button may also need a default value. Image tiles require a description of the image to be displayed, and list boxes and popdown lists require that lists of options be supplied. All of the physical layout parameters and many of the default values or options are specified in a DCL file using Dialog Control Language. Tools for working with Programmable Dialog Boxes are referred to as the *AutoCAD PDB facility.*

DCL FILE FORMATS

Similar to AutoLISP, a DCL file must be in the form of an ASCII text file. DCL filenames for the Windows 95 and Windows NT environments can consist of any valid alphanumeric characters (up to 256 characters), but the extension must be .DCL. Windows 3.x and DOS filenames are limited to 8 characters, plus the .DCL extension. The DCL language is an easy language to understand and write—many of the components of a DCL file are represented using common English words.

The components of a dialog box are referred to as *tiles.* The tile *definitions* are created by specifying values for various *attributes.* Each applicable attribute controls a specific characteristic of the tile being defined, such as size, location, and default values. In addition, *prototypes* and *subassemblies* can be defined and *referenced* by a DCL file similar to the way a BLOCK or an XREF object is referenced by an AutoCAD drawing. This means that you can include a definition once and reference that definition as many times as needed instead of generating the overhead required by defining an object locally for each and every occurrence.

Unlike programming in AutoLISP, when writing a DCL file you do not use parentheses. To define a dialog box or tile, all of the required attributes for a tile definition are placed within *curly braces* {}. Indentation is used to help make a DCL file more readable. As with AutoLISP, indentation helps to visually separate individual elements of a file. Semicolons are used to indicate the end of a field definition. Comments can be indicated by using two forward slashes (//). Each of these topics will be discussed in this chapter.

For a good example of Dialog Control Language code, view the ACAD.DCL and BASE.DCL files. (Both of these files are typically found in AutoCAD's SUPPORT subdirectory.) The ACAD.DCL file contains definitions for all of the dialog boxes used by AutoCAD, while the BASE.DCL contains standard prototype definitions. It is not recommended that you edit either one of these files, since altering them can cause AutoCAD's built-in dialog interface to fail.

DIALOG BOX COMPONENTS

The individual components within a dialog box are known as *tiles*. Each type of tile provides specialized ways of displaying and acquiring information. In addition, each type of tile has specific attributes that can be set to control its appearance and function. Fig. 17-2 shows examples of several different types of tiles.

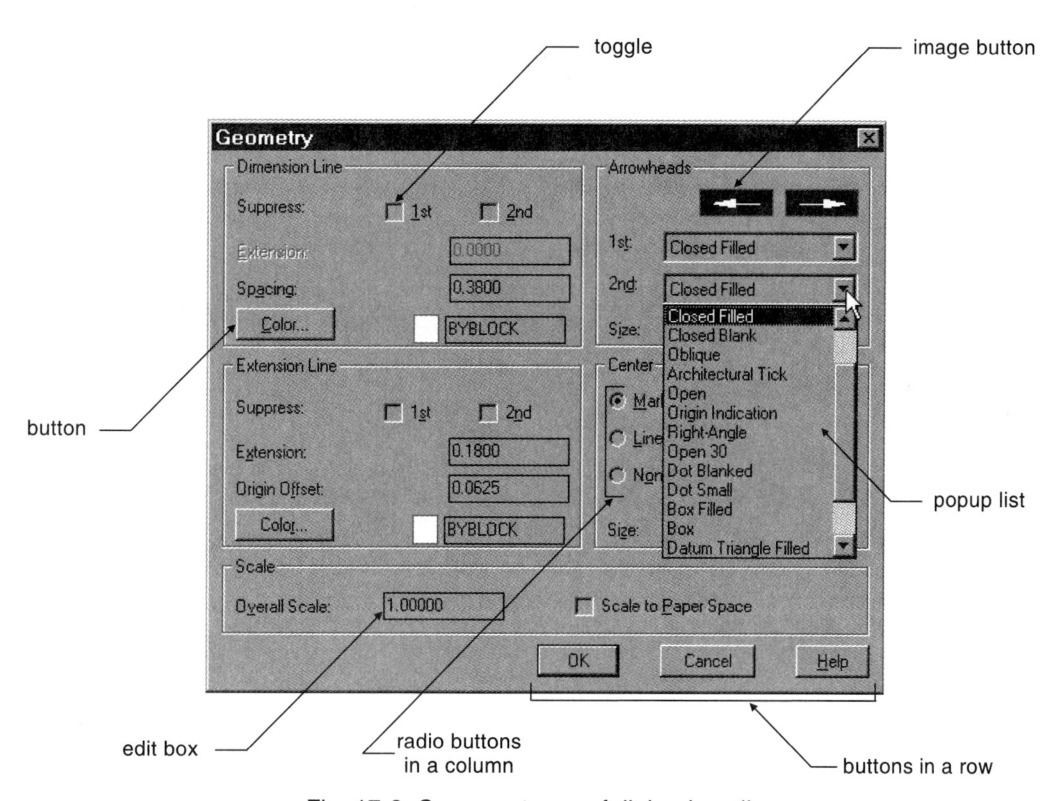

Fig. 17-2. Common types of dialog box tiles.

The construction of a dialog box is *constraint based*. In other words, the size of the dialog box and the layout of its components is done automatically, requiring little information from you. Therefore, it is not necessary to specify the exact location or size of each component tile. However, size and appearance can be customized when the default appearance is not acceptable.

It should be noted that dialog boxes are interactive devices, requiring a user to supply some type of input. Using a script file, you can start a dialog box. However, you cannot directly affect the dialog box itself with the script. Also, the AutoLISP COMMAND function cannot be used to control or provide input to dialog boxes.

The AutoCAD PDB facility provides built-in definitions for each of the types of basic tiles. This set of predefined tiles can be categorized into the following areas: Predefined Active Tiles, Tile Clusters, Decorative and Informative Tiles, Text Clusters, and Exit Buttons and Error Tiles. The table in Fig. 17-3 shows the available tiles in each of their respective categories.

Predefined Active Tiles	Tile Clusters	Decorative & Informative	Text Clusters	Exit Buttons and Error Tile
button	boxed_column	image	concatenation	err_tile
edit_box	boxed_radio_column	text	paragraph	ok_only
image_button	boxed_radio_row	spacer	text_part	ok_cancel
list_box	boxed_row	spacer_0		ok_cancel_help
popup_list	column	spacer_1		ok_cancel_help_errtile
radio_button	dialog			ok_cancel_help_info
slider	radio_column			
toggle	radio_row			
	row			

Fig. 17-3. The AutoCAD PDB facility provides built-in definitions for each of these types of tiles.

Predefined active tiles are, by default, both active and selectable. These tiles are the basis for complex tiles or clusters, and supply most of the functionality of a dialog box.

The *tile clusters* are used to group sets of tiles into rows or columns called *clusters* or *subassemblies*. When laying out your dialog box, these clusters behave as a single tile, which can greatly simplify the layout and editing process.

Decorative and informative tiles are used to enhance the appearance of a dialog box. Informative text and representative images can be displayed and tile positioning can be adjusted to achieve the best possible appearance.

Text clusters are used for greater flexibility in formatting and laying out text in a dialog box.

Every dialog box requires an *exit tile*. This is a tile that dismisses the dialog box and returns to the current application. The most common exit tiles are the OK and the Cancel buttons, but custom exit buttons can be designed as well. The AutoCAD PDB facility provides a variety of predefined tiles and subassemblies for exiting (or *retiring*) a dialog box. Referring again to Fig. 17-2, you will notice three buttons in a row along the bottom of the dialog box that are labeled OK, Cancel, and Help. This is a very common subassembly and is defined in the BASE.DCL file. There are many such subassemblies available for use in custom dialog boxes. This allows your time to be more productive, and keeps you from having to "re-invent the wheel" each time a new dialog box is designed.

The *error tile* is an area in the lower-left corner of the dialog box that can be used to display an error message when incorrect or incomplete data is supplied to the dialog box.

PROFESSIONAL TIP

There are some tiles which are considered restricted tiles. These are the base tiles which comprise the foundation of many of the built-in tile definitions used by the AutoCAD PDB facility. The restricted tiles should not be used in your DCL files, and include cluster and tile. Also, you should not use the basic exit button types unless you first redefine the standard exit tile subassemblies. The basic exit button types include: ok_button, cancel_button, help_button, and info_button.

DIALOG DEFINITION TREE STRUCTURES

In a DCL file, the *dialog* is defined by specifying the particular tiles that will be present and subsequently defining the attributes for each of these tiles. The basic format for the dialog definition uses a *tree* structure. This can be compared to a Windows directory tree, where each element (directories, subdirectories, files, etc.) branches off another element or off the *root*.

A sample dialog box tree structure is shown in Fig. 17-4. Note that the top (or root) of the tree is always a *dialog*. Dialogs and subassemblies have very definitive *parent* and *child* relationships. All of the top level tiles within a dialog box are children of the *dialog* itself. The term *top level* is used here to indicate tiles that are defined along the trunk of the dialog tree; these could also be referred to as *branches*. In Fig. 17-4, the top level tiles are the toggle, the boxed_column, and row clusters. The various tiles within any cluster are considered children of that cluster.

It is important to understand the concept of parent/child relationships in DCL. It is common to specify the attributes for a cluster's children within the attributes of the cluster itself. Also, when you create new dialogs or subassemblies, you can use the parent/child relationships to your advantage to simplify the dialog definition process.

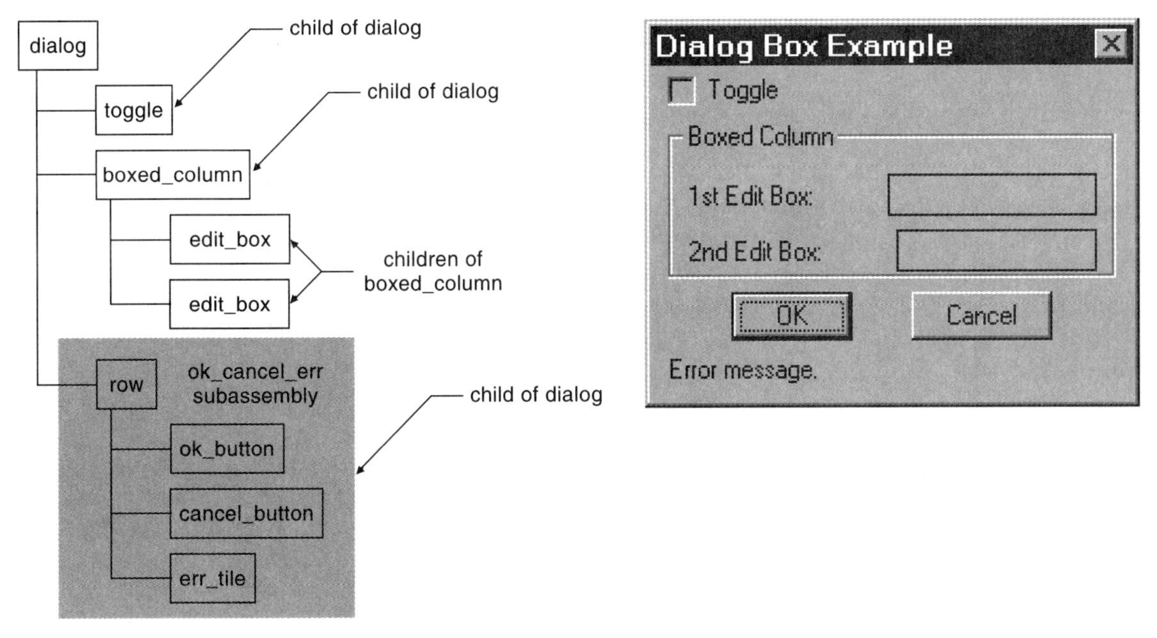

Fig. 17-4. Sample dialog tree structure showing parent-child relationships and the dialog box being defined.

DEFINING TILES IN DCL

All tiles and subassemblies reference specific *attributes* that control their layout, appearance, and behavior. These attributes are set in the tile definition within a DCL file. As an example, every dialog box has a string of text that appears across the top bar. This text is specified by assigning a value to the *label* attribute for the *dialog* tile cluster. The initial values for *toggles,* the graphic that appears in an *image,* and the tile that has the initial focus are all examples of attribute values in a DCL file. As an example, the following DCL code defines the dialog box shown in Fig. 17-4:

```
// Sample Dialog Box Code for Fig. 17-4

sample : dialog {
        label            = "Dialog Box Example";
        : toggle {
          label          = "Toggle";
          value          = "1";
        }
        : boxed_column {
          label          = "Boxed Column";
          : edit_box {
            label        = "1st Edit Box:";
            key          = "edit_1";
          }
          : edit_box {
            label        = "2nd Edit Box:";
            key          = "edit_2";
          }
        }
        ok_cancel_err;
}
```

Compare the DCL code above with the dialog box example in Fig. 17-4 to get a basic idea of the function of tile attributes. Notice, for example, how the *label* attributes are supplied. The *key* attribute is used by AutoLISP to access a tile, and is also explained later in this chapter. Note also the *ok_cancel_err* subassembly call. Since this is a predefined subassembly, no further definition is necessary here. A full discussion of DCL code is also presented later in this chapter.

Many attributes can be applied to a variety of tiles. For example, the *label* attribute is common to many different tiles. Other attributes, such as *width* can apply to any type of tile. Still others apply only to specific types of tiles. For example, the *color* attribute applies only to image tiles. The table in Fig. 17-5 lists the available attributes and the types of tiles to which they can be applied. Note that two of the attributes are used only in Windows and Windows NT, and cannot be used in AutoCAD for DOS applications.

Attribute Name	Applicable Tiles	Description (if Specified or True)
action	all active tiles	AutoLISP expression specifying action associated with this tile
alignment	all tiles	horizontal or vertical position in a cluster
allow_accept	edit_box, image_button, list_box	activates button specified as *is_default* when this tile is selected
aspect_ratio	image, image_button	aspect ratio of a tile (ratio of horizontal to vertical size)
big_increment	slider	incremental distance moved by picking the slider bar
children_alignment	row, column, radio_row, radio_column, boxed_row, boxed_column, boxed_radio_row, boxed_radio_column	controls the alignment of a cluster's children
children_fixed_height	row, column, radio_row, radio_column, boxed_row, boxed_column, boxed_radio_row, boxed_radio_column	the height of a cluster's children doesn't grow during layout
children_fixed_width	row, column, radio_row, radio_column, boxed_row, boxed_column, boxed_radio_row, boxed_radio_column	the width of a cluster's children doesn't grow during layout
color	image, image_button	the background fill color of an image
edit_limit	edit_box	controls the maximum number of characters that a user can enter
edit_width	edit_box, popup_list	width of the edit portion of the tile
fixed_height	all tiles	height of tile doesn't grow during layout
fixed_width	all tiles	width of tile doesn't grow during layout
fixed_width_font	list_box, popup_list	displays text in a fixed pitch font (Windows/Windows NT only)
height	all tiles	height of a tile
initial_focus	dialog	specifies which tile has the focus when the dialog starts

Continued

Fig. 17-5. Available attributes and applicable tiles to which they can be assigned.

Attribute Name	Applicable Tiles	Description (if Specified or True)
is_bold	text	text is displayed as bold (on platforms supporting bold text)
is_cancel	button	button cancels the dialog box
is_default	button	button is activated when [ENTER] is pressed
is_enabled	all active tiles	tile is enabled when dialog starts
is_tab_stop	all active tiles	when the TAB key is used to move between tiles, this tile is one of the stops
key	all active tiles	the name used to access the tile
label	boxed_row, boxed_column boxed_radio_row, button, boxed_radio_column, text, dialog, edit_box, list_box, popup_list, radio_button, toggle	text label associated with the tile
layout	slider	controls horizontal or vertical layout
list	list_box, popup_list	initial values to be displayed in the list
max_value	slider	upper value limit
min_value	slider	lower value limit
mnemonic	all active tiles	mnemonic character to activate tile
multiple_select	list_box	allows multiple selections from list
password_char	edit_box	specifies the password character
small_increment	slider	incremental distance moved by picking slider arrow
tabs	list_box, popup_list	tab locations for column style lists
tab_truncate	list_box, popup_list	maintains tab positions by truncating list items when necessary (Windows/Windows NT only)
value	text, active tiles (except button and image_button)	initial tile value when dialog starts
width	all tiles	width of the tile

Fig. 17-5. Continued.

Similar to arguments for AutoLISP functions, the values specified for tile attributes in a DCL file must be of a specific data *type*. There are four basic data types used in DCL: *integer, real, string,* and *reserved word*. The first three data types are handled exactly as in AutoLISP– integers have no decimal, reals must have a leading digit, and strings are enclosed in double quotes. The string data values are case-sensitive, meaning that in the case of the DCL code for Fig. 17-4, referencing a key named "Edit_1" would not access the edit box tile with the key "edit_1".

Reserved words are a special data type made up of alphanumeric characters that are *not* enclosed in double quotes. Reserved words are used for many different attributes for various tiles. For example, the *layout* attribute of a slider can be specified as either *horizontal* or *vertical*. Many attributes are simply switches that use *true* or *false* as their values. It is important to remember that reserved words are case-sensitive, and *True* or *TRUE* are not recognized as *true*.

Similar to the case sensitivity that applies to strings and reserved words, attribute names themselves are also case-sensitive. Therefore, trying to assign a value to an attribute indicated as *Color* would not set the *color* of an image tile. All attribute names are written using lowercase characters and underscore characters (_).

Attribute value specifications are considered optional when defining dialog boxes and tiles. For most attributes when no value is specified, a default value is used. In some cases, however, not specifying certain attributes will render a tile useless. For example, without a *key* attribute, your AutoLISP application cannot access a tile to retrieve or set a value. Even without the key, the tile will display properly when the dialog is loaded, so it is optional as far as the DCL code is concerned, but it may still be required by your application.

There are many attributes which are specific to certain tile types. For example, the *color* attribute applies only to *image* and *image button* tiles. If a *color* attribute is specified for a different tile type (i.e., edit box, toggle, etc.), AutoCAD may report an error when the DCL file is loaded. In some cases, the irrelevant attribute is simply ignored.

PROFESSIONAL TIP

As with restricted tiles, there are also *restricted attributes*. These three attributes should *not* be used in your DCL files:

- horizontal_margin
- vertical_margin
- type

Let's Review...

1. Programmable dialog boxes provide an interface which is more intuitive than text prompts at the command line.
2. DCL code describes the layout and appearance of a dialog box by specifying attributes such as labels, locations, and defaults for each tile.
3. DCL files must be in the form of an ASCII text file, and the expected file extension is .DCL.
4. Semicolons are used in DCL files to indicate the end of a field definition.
5. Comments in a DCL file are indicated by using two forward slashes.
6. Every dialog box requires an exit tile.
7. Dialogs and subassemblies have a very definitive parent and child relationship that can be used to your advantage by simplifying the dialog definition process.
8. DCL tile attributes require the use of specific data types, and those using string data are case-sensitive.

DCL TILES

One of the biggest reasons for using a dialog interface over sequential text prompts is the capability for better communication with the user. This, coupled with the fact that AutoCAD users are largely graphic communicators, provides an excellent reason to use graphics to enhance and speed up communications in a dialog session.

Predefined Active Tiles

Predefined active tiles are the basis for most dialog definitions. These are combined as needed into clusters and subassemblies that define a dialog box. It is important to be familiar with each of the available dialog box components. The following section shows an example of each tile type and a brief description of how it is used, along with a listing of the primary attributes associated with it. Attribute functionality specific to the tile being described is also described. *Note that any combination of attributes may be specified, ranging from none to all of the available attributes, depending on the specific needs for each individual tile.*

Dialog

```
: dialog {
  initial_focus   label   value   key
}
```

The *dialog* tile is the primary tile of a dialog box. It is laid out in column format, with each tile encountered in the dialog box description being placed below the previous tile. All other tile descriptions occur within the dialog description.

initial_focus — *the key of the tile that is initially highlighted, or the key that will be activated if the user presses [ENTER]*

label — *a text string for the optional title appearing in the dialog title bar*

value — *Another means of specifying the title, usually used at run time. Since this value can be changed, it is not inspected when the layout takes place. This means that if the dialog box is not wide enough, that the text may be truncated.The term "run time" indicates the time that the dialog box is active and running.*

Button

OK

```
: button {
  action   alignment   fixed_height   fixed_width
  height   is_cancel   is_default   is_enabled   key
  is_tab_stop   label   mnemonic   width
}
```

A *button* tile resembles a mechanical pushbutton both in appearance and in action. When this tile is being picked, its shaded border reverses orientation, giving the illusion of going from a projected state to a depressed state. All dialogs require at least one button which serves as a *retirement* button. This can be an OK button or a user-defined button that is the equivalent to an OK button. Most dialogs also include a Cancel button.

label — *specifies the text to be displayed on the button*

Edit Box

Linetype Scale: 1.0000

```
: edit_box {
  action  alignment  allow_ac-
 cept  fixed_height
   edit_limit  edit_width
 fixed_width
  height  is_enabled
 is_tab_stop  key  label
   mnemonic  password_char
 value  width
 }
```

An *edit_box* allows a user to both enter and edit a single line of text in a dialog box. The optional label can be used to inform the user of what information should be entered. When the *edit_limit* is greater than the *edit_width*, the edit box scrolls horizontally as needed to display the additional text during an editing operation.

label — *The title of the edit_box. An edit_box label is left-justified within the width of the tile.*

value — *Text string specifying the initial contents of the edit_box. The AutoCAD documentation states that a null character is appended to the string under certain circumstances. As implied by the term "null," the null character does not produce an actual ASCII character, so no character is actually appended. This means that the string or its length does not change.*

Image Button

```
: image_button {
 action  alignment  allow_accept  aspect_ratio
 color  fixed_height  fixed_width  height  is_enabled
 is_tab_stop  key  label  mnemonic  width
}
```

The *image_button* tile displays a graphic image, the source being either an AutoCAD slide file or a series of specified vectors. This tile works like a button, in that simply picking the tile causes its specified action to take place. When an image button is picked, the coordinates of the point picked can be determined. An application program can use this information to vary the results of picking an image button based on where the user picked it. An example of this is found when using the DDVPOINT command in which a small drawing is displayed that allows the user to pick the appropriate location in the button to achieve the desired results.

An image tile requires either that an exact width and height are specified, or that a height or a width is specified along with an aspect_ratio attribute.

List Box

```
: list_box {
  action   alignment   allow_accept   fixed_height
  fixed_width_font   tabs   fixed_width   height   is_enabled
  is_tab_stop   key   label   list   mnemonic   multiple_select
  tab_truncate   value   width
}
```

The *list_box* is used to present the user with a list of text strings arranged in rows. When more strings are specified in the list than can be displayed in the list box, the scroll bar activates for moving up and down through the list.

label — *the title appearing above the tile*

value — *A quoted string containing a zero or more integers specifying the list items that are initially selected. The numbers correspond to the position in the list of the selected items. This works on a zero-based system similar to the way the nth function references items in a list. The first item is item 0, the second is item 1, and so on. If the value string contains no integers, no items are initially selected.*

Popup List

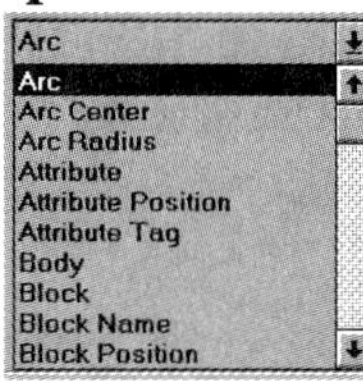


```
: popup_list {
  action   alignment edit_width fixed_height   fixed_width_font
  tabs   fixed_width   height   is_enabled   is_tab_stop
  key   label   list   mnemonic   tab_truncate   tabs_value
  width
}
```

The *popup_list* works exactly like a list_box, except that the list itself is initially hidden until either the current text value or the downward pointing arrow on the right side is selected. Note that the popup list does not allow multiple selections.

label — *specifies the title appearing to the left of the popup_list*

edit_width — *The width of the text part of the list. (This does not include the label, popup arrow, or scroll bar.) The value can be specified as a real or as an integer.*

value — *a quoted string containing an integer specifying the initial value (like the list_box) using a zero-based index*

Radio Button

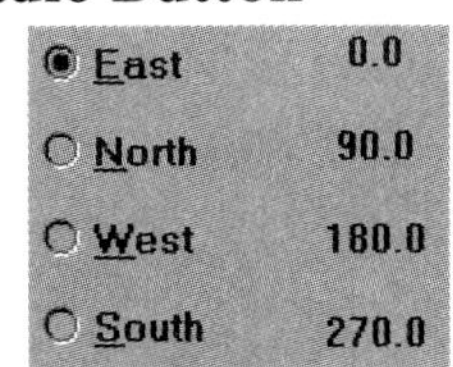


```
: radio_button {
  action  alignment fixed_height  fixed_width  height
  is_enabled  is_tab_stop  key  label  list  mnemonic
  value  width
}
```

The *radio button* allows a number of options to be presented, and only one to be selected at a given time. A radio button is so named because, like the buttons on an old car radio, pressing one button switches to the new setting, turning all the others off in the process. Note that a radio button can only be placed within a *radio_row* or a *radio_column*. Attempting to place a radio button elsewhere will cause the PDB facility to report an error message.

label — *the text that appears to the right of the button*

value — *A quoted string containing an integer that specifies the initial state of the button. For example, the value "0" means the radio_button is off. All other values indicate that the tile is on.*

Slider

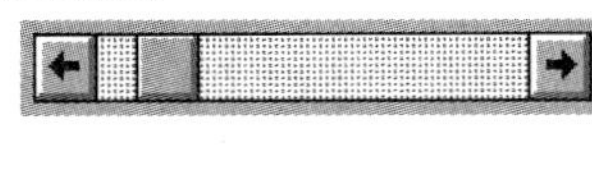

```
: slider {
  action  alignment big_increment fixed_height
  fixed_width  height  key  label  layout  max_value
  min_value  mnemonic  small_increment value  width
}
```

The *slider* functions similar to any scroll bar. Picking the arrow moves the slider by a small incremental value and picking the scroll bar moves it by a big incremental value. Also, the slider button can be picked and moved directly. The slider obtains a 16-bit signed integer value that it returns to the application as a string. Since the value is 16-bit, the maximum possible range of a slider is between –32,768 and 32,767. If a wider range is required, the application can scale the value returned by the slider.

value — *a quoted string containing an integer specifying the initial value of the slider*

Toggle

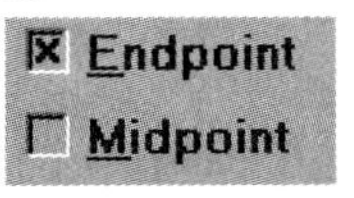


```
: toggle {
  action  alignment  fixed_height  fixed_width
  height  is_enabled  is_tab_stop  label  width
}
```

A *toggle* works like a light switch; it is either on or it is off. Picking the switch causes the value to be changed. When a toggle is on, there is an X in the box. When it is off, the box will be empty.

label — *the text displayed to the right of the toggle*

value — *a quoted string with a value of either "0" (off) or "1" (on), specifying the initial state of the toggle*

Tile Clusters

Tile clusters provide a way of grouping related tiles together for better organization within a dialog box. The clusters themselves cannot be selected, only the tiles they contain can be selected. With the exception of *radio_rows* and *radio_columns*, clusters cannot have assigned actions. The following sections describes the available tile clusters.

Column

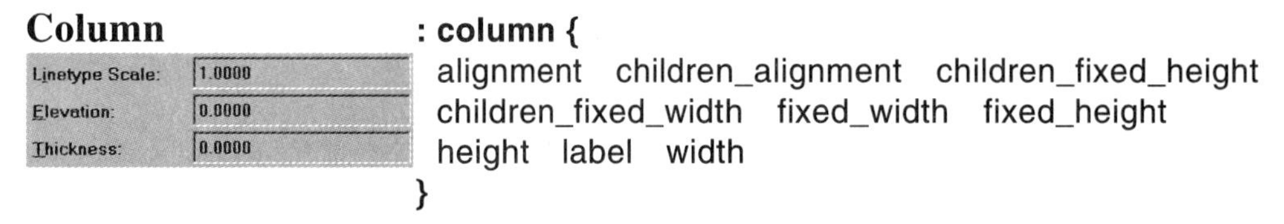


```
: column {
  alignment   children_alignment   children_fixed_height
  children_fixed_width   fixed_width   fixed_height
  height   label   width
}
```

Tiles within a *column* are stacked vertically as they are encountered within the DCL description of the column, with the first tile listed being placed at the top of the column. All tiles in a column description are considered to be *children* of the column tile. Therefore, the attributes such as *children_alignment* apply to the tiles that are placed within the column. A column can contain any kind of tile (with the exception of a single radio button), including rows and other columns.

PROFESSIONAL TIP

If a *label* attribute is supplied, a box is automatically drawn around the extents of the column tile. On some platforms, the box may be drawn incorrectly. If you need a label, it is best to use a *boxed_column*.

Boxed Column

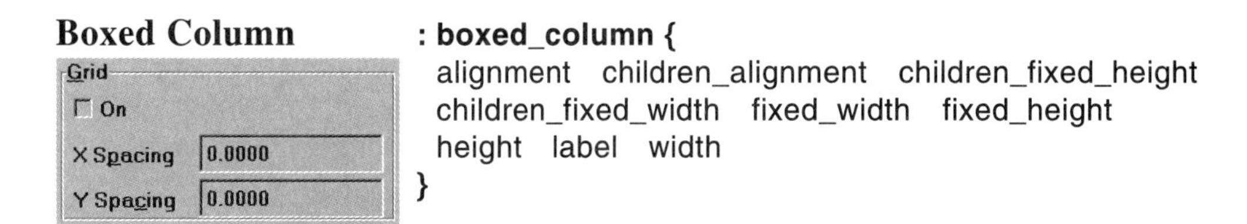


```
: boxed_column {
  alignment   children_alignment   children_fixed_height
  children_fixed_width   fixed_width   fixed_height
  height   label   width
}
```

A *boxed_column* functions in a manner similar to a simple column, but it offers a means of providing a more segregated grouping of related tiles. A box is drawn to encompass all of the children, and a label can be specified. The label can be text characters, a space (" ") can be supplied to indicate a blank label, or a null label ("") can be used. Blank and null labels can be used to adjust alignment and positioning of boxed columns when necessary.

Row

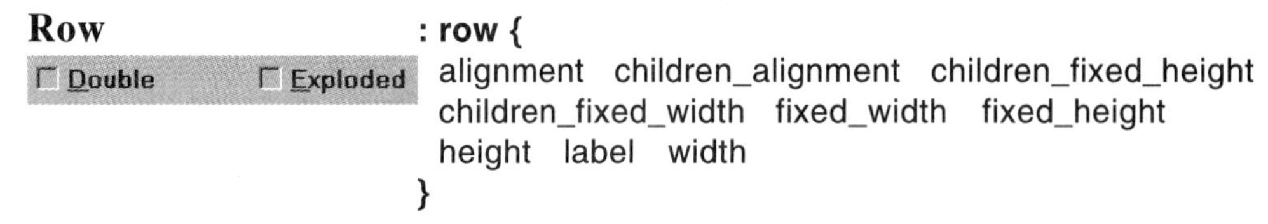


```
: row {
  alignment   children_alignment   children_fixed_height
  children_fixed_width   fixed_width   fixed_height
  height   label   width
}
```

A *row* functions exactly the same as a column, except that its layout is horizontal rather than vertical. The layout is from left to right as encountered in the DCL listing.

Boxed Row

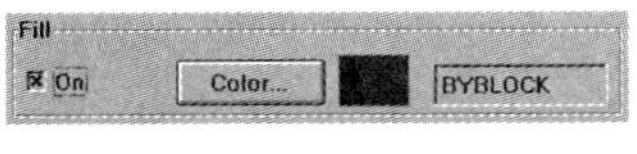


```
: boxed_row {
  alignment  children_alignment  children_fixed_height
  children_fixed_width  fixed_width  fixed_height
  height  label  width
}
```

A *boxed_row* functions in a manner similar to a simple row, but it offers a means of providing a more segregated grouping of related tiles. A box is drawn to encompass all of the children, and a label can be specified. Text characters can be used as a label, a space (" ") can be supplied to indicate a blank label, or a null label ("") can be used. Blank and null labels can be used to adjust alignment and positioning of boxed rows when necessary.

Radio Column

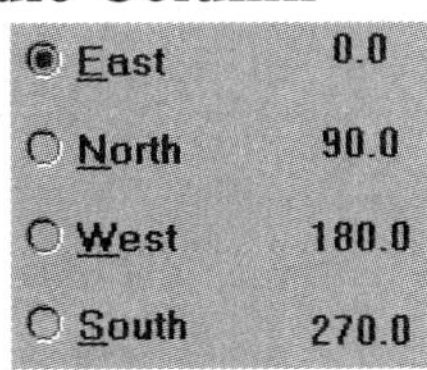


```
: radio_column {
  alignment  children_alignment  children_fixed_height
  children_fixed_width  fixed_width  fixed_height
  height  label  width
}
```

The *radio_column* is one of the cluster configurations provided for holding radio button tiles. The buttons are laid out vertically similar to a standard column. An action can be assigned to a radio column.

value *a quoted string representing the key of the radio button that currently has a value of "1" (on)*

Boxed Radio Column

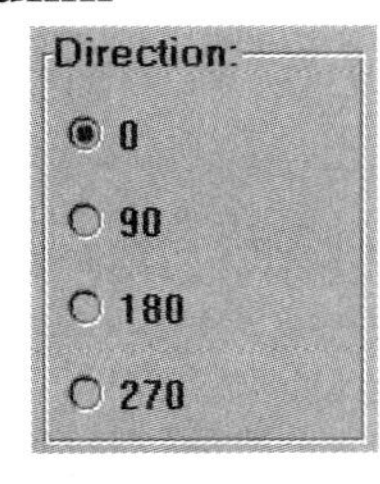


```
: boxed_radio_column {
  alignment  children_alignment  children_fixed_height
  children_fixed_width  fixed_width  fixed_height
  height  label  width
}
```

The *boxed_radio_column* has the same functionality as a radio column, except that a box is drawn around the children.

value *a quoted string representing the key of the radio button that currently has a value of "1" (on)*

Radio Row

```
: radio_row {
  alignment  children_alignment  children_fixed_height
  children_fixed_width  fixed_width  fixed_height
  height  label  width
}
```

A *radio_row* is one of the cluster configurations provided for holding radio button tiles. The buttons are laid out horizontally, similar to a standard row. An action can be assigned to a radio row. A radio column is usually more convenient to use than a radio row because the compact structure minimizes cursor movement. As a rule, it is best to use radio columns where possible.

value *a quoted string representing the key of the radio button that currently has a value of "1" (on)*

Boxed Radio Row

```
: boxed_radio_row {
  alignment  children_alignment  children_fixed_height
  children_fixed_width  fixed_width  fixed_height
  height  label  width
}
```

The *boxed_radio_row* has the same functionality as a radio row, except that a box is drawn around the children. It is preferable to use a boxed_radio_column over a boxed_radio_row to minimize cursor movement.

value *a quoted string representing the key of the radio button that currently has a value of "1" (on)*

Informative Tiles

The principle reason for using a dialog interface over sequential text prompts is the capability for more effective communication with the user. Combine this with the fact that AutoCAD users are primarily graphic communicators, and you will find an excellent reason to use graphics to clarify concepts and enhance communications in a dialog session. Graphic images with supplementary text where appropriate provides a smooth and efficient interface.

The AutoCAD PDB facility provides the capability to place images and text on a dialog box that are for information only. These informative tiles are not selectable, and perform no action. Their sole purpose is to provide information to the user.

Image

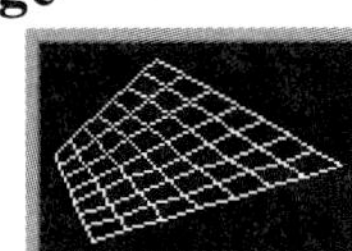

```
: image {
  action  alignment  aspect_ratio  color  fixed_height
  fixed_width  height  is_enabled  is_tab_stop  key
  label  mnemonic  width
}
```

Either a slide file or a specified set of vectors can be displayed in an *image*. Slide files can be used as is, or as part of a slide library. Describing complex geometry by individual vector specifications can be difficult and tedious. It is usually much faster to draw the geometry in AutoCAD and create a slide image to use. If a simple illustration is all that is needed, you may wish to specify vectors. The vector specifications are used to describe the coordinate locations of the vector endpoints and their color.

An image tile requires either that an exact width and height are specified, or that the height or the width is specified along with an aspect_ratio attribute.

Text

c:\Program Files\AutoCAD R14\Support

```
: text {
  alignment  fixed_height  fixed_width  height
  is_bold  key  label  value  width
}
```

The *text* tile is used to display a text string in a dialog box. Text tiles can be used as titles, or as informative text. In most cases, however, a *label* attribute is used to display titles–unless the standard positioning of a label is not acceptable. Text tiles are most commonly used to display dynamic information regarding the current dialog session. For example, in a file dialog box a text string is displayed that represents the current directory path location. The string is immediately updated each time the user selects a different directory. The updates are performed by the application, but the DCL text tile is used to display the results.

In most cases, text tiles should not be used to display error messages. AutoCAD's standard is to use the predefined error tile, located in the lower-left corner of the dialog box. Since this is where most users are accustomed to seeing error messages appear, an error message located elsewhere in the dialog box might be overlooked.

label — *One means of specifying the text to display. A text tile's width attribute is compared to the length of the label, and the greater of the two is used for the actual width. At least one of these attributes must be present.*

value — *The second means of specifying the text to display. This means is usually used when the text is to be changed at run time. Note that the value attribute does not affect the width of the text tile. As a general rule, the label attribute is used for static text and the value attribute for dynamic text that may change at run time.*

Text Part

text

```
: text_part {
  label
}
```

A *text_part* is used to construct larger pieces of text. Unlike a text tile, a text part has no margins to cause uneven spacing between words in a *paragraph* or *concatenation*. Text parts are also used for dynamically updating text, where only part of the text is dynamic and the rest remains static.

Concatenation

```
: concatenation {
}
```

text part 1 and text part 2

The *concatenation* is a single line of text composed of one or more text_part tiles. After the text parts are assembled into a single text string, standard margins are applied to the concatenation.

Paragraph

```
: paragraph {
}
```

text_parts and
concatenations.

A *paragraph* is very similar to a *column* cluster. It is a cluster of text part or concatenation tiles arranged vertically. Each tile is added on a new line below the previous tile. When it is necessary to have multiple text parts on a single line as part of a paragraph, they must first be placed within a concatenation.

Spacer

```
: spacer {
  alignmment   fixed_height   fixed_width
  height   width
}
```

The AutoCAD PDB facility automatically handles spacing of tiles within a dialog box. Allowing the PDB facility to manage spacing helps to ensure consistency between dialog boxes. Sometimes, however, the PDB facility may not lay out the tiles according to the specific appearance you are trying to achieve. In such a case, the spacer tile can be used to adjust the size and layout of adjacent tiles. The spacer is actually a blank tile; it is not visible on the dialog box and cannot be selected by the user.

Spacer 0

```
spacer_0;
```

Many tiles and clusters are "stretched" during layout. This means that the intended sizing and positioning of the cluster's children may change to accommodate the PDB default layout. The spacer tile is provided to allow the programmer to adjust this default layout. The spacer_0 tile is a predefined configuration of the standard spacer tile that normally has no width. When placed in a row or column of tiles, it indicates where space is to be inserted when a layout is stretched.

The spacer_0 tiles can be used in various combinations to produce the exact layout you require. Fig. 17-6A shows four buttons being stretched to fill the width of the dialog box. Note the width of the button tiles. Example B shows a single spacer_0 being used between button #3 and button #4. Finally, example C shows one spacer_0 between buttons #1 and #2, two spacer_0 tiles between #2 and #3 and three between #3 and #4. This example demonstrates that spacer_0 tiles can be used as needed to generate the layout appearance you want in your dialog boxes.

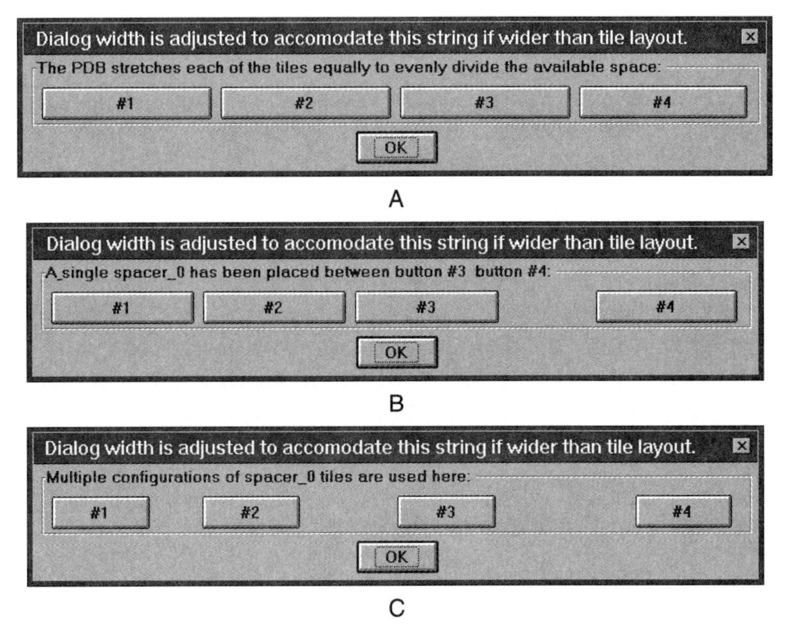

Fig. 17-6. Example of spacer_0 tile effects.

Spacer 1 spacer_1;

The spacer_1 tile is also used for layout purposes. It has a preset height and width of 1. It represents the smallest spacer configuration which is obvious to the user. In the examples in Fig. 17-7, you may notice that the spacer_0 can virtually disappear, whereas the spacer_1 tile cannot be collapsed to a zero width. Other spacer requirements can be met by specifying a width to a standard spacer tile.

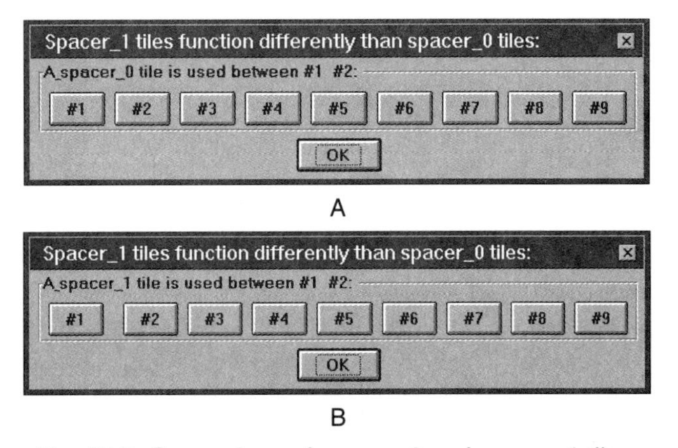

Fig. 17-7. Comparison of spacer_0 and spacer_1 tiles.

ERROR AND EXIT TILES

Every dialog box has to have at least one exit tile. Most dialog boxes will have two exit tiles–an OK button and a Cancel button. These are referred to as *retirement buttons*, and are predefined tiles. The error tile is a text tile appearing at the bottom of a dialog box. It can be used by the programmer to display an error message to the user when incorrect or incomplete data is supplied to a tile.

Since retirement buttons and error tiles are standard equipment for every dialog box, the PDB facility provides many predefined subassemblies in a variety of configurations. Also provided is a predefined *help* tile prototype, which can be used to display information contained in a help file. These predefined subassemblies do not require attribute specifications, therefore they are not followed by attributes within curly braces.

Errtile **errtile;**

Invalid input value.

The errtile (error tile) is found at the lower-left corner of a dialog box. This provides an easy means of "forgiving" errors and supplying the user with error messages or additional information as required. The key for this tile is *"error";* it is best to use the errtile for error messages to be consistent with AutoCAD's built-in dialog boxes.

Ok Only **ok_only;**

OK

The OK button is most commonly used by itself on an "information only" type dialog. This can include dialogs that supply instructions, information, or critical error messages. The ok_only tile asks the user only for acknowledgment to the displayed information or message, and does not provide a button for canceling the operation. As an example, the AutoCAD ALERT dialog boxes have only an OK button.

Since the OK button itself is predefined in BASE.DCL, it already has a key assignment. The key for the OK button is *accept.*

Ok, Cancel **ok_cancel;**

This subassembly is used on dialog boxes where it is desirable to provide the user with an easy way to cancel the operation in progress or even the entire application. This uses the standard OK button, therefore the key is still *"accept"*. The key for the predefined CANCEL button (in *any* subassembly) is *"cancel"*. It is recommended that all dialog boxes that can originate changes to application or drawing data have a Cancel button.

Ok, Cancel, Help **ok_cancel_help;**

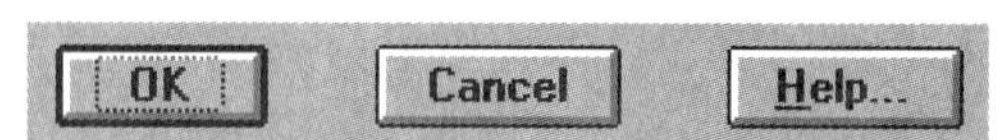

The ok_cancel_help subassembly provides the standard OK and Cancel options, plus a Help button. The key for the help button is *"help"*. Complex dialog boxes and the main dialog box for an application are logical places to include a help feature. The AutoLISP code that handles the help button can be used to display the standard AutoCAD HELP dialog box with context-oriented help information using the AutoLISP "HELP" function.

Ok, Cancel, Help, Errtile **ok_cancel_help_errtile;**

OK Cancel Help...
Invalid input value.

This subassembly combines an errtile with the standard ok_cancel_error tile for convenience in defining all four tiles at the same time.

Ok, Cancel, Help, Info **ok_cancel_help_info;**

OK Cancel Help... Info...

An Info button is commonly used by third-party developers to display application specific information. Such information might include company logo, address, etc., a software version number, or possibly directions for obtaining technical support. The message is usually displayed in a subsequent dialog box or even a simple ALERT box. In either case, since this is typically an information feature only, if you are not using an ALERT box, then it is best to specify an ok_only retirement button from the dialog displayed by the info button. The key for the info button is *"info"*.

TILE ATTRIBUTES

The PDB facility references various attributes associated with each type of tile to determine the layout and functionality of the tile. If attributes are not specified, the default value is used for that property. The following section provides a more detailed look at each of the available attributes and how they are handled.

Data types for attribute values are shown in their actual format by the examples. Remember, there are four basic data types used in DCL: *integer, real, string,* and *reserved word*. The first three data types are handled exactly as in AutoLISP–integers have no decimal and are a whole number, reals must have a leading digit and a decimal point, and strings are enclosed in double quotes. Reserved words are a special data type made up of alphanumeric characters that are *not* enclosed in double quotes. Reserved words are used for many different attributes.

action = "(setq VAR 3)";

The action attribute is one way to specify a *callback*, or action to be performed when the tile is activated. This option is primarily used for short, single line AutoLISP expressions. More detailed actions are usually defined in the AutoLISP application that handles the dialog box using the *action_tile* function.

When specified here, the AutoLISP expression needs to be enclosed in quotation marks as shown above. The semicolon is a line terminator, and is discussed later in this chapter.

alignment = left;

The alignment attribute specifies the horizontal or vertical positioning of a child tile within its cluster. The value is entered as a reserved word, and the possible values depend on the type of cluster the tile is contained within. For example, if the tile is in a row the possible values are top, centered, and bottom. However, if the tile is in a column, the possible values are left, centered, and right. In either case, the default is centered.

Note that it is not possible to specify the alignment along the long axis of a cluster. For example, the tiles in a column can be aligned in a left/right fashion, but not vertically. By default, the long axis alignment for a row or a column is done as follows: the first and last tiles are aligned to the ends and all the rest are evenly spaced in between. To realign tiles along the long axis, use spacer tiles.

allow_accept = true;

The allow_accept attribute default is false. When the value of allow_accept is *true:*

- the tile is active when the [ENTER] key is pressed, or
- the tile is double clicked (where a double-click is supported), then

A. The tile is activated and its action expression evaluated, and
B. The tile whose key is "*accept*" is activated, dismissing the dialog and returning to the application.

aspect_ratio = 1.0;

This controls the ratio of width to height of an image, the actual real number value is equal to the width divided by the height. When a 0.0 value is specified, the tile is fitted to the size of the image. (Image sizes are specified by the AutoLISP application handling the dialog.) This attribute has no default value, because if it is not used, then both an explicit height and width value must be specified.

big_increment = 10;

Specifies the slider's incremental control value for situations when the slider bar itself is picked to cause a "page-at-a-time" style movement. The default value is one-tenth the total range as specified by the *max_value* and *min_value* attributes for the slider.

children_alignment = right;

If the children tiles of a cluster do *not* have explicit alignment values specified, this attribute controls their horizontal and vertical positioning. The value is entered as a reserved word, and the possible values depend on the type of cluster the tile is contained within. For example, if the tile is in a row the possible values are *top, centered,* and *bottom*. However, if the tile is in a column, the possible values are *left, centered,* and *right*. In either case, the default is *centered.*

Remember that it is not possible to specify the alignment along the long axis of a cluster. See the *alignment* attribute explanation for more information.

children_fixed_height = true;
children_fixed_width = true;

These attributes prevent a tile that is a child of the cluster from growing into any extra space that becomes available in the layout process (as in Fig. 17-6). If a child tile has an explicit value given for height or width, the corresponding *fixed_* attribute has no effect on its size. The possible values are either *true* or *false*, and are indicated as reserved words. Care should be taken when overriding the PDB facility's layout defaults to insure consistent layouts.

color = dialog_background;
color = white;

This attribute specifies the background fill color for an image tile. Either a specific color can be used, or the current dialog or graphics screen colors can be indicated. The table in Fig. 17-8 shows the possible values and their meanings.

Note that if an incompatible color scheme is selected and the image vectors are the same color as the background, the image will not be visible.

Reserved Word Value	Meaning
dialog_line	Current dialog box line color
dialog_foreground	Current dialog box foreground color
dialog_background	Current dialog box background color
graphics_foreground	Current graphics screen foreground color
graphics_background	Current graphics screen background color
black	AutoCAD color 0 (*black* or *white* depending on current AutoCAD screen configuration)
red	AutoCAD color 1
yellow	AutoCAD color 2
green	AutoCAD color 3
cyan	AutoCAD color 4
blue	AutoCAD color 5
magenta	AutoCAD color 6
white	AutoCAD color 7 (*black* or *white* depending on current AutoCAD screen configuration)

Fig. 17-8. Possible color attribute values and their meanings.

edit_limit = 32;

This integer attribute controls the maximum number of characters that can be entered into an edit_box. The default value is 132 characters, and the maximum allowable value is 256. If the edit_limit is greater than the edit_width, then the text can be scrolled as needed for editing.

edit_width = 16;

The edit_width specifies the width, in character positions, of the *box* portion of an edit_box. If not specified, or if the value is zero, the box simply expands to fill the available space. If an edit_box tile that has an explicit edit_width specified needs to be "stretched" at *layout time*, the additional space is inserted between the edit_box and its label. This value can be specified either as a real or an integer. (The term *layout time* refers to when the dialog box in being constructed on-screen.)

fixed_height = true;
fixed_width = true;

These attributes prevent a tile from "growing" into any extra space that becomes available in the layout process (as in Fig. 17-6). If a tile has an explicit value given for height or width, the corresponding *fixed_* attributes have no effect on its size. The possible values are either *true* or *false*, and are indicated as reserved words.

fixed_width_font = true;

When *true*, this attribute forces list boxes and popup lists to display text in a fixed pitch font. This means that each character will have the same width, and allows for easier tab alignment and spacing in the list. This attribute is available only in Windows and Windows NT.

height = 3;

This specifies an exact height for a tile in character height units (the height of the screen characters including line spacing). This attribute can be specified as an integer or a real. Image tiles and buttons must have a specified height, either through the height attribute or with the width and aspect_ratio attributes. Note that this attribute specifies the minimum height of the tile.

initial_focus = "tile_key";

The tile on a dialog box that is to have the initial keyboard focus is set with the initial_focus attribute. The string value indicates the key of the tile that is to have the initial focus. This means that when a dialog box is opened, keyboard entries are received by this tile. For example, if an edit_box were the initial focus, text entered would be placed within that edit_box. If a button had the initial focus, striking [ENTER] would have the effect of pressing the button. (The term *keyboard* focus indicates that the tile is "active" and any keyboard entries will be applied to the tile.)

is_bold = true;

On platforms that support bold display text, this attribute causes text to be displayed as bold when the value is true.

is_cancel = true;

If this attribute is true, then the tile is activated when the cancel key (Escape or Control+C) is pressed. If the action expression for the tile doesn't exit the dialog, it is automatically terminated after the action has been evaluated. The default value for is_cancel is false.

is_default = true;

This specifies which tile is activated when the accept key ([ENTER]) is pressed. Only one tile in a dialog box can have this attribute set to *true* The default value is *false*.

is_enabled = false;

This attribute is used to initially disable (and "grey-out") a tile. The default value for this is *true;* the *false* setting disables a tile. This specifies the initial state only, and can be enabled at run time by the handling application.

is_tab_stop = true;

The is_tab_stop attribute allows a tile to be removed from the tab stop "trail." While a dialog box is running, pressing the tab key shifts the keyboard focus from each applicable tile to the next. To prevent a tile from receiving keyboard focus in this manner, set the attribute value to false. The default value of is_tab_stop is true.

key = "key_name";

The key is, as the name might imply, the fundamental means of accessing a tile at run time to obtain or change its value or mode. The key name for each tile within a dialog box should be unique. The data type for a key is a string–remember that key values are case-sensitive, and the values key_1 and Key_1 are not the same.

label = "Label text";

This specifies the contents of the text string displayed with the tile. Depending on the type of tile, this string might be displayed within or near the tile. A mnemonic character can be specified to provide quick keyboard access to a tile. To indicate a mnemonic character, place an ampersand (&) in the character position to the left of the desired mnemonic:

label = "Label te&xt" *produces the label* *Label te<u>x</u>t*

(The mnemonic character of a label string can also be set by the *mnemonic* attribute.)

layout = vertical;

This indicates the orientation of a slider bar. The default is *horizontal.*

list = "List_item1\nList_item2\nList_item3";

The *list* attribute is a string used to specify the initial contents of a list_box or popup_list tile. All list items are placed within one string with line separation indicated by a newline character "\n". Tab characters "\t" can be within a list string.

max_value = 1000;
min_value = 1;

These two attributes specify the largest and smallest possible values for a slider. The defaults are *max_value* = 1000, and *min_value* = 0. The value of each must be between –32768 and 32767 (a signed, 16-bit integer).

mnemonic = "d";

This is an alternate way to specify a mnemonic character for a label string. The primary means of setting a keyboard mnemonic is with the *label* attribute.

multiple_select = true;

The list_box tile uses this attribute to determine whether or not multiple items within a list can be simultaneously selected and highlighted. The default value is *false.*

password_char = "*";

In some cases, it may be desirable to institute security measures in an application. Protection of confidential data or limiting access to destructive program options are possible reasons for providing password protection to applications or application features. When a program asks for the user to enter a password, it is typical that the password is not displayed on the screen for others to see. In many cases, alternate characters (such as dashes "-" or asterisks "*") are displayed when the password is entered. The *password_char* attribute allows specification of an alternate character to appear in an edit box rather than the actual characters typed by the user.

small_increment = 1;

Specifies the slider's incremental control value for the slider arrow. The default value is one-hundredth the total range as specified by the max_value and min_value attributes for the slider.

tabs = "4 8 12 16";

Tabs can be placed in list strings for list_boxes and popup_lists to achieve a desired vertical alignment of columns of the text. The value is specified as a string containing integers or real numbers separated by spaces. Each number indicates the position, in character width units, of each tab in the list.

tab_truncate = true;

When *true*, this protects the tab alignment of a list box or popup list by truncating the strings when they are larger than the associated tab stop. This attribute is available only in Windows and Windows NT.

value = "1";

The value attribute specifies the initial value of a tile. Different tiles will require different types of values, but they are always presented in a string. For example, a toggle uses an integer string value ("1" or "0") and a radio_column specifies a key string ("key_name") value.

width = 8;

This represents the minimum width of a tile in character width units, and can be an integer or a real. Image tiles and buttons must have a specified width, either through the *width* attribute or with the *height* and *aspect_ratio* attributes.

USING DIALOG CONTROL LANGUAGE

The first step in creating a dialog box is to specify the content and layout of a dialog box using Dialog Control Language within a .DCL file. To prepare for this task, you should first sketch the desired dialog box either using AutoCAD, or even just using a pencil and paper. This gives you a chance to design and revise your dialog box layout and appearance as needed without having to change your DCL code. Once you have decided on the layout, use a text editor to create a text file with any desired name and a .DCL file extension. One or more dialog box descriptions can be put into this one DCL file. A DCL file can also be created that contains prototypes and subassemblies to be referenced by other DCL files.

PROFESSIONAL TIP

A new DCL file will automatically have access to the tiles defined in the BASE.DCL file, but can access other DCL files by specifying an *include directive*:

```
@include "filename.dcl"
```

This has the effect of *including* the specified file in the dialog loading process so that the external tile definitions can be utilized. If a directory path is not indicated, the ACAD library path is searched for the specified files. Include directives are usually placed near the top of the DCL file before the dialog definitions.

Defining a Tile

Each dialog box definition begins with the name of the dialog tile and a dialog tile specification separated by a colon : with a space on each side. The curly braces are next. They contain all of the children tile definitions and the attributes of the dialog. Children tiles are not named as is the dialog box, but each specification is preceded by a colon and the attributes and children are contained in the curly braces. The example shown in Fig. 17-9 is a dialog box definition that contains a text tile and an ok_only tile. The shown DCL code defines the dialog box shown in Fig. 17-10.

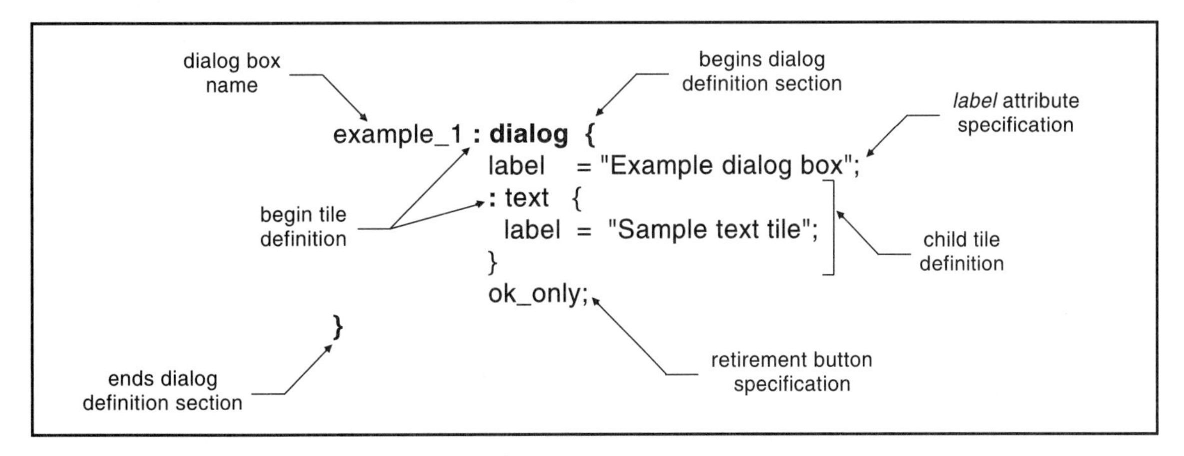

Fig. 17-9. Dialog definition DCL code.

Fig. 17-10. Dialog box defined by DCL code in Fig.17-9.

Remember that a dialog box definition must be loaded and handled by AutoLISP to be displayed. The DCL definition cannot, by itself, run a dialog session.

Just as the children tiles of a dialog are enclosed in the curly braces that enclose the dialog definition, children of other tiles are defined within the definition of the parent tile. The block diagram tree shown in Fig. 17-11 shows the parent-child relationships for a dialog box that has various tiles defined within two *columns* that are children of a *boxed_row* tile, and an ok_cancel retirement button specification.

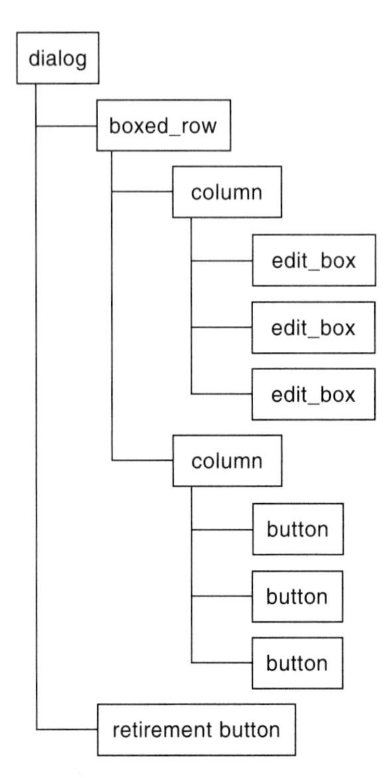

Fig. 17-11. Dialog tree structure block diagram.

Compare the tree diagram with the actual DCL code shown in Fig. 17-12. Note the overall tree structure and the placement of children within the curly braces. (Clusters containing nested tiles are shown with bold braces.)

```
example_2 : dialog {
          label   =   "Example dialog box #2";
          : boxed_row {
           label   =   "Boxed Row Label";
           : column {
            : edit_box {
             label   =   "Edit Box 1: ";
             edit_width   =   8;
             key   =   "ebox_1";
            }
            : edit_box {
             label   =   "Edit Box 2: ";
             edit_width   =   16;
             key   =   "ebox_2";
             value   =   "Default value";
            }
            : edit_box {
             label   =   "Edit Box 3: ";
             edit_width   =   4;
             key   =   "ebox_3";
            }
           }
           : column {
            : button {
             label   =   "button_1";
             key   =   "btn_1";
            }
            : button {
             label   =   "button_2";
             key   =   "btn_2";
            }
            : button {
            : label   =   "button_3";
            : key   =   "btn_3";
            }
           }
          }
          ok_cancel;
}
```

children of dialog

child of *boxed_row*

children of *column*

child of *boxed_row*

children of *column*

Fig. 17-12. DCL code example.

Fig. 17-13 shows the dialog box defined by the code in Fig. 17-12. Note the effects of the associated attribute values for each of the tiles.

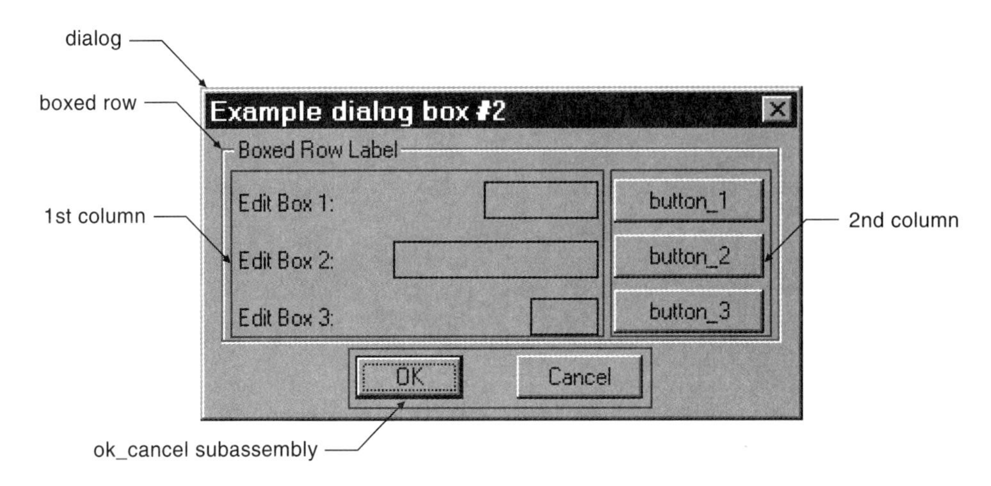

Fig. 17-13. Dialog box defined by Fig. 17-12.

DCL FILE FORMAT AND SYNTAX

The previous examples show the basic structure and format for a DCL file. While indentation is used within DCL files, it is somewhat different than the style used in AutoLISP programming. Even so, nested levels are indented. A brief study of Fig. 17-12 shows that a tile's attributes and children are indented to the same column as the tile specification. Spaces outside of a string (not enclosed in quotation marks) are ignored, similar to an AutoLISP program file. Attributes are separated from values by an equal sign (=) and attribute lines are terminated with a semicolon. A missing bracket or semicolon makes a DCL file unusable. Remember that attribute names are case-sensitive, so attributes named *Width* or *WIDTH* will not have an effect on the *width* attribute of a tile.

Instead of using a semicolon for comments (as you do with AutoLISP), a DCL file uses a double-forward slash arrangement for full line comments. The PDB facility ignores anything preceded with //. In-line comments are also possible by typing /* to indicate the start of the comment and */ to indicate the end. Such comments can span multiple lines if necessary. The following example shows various comment styles and syntax.

```
// Example dialog box for AutoLISP, Chap. 17
example_3 : dialog {          // begin dialog definition
            label = "Example dialog box #2";
            : slider  {
              big_increment = /*Default would be 10*/  5;
```

Try to format your DCL files like the examples shown in this chapter. For additional reference, open some of AutoCAD's DCL files in the SUPPORT and SAMPLE subdirectories and browse through them. Remember not to change these files directly, since it could cause some of AutoCAD's own built-in features to run incorrectly.

Exercise 17-1

☐ Create a dialog box definition in a file named EX17-1.DCL to match the sketch below. Assign keys to each applicable tile, and set other attributes to match the appearance of this example. The name of the dialog should be "dlg_1". Include comments in the DCL file as appropriate.

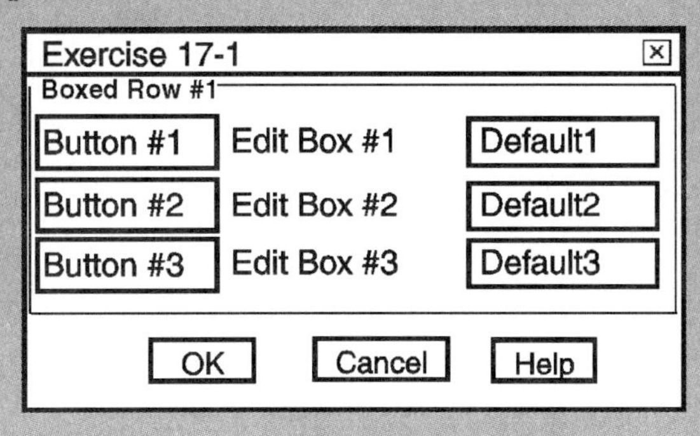

Now that you have created your first DCL file and defined your first dialog box, you need to write the AutoLISP code that runs the dialog box. This information is covered in detail in Chapter 18, but for now, so you can test the code you just generated in Exercise 17-1. Create an AutoLISP file named EX17-1.LSP and place the following AutoLISP code in it:

```
(load_dialog "EX17-1.DCL")
(new_dialog "dlg_1")
(start_dialog)
```

If this does not work as shown, you may need to specify the correct directory path in the file name field. As always, with AutoLISP, use either "\\" or "/" for directory path delimiters. None of the tiles will have any associated action, but the predefined OK and CANCEL buttons will dismiss the dialog box when you are done viewing it.

Chapter 18 will demonstrate the use of AutoLISP and DCL together in an application for obtaining user input. Note that ADS (AutoCAD Development System) applications can also handle dialog boxes. See the *AutoCAD Customization Guide* if you would like more information on ADS.

Let's review...

1. Predefined active tiles are the basis for most dialog definitions, and are combined as needed into clusters and subassemblies to define a dialog box.
2. Any combination of attributes can be used to define a tile, ranging from none to all of the available attributes, depending on the specific needs for each tile.
3. Most dialogs have two retirement buttons (exit tiles), typically labelled OK and Cancel. Every dialog requires at least one retirement button.
4. Error tiles appear at the bottom of the dialog box and allow the programmer to display an error message to the user.
5. Predefined subassemblies do not require attribute specifications, and therefore, are not followed by attibutes within curly braces.
6. Externally defined subassemblies can be referenced by the use of an include directive.
7. Dialog control language cannot run a dialog box by itself, but requires a handling application. The controlling application can be created using ADS or AutoLISP.

CHAPTER TEST

Write your answers in the spaces provided.

1. Why are dialog boxes often a more efficient means of obtaining user input?

 ____

 ____

2. How does the computer operating system you are using affect the appearance of dialog boxes?

 ____

 ____

3. What is the name of the language that is used to define dialog boxes and what type of files are used to store these definitions?

 ____

4. The components of a dialog box are called __________.
5. What is the name of the DCL file that contains most of the basic predefined tile definitions?

 ____

6. Which DCL file contains the definitions for AutoCAD's built-in dialog boxes?

 ____

7. What controls the appearance of tiles within a dialog box?

 ____

 ____

8. The tools provided for working with dialog boxes are referred to as:

____

9. What is meant by the term "predefined active tile"?

____

____

10. What are decorative and informative tiles primarily used for?

____

____

11. What advantages are given when using tile clusters instead of individual tiles in a dialog box?

____

____

____

12. What is an "exit" tile? Give two examples of common exit buttons.

____

____

13. Why is it usually best to use the predefined error tile to display error messages to the user?

____

____

14. Define the term "subassembly" as it applies to DCL.

____

____

____

15. Tiles nested within another tile are referred to as its __________.
16. What are the four available data types for specifying attribute values?

____

____

____

17. Describe the difference between a string and a reserved word.

____

____

18. Which attribute is necessary in order for your AutoLISP application to access a tile?

____

19. What is a retirement button, and what dialog boxes use a retirement button?

____

____

____

```
; IMGTOGL.lsp
; Author: Flip D. Pitcher
; Purpose: Demonstration of dynamic updating of an image tile based on user input.
:    This controls a dialog box that displays a single image tile that, when picked, toggles to
;    another image and updates a text description.  Picking OK starts the command
;    represented by the current picture, Picking Cancel aborts.
;
;Support Files required (All support files to be located in the support path):
;    SLIDE files to match the names in IMAGE_LIST local symbol.
;    IMAGE_TOGL.DCL file to define the dialog box.
;Assumptions: The DCL file and all slide files exist on the AutoCAD support path.
;Initialization section: Sets up fundamental symbols
;
(setq IMAGE_COUNTER 0        ;Counter variable initialized at 0, then define image list
      IMAGE_LIST (list "LINE" "ARC" "CIRCLE" "POLYLINE" "POLYGON" "RECTANGL")
      IMAGE_CURRENT (nth IMAGE_COUNTER IMAGE_LIST) ;Initial item is first image in list.
      DESCR_LIST (list "Line" "Arc" "Circle" "Polyline" "Polygon" "Rectangle") ;Define text values
      OPTION (car DESCR_LIST)  ;OPTION set to current image, incase OK is picked first.
)
;
;Utility Function Definition: Code to update image and text at run-time.  This NXTIMG function
; is called as the action associated with the IMAGE_BUTTON labeled "_dlgimg".
;
(defun NXTIMG ()
  (if (= 5 IMAGE_COUNTER)                         ;Has the end of the list been reached?
     (setq IMAGE_COUNTER 0)                       ;If so, THEN reset counter to first position in list
     (setq IMAGE_COUNTER (1+ IMAGE_COUNTER)) ;Or ELSE increment the counter.
  )                                                ;End IF
  (start_image "_dlgimg")                                        ;Open the slide tile for definition
  (fill_image 0 0 (dimx_tile "_dlgimg")(dimy_tile "_dlgimg") -15)  ;Set image background color to
                                                                  ; match dialog box background.
  (slide_image 0 0                                               ;Display slide image
          (dimx_tile "_dlgimg")(dimy_tile "_dlgimg")
          (nth IMAGE_COUNTER IMAGE_LIST)


  )
  (end_image)                                                    ;Close image tile definition
  (set_tile "_descr" (nth IMAGE_COUNTER DESCR_LIST)) ;Set value for text tile.
  (setq OPTION (nth IMAGE_COUNTER DESCR_LIST))     ;Update OPTION value
)                                                                ;End DEFUN
(setq DCL_ID (load_dialog "IMG_TOGL.DCL"))     ;Read DCL code from file
(new_dialog "main" DCL_ID)                     ;Initialize dialog box.
(start_image "_dlgimg")                        ;Open image tile for initial definition
(slide_image 0 0 (dimx_tile "_dlgimg")(dimy_tile "_dlgimg") "LINE")  ;Set initial slide image
(end_image)                                    ;Close image tile definition
(set_tile "_descr" "Line")                     ;Set initial text tile value
(action_tile "_dlgimg" "(NXTIMG)")             ;Assign action for image tile.
(setq CODE (start_dialog))                     ;Start dialog session and determine exit mode
(unload_dialog DCL_ID)        ;removes DCL code from memory
(cond       ;Evaluated after exiting dialog session, determines proper action
```

```
  ((zerop CODE) (princ "\n*Cancel*\n"))  ;If CODE is 0, user selected Cancel.  Display message.
  ((= "Line" OPTION) (command "._LINE"))
  ((= "Arc" OPTION) (command "._ARC"))
  ((= "Circle" OPTION) (command "._CIRCLE"))
  ((= "Polyline" OPTION) (command "._PLINE"))
  ((= "Polygon" OPTION) (command "._POLYGON"))
  ((= "Rectangle" OPTION) (princ "Rectangle...")(C:RECTANG)) ;calls predefined AutoLISP
                                                              ;function
)
(princ)  ;quiet exit
;
;
//  IMG_TOGL.DCL
//  Author: Flip D. Pitcher
//  DCL definition file for img_togl.lsp.
//  Defines a dialog session that uses one image button, a text tile and an
//  OK_CANCEL subassembly.
//
main : dialog {
    label = "Image Toggling Example";
    children_alignment = centered;     // Sets alignment for image, text & ok_cancel tiles
    : image_button {
      color = dialog_background;
      width = 10;
      fixed_width = true;     // Prevents image size expansion to fit tile
      aspect_ratio = 1;       // Keeps image square
      key = "_dlgimg";
}                             // End of Image button definition
    : text_part {
      key = "_descr";
      width = 18;
}
    ok_cancel;
}
```

Chapter 18

Programmable Dialog Box Functions

Learning Objectives

After completing this chapter, you will be able to:

- ☐ Use AutoLISP expressions to manage dialog sessions.
- ☐ Load and unload descriptive DCL files.
- ☐ Design and control tile functionality.
- ☐ Dynamically update dialog box contents.
- ☐ Retrieve entered data for use by an AutoLISP application.
- ☐ Display image tiles in a dialog box.
- ☐ Incorporate sliders into a dialog box.

AutoLISP provides a specialized set of functions for handling dialog sessions. These functions are used for loading DCL code, controlling tile functionality, displaying and updating images and text, obtaining user specified values, and ending dialog sessions. A sequence of AutoLISP code written for controlling a dialog session will always have the same basic form. The steps for starting, controlling, and ending a dialog session are shown in the block diagram in Fig. 18-1. Each dialog box will have its own specialized requirements, but the figure shows the general steps followed.

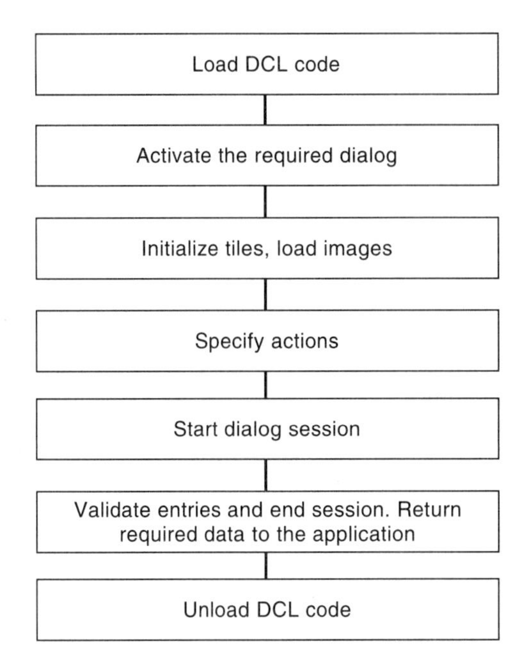

Fig. 18-1. Block diagram showing fundamental steps in running a dialog session.

DIALOG BOX CONTROL FUNCTIONS

Several dialog box control functions are available to programmers. These include:

- LOAD_DIALOG
- NEW_DIALOG
- START_DIALOG
- DONE_DIALOG
- TERM_DIALOG
- UNLOAD_DIALOG

These functions are covered in the following sections.

The LOAD_DIALOG Function

All dialog boxes are inherently dependent on the files containing the descriptive DCL code. This descriptive code must be loaded into memory before AutoLISP can use it to display and control a dialog box. The *LOAD_DIALOG function* opens a DCL file and reads the description for the dialog boxes and tiles described within. Note that any number of dialog component descriptions may be found within a single DCL file. These dialog components include dialog boxes, subassemblies, and prototypes.

The syntax for the LOAD_DIALOG function is:

```
(load_dialog DCLFILE)
```

Similar to loading an AutoLISP file, the filename argument, DCLFILE, is specified as a string. If the file extension is not specified, it defaults to .DCL. A DCL file can have other file extensions, but in most cases it is best to use the .DCL extension in order to maintain consistency with industry standards.

Evaluation of a LOAD_DIALOG expression returns an incremental positive integer if successful and a negative integer (–1) if the specified DCL file cannot be opened. The positive integer returned is raised by 1 each time a DCL file is successfully loaded, but the negative integer is always –1. Possible reasons why a DCL file won't load include errors in the DCL code or a "file not found" condition. If the file is not located on the library path, then the directory path needs to be specified.

After the DCL file is successfully loaded, the returned integer is used by AutoLISP to reference the DCL code contained in the loaded file. Now that this file is loaded, all of the DCL definitions within it are accessible by your application.

The NEW_DIALOG Function

The *NEW_DIALOG function* activates a user-specified dialog definition found within the indicated file. The syntax for a NEW_DIALOG expression is as follows:

```
(new_dialog DLGNAME DCL_ID [ACTION-EXPRESSION [SCREEN-PT]])
```

The two required arguments are DLGNAME, which specifies the name of the dialog to activate, and DCL_ID, which indicates the integer identifier returned by the preliminary LOAD_DIALOG expression. The optional ACTION-EXPRESSION is a string containing AutoLISP expressions (if any) that perform default actions, and must be specified when the SCREEN-PT argument is used. At run time, active tiles that do not have specific actions associated with them will perform the default action specified in the NEW_DIALOG expression.

The SCREEN-PT argument allows specification of the initial location of the dialog box, according to platform-specific rules. The format for specification is exactly like a standard point coordinate list, but refers to the screen coordinates used by the operating system, not to AutoCAD's coordinate system. In Windows, the '(0 0) point is the upper-left corner of the screen, and the insertion point for the dialog box is at its upper-left corner. In DOS, the '(0 0) point is at the lower-left corner of the screen, and the insertion point is at the lower-left corner of the dialog box. The upper values depend on screen resolution, so this may affect the placement of your dialog boxes. In DOS and Windows, if you inadvertently specify a value that will cause part of the dialog to disappear off the edge of the screen, then the PDB facility will ignore the SCREEN-PT argument and place the dialog in the center of the screen. It is seldom necessary to place a dialog box in a specific location; the default location of the center of the screen is adequate for all but very specialized needs.

Once the supportive DCL code has been loaded and the new dialog box has been activated, the initial state, value, and functionality of the tiles must be provided. In many cases, some or all of this information is specified in the DCL file using action and value attributes. Other applications may use a generic dialog box definition that requires all of these specifications be made using AutoLISP. These tile-handling functions are discussed in a later section of this chapter.

The START_DIALOG Function

The *START_DIALOG function* forces the current dialog box (defined by the preceding NEW_DIALOG expression) to be displayed and starts the actual dialog session. This function uses no arguments:

```
(start_dialog)
```

The value returned by START_DIALOG depends on the subsequent DONE_DIALOG expression, and is therefore, explained in the DONE_DIALOG section. The dialog box activated by the START_DIALOG expression will remain active until an action expression ends the session. When nested dialog boxes are activated without ending the current session, the current dialog is put on "hold" and will reactivate once the subdialog session is complete.

The DONE_DIALOG Function

Once all of the required data has been obtained by the dialog box and it is time for the application to proceed, it is necessary to dismiss the current dialog box. The *DONE_DIALOG function* dismisses the currently active dialog box. A DONE_DIALOG expression must be called from within an action expression or a callback function. Action expressions and callback functions are defined and their use explained in the ACTION_TILE discussion later in this chapter.

The predefined OK and CANCEL exit tiles will automatically issue a DONE_DIALOG, but a DONE_DIALOG expression can also be assigned as part of the action expression for other tiles within a dialog box. The syntax for such an expression is:

```
(done_dialog [STATUS])
```

The most common means for a user to exit a dialog session is to pick either the OK or the CANCEL button. When the optional STATUS argument is not used, the START_DIALOG expression that this DONE_DIALOG expression closes will return the integer 1 if OK was picked, and 0 if the CANCEL button was used. The STATUS argument can be any integer, and is returned instead of the standard 0 or 1 when specified. When it is necessary to track more than just the exit method, the STATUS argument can be used to report the status of the dialog box to your application. One common application is to reference a bit style value that is set based on entries to specific tiles in your dialog box. Once the dialog session is done and the application is resumed, decisions can be made based on the returned value. Remember, the STATUS argument is returned by the START_DIALOG function, not the DONE_DIALOG function.

The DONE_DIALOG expression itself will return a X,Y point coordinate list that indicates the location on the screen of the dialog box when the user exits. If the dialog box must be reopened, this value can be referenced by the subsequent NEW_DIALOG expression to place the dialog box in the exact same position it was in the previous session.

PROFESSIONAL TIP

It is very important to be aware that if you redefine the action for the buttons whose keys are "*accept*" or "*cancel*" (OK and CANCEL by default), then it is necessary that your new definition calls the DONE_DIALOG expression. Failing to provide a means to terminate the dialog can trap the user, sometimes requiring a system boot to finally terminate the dialog. Also, since a keyboard cancellation actually activates the tile whose key is "cancel", even this will not dismiss a dialog if a DONE_DIALOG expression is not associated with the tile.

The TERM_DIALOG Function

The *TERM_DIALOG function* is used to dismiss all current dialog boxes—active or not—as if each had been canceled by the user. This function always returns nil, and is commonly used for aborting a series of nested dialog boxes. In most cases, however, canceling a nested dialog box should return to the previous dialog box.

```
(term_dialog)
```

The UNLOAD_DIALOG Function

The *UNLOAD_DIALOG function* helps prevent possible conflicts between tile definitions in subsequently loaded DCL files that reference previously defined tile names.

```
(unload_dialog DCL_ID)
```

Let's Review...

1. Each dialog session requires the same fundamental approach in the controlling application:
   A) Load the dialog definition file.
   B) Activate the desired dialog definition.
   C) Initialize tiles and load images.
   D) Specify actions.
   E) Start dialog session.
   F) Return validated entries to the application and end dialog session.
   G) Unload dialog definition file.
2. Loading a DCL file provides access to each of the dialog definitions it contains.
3. The NEW_DIALOG call activates a specified dialog box definition. The START_DIALOG function begins the dialog session. All application specific tile definitions take place between the NEW_DIALOG and START_DIALOG expressions.
4. The DONE_DIALOG function dismisses the currently active dialog box, whereas the TERM_DIALOG dismisses all currently visible dialog boxes–active or not.
5. Unloading the DCL code when the dialog session is complete helps prevent possible conflicts between tile definitions.

STARTING YOUR FIRST DIALOG SESSION

With the functions discussed to this point, it is possible to start your first dialog session. The first step is to create a dialog box description in a DCL file. Next, you will create an AutoLISP file to handle the dialog session. This first exercise will use a text tile to display a message and an ok_only tile as a retirement button. Like each of the predefined OK and Cancel buttons, the ok_only tile has a DONE_DIALOG expression assigned as its action.

Follow these steps to define and run your first dialog session:

1. Using your text editor, create an ASCII text file named DDFIRST.DCL. (This filename uses AutoCAD's standard naming criteria of preceding a dialog support file name with "DD".) Note: The following exercise assumes that both files are found on the AutoCAD library path.
2. Place the following dialog description in DDFIRST.DCL:

```
//DDFIRST.DCL                                                    // [1]
//Displays the message: Dialog session example 1
first : dialog {                              // [2]
      label          = "Dialog Handling Example";
      : text  {                               // [3]
        label        = "Dialog session example 1";
      }
      ok_only;                                // [4]
}
```

3. Save and exit the file DDFIRST.DCL, and open a new text file named DDFIRST.LSP that contains the following AutoLISP code:

```
;;DDFIRST.LSP                                                   ; [5]
;;Handles the dialog box named  - first  -  defined in DDFIRST.DCL
(defun C:GOFIRST ( / dcl_id )                                   ; [6]
  (setq DCL_ID (load_dialog "DDFIRST.DCL"))                     ; [7]
  (if (not (new_dialog "first" DCL_ID)) (exit))                 ; [8]
  (start_dialog)                                                ; [9]
  (unload_dialog DCL_ID)                                        ; [10]
  (princ)                                                       ; [11]
)
```

4. At the AutoCAD Command: prompt, type the following LOAD expression to load the AutoLISP file:

   Command: **(load "DDFIRST")** ↵

5. After loading the file, type GOFIRST at the Command: prompt to start the dialog session. The dialog box shown in Fig. 18-2 is displayed.

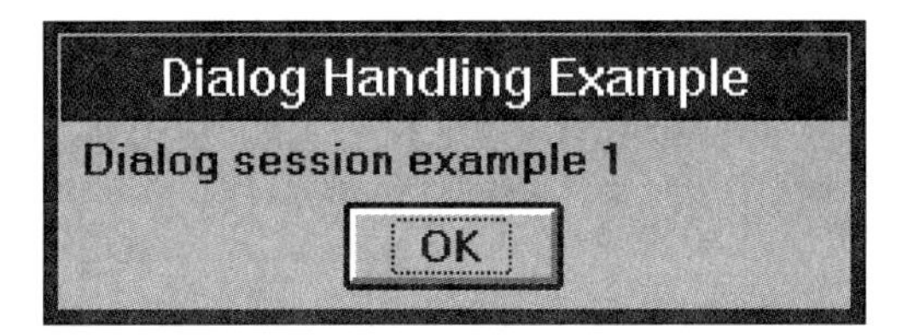

Fig. 18-2. The DDFIRST dialog box.

Now that you have run your first dialog session, let's take a closer look at the code used to describe and handle the session. The DCL code is explained below:

[1] **//DDFIRST.DCL**
//Displays the message: Dialog session example 1 These are comments. The double-forward slash characters (//) cause the PDB facility to ignore the text that follows on the same line.

[2] **first : dialog {**
label = "Dialog Handling Example"; This code defines the dialog box name and assigns the label attribute value. While alternate indentation formats can be used, the style shown provides an easy-to-read format to simplify the process of matching opening and closing brackets. Note that attribute definitions are terminated with a semicolon.

[3] **: text {**
label = "Dialog session example 1";
{ The text tile is described here, and its primary attribute (label) is assigned a value.

[4] **ok_only;** This predefined tile is used as a retirement button. It is a requirement to have some type of a retirement button in every dialog. Predefined tiles can be used or custom tiles can be defined to handle special circumstances.

The associated AutoLISP code is explained as follows:

[5] **;;DDFIRST.LSP**
;;Handles the dialog box named – first – defined in DDFIRST.DCL These are AutoLISP file comments.

[6] **(defun C:GOFIRST (/ dcl_id)** The DEFUN expression defines the command line function, C:GOFIRST, and declares the symbol DCL_ID to be local.

[7] **(setq DCL_ID (load_dialog "DDFIRST.DCL"))** The file handle returned by the load_dialog expression is assigned to the symbol DCL_ID. Although the symbol name DCL_ID is commonly used to reference a DCL file handle, any valid symbol name can be used.

[8] **(if (not (new_dialog "first" DCL_ID)) (exit))** This is a common widget (special-purpose tool) used to handle certain load time error situations. If the specified dialog cannot be initialized, the exit expression prohibits further evaluation of the AutoLISP code.

[9] **(start_dialog)** The dialog box indicated by the preceding new_dialog expression is displayed and the dialog session starts. Note that until the user exits the dialog session by some means, no further evaluation of the AutoLISP code will occur.

[10] **(unload_dialog DCL_ID)** Once the user ends the dialog session—either by selecting the OK button or by pressing the ESC key on the keyboard—evaluation of the AutoLISP code continues. This expression unloads the DCL code contained in the file referenced by DCL_ID.

[11] **(princ)** Standard "quiet" exit.

The previously demonstrated AutoLISP code represents the core functionality of every AutoLISP program written to control a dialog session. The DCL code is loaded, a new dialog is specified and started, and the DCL code is unloaded when the session is done. The next section covers the tile handling functions that provide the tools for defining the initial state, value, and functionality of the tiles in your dialog box.

Exercise 18-1

☐ Using the previous example as a model, create a DCL file named DDEX18-1.DCL. Create an AutoLISP file named DDEX18-1.LSP to display the text message of your choice. Use an ok_only button to exit the dialog box.

WORKING WITH TILES

Defaults values, initial states, and tile actions are sometimes specified in the DCL code using attributes such as VALUE, IS_ENABLED, and ACTION. This works well for some specialized dialog boxes, but may not be suitable for every situation. For example, default values indicated may depend on current settings of AutoCAD system variables or other variable parameters within the active drawing session. An example can be found in the Units Control (DDUNITS) dialog box, where the dialog is initialized with the current units settings displayed. Such parameters might also affect the relevance of various tiles. A good example of this situation is found in the Boundary Hatch (BHATCH) dialog box, where option buttons may be enabled or disabled based on their relevance to the current hatch pattern name.

The following section discusses the AutoLISP functions provided for DCL tile handling.

Initializing Tiles

The process of initializing a tile for a dialog session can include supplying a default value, giving a tile the initial keyboard focus, enabling or disabling the tile, or highlighting its contents. Note that when changing the value or state of a tile, it is necessary to reference the key attribute of the tile. Therefore, all tiles that are to be accessible by AutoLISP must have an assigned key attribute set within the DCL descriptive code.

The *SET_TILE function* can be used for setting the initial value of a tile or for changing the value at run time. The syntax for the SET_TILE function is:

```
(set_tile KEY VALUE)
```

The KEY argument references the value assigned to the tile's key attribute within the DCL file. The VALUE argument is a string that specifies the new value to assign. The following example demonstrates the use of SET_TILE using an edit box to display the current value of the FILLETRAD system variable.

1. Create a DCL file named DDSECOND.DCL that contains the following DCL code:

```
//DDSECOND.DCL
//Displays the current value of FILLETRAD
second : dialog {                              // [1]
          label          = "Tile Handling Example";
        : text  {                              // [2]
          label          = "Current Drawing Settings";
          alignment      = centered;
        }
        : edit_box {                           // [3]
          label          = "Fillet Radius:";
          edit_width     = 6;
          key            = "f_rad";
        }
        ok_only;                               // [4]
}
```

2. Create an AutoLISP file named DDSECOND.LSP that contains the following AutoLISP code:

```
(defun C:GOSEC ( / dcl_id )
  (setq DCL_ID (load_dialog "DDSECOND.DCL"))
  (if (not (new_dialog "second" DCL_ID)) (exit))
  (set_tile "f_rad" (rtos (getvar "FILLETRAD")))
  (start_dialog)
  (unload_dialog DCL_ID)
  (princ)
)
```

3. At the AutoCAD Command: prompt, type the following LOAD expression to load the AutoLISP file:

   Command: **(load "DDSECOND")** ↵

4. After loading the file, type GOSEC at the Command: prompt to start the dialog session. The dialog box shown in Fig. 18-3 is displayed:

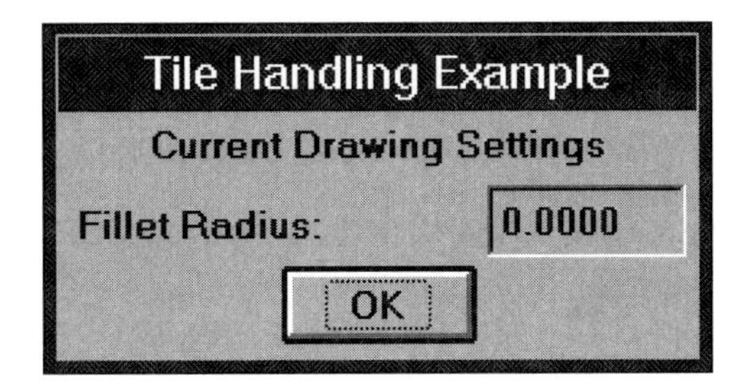

Fig. 18-3. The DDSECOND dialog box.

Now let's take a closer look at the code used to generate this dialog session:

[1] **//DDSECOND.DCL**
//Displays the current value of FILLETRAD
second : dialog {
label = "Tile Handling Example"; The comments briefly describe the DCL file. The dialog name is "second" and a label is specified.

[2] **: text {**
label = "Current Drawing Settings";
alignment = centered;
} The text tile has a label attribute assigned, and includes an alignment variable. Notice the difference in the placement of the text in Fig. 18-2 and Fig. 18-3.

[3] **: edit_box {**
label = "Fillet Radius:";
edit_width = 6;
key = "f_rad";
} Since the edit_box must be accessible by AutoLISP, a key attribute has been specified. Remember that references to this key are case-sensitive. The edit_width attribute controls the width of the edit portion of the tile at layout time. The label informs the user about the contents of the tile.

[4] **ok_only;**
} An ok_only retirement button is often used when the dialog session is not able to effect changes in the environment or content of the current drawing.

This dialog session has no actions associated with any of the tiles except for the default action associated with the retirement button. Even though it is possible to change the contents of the edit box, such changes have no effect on the current drawing session.

The ACTION_TILE Function. To give a tile the capability to actually do something requires an action expression. Action expressions are defined using the *ACTION_TILE function*.The syntax for an ACTION_TILE expression is:

```
(action_tile KEY ACTION-EXPRESSION)
```

The KEY argument is a text string indicating which tile is to be assigned the action defined by the ACTION-EXPRESSION argument. The ACTION-EXPRESSION argument is an AutoLISP expression presented as a string by enclosing the entire expression in quotation marks. Since the AutoLISP expression is a string, it is necessary to precede each quotation mark with a backslash character when using an AutoLISP expression that also contains quotation marks.

The following example shows how an action might be applied to the edit box in the dialog box shown in Fig. 18-3:

```
(defun C:GOSEC ( / dcl_id )
  (setq DCL_ID (load_dialog "DDSECOND.DCL"))
  (if (not (new_dialog "second" DCL_ID)) (exit))
  (set_tile "f_rad" (rtos (getvar "FILLETRAD")))
  (action_tile "f_rad" "(setvar \"FILLETRAD\" (atof $value))")
  (start_dialog)
  (unload_dialog DCL_ID)
  (princ)
)
```

Insert the expression printed in bold type as shown and run this dialog session again. Notice how the data entered in the edit box is accessed by using the $value symbol to extract the current value of the tile. This variable is available along with $key, $data, $reason, $x, and $y. Action expression variables provide information about the tile interaction at run time. A description of each variable is shown in Fig. 18-4.

Variable name	Description
$key	This holds the value of the key of the selected tile.
$value	The current value referenced by the tile is available using *$value.* This value is always returned as a string.
$data	Application managed data set after the last *new_dialog* using *client_data_tile.*
$reason	Code indicating what the user did to initiate the action. This variable is used with *edit_box, list_box, image_button* and *slider* tiles. 1 = User selected tile 2 = User exited edit_box but has not made a final selection 3 = User changed value of slider but has not made a final selection 4 = For list boxes, the user pressed enter when a list item was highlighted.
$x $y	These symbols allow access to the point coordinates of the position the user picked on an image_button tile.

Fig. 18-4. Action expression variables provide information about the tile interaction at run time.

PROFESSIONAL TIP

The callback reasons returned by $reason may vary slightly from one platform to the next. It is easy to verify the callback reasons returned by each action; simply use an ALERT expression that displays the callback reason at run time. The following action expression can be used by substituting the key of the tile to check for the *key* argument below:

```
(action_tile "key" "(alert (strcat \"Callback reason code: \" (itoa $reason)))")
```

Note that this could be further modified to display any of the return codes that need to be checked, by placing a representative string in place of *(itoa $reason)* in the ACTION_TILE expression, for example $key or $value.

Action expressions can contain a variety of AutoLISP functions, but any functions which change the display or require user input outside of the dialog interface cannot be used while a dialog box is active. These functions are listed below:

command	getdist	grclear	prompt
entdel	getint	grdraw	redraw
entmake	getkword	grread	ssget (interactive)
entmod	getorient	grtext	textpage
entsel	getpoint	grvecs	textscr
entupd	getreal	menucmd	
getangle	getstring	nentsel	
getcorner	graphscr	osnap	

An action expression can include any desired AutoLISP code. When the desired action requires a large amount of AutoLISP code, it is best to define a function to perform the required tasks and call the defined function within the action expression.

The MODE_TILE Function. The initial state of a tile can be set in the DCL file or in the controlling application. Changes at run time in the state of a tile can be made using the *MODE_TILE function.* Frequently, the validity of a tile may change based on the setting of other tiles in the dialog session. For example, in the Boundary Hatch dialog box, many of the tiles are disabled at any one time, depending on whether or not they are currently applicable. Notice that the Custom Pattern: edit box is only enabled when the Pattern Type popdown list is set to Custom; the Apply button is only enabled after enough information has been supplied to create a hatch pattern. Several buttons will toggle from active to inactive, or inactive to active as you change the settings of other tiles in the dialog box. Other functions of MODE_TILE include setting the keyboard focus to a tile, selecting the contents of an edit box, or turning image highlighting on or off. Setting the focus to a specific tile helps to guide the user through the dialog session. For example, in the DDSECOND file used earlier in this chapter, a logical addition to the current functionality of this dialog would be to set the keyboard focus to the OK button after the user enters a value in the edit box.

The following example shows the addition of a MODE_TILE expression in the action expression that sets the focus to the OK button:

```
(defun C:GOSEC ( / dcl_id )
 (setq DCL_ID (load_dialog "DDSECOND.DCL"))
 (if (not (new_dialog "second" DCL_ID)) (exit))
 (set_tile "f_rad" (rtos (getvar "FILLETRAD")))
 (action_tile "f_rad"
  "(setvar \"FILLETRAD\" (atof $value))(mode_tile \"accept\" 2")"
 )
```

```
  (start_dialog)
  (unload_dialog DCL_ID)
  (princ)
)
```

Run this dialog to see the effects of the MODE_TILE expression. Notice that the OK button becomes highlighted after a value has been set. This indicates that the keyboard focus has been transferred to this tile. On the surface, this use of the MODE_TILE function seems to work well—but there is an inherent problem with the way that the expression has been utilized.

Some tiles may evaluate their action expressions for different reasons. A button tile performs its action when picked; this never changes. Some tiles, however, have different reasons for evaluating the action expression. For example, depending on the platform, an edit box may evaluate its action when picked or when an [ENTER] is pressed while the edit box is the current tile. With the previous code loaded in Release 12 for Windows or Release 13(c2) for Windows, it is impossible to return to the edit box after the first time the focus is reset to the OK button. The reason for this is because when the tile is picked, the action expression is evaluated and the focus is reset to the OK button. A situation like this makes it necessary to first evaluate the reason for the action expression evaluation before deciding what action to perform.

Using the $reason variable, it can instantly be determined what the reason was for evaluating the action expression. Note that the only tile types that you need to check for callback reasons are the edit_box, list_box, image_button, and slider.

Alter the AutoLISP code as shown below to add a test. The test will check to see if the user pressed [ENTER] to accept the value in the edit box, and will only set the focus to the OK button if this is the case.

```
(defun C:GOSEC ( / dcl_id )
  (setq DCL_ID (load_dialog "DDSECOND.DCL"))
  (if (not (new_dialog "second" DCL_ID)) (exit))
  (set_tile "f_rad" (rtos (getvar "FILLETRAD")))
  (action_tile "f_rad"
    "(setvar \"FILLETRAD\" (atof $value))(if (= 1 $reason) (mode_tile \"accept\" 2))"
  )
  (start_dialog)
  (unload_dialog DCL_ID)
  (princ)
)
```

Another common use for MODE_TILE is to disable or enable tiles based on user input. The next example demonstrates this capability along with the functions for setting and retrieving tile values: SET_TILE and GET_TILE.

To prepare the dialog definition referenced by this example, save the following DCL code as DDTHIRD.DCL. This defines a dialog box for changing GRID settings.

```
//DDTHIRD.DCL
//
third : dialog {
        label             = "Grid Setup";
        : toggle {
          label           = "Grid On";
          mnemonic        = "O";
          key             = "gr_tog";
        }
```

```
        : edit_box {
          label          = "X Spacing:";
          edit_width     = 6;
          key            = "gr_x";
          mnemonic       = "X";
        }
        : edit_box {
          label          = "Y Spacing:";
          edit_width     = 6;
          key            = "gr_y";
          mnemonic       = "Y";
        }
        ok_cancel_err;
}
```

The GET_TILE Function. Run time checking and setting of tile values is necessary in many dialog sessions. The SET_TILE function allows a tile value to be set (as described earlier in this chapter). The complement of this function is the GET_TILE function. The *GET_TILE function* retrieves the current value of the tile indicated by the key argument:

```
(get_tile KEY)
```

The following code controls the dialog box described by the previous DCL code, which defines a situation where some of the tiles may not be applicable depending on the settings of other tiles. If the grid is off, there is no reason to set the X and Y spacing values. An application should always take such things into consideration and adjust the state of tiles according to their validity. Also demonstrated in this example is the technique for handling longer action expressions. Defining functions to be called by the action expression allows more complex and extensive actions to be developed. Each of the action expressions in the following code use this method. Notice how the functions can use the $value and $reason variables as arguments to provide decision-making criteria to the functions.

The action for the Grid On toggle will use the GRIDMODE variable to toggle the status of the grid, and it will use a MODE_TILE expression as part of its action. If the grid is off, it will disable the edit boxes, otherwise, it will enable the boxes and make the X Spacing box current. Note also that accepting the value in the X Spacing edit box will make the Y Spacing current and accepting the Y Spacing sets the focus to the OK button. This is also done using MODE_TILE expressions. Carefully examine the following code to see what tests are performed to determine the proper course of action, and how the modes are set. The application may appear a bit lengthy for such a small dialog, but there are several factors of the dialog that must be properly controlled in order to maintain the type of functionality found in AutoCAD's built-in dialog boxes. Each line of the code will be explained in the text following this example:

```
;;DDTHIRD.LSP
;;
(defun GRID_TOG (val)                    ; [1]
  (if (zerop (atoi VAL))                 ; [2]
    (progn
      (mode_tile "gr_x" 1)               ; [3]
      (mode_tile "gr_y" 1)               ; [4]
      (mode_tile "accept" 2)             ; [5]
    )
```

```
    (progn
      (mode_tile "gr_x" 0)                        ; [6]
      (mode_tile "gr_y" 0)                        ; [7]
      (mode_tile "gr_x" 2)                        ; [8]
      (mode_tile "gr_x" 3)                        ; [9]
))  )

(defun SET_GRX (why)                              ; [10]
  (if (= WHY 1)                                   ; [11]
    (progn
      (set_tile "gr_x" (rtos (atof (get_tile "gr_x"))))    ; [12]
      (mode_tile "gr_y" 2)                        ; [13]
      (mode_tile "gr_y" 3)                        ; [14]
))  )
(defun SET_GRY (why)                              ; [15]
  (if (= WHY 1)                                   ; [16]
     (progn
       (set_tile "gr_y" (rtos (atof (get_tile "gr_y"))))   ; [17]
       (mode_tile "accept" 2)                     ; [18]
))  )
(defun CHECKOUT ()                                ; [19]
  (if (zerop (atoi (get_tile "gr_tog")))          ; [20]
     (setvar "GRIDMODE" 0)                        ; [21]
     (progn
       (setvar "GRIDMODE" 1)                      ; [22]
       (setvar "GRIDUNIT" (list (atof (get_tile "gr_x")) (atof (get_tile "gr_y"))))     ; [23]
))  )
(defun C:GOTHR ()                                 ; [24]
  (setq DCL_ID (load_dialog "DDTHIRD.DCL"))             ; [25]
  (if (not (new_dialog "third" DCL_ID)) (exit))         ; [26]
  (set_tile "gr_tog" (rtos (getvar "GRIDMODE")))        ; [27]
  (set_tile "gr_x" (rtos (car (getvar "GRIDUNIT"))))    ; [28]
  (set_tile "gr_y" (rtos (cadr (getvar "GRIDUNIT"))))   ; [29]
  (if (zerop (getvar "GRIDMODE"))                 ; [30]
     (progn
       (mode_tile "gr_x" 1)                       ; [31]
       (mode_tile "gr_y" 1)                       ; [32]
  ) )
  (action_tile "gr_tog" "(GRID_TOG $value)")            ; [33]
  (action_tile "gr_x" "(SET_GRX $reason)")              ; [34]
  (action_tile "gr_y" "(SET_GRY $reason)")              ; [35]
  (action_tile "accept" "(CHECKOUT)(done_dialog)") ; [36]
  (start_dialog)                                  ; [37]
  (unload_dialog DCL_ID)                          ; [38]
  (command "redraw")                              ; [39]
  (princ)                                         ; [40]
)
```

Documentation for DDTHIRD.LSP

[1] **(defun GRID_TOG (val)** Defines a function to be called by the Grid On toggle.

[2] **(if (zerop (atoi VAL))** If the toggle is off, the value will be zero. The then and else expressions are as follows:

[3] **(mode_tile "gr_x" 1)** Disable X Spacing edit box.

[4] **(mode_tile "gr_y" 1)** Disable Y Spacing edit box.

[5] **(mode_tile "accept" 2)** Set focus to OK button.

(Lines [3]–[5]: THEN)

[6] **(mode_tile "gr_x" 0)** Enable X-Spacing edit box.

[7] **(mode_tile "gr_y" 0)** Enable Y-Spacing edit box.

[8] **(mode_tile "gr_x" 2)** Set focus to X Spacing edit box.

[9] **(mode_tile "gr_x" 3)** Select contents of X spacing edit box.

(Lines [6]–[9]: ELSE)

[10] **(defun SET_GRX (why)** Defines function to be called by X Spacing edit box; uses $reason variable assigned to argument WHY.

[11] **(if (or (= WHY 1) (= WHY 2))** If the user accepts the value (1) or exits the edit box by picking another tile (2), then do the following:

[12] **(set_tile "gr_x" (rtos (atof (get_tile "gr_x"))))** Reset tile value using RTOS defaults.

[13] **(mode_tile "gr_y" 2)** Set focus to Y Spacing edit box.

[14] **(mode_tile "gr_y" 3)** Select contents of Y Spacing edit box.

[15] **(defun SET_GRY (why)** Defines function to be called by Y Spacing edit box, uses $reason variable assigned to argument WHY.

[16] **(if (= WHY 1)** If the user accepted the value, then do the following:

[17] **(set_tile "gr_y" (rtos (atof (get_tile "gr_y"))))** Reset tile value using RTOS defaults.

[18] **(mode_tile "accept" 2)** Set focus to OK button.

[19] **(defun CHECKOUT ()** Defines function to be called by the OK button. The key of the OK button is always "accept". The purpose here is to retrieve the values of the tiles as required and set the appropriate AutoCAD system variables.

[20] **(if (zerop (atoi (get_tile "gr_tog")))** The final course of action is decided here by the values of the tiles at the time the OK button is selected. If the value of the toggle is 0, then the grid is turned off. When the value is 1, then the grid is turned on and the values found in the X Spacing and Y Spacing edit boxes are used to set the new spacing for the grid.

[21] **(setvar "GRIDMODE" 0)** Turns the grid off.

[22] **(setvar "GRIDMODE" 1)** Turns the grid on.

[23] **(setvar "GRIDUNIT"**
(list
(atof (get_tile "gr_x"))
(atof (get_tile "gr_y")) Sets the value for grid spacing to the list composed of the converted value of strings shown in the *X* and *Y* Spacing edit boxes.

[24] **(defun C:GOTHR ()** This is the primary function, defined with command line access.

[25] **(setq DCL_ID (load_dialog "DDTHIRD.DCL"))** Loads the dialog definition code found in DDTHIRD.DCL.

[26] **(if (not (new_dialog "third" DCL_ID)) (exit))** Error trap that loads the dialog box named "third" successfully or exits.

[27] **(set_tile "gr_tog" (rtos (getvar "GRIDMODE")))** Sets the Grid On toggle to according to the current status of the grid.

[28] **(set_tile "gr_x" (rtos (car (getvar "GRIDUNIT"))))** Sets the X Spacing dialog to the current X spacing value.

[29] **(set_tile "gr_y" (rtos (cadr (getvar "GRIDUNIT"))))** Sets the Y Spacing dialog to the current Y spacing value.

[30] **(if (zerop (getvar "GRIDMODE"))** If the grid is not currently on, do the following:

[31] **(mode_tile "gr_x" 1)** Disable the X Spacing edit box.

[32] **(mode_tile "gr_y" 1)** Disable the Y Spacing edit box.

[33] **(action_tile "gr_tog" "(GRID_TOG $value)")** Defines the action for the Grid On toggle: calls GRID_TOG using the current value of the $value variable.

[34] **(action_tile "gr_x" "(SET_GRX $reason)")** Defines the action for the X Spacing edit box: calls SET_GRX using the current value of the $reason variable.

[35] **(action_tile "gr_y" "(SET_GRY $reason)")** Defines the action for the Y Spacing edit box: calls SET_GRY using the current value of the $reason variable.

[36] **(action_tile "accept" "(CHECKOUT)(done_dialog)")** Defines the action for the OK button: calls the CHECKOUT function and issues a done_dialog to end the dialog session. Note that when redefining the OK button, a done_dialog expression must be specified in order for the button to properly end the dialog session.

[37] **(start_dialog)** Starts the dialog session.

[38] **(unload_dialog DCL_ID)** After the session is complete, unloads no longer needed DCL definition code.

[39] **(command "redraw")** Redraws the screen to refresh the grid display.

[40] **(princ)** A quiet exit and a close to the function definition code.

The code in the previous section demonstrates some of the functionality that can be expected in a dialog box by every level of AutoCAD user. It is important to both maintain control and provide a great degree of flexibility for the user to move freely to applicable tiles as desired. An additional aspect, however, is error checking and control. Most applications will work well as long as the user enters appropriate values in the edit boxes. However, the edit box is a very flexible medium, and without run time validation of data, may allow the user to enter inappropriate data. Unfortunately, functions such as INITGET and GETKWORD cannot be utilized in a dialog session. The following sequence demonstrates one possible way of handling data validation at run time in the DDTHIRD dialog.

1. Change the *ok_cancel;* specification in DDTHIRD.DCL to *ok_cancel_err;*.

2. Now that an error tile exists, the key "*error*" can be referenced to display error messages at the bottom of the dialog box in the error tile (*errtile*). The SET_TILE function is used to set the value of this tile as well. To first test for the appropriate value for errtile, a validation function can be defined in DDTHIRD.LSP. Such a function would be called instead of the current function calls in the action expressions. Note that the $value, $reason, and $key variables are expected and therefore, must be passed by the calling expressions.

```
(defun VALIDATE (val why key)             ; uses $value, &reason, and $key
  (if (= "." (substr VAL 1 1)) (setq VAL (strcat "0" VAL)))     ; error trap
  (if (not
        (or
           (= (type (read VAL)) 'REAL)    ; is it a real number?
           (= (type (read VAL)) 'INT)     ; is it an integer?
     ) )
        (progn                            ;THEN it wasn't a number!
          (mode_tile KEY 3)               ; return focus to tile being checked
          (set_tile "error" "Invalid entry") ; sets error tile value
        )
        (progn                            ; ELSE it was a number!
          (set_tile "error" "")           ; blanks out error tile
          (if (= KEY "gr_x")              ; if this was the X tile,
             (SET_GRX WHY)                ; THEN call action for setting the grid X spacing.
             (SET_GRY WHY)                ; ELSE call action for setting the grid Y spacing.
))      ) )
```

3. In the ACTION_TILE action expressions, change the current call to the SET_GRX and SET_GRY functions to a call to the VALIDATE function with the appropriate variables passed as arguments. The VALIDATE function will call these functions when the data found in the edit box is validated.

Let's Review...

1. The SET_TILE function is used to specify default values for tiles within a dialog box.
2. All tiles that are required to do something when picked or given a value should have an action defined using ACTION_TILE expression.
3. The KEY attribute is required to be able to work with a given tile. The key attribute is a case-sensitive text string.
4. Any functions which change the display or require user input outside of the dialog interface cannot be used while a dialog box is active.
5. The MODE_TILE function can be used to set the state of a tile.
6. Run-time variables associated with dialog box tiles include *$key, $value, $data, $reason, $x,* and *$y*.
7. Run time validation of data entries in a dialog box can be critical to the proper functioning of your application.

LIST BOXES AND POPUP LISTS

Multiple choice has always been the easiest method of selection and decision making. The list box provides a multiple choice-style interface where a list of available selections for any given data specification are presented to the user, allowing selection only from the list. The two types of lists available are the list_box and the popup_list. Refer back to chapter 17 for information on how each are used. There are three AutoLISP functions associated only with lists—START_LIST, ADD_LIST, and END_LIST.

The START_LIST Function

The *START_LIST function* starts the process of building a list. It specifies to the PDB facility the key of the list which is being defined or manipulated in subsequent code, and what type of operation is being performed. The syntax for the START_LIST function is:

```
(start_list  KEY [OPERATION [INDEX]])
```

As stated, the KEY argument specifies the key of the list being worked with. The optional OPERATION argument indicates what is being done to the list as shown in Fig. 18-5.

Value	Meaning
1	Change selected list contents
2	Append new list entry
3	Delete old list and create new list

Fig. 18-5. Possible values of the optional OPERATION argument.

Note that if no OPERATION argument is specified, the default is 3. The optional INDEX is used only when the OPERATION argument is specified and then only when the value of OPERATION is 1. An append automatically occurs at the end of a list and the OPERATION argument deletes the existing contents and starts over again. The INDEX argument is used to tell the PDB which member of the list is being changed. It is important to remember that the INDEX argument for this list is used as a zero-based index. As with the nth function, this means that the first item in the list is index number 0, the second is index number 1, etc.

The ADD_LIST Function

Once a list has been "opened" by START_LIST, the subsequent ADD_LIST expressions are used to make changes or additions to the list. Since the key of the list being worked with is already known, the only information that needs to be provided to ADD_LIST is a string specifying the item to add. The syntax for ADD_LIST is:

```
(add_list ITEM)
```

In the event that the operation specified is 1, only one ADD_LIST is necessary, and its item argument is used to replace the current item at the position specified by index. In the event that no index position is specified for a change operation, it defaults to 0. For operation numbers 2 and 3, any number of ADD_LIST expressions can be evaluated. If a large number or variable number of items need to be added to the list, it can be a redundant task to individually specify each item with its own ADD_LIST expression. It is much easier to use some of the available advanced list-handling functions. In this case, the MAPCAR function works well. By using MAPCAR to process the function and specifying each item in a list, the entire process can be greatly simplified. For example:

```
(mapcar 'add_list (list "A" "B" "C" "D"))
```

This expression would add the text items "A","B", "C", and "D" to the list that is currently open.

The END_LIST Function

Once all of the required items have been added to a list, it is necessary to end the list creation process by using the *END_LIST function*. This function is called with no arguments and closes the list that is currently open. The syntax for END_LIST is:

```
(end_list)
```

Once the current list is ended with END_LIST, construction of the list is halted. The following code demonstrates the use of the DCL list operators. Remember that the same three functions apply to both list boxes and popup lists. This example uses a popup list.

```
//DDFOURTH.DCL
// Presents a list of layers to the user.
fourth : dialog {
        label           = "Select Layer";
        : popup_list {
          label         = "New Current Layer:";
          mnemonic      = "N";
          key           = "lyr_pop";
          allow_accept  = true;
          width         = 32;
        }
        ok_cancel;
}
```

Study the controlling code for this dialog shown below; then review the explanatory section that follows.

```
;;DDFOURTH.LSP
;;
(defun CHECKOUT ()                                          ; [1]
  (setq LD (tblsearch "LAYER" (nth (atoi (get_tile "lyr_pop")) LL))     ; [2]
        LN (cdr (assoc 2 LD))                               ; [3]
        LS (cdr (assoc 70 LD))                              ; [4]
  )
  (if (and                                                  ; [5]
       (/= 1 LS)
       (/= 65 LS)
     )
     (progn                                                 ; [6]
```

```
        (setvar "CLAYER" (nth (atoi (get_tile "lyr_pop")) LL))      ; [7]
        (done_dialog)                                               ; [8]
      )
      (alert "Selected layer is frozen!")                           ; [9]
) )
  (defun C:GOFOR ()                                                 ; [10]
   (setq DCL_ID (load_dialog "DDFOURTH.DCL"))                       ; [11]
   (if (not (new_dialog "fourth" DCL_ID)) (exit))
   (start_list "lyr_pop")                                           ; [12]
   (setq LL '()                                                     ; [13]
         NL (tblnext "LAYER" T)
         IDX 0
   )                                                                ; [14]
   (while NL                                                        ; [15]
          (if (= (getvar "CLAYER") (cdr (assoc 2 NL)))              ; [16]
             (setq CL IDX)                                          ; [17]
             (setq IDX (1+ IDX))
          )                                                         ; [18]
          (setq LL (append LL (list (cdr (assoc 2 NL))))            ; [19]
                NL (tblnext "LAYER"))                               ; [20]
   )      )
   (mapcar 'add_list LL)                                            ; [21]
   (end_list)                                                       ; [22]
   (set_tile "lyr_pop" (itoa CL))                                   ; [23]
   (action_tile "lyr_pop" "(if (= $reason 4) (mode_tile \"accept\" 2))")  ; [24]
   (action_tile "accept" "(CHECKOUT)")                              ; [25]
   (start_dialog)                                                   ; [26]
   (unload_dialog DCL_ID)                                           ; [27]
   (princ)                                                          ; [28]
)
```

Documentation for DDFOURTH

[1] (defun CHECKOUT () Defines the CHECKOUT function called by the OK button.

[2] (setq LD (tblsearch "LAYER" (nth (atoi (get_tile "lyr_pop")) LL)) The variable LD is set to the symbol table data for the layer name found in the popup list.

[3] LN (cdr (assoc 2 LD)) Sets LN to the Layer Name

[4] LS (cdr (assoc 70 LD)) Sets LS to the Layer Status

[5] (if (and If both of these conditions are met...
(/= 1 LS) LS setting of 1 means layer is frozen.
(/= 65 LS) LS setting of 65 means layer is frozen.
) and

[6] (progn If test returned T, then layer is not frozen.

[7] (setvar "CLAYER" LN) Set the specified layer to current.

[8] (done_dialog) End the dialog session.

[9] (alert "Selected layer is frozen!") Or else, issue alert and resume dialog.

[10] **(defun C:GOFOR ()** Defines main function.

[11] **(setq DCL_ID (load_dialog "DDFOURTH.DCL"))**
(if (not (new_dialog "fourth" DCL_ID)) (exit)) This code loads the DCL file and specified dialog definition.

[12] **(start_list "lyr_pop")** Begins the definition for the list with the key "lyr_pop".

[13] **(setq LL '()** LL is the list that will hold layer names.
NL (tblnext "LAYER" T) NL is the NextLayer name.
IDX 0 IDX is an index symbol for position tracking.

[14] **)** Ends SETQ.

[15] **(while NL** While there is a new layer name to process, NL has value. NL will be nil when the last layer name has been processed.

[16] **(if (= (getvar "CLAYER") (cdr (assoc 2 NL)))** On each iteration, NL is checked to see if it is the current layer.

[17] **(setq CL IDX)**
(setq IDX (1+ IDX)) If so, CL holds the current IDX value. Or else, increment the index value.

[18] **)** Ends IF.

[19] **(setq LL (append LL (list (cdr (assoc 2 NL)))))** Adds the new layer name to the list LL.

[20] **NL (tblnext "LAYER")** Sets NL to the next layer.

[21] **(mapcar 'add_list LL)** Applies ADD_LIST to each element of LL, adding the items to the open list "lyr_pop".

[22] **(end_list)** Closes the list "lyr_pop".

[23] **(set_tile "lyr_pop" (itoa CL))** Sets the current value of the list "lyr_pop" to the current layer name using the held IDX value.

[24] **(action_tile "lyr_pop" "(if (= $reason 4) (mode_tile \"accept\" 2))")** The action expression for the list. If the user presses [ENTER] while a list item is highlighted (callback code 4), then the keyboard focus is shifted to the OK button.

[25] **(action_tile "accept" "(CHECKOUT)")** The OK button is redefined to run the CHECKOUT function. This enables testing and validating of data while the dialog is still active.

[26] **(start_dialog)** Starts the dialog session.

[27] **(unload_dialog DCL_ID)** Unloads the dialog definition data from memory.

[28] **(princ)** Quiet exit.

IMAGES AND IMAGE BUTTONS

Images and image buttons provide the capability to incorporate graphics into your dialog boxes. Graphic images greatly enhance your ability to communicate with the user. Such images can be used purely as ornamentation. For example, you might decide to place your company logo on a dialog box. More useful applications might include showing the current status of settings in the dialog session—similar to the aperture size display on the Running Object Snap dialog box. Images can also be used as buttons, allowing the user to quickly select an easily recognizable image in a dialog session. When used as buttons, either the entire image can respond as a single button or an image can be used to provide multiple options to the user. The coordinates of the point on the image that the user actually picked can be referenced to produce different results based on what part of the image the user actually selected. A good example of this is provided in AutoCAD's Viewpoint Presets dialog box.

The graphics portion of the image can be created either as an AutoCAD slide file (.SLD) using the MSLIDE command or the vectors can be described individually and drawn directly on the image tile.

The START_IMAGE Function

Producing and controlling an image tile requires several steps. First, the image must be opened (similar to list boxes). To open an image, the *START_IMAGE function* is used:

```
(start_image KEY)
```

The KEY argument is a string referring to the key of the image being constructed. The base image will be blank, but will have an assigned size as specified by the DCL file. The default color of this blank image is sensitive to the current color of the AutoCAD graphics screen background. The default image color depends on the platform and the current color scheme, so it is usually desirable to set the background color of the image to a color compatible with the image shown on the tile. Obviously, vectors drawn the same color as the background will not be visible. Therefore, the next step is often generating the desired color of background.

The FILL_IMAGE Function

The *FILL_IMAGE function* allows a filled rectangle to be drawn in any color in the current tile. It can be drawn in any size that fits within the available space, up to and including the entire tile. The syntax for the FILL_IMAGE function is as follows:

```
(fill_image X Y WID HGT COLOR)
```

Similar to the list box, the image key is only required for opening the image and is specified in the START_IMAGE expression. Any image tile-related functions used between the START_IMAGE and a subsequent END_IMAGE function are automatically applied to the image that is currently open. The first two arguments—X and Y—specify the X axis and Y axis start point for the filled rectangle. The next two arguments—WID and HGT—specify the width and height of the filled area. Finally, the COLOR argument specifies the color of the filled area. It is important to remember that the starting point for a FILL_IMAGE function is always interpreted as the upper-left corner, and the direction of construction is down and to the right. Image tiles use a Cartesian coordinate system like AutoCAD, but the point of origin (0,0) is found at the upper-left of the image rather than the lower-left, and the positive Y direction is toward the bottom of the image. The positive X direction is still to the right of the image.

The upper coordinate values for a particular image are based on the specified dimensions of the tile as described in the DCL file, the platform you are using and the characteristics of the current system font. They can be retrieved from the currently open image by using the DIMX_TILE and DIMY_TILE functions:

```
(dimx_tile KEY)
(dimy_tile KEY)
```

Both of these functions return their respective dimensions from the specified image in tile unit coordinates. This is useful for setting a background color for a specific image. To fill a blank image, use the FILL_IMAGE function with the desired fill color. Since a FILL_IMAGE expression requires the point coordinates for two of the corners to fill an image completely, you can use 0,0 as the first corner and the values returned by DIMX_TILE and DIMY_TILE for the other corner:

```
(setq WID (dimx_tile "imagekey")
      HGT (dimy_tile "imagekey")
      CLR 4
)
(fill_image 0 0 WID HGT CLR)
```

This has the effect of filling in the entire image area of the tile with the key imagekey with color number 4 (cyan). Overriding system color schemes with specific background colors in an image tile can prevent unexpected results.

PROFESSIONAL TIP

It can be difficult to provide absolute coordinates for an image that will produce the same results on all platforms (Windows, DOS, Windows NT, etc.) because coordinate values used may vary depending on current system settings. It can be most efficiently accomplished by analyzing the current coordinate extents and specifying distances as a *percentage* of the overall image. In order to determine the overall dimensions of an image tile in terms of image units, utilize the DIMX_TILE and DIMY_TILE functions, then specify the required vectors as a percentage of this number.

This next example uses absolute tile coordinates to define the image for the tile. Create these files as shown and run the dialog session. The controlling AutoLISP code is explained following the program code.

```
//DDFIFTH.DCL
//Image tile example.
fifth : dialog {
      label           = "Image Tile Dialog Example";
      : row {
        : image {
          key           = "logo";
          width         = 14;
          fixed_width   = true;
          fixed_height  = true;
          aspect_ratio  = 1;
        }
```

```
        : boxed_column {
          width              = 16;
          : paragraph {
            : text_part {
              value          = "LISP-r-us, Inc.";
            }
            : text_part {
              value          = "  Quality Code...";
            }
            : text_part {
              value          = "    While-u-wait";
            }
            : text_part {
              value          = "       (and wait...)";
            }
        }}
      }
      ok_only;
}
```

Now create the AutoLISP file DDFIFTH.LSP as shown here:

```
;;DDFIFTH.LSP
;;
(defun C:GOFIF ()                                                  ; [1]
  (setq DCL_ID (load_dialog "DDFIFTH.DCL"))                        ; [2]
  (new_dialog "fifth" DCL_ID)
  (start_image "logo")                                             ; [3]
  (fill_image 0 0 (dimx_tile "logo")(dimy_tile "logo") 7)          ; [4]
  (mapcar 'fill_image                                              ; [5]
          (list 91 94 97 100 103 91 91 114 114)
          (list 3 6 9 12 15 26 3 26 3)
          (list 32 26 20 14 8 9 9 9 9)
          (list 32 26 20 14 8 9 9 9 9)
          (list 1 2 5 1 7 3 6 6 3)
  )
  (mapcar 'vector_image                                            ; [6]
          (list 10 10 22 28 34 34 28 28 39 39 45 45)
          (list 10 20 20 20 20 15 15 10 20 10 10 15)
          (list 10 17 22 34 34 28 28 34 39 45 45 39)
          (list 20 20 10 20 15 15 10 10 10 10 15 15)
          (list 1 1 1 1 1 1 1 1 1 1 1 1)
  )
  (mapcar 'vector_image                                            ; [7]
          (list 45 45 65 65 52  83  83  89  99  93  93  99 99)
          (list 36 36 36 60 60 106 116 116 106 106 111 111 116)
          (list 45 65 65 45 65  83  89  89  93  93  99  99 93)
          (list 86 36 60 60 86 116 116 106 106 111 111  116 116)
          (list 1 1 1 1 1 1 1 1 1 1 1 1 1)
  )
  (end_image)                                                      ; [8]
  (start_dialog)                                                   ; [9]
)
```

Documentation for DDFIFTH.LSP

[1] **(defun C:GOFIF ()** Defines the command line function GOFIF.

[2] **(setq DCL_ID (load_dialog "DDFIFTH.DCL"))**
(new_dialog "fifth" DCL_ID) These lines load the DCL file and the dialog description.

[3] **(start_image "logo")** Opens the image "logo".

[4] **(fill_image 0 0 (dimx_tile "logo")(dimy_tile "logo") 7)** Sets the image background to color 7 (black or white, depending on the current AutoCAD graphics screen background color).

[5] **(mapcar 'fill_image**
(list 91 94 97 100 103 91 91 114 114)
(list 3 6 9 12 15 26 3 26 3)
(list 32 26 20 14 8 9 9 9 9)
(list 32 26 20 14 8 9 9 9 9)
(list 1 2 5 1 7 3 6 6 3)
) These fill_image calls generate the design in the upper-right corner. The use of mapcar here is similar to the explanation below in the vector_image description.

[6] **(mapcar 'vector_image**
(list 10 10 22 28 34 34 28 28 39 39 45 45)
(list 10 20 20 20 20 15 15 10 20 10 10 15)
(list 10 17 22 34 34 28 28 34 39 45 45 39)
(list 20 20 10 20 15 15 10 10 10 10 15 15)
(list 1 1 1 2 3 4 5 6 1 1 1 1)
) This expression draws vectors on the open image to form the word LISP. Notice the use of the mapcar function to consolidate 12 separate vector_image expressions. (All 25 vector descriptions in this example could be placed in the same mapcar expression. They are separated here to enhance readability). Large amounts of data can be much more manageable when contained in lists, and processed with list operators.

[7] **(mapcar 'vector_image**
(list 45 45 65 65 52 83 83 89 99 93 93 99 99)
(list 36 36 36 60 60 106 116 116 106 106 111 111 116)
(list 45 65 65 45 65 83 89 89 93 93 99 99 93)
(list 86 36 60 60 86 116 116 106 106 111 111 116 116)
(list 1 1 1 1 1 1 1 1 2 3 4 5 6)
) The second half of the mapcar above. In each of these expressions, notice the last list–this supplies the color argument. Each S is drawn using colors 2 through 6. All of the other vectors are drawn using color number 1.

[8] **(end_image)** Closes the current image, ending its definition.

[9] **(start_dialog)** Start the dialog session.

PROFESSIONAL TIP

When developing the previous application program, it was necessary to determine what coordinates were to be used to generate the characters as shown. For speed and convenience, during the development phase the image tile was specified in the DCL file as being an *image_button* rather than just an *image*. Image buttons provide interactivity not available with an image. By assigning an action using the ALERT function and the $X and $Y variables, the selected coordinates can be displayed on-screen:

```
(action_tile "logo" "(alert (strcat (itoa $X) \",\" (itoa $Y)))")
```

Use this technique to determine the coordinates necessary to produce the desired image. When you are finished developing the application, change the specification in the DCL file back to image from image_button, and remove the ACTION_TILE expression from the AutoLISP file.

Simple image tiles are for display only, and usually require no handling beyond the definition of the image unless the image is to be updated based on current user settings within the dialog. When an image is created using an image_button tile, the image itself can be interactive with the user. Picking an image tile with the cursor will start the action associated with the tile, and updates the $X and $Y variables. The following example uses these returned coordinates to determine the action by using a cond expression that tests the $x and $y values. Enter the following descriptive DCL code into a file named DDSIXTH.DCL:

```
//DDSIXTH.DCL
//
sixth : dialog {
        label                = "Image Button Example";
        : row {
          : image_button {
            key              = "boxes";
            width            = 14;
            fixed_width      = true;
            fixed_height     = true;
            aspect_ratio     = 1;
          }
        }
        : row {
          spacer_1;
          : image {
            key              = "col_swatch";
            width            = 6;
            fixed_width      = true;
            fixed_height     = true;
            aspect_ratio     = 1;
          }
        }
        ok_only;
}
```

Now, enter the AutoLISP code below into a file named DDSIXTH.LSP:

```
;;DDSIXTH.LSP
;;
(defun PICK_COL (X Y)                                ; [1]
  (start_image "col_swatch")                         ; [2]
  (cond                                              ; [3]
    ( (and (<= X 63) (<= Y 63))
      (fill_image 0 0 (dimx_tile "col_swatch")(dimy_tile "col_swatch") 1)
    )
    ( (and (> X 63) (<= Y 63))
      (fill_image 0 0 (dimx_tile "col_swatch")(dimy_tile "col_swatch") 2)
    )
    ( (and (<= X 63) (> Y 63))
      (fill_image 0 0 (dimx_tile "col_swatch")(dimy_tile "col_swatch") 3)
    )
    ( (and (> X 63) (> Y 63))
      (fill_image 0 0 (dimx_tile "col_swatch")(dimy_tile "col_swatch") 4)
    )
  )
  (end_image)                                        ; [4]
)
(defun C:GOSIX ()                                    ; [5]
  (setq DCL_ID (load_dialog "DDSIXTH.DCL"))          ; [6]
  (new_dialog"2sixth" DCL_ID)
  (start_image "boxes")                              ; [7]
  (fill_image 0 0 (dimx_tile "boxes") (dimy_tile "boxes") 7)
  (mapcar 'fill_image                                ; [8]
          (list 0 63 0 63)
          (list 0 0 63 63)
          (list 63 62 63 62)
          (list 63 63 62 62)
          (list 1 2 3 4)
  )
  (end_image)                                        ; [9]
  (start_image "col_swatch")                         ; [10]
  (fill_image 0 0 (dimx_tile "col_swatch")(dimy_tile "col_swatch") -15)
  (end_image)
  (action_tile "boxes" "(PICK_COL $x $y)")           ; [11]
  (start_dialog)                                     ; [12]
)                                                    ; [13]
```

Documentation for DDSIXTH.LSP

[1] (defun PICK_COL (X Y) Defines the function called by the action expression for the "boxes" image tile.

[2] (start_image "col_swatch") Begins run time redefinition of the "col_swatch" image tile.

[3] **(cond**
((and ((<= X 63) ((<= Y 63))
(fill_image 0 0 (dimx_tile "col_swatch")(dimy_tile "col_swatch") 1)
)
((and (> X 63) ((<= Y 63))
(fill_image 0 0 (dimx_tile "col_swatch")(dimy_tile "col_swatch") 2)
)
((and ((<= X 63) (> Y 63))
(fill_image 0 0 (dimx_tile "col_swatch")(dimy_tile "col_swatch") 3)
)
((and (> X 63) (> Y 63))
(fill_image 0 0 (dimx_tile "col_swatch")(dimy_tile "col_swatch") 4)
)
) This COND expression determines the location of the user pick and recolors the "col_swatch" tile accordingly.

[4] **(end_image)** Ends the image definition and the PICK_COL definition.

[5] **(defun C:GOSIX ()** Begins the primary function definition.

[6] **(setq DCL_ID (load_dialog "DDSIXTH.DCL"))**
(new_dialog "sixth" DCL_ID) Standard DCL definition loading expressions.

[7] **(start_image "boxes")** Starts the image definition for the "boxes" tile.

[8] **(mapcar 'fill_image**
(list 0 63 0 63)
(list 0 0 63 63)
(list 63 62 63 62)
(list 63 63 62 62)
(list 1 2 3 4)
) Places four colored rectangles on the image.

[9] **(end_image)** Ends the image definition.

[10] **(start_image "col_swatch")**
(fill_image 0 0 (dimx_tile "col_swatch")(dimy_tile "col_swatch") -15)
(end_image) This section defines the "col_swatch" image tile as being the same color as the current dialog background.

[11] **(action_tile "boxes" "(PICK_COL $x $y)")** Calls PICK_COL when the user picks the image button.

[12] **(start_dialog)** Starts the dialog session.

[13]) Ends the C:GOSIX function definition.

The previous example uses a reference to color number -15 to specify the color of the dialog background. The table in Fig. 18-6 shows the available numeric codes for accessing current system color values.

Color Number	Definition
–2	Current background color of AutoCAD's graphics screen.
–15	Current dialog box background color.
–16	Current color of dialog text (foreground color).
–18	Current dialog box line color.

Fig. 18-6. Available numeric codes for accessing current system color values.

While vectors and fill areas can be used to create simple images, complex images may be difficult to create using these tools. It may be easier to create the image in AutoCAD using familiar drawing tools, then create a slide file that can be displayed in the image tile. A slide file is displayed using the *SLIDE_IMAGE function:*

```
(slide_image X1 Y1 WID HGT SLDNAME)
```

The X1 and Y1 arguments are used to specify the tile coordinate location of the upper-left corner of the slide. The WID and HGT specify the size of the area the slide will be displayed in within the tile. Multiple slides can be displayed on a single tile if necessary, but positioning must be carefully planned so the images do not overlay each other. Also, when displaying a subsequent slide the first slide will only be overwritten by vectors on the second slide, not by the background. This will cause both slides to be visible at the same time. The best approach is to first overwrite the existing image on the tile with a FILL_IMAGE expression, then display the subsequent slide.

NOTE

Slides are displayed in the same format as they are created. This is especially important to Windows users, since you can change the aspect ratio of the AutoCAD for Windows graphics screen. When AutoCAD is maximized, the graphics window area is a rectangle, which is much wider than it is tall. If a slide created as a rectangle is displayed in a square tile, the image will not fit the tile well and will tend to be too small. This can be corrected by resizing the AutoCAD graphics window to a shape that is proportional to the image tile. Then, zoom the display so that the slide geometry fills the screen and create the slide.

PROFESSIONAL TIP

Solid fill areas, including wide polylines, will be displayed as outlines in a slide image. Hatch patterns dense enough to appear solid on an image can be slow to display. This problem is best handled by using AutoCAD's SHADE command before creating the slide. All solid fill areas are shaded in along with any existing 3D geometry, and shading *can* be displayed properly in an image tile.

To see how the SLIDE_IMAGE function is used, the following example provides a dialog box with an image tile that toggles through a set of three slides, and performs a command as depicted by the slide. Enter the following DCL code into a file named DDSEVEN.DCL:

```
//DDSEVEN.DCL
//
seven : dialog {
        label                  = "Slide Image Example";
        : row {
          spacer_0;
         : image_button {
           color               = dialog_background;
           width               = 10;
           aspect_ratio        = 1;
           key                 = "_dlgimg";
           alignment           = centered;
         }
         spacer_0;
       }
       ok_cancel;
}
```

Now, enter the following AutoLISP code into a file named DDSEVEN.LSP:

```
;;DDSEVEN.LSP
;;
;; First, define an image toggler...
(defun NXTIMG ()
  (if (= 2 IMAGE_COUNTER)                                              ;[1]
     (setq IMAGE_COUNTER 0)                                            ;[2]
     (setq IMAGE_COUNTER (1+ IMAGE_COUNTER))                           ;[3]
  )
  (start_image "_dlgimg")                                              ;[4]
  (fill_image 0 0 (dimx_tile "_dlgimg") (dimy_tile "_dlgimg") -15)     ;[5]
  (slide_image 0 0 (dimx_tile "_dlgimg") (dimy_tile "_dlgimg")         ;[6]
           (nth IMAGE_COUNTER IMAGE_LIST)                              ;[7]
  )
  (end_image)                                                          ;[8]
  (setq OPTION (nth IMAGE_COUNTER IMAGE_LIST))                         ;[9]
)
;;
;;Now, a function to setup and display dialog box...
(defun C:GOSEV ()
  (setq IMAGE_COUNTER 0                                                ;[10]
        IMAGE_LIST (list "LINE" "ARC" "CIRCLE")                        ;
        IMAGE_CURRENT (nth IMAGE_COUNTER IMAGE_LIST)                   ;
        OPTION (car IMAGE_LIST)                                        ;
  )
  (setq DCL_ID (load_dialog "DDSEVEN.DCL"))                            ;[11]
  (new_dialog "seven" DCL_ID)                                          ;
  (start_image "_dlgimg")                                              ;[12]
  (slide_image 0 0 (dimx_tile "_dlgimg") (dimy_tile "_dlgimg") "LINE") ;[13]
```

```
(end_image)                                          ;[14]
(action_tile "_dlgimg" "(NXTIMG)")                   ;[15]
(start_dialog)                                       ;[16]
(cond                                                ;[17]
 ((= "LINE" OPTION)
  (command "._LINE")
 )
 ((= "ARC" OPTION)
  (command "._ARC")
 )
 ((= "CIRCLE" OPTION)
  (command "._CIRCLE")
 )
)
)
```

Documentation for DDSEVEN.LSP

[1] **(if (= 2 IMAGE_COUNTER)** Checks to see the counter on last item.

[2] **(setq IMAGE_COUNTER 0)** If so, then reset to 0.

[3] **(setq IMAGE_COUNTER (1+ IMAGE_COUNTER))** Else, increment counter.

[4] **(start_image "_dlgimg")** Starts image definition.

[5] **(fill_image 0 0 (dimx_tile "_dlgimg") (dimy_tile "_dlgimg") -15)** Cover any previous image with the background color.

[6] **(slide_image 0 0 (dimx_tile "_dlgimg") (dimy_tile "_dlgimg")** Locates and sizes the slide image described in [7].

[7] **(nth IMAGE_COUNTER IMAGE_LIST)** Gets the slide file using the name stored in the image_counter position, in the list image_list.

[8] **(end_image)** Ends the image tile definition.

[9] **(setq OPTION (nth IMAGE_COUNTER IMAGE_LIST))** Updates the OPTION variable to reflect the current image.

[10] **(setq IMAGE_COUNTER 0)**
IMAGE_LIST (list "LINE" "ARC" "CIRCLE")
IMAGE_CURRENT (nth IMAGE_COUNTER IMAGE_LIST)
OPTION (car IMAGE_LIST)
) This sequence initializes all of the required variables.

[11] **(setq DCL_ID (load_dialog "DDSEVEN.DCL"))**
(new_dialog "seven" DCL_ID) Standard DCL definition loading expression.

[12] **(start_image "_dlgimg")** Starts initial definition of image "_dlgimg".

[13] **(slide_image 0 0 (dimx_tile "_dlgimg") (dimy_tile "_dlgimg") "LINE")** Initializes image tile with slide image for "LINE".

[14] **(end_image)** Ends the image definition.

[15] **(action_tile "_dlgimg" "(NXTIMG)")** Calls NXTIMG when you pick the image button.

[16] **(start_dialog)** Starts the dialog session.

[17] **(cond ...**

```
  ((= "LINE" OPTION)
    (command "._LINE")
  )
  ((= "ARC" OPTION)
    (command "._ARC")
  )
  ((= "CIRCLE" OPTION)
    (command "._CIRCLE")
  )
) Performs action based on OPTION value.
```

Let's Review...

1. The AutoLISP functions used only for controlling lists and popup lists include START_LIST, ADD_LIST, and END_LIST.
2. Images greatly enhance your ability to communicate with the user.
3. The START_IMAGE function opens an image tile for the definition process.
4. The FILL_IMAGE function can be used to set the color for all or part of an image tile.
5. The DIMX_TILE and DIMY_TILE provide a convenient means of finding the height and width of an image.
6. The SLIDE_IMAGE function is used to display a standard AutoCAD slide file in a dialog box, but simple line images can be drawn directly on the tile by using the VECTOR_IMAGE function.

USING SLIDERS

Sliders provide a fast and easy way to adjust numerical values on a relative scale. Incorporating sliders in your dialog boxes, where appropriate, can increase functionality and user friendliness. The slider, like most other tiles, can be assigned an action. A common dynamic application for a slider action is to update another tile on the dialog box.

In the following example, a slider is created that allows the user to select a number between 0 and 100. The current value of the slider is displayed in a TEXT_PART TILE, and it is dynamically updated with the movement of the slider. Enter the following descriptive DCL code into a file named DDEIGHT.DCL:

```
//DDEIGHT.DCL
//
eight : dialog {
      label = "Interactive Slider Example";
      : column {
        : row {
          : text_part {
            value = "The Slider Number is: ";
          }
          : text_part {
            value = "50";
            key = "_numtxt";
          }
        }
        :row {
        spacer_0;
          : text_part {
            value = "0";
            align = right;
          }
          : slider {
            key = "_slider";
            value = "50";
            max_value = 100;
            min_value = 0;
            big_increment = 10;
            small_increment = 1;
            fixed_width = true;
            width = 20;
          }
          : text_part {
            value = "100";
            align = left;
          }
        }
      }
      ok_only;
}
```

Now, create a file named DDEIGHT.LSP using the following code:

```
;;DDEIGHT.LSP
;;
(defun C:DDEIGHT ()
  (setq DCL_ID (load_dialog "DDEIGHT.DCL"))
  (new_dialog "eight" DCL_ID)
  (action_tile "_slider" "(set_tile \"_numtxt\" (setq VAL $value))")
  (start_dialog)
  (alert (strcat "Your final slider value was: " VAL))
  (princ)
)
```

In this example, the ACTION_TILE statement deserves some additional explanation. Here, the action is defined as a SET_TILE expression that assigns the current value of the slider to be the current value of the TEXT_PART whose key is "_numtxt". Each time the slider is moved, the text is instantly updated. At the same time, the $value is stored in a variable named VAL for use after the dialog session ends (in this case, by an ALERT expression).

By combining a slider with an edit box, versatility is increased because input can be supplied at either end, with both tiles automatically updating the other. In the following example, this concept is demonstrated. Create a DCL file named DDNINTH.DCL using the following code:

```
//DDNINTH.DCL
//
nine : dialog {
        label = "2nd Interactive Slider Example";
        : column {
          : row {
            : edit_box {
              label  = "The Slider Number is: ";
              value = "50";
              key    = "_ebox";
            }
          }
          :row {
          spacer_0;
            : text_part {
              value = "0";
              align  = right;
            }
            : slider {
              key = "_slider";
              value = "50";
              max_value = 100;
              min_value = 0;
              big_increment = 10;
              small_increment = 1;
              fixed_width = true;
              width = 20;
            }
            : text_part {
              value = "100";
              align  = left;
            }
          }
        }
        ok_only;
}
```

Next, create an AutoLISP program file named DDNINTH.LSP with the following code:

```
(defun C:GONINE ()
  (setq DCL_ID (load_dialog "DDNINTH.DCL"))
  (new_dialog "nine" DCL_ID)
  (action_tile "_slider" "(set_tile \"_ebox\" (setq VAL $value))")
  (action_tile "_ebox" "(set_tile \"_slider\" (setq VAL $value))")
  (start_dialog)
  (alert (strcat "Your final slider value was: " VAL))
)
```

Notice that this example provides complimentary action statements that automatically update the other tile. If desired, error checking could be built in to prevent the user from entering values less than 0 or greater than 100 in the edit box. This example provides no such error checking.

DIALOG DESIGN CONSIDERATIONS

When designing a dialog box, the primary concern is that your dialog box presents the user with the same style of interface provided by AutoCAD's built-in dialog boxes. Basic functionality should be the same, with tab stops and mnemonics carefully planned. The layout of a dialog box is important as well. A clean and sensible appearance makes a dialog session easier for the user. The following section briefly discusses techniques for getting the most out of your dialog sessions.

Keyboard Mnemonics

Keyboard mnemonics are a familiar tool for most computer users and should be made available whereever appropriate. Remember that different users have different preferences regarding keyboard and pointing devices. While some users may prefer to point each time they want to change the keyboard focus, others might wish to keep their hands on the keyboard. Providing keyboard mnemonics generates no significant overhead and takes only seconds to put into place, so it is always best to include them in your dialog sessions.

Sound planning of your mnemonics is very important. Depending on the number of user tiles in your dialog session, you may need to provide several mnemonic options. Where possible, a unique letter should be used. Note the letters X and Y in the sample program DDTHIRD. This makes them prime candidates for selection as mnemonics. In some cases, however, you may not have an adequate selection of unique characters. You may need to be a bit more creative in your selection of mnemonics for such a dialog box. A good example of this is provided in AutoCAD's built-in Drawing Aids dialog box (accessed with the DDRMODES command). Note the handling of mnemonics with the tiles referencing X and Y values.

Although it is possible for more than one tile to use the same mnemonic, it is not recommended to do so. The effect of doing so is that the tiles are brought into focus in the order in which they are defined in the dialog descriptive code. This can be confusing, especially to new users.

Tab Stops

The user has the ability to cycle the focus through all of the available tiles by pressing the Tab key. All active user tiles are tab stops unless the is_tab_stop attribute has been set to false.

Typically, the tab stop order is the same order in which the tile definitions are encountered in the DCL description. In some cases, this may not be a logical order of presentation.

To change the order of presentation of the tab stops in your dialog session, reference the callback reason at run time to determine to where the focus should move from the current tile. This is done in the action expression for the tile by checking the value of $reason. Based on the current settings in the dialog session, the action expression can determine where to take the user next and then implement the MODE_TILE function to switch keyboard focus.

Be very careful, however, that movement within the dialog is not too restricted. While it is good to guide the user through your dialog where possible, it is also necessary to allow freedom of movement. After all, the most attractive feature of a dialog box is that data can be entered and edited freely without having to enter data in a linear prompt sequence. Keep this in mind as you design your dialog sessions.

Error Control

Validity checking for user input is a necessary feature of any dialog that employs edit boxes. The edit box accepts any text that the user enters, which makes it possible to enter a text string where a numerical value is expected. Then, any later expressions referencing that value may cause an unexpected error because an improper data type was entered by the user. Therefore, it is critical to check data from edit boxes before ending the dialog session.

The method used by some of AutoCAD's built-in dialog boxes is very forgiving, yet inflexible. While the dialog session is active, the user can enter improper data types in edit boxes. The error tile then displays a message, but the user is not restricted in any way from moving around the dialog box. That is, until the OK button is picked. Once the OK button is picked, final validity checking is done and when invalid data is encountered, the data in the tile is selected and the error tile message is updated. To experience this first hand, open the Drawing Aids dialog box, and type something like "hello" in the Snap X Spacing edit box. Observe how this dialog handles your incorrect entry.

In some cases, more critical errors may be handled with an alert box. The alert box requires immediate attention from the user, since the OK button has to be picked to continue with the dialog session. This enables the programmer to be sure that the user is immediately aware of the error message or other information delivered in the alert box.

Also, be sure to monitor the errtile, and clear away error messages that are no longer valid by setting the tile to an empty string.

Basic Layout Considerations

When laying out a dialog box, the tiles should fit together well to present a clean appearance. Alignment conventions should be consistent throughout the dialog, and spacers should be used where necessary to maintain a visual balance within the dialog box. The layout should present all of the tiles in a sensible and logical manner, so that it is easy for the user to understand the interface.

The most frequently used tiles should be prominent within the dialog box. It should be easy to move between tiles, especially related tiles.

In addition, arrange tile clusters in the most presentable manner. For example, radio buttons are easiest to work with in a column. This brings the tiles close to each other so that the user doesn't need to move the cursor all the way across the dialog box to make another selection. Although the radio row is an available cluster, it is not recommended to use one except when it contains few buttons or is necessary for the current dialog box design.

When laying out text on a dialog box, use the standards followed by AutoCAD's built-in dialog boxes. Headings and labels commonly use what is known as "headline" capitalization, where the initial letters of the major words are capitalized. Do not use periods at the end of labels. Text box and pop-up list labels should end in a colon. All prompts and messages should utilize sentence-style capitalization.

Ending a Dialog Session

A dialog box should not take any action that affects the drawing or the drawing environment until the user picks the OK button. For example, what if the Drawing Aids dialog box changed the associated system variables as the values were entered in the dialog box? If the user began to make changes, decided not to change anything after all, and then pressed the CANCEL button, it would be too late because the changes would have already been made. If the user selects the CANCEL button, the dialog box should do nothing at all.

Providing Help

The level of on-line help you provide in a dialog session depends on how much information the user may need. A simple dialog session may require little or no help, whereas a complex dialog may need to provide a comprehensive help facility.

Help can be provided in a number of ways. In a simple dialog session, a single alert box may be able to provide all of the information that the user needs. If possible, it is best to display the standard AutoCAD Help dialog box using the AutoLISP help function. Context-sensitive help can be applied to assist the user through complex dialog sequences.

Programming Considerations

Reusable code is one of the most valuable tools available to any programmer. With dialog boxes, there are many ways to reuse code. Every programmer should develop a documented collection of various tools and widgets to reuse in day-to-day programming. Working with dialog boxes provides a basic set of flexible tools that can be customized to meet almost any needs. Within this area are given sets of tiles that will be required again and again. For example, some of the built-in subassemblies such as ok_cancel and spacer_0 are encountered in a variety of dialog boxes. If no such subassemblies existed, they would have to be defined in the source DCL code each time they were needed. You can create your own library of predefined subassemblies so that they can be called quickly and easily.

In addition, various "chunks" of AutoLISP code can be reused if designed correctly. As an example, consider a dialog session with multiple dialog boxes and one or more slides to be displayed in each dialog session. Displaying each slide individually would require the following code to be written once for each slide image used in the dialog sequence:

```
(start_image "image1")
(slide_image 0 0 (dimx_tile "image1")(dimy_tile "image1") "slide1")
(end_image)
```

A much simpler tool for displaying slide images could be developed as shown here:

```
(defun _SLIDE (key sldnam)
  (start_image key)
  (slide_image 0 0 (dimx_tile key) (dimy_tile key) sldnam)
  (end_image)
)
```

Now, to display each slide only one expression would be required:

```
(_SLIDE "image1" "slide1")
```

Such widgets and tools can be developed for any redundant tasks such as loading dialogs, adding items to lists, handling images, etc. Use this capability to your advantage as you begin working with dialog boxes.

PROFESSIONAL TIP

When a specific application uses a variety of defined subassemblies across multiple dialog boxes, it may be best to put all of the subassembly definitions into a single DCL file. Any DCL file can use tools defined in another DCL file using an *@include* directive to load the definition file. For example, to load the tile definitions in a file named WIDGETS.DCL, you would use the following:

```
@include "widgets.dcl"
```

Note that no semicolon is used to terminate this line.

Understanding DCL errors

The most common error you are likely to encounter while working with DCL files is a missing line termination (;), which is similar to AutoLISP's own "malformed list." Other missing characters, such as missing curly braces and colons, can also cause problems. Common AutoLISP errors associated with DCL tiles includes misspelled key names, and malformed strings resulting from missing backslashes preceding quotation marks within an action expression.

The primary troubleshooting tool provided by the PDB facility is the *semantic auditing.* This auditing tool checks the DCL file being loaded for various levels of semantic errors. The term semantic error indicates an error in the descriptive wording or syntax within the file. There are four levels of checking as described in Fig. 18-7.

Level	Description
0	No checking. This is used when the DCL file has already been audited, and has not been edited since the last audit.
1	Display Error Messages. This is the default level of checking, and produces almost no delay in the DCL loading process. This level of auditing finds errors that may cause AutoCAD to terminate.
2	Display Warning Messages. This level finds less serious mistakes, such as missing and inappropriately valued attributes. Any modified DCL file should be subjected to this level of auditing.
3	Display Hints. This level of checking is for fine tuning your DCL code. It will check attribute definitions very closely, finding any redundant definitions.

Fig. 18-7. Levels of error checking.

To set the level of semantic auditing for a DCL file, include the following line in your DCL file:

```
dcl_settings : default_dcl_settings { audit_level = 3; }
```

Substitute the new desired audit level for the number three in the example. Remove the auditing statements from the file before the application is released for use.

Run Time Symbol Checking

One of the biggest hurdles in troubleshooting a dialog box is knowing what value a variable has at run time, or what callback reason or value is being returned to the application by a specific tile during a specific user activity. The alert function can be a very handy tool for momentarily interrupting the dialog flow and displaying a critical message. For example, to find out what value a tile is returning to the application, something similar to the following expression can be used:

```
(action_tile "tile_nam" "(alert (strcat \"$VALUE = \" $value))")
```

Be sure to adjust this model for the appropriate data type to be tested for.

A FINAL WORD REGARDING DIALOG BOXES

The dialog box is considered the preferred interface style for all but the simplest of applications. Using dialog boxes not only gives your application a new level of usability, it also provides a built-in look and feel. This helps new users feel comfortable from the first time they use the application. Users of every experience level will usually prefer an intuitive and well-designed dialog box to a series of command line prompts.

CHAPTER TEST

Write your answers in the spaces provided.

1. Describe the basic sequence of AutoLISP code for controlling a dialog session.

____

____

____

____

2. What AutoLISP function is used to load a DCL file and what is its primary argument?

____

3. Detail the use of the NEW_DIALOG function.

____

____

____

____

4. What function forces the current dialog box to be displayed and begins the dialog session?

5. What is the difference between DONE_DIALOG and TERM_DIALOG?

6. Why should DCL code that is no longer being used be unloaded from memory?

7. What can be included in the process of initializing a tile for a dialog session?

8. Describe the two required arguments for the SET_TILE function.

9. Write an action expression for a tile whose key is _KEY1 that uses the alert box to display the message "You picked the KEY1 tile".

10. List the six run-time variables associated with dialog tiles.

11. What types of AutoLISP functions cannot be used while a dialog box is active?

12. What AutoLISP function is used to enable or disable a tile, or to set it as the current tile?

13. What is meant by "run time validation" of data?

14. Write the code required to display the message "Invalid entry." in the error tile.

15. What is the run time variable that is used to determine the reason for an action?

16. What are the three functions associated with managing lists and popup lists?

17. Describe the three possible values for the OPERATION argument in the ADD_LIST function.

18. What function is used to indicate the beginning of an image tile definition?

19. Describe the purpose of the FILL_IMAGE function.

20. What two functions can be used to determine the size of an image tile?

21. What function best facilitates the placement of a complex image within an image tile?

22. Simple images can be drawn directly on an image tile with what function?

23. What is the purpose of a slider?

24. Where should keyboard mnemonics be used in a dialog box?

25. When is a tile a "tab stop"?

26. How is the DCL file semantic audit level changed?

PROGRAMMING PROBLEMS

1. Write the DCL and AutoLISP code required to generate and control the dialog box shown. Upon selecting a button, the dialog should be dismissed and the appropriate command entered.

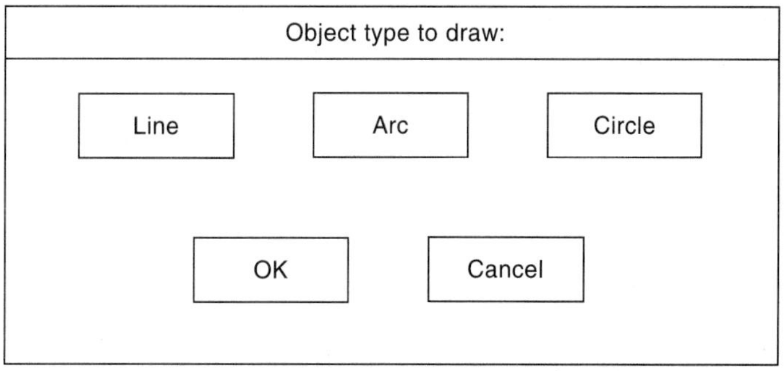

Object type to draw:

Line Arc Circle

OK Cancel

2. Redesign the dialog box in problem 1 to use appropriate image buttons for the LINE, ARC, and CIRCLE options.
3. Open the program file PARA2.LSP created in Chapter 9 Programming Problems (P9-3) and design a dialog interface. It should display a slide image showing the lettered dimensions and have an edit box for each dimension. Be sure to include run time validation of data and error handling as appropriate.

Chapter 19

Programming and Debugging Techniques

Learning Objectives

After completing this chapter, you will be able to:

- ☐ Describe how to write program code in an easy-to-read format.
- ☐ Explain common techniques for effectively debugging a program.
- ☐ Use AutoLISP's built-in function tracer.
- ☐ Utilize AutoLISP memory-management procedures.

PROGRAMMING AND DEBUGGING

Similar to any other programming language, AutoLISP requires a great deal of *debugging* (working the *bugs* out). For a novice, it is reasonable to estimate that at least 75% of the total time required to generate a working application is spent figuring out what went wrong. As you become more knowledgeable and efficient this might drop to around 40-50%, with only the short and simple applications consistently requiring less troubleshooting.

Since so much time and cost is involved in debugging, it is important to become an effective debugger. The first part of this chapter discusses many of the finer points of finding the "bugs" within a program. Mastering these techniques will greatly increase programming productivity, thus saving time and expense.

DEBUGGING EFFECTIVELY

One of the most important aspects of debugging a program is being able to easily read it. When a program is difficult to follow, debugging it naturally takes much longer. The following techniques can be put into practice to make an AutoLISP program file much easier to read and, therefore, easier to debug.

Indentation

Indentation serves the greatest purpose when it is used to track nesting levels within a program. While many expressions may be nested only a few levels deep, a complicated application may require extensive nesting.

Within a set of nested expressions, the closing parenthesis should be found in the same column as the opening parenthesis. Indenting only one column may not be enough to clearly distinguish levels of nesting; two-column indentation is used in many examples in this text. The example in Fig. 19-1 uses this method.

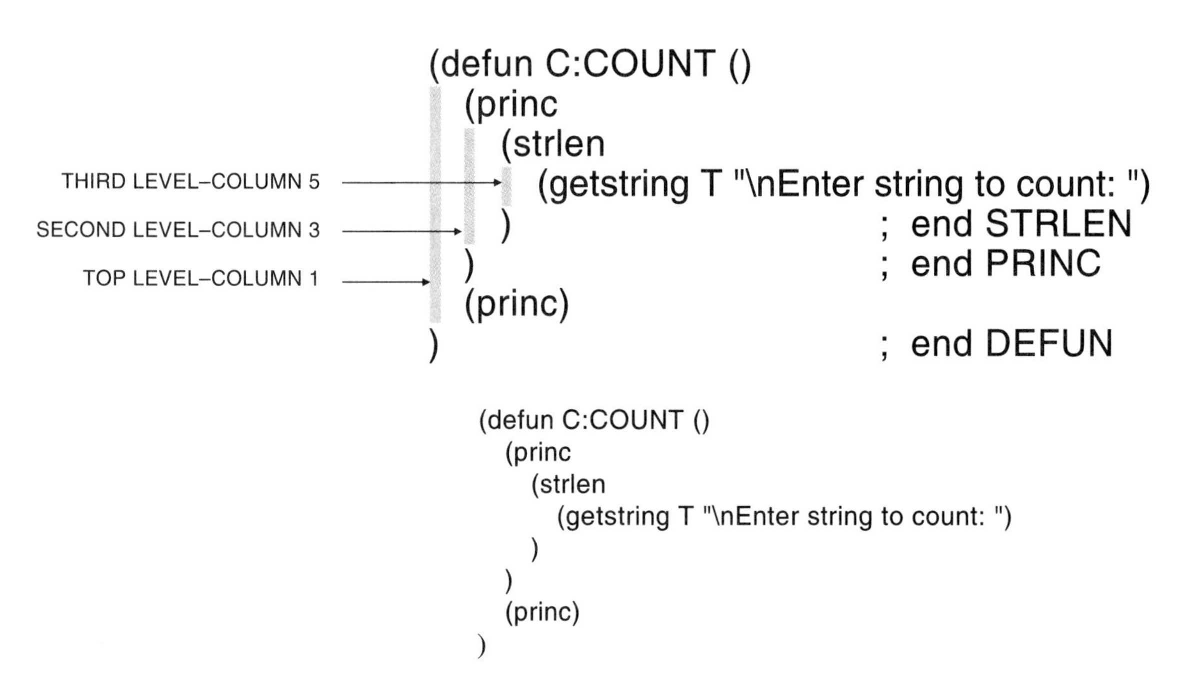

Fig. 19-1. Proper indentation is one of the keys to efficient debugging and troubleshooting.

Notice in Fig. 19-1 how the nesting levels become much easier to track when indentation is properly used. Within a text editor, the cursor can be placed directly on an opening parenthesis and moved straight down to find its closing parenthesis. Mastering indentation techniques gives the programmer a distinct advantage in locating missing or extra parentheses.

When an expression is short enough to begin and end on the same line, and has only two or three levels of nesting, it may be easier to read if the expression is left on a single line. For example:

```
(defun DTR (a) (* pi (/ 180.0 a)))
```

Many times, whether to drop a nested expression to the next line and indent is merely a judgment call. The method that best enhances readability should be used.

The example in Fig. 19-2 has some deeper levels of nesting, with opening and closing parentheses levels shown. As shown in Fig. 19-1, lines are used to connect opening and closing parentheses.

```
(DEFUN PARSE (STR / REF N CHAR LSTR LADD LST)(SETQ REF (STRLEN STR) N
1)(WHILE (>= REF N)(SETQ CHAR (SUBSTR STR N 1))(WHILE (AND (/= CHAR ",")(/=
CHAR "")(/= CHAR " "))(IF (NULL LSTR)(SETQ LSTR CHAR)(SETQ LSTR (STRCAT LSTR
CHAR)))(SETQ N (1+ N))(SETQ CHAR (SUBSTR STR N 1)))(SETQ LADD LSTR LSTR
NIL)(SETQ N (1+ N))(IF (/= LADD NIL)(SETQ LST (APPEND LST (LIST LADD))))))
```

```
; PARSE.LSP by Paul Amout
;
; Date:  February 1, 19xx
;
; The PARSE routine will read a CDF (Comma Delimited Format) or SDF (Space
; Delimited Format) string and returns a list. Each field is an element of the
; returned list. Example:
;
; Example (PARSE "Hello, Goodbye") returns ("Hello" "Goodbye")
;
(defun PARSE (STR / REF N CHAR LSTR LADD LST)
  (setq REF (strlen STR) N 1)
  (while (>= REF N)
    (setq CHAR (substr STR N 1))
    (while
      (and
        (/= CHAR ",")
        (/= CHAR "")
        (/= CHAR " ")
      )                                      ; ---------------- end AND
      (if
        (null LSTR)
        (setq LSTR CHAR)
        (setq LSTR (strcat LSTR CHAR))
      )                                      ; ----------------- end IF
      (setq N (1+ N))
      (setq CHAR (substr STR N 1))
    )                                        ; ----------------- end WHILE
    (setq LADD LSTR LSTR nil)
    (setq N (1+ N))
    (if
      (/= LADD nil)
      (setq LST (append LST
                  (list LADD)
                )                            ; ------------ end APPEND
      )                                      ; ------------ end SETQ
    )                                        ; ----------- end IF
  )                                          ; ----- end WHILE
)                   ; – end DEFUN
```

Fig. 19-2. Compare the difference between these two versions of the same program. This program is quite simple to follow when written using proper documentation, indentation, and capitalization techniques.

When no indentation is used in a program, it is extremely difficult to read. Since missing or extra parentheses are two of the most common errors within AutoLISP, it is important to be able to quickly locate the beginning and end of all nested expressions. Indentation is an invaluable tool for this purpose.

Uppercase and Lowercase Characters

Using both uppercase and lowercase letters adds contrast within the body of a program. This is clearly demonstrated by comparing both versions of PARSE.LSP in Fig. 19-2. If all uppercase or all lowercase characters are used in a program, it is more difficult to find specific expressions or elements within it.

A critical aspect of debugging a program is being able to quickly locate symbols. The convention used throughout this text displays all built-in AutoLISP function names in lowercase characters. All other symbols and arguments are shown in uppercase characters, which makes them stand out from the rest of the program code. Any text strings are written exactly as they are to be printed, at the programmer's discretion. In a few cases, such as the OPEN function, lowercase characters are critical in a program.

Re-examine PARSE.LSP and see how easy the defined symbols are to locate within the program:

```
PROGRAM CODE                                          SYMBOLS ON THIS LINE
(defun PARSE (STR / REF N CHAR LSTR LADD LST)         PARSE (plus an argument)
    (setq REF (strlen STR) N 1)                       REF STR N
    (while
    (>= REF N)                                        REF N
      (setq CHAR (substr STR N 1))                    CHAR STR N
      (while
        (and
          (/= CHAR ",")                               CHAR
          (/= CHAR "")                                CHAR
          (/= CHAR " ")                               CHAR
        )
        (if
          (null LSTR)                                 LSTR
          (setq LSTR CHAR)                            LSTR CHAR
          (setq LSTR (strcat LSTR CHAR))              LSTR CHAR
        )
        (setq N (1+ N))                               N
        (setq CHAR (substr STR N 1))                  CHAR STR N
      )
      (setq LADD LSTR LSTR nil)                       LADD LSTR
      (setq N (1+ N))                                 N
      (if
        (/= LADD nil)                                 LADD
        (setq LST (append LST                         LST
                  (list LADD)                         LADD
        )
      )
    )
)
```

Likewise, all built-in function names are easily recognized since they are displayed in lowercase characters. The key here is the contrast within the code–another powerful tool for simplifying the debugging process.

Recognizing Error Messages

In addition to using proper writing techniques, the programmer needs to be familiar with error messages. Many specific error messages will be encountered. Some of the most common error messages encountered by new programmers are listed in Fig. 19-3. The explanations point out the most common reason for the error message, but not necessarily the only possible cause.

While you will encounter other error messages from AutoLISP, these are likely to be the most common ones. The full listing of error messages is given in Appendix C.

Error Message	Possible Reason for the Message
malformed list	Missing closing parenthesis.
malformed string	Missing closing quotation mark.
bad argument type	Argument supplied to function was not of the data type required.
bad function	Function name specified is not recognized. Commonly due to a typographical or spelling error.
null function	Same as a "bad function," except the function name supplied evaluates to nil.
too many arguments	As implied, a function has been given more arguments than are allowed.
too few arguments	A required argument has been omitted.
incorrect number of arguments to a function.	A user-defined function has been called with the wrong number of arguments.
extra right parenthesis	Either a missing left parenthesis, or an extra right parenthesis

Fig. 19-3. Common error messages.

LOCATING PROGRAMMING ERRORS

AutoLISP provides several tools for the programmer to use to locate the source of programming errors. When an error occurs, the program ceases evaluation and the erroneous expression is returned to the screen. Many lines of code may follow this expression, depending on the complexity of the program. The purpose of this additional code is to help you identify the exact location of the faulty expression by showing the expressions in which it is nested. The following example demonstrates this concept:

```
(defun C:DRAWBOX (/ P1 D P4 P3 P2)
  (setq P1 (getpoint "\nLower left corner: "))
  (setq D  (getdist "\nLength of one side: "))
  (setq P4
    (polar
      (setq P3
        (polar
          (setq P2
            (polar P1 0 DD)
          )
          (* 0.5 pi)
          D
        )
      )
      pi
      D
    )
  )
  (command "LINE" P1 P2 P3 P4 "C")
  (princ)
)
```

Symbol D, typed as DD, is the source of the error.

The error messages that are produced:

Command: **(LOAD "DRAWBOX")** ↵
C:DRAWBOX

Command: **DRAWBOX** ↵
Lower left corner: *(pick a point)*
Length of one side: **2** ↵

error: bad argument type	*Error type displayed.*
(POLAR P1 0 DD)	*Offending expression is shown first.*
(SETQ P2 (POLAR P1 0 DD))	*Next upward level of nesting shown.*
(POLAR (SETQ P2 (POLAR P1 0 DD)) (* 0.5 PI) D)	*Next upward level of nesting... (and so on)*
(SETQ P3 (POLAR (SETQ P2 (POLAR P1 0 DD)) (* 0.5 PI) D) PI D)	
(POLAR (SETQ P3 (POLAR (SETQ P2 (POLAR P1 0 DD)) (* 0.5 PI) D)) PI D)	
(SETQ P4 (POLAR (SETQ P3 (POLAR (SETQ P2 (POLAR P1 0 DD)) (* 0.5 PI) D)) PI D))	
(C:DRAWBOX)	*Top level expression in which the error occurred; typically a function call.*
Cancel	

PROFESSIONAL TIP

When an error occurs deep within a large application, the code can often scroll by much too fast to be able to see where the problem occurred. In a Windows environment, this is not a problem. Press the F2 key to display the text screen and use the scroll bars to review the code that was dumped to the screen. If necessary, the number of lines stored in memory can be increased by using the Preferences command.

In a DOS environment (Release 13 and previous releases), this approach is not possible. One option is to run the application again, holding your finger over the PAUSE key on your keyboard. The PAUSE button stops the scrolling, and if you are fast enough, you can see the offending expression. If the application can be run in a text screen mode you will have a better chance of identifying the error.

Further interrogation of the program is possible by evaluating symbols used within a routine. It is important to remember that if a symbol is declared as local to a function, it loses its value after the function is halted.

To retain the values of all variables, the symbols must be excluded from the argument list. In most cases, local symbols are not declared until the program is found to run properly. If the argument list has already been defined, simply insert a new closing parenthesis followed by a semicolon as shown below:

```
(defun C:DRAWBOX () ;/ P1 D P4 P3 P2)
```

This has the effect of causing all local variable symbol declarations to be ignored as a comment, thus preserving their assigned values. Now, all symbols used in this function can be evaluated. Once the problem has been solved, the argument list can be changed back.

All interrogations of an AutoLISP routine typically begin with the offending expression. In the case of the DRAWBOX.LSP program, a "bad argument type" is cited as the cause of the problem. The first step, therefore, is to research the use of the function. In this case, the research reveals the syntax of the POLAR function is:

```
(polar PT ANGLE DISTANCE)
```

The PT argument must be a point coordinate. In the POLAR expression, the variable P1 is supplied for the base point argument. Check its value using the exclamation point:

```
Command: !P1 ↵
(3.4601 4.335 0.0)                    point that was picked
```

Since P1 is the proper data type, further interrogation is necessary. The ANGLE argument also requires a numeric argument. The value of 0 is a suitable data type. Be sure it is a zero and not the letter "O." That leaves only one more argument to check:

```
Command: !DD ↵
nil
```

The DISTANCE argument is required to be a numeric value, but is not. This shows the programmer that the DISTANCE argument is indeed the bad argument type. Now it is necessary to find out why. The problem in this example is simple; since the symbol DD is not defined in this program it has a value of nil. Replace the incorrect symbol name with the correct one, and the routine runs properly.

In other cases, however, it might be due to an incorrect equation, or improperly setting variable values in another area of the program. Knowing the name of a variable that is not being set to the proper value is the first step in finding out the real source of the problem.

FUNCTION DESIGN CONSIDERATIONS

Working in larger applications is typically when debugging ceases to be "challenging" and can be classified as "difficult". The problem is that there is so much code being evaluated, and so many places for errors to hide. It takes much longer to read through all of the additional code to finally locate a problem. A large application can quickly become unmanageable and fraught with errors. Trying to locate a small problem in a huge application can be a very frustrating and time-consuming task.

The best way to handle large programs is to construct them as a collection of many smaller functions. Creating many small functions helps reduce the amount of code repetition in your program file. Additionally, it localizes program functionality, meaning that it reduces the size of the area of code that needs to be examined when searching for errors.

For example, the following routine draws a multicolored line. In the *entmake* expression, an intentional error has been inserted to demonstrate the error message returned.

```
(defun C:CLINE ()
 (setq FPT (getpoint "\nFrom point: ")
       CLR 1
 )
 (while (and
          FPT
          (setq TPT (getpoint FPT "\nTo point: "))
        )
        (entmark (list '(0 . "LINE") (cons 10 FPP) (cons 11 TPT) (cons 62 CLR)))
        (if ( < CLR 16)
           (setq CLR (1+ CLR))
           (setq CLR 1)
        )
        (setq FPT TPT)
 )
 (princ)
)
```

```
Command: CLINE ↵

From point:
To point: error: null function
(ENTMARK (LIST (QUOTE (0 . "LINE")) (CONS 10 FPP) (CONS 11 TPT) (CONS 62 CLR)))
(WHILE (AND FPT (SETQ TPT (GETPOINT FPT "\nTo point: "))) (ENTMARK (LIST (QUOTE
(0 . "LINE")) (CONS 10 FPP) (CONS 11 TPT) (CONS 62 CLR))) (IF ( <CLR 16) (SETQ
CLR (1+ CLR)) (SETQ CLR 1)) (SETQ FPT TPT))
(C:CLINE)
*Cancel*
```

Notice that within the error message, the function in which the erroneous expression is located is printed to the screen. In this case, the file is small and the expression is easy to locate. The point is, however, that this code could occur *anywhere* within the C:CLINE function definition. In a larger application, you might have to look through hundreds of lines of AutoLISP code to find the problematic expression. By breaking the routine into smaller functions, you can narrow down the search requirements for debugging this code.

One example of this approach can be found in the following sample of the same program, where the functional parts of the program are written as separate functions to be called by the primary function.

```
;;DRAWCLINE function draws a line between two specified points (P1 & P2)
;; in the color value specified by CV.

(defun DRAWCLINE (P1 P2 CV)
 (entmark (list '(0 . "LINE") (cons 10 P1) (cons 11 P2) (cons 62 CV)))
)

;;LOOPINC function returns its NUM argument incremented by one, unless the
;; number exceeds MAXVAL, in which case it is reset to 1.

(defun LOOPINC (NUM MAXVAL)
 (if ( < NUM MAXVAL)
    (setq NUM (1+ NUM))
    (setq NUM 1)
))

;;C:CLINE function provides command line access and user interface for drawing
;; a multicolored line.

(defun C:CLINE ()
 (setq FPT (getpoint "\nFrom point: ")
       CLR 1
 )
 (while (and
            FPT
            (setq TPT (getpoint FPT "\nTo point: "))
        )
        (DRAWCLINE FPT TPT CLR)                    ;;calls DRAWCLINE
        (setq CLR (LOOPINC CLR 16)                 ;;calls LOOPINC
              FPT TPT
        )
 )
 (princ)
)
```

Command: **CLINE** ↵

From point:
To point: error: null function
(ENTMARK (LIST (QUOTE (0 . "LINE")) (CONS 10 P1) (CONS 11 P2) (CONS 62 CV)))
(DRAWCLINE FPT TPT CLR)
(WHILE (AND FPT (SETQ TPT (GETPOINT FPT "\nTo point: "))) (DRAWCLINE FPT TPT CLR) (SETQ CLR (LOOPINC CLR 16) FPT TPT))
(C:CLINE)
Cancel

While this program works the same whether it is written in "chunks" as shown here or as a single larger application, it is much easier to locate specific expressions in smaller "chunks." Note that the error code displayed shows that the problem occurred in an *entmake* expression that is found when the DRAWCLINE function is called. This tells you that the problem exists within the function definition or the function call. Since this represents a much smaller "chunk" of code, it becomes quicker and easier to debug.

As a note, the problem with the code above is in the fact that *entmake* was incorrectly spelled as *entmark*.

EXERCISE 19-1

☐ Using the techniques previously described, rewrite the following program in a readable manner. Then troubleshoot the program to determine the error it contains.

```
; LP.LSP Al Jess Pickett
;
; Date: January 15, 19xx
;
; This program allows the user to pick any entity to make current the layer on
; which that entity resides.
;
(defun c:lp (/ nl) (prompt "\nSelect entity on target layer: ")(if (setq es (entsel
))(progn (setq nl (cdr (assoc 8 (entget (cdr es)))))(command "layer" "s" nl
""))(princ "\nNo entities selected!")(princ))
```

USING A FUNCTION TRACER

An additional debugging tool provided within AutoLISP is the TRACE function. TRACE allows AutoLISP functions to be "traced," so that each time the function is entered the programmer is informed and shown the results of the evaluation. This is valuable when a specific program calls one or more outside functions in the course of its evaluation.

The TRACE Function

The *TRACE function* is AutoLISP's primary function for assisting the programmer in debugging a program. The syntax for the TRACE function is:

```
(trace FUNCTION ...)
```

Any number of FUNCTION names can be specified; the name of the last one is returned by the TRACE expression. Once the trace flag is set for a given function, each use of the function is reported by AutoLISP along with the result returned by it. The next program example uses an incorrectly defined DTR (Degrees To Radians) user function:

```
(defun dtr (a)
  (/ pi (* a 180))
)
```

```
(defun C:BOXES ()
  (setq SZ (getdist "\nLength of one side of box: "))
  (setq P1 (getpoint "\nLower left corner: "))
  (setq ANG (getreal "\nAngle for box: "))
  (setq P2 (polar P1 (dtr ANG) SZ))
  (setq P3 (polar P2                       ; Note: The arguments for the POLAR
              (+ (dtr ANG) (* pi 0.5)) ;   function have been separated for
              SZ                       ;   additional clarity. Each argument
           )                           ;   is at the same nesting level.
  )
  (setq P4 (polar P3
              (+ (dtr ANG) pi)
              SZ
           )
  )
  (command ".LINE" P1 P2 P3 P4 "C")
  (princ)
)
```

Command: **(LOAD "BOXES")** ↵
C:BOXES
Command: **BOXES** ↵
Length of one side of box: **1** ↵
Lower left corner: *(pick a point)*
Angle for box: **45** ↵
Command:

Using this routine as shown draws a box, but not at 45° as specified. Since the angle provided in the routine is incorrect, the first step is to troubleshoot the function that derives this angle. One method is to use the TRACE function:

Command: **(trace DTR)** ↵
DTR

Command: **BOXES** ↵
Length of one side of box: **1** ↵
Lower left corner: *(pick a point)*
Angle for box: **45** ↵
  Entering DTR: 45.0
  Result: 0.000387851
    Entering DTR: 45.0
    Result: 0.000387851
    Entering DTR: 45.0
    Result: 0.000387851
Command:

TRACE shows the function DTR being entered and the result for the TRACE function indents one column for each level of nesting

Now it is simple to determine the cause of the error. Since 45° expressed in radians should be 0.25 x pi (about 0.785), it is apparent that the conversion function is incorrect.

The UNTRACE Function

Once a function no longer requires tracing, the *UNTRACE function* removes the trace flag from the specified functions. The syntax for UNTRACE is:

```
(untrace FUNCTION ...)
```

As with TRACE, the name of the last FUNCTION argument is returned. An example of the UNTRACE function follows:

```
(untrace DTR)        returns  DTR
```

The DTR function will no longer be traced.

USING ALERT AS A DEBUGGING TOOL

One of the primary problems with debugging large AutoLISP applications is determining *where* within the program an error is occurring. It is often helpful to verify how far the program progressed before it crashed. An effective tool for this verification is the ALERT function.

The ALERT function pauses for user input, requiring that the OK tile be picked before it will continue. Since this can be used both for issuing a message and for pausing the evaluation of a program, the ALERT function provides two valuable purposes for the programmer.

Displaying Changing Symbol Values

When a program is running, but is running incorrectly, it is often necessary to check symbol values at run time. This helps you track changing values. Otherwise, after the program runs, all you can check by conventional means is the final value of the symbol. For example, the following code uses the C:CLINE routine defined earlier in this chapter to demonstrate this principle. The *null function* error occurring previously has been fixed, but a new error replaces the old one. The new problem with the program is that it runs, but the line is only drawn in red. Here is the revised code:

```
;;DRAWCLINE function draws a line between two specified points (P1 & P2)
;; in the color value specified by CV.

(defun DRAWCLINE (P1 P2 CV)
 (entmake (list '(0 . "LINE") (cons 10 P1) (cons 11 P2) (cons 62 CV)))
)

;;LOOPINC function returns its NUM argument incremented by one, unless the
;; number exceeds MAXVAL, in which case it is reset to 1.

(defun LOOPINC (NUM MAXVAL)
 (if ( < NUM MAXVAL)
    (setq NUM (1+ NUM))
    (setq NUM 1)
))
```

```
;;C:CLINE function provides command line access and user interface for drawing
;; a multicolored line.

(defun C:CLINE ()
 (setq FPT (getpoint "\nFrom point: ")
       CLR 1
 )
 (while (and
          FPT
           (setq TPT (getpoint FPT "\nTo point: "))
        )
        (DRAWCLINE FPT TPT CLR)                    ;;calls DRAWCLINE
        (setq CLR (LOOPINC CLR 1)                  ;;calls LOOPINC
              FPT TPT
 )      )
 (princ)
)
```

Since the color isn't changing, the first area to be suspect is the LOOPINC function. To check the incrementing at run time, and verify both the value coming into LOOPINC as well as going out, revise the code using two alert expressions to report the symbol values:

```
(defun LOOPINC (NUM MAXVAL)
 (alert (strcat "Entering LOOPINC, NUM = " (itoa NUM) "MAXVAL = " (itoa MAXVAL)))
 (if ( < NUM MAXVAL)
    (setq NUM (1+ NUM))
    (setq NUM 1)
 )
 (alert (strcat "Leaving LOOPINC, NUM = " (itoa NUM) "MAXVAL = " (itoa MAXVAL)))
 (eval NUM)    ;;LOOPINC must return value of NUM to C:CLINE
)
```

Note that since the value of NUM must be returned by LOOPINC, an expression returning this value must be the final expression in the function definition.

Running this revised code causes the value of NUM and MAXVAL to be displayed both before and after each attempted incrementation. This makes it easy to see that the incrementing is failing because NUM is already equal to MAXVAL, so it is reset to 1 each time. A closer look at the calling expression reveals that the MAXVAL argument is passed with a 1 value rather than the desired 16.

Creating Run-time Checkpoints

Checking the progress of a program that crashes can help speed the process of finding the problem. One means of monitoring the progress of your program is to insert run-time checkpoints. The ALERT function makes this very easy to do.

Load time crashes are common. Malformed lists and extra right parentheses are some of the most frequent causes. The following example shows an excerpt from an AutoLISP file that defines a number of command line functions. Trying to load the program returns a malformed list, but provides no information about the location of the error.

```
(defun C:AR () (command "ARRAY") (princ))
(defun C:B () (command "BREAK") (princ))
;; BREAK–@ allows you to select a line to break, and an intersection
;; to break it at...
 (defun C:BA (/ SS BP)
  (setvar "osmode" 512)
  (setq SS (getpoint "Select line to break: "))   ;select line
  (redraw (ssname (setq SST (ssget SS)) 0) 3)      ;highlight selected line
  (if (not (or (= "LINE" (cdr (assoc 0 (entget (ssname SST 0)))))
               (= "ARC" (cdr (assoc 0 (entget (ssname SST 0)))))
               (= "POLYLINE" (cdr (assoc 0 (entget (ssname SST 0)))))
     )  )
     (progn
         (redraw (ssname SST 0) 1)
         (princ "\nCan't BREAK–@ that entity.")
     )
     (progn
         (setvar "OSMODE" 32)                          ;osnap INT
         (setq BP (getpoint "Intersection to BREAK–@: ")) ;pick INT
         (command "BREAK" SS "F" BP "@")              ;break line
         (setvar "osmode" 0) (SETVAR "HIGHLIGHT" 1) (PRINC) ;osnap NONE
  ) )
(princ))
;;
(defun C:BYL (/ SS)          ;Changes selected entities to BYLAYER setting
  (if (setq SS (ssget))        ;for both COLOR and LINETYPE
   (command "CHANGE" SS "" "P" "C" "BYL" "LT" "BYLAYER" "")
   (princ "\nNo entities selected!")
  )
  (princ)
)
;;
(defun C:CG () (command "CHANGE") (princ)
(defun C:CX ()  (command "COPY") (princ))
(defun C:EX ()  (command "EXTEND") (princ))
(defun C:F () (command "FILLET") (princ))
(defun C:FR (/ r) (setq r (getdist "\nFillet radius: ")) ;set radius value,
 (command "FILLET" "R" r)(C:F)                       ;Invoke FILLET macro
)
(defun C:FX () (command "FILLET" "R" "0")(C:F))     ;FILLET 0 radius
(defun C:HO ()  ;;Half Offset, for offsetting diameter values
 (initget 3)
 (setq OV (getreal "\nOffset to halve: "))
 (command ".OFFSET" (* 0.5 OV))
)
(defun C:M ()  (command "MOVE") (princ))
(defun C:MI ()  (command "MIRROR" "AU") (princ))
(defun C:O ()  (command "OFFSET") (princ))
```

The load attempt looks like this:

```
Command: (load "fastkeys") ↵
error: malformed list
(LOAD "fastkeys")
*Cancel*
```

Now, inserting the ALERT expressions as checkpoints provides a quick way to narrow down the search area:

```
(defun C:AR () (command "ARRAY") (princ))
(defun C:B () (command "BREAK") (princ))
(alert "Checkpoint 1")
;; BREAK–@ allows you to select a line to break, and an intersection
;; to break it at...
 (defun C:BA (/ SS BP)
  (setvar "osmode" 512)
  (setq SS (getpoint "Select line to break: "))   ;select line
  (redraw (ssname (setq SST (ssget SS)) 0) 3)      ;highlight selected line
  (if (not (or (= "LINE" (cdr (assoc 0 (entget (ssname SST 0)))))
               (= "ARC" (cdr (assoc 0 (entget (ssname SST 0)))))
               (= "POLYLINE" (cdr (assoc 0 (entget (ssname SST 0)))))
     )  )
     (progn
          (redraw (ssname SST 0) 1)
          (princ "\nCan't BREAK–@ that entity.")
     )
     (progn
          (setvar "OSMODE" 32)                              ;osnap INT
          (setq BP (getpoint "Intersection to BREAK–@: ")) ;pick INT
          (command "BREAK" SS "F" BP "@")                   ;break line
          (setvar "osmode" 0) (SETVAR "HIGHLIGHT" 1) (PRINC) ;osnap NONE
  ) )
(princ))
;;
(defun C:BYL (/ SS)         ;Changes selected entities to BYLAYER setting
 (if (setq SS (ssget))         ;for both COLOR and LINETYPE
   (command "CHANGE" SS "" "P" "C" "BYL" "LT" "BYLAYER" "")
   (princ "\nNo entities selected!")
 )
 (princ)
)
;;
(alert "Checkpoint 2")
(defun C:CG () (command "CHANGE") (princ)
(defun C:CX ()  (command "COPY") (princ))
(defun C:EX ()  (command "EXTEND") (princ))
(defun C:F () (command "FILLET") (princ))
(defun C:FR (/ r) (setq r (getdist "\nFillet radius: ")) ;set radius value,
   (command "FILLET" "R" r)(C:F)                    ;Invoke FILLET macro
)
(defun C:FX () (command "FILLET" "R" "0")(C:F))     ;FILLET 0 radius
```

```
(defun C:HO () ;;Half Offset, for offsetting diameter values
  (initget 3)
  (setq OV (getreal "\nOffset to halve: "))
  (command ".OFFSET" (* 0.5 OV))
)
(defun C:M () (command "MOVE") (princ))
(defun C:MI () (command "MIRROR" "AU") (princ))
(defun C:O () (command "OFFSET") (princ))
(alert "Checkpoint 3")
```

Although the error message is the same when loading the revised code, the ALERT functions are encountered before the errors are evaluated. Since Checkpoint 2 was reached, but not Checkpoint 3, you know the error occurred somewhere between these two expressions. From this point, the code between the checkpoints could be debugged, or the checkpoints could be moved closer to each other as needed until the remaining code was in a small enough area to be easily searched.

As it turns out, the error here is within the function definition for C:CG—a missing closing paren for the DEFUN expression. Once the program code is corrected, remove the checkpoints as needed.

MEMORY MANAGEMENT

Besides knowing the AutoLISP language, you must also have a keen knowledge of the environment in which applications must run. Since AutoLISP is an *interpreted language* as opposed to a *compiled language,* memory management becomes much easier. It is not necessary to specifically allocate memory segments for the variables used since this is done by the interpreter. It is, however, essential in some environments to carefully manage overall memory usage.

With AutoCAD, data storage space for programs and AutoLISP data have virtually no limits. This can be attributed to the fact that when regular memory is filled, pages of memory are written to disk to make more room in physical memory. These pages can then be swapped in and out of physical memory as needed. Thus, in this environment, AutoCAD and AutoLISP use what is termed as *virtual memory*–and there is little need for concern of running out of memory.

640K DOS Systems and Environmental Variables

When an application must run on an older 640K DOS version of AutoCAD using either regular AutoLISP or Extended AutoLISP, certain considerations must be made. It is important to remember that every AutoLISP function, every user-defined function, and every assigned symbol requires a certain amount of memory to hold its value or definition. The amount of memory available for AutoLISP applications in these environments is controlled by the setting of DOS environmental variables. These are the LISPHEAP and LISPSTACK variables.

The *LISPHEAP,* also called *node space,* is the area of memory used to store all functions and variables. The *LISPSTACK* is the "working" memory, which holds function arguments and any partial results.

The setting of these variables is done in DOS, prior to entering AutoCAD. It is most convenient to set these variables using a batch file. (See your DOS manual and the *AutoCAD Installation and Performance Guide* for additional information.) The default values are:

```
LISPHEAP=40000
LISPSTACK=3000
```

These values can be adjusted as required, but the total of the two settings cannot exceed 45000 bytes. If Extended AutoLISP is used, a LISPHEAP setting is ignored because it references the LISPXMEM variable for its setting.

Memory-Management Techniques

One effective memory-management tool is the argument list for function definitions. By declaring all variables used as local, they no longer occupy node space. Any variables not specifically declared as local will retain their last assigned value for the remainder of the drawing session.

When a defined function is no longer needed, its symbol can be reassigned to nil to release it from memory. To release the node space currently holding the PARSE function previously defined, use the following expression:

```
(setq PARSE nil)
```

The ATOMLIST Function. The *atomlist* is a list maintained by AutoLISP in versions of AutoCAD prior to Release 12, which holds defined functions and symbols. Although this function is not used in Release 12, some of your applications may need to run on prior versions of AutoCAD. In such a case, it will be helpful to be familiar with the atomlist and related material. When first entering the drawing editor, this list contains only the built-in function and symbol names. Each new function definition and symbol assignment is added to the front of this list.

If the next application to be loaded is large and requires much node space, it may be useful to first empty the atomlist of all user-defined functions and symbols. The *AutoCAD Customization Guide* provides a function definition used for this purpose.

```
(defun C:CLEAN (/ I ITEM)
  (setq I 0)
  (while (not (equal (setq ITEM (nth I atomlist)) 'C:CLEAN))
    (if (= (type (eval ITEM)) 'FILE)
      (close (eval ITEM))
    )
    (setq I (1+ I))
  )
  (setq atomlist (member 'C:CLEAN atomlist))
                         'DONE
)
```

This function cleans out all functions and symbols from the atomlist that were defined *after* the CLEAN function. Therefore, the most effective way in which to use this function is within the ACADR14.LSP file. Doing so ensures that the CLEAN.LSP routine is loaded in every drawing session. Also, it can be positioned within the ACADR14.LSP file so that functions that must not be lost are defined prior to invoking CLEAN.

Virtual Function Paging

This function, although not used in Release 12, 13, or 14, is very useful in older versions of AutoCAD. It has no functionality for Releases 12–14, but is still a valid function in order to maintain compatability with older programs. In Release 11 and earlier versions, when an application is so large as to exceed the total amount of node space available, virtual function paging can be used. The *VMON function* enables virtual function paging for all subsequently defined functions. The syntax for this function is:

```
(vmon)
```

Any functions defined prior to the VMON call are not paged out, so this should be at the top of an application. When node space is full, infrequently used functions are paged out. Then, as needed, these functions can be read back into memory.

Note that only functions are paged. All symbols within an application must still fit within available node space. This is especially important when working with large data lists, where one symbol holds much more than just one value.

OVERALL PROGRAM APPEARANCE

The programmer's goal for each application should be not only that it works properly, but also that the application is presented in a professional manner. Every program should have the look and feel of being a built-in function of AutoCAD. This is most important when an application may end up being used by an inexperienced user. If the prompts are similar in format to those provided by AutoCAD, and the program's performance is fairly transparent, users feel much more comfortable using the application.

The term *transparent* in this sense, indicates that an application should not display code across the command line during its evaluation. Remember that this is controlled by the CMDECHO variable. As an application loads, one of the first expressions should be:

```
(setvar "CMDECHO" 0)
```

This also enables an application to run much faster, since it is not necessary to constantly print to the screen.

It can also be helpful to provide default answers with a prompt. A very basic method of providing a default is with the use of the INITGET and GETKWORD functions. Since GETKWORD returns nil when the user strikes the ENTER key without providing a response (note that null input must be allowed by INITGET), a simple test statement can follow. An IF expression could check for a nil value and thereby assign a default. Here is an example:

```
(initget "Yes No")
(setq ANS (getkword "\nOK to proceed? <Y>: "))
(if (null ANS) (setq ANS "Yes"))
```

Another helpful hint for creating a professional application is to use ANSI escape code sequences in prompts and messages when possible. Remember that the line:

```
DEVICE=ANSI.SYS
```

must be included in the CONFIG.SYS file for these to be recognized. In addition, ANSI escape code sequences can only be used when the DOS *text screen* is showing; the graphics screen environment does not recognize ANSI escape codes. When using these codes properly, it is possible to print bold or even colored text strings. This can be a very effective tool for drawing special attention to items of particular importance.

Using Supporting Menus

For almost every standard AutoCAD command, there is a supporting menu. When an editing command is picked from the menu, a submenu facilitating the selection process is invoked. This makes AutoCAD much more "user friendly" by increasing the user's options for input. Although frequent keyboard input is required, AutoCAD is primarily menu driven. Giving your program the capability to invoke screen or icon menus makes it feel more "built in".

As discussed in earlier chapters, the MENUCMD function is used to invoke an AutoCAD menu. It can invoke either a standard AutoCAD menu, or a custom menu of your own design. Often, an existing menu can be useful to your program. One of the most common needs is to select a set of AutoCAD entities. AutoCAD's own selection menus provide options for WINDOW, CROSSING, etc. When your program requires a selection process, the following menu call would be appropriate:

```
(menucmd "S=OSELECT1")
```

If no existing menu provides the options your program needs, then design your own custom screen or icon menu. (For more information on menu customization, see **AutoCAD and its Applications–Advanced** by Shumaker and Madsen, or the *AutoCAD Customization Guide*.)

ERROR HANDLING

Proper error handling is probably the most critical aspect of giving a program the "built-in" look and feel. By default, AutoLISP prints an error message and follows it up by "spitting out" LISP code all over the screen. This particular event can be very frightening to new users of an application.

Programmers can prevent this type of error reporting from occurring by defining custom error handlers. If the symbol *error* evaluates to nil, errors produce the standard results. If the symbol value is non-nil, it is executed as a function and passed as an argument by AutoLISP. Since the symbol is executed as a function, it must be DEFUNed first:

```
(defun *error* (msg)
  (princ "\nError: ")
  (princ msg)
  (princ)
)
```

Having defined an error handler, observe the results:

```
Command: (+ 5 "A") ↵
Error: bad argument type
```

Errors can be defined in any fashion to perform a limited number of tasks. The most common use (as previously shown) is to simply print the error message to the screen and prevent AutoLISP from scrolling LISP code across the screen.

It may be obvious, however, that it is not in the programmer's best interest to prevent the display of LISP code *while* programming. Since the scrolling of the code helps locate the source of the error, it is useful and should be used to your advantage. If an error handler has already been defined, it can be undefined even easier:

```
(setq *error* nil)
```

This returns error handling to AutoLISP's internal mechanism.

The most effective method of handling errors is to prevent them. One common cause of errors is inappropriate user input. All user responses should be controlled. If they cannot be directly controlled using INITGET, then the validity of the response should be checked using some other means.

If a program requires specific circumstances, such as the selection of a particular entity type, the user should be locked in a loop until a valid response is given. For example:

```
(setq ES (entsel "\nSelect a circle: "))
(while
  (or
    (null ES)
    (/= "CIRCLE" (cdr (assoc 0 (entget (car ES)))))
  )
  (princ "\nInvalid selection. Try again...")
  (setq ES (entsel "\nSelect a circle: "))
)
```

Loops like this can prevent many problems by requiring a valid selection before proceeding.

In conjunction with controlling input, it is necessary to report problems to the user in an obvious manner. One means of doing this is provided in the form of the alert dialogue box. The ALERT function displays a dialogue box with a specified message. The syntax for ALERT is:

```
(alert STRING)
```

The string can be any specified message. Note that the line length and overall number of lines displayed are platform, device and window dependent. Subject only to these limitations, any message can be displayed. An alert box can be a more effective way of delivering important messages to the user than by printing them to the command line, since an "OK" button must be picked to dismiss the box and continue. In the next example, an entity selection loop is shown, using an ALERT expression for the user error message:

```
(while
  (null
    (setq EN (entsel "\nPick an entity: "))
  )
  (alert "Requires selection of an entity!")
)
```

Now, when the entity selection is not successful, the dialogue box shown in Fig. 19-4 appears on the screen:

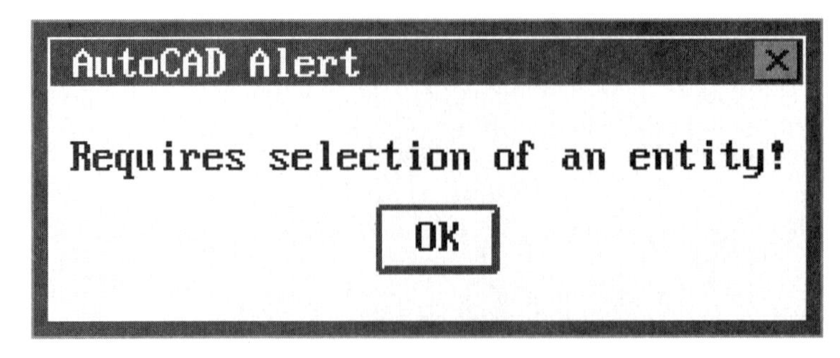

Fig. 19-4. Alert box issued by AutoCAD.

Let's Review...

The programming techniques discussed in this chapter and throughout this text must be used together for the most effective programming results. Here is a list of helpful guidelines for achieving the highest level of productivity in AutoLISP programming:

1. **Create an Outline**
   Before beginning to write the actual program code, a programmer should first generate a short outline to help organize the approach. This outline should describe the overall intent of the program, then describe anticipated subroutines (smaller tasks necessary to achieve the overall goal). This helps the programmer take a more structured approach to writing, thereby making programming time more effective.
2. **Be an Open-Book Programmer**
   No matter how simple the program to be written, it is always advisable to have the *AutoLISP Programmer's Reference* or *Customization Guide* open to the function being used. Even experienced programmers must refer to the documentation regularly. Having it open to verify the proper use and syntax of each function will eliminate many common errors in programming, thus increasing productivity.
3. **Write Many Small Routines Instead of One Large Program**
   When one large program is written as many small subroutines, everything is simplified. First, it is easier to write a small program than a large one. In addition, each subroutine can be tested by itself to ensure that it works before incorporating it into the whole program. Troubleshooting is easier because when an error occurs, it can be isolated into one small subroutine instead of searching the entire program.
4. **Write an Easy-to-Read Program**
   When indentation is properly used to indicate levels of nesting, and capitalization is used to create contrast within the program code, the program is much easier to read. In addition, all program code should be thoroughly documented. These steps require only a few extra minutes, but can save many hours when troubleshooting or revising a program.
5. **When Possible, Do Not Declare Local Symbols Until the Program is Operable**
   Leaving symbols global makes it possible to check the value of each one. In this manner, it can be determined how far a routine made it before an error occurred. After an application is found to work, then make the declarations of local symbols as required.
6. **Be Familiar with the Common Error Messages**
   Familiarity with the causes of common error messages makes it easier to find a problem area. Several of these are listed in Fig. 19-3, but the most common error messages are "bad argument type" and "malformed list."
7. **Use Appropriate Error Handling**
   When writing an application, AutoLISP's internal error handler is typically most useful. Once an application is complete, custom error handling should be in place to handle any unforeseen possibilities for errors. Preventing user-caused errors can be accomplished by effectively controlling the user's input options. When this cannot be accomplished by using the INITGET function, tests and loops can be used.

CHAPTER TEST

Write your answers in the spaces provided.

1. What aspect of programming provides a great deal of overhead when writing a program?

 ____

2. How does proper program indentation help to decrease debugging time?

 ____

 ____

 ____

3. What is the recommended number of spaces for indentation when programming in AutoLISP?

 ____

4. In a program, what is the recommended standard regarding the use of upper- and lowercase characters? Explain why this standard is useful.

 ____

 ____

 ____

 ____

 ____

5. What is indicated by the error message "malformed list"?

 ____

6. What does the error message "bad argument type" indicate?

 ____

 ____

7. What technique can be used to locate the source of a "bad argument type" message?

 ____

 ____

 ____

8. Why should the local variables typically not be declared until your program is running successfully?

 ____

 ____

 ____

9. Explain the usage of the TRACE function.

 ____

 ____

 ____

10. Describe the use of the UNTRACE function.

11. Define the term "virtual memory".

12. On 640K DOS systems using Release 11 and prior releases, what are the LISPHEAP and the LISPSTACK values?

13. Why are LISPHEAP and LISPSTACK no longer used in Release 12 and 13?

14. How can the argument list be an effective memory-management tool?

15. How can a function definition be released from memory?

16. What is the purpose of the VMON function and why is it still supported (although not used) after Release 11?

17. Why should a program's operation be as "transparent" as possible?

18. What line must be in your CONFIG.SYS file to be able to use ANSI escape sequences for altering text appearance?

19. Detail the use of the MENUCMD function.

____

____

____

20. How can the internal error handler in AutoLISP be customized?

____

____

____

PROGRAMMING PROBLEMS

1. Edit all of the programs you created in the programming problems of Chapters 13, 14, 15, and 16 using the techniques described in this chapter. Incorporate custom error handlers, check the upper- and lowercase text use and ensure proper indentation and documentation. Also, make the programs run as transparently as possible and have a real "built-in" look and feel. In appropriate places (such as an SSGET expression) make appropriate menu calls for program support.

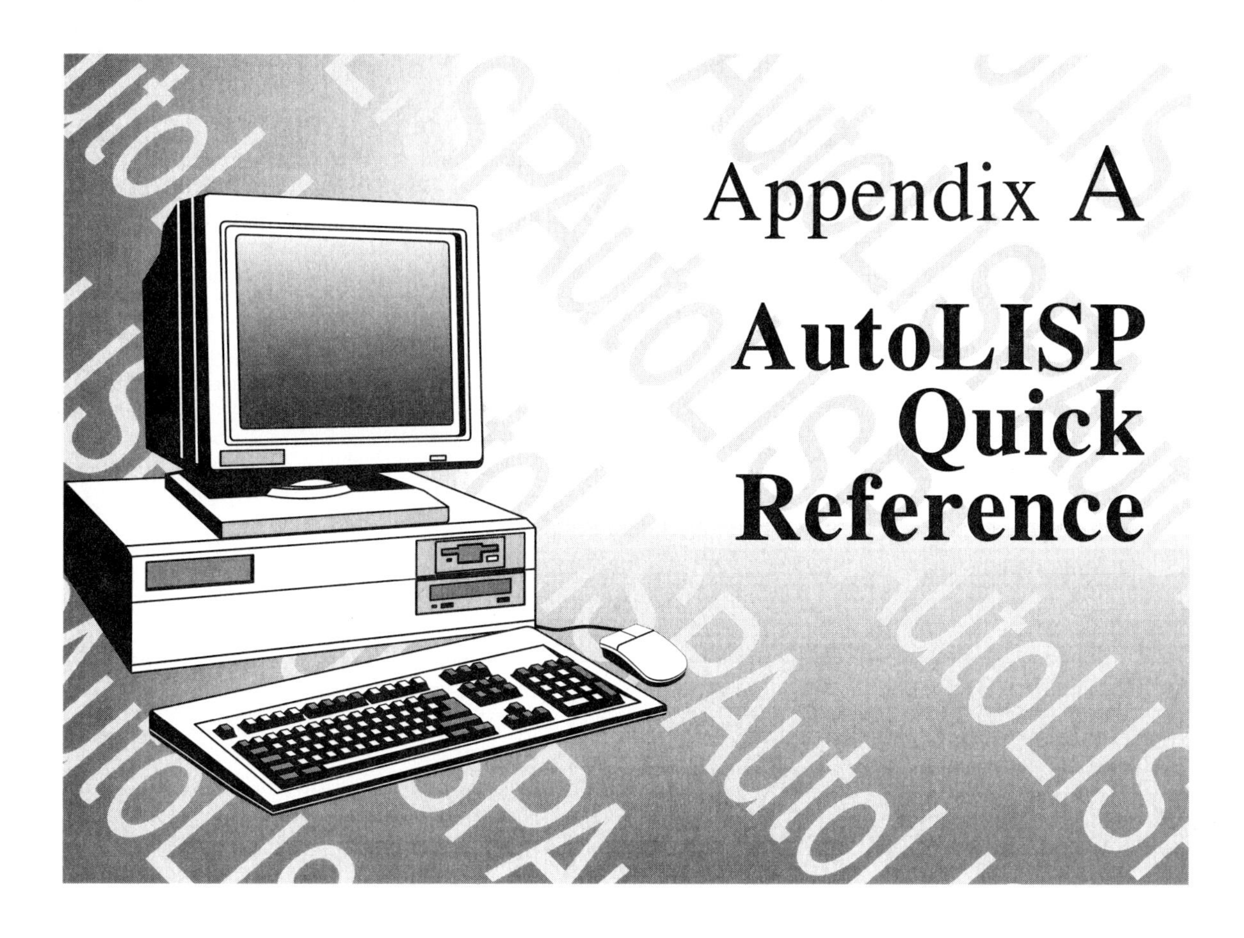

Appendix A

AutoLISP Quick Reference

This section is designed to be a quick reference tool for checking function syntax. In Table A-1, the functions are presented in tabular format, which includes the function name in alphabetical order, a brief description, the AutoCAD version number indicating where the function first appeared, and a corresponding textbook page number where information about the function is located. Table A-2 shows AutoLISP function names grouped into categories of related functions. This table can be helpful when you are looking for information on a function when you are not sure of its name.

Table A-1 includes several pieces of information for each function. First, the correct syntax for each function is supplied. In the column to the right, a description of each function is provided. Directly below the syntax, two numbers appear. The number in the lower-left corner is the release or version number in which the function was initially valid. This is useful when writing AutoLISP applications that need to be compatible with older releases of AutoCAD. Where applicable, the number in the lower-right corner refers you to the page number in the text where the function is thoroughly discussed. See the following illustration to determine the exact placement of these items.

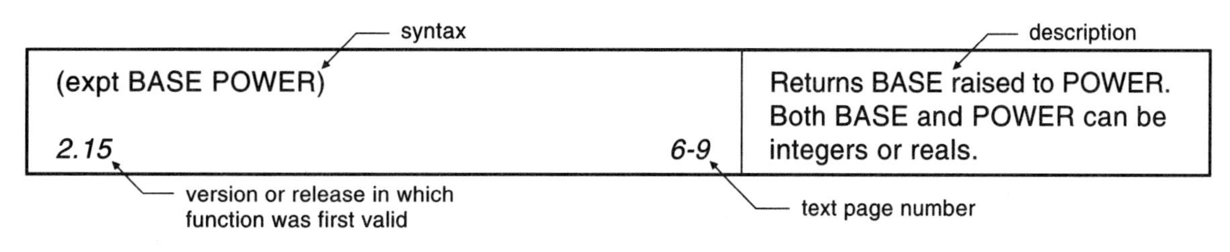

Table A-1. AutoLISP Function Compendium

AutoLISP Function	Description
(– [NUMBER NUMBER] ...) *2.15* *1-6*	Subtracts the sum of the second through the last NUMBERs from the first NUMBER and returns the difference. NUMBERs may be integers or reals.
(* [NUMBER NUMBER] ...) *2.15* *1-6*	Multiplies all NUMBERs and returns the product. NUMBERs may be integers or reals.
(*error* STRING) *2.18* *19-19*	Allows a new error handler to be defined when used within a DEFUN expression.
(+ [NUMBER NUMBER] ...) *2.15* *1-5*	Returns the sum of all NUMBERs supplied to it. NUMBERs may be integers or reals.
(/ [NUMBER NUMBER] ...) *2.15* *1-7*	Divides the first NUMBER by the product of the second through the last NUMBERs and returns the quotient. NUMBERs may be integers or reals.
(/= ATOM ATOM ...) *2.15* *8-4*	Returns T if all arguments are not equal. Arguments can be reals, integers, or strings.
(< ATOM ATOM ...) *2.15* *8-4*	Returns T if each argument is less than the argument to its right. Arguments can be reals, integers, or strings.
(<= ATOM ATOM ...) *2.15* *8-4*	Returns T if each argument is less than or equal to the argument to its right. Arguments can be reals, integers, or strings.
(= ATOM ATOM ...) *2.15* *8-2*	Returns T if all arguments are equal. Arguments can be reals, integers, or strings.
(> ATOM ATOM ...) *2.15* *8-4*	Returns T if each argument is greater than the argument to its right. Arguments can be reals, integers, or strings.
(>= ATOM ATOM ...) *2.15* *8-4*	Returns T if each argument is greater than or equal to the argument to its right. Arguments can be reals, integers, or strings.

AutoLISP Function	Description
(~ NUMBER) *2.15*	Returns the bitwise NOT (one's complement) of NUMBER. NUMBER must be an integer.
(abs NUMBER) *2.15* *6-3*	Returns the absolute value of NUMBER. NUMBER may be an integer or a real.
(acad_colordlg COLORNUM [FLAG]) *13* *4-12*	Displays the standard AutoCAD color selection dialog box.
(acad_helpdlg HELPFILE TOPIC) *13*	Invokes the help facility on all platforms (obsolete).
(acad_strlsort LIST) *13* *7-19*	Sorts a list of strings by alphabetical order.
(action_tile KEY ACTION-EXPRESSION) *12* *18-10*	Associates the specified tile with an ACTION-EXPRESSION or callback.
(add_list ITEM) *12* *18-18*	Adds the specified string to the current list.
(ads) *11*	Returns a list of all currently loaded AutoCAD Development System (ADS) applications.
(alert STRING) *12* *19-20*	Displays STRING in an alert box, and requires the user to pick the OK button to clear the box.
(alloc NUMBER) *2.18*	Sets the segment size to NUMBER nodes. NUMBER must be an integer.
(and EXPRESSION ...) *2.15* *8-11*	Returns T if all EXPRessions evaluate to non-nil values.
(angle PT1 PT2) *2.15* *5-4*	Returns the angle between PT1 and PT2 in radians.
(angtof STRING [MODE]) *12* *7-8*	Returns STRING converted into a real number denoting an angle. MODE, when present, indicates the system of angular measurement.
(angtos ANGLE [MODE [PRECISION]]) *2.18* *7-7*	Returns ANGLE as a string as specified by integer values of MODE and PRECISION (when present).

AutoLISP Function	Description
(append EXPR ...) *2.15* *9-5*	Takes any number of lists and combines the elements of each into one list.
(apply FUNCTION LIST) *2.18* *10-13*	Evaluates FUNCTION using the elements of LIST as its arguments.
(arx) *13*	Returns currently loaded ARX applications as quoted strings within a list.
(arxload APPLICATION [ONFAILURE]) *13*	Loads the specified ARX APPLICATION, or returns ONFAILURE if the load was not successful. APPLICATION must be a string.
(arxunload APPLICATION [ONFAILURE]) *13*	Unloads the specified ARX APPLICATION, or returns ONFAILURE if the load was not successful. APPLICATION must be a string.
(ascii STRING) *2.15* *7-9*	Returns the conversion of the first character of STRING into its ASCII character code.
(ase_docmp OBJ_PATH1 OBJ_PATH2 [NAME_CODE]) *13*	Compares OBJ_PATH1 and OBJ_PATH2 as specified by NAME_CODE, returns T if path arguments are similar, and NIL otherwise.
(ase_docurrent) *13*	Returns the current ASE settings or nil if there is no current database object reference.
(ase_dolist [OBJ_PATH [ATTR]]) *13*	Returns a list of database object paths as specified by the ATTR bit value.
(ase_dopathcode OBJ_PATH) *13*	Returns database object definition code for the specified OBJ_PATH.
(ase_dopathmake ENV_NAME [CAT_NAME [SCHEMA_NAME [TABLE_NAME [LP_NAME]]]]) *13*	Returns full object database path from atomic names.
(ase_dopathname OBJ_PATH NAME_CODE) *13*	Returns the name as specified by NAME_CODE from the database object path.

AutoLISP Function	Description
(ase_dostatus [OBJ_PATH]) *13*	Returns an integer indicating current status of the current or specified object path.
(ase_errcode ERR_NUM) *13*	Returns the ASE error code.
(ase_errdsc ERR_NUM) *13*	Indicates the cause of the error descriptor number ERR_NUM.
(ase_errmsg ERR_NUM) *13*	Returns the error message for the error descriptor number ERR_NUM.
(ase_errqty) *13*	Returns the number of error descriptors, or 0 if there are no errors.
(ase_linkcreate LINK_DATA) *13*	Creates a new link based on the LINK_DATA description.
(ase_linkget LINK_DATA) *13*	Returns the link data for specified link.
(ase_linkremove LINK_ID) *13*	Removes specified link.
(ase_linkupdate LINK_DATA) *13*	Updates an existing link.
(ase_lpcreate TABLE_PATH LP_NAME KEY) *13*	Creates a new link path.
(ase_lperase LP_NAME) *13*	Erases specified link path.
(ase_lpkey LP_NAME) *13*	Returns the key column names for the specified link table.
(ase_lplist [OBJ_PATH]) *13*	Returns a list of the path names related to the specified database object reference.
(ase_lppath LP_NAME) *13*	Returns the table path or the specified link path name.
(ase_lprename LP_OLDNAME LP_NEWNAME) *13*	Renames a link path as specified.

AutoLISP Function	Description
(ase_lpisupdatable LP_NAME) *13*	Returns T if the link path is updatable, and NIL otherwise.
(ase_lsadd LINK_SEL LINK_ID) *13*	Adds link identifier LINK_ID to the link selection LINK_SEL.
(ase_lscmp LINK_SEL1 LINK_SEL2) *13*	Returns T if LINK_SEL1 and LINK_SEL2 are similar, and NIL otherwise.
(ase_lscopy LINK_SEL) *13*	Copies the link selection into a new one.
(ase_lscreate LINK_FILTER) *13*	Creates a link selection base on the LINK_FILTER.
(ase_lsdel LINK_SEL LINK_NUM) *13*	Deletes a link position from the specified link selection.
(ase_lsentsel LINK_SEL) *13*	Returns a selection set of entities related to the links in the link selection LINK_SEL.
(ase_lserase LINK_SEL) *13*	Erases the links and clears the link selection.
(ase_lsfree LINK_SEL) *13*	Frees the link selection.
(ase_lsget LINK_SEL LINK_NUM) *13*	Returns the link identifier for the position LINK_NUM in the link selection LINK_SEL.
(ase_lsintersect LINK_SEL LINK_SEL_INTERSECT) *13*	Deletes all link identifiers from a link selection *except* those specified in LINK_SEL_INTERSECT.
(ase_lsintersectfilter LINK_FILTER) *13*	Removes link identifiers from a link selection that are not related to the specified link filter.
(ase_lsisupdatable LINK_SEL) *13*	Returns T if all links in the link selection are updatable.

AutoLISP Function	Description
(ase_lslpnames LINK_SEL) *13*	Returns a list of all related link path names from the link selection.
(ase_lsmemb LINK_SEL LINK_ID) *13*	Checks whether a link identifier is a member of the link selection.
(ase_lsqty LINK_SEL) *13*	Returns the number of links in the link selection LINK_SEL.
(ase_lssubtract LINK_SEL LINK_SEL_SUBTRACT) *13*	Deletes all link identifiers specified in LINK_SEL_SUBTRACT from a link selection.
(ase_lsunite LINK_SEL LINK_SEL_UNION) *13*	Adds a link selection specified in LINK_SEL_UNION to the one specified in LINK_SEL.
(ase_lsxnames LINK_SEL) *13*	Returns a list of related block or xref names from LINK_SEL.
(ase_version) *13*	Returns the current ASE version.
(assoc ITEM ALIST) *2.18* *10-3*	Searches the association list (ALIST) for the key ITEM and returns the associated data.
(atan NUM1 [NUM2]) *2.15* *6-7*	Returns the arctangent of NUMBER in radians. NUMBER may be an integer or a real.
(atof STRING) *2.18* *7-2*	Returns the conversion of STRING into a real number value.
(atoi STRING) *2.15* *7-4*	Returns the conversion of STRING into an integer.
(atom ITEM) *2.15* *8-5*	Returns T if ITEM is an atom (not a list).
(atoms-family FORMAT [SYMLIST]) *12* *12-32*	Returns a list of previously defined symbols. FORMAT is an integer with a value of 0 or 1, and SYMLIST is an optional list of symbols to search for.

AutoLISP Function	Description
(autoarxload FILENAME CMDLIST) *13*	The .ARX file name specified is loaded when any of the commands defined by CMDLIST is entered.
(autoload FILENAME CMDLIST) *13*	The .LSP file name specified is loaded when any of the commands defined by CMDLIST is entered.
(autoxload FILENAME CMDLIST) *13*	The ADS application file name specified is loaded when any of the commands defined by CMDLIST is entered.
(Boole FUNC INT1 INT2 ...) *2.18*	A general bitwise Boolean function.
(boundp ATOM) *2.15* *8-7*	Returns T if ATOM is bound to a value.
(caar LIST), (cadr LIST), (cddr LIST), (cadar LIST), etc. *2.18* *3-9*	Returns the specified element or portion of LIST. Up to four levels of concatenation are supported.
(car LIST) *2.15* *3-5*	Returns the first element of LIST.
(cdr LIST) *2.15* *3-6*	Returns LIST without the first element.
(chr INTEGER) *2.15* *7-10*	Returns the conversion of the specified INTEGER ASCII code into the character it represents.
(client_data_tile KEY CLIENTDATA) *12*	Associates application-managed data with the specified tile.
(close FILE-DESC) *2.18* *14-6*	Closes the open file specified by FILE-DESC. FILE-DESC is the file handle returned when the file was opened.
(command [ARGUMENTS] ...) *2.18* *2-15*	Executes one or more AutoCAD commands as specified by the ARGUMENTS.

AutoLISP Function		Description
(cond (TEST1 RESULT1 ...) ...) *2.15*	*8-18*	The primary conditional function in AutoLISP. The first non-nil TEST causes the corresponding RESULT to be evaluated.
(cons NEW-FIRST-ELEMENT LIST) *2.15*	*10-4*	Returns LIST with NEW-FIRST-ELEMENT added to the beginning.
(cos ANGLE) *2.15*	*6-7*	Returns the cosine of ANGLE, where ANGLE is expressed in radians. ANGLE may be an integer or a real.
(cvunit VALUE FROM TO) *11*	*5-3*	Returns the conversion of VALUE in FROM units into TO units.
(defun SYM ARGUMENT-LIST EXPR ...) *2.18*	*2-19*	Defines a new function name, where SYM is the name. Any number of EXPRessions are evaluated using any supplied arguments as indicated in ARGUMENT-LIST.
(dictadd ENAME SYMBOL NEWOBJ) *13*	*15-29*	Adds a nongraphical object to the specified dictionary.
(dictnext ENAME SYMBOL [REWIND]) *13*	*15-21*	The ENAME dictionary object is searched incrementally or for the item SYMBOL. Using the non-nil argument REWIND returns to the first entry.
(dictremove ENAME SYMBOL) *13*	*15-32*	Removes an entry from the specified dictionary.
(dictrename ENAME OLDSYM NEWSYM) *13*	*15-25*	Renames a dictionary entry.
(dictsearch ENAME SYMBOL [SETNEXT]) *13*	*15-23*	The ENAME dictionary object is searched for SYMBOL. Successful searches reset the position of the *dictnext* marker.
(dimx_tile KEY) (dimy_tile KEY) *12*	*18-23*	Returns the X or Y dimensions of the specified tile.
(distance PT1 PT2) *2.15*	*5-5*	Finds the distance between PT1 and PT2.

AutoLISP Function			Description
(distof STRING [MODE])	*12*	*7-3*	Returns the conversion of STRING into a real value according to the integer argument MODE.
(done_dialog [STATUS])	*12*	*18-4*	Terminates the current dialogue box and removes it from the display. This can only be called from within an action expression or a callback function.
(end_image)	*12*	*18-26*	Ends the creation of the currently active image.
(end_list)	*12*	*18-19*	Ends processing of the current list.
(entdel ENAME)	*2.5*		Deletes or undeletes the entity whose name is ENAME.
(entget ENAME [APPLIST])	*2.5*	*13-4*	Gets the database record for a specified entity name ENAME. The optional APPLIST argument causes the associated extended entity data to be returned as well.
(entlast)	*2.5*	*13-10*	Returns the name of the last main entity listing in the drawing database.
(entmake [ELIST])	*11*	*13-25*	Appends a new entity definition to the drawing database.
(entmakex [ELIST])	*13*		Makes a new object or entity, giving it a handle and entity name.
(entmod ELIST)	*2.5*	*13-21*	Updates the drawing database records using the entity data record ELIST.
(entnext [ENAME])	*2.5*	*13-2*	With no arguments, this function returns the name of the first entity in the drawing database. Otherwise, this function returns the name of the entity whose record is found directly after ENAME in the database.

AutoLISP Function			Description
(entsel [PROMPT])	*2.5*	*13-11*	Prompts user to select an entity and returns the entity name and the point picked.
(entupd ENAME)	*2.5*	*13-22*	Updates the screen image of a modified entity.
(eq EXPR1 EXPR2)	*2.15*	*8-3*	Returns T if the two expressions (EXPR1 and EXPR2) are identical. Reals, integers, strings, or lists are valid arguments.
(equal EXPR1 EXPR2 [FUZZ])	*2.15*	*8-3*	Returns T if both expressions (EXPR1 and EXPR2) evaluate to the same thing. Reals, integers, strings, or lists are valid arguments. FUZZ represents the maximum numeric amount by which EXPR1 and EXPR2 can vary and still be considered equal.
(eval EXPR)	*2.18*	*9-9*	Evaluates any EXPRession and returns the result.
(exit)	*12*		Forces the current AutoLISP application to quit.
(exp NUMBER)	*2.15*	*6-10*	Returns the constant *e* raised to the NUMBER power (natural antilog). NUMBER may be an integer or a real.
(expand NUMBER)	*2.18*		Allocates node space by requesting a specified NUMBER of segments.
(expt BASE POWER)	*2.15*	*6-9*	Returns BASE raised to POWER. Both BASE and POWER can be integers or reals.
(fill_image X1 Y1 WID HGT COLOR)	*12*	*18-22*	Draws a filled rectangle in the currently active tile.
(findfile FILENAME)	*10*	*14-2*	Searches for FILENAME. If no path is specified, the library path is searched.

AutoLISP Function		Description
(fix NUMBER) *2.15*	*6-2*	Returns NUMBER converted into an integer. A real number is expected, but if an integer is supplied it is returned unchanged.
(float NUMBER) *2.15*	*6-2*	Returns NUMBER promoted to a real. An integer is expected, but if a real is supplied, it is returned unchanged.
(foreach NAME LIST EXPR ...) *2.18*	*9-8*	Loops once "for each" element of LIST, evaluating all EXPRessions, and assigning NAME to the current element.
(gc) *2.15*	*12-3*	Forces a garbage collection.
(gcd NUM1 NUM2) *2.15*	*6-4*	Returns the greatest common denominator of two numbers (NUM1 and NUM2). Both numbers must be integers.
(get_attr KEY ATTRIBUTE) *12*		Returns the DCL value of the specified ATTRIBUTE.
(get_tile KEY) *12*	*18-13*	Returns the run–time value of the specified tile.
(getangle [PT] [PROMPT]) *2.15*	*5-6*	PROMPTs for user input of an angle. The optional point (PT) argument can be specified as a base point for the angle to be measured from.
(getcfg CFGNAME) *13*	*14-13*	Returns application data from AppData section of ACAD.CFG for specified CFGNAME.
(getcname CNAME) *13*	*7-21*	Retrieves the localized or English name of an AutoCAD command.
(getcorner PT [PROMPT]) *2.6*	*3-13*	PROMPTs for user input of a point (PT), drawing a dynamic rectangle until the point is picked.
(getdist [PT] [PROMPT]) *2.15*	*5-10*	PROMPTs for user input of a distance. The optional point (PT) argument is a base point and causes a rubberband line to be maintained until a point is picked.

AutoLISP Function	Description
(getenv VARIABLE-NAME) *10* *14-14*	Returns the current value of the environmental variable name.
(getfiled TITLE DEFAULT EXT FLAGS) *12* *14-3*	Prompts the user to select a filename using the standard AutoCAD File dialogue box. The TITLE argument specifies a label for the dialogue box. DEFAULT specifies a filename to use, while EXT is the DEFAULT filename extension. Finally, the FLAGS argument controls the behavior of the dialogue box.
(getint [PROMPT]) *2.15* *4-2*	Prompts user for input of an integer. Only integer input is valid.
(getkword [PROMPT]) *2.6* *4-8*	Prompts user for input of a keyword as specified by a preceding initget expression.
(getorient [PT] [PROMPT]) *2.5* *5-8*	PROMPTs for user input of an angle, but the returned angle is not based on the current settings of ANGBASE and ANGDIR. The optional point argument (PT) can be specified as a base point for the angle to be measured from.
(getpoint [PT] [PROMPT]) *2.15* *3-3*	PROMPTs for user input of a point. If the optional point (PT) argument is used, a rubberband line is maintained until the point is picked.
(getreal [PROMPT]) *2.15* *4-3*	Prompts user for input of a real number. Integers are also acceptable input and are returned as reals.
(getstring [CR] [PROMPT]) *2.15* *4-5*	PROMPTs user for input of a string. If the optional non-nil argument is used for CR, spaces are allowed in the string.

AutoLISP Function		Description
(getvar VARNAME) *2.15*	*4-10*	Returns the current setting of VARNAME, where VARNAME is an AutoCAD system variable. The VARNAME argument must be a string.
(graphscr) *2.15*	*16-2*	Displays the current graphics screen.
(grclear) *2.5*	*16-14*	Clears the graphics screen.
(grdraw FROM TO COLOR [HIGHLIGHT]) *2.5*	*16-15*	Draws a vector between the FROM and TO points in the current viewport. The color and condition of the vector depends on the COLOR and HIGHLIGHT settings.
(grread [TRACK] [ALLKEYS [CURTYPE]]) *2.5*	*16-26*	Reads input from an input device, subject to the settings of TRACK and ALLKEYS. The cursor type is controlled by the CURTYPE argument.
(grtext [BOX TEXT [HIGHLIGHT]]) *2.5*	*16-22*	Displays text in the menu, status, and/or mode areas of the graphics screen. If BOX is called, then the string argument TEXT is displayed in the BOX. If HIGHLIGHT is specified, grtext highlights the TEXT in the BOX.
(grvecs VLIST [TRANS]) *12*	*16-18*	Draws multiple vectors in the current viewport. The optional TRANS argument uses a transformation matrix to change the location or proportion of the vectors defined in VLIST.
(handent HANDLE) *10*	*13-10*	Returns the name of the entity whose handle is HANDLE.
(help [HELPFILE [TOPIC [COMMAND]]]) *13*		Starts the AutoCAD Help Facility using optional filtering arguments.

AutoLISP Function		Description
(if TESTEXPR THENEXPR [ELSEEXPR]) *2.18*	*8-8*	Evaluates THENEXPR if TESTEXPR is non-nil. If TESTEXPR is nil and ELSEEXPR is present, ELSEEXPR is evaluated instead.
(initget [BITS] [STRING]) *2.6*	*4-7*	Controls user input for the next GETxxxx function as defined by BITS and STRING.
(inters PT1 PT2 PT3 PT4 [ONSEG]) *2.6*	*5-17*	Returns the point at which an imaginary line with endpoints PT1 and PT2 intersects another imaginary line with endpoints PT3 and PT4. If the optional ONSEG argument is present and nil, the lines are considered to be infinite in length.
(itoa INTEGER) *2.15*	*7-6*	Returns INTEGER as a string.
(lambda ARGUMENTS EXPR ...) *2.18*	*10-15*	Defines an anonymous function.
(last LIST) *2.18*	*3-15*	Returns the last element in LIST. The LIST argument cannot be nil.
(length LIST) *2.18*	*3-15*	Returns an integer that indicates the number of elements within LIST.
(list EXPRESSION ...) *2.15*	*3-2*	Returns a list containing all EXPRessions.
(listp ITEM) *2.15*	*8-6*	Returns T if ITEM is a list.
(load FILENAME [ONFAILURE]) *2.18*	*2-6*	Loads the specified AutoLISP FILENAME, or returns ONFAILURE if the load was not successful. FILENAME must be a string.
(load_dialog DCLFILE) *12*	*18-2*	Loads the specified Dialogue Control Language (DCL) file.

AutoLISP Function	Description
(log NUMBER) *2.15* *6-10*	Returns the natural log of NUMBER. NUMBER may be an integer or a real.
(logand NUMBER NUMBER ...) *2.15*	Returns the logical bitwise AND of all NUMBERs. NUMBERs must be integers.
(logior INTEGER ...) *2.15*	Returns the logical bitwise inclusive OR of all NUMBERs. Only integer arguments are accepted.
(lsh NUM1 NUMBITS) *2.18*	Returns the logical bitwise shift of NUM1 by a given number of bits (NUMBITS). Only integer arguments are accepted.
(mapcar FUNCTION LIST1 ... LISTN) *2.18* *10-14*	Returns a list as a result of evaluating FUNCTION with the elements of the supplied LISTs.
(max NUMBER NUMBER ...) *2.15* *6-5*	Returns the largest of the supplied NUMBERs. Accepts integer and/or real numbers as arguments.
(mem) *2.15*	Displays the current status of AutoLISP's memory.
(member EXPR LIST) *2.15* *10-5*	Returns a list beginning with EXPR if it is found within LIST.
(menucmd STRING) *2.5* *16-6*	Invokes the menu indicated by STRING.
(menugroup GROUPNAME) *14* *16-11*	Verifies that a menugroup is loaded.
(min NUMBER NUMBER ...) *2.15* *6-5*	Returns the smallest of the supplied NUMBERs. Accepts integer and/or real numbers as arguments.

AutoLISP Function		Description
(minusp ITEM) *2.15*	*8-6*	Returns T if ITEM is a real or an interger and evaluates to a negative value.
(mode_tile KEY MODE) *12*	*18-11*	Sets the MODE of the tile having the key assignment KEY.
(namedobjdict) *13*	*15-18*	Returns the entity name of the current named object dictionary.
(nentsel [PROMPT]) *11*	*13-12*	Returns the name of a selected subentity and a 4x3 model to world coordinate transformation matrix.
(nentselp [PROMPT] [PT]) *12*	*13-18*	Returns the name of a selected subentity and a 4x4 model to world coordinate transformation matrix. The optional PT argument can be used to make an automatic selection.
(new_dialog DLGNAME DCL_ID [ACTION-EXPRESSION [SCREEN-PT]]) *12*	*18-3*	Initializes a new dialogue box as specified and displays it on screen.
(not ITEM) *2.15*	*8-12*	Returns T if ITEM evaluates to nil.
(nth N LIST) *2.15*	*10-9*	Returns the Nth element of LIST.
(null ITEM) *2.15*	*8-7*	Returns T if ITEM is bound to nil.
(numberp ITEM) *2.15*	*8-6*	Returns T if ITEM evaluates to a number (real or integer).

AutoLISP Function		Description
(open FILENAME MODE) *2.18*	*14-4*	Opens a file specified by FILENAME for reading, writing, or appending as indicated by MODE. FILENAME must be a string and MODE must be a lowercase string.
(or EXPRESSION ...) *2.15*	*8-12*	Returns T if any of the EXPRessions evaluate to a non-nil value.
(osnap PT MODE-STRING) *2.15*	*5-13*	Returns a point resulting from applying the MODE-STRING object snap modes to PT.
pi *2.15*	*5-2*	Evaluates to the constant *pi* (3.14159).
(polar PT ANGLE DISTANCE) *2.15*	*5-5*	Returns the point found DIST units from PT at ANGLE direction.
(prin1 [EXPR [FILE-DESC]]) *2.15*	*7-13*	Prints EXPR to the screen or to the open file specified by FILE-DESC.
(princ [EXPR [FILE-DESC]]) *2.15*	*7-14*	Prints EXPR to the screen or to the open file specified by FILE-DESC.
(print [EXPR [FILE-DESC]]) *2.15*	*7-15*	Prints EXPR to the screen or to the open file specified by FILE-DESC.
(progn EXPRESSION ...) *2.18*	*8-10*	Evaluates each EXPRession sequentially, and allows more than one EXPRession to be evaluated where only one EXPRession is expected.
(prompt MESSAGE) *2.15*	*2-13*	Displays MSG on the prompt line.
(quit) *12*		Forces the current AutoLISP application to quit.

AutoLISP Function		Description
(quote EXPR ...) *2.15*	*2-10*	Returns an EXPRession unevaluated.
(read STRING) *2.18*	*7-11*	Returns the first list or atom obtained from STRING.
(read-char [FILE-DESC]) *2.18*	*14-10*	Reads one character from keyboard input or from the open file specified by FILE-DESC, and returns the ASCII numeric value for that character.
(read-line [FILE-DESC]) *2.18*	*14-5*	Reads one line of input from the keyboard or from the open file specified by FILE-DESC and returns the string.
(redraw [ENAME [MODE]]) *2.15*	*16-4*	Redraws the entity specified by ENAME in the indicated MODE. If no arguments are given, the current viewport is redrawn.
(regapp APPLICATION) *11*		Registers the APPLICATION's extended entity data.
(rem NUMBER NUMMBER...) *2.15*	*6-4*	Divides the first number (NUM1) by the second number (NUM2) and returns the remainder. Either integers or reals are valid arguments.
(repeat NUMBER EXPR ...) *2.18*	*9-2*	Evaluates all EXPRessions NUMBER times. NUMBER must be an integer.
(reverse LIST) *2.15*	*10-7*	Returns LIST in reverse order.
(rtos NUMBER [MODE [PRECISION]]) *2.18*	*7-4*	Returns NUMBER converted to a string as specified by the integer arguments MODE and PRECISION.
(set SYM EXPR) *2.18*	*9-8*	Sets the value of a quoted SYMbol to that of an EXPRession.

AutoLISP Function			Description
(set_tile KEY VALUE)	*12*	*18-8*	Sets the run–time value of the specified tile.
(setcfg CFGNAME CFGVAL)	*13*	*14-12*	Writes application data to the AppData section of ACAD.CFG.
(setfunhelp C:FNAME [HELPFILE [TOPIC [COMMAND]]])	*13*		Registers a user defined command name with the AutoCAD Help Facility.
(setq SYM1 EXPR1 [SYM2 EXPR2] ...)	*2.15*	*1-12*	Sets the value of any number of SYMbols to the value of the specified EXPRession(s).
(setvar VARNAME VALUE)	*2.15*	*4-10*	Sets the value of an AutoCAD system variable VARNAME to the VALUE setting.
(setview VIEW_DESCRIPTOR [VPORT_ID])	*13*	*15-41*	Establishes a view for a specified viewport.
(sin ANGLE)	*2.15*	*6-6*	Returns the sine of ANGLE. ANGLE must be expressed in radians.
(slide_image X1 Y1 WID HGT SLDNAME)	*12*	*18-29*	Draws an AutoCAD slide in the currently active image.
(snvalid SYM_NAME [FLAG])	*13*	*15-12*	Checks the symbol table for valid characters.
(sqrt NUMBER)	*2.15*	*6-9*	Returns the square root of NUMBER. The NUMBER may be either an integer or a real.
(ssadd [ENAME [SS]])	*2.5*	*12-31*	Adds the entity ENAME to the selection set (SS), or can be used to create a new selection set.
(ssdel ENAME SS)	*2.5*	*12-35*	Removes the entity ENAME from selection set SS.

AutoLISP Function	Description
(ssget [MODE] [PT1 [PT2]] [PT-LIST] [FILTER-LIST]) *2.5 and 9* *12-2*	Creates a selection set based on the selection modes, points, and filters specified.
(ssgetfirst) *13* *12-21*	Determines which objects are selected and gripped.
(sslength SS) *2.5* *12-23*	Returns the number of entities in selection set SS.
(ssmemb ENAME SS) *2.5* *12-36*	Returns ENAME if the entity name is found in selection set SS.
(ssname SS INDEX) *2.5* *12-25*	Returns the name of the entity found at position number INDEX in the selection set SS.
(ssnamex SS [INDEX]) *13* *12-27*	Returns information about how a selection set was created.
(sssetfirst GRIPSET [PICKSET]) *13* *12-23*	Sets which objects are selected and gripped.
(start_dialog) *12* *18-3*	Begins accepting user input from the dialogue box initialized by the new_dialog call.
(start_image KEY) *12* *18-22*	Starts creating the specified image.
(start_list KEY [OPERATION [INDEX]]) *12* *18-18*	Starts processing the specified list box or popup list.
(startapp APPCMD FILE) *13*	Executes the Windows application APPCMD using the filename FILE.
(strcase STRING [WHICH]) *2.5* *7-16*	Returns STRING with all characters in upper- or lowercase as specified by the WHICH argument.

AutoLISP Function	Description
(strcat STRING1 [STRING2] ...) *2.15* *7-17*	Returns a string formed by concatenating one or more STRING arguments.
(strlen [STRING] ...) *2.15* *7-18*	Returns an integer indicating the total number of characters contained in all of the STRING arguments.
(subst NEWitem OLDitem LIST) *2.15* *13-20*	Returns LIST with NEW-ITEM substituted for each occurrence of OLD-ITEM.
(substr STRING START [LENGTH]) *2.15* *7-18*	Returns a portion of STRING as specified by the integer arguments START and LENGTH.
(tablet CODE [ROW1 ROW2 ROW3 DIRECTION]) *12* *16-11*	Controls digitizer calibration.
(tblnext TABLE-NAME [REWIND]) *2.6* *15-2*	Returns the next item in the specified TABLE-NAME. If the optional non-nil argument REWIND is used, then tblnext goes back to the beginning of the table.
(tblobjname TABLE-NAME SYMBOL) *13* *15-11*	Returns the entity name of the specified symbol table entry.
(tblsearch TABLE-NAME SYMBOL [SETNEXT]) *2.6* *15-9*	Searches for SYMBOL in TABLE-NAME. The optional non-nil argument SETNEXT causes the next use of tblnext to return the entry after this one.
(term_dialog) *12* *18-4*	Terminates all current dialogue boxes and removes them from the display as if the user had canceled them.
(terpri) *2.15*	Prints a newline on the screen.

AutoLISP Function		Description
(textbox ELIST) *12*	*13-30*	Returns the displacement of the lower-left and upper-right corners of the bounding box for a text entity from the insertion point.
(textpage) *11*	*16-2*	Displays the current text screen and clears it.
(textscr) *2.15*	*16-2*	Displays the current text screen.
(trace FUNCTION ...) *2.18*	*19-10*	Traces the evaluation of each FUNCTION, reporting when each begins and showing the results of the evaluation.
(trans PT FROM TO [DISP]) *10*		Returns PT translated between the FROM coordinate system and the TO coordinate system. The optional DISP argument causes the 3D point to be treated as a displacement.
(type ITEM) *2.18*	*8-16*	Returns the data type of ITEM.
(unload_dialog DCL_ID) *12*	*18-5*	Unloads the specified DCL file.
(untrace FUNCTION ...) *2.18*	*19-12*	Discontinues the trace for specified FUNCTIONs.
(vector_image X1 Y1 X2 Y2 COLOR) *12*		Draws a vector in the currently active image.
(ver) *2.18*	*14-13*	Returns the current AutoLISP version number in a string.
(vmon) *2.5*	*19-18*	Allows virtual function paging.

AutoLISP Function		Description
(vports) *10*	*15-35*	Returns a list of viewport descriptors for the current viewport configuration.
(wcmatch STRING PATTERN) *11*	*15-14*	Matches a STRING to a specified wild card PATTERN.
(while TESTEXPR EXPR ...) *2.18*	*9-3*	Repeats evaluation of all EXPRessions until TESTEXPR evaluates to nil.
(write-char NUM [FILE-DESC]) *2.18*	*14-11*	Writes one character specified as a ASCII numeric code either to the screen or to the open file indicated by FILE-DESC.
(write-line STRING [FILE-DESC]) *2.18*	*14-6*	Writes STRING to the screen or to the open file indicated by FILE-DESC.
(xdroom ENAME) *11*		Returns the amount of available memory (in bytes) that an entity has for extended entity data.
(xdsize LIST) *11*		Returns the amount of memory (in bytes) that a list of extended entity data will require.
(xload APPLICATION [ONFAILURE]) *11*		Loads an ADS application or returns ONFAILURE if it is not successful.
(xunload APPLICATION [ONFAILURE]) *11*		Unloads an ADS application or returns ONFAILURE if it is unsuccessful.
(zerop ITEM) *2.15*	*8-7*	Returns T if ITEM evaluates to a real or an integer, and has a value of zero.
(1+ NUMBER) *2.15*	*9-6*	Returns the value of NUMBER increased by one. NUMBER may be an integer or a real.
(1– NUMBER) *2.15*	*9-6*	Returns the value of NUMBER decreased by one. NUMBER may be an integer or a real.

Table A-2. AutoLISP Functions Grouped by Related Functions

Category	Related Functions	
ARITHMETIC	+ – * / ~ 1+ 1– abs atan cos exp expt	gcd log logand logior lsh max min pi rem sin sqrt
ARX HANDLING	arx arxload	arxunload autoarxload
ASE HANDLING	ase_docmp ase_docurrent ase_dolist ase_dopathcode ase_dopathmake ase_dopathname ase_dostatus ase_errcode ase_errdsc ase_errmsg ase_errqty ase_linkcreate ase_linkget ase_linkremove ase_linkupdate ase_lpcreate ase_lperase ase_lpisupdatable ase_lpkey ase_lplist ase_lppath	ase_lprename ase_lsadd ase_lscmp ase_lscopy ase_lscreate ase_lsdel ase_lsentsel ase_lserase ase_lsfree ase_lsget ase_lsintersect ase_lsintersectfilter ase_lsisupdatable ase_lslpnames ase_lsmemb ase_lsqty ase_lssubtract ase_lsunite ase_lsxnames ase_version
SYMBOL HANDLING	atoms-family quote set	setq type
STRING HANDLING	acad_strlsort read read-char read-line strcase	strcat strlen substr write-char write-line

Category	Related Functions	
CONVERSIONS	angtos	distof
	angtof	fix
	ascii	float
	atof	itoa
	atoi	rtos
	chr	trans
	cvunit	
PREDICATES/CONDITIONALS/LOOPS	=	equal
	/=	if
	<	listp
	<=	minusp
	>	not
	>=	null
	and	numberp
	atom	or
	Boole	progn
	boundp	repeat
	cond	while
	eq	zerop
LIST MANIPULATION	append	cdaadr
	apply	cadaar
	assoc	caddar
	car	cadadr
	cdr	caadar
	caar	caaddr
	cadr	cdddar
	cdar	cddadr
	cddr	cdaddr
	caaar	cadddr
	caadr	cddddr
	cadar	cons
	cdaar	foreach
	caddr	last
	cdadr	length
	cddar	list
	cdddr	mapcar
	caaaar	member
	cdaaar	nth
	cddaar	reverse
	cdadar	subst
NAMED OBJECT HANDLING	dictadd	dictsearch
	dictnext	entmakex
	dictremove	namedobjdict
	dictrename	

Category	Related Functions	
HELP FACILITY MANAGEMENT	acad_helpdlg help	setfunhelp
FILE HANDLING	autoload close findfile getfiled load open	read read-char read-line startapp write-char write-line
FUNCTION HANDLING	apply defun eval exit lambda mapcar	progn quit setfunhelp trace untrace
DISPLAY CONTROL/GRAPHICS	acad_colordlg graphscr grclear grdraw grread grtext grvecs menucmd menugroup prin1	princ print prompt redraw setview terpri textpage textscr vports
WILD CARD MATCHING	wcmatch	
USER INPUT	getangle getcname getcorner getdist getint getkword	getorient getpoint getreal getstring initget
GEOMETRIC UTILITIES	angle distance inters	osnap polar textbox
QUERIES AND COMMANDS	command findfile getfiled	getvar setvar
APPLICATION DATA	getcfg	setcfg

Category	Related Functions	
ERROR HANDLING	alert *error* exit	quit trace untrace
SELECTION SETS	ssadd ssdel ssget ssgetfirst sslength	ssmemb ssname ssnamex sssetfirst
ENTITY HANDLING	entdel entget entlast entmake entmod entnext	entsel entupd handent nentsel nentselp
EXTENDED ENTITY DATA	regapp xdsize	xdroom
SYMBOL TABLES	snvalid tblnext	tblobjname tblsearch
ADS APPLICATION HANDLING	ads autoxload	xload xunload
MEMORY MANAGEMENT	alloc expand gc	mem vmon
MISCELLANEOUS	getenv tablet	ver
DCL FILE HANDLING	load_dialog	unload_dialog
DIALOG BOX CONTROL	action_tile client_data_tile done_dialog get_attr mode_tile	new_dialog set_tile start_dialog term_dailog
LIST BOXES AND POPUP LISTS	add_list end_list	start_list
HANDLING IMAGE TILES	dimx_tile dimy_tile end_image fill_image	slide_image start_image vector_image

Appendix B DXF Group Codes

The following DXF group codes are used in the entity-definition records in the drawing database. All optional codes are noted with their standard default values.

Table B-1 is a generic listing of DXF group codes that are presented in numerical order. For specific usages of these codes, refer to the listings of DXF group codes by entity type in Tables B-2 and B-3.

The group codes found in Table B-2 are common to all entities and are used in conjunction with the entity-specific codes listed in Table B-3.

Table B-3 lists the precise meaning of each code when used to define a specific entity type. Remember that the codes in this table are not necessarily sufficient for a complete entity definition; the codes in Table B-2 must be considered as well. The listings are presented so that required fields are shown first, followed by optional fields.

Codes noted as “fixed” indicate that the field always has the same purpose. Those that are not “fixed” may have different meanings depending upon the entity they define.

Table B-1. Group Codes

Group Code	Description
–5	Application: Persistent reactor chain
–4	Application: Conditional operator (used only with ssget)
–3	Application: Extended entity data (XDATA) sentinel; (fixed)
–2	Application: Entity name reference; (fixed)
–1	Application: Entity name. Changes each time a drawing is opened; never saved; (fixed)
0	Starts an entity. Text string indicates the entity type (fixed)
1	The primary text value for an entity
2	Name: Attribute tag, block name, etc.
3-4	Other textual or name values
5	Entity handle expressed as a hexadecimal string; (fixed)
6	Linetype name; (fixed)
7	Text style name; (fixed)
8	Layer name; (fixed)
9	Variable name identifier
10	Primary point (start point of a line or text entity, center of a circle, etc.)
11-18	Other points
20	Y value of the primary point
21-28	Y value of other points
30	Z value of the primary point
31-37	Z value of other points
38	Entity elevation (if nonzero; only in versions prior to AutoCAD Release 11)
39	Entity's thickness if non-zero: (fixed)
40-48	Floating point values (text height, scale factors, etc.)
48	Linetype scale
49	Repeated value (for example, dash lengths in LTYPE table)
50-58	Angles
60	Entity visibility (0 = visibility; 1 = invisibility)
62	Color number; (fixed)
66	"Entities follow" flag; (fixed)

Group Code	Description
67	Model or Paper space; (fixed)
68	Application: Viewport is on but fully off screen, is not active, or is off
69	Application: Viewport identification number
70-78	Integer values (repeat counts, flag bits, modes)
90-99	32-bit integer values
100	Subclass data marker
102	Control string followed by "{⟨arbitary name⟩" or "}"
105	DIMVAR symbol table entry object handle
210	Extrusion direction; (fixed)
220	Y value of the extrusion direction
230	Z value of the extrusion direction
280-289	8-bit integer values
300-309	Arbitrary text strings
310-319	Arbitrary binary chunks
320-329	Arbitrary object handles
330-339	Soft-pointer handle
340-349	Hard-pointer handle
350-359	Soft-owner handle
360-369	Hard-owner handle
999	Comments
1000	An ASCII string in XDATA (up to 255 bytes in length)
1001	Registered application name for XDATA; (fixed)
1002	XDATA control string ("{" or "}"); (fixed)
1003	Layer name in XDATA
1004	Chunk of bytes in XDATA (up to 127 bytes in length)
1005	Entity handle in XDATA
1010	A point in XDATA
1020	Y value of a point
1030	Z value of a point
1011	A 3D World space position in XDATA
1021	Y value of a World space position
1031	Z value of a World space position
1012	A 3D World space displacement in XDATA

Group Code	Description
1022	Y value of a World space displacement
1032	Z value of a World space displacement
1013	A 3D World space direction in XDATA
1023	Y value of a World space direction
1033	Z value of a World space direction
1040	Floating point value in XDATA
1041	Distance value in XDATA
1042	Scale factor in XDATA
1070	16-bit signed integer in XDATA
1071	32-bit signed long integer in XDATA

Table B-2. Group Codes Common to All Entities

Group Code	Meaning	Default (if omitted)
–1	Entity name (may change each time drawing is opened)	Not omitted
0	Entity type	Not omitted
5	Handle	Not omitted
100	Subclass marker (AcDbEntity)	Not omitted
67	Space (Absent or zero indicates model space. A value of one indicates paper space.)	0
8	Layer name	Not omitted
6	Linetype name (present if not "BYLAYER")	"BYLAYER"
62	Color number (present if not 256, [BYLAYER])	"BYLAYER"
48	Linetype scale	1.0
60	Object visibility (0 = visible; 1 = invisible)	0
90	ADELOCK	
102	Start of application defined group "{application_name"	Not omitted
102	End of group, "}"	No default

The following table shows the group codes that are output if persistent reactors have been attached to an entity.

ACAD_REACTORS Records	
Group Code	**Meaning**
102	Start of application defined group "{application_name" ("{ACAD_REACTORS")
330	Soft pointer ID/handle to owner dictionary
102	End of group, "}"

The following table shows the group codes that are output if an extension dictionary has been attached to an entity.

ACAD_XDICTIONARY Records	
Group Code	**Meaning**
102	Start of application defined group "{application_name" ("{ACAD_XDICTIONARY")
360	Hard owner ID/handle to owner dictionary
102	End of group, "}"

Table B-3. Entity-Specific Codes

Entity Type	Group Code	Meaning
3DFACE	100	Subclass marker (AcDbFace)
	10	First corner (in WCS)
	20	Y value of first corner (in WCS)
	30	Z value of first corner (in WCS)
	11	Second corner (in WCS)
	21	Y value of second corner (in WCS)
	31	Z value of second corner (in WCS)
	12	Third corner (in WCS)
	22	Y value of third corner (in WCS)
	32	Z value of third corner (in WCS)
Continued	13	Fourth corner (in WCS)

Table B-3. Entity-Specific Codes

Entity Type	Group Code	Meaning
3DFACE	23	Y value of fourth corner (in WCS)
	33	Z value of fourth corner (in WCS)
	70	Invisible edge flags (default = 0) 1 = First edge is invisible 2 = Second edge is invisible 4 = Third edge is invisible 8 = Fourth edge is invisible
3DSOLID	100	Subclass marker (AcDbModelerGeometry)
	70	Modeler format version number
	1	Proprietary data (multiple lines ⟨255 characters each)
	3	Additional lines (group 1 string is greater than 255 characters)
ACAD_PROXY_ENTITY	100	DXF: AcDbProxyEntity
	90	DXF: Proxy entity class ID
	91	DXF: Actual application entity's class ID
	92	DXF: Size of graphics data (in bytes)
	310	DXF: Binary graphics data
	93	DXF: Size of entity data (in bits)
	310	DXF: Binary entity data
	330	DXF: An object ID
	340	DXF: An object ID
	350	DXF: An object ID
	360	DXF: An object ID
	94	DXF: 0 (End of object ID section)
ARC	100	Subclass marker (AcDbCircle)
	39	Thickness (default = 0)
	10	Center point (in OCS)
	20	Y value of center point (in OCS)
Continued	30	Z value of center point (in OCS)

Entity Type	Group Code	Meaning
ARC	40	Radius
	100	Subclass marker (AcDbArc)
	50	Start angle
	51	End angle
	210	Extrusion direction (default = 0,0,1)
	220	Y value of extrusion direction
	230	Z value of extrusion direction
ATTDEF	100	Subclass marker (AcDbText)
	39	Thickness (optional; default = 0)
	10	Text start point (in OCS)
	20, 30	Y and Z values of text start point (in OCS)
	40	Text height
	1	Default value (string)
	100	Subclass marker (AcDbAttributeDefinition)
	50	Text rotation (optional; default = 0)
	41	Relative X scale factor (optional; default = 1)
	51	Oblique angle (optional; default = 0)
	7	Text style name (optional: default = "STANDARD")
	71	Text generation flags (optional; default = 0). See TEXT.
	72	Horizontal text justification type (optional; default = 0). See TEXT.
	11	Second alignment point (in OCS). (optional; present only if 72 or 74 group values are present and nonzero)
	21, 31	Y and Z values of second alignment point (in OCS)
	210	Extrusion direction (optional: default = 0, 0, 1)
	220, 230	Y and Z values of extrusion direction
	100	Subclass marker (AcDbAttributeDefinition)
Continued	3	Prompt string

Entity Type	Group Code	Meaning
ATTDEF	2	Tag string
	70	Attribute flags 1 = Invisible 2 = Constant 4 = Verify 8 = Preset
	73	Field length (optional; default = 0)
	74	Vertical text justification type (optional, default = 0). See TEXT.
ATTRIB	100	Subclass marker (AcDbText)
	39	Thickness (optional; default = 0)
	10	Text start point (in OCS)
	20, 30	Y and Z values of text start point (in OCS)
	40	Text height
	1	Value (string)
	100	Subclass marker (AcDbAttribute)
	2	Attribute tag (string)
	70	Attribute flags 1 = Invisible 2 = Constant 4 = Verification 8 = Preset
	73	Field length (optional; default = 0)
	50	Text rotation (optional; default = 0)
	41	Relative X scale factor (optional; default = 1)
	51	Oblique angle (optional; default = 0)
	7	Text style name (optional, default = "STANDARD")
	71	Text generation flags (optional, default = 0). See TEXT.
	72	Horizontal text justification type (optional, default = 0). See TEXT.
Continued	74	Vertical text justification type (optional, default = 0). See TEXT.

Entity Type	Group Code	Meaning
ATTRIB	11	Alignment point (in OCS) (optional; present only if 72 or 74 group values are present and nonzero)
	21, 31	Y and Z values of alignment point (in OCS)
	210	Extrusion direction (optional; default = 0, 0, 1)
	220, 230	Y and Z values of extrusion direction
BODY	100	Subclass marker (AcDbModelerGeometry)
	70	Modeler format version number (currently = 1)
	1	Proprietary data (multiple lines <255 characters each)
	3	Additional lines of proprietary data
CIRCLE	10	Center point
	40	Radius
	210	Extrusion direction if not parallel to World Z axis
DIMENSION	100	Subclass marker (AcDbDimension)
	1	Dimension text entered by user (default = actual measurement)
	2	Name of pseudo-block containing dimension picture
	3	Dimension style name
	10	Definition point (in WCS)
	11	Middle point of dimension text
	12	Insertion point for clones of a dimension (Baseline and Continue)
	13	Definition point for linear and angular dimensions
	14	Definition point for linear and angular dimensions
	15	Definition point for diameter, radius, or angular dimensions
Continued	16	Point defining dimension arc for angular dimensions

Entity Type	Group Code	Meaning
DIMENSION	20	Y value of definition point (WCS)
	30	Z value of definition point (WCS)
	21	Y value of middle point of dimension text (in OCS)
	31	Z value of middle point of dimension text (in OCS)
	22	Y value of insertion point for clones of a dimension. Baseline and Continue (in OCS)
	32	Z value of insertion point for clones of a dimension. Baseline and Continue (in OCS)
	23	Y value of definition point for linear and angular dimensions (in WCS)
	33	Z value of definition point for linear and angular dimensions (in WCS)
	24	Y value of definition point for linear and angular dimensions (in WCS)
	34	Z value of definition point for linear and angular dimensions (in WCS)
	25	Y value of definition point for diameter, radius, and angular dimensions (in WCS)
	35	Z value of definition point for diameter, radius, and angular dimensions (in WCS)
	26	Y value of point defining dimension arc for angular dimensions (in OCS)
	36	Z value of point defining dimension arc for angular dimensions (in OCS)
	40	Leader length for radius and diameter dimensions
	50	Angle for rotated, horizontal, or vertical linear dimensions
	51	Horizontal direction
	52	Extension line angle for oblique linear dimensions
Continued	53	Rotation angle for dimension text

Entity Type	Group Code	Meaning
DIMENSION	70	Dimension type (0-6 Integer codes; 32-128 Bit codes) 0 = Rotated, horizontal, or vertical 1 = Aligned 2 = Angular 3 = Diameter 4 = Radius 5 = Angular 3 point 6 = Ordinate 32 = Block reference 64 = X-type ordinate and default location 128 = X-type ordinate at a user-defined location
	210	Extrusion direction (default = 0, 0, 1)
	220	Y value of extrusion direction
	230	Z value of extrusion direction
	–3	Application: ID "ACAD", begins section of XDATA containing hatch properties
ELLIPSE	100	Subclass marker (AcDbEllipse)
	10	Center point (in WCS)
	20	Y value of center point (in WCS)
	30	Z value of center point (in WCS)
	11	Endpoint of major axis relative to the center
	21	Y value of endpoint of major axis relative to the center
	31	Z value of endpoint of major axis relative to the center
	210	Extrusion direction (default = 0, 0, 1)
	220	Y value of extrusion direction
	230	Z value of extrusion direction
	40	Ratio of minor axis to major axis
	41	Start parameter (0.0 = full ellipse)
	42	End parameter (2π= full ellipse)
HATCH	100	Subclass marker (AcDbHatch)
Continued	10	Elevation point (in OCS)

Entity Type	Group Code	Meaning
HATCH	20	Y value of elevation point (in OCS)
	30	Z value of elevation point (in OCS)
	210	Extrusion direction (default = 0, 0, 1)
	220	Y value of extrusion direction
	230	Z value of extrusion direction
	2	Hatch pattern name
	70	Solid fill flag (solid fill = 1; pattern fill = 0)
	71	Associativity flag (associative = 1; non-associative = 0)
	91	Number of boundary paths
	92	Boundary path type flag 0 = Default 1 = External 2 = Polyline 4 = Derived 8 = Textbox 16 = Outermost
	93	Number of edges in this boundary path
	72	Edge type 1 = Line 2 = Circular arc 3 = Elliptic arc 4 = Spline
	97	Number of source boundary objects
	340	Hard reference to source boundary objects
	75	Hatch style 0 = Normal style 1 = Outer style 2 = Ignore style
	76	Hatch pattern type 0 = User-defined 1 = Predefined 2 = Custom
	52	Hatch pattern angle
Continued	41	Hatch pattern scale or spacing

Entity Type	Group Code	Meaning
HATCH	77	Hatch pattern double flag (double = 1, not double = 0)
	78	Number of pattern definition lines
	53	Pattern line angle
	43	Pattern line base point, X component
	44	Pattern line base point, Y component
	45	Pattern line offset, X component
	46	Pattern line offset, Y component
	79	Number of dash length items
	49	Dash length
	47	Pixel size
	98	Number of seed points
IMAGE	100	Subclass marker (AcDbRasterImage)
	90	Class version
	10	Insertion point (in OCS)
	20	Y value of insertion point (in OCS)
	30	Z value of insertion point (in OCS)
	11	U-vector of a single pixel (in OCS)
	21	Y value U-vector (in OCS)
	31	Z value U-vector (in OCS)
	12	V-vector of a single pixel (in OCS)
	22	Y value of V-vector (in OCS)
	32	Z value of V-vector (in OCS)
	13	Image size in pixels (U and V values)
	23	V value of image size in pixels
	340	Hard reference to imagedef object
Continued	70	Image display properties 1 = Show image 2 = Show image when not aligned with screen 4 = Use clipping boundary 8 = Transparency is on

Entity Type	Group Code	Meaning
IMAGE	280	Clipping state: 0 = off, 1 = on
	281	Brightness value (0-100; default = 50)
	282	Contrast value (0-100; default = 50)
	283	Fade value (0-100; default = 0)
	360	Hard reference to imagedef_reactor object
	71	Clipping boundary type (1 = rectangular, 2 = polygonal)
	91	Number of clip boundary vertices
	14	Clip boundary vertex (in OCS)
INSERT	100	Subclass marker (AcDbBlockReference)
	2	Block name
	10	Insertion point (in OCS)
	20	Y value of insertion point (in OCS)
	30	Z value of insertion point (in OCS)
	41	X scale factor (default = 1)
	42	Y scale factor (default = 1)
	43	Z scale factor (default = 1)
	44	Column spacing (default = 0)
	45	Row spacing (default = 0)
	50	Rotation angle (default = 0)
	66	Variable attributes-follow flag (default = 0)
	70	Column count (default = 1)
	71	Row count (default = 1)
	210	Extrusion direction (default = 0, 0, 1)
	220	Y value of extrusion direction
	230	Z value of extrusion direction
	–3	Application: ID "ACAD"; begins section in XDATA containing hatch properties

Entity Type	Group Code	Meaning
LEADER	100	Subclass marker (AcDbLeader)
	3	Dimension style name
	71	Arrowhead flag (0 = disabled; 1 = enabled)
	72	Leader path type (0 = straight line segments; 1 = spline)
	73	Leader creation flag (default = 3) 0 = Leader created with text annotation 1 = Created with tolerance annotation 2 = Created with block reference annotation 3 = Created without any annotation
	74	Hookline direction flag 0 = Opposite direction from the horizontal vector 1 = Same direction as horizontal vector
	75	Hookline flag (0 = no hookline; 1 = has a hookline)
	40	Text annotation height
	41	Text annotation width
	76	Number of vertices in leader
	10	Vertex coordinates
	20	Y value of vertex coordinates
	30	Z value of vertex coordinates
	77	Color (DIMCLRD = BYBLOCK)
	340	Hard reference to associated annotation (mtext, tolerance, or insert entity)
	210	Normal vector
	220	Y value of normal vector
	230	Z value of normal vector
	211	"Horizontal" direction for leader
	221	Y value of "horizontal" direction for leader
	231	Z value of "horizontal" direction for leader
	212	Block reference insertion point offset from last leader vertex
Continued	222	Y value of block reference insertion point offset from last leader vertex

Entity Type	Group Code	Meaning
LEADER	232	Z value of block reference insertion point offset from last leader vertex
	213	Annotation placement point offset from last leader vertex
	223	Y value of annotation placement point offset from last leader vertex
	233	Z value of annotation placement point offset from last leader vertex
LINE	100	Subclass marker (AcDbLine)
	39	Thickness (default = 0)
	10	Start point (in WCS)
	20	Y value of start point (in WCS)
	30	Z value of start point (in WCS)
	11	End point (in WCS)
	21	Y value of end point (in WCS)
	31	Z value of end point (in WCS)
	210	Extrusion direction (default = 0, 0, 1)
	220	Y value of extrusion direction
	230	Z value of extrusion direction
LWPOLYLINE	100	Subclass marker (AcDbPolyline)
	90	Number of vertices
	70	Polyline flag (default = 0) 1 = Closed 128 = Plinegen
	43	Constant width (default = 0)
	38	Elevation (default = 0)
	39	Thickness (default = 0)
	10	Vertex coordinates (in WCS)
	20	Y value of vertex coordinates (in WCS)
	40	Starting width (default = 0; multiple entries)
Continued	41	End width (default = 0; multiple entries)

Entity Type	Group Code	Meaning
LWPOLYLINE	42	Bulge (default = 0)
	210	Extrusion direction (default = 0,0,1)
	220	Y value of extrusion direction
	230	Z value of extrusion direction
MLINE	100	Subclass maker (AcDbMline)
	2	Mline style name (32 characters max.)
	340	Pointer-handle/ID of MLINESTYLE dictionary
	40	Scale factor
	70	Justification (0 = top, 1 = zero, 2 = bottom)
	71	Open/closed flag 1 = Open 3 = Closed
	72	Number of vertices
	73	Number of elements in MLINESTYLE definition
	10	Start point (in WCS)
	20	Y value of start point (in WCS)
	30	Z value of start point (in WCS)
	210	Extrusion direction (default = 0, 0, 1)
	220	Y value of extrusion direction
	230	Z value of extrusion direction
	11	Vertex coordinates
	21	Y value of vertex coordinates
	31	Z value of vertex coordinates
	12	Direction vector of segment starting at this vertex
	22	Y value of direction vector of segment starting at this vertex
	32	Z value of direction vector of segment starting at this vertex
Continued	13	Direction vector of miter at this vertex

Entity Type	Group Code	Meaning
MLINE	23	Y value of direction vector of miter
	33	Z value of direction vector of miter
	74	Number of parameters for this element
	41	Element parameters
	75	Number of area fill parameters for this element
	42	Area fill parameters
MTEXT	100	Subclass marker (AcDbMText)
	10	Insertion point
	20	Y value of insertion point
	30	Z value of insertion point
	40	Default text height
	41	Reference rectangle width
	71	Attachment point 1 = Top left 2 = Top center 3 = Top right 4 = Middle left 5 = Middle center 6 = Middle right 7 = Bottom left 8 = Bottom center 9 = Bottom right
	72	Drawing direction 1 = Left to right 2 = Right to left 3 = Top to bottom 4 = Bottom to top
	1	Text string
	3	Additional text (always in 250 character increments)
	7	Text style name (default = STANDARD)
	210	Extrusion direction (default = 0,0,1)
Continued	220	Y value of extrusion direction

Entity Type	Group Code	Meaning
MTEXT	230	Z value of extrusion direction
	11	X-axis direction vector (in WCS)
	21	Y value of X-axis direction vector (in WCS)
	31	Z value of X-axis direction vector (in WCS)
OLEFRAME	100	Subclass marker (AcDbOleFrame)
	70	OLE version number
	90	Length of binary data
	310	Binary data
	1	End of Ole data
OLE2FRAME	100	Subclass marker (AcDbOle2Frame)
	70	OLE version number
	3	Length of binary data
	10	Upper left corner (in WCS)
	20	Y value of upper left corner (in WCS)
	30	Z value of upper left corner (in WCS)
	11	Lower right corner (in WCS)
	21	Y value of lower right corner (in WCS)
	31	Z value of lower right corner (in WCS)
	71	OLE object type 1 = Link 2 = Embedded 3 = Static
	72	Tile mode descriptor 0 = Tiled model space viewport 1 = Non-tiled paper space viewport
	90	Length of binary data
	310	Binary data
	1	End of OLE data
POINT	100	Subclass marker (AcDbPoint)
Continued	10	Point location (in WCS)

Entity Type	Group Code	Meaning
POINT	20	Y value of point location (in WCS)
	30	Z value of point location (in WCS)
	39	Thickness (default = 0)
	210	Extrusion direction (default = 0,0,1)
	220	Y value of extrusion direction
	230	Z value of extrusion direction
	50	Angle of UCS X axis in effect when drawn (default = 0)
POLYLINE	100	Subclass marker (AcDb2dPolyline or AcDb3dPolyline)
	10	Always 0
	20	Always 0
	30	Polyline's elevation (2D = OCS, 3D = WCS)
	39	Thickness (default = 0)
	70	Polyline flag (bit-coded; default = 0) 1 = Closed 2 = Curve-fit vertices added 4 = Spline-fit vertices added 8 = 3D polyline 16 = 3D polygon mesh 32 = Polygon mesh is closed in the N direction 64 = Polyface mesh 128 = Linetype pattern generated continuously around the vertices of this polyline
	40	Default starting width (default = 0)
	41	Default ending width (default = 0)
	71	Polygon mesh M vertex count (default = 0)
	72	Polygon mesh N vertex count (default = 0)
	73	Smooth surface M density (default = 0)
Continued	74	Smooth surface N density (default = 0)

Entity Type	Group Code	Meaning
POLYLINE	75	Curves and smooth surface type (default = 0) Integer codes, not bit-coded: 0 = None 5 = Quadratic B-spline surface 6 = Cubic B-spline surface 8 = Bezier surface
	210	Extrusion direction (default = 0,0,1)
	220	Y value of extrusion direction
	230	Z value of extrusion direction
RAY	100	Subclass marker (AcDbRay)
	10	Start point (in WCS)
	20	Y value of start point (in WCS)
	30	Z value of start point (in WCS)
	11	Unit direction vector (in WCS)
	21	Y value of unit direction vector (in WCS)
	31	Z value of unit direction vector (in WCS)
REGION	100	Subclass marker (AcDbModelerGeometry)
	70	Modeler format version number (currently =1)
	1	Proprietary data (multiple lines <255 characters each)
	3	Additional lines of porprietary data
SEQEND	–2	Name of entity beginning sequence
SHAPE	100	Subclass marker (AcDbShape)
	39	Thickness (default = 0)
	10	Insertion point (in WCS)
	20	Y value of insertion point (in WCS)
	30	Z value of insertion point (in WCS)
	40	Size
	2	Shape name
	50	Rotation angle (default = 0)
	41	Relative X scale factor (default =1)
Continued	51	Oblique angle (default =0)

Entity Type	Group Code	Meaning
SHAPE	210	Extrusion direction (default = 0,0,1)
	220	Y value of extrusion direction
	230	Z value of extrusion direction
SOLID	100	Subclass marker (AcDbSolid)
	10	First corner
	20	Y value of first corner
	30	Z value of first corner
	11	Second corner
	21	Y value of second corner
	31	Z value of second corner
	12	Third corner
	22	Y value of third corner
	32	Z value of third corner
	13	Fourth corner
	23	Y value of fourth corner
	33	Z value of fourth corner
	39	Thickness (default = 0)
	210	Extrusion direction (default = 0, 0, 1)
	220	Y value of extrusion direction
	230	Z value of extrusion direction
SPLINE	100	Subclass marker (AcDbSpline)
	210	Normal vector (omitted if the spline is nonplanar)
	220	Y value of normal vector
	230	Z value of normal vector
Continued	70	Bit Value Spline flag 1 = Closed spline 2 = Periodic spline 4 = Rational spline 8 = Planar 16 = Linear (Planar bit also set)

Entity Type	Group Code	Meaning
SPLINE	71	Degree of the spline curve
	72	Number of knots
	73	Number of control points
	74	Number of fit points
	42	Knot tolerance (default = 0.0000001)
	43	Control-point tolerance (default = 0.0000001)
	44	Fit tolerance if a fit spline (default = 0.0000000001)
	12	Start tangent (in WCS)
	22	Y value of start tangent (in WCS)
	32	Z value of start tangent (in WCS)
	13	End tangent (in WCS)
	23	Y value of end tangent (in WCS)
	33	Z value of end tangent (in WCS)
	40	Knot values
	41	Weight (if not 1)
	10	Control points (in WCS)
	20	Y value of control points (in WCS)
	30	Z value of control points (in WCS)
	11	Fit points (in WCS)
	21	Y value of fit points (in WCS)
	31	Z value of fit points (in WCS)
TEXT	100	Subclass marker (AcDbText)
	10	First alignment point (in OCS)
	20	Y value of first alignment point (in OCS)
	30	Z value of first alignment point (in OCS)
	39	Thickness (default = 0)
	40	Height
Continued	1	Text value (the string itself)

Entity Type	Group Code	Meaning
TEXT	50	Rotation (default = 0)
	41	Relative X-scale factor (default = 1)
	51	Oblique angle (default = 0)
	7	Text style name (default = "STANDARD")
	71	Text generation flags (default = 0) 2 = Backward (mirrored in X) 4 = Upside down (mirrored in Y)
	72	Horizontal text justification type (default = 0) Integer codes (not bit-coded) 0 = Left 1 = Center 2 = Right 3 = Aligned (if vertical alignment = 0) 4 = Middle (if vertical allignment = 0) 5 = Fit (if vertical alignment = 0)
	73	Vertical text justification type (default = 0) Integer codes (not bit-coded) 0 = Baseline 1 = Bottom 2 = Middle 3 = Top
	11	Alignment point (in OCS)
	21	Y value of second alignment point (in OCS)
	31	Z value of second alignment point (in OCS)
	210	Extrusion direction (default =0, 0, 1)
	220	Y value of extrusion direction
	230	Z value of extrusion direction
TOLERANCE	100	Subclass marker (AcDbFcf)
	3	Dimension style name
	10	Insertion point (in WCS)
	20	Y value of insertion point (in WCS)
	30	Z value of insertion point (in WCS)
	11	X-axis direction vector (in WCS)
Continued	21	Y value of X-axis direction vector (in WCS)

Entity Type	Group Code	Meaning
TOLERANCE	31	Z value of X-axis direction vector (in WCS)
	210	Extrusion direction (default = 0, 0, 1)
	220	Y value of extrusion direction
	230	Z value of extrusion direction
TRACE	100	Subclass marker (AcDbTrace)
	10	First corner (in OCS)
	20	Y value of first corner (in OCS)
	30	Z value of first corner (in OCS)
	11	Second corner (in OCS)
	21	Y value of second corner (in OCS)
	31	Z value of second corner (in OCS)
	12	Third corner (in OCS)
	22	Y value of third corner (in OCS)
	32	Z value of third corner (in OCS)
	13	Fourth corner (in OCS)
	23	Y value of fourth corner (in OCS)
	33	Z value of fourth corner (in OCS)
	39	Thickness (default = 0)
	210	Extrusion direction (default = 0, 0, 1)
	220	Y value of extrusion direction
	230	Z value of extrusion direction
VERTEX	100	Subclass marker (AcDbVertex)
	100	Subclass marker (AcDb2dVertex or AcDb3dPolyline Vertex)
	10	Location point (OCS when 2D; WCS when 3D)
	20	Y value of location point (OCS when 2D; WCS when 3D)
Continued	30	Z value of location point (OCS when 2D; WCS when 3D)

Entity Type	Group Code	Meaning
VERTEX	40	Starting width (default is 0)
	41	Ending width (default is 0)
	42	Bulge (default is 0)
	70	Vertex flags (default is 0) 1 = Extra vertex created by curve-fitting 2 = Curve-fit tangent 4 = Not used 8 = Spline vertex created by spline-fitting 16 = Spline frame control point 32 = 3D polyline vertex 64 = 3D polygon mesh vertex 128 = Polyface mesh vertex
	50	Curve fit tangent direction
	71	Polyface mesh vertex index (present only if non-zero)
	72	Polyface mesh vertex index (present only if non-zero)
	73	Polyface mesh vertex index (present only if non-zero)
	74	Polyface mesh vertex index (present only if non-zero)
VIEWPORT	100	Subclass marker (AcDbViewport)
	10	Center point (in WCS)
	20	Y value of center point (in WCS)
	30	Z value of center point (in WCS)
	40	Width in paper space units
	41	Height in paper space units
	68	Viewport status field: 1 = On (but is fully off screen, or is one of the viewports not active because the $MAXACTVP count is exceeded) 0 = Off ⟨positive value⟩ = On and active (viewport stacking is ordered)
Continued	69	Viewport ID (changes each time a drawing is opened; never saved)

Entity Type	Group Code	Meaning
VIEWPORT xdata group codes (Order is important)	1001	Application ID ("ACAD"). Begins a section of xdata that describes the viewport.
	1000	Begin viewport data. Field is always the string MVIEW.
	1002	Begin window descriptor data.
	1070	Extended data version number (always integer 16)
	1010	View target point (in WCS)
	1020	Y value of view target point (in WCS)
	1030	Z value of view target point (in WCS)
	1010	View direction vector (in WCS)
	1020	Y value of view direction vector (in WCS)
	1030	Z value of view direction vector (in WCS)
	1040	View twist angle
	1040	View height
	1040	View center point X value (in DCS)
	1040	View center point Y value (in DCS)
	1040	Perspective lens length
	1040	Front clip plane Z value
	1040	Back clip plane Z value
	1070	View mode
	1070	Circle zoom
	1070	Fast zoom setting
	1070	UCSICON setting
	1070	Snap ON/OFF
	1070	Grid ON/OFF
	1070	Snap style
	1070	Snap ISOPAIR
	1040	Snap angle
	1040	Snap base point UCS – X value of coordinate
Continued	1040	Snap base point UCS – Y value of coordinate

Entity Type	Group Code	Meaning
VIEWPORT xdata group codes (Order is important)	1040	Snap X spacing
	1040	Snap Y spacing
	1040	Grid X spacing
	1040	Grid Y spacing
	1070	Hidden in plot flag
	1002	Begin frozen layer list (field is always the string "{")
	1003	Names of layers frozen in this viewport
	1002	End frozen layer list (field is alway the string "}")
	1002	End viewport data (field is always the string "}")
XLINE	100	Subclass marker (AcDbXline)
	10	First point (in WCS)
	20	Y value of first point (in WCS)
	30	Z value of first point (in WCS)
	11	Direction vector (in WCS)
	21	Y value of direction vector (in WCS)
	31	Z value of direction vector (in WCS)

Non-Graphical Entities

Most of AutoCAD's database records present a graphical representation within the drawing editor, but there are some records that do not directly define a visible object. The following listing shows the applicable DXF group codes for AutoCAD's non-graphical entities. This first table shows group codes applying to all non-graphical entities.

Table B-4. Group Codes Common to All Non-Graphical Entities

Group Code	Meaning	Default
–1	Entity name (Changes each drawing session)	Not omitted
0	Entity type	Not omitted
5	Entity handle	Not omitted
70	Flag values 16 = Table entry dependent on an XREF 32 = Externally dependent XREF has been resolved 64 = Table entry was referenced by at least one entity when the drawing was last edited	
90	ADE Lock	

Table B-5. Dictionary Group Codes

Entity Type	Group Code	Meaning
DICTIONARY	100	Subclass marker (AcDbDictionary)
	3	Entry name (one per entry)
	350	Handle of entry object (one per entry)
ACAD_GROUP	5	Handle
	102	Start of persistent reactors group; always "{ACAD_REACTORS"
	330	Soft-pointer ID/handle to owner dictionary
Continued	102	End of persistent reactors group, always "}"

Entity Type	Group Code	Meaning
ACAD_GROUP	100	Subclass marker (AcDbGroup)
	300	Group description
	70	"Unnamed" flag: 1 = unnamed; 0 = named
	71	Selectability flag: 1 = selectable; 0 = not selectable
	340	Entity group handle
ACAD_MLINESTYLE	0	Object name
	5	Handle
	102	Start of persistent reactors group; always "{ACAD_REACTORS"
	330	Soft-pointer ID/handle to owner dictionary
	102	End of persistent reactors group; always "}"
	100	Subclass marker (AcDbMlineStyle)
	2	Mline style name
	70	Bit value flage 1 = fill on 2 = display miters 16 = Start square end (line) cap 32 = Start inner arcs cap 64 = Start round (outer arcs) cap 256 = End square (line) cap 512 = End inner arcs 1024 = End round (outer arcs) cap
	3	Style description
	62	Element fill color
	51	Start angle
	52	End angle
	71	Number of elements
	49	Element offsets
	62	Element colors
	6	Element linetypes

Entity Type	Group Code	Meaning
ACAD_PROXY_OBJECT	100	AcDbProxyObject
	90	Proxy object class ID
	91	Actual application object's class ID
	93	Size of object data (in bits)
	310	Binary object data
	330	An object ID
	340	An object ID
	350	An object ID
	360	An object ID
	94	End of object ID section (default = 0)
XRECORD	100	Subclass marker (AcDbXrecord)
	1-369 (except 5 and 105)	These values can be used by an application in any way

Table B-6. Group Codes Common to All Symbol Tables

Group Code	Meaning
–1	Entity name (Changes each drawing session)
0	Entity type (For TABLE)
2	Table name
5	Handle
100	Subclass marker (AcDbSymbolTable)
70	Maximum number of entries in table

Table B-7. Block and Symbol Table Group Codes

Entity Type	Group Code	Meaning
APPID	100	Subclass marker (AcDbRegAppTableRecord)
	2	User registered application name
	70	Standard flag values

Entity Type	Group Code	Meaning
BLOCK	100	Subclass marker (AcDbBlockTableRecord)
	2	Block name
	70	Bit value type flag 1 = Anonymous block 2 = Variable attributes follow 4 = XREF 8 = (not used) 16 = Externally dependent 32 = Resolved XREF or a dependent of an XREF 64 = Definition is referenced
	1	XREF path name
DIMSTYLE	100	Subclass marker (AcDbDimStyleTableRecord)
	2	Dimension style name
	70	Standard flag values
	170	DIMALT
	171	DIMALTD
	143	DIMALTF
	274	DIMALTTD
	286	DIMALTTZ
	273	DIMALTU
	285	DIMALTZ
	4	DIMAPOST
	41	DIMASZ
	275	DIMAUNIT
	5	DIMBLK
	6	DIMBLK1
	7	DIMBLK2
	141	DIMCEN
	176	DIMCLRD
	177	DIMCLRE
	178	DIMCLRT
Continued	271	DIMDEC

Entity Type	Group Code	Meaning
DIMSTYLE	46	DIMDLE
	43	DIMDLI
	44	DIMEXE
	42	DIMEXO
	287	DIMFIT
	147	DIMGAP
	280	DIMJUST
	144	DIMLFAC
	72	DIMLIM
	3	DIMPOST
	45	DIMRND
	173	DIMSAH
	40	DIMSCALE
	281	DIMSD1
	282	DIMSD2
	75	DIMSE1
	76	DIMSE2
	175	DIMSOXD
	77	DIMTAD
	272	DIMTDEC
	146	DIMTFAC
	73	DIMTIH
	174	DIMTIX
	48	DIMTM
	172	DIMTOFL
	74	DIMTOH
	71	DIMTOL
	283	DIMTOLJ
	47	DIMTP
Continued	142	DIMTSZ

Entity Type	Group Code	Meaning
DIMSTYLE	145	DIMTVP
	340	DIMTXSTY
	140	DIMTXT
	284	DIMTZIN
	270	DIMUNIT
	288	DIMUPT
	78	DIMZIM
LAYER	100	Subclass marker (AcDbSymbolTableRecord)
	2	Layer name
	70	Standard flags 1 = Frozen 2 = Frozen by default for new viewports 4 = Locked
	62	Color number
	6	Linetype
LTYPE	100	Subclass marker (AcDbLinetypeTableRecord)
	2	Linetype name
	70	Standard flags values
	3	Descriptive text for linetype
	72	Alignment code (always 65, the ASCII code for A)
	73	Number of dash length elements
	40	Total pattern length
	49	Dash, dot or space length
	74	Complex linetype element type 0 = Not complex 2 = Embedded text string 4 = Embedded shape
	75	Complex shape code
	340	Pointer to STYLE object
	46	S = Scale value
Continued	50	R = Rotation value

Entity Type	Group Code	Meaning
LTYPE	44	X = X offset value
	45	Y = Y offset value
	9	Text string
STYLE	100	Subclass marker (AcDbTextStyleTableRecord)
	2	Style name
	70	Standard flag values 1 = Describes a shape 4 = Vertical text
	40	Fixed text height
	41	Width factor
	50	Oblique angle
	71	Text generation flags 2 = Backward 4 = Upside down
	42	Last height used
	3	Primary font filename
	4	Big font filename
UCS	100	Subclass marker (AcDbUCSTableRecord)
	2	UCS name
	70	Standard flag values
	10	Origin in WCS
	20, 30	Y and Z values of origin (in WCS)
	11	WCS X-axis direction
	21, 31	Y and Z values of X-axis direction (in WCS)
	12	WCS Y-axis direction
	22, 32	Y and Z values of Y-axis direction (in WCS)
VIEW	100	Subclass marker (AcDbViewTableRecord)
	2	View name
	70	View flag values (1 = Paper Space)
Continued	40	View height

Entity Type	Group Code	Meaning
VIEW	10	2D Center point (in DCS)
	20	Y value of view center point (in DCS)
	41	View width (in DCS)
	11	View direction from target (in WCS)
	21, 31	Y and Z values of view direction from target (in WCS)
	12	Target point (in WCS)
	22, 32	Y and Z values of target point (in WCS)
	42	Lens length
	43	Front clipping plane
	44	Back clipping plane
	50	Twist angle
	71	View mode
VPORT	100	Subclass marker (AcDbViewportTableRecord)
	2	Viewport name
	70	Standard flag values
	10	2D lower-left corner
	20	Y value of lower-left corner
	11	2D upper-right corner
	21	Y value of upper-right corner
	12	2D center point (in DCS)
	22	Y value of center point (DCS)
	13	2D snap base point
	23	Y value of snap base point
	14	Snap spacing, X & Y
	24	Y value of snap spacing, X & Y
	15	Grid spacing, X & Y
	25	Y value of grid spacing, X & Y
Continued	16	Direction from target point (in WCS)

Entity Type	Group Code	Meaning
VPORT	26	Y value of view direction from target point (in WCS)
	36	Z value of view direction from target point (in WCS)
	17	Target point (in WCS)
	27	Y value of target point (in WCS)
	37	Z value of target point (in WCS)
	40	Height
	41	Viewport aspect ratio
	42	Lens length
	43	Front clipping plane
	44	Back clipping plane
	50	Snap rotation angle
	51	Twist angle
	68	Application: Status field
	69	Application: ID
	71	View mode
	72	Circle zoom percent
	73	Fast zoom setting
	74	UCSICON setting
	75	Snap on/off
	76	Grid on/off
	77	Snap style
	78	Snap isopair

Appendix C
AutoLISP Error Codes

Table C-1 shows the error code values passed to the AutoCAD ERRNO system variable when an AutoLISP error occurs. *Note that not all AutoLISP errors will produce an error code.* To retrieve the error code value, use the GETVAR function as follows:

```
(getvar "ERRNO")
```

The ERRNO variable is not always reset to zero; therefore, if its value is not retrieved immediately after the error occurs, the value may be misleading. In addition, this variable always has a value of zero when entering the drawing editor.

The *AutoLISP Programmer's Reference Manual* cautions that these values may change in future releases of AutoCAD. Keep this in mind as you use this tool in developing your programs.

NOTE

Error codes 2, 5, and 6 may be reported by any one of several AutoLISP functions including: ENTDEL, ENTGET, ENTMOD, ENTNEXT, ENTUPD, REDRAW, REGAPP, SSADD, SSDEL, SSMEMB, TRANS, and XDROOM. The AutoLISP Function field for these codes is listed as "*Several functions."

Table C-1. Error Codes

Value	Meaning	AutoLISP Function(s)
1	Invalid symbol table name	entmake; regapp; entmod
2	Invalid entity or selection set name	*Several functions
3	Exceeded maximum number of selection sets	ssget
4	Invalid selection set	ssget
5	Improper use of block definition entity	*Several functions
6	Improper use of XREF entity	*Several functions
7	Entity selection: pick failed	entsel; nentsel
8	End of entity file	entnext; entupd
9	End of block definition file	entnext
10	Failed to find last entity	entlast
11	Illegal attempt to delete viewport entity	entdel
12	Operation not allowed during Pline	(not currently used)
13	Invalid handle	handent
14	Handles not enabled	handent
15	Invalid arguments in coordinate transform request	trans
16	Invalid space in coordinate transform request	trans
17	Invalid use of deleted entity	entmod; trans
18	Invalid table name	tblnext; tblsearch
19	Invalid table function argument	tblnext; tblsearch
20	Attempt to set a read-only variable	setvar
21	Zero value not allowed	setvar
22	Value out of range	setvar
23	Complex REGEN in process	entmake; entmod; entupd
24	Attempt to change an entity type	entmake; entmod
25	Bad layer name	entmake; entmod

Value	Meaning	AutoLISP Function(s)
26	Bad linetype name	entmake; entmod
27	Bad color name	entmake; entmod
28	Bad text style name	entmake
29	Bad shape name	entmake
30	Bad field for entity type	entmake; entmod
31	Attempt to modify deleted entity	entmod
32	Attempt to modify a SEQEND subentity	entmod
33	Attempt to change handle	entmod
34	Attempt to change viewport visibility	entmake; entmod
35	Entity on locked layer	entmake; entmod
36	Bad entity type	entmake
37	Bad Polyline entity	entmake
38	Incomplete complex entity in block	entmake
39	Invalid block name field	(not currently used)
40	Duplicate block flag fields	entmake
41	Duplicate block name fields	entmake
42	Bad normal vector	entmake
43	Missing block name	entmake
44	Missing block flags	entmake
45	Invalid anonymous block	entmake
46	Invalid block definition entity	entmake
47	Mandatory field missing	entmake
48	Unrecognized XDATA type	entmake; entmod
49	Improper nesting of list in XDATA	entmake; entmod
50	Improper location of APPID field	entmake; entmod
51	Exceeded maximum XDATA size	entmake; entmod
52	Entity selection: null response	entsel; nentsel; nentselp

Value	Meaning	AutoLISP Function(s)
53	Duplicate APPID	entmake; entmod
54	Attempt to make or modify viewport entity	entmake; entmod
55	Attempt to make or modify an Xref, Xdef, or Xdep	entmake; entmod
56	SSGET filter: unexpected end of list	ssget
57	SSGET filter: missing test operand	ssget
58	SSGET filter: invalid opcode (–4) string	ssget
59	SSGET filter: improper nesting or empty conditional clause	ssget
60	SSGET filter: mismatched begin and end of conditional clause	ssget
61	SSGET filter: wrong number of arguments in conditional clause (for NOT or XOR)	ssget
62	SSGET filter: exceeded maximum nesting limit	ssget
63	SSGET filter: invalid group code	ssget
64	SSGET filter: invalid string test	ssget
65	SSGET filter: invalid vector test	ssget
66	SSGET filter: invalid real test	ssget
67	SSGET filter: invalid integer test	ssget
68	Digitizer isn't a tablet	tablet
69	Tablet is not calibrated	tablet
70	Invalid arguments	tablet
71	ADS error: Unable to allocate new result buffer	
72	ADS error: Null pointer detected	
73	Can't open executable file	xload
74	Application is already loaded	xload
75	Maximum number of applications already loaded	xload

Value	Meaning	AutoLISP Function(s)
76	Unable to execute application	xload
77	Incompatible version number	xload
78	Unable to unload nested application	xunload
79	Application refused to unload	xunload
80	Application is not currently loaded	xunload
81	Not enough memory to load application	xload
82	ADS error: invalid transformation matrix	
83	ADS error: invalid symbol name	
84	ADS error: invalid symbol value	
85	AutoLISP/ADS operation prohibited while a dialogue box is displayed	

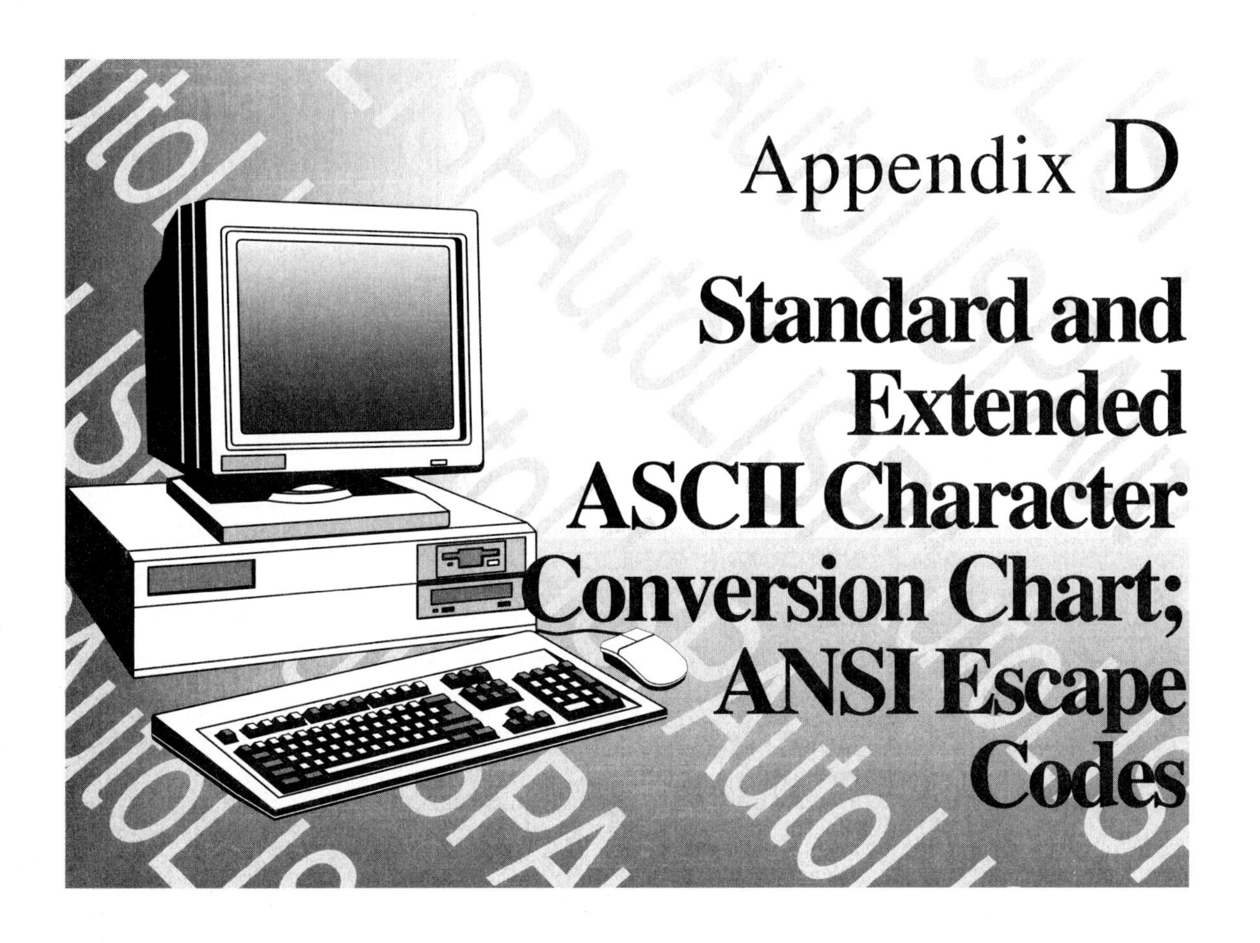

Table D-1 is a conversion chart that contains standard and extended ASCII characters. These special characters are used to enhance the appearance and functionality of an AutoLISP program in a DOS environment, thus providing a "built-in" look and feel.

AutoLISP uses two different methods for displaying these characters. The first method uses octal codes. These octal codes are used as arguments for any of AutoLISP's printing functions. For example, in order to produce a beeping sound from the computer, octal code 7 is used:

```
(princ "\007")                    emits a "beep" sound
```

Another means of utilizing these characters is by combining the desired ASCII code with the AutoLISP CHR function. For example, to print a "smiling face" to the screen, the following expression can be used:

```
(princ (chr 1))                   produces a "smiling face" character
```

NOTE

Some special characters will not print properly when using AutoCAD for Windows. In a non-Windows version of AutoCAD, using these characters in the AutoCAD text screen will yield the best results.

Table D-1. Character Conversion Chart

Decimal values through 127 are the standard low bit character set. Decimal values above 127 are the IBM extended high bit character set.

00 NUL CTRL@ 0	10 ▶ DLE CTRL P 16	20 SP 32	30 0 48	40 @ 64	50 P 80	60 ` 96	70 p 112
01 ☺ SOH CTRL A 1	11 ◀ DC1 CTRL Q 17	21 ! 33	31 1 49	41 A 65	51 Q 81	61 a 97	71 q 113
02 ☻ STX CTRL B 2	12 ↕ DC2 CTRL R 18	22 " 34	32 2 50	42 B 66	52 R 82	62 b 98	72 r 114
03 ♥ ETX CTRL C 3	13 ‼ DC3 CTRL S 19	23 # 35	33 3 51	43 C 67	53 S 83	63 c 99	73 s 115
04 ♦ EOT CTRL D 4	14 ¶ DC4 CTRL T 20	24 $ 36	34 4 52	44 D 68	54 T 84	64 d 100	74 t 116
05 ♣ ENQ CTRL E 5	15 § NAK CTRL U 21	25 % 37	35 5 53	45 E 69	55 U 85	65 e 101	75 u 117
06 ♠ ACK CTRL F 6	16 ▬ SYN CTRL V 22	26 & 38	36 6 54	46 F 70	56 V 86	66 f 102	76 v 118
07 • BEL CTRL G 7	17 ↨ ETB CTRL W 23	27 ' 39	37 7 55	47 G 71	57 W 87	67 g 103	77 w 119
08 ◘ BS CTRL H 8	18 ↑ CAN CTRL X 24	28 (40	38 8 56	48 H 72	58 X 88	68 h 104	78 x 120
09 ○ HT CTRL I 9	19 ↓ EM CTRL Y 25	29) 41	39 9 57	49 I 73	59 Y 89	69 i 105	79 y 121
0A ◙ LF CTRL J 10	1A → SUB CTRL Z· 26	2A * 42	3A : 58	4A J 74	5A Z 90	6A j 106	7A z 122
0B ♂ VT CTRL K 11	1B ← ESC CTRL [27	2B + 43	3B ; 59	4B K 75	5B [91	6B k 107	7B { 123
0C ♀ FF CTRL L 12	1C ∟ FS CTRL \ 28	2C , 44	3C < 60	4C L 76	5C \ 92	6C l 108	7C ¦ 124
0D ♪ CR CTRL M 13	1D ↔ GS CTRL] 29	2D - 45	3D = 61	4D M 77	5D] 93	6D m 109	7D } 125
0E ♫ SO CTRL N 14	1E ▲ RS CTRL ∧ 30	2E . 46	3E > 62	4E N 78	5E ∧ 94	6E n 110	7E ~ 126
0F ☼ SI CTRL O 15	1F ▼ US CTRL _ 31	2F / 47	3F ? 63	4F O 79	5F — 95	6F o 111	7F DEL △ 127

LEGEND

Hex	0D	CR	ASCII Name
	♪		Display Character
Key	CTRL M	13	Decimal

Table D-1. Character Conversion Chart

80 Ç 128	90 É 144	A0 á 160	B0 ░ 176	C0 └ 192	D0 ╨ 208	E0 α 224	F0 ≡ 240
81 ü 129	91 æ 145	A1 í 161	B1 ▒ 177	C1 ┴ 193	D1 ╤ 209	E1 ß 225	F1 ± 241
82 é 130	92 Æ 146	A2 ó 162	B2 ▓ 178	C2 ┬ 194	D2 ╥ 210	E2 Γ 226	F2 ≥ 242
83 â 131	93 ô 147	A3 ú 163	B3 │ 179	C3 ├ 195	D3 ╙ 211	E3 π 227	F3 ≤ 243
84 ä 132	94 ö 148	A4 ñ 164	B4 ┤ 180	C4 ─ 196	D4 ╘ 212	E4 Σ 228	F4 ⌠ 244
85 à 133	95 ò 149	A5 Ñ 165	B5 ╡ 181	C5 ┼ 197	D5 ╒ 213	E5 σ 229	F5 ⌡ 245
86 å 134	96 û 150	A6 ª 166	B6 ╢ 182	C6 ╞ 198	D6 ╓ 214	E6 µ 230	F6 ÷ 246
87 ç 135	97 ù 151	A7 º 167	B7 ╖ 183	C7 ╟ 199	D7 ╫ 215	E7 τ 231	F7 ≈ 247
88 ê 136	98 ÿ 152	A8 ¿ 168	B8 ╕ 184	C8 ╚ 200	D8 ╪ 216	E8 Φ 232	F8 ° 248
89 ë 137	99 Ö 153	A9 ⌐ 169	B9 ╣ 185	C9 ╔ 201	D9 ┘ 217	E9 Θ 233	F9 ● 249
8A è 138	9A Ü 154	AA ¬ 170	BA ║ 186	CA ╩ 202	DA ┌ 218	EA Ω 234	FA • 250
8B ï 139	9B ¢ 155	AB ½ 171	BB ╗ 187	CB ╦ 203	DB █ 219	EB δ 235	FB √ 251
8C î 140	9C £ 156	AC ¼ 172	BC ╝ 188	CC ╠ 204	DC ▄ 220	EC ∞ 236	FC n 252
8D ì 141	9D ¥ 157	AD ¡ 173	BD ╜ 189	CD ═ 205	DD ▌ 221	ED ∅ 237	FD 2 253
8E Ä 142	9E ₧ 158	AE « 174	BE ╛ 190	CE ╬ 206	DE ▐ 222	EE ∈ 238	FE ▮ 254
8F Å 143	9F ƒ 159	AF » 175	BF ┐ 191	CF ╧ 207	DF ▀ 223	EF ∩ 239	FF BLANK 'FF' 255

LEGEND

Hex	0D	CR	ASCII Name
	♪		Display Character
Key	CTRL M	13	Decimal

ANSI Escape Codes

Table D-2 shows the ANSI escape codes. These codes are useful for creating bold text in a user prompt, changing text color, and for positioning the cursor around the text screen. In addition, it is possible to assign new values to keys on your keyboard. The most commonly used keys are the function keys, but it is also possible to provide values to specified [ALT] keystrokes (hold down the [ALT] key while pressing another key). In order to use these escape codes, the ANSI.SYS file must be present, and the following line must be included in your CONFIG.SYS file:

```
DEVICE=ANSI.SYS
```

Be sure to indicate the directory path to this file if it is not in your root directory. For example:

```
DEVICE=C:\DOS\ANSI.SYS
```

These escape codes are used by AutoLISP's printing functions. The code numbers themselves follow the escape code, which is shown below:

```
\e[
```

The numerical codes are then followed by a lowercase "m" to specify setting of graphics mode. For example, to force the text to be printed in bold characters, the following expression can be used:

```
(princ "\e[1m")
```

All text from this point on will be bold. The numerical codes can be used together if they are separated by a semicolon. The following expression changes text to be both bold and magenta in color:

```
(princ "\e[1;35m")
```

To reset the text to its default setting, use this expression:

```
(princ "\e[0m")
```

NOTE

Similar to the ASCII characters shown in Table D-1, the ANSI escape codes are valid only while AutoCAD's text screen is visible. In addition, the escape codes do not work in AutoCAD for Windows. Table D-2 shows the graphics-related numerical codes for ANSI escape sequences.

Table D-2. ANSI Escape Codes

TEXT FORMAT	
Escape Codes	**Description**
0	Default (reset)
1	Bold
4	Underscored (monochrome monitors only)
5	Blinking
7	Reverse video (black text/white background)
8	Hidden (prevent display of text)
TEXT COLOR	
Escape Codes	**Description**
30	Black
31	Red
32	Green
33	Yellow
34	Blue
35	Magenta
36	Cyan
37	White
BACKGROUND COLOR	
Escape Codes	**Description**
40	Black
41	Red
42	Green
43	Yellow
44	Blue
45	Magenta
46	Cyan
47	White

Table D-2. ANSI Escape Codes

CURSOR CONTROL	
Escape Codes	**Description**
A	Move cursor up
B	Move cursor down
C	Move cursor right
D	Move cursor left
H	Move cursor to specified location
f	Move cursor to specified position
s	Save cursor position
u	Return cursor to saved position
MISCELLANEOUS	
Escape Codes	**Description**
2J	Clear screen
K	Erase from cursor position to end of line

ANSI escape code applications are shown in the following examples. Note how they are integrated within the AutoLISP programs.

To display a bold, red, and blinking "WARNING!" on a blue background, and then reset the display to its default, use the following expression:

```
(princ "\e[44;31;1;5mWARNING!\e[0m")
```

When processing large amounts of data, it is helpful to allow the user to know the status of the process. The following routine uses ASCII characters and ANSI escape codes to perform this task.

```
(defun CLICK ()
  (mapcar
    'princ
    (list
    "\e[D"                           ; Left one column
    "\e[1m"                          ; Bold text
    "\e[34m"                         ; Blue text
    "\262"                           ; Octal code for ASCII character
    "\e[0m"                          ; Normal text
    "\e[31m"                         ; Red text
    "\262"                           ; Octal code for ASCII character
    "\e[s"                           ; Save cursor position
    "\e[24;1f"                       ; Move cursor to Row 24, Column 1
    "\e[0m"                          ; Normal text
    (strcat (itoa INCR) "%")         ; Write INCR percent to screen
    "\e[u"                           ; Return cursor to saved position
    )
  )
)
```

To apply the CLICK function, a value must be assigned to the symbol INCR. The CLICK function is then called from within a loop in another function. The following routine uses a loop to demonstrate the CLICK function. The COUNTER in the loop is for a visible delay.

```
(textpage)                           ; Clears the text screen
(princ "\e[25;3H")                   ; Places the cursor at Row 25, Column 3
(setq INCR 0                         ; INCR symbol created
      COUNTER 0                      ; COUNTER symbol created
)
(repeat 51                           ; First click is 0, therefore, 51 are needed
  (CLICK)                            ; Call CLICK function
  (repeat 1000                       ; This loop is for a visible delay...
    (setq COUNTER (1+ COUNTER))      ; ...and is for demonstration purposes only
  )
  (setq COUNTER 0                    ; Reset COUNTER to 0
        INCR (+ 2 INCR)              ; Increment INCR by 2
  )
)
(princ)                              ; "Quiet" exit
```

Note that since there are only 80 columns of text on AutoCAD's text screen, it is not possible for this routine to increment by 1 without special considerations for dropping to the next line to continue the bar display.

Redefining the Keyboard

Another useful capability of the ANSI escape codes is to redefine your keyboard. Specific keystrokes can be assigned new functions to enhance productivity. In order to reassign these keys, AutoLISP's printing functions are used.

All keys on the keyboard are addressed by a *scan-code sequence.* The scan-code sequence is used to redefine the functions they perform. Table D-3 lists the function keys and their scan-code assignments.

Table D-3. Scan-Code Sequences

Function Key	Scan-Code Sequences
F1	Do not reassign this key, especially when novice users will be using new key assignments.
F2	0;60
F3	0;61
F4	0;62
F5	0;63
F6	0;64
F7	0;65
F8	0;66
F9	0;67
F10	0;68
F11	0;133
F12	0;134

To reassign these keys, an escape code is printed, followed by the scan-code and the new function. This should then be finalized with a carriage return (code 13). Each key reassignment is followed by a lowercase "p".

The following escape sequence redefines the function keys to object snap modifiers. The apostrophes are required as delimiters.

```
(setvar "CMDECHO" 0)
(textscr)
; F2
; ESCAPE    SCAN-CODE      NEW FUNCTION
; ------    ---------      ----------
;     |          |                |
;     |          |                |
;     |          |                |
;     |          |      ----------
;     |          |     |
;     |          |     |    CARRIAGE RETURN
;     |          |     |    ------------
;     |          |     |           |
;     --      ----     |        ----
;       |    |         |       |
(princ "\e[0;60;'INTERSECTION';13p")
(princ "\n")
; F3
(princ "\e[0;61;'ENDPOINT';13p")
(princ "\n")
; F4
(princ "\e[0;62;'MIDPOINT';13p")
(princ "\n")
; F5
(princ "\e[0;63;'CENTER';13p")
(princ "\n")
; F6
(princ "\e[0;64;'PERPENDICULAR';13p")
(princ "\n")
; F7
(princ "\e[0;65;'TANGENT';13p")
(princ "\n")
; F8 – ORTHO not redefined!
(princ "\e[0;66;0;66p")
(princ "\n")
; F9
(princ "\e[0;67;'QUADRANT';13p")
(princ "\n")
; F10
(princ "\e[0;68;'NODE';13p")
(princ "\n")
; F11 – No carriage return is desired here for using "QUICK"
(princ "\e[0;133;'QUICK,'p")
(princ "\n")
; F12
(princ "\e[0;134;'NEAREST';13p")
(princ "\n")
;
; The following allows access to original function key values by
```

```
; pressing [SHIFT]+[FUNCTION KEY]. Doing this allows access to
; the COORDS toggle, SNAP toggle, etc.
;
; SHIFT+F2
; ESCAPE   SCAN-CODE    ORIGINAL SCAN-CODE
; -----    ---------    -------------
;    |_         _|   _______________|
;      |       |    |
(princ "\e[0;85;0;60p")
; SHIFT+F3
(princ "\e[0;86;0;61p")
; SHIFT+F4
(princ "\e[0;87;0;62p")
; SHIFT+F5
(princ "\e[0;88;0;63p")
; SHIFT+F6
(princ "\e[0;89;0;64p")
; SHIFT+F7
(princ "\e[0;90;0;65p")
; SHIFT+F9
(princ "\e[0;92;0;67p")
; SHIFT+F10
(princ "\e[0;93;0;68p")
(princ)
```

Remember that the “e” in the escape code and the trailing “p” must be lowercase characters.

In a similar fashion, it is also possible to assign [ALT]+[KEY] combinations. The scan codes for these keystrokes are shown in Table D-4.

Table D-4. Scan-Codes for [ALT]+[KEY] Combinations

Scan-Code Assignment	Keystroke ([ALT]+[KEY])
0;120	1
0;121	2
0;122	3
0;123	4
0;124	5
0;125	6
0;126	7
0;127	8
0;128	9
0;129	0

Continued.

Table D-4. Scan-Codes for [ALT]+[KEY] Combinations

Scan-Code Assignment	Keystroke ([ALT]+[KEY])
0;130	–
0;131	=
0;16	Q
0;17	W
0;18	E
0;19	R
0;20	T
0;21	Y
0;22	U
0;23	I
0;24	O
0;25	P
0;30	A
0;31	S
0;32	D
0;33	F
0;34	G
0;35	H
0;36	J
0;37	K
0;38	L
0;44	Z
0;45	X
0;46	C
0;47	V
0;48	B
0;49	N

Continued.

Table D-4. Scan-Codes for [ALT]+[KEY] Combinations

Scan-Code Assignment	Keystroke ([ALT]+[KEY])
0;50	M
0;104	F1
0;105	F2
0;106	F3
0;107	F4
0;108	F5
0;109	F6
0;110	F7
0;111	F8
0;112	F9
0;113	F10

To assign the LINE command to the [ALT]+[L] keystroke, the following expression can be used:

```
(princ "\e[0;38;'LINE';13p")
```

It is also possible to reassign values to the [CTRL]+[KEY] combinations. These scan-codes differ slightly in format for the basic keys. The preceding "0;" is not used for the A through Z keys or the numeric keypad 0 through 9 keys. For example:

```
(princ "\e[12;'LINE';13p")
```
assigns [CTRL]+[L] to the LINE command

When reassigning key values, two points of caution should be carefully observed. First, do not reassign base values, such as the alphanumeric keystrokes of [H] or [7]. It may be necessary to reboot your computer if you reassign the wrong keys. For example, if you reassign the [1] key, it affects both of the [1] keys on your keyboard. Another example is when you reassign the value of the [L] key; you could no longer load an AutoLISP file.

The second point of caution is not to reassign AutoCAD's standard [CTRL] keystokes (such as [CTRL]+[C]).

The entire set of codes for the [CTRL]+[KEY] combination are shown in Table D-5.

Table D-5. Scan-Codes for [CTRL]+[KEY] Combinations

Scan-Code Assignment	Keystroke ([CTRL]+[KEY])
1	A
2	B
3	C
4	D
5	E
6	F
7	G
8	H
9	I
10	J
11	K
12	L
13	M
14	N
15	O
16	P
17	Q
18	R
19	S
20	T
21	U
22	V
23	W
24	X
25	Y
26	Z

Continued.

Table D-5. Scan-Codes for [CTRL]+[KEY] Combinations

Scan-Code Assignment	Keystroke ([CTRL]+[KEY])
0;94	F1
0;95	F2
0;96	F3
0;97	F4
0;98	F5
0;99	F6
0;100	F7
0;101	F8
0;102	F9
0;103	F10

RESETTING MODIFIED KEY VALUES

Any key value can be reset to its standard value by assigning it to its original scan-code. For example, to reset the [F2] key, the following expression can be used:

```
(princ "\e[0;62;0;62p")
```

Remember to reset all key values before exiting AutoCAD so that the keys function normally in your other applications. This can be done by redefining your END and QUIT commands, forcing them to load an AutoLISP file that resets all key values.

It is also possible to assign and reset key values in DOS. The DOS PROMPT command is used, with the ANSI escape code for DOS being "$e[". For example, to reset the [F2] key to the AutoCAD PLINE command, input the following sequence at the DOS prompt:

```
prompt=$e[0;60;"PLINE";13p
```

Notice that the delimiters for the command are quotation marks instead of apostrophes.

To automate the process of setting keys in DOS, a batch file can be used. A *batch file* is a file with a .BAT extension, and contains a list of DOS commands. For example, a batch file that makes the same assignment as the function keys shown earlier appears as follows:

```
prompt $e[0;60;"INTERSECTION";13p
prompt $e[0;61;"ENDPOINT";13p
prompt $e[0;62;"MIDPOINT";13p
prompt $e[0;63;"CENTER";13p
prompt $e[0;64;"PERPENDICULAR";13p
prompt $e[0;65;"TANGENT";13p
prompt $e[0;66;;66p
prompt $e[0;67;"QUADRANT";13p
prompt $e[0;68;"NODE";13p
prompt $e[0;133;"QUICK";13p
prompt $e[0;134;"NEAREST";13p
@rem – –〉 The last line should reset the DOS prompt to normal.
@rem – –〉 The line below sets the prompt to show the path (e.g. C:\ACAD13〉).
prompt=$P$G
```

Resetting the keys in DOS is accomplished in the same manner as in AutoLISP. For example to reset the [F2] key, the following DOS command is used:

```
prompt $e[0;60;0;60p
```

This can also be placed in a batch file along with any other keys that need to be reset. ASCII characters and ANSI escape codes are very useful for giving a program the "built-in" look and feel. In addition, they assist the programmer in focusing the user's attention on the most important part of a message. While it may not be wise to present your standard prompts in multicolor text, limited use of bold and colored text can greatly enhance the user interface value of your program. The reassignment of key values can also be a great productivity tool. When changing the value of function keys, it is best to create a template with labels for the new key assignments.

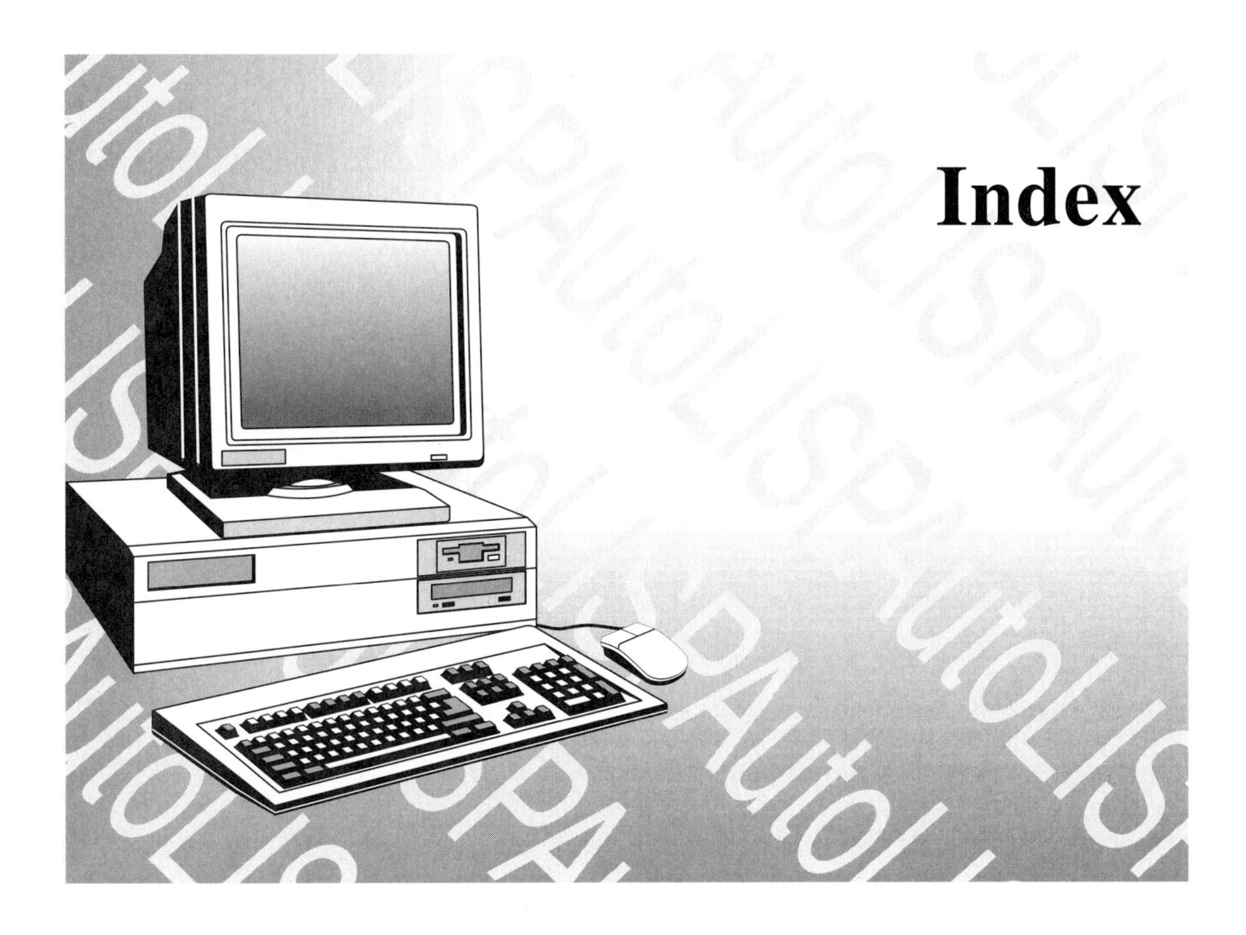

A

*Page numbers in **bold** indicate where function syntax and description are found in the text.*

Page numbers in **bold** *indicate where function syntax and description are found in the text.*

B

C

Page numbers in **bold** *indicate where function syntax and description are found in the text.*

D

E

F

G

H

I

K

L

M

N

O

P

Page numbers in **bold** *indicate where function syntax and description are found in the text.*

Q

R

S

T

U

V

W

Z

Page numbers in **bold** *indicate where function syntax and description are found in the text.*